FIRST EDITION

READINGS ON THE
MORAL FOUNDATIONS OF POLITICS

EDITED BY IAN SHAPIRO
YALE UNIVERSITY

Bassim Hamadeh, CEO and Publisher
Michael Simpson, Vice President of Acquisitions
Jamie Giganti, Senior Managing Editor
Miguel Macias, Graphic Designer
Mieka Porter, Senior Acquisitions Editor
Sean Adams, Project Editor
Michael Skinner, Senior Licensing Specialist
Rachel Singer, Interior Designer

Copyright © 2016 by Cognella, Inc. All rights reserved. No part of this publication may be reprinted, reproduced, transmitted, or utilized in any form or by any electronic, mechanical, or other means, now known or hereafter invented, including photocopying, microfilming, and recording, or in any information retrieval system without the written permission of Cognella, Inc.

First published in the United States of America in 2016 by Cognella, Inc.

Trademark Notice: Product or corporate names may be trademarks or registered trademarks, and are used only for identification and explanation without intent to infringe.

Printed in the United States of America

ISBN: 978-1-63487-697-1 (pbk) / 978-1-63487-698-8 (br)

www.universityreaders.com   800-200-3908

Contents

CHAPTER 1
EICHMANN IN JERUSALEM (SELECTIONS)   2
BY HANNAH ARENDT

CHAPTER 2
JEREMY BENTHAM'S ECONOMIC WRITINGS,
VOL. III (SELECTIONS)   38
BY JEREMY BENTHAM

CHAPTER 3
SHOULD MARXISTS BE INTERESTED IN
EXPLOITATION?   40
BY JOHN ROEMER

CHAPTER 4
A THEORY OF JUSTICE, CHAPTERS 1 AND 2   70
BY JOHN RAWLS

CHAPTER 5

*SOCIAL UNITY AND PRIMARY GOODS,
SECTIONS IV AND V*   90
BY JOHN RAWLS

CHAPTER 6

A THEORY OF JUSTICE, CHAPTERS 3 AND 4   98
BY JOHN RAWLS

CHAPTER 7

*JUSTICE AS FAIRNESS: POLITICAL NOT
METAPHYSICAL* (SELECTIONS)   122
BY JOHN RAWLS

CHAPTER 8

*RESOURCES, CAPACITIES, AND OWNERSHIP:
THE WORKMANSHIP AND DISTRIBUTIVE JUSTICE*   142
BY IAN SHAPIRO

CHAPTER 9

ANARCHY, STATE AND UTOPIA, CHAPTERS 1–3
(SELECTIONS)   166
BY ROBERT NOZICK

CHAPTER 10

ANARCHY, STATE AND UTOPIA, CHAPTERS 4
AND 5 (SELECTIONS)   184
BY ROBERT NOZICK

CHAPTER 11
ANARCHY, STATE AND UTOPIA, CHAPTER 7
(SELECTIONS)   208
BY ROBERT NOZICK

CHAPTER 12
MORALS AND THE CRIMINAL LAW   228
BY PATRICK DEVLIN

CHAPTER 13
AFTER VIRTUE, CHAPTERS 1–3   246
BY ALASDAIR MACINTYRE

CHAPTER 14
AFTER VIRTUE, CHAPTER 5   278
BY ALASDAIR MACINTYRE

CHAPTER 15
LIBERALISM AGAINST POPULISM, CHAPTER 5   290
BY WILLIAM H. RIKER

CHAPTER 16
THREE NORMATIVE MODELS OF DEMOCRACY   300
BY JÜRGEN HABERMAS

CHAPTER 17
*DELIBERATIVE POLLING: TOWARD A
BETTER-INFORMED DEMOCRACY*   312
BY JAMES S. FISHKIN

CHAPTER 18
CAPITALISM, SOCIALISM, AND DEMOCRACY, CHAPTERS 21 AND 22   328
BY JOSEPH SCHUMPETER

CHAPTER 19
THE CALCULUS OF CONSENT, CHAPTER 6   352
BY JAMES M. BUCHANAN AND GORDON TULLOCK

CHAPTER 20
JOHN LOCKE'S DEMOCRATIC THEORY   362
BY IAN SHAPIRO

CHAPTER 21
THE LIMITS OF CONSENSUAL DECISION   384
BY DOUGLAS W. RAE

CHAPTER 22
ELEMENTS OF DEMOCRATIC JUSTICE   430
BY IAN SHAPIRO

NOTE TO STUDENTS

The Moral Foundations of Politics course draws on some readings that are in the public domain and some that are not. This reader contains the *non-public domain* readings for both the Yale University and Coursera versions of the course. *Public domain* readings can be downloaded, free of charge, from mofopo.com.

EICHMANN IN JERUSALEM

(SELECTIONS)

BY HANNAH ARENDT

Hannah Arendt, *Eichmann in Jerusalem: A Report on the Banality of Evil*, pp. 21-55, 135-150. Copyright © 2006 by Penguin Group USA. Reprinted with permission.

ONE

THE ACCUSED

Otto Adolf, son of Carl Adolf Eichmann and Maria née Schefferling, caught in a suburb of Buenos Aires on the evening of May 11, 1960, flown to Israel nine days later, brought to trial in the District Court in Jerusalem on April 11, 1961, stood accused on fifteen counts: "together with others" he had committed crimes against the Jewish people, crimes against humanity, and war crimes during the whole period of the Nazi regime and especially during the period of the Second World War. The Nazis and Nazi Collaborators (Punishment) Law of 1950, under which he was tried, provides that "a person who has committed one of these ... offenses ... is liable to the death penalty." To each count Eichmann pleaded: "Not guilty in the sense of the indictment."

In what sense then did he think he was guilty? In the long cross-examination of the accused, according to him he "the longest ever known," neither the defense nor the prosecution nor, finally, any of the three judges ever bothered to ask him this obvious question. His lawyer, Robert Servatius of Cologne, hired by Eichmann and paid by the Israeli government (following the precedent set at the Nuremberg Trials, where all attorneys for the defense were paid by the Tribunal of the victorious powers), answered the question in a press interview: "Eichmann feels guilty before God, not before the law," but this answer remained without confirmation from the accused himself. The defense would apparently have preferred him plead not guilty on the grounds that under the then existing Nazi legal system he had not done anything wrong, that what he was accused of were not crimes but "acts of state," over which no other state has jurisdiction (*par in parem imperium non habet*), that it had been his duty to obey and that, a Servatius' words, he had committed acts "for which you are decorated if you win and go to the gallows if you lose." (Thus

Goebbels had declared in 1943: "We will go down in history as the greatest statesmen of all times or as their greatest criminals.") Outside Israel (at a meeting of the Catholic Academy in Bavaria, devoted to what the *Rheinischer Merkur* called "the ticklish problem" of the "possibilities and limits in the coping with historical and political guilt through criminal proceedings"), Servatius went a step farther, and declared that "the only legitimate criminal problem of the Eichmann trial lies in pronouncing judgment against his Israeli captors, which so far has not been done"—a statement, incidentally, that is somewhat difficult to reconcile with his repeated and widely publicized utterances in Israel, in which he called the conduct of the trial "a great, spiritual achievement," comparing it favorably with the Nuremberg Trials.

Eichmann's own attitude was different. First of all, the indictment for murder was wrong: "With the killing of Jews I had nothing to do. I never killed a Jew, or a non-Jew, for that matter—I never killed any human being. I never gave an order to kill either a Jew or a non-Jew; I just did not do it," or, as he was later to qualify this statement, "It so happened ... that I had not once to do it"—for he left no doubt that he would have killed his own father if he had received an order to that effect. Hence he repeated over and over (what he had already stated in the so-called Sassen documents, the interview that he had given in 1955 in Argentina to the Dutch journalist Sassen, a former S.S. man who was also a fugitive from justice, and that, after Eichmann's capture, had been published in part by *Life* in this country and by *Der Stern* in Germany) that he could be accused only of "aiding and abetting" the annihilation of the Jews, which he declared in Jerusalem to have been "one of the greatest crimes in the history of Humanity." The defense paid no attention to Eichmann's own theory, but the prosecution wasted much time in an unsuccessful effort to prove that Eichmann had once, at least, killed with his own hands (a Jewish boy in Hungary), and it spent even more time, and more successfully, on a note that Franz Rademacher, the Jewish expert in the German Foreign Office, had scribbled on one of the documents dealing with Yugoslavia during a telephone conversation, which read: "Eichmann proposes shooting." This turned out to be the only "order to kill," if that is what it was, for which there existed even a shred of evidence.

The evidence was more questionable than it appeared to be during the trial, at which the judges accepted the prosecutor's version against Eichmann's categorical denial—a denial that was very ineffective, since he had forgotten the "brief incident [a mere eight thousand people] which was not so striking," as Servatius put it. The incident took place in the autumn of 1941, six months after Germany had occupied the Serbian part of Yugoslavia. The Army had been plagued by partisan warfare ever since, and it was the military authorities who decided to solve two problems at a stroke by shooting a hundred Jews and Gypsies as hostages for every dead German soldier. To be sure, neither Jews nor Gypsies were partisans, but, in the words of the responsible civilian officer in the military government, a certain Staatsrat Harald Turner, "the Jews we had in the camps [anyhow]; after all, they too are Serb nationals, and besides, they have to disappear" (quoted by Raul Hilberg in *The Destruction of the European Jews*, 1961). The camps had been set up by General Franz Böhme, military governor of the region, and they housed Jewish males only. Neither General Böhme nor Staatsrat Turner waited for Eichmann's approval before starting to shoot Jews and Gypsies by the thousand. The trouble began when Böhme, without consulting the appropriate police and S.S. authorities, decided to *deport* all his Jews, probably in order to show that no special troops, operating under a different command, were required to make Serbia *judenrein*. Eichmann was informed, since it was a matter of deportation, and he refused approval because the move would interfere with other plans; but it was not Eichmann but Martin Luther, of the Foreign Office, who reminded General Böhme that "In other territories [meaning Russia] other military commanders have taken care of considerably greater numbers of Jews without even mentioning it." In any event, if Eichmann actually did "propose shooting," he told the military only that they should go on doing what they had done all along, and that the question of hostages was entirely in their own competence. Obviously, this was an Army affair, since only males were involved. The implementation of the Final Solution in Serbia started about six months later, when women and children were rounded up and disposed of in mobile gas vans. During cross-examination, Eichmann, as usual, chose the most complicated and least likely explanation: Rademacher had needed the support of the Head Office for Reich Security, Eichmann's outfit, for his own stand on the matter in the Foreign Office, and therefore had forged the document. (Rademacher himself explained the incident much more reasonably at his own trial, before a West German court in 1952: "The Army was responsible for order in Serbia and had to kill rebellious Jews by shooting." This sounded more plausible but was a lie, for we know—from Nazi sources—that the Jews were not "rebellious.") If it was difficult to interpret a remark made over the phone as an order, it was more difficult to believe that Eichmann had been in a position to give orders to the generals of the Army.

Would he then have pleaded guilty if he had been indicted as an accessory to murder? Perhaps, but he would have made important qualifications. What he had done was a crime only in retrospect, and he had always been a law-abiding citizen, because Hitler's orders, which he had certainly executed to the best of his ability, had possessed "the force of law" in the Third Reich. (The defense could have quoted in support of Eichmann's thesis the testimony of one of the best-known experts on constitutional law in the Third Reich, Theodor Maunz, currently Minister of Education and Culture in Bavaria, who stated in 1943 [in *Gestalt und Recht der Polizei*]: "The command of the Führer ... is the absolute center of the present legal order.") Those who today told Eichmann that he could have acted differently simply did not know, or had forgotten, how things had been. He did not want to be one of those who now pretended that "they had always been against it," whereas in fact they had been very eager to do what they were told to do. However, times change, and he, like Professor Maunz, had "arrived at different insights." What he had done he had done, he did not want to deny it; rather, he proposed "to hang myself in public as a warning example for all anti-Semites on this earth." By this he did not mean to say that he regretted anything: "Repentance is for little children." (*Sic!*)

Even under considerable pressure from his lawyer, he did not change this position. In a discussion of Himmler's offer in 1944 to exchange a million Jews for ten thousand trucks, and his own role in this plan, Eichmann was asked: "Mr. Witness, in the negotiations with your superiors, did you express any pity for the Jews and did you say there was room to help them?" And he replied: "I am here under oath and must speak the truth. Not out of mercy did I launch this transaction"—which would have been fine, except that it was not Eichmann who "launched" it. But he then continued, quite truthfully: "My reasons I explained this morning," and they were as follows: Himmler had sent his own man to Budapest to deal with matters of Jewish emigration. (Which, incidentally, had become a flourishing business: for enormous amounts of money, Jews could buy theix way out. Eichmann, however, did not mention this.) It was the fact that "here matters of emigration were dealt with by a man who did not belong to the Police Force" that made him indignant, "because I had to help and to implement deportation, and matters of emigration, on which I considered myself an expert, were assigned to a man who was new to the unit. ... I was fed up. ... I decided that I had to do something to take matters of emigration into my own hands."

Throughout the trial, Eichmann tried to clarify, mostly without success, this second point in his plea of "not guilty in the sense of the indictment." The indictment implied not only that he had acted on purpose, which he did not deny, but out of base motives and in full knowledge of the criminal nature of his deeds. As for the base motives, he was perfectly sure that he was not what he called an *innerer Schweinehund,* a dirty bastard in the depths of his heart; and as for his conscience, he remembered perfectly well that he would have had a bad conscience only if he had not done what he had been ordered to to—to ship millions of men, women, and children to their death with great zeal and the most meticulous care. This, admittedly, was hard to take. Half a dozen psychiatrists had certified him as "normal"—"More normal, at any rate, than I am after having examined him," one of them was said to have exclaimed, while another had found that his whole psychological outlook, his attitude toward his wife and children, mother and father, brothers, sisters, and friends, was "not only normal but most desirable"—and finally the minister who had paid regular visits to him in prison alter the Supreme Court had finished hearing his appeal reassured everybody by declaring Eichmann to be "a man with very positive ideas." Behind the comedy of the soul experts lay the hard fact that his was obviously no case of moral let alone legal insanity, (Mr. Hausner's recent revelations in the *Saturday Evening Post* of things he "could not bring out at the trial" have contradicted the informatioi given informally in Jerusalem. Eichmann, we are now told, had been alleged by the psychiatrists to be "a man obsessed with a dangerous and insatiable urge to kill," "a perverted, sadistic personality." In which case he would have belonged in an insane asylum.) Worse, his was obviously also no case of insane hatred of Jews, of fanatical anti-Semitism or indoctrination of any kind. He "personally" never had anything whatever against Jews; on the contrary, he had plenty of "private reasons" for not being a Jew hater. To be sure, there were fanatic anti-Semites among his closest friends, for instance László Endre, State

Secretary in Charge of Political (Jewish) Affairs in Hungary, who was hanged in Budapest in 1946; but this, according to Eichmann, was more or less in the spirit of "some of my best friends are anti-Semites."

Alas, nobody believed him. The prosecutor did not believe him, because that was not his job. Counsel for the defense paid no attention because he, unlike Eichmann, was, to all appearances, not interested in questions of conscience. And the judges did not believe him, because they were too good, and perhaps also too conscious of the very foundations of their profession, to admit that an average, "normal" person, neither feeble-minded nor indoctrinated nor cynical, could be perfectly incapable of telling right from wrong. They preferred to conclude from occasional lies that he was a liar—and missed the greatest moral and even legal challenge of the whole case. Their case rested on the assumption that the defendant, like all "normal persons," must have been aware of the criminal nature of his acts, and Eichmann was indeed normal insofar as he was "no exception within the Nazi regime." However, under the conditions of the Third Reich only "exceptions" could be expected to react "normally." This simple truth of the matter created a dilemma for the judges which they could neither resolve nor escape.

He was born on March 19, 1906, in Solingen, a German town in the Rhineland famous for its knives, scissors, and surgical instruments. Fifty-four years later, indulging in his favorite pastime of writing his memoirs, he described this memorable event as follows: "Today, fifteen years and a day after May 8, 1945, I begin to lead my thoughts back to that nineteent of March of the year 1906, when at five o'clock in the morning I entered life on earth in the aspect of a human being." (The manuscript has not been released by the Israeli authorities. Harry Mulisch succeeded in studying this autobiography "for half an hour," and the German-Jewish weekly *Der Aufbau* was able to publish short excerpts from it.) According to his religious beliefs, which had not changed since the Nazi period (in Jerusalem Eichmann declared himself to be a *Gottgläubiger*, the Nazi term for those who had broken with Christianity, and he refused to take his oath on the Bible), this event was to be ascribed to "a higher Bearer of Meaning," in entity somehow identical with the "movement of the universe," to which human life, in itself devoid of "higher meaning," is subject. (The terminology is quite suggestive. To call God a *Höheren Sinnesträger* meant linguistically to give him some place in the military hierarchy, since the Nazis had changed the military "recipient of orders," the *Befehlsempfänger*, into a "bearer of orders," a Befehls*träger*, indicating, as in the ancient "bearer of ill tidings," the burden of responsibility and of importance that weighed supposedly upon those who had to execute orders. Moreover, Eichmann, like everyone connected with the Final Solution, was officially a "bearer of secrets," a *Geheimnisträger*, as well, which as far as self-importance went certainly was nothing to sneeze at.) But Eichmann, not very much interested in metaphysics, remained singularly silent on any more intimate relationship between the Bearer of Meaning and the bearer if orders, and proceeded to a consideration of the other possible cause of his existence, his parents: "They would hardly have been so overjoyed at the arrival of their first-born had they been able to watch how in the hour of my birth the Norn of misfortune, to spite the Norn of good fortune, was already spinning threads of grief and sorrow into my life. But a kind, impenetrable veil kept my parents from seeing into the future."

The misfortune started soon enough; it started in school. Eichmann's father, first an accountant for the Tramways and Electricity Company in Solingen and after 1913 an official of the same corporation in Austria, in Linz, had five children, four sons and a daughter, of whom only Adolf the eldest, it seems, was unable to finish high school, or even to graduate from the vocational school for engineering into which he was then put. Throughout his life, Eichmann deceived people about his early "misfortunes" by hiding behind the more honorable financial misfortunes of his father. In Israel, however, during his first sessions with Captain Avner Less, the police examiner who was to spend approximately 35 days with him and who produced 3,564 typewritten pages from 76 recorder tapes, he was in an ebullient mood, full of enthusiasn about this unique opportunity "to pour forth everything ... I know" and, by the same token, to advance to the rani of the most cooperative defendant ever. (His enthusiasm was soon dampened, though never quite extinguished when he was confronted with concrete questions based on irrefutable documents.) The best proof of his initial boundless confidence, obviously wasted on Captain Less (who said to Harry Mulisch: "I was Mr. Eichmann's father confessor"), was that for the first time in his life he admitted his early disasters, although he must have been aware of the fact that he thus contradicted himself on several important entries in all his official Nazi records.

Well, the disasters were ordinary: since he "had not exactly been the most hard-working" pupil—or, one may add, the most gifted—his father had taken him first from high school and then from vocational school, long before graduation. Hence, the profession that appears on all his official documents: construction engineer, had about as much connection with reality as the statement that his birthplace was Palestine and that he was fluent in Hebrew and Yiddish—another outright lie Eichmann had loved to tell both to his S.S. comrades and to his Jewish victims. It was in the same vein that he had always pretended he had been dismissed from his job as salesman for the Vacuum Oil Company in Austria because of membership in the National Socialist Party. The version he confided to Captain Less was less dramatic, though probably not the truth either: he had been fired because it was a time of unemployment, when unmarried employees were the first to lose their jobs. (This explanation, which at first seems plausible, is not very satisfactory, because he lost his job in the spring of 1933, when he had been engaged for two full years to Veronika, or Vera, Liebl, who later became his wife. Why had he not married her before, when he still had a good job? He finally married in March, 1935, probably because bachelors in the S.S., as in the Vacuum Oil Company, were never sure of their jobs and could not be promoted.) Clearly, bragging had always been one of his cardinal vices.

While young Eichmann was doing poorly in school, his father left the Tramway and Electricity Company and went into business for himself. He bought a small mining enterprise and put his unpromising youngster to work in it as an ordinary mining laborer, but only until he found him a job in the sales department of the Oberösterreichischen Elektrobau Company, where Eichmann remained for over two years. He was now about twenty-two years old and without any prospects for a career; the only thing he had learned, perhaps, was how to sell. What then happened was what he himself called his first break, of which, again, we have two rather different versions. In a handwritten biographical record he submitted in 1939 to win a promotion in the S.S., he described it as follows: "I worked during the years of 1925 to 1927 as a salesman for the Austrian Elektrobau Company. I left this position of my own free will, as the Vacuum Oil Company of Vienna offered me the representation for Upper Austria." The key word here is "offered," since, according to the story he told Captain Less in Israel, nobody had offered him anything. His own mother had died when he was ten years old, and his father had married again. A cousin of his stepmother—a man he called "uncle"—who was president of the Austrian Automobile Club and was married to the daughter of a Jewish businessman in Czechoslovakia, had used his connection with the general director of the Austrian Vacuum Oil Company, a Jewish Mr. Weiss, to obtain for his unfortunate relation a job as traveling salesman. Eichmann was properly grateful; the Jews in his family were among his "private reasons" for not hating Jews. Even in 1943 or 1944, when the Final Solution was in full swing, he had not forgotten: "The daughter of this marriage, half-Jewish according to the Nuremberg Laws, ... came to see me in order to obtain my permission for her emigration into Switzerland. Of course, I granted this request, and the same uncle came also to see me to ask me to intervene for some Viennese Jewish couple. I mention this only to show that I myself had no hatred for Jews, for my whole education through my mother and my father had been strictly Christian; my mother, because of her Jewish relatives, held different opinions from those current in S.S. circles." He went to considerable lengths to prove his point: he had never harbored any ill feelings against his victims, and, what is more, he had never made a secret of that fact. "I explained this to Dr. Löwenherz [head of the Jewish Community in Vienna] as I explained it to Dr. Kastner [vice president of the Zionist Organization in Budapest]; I think I told it to everybody, each of my men knew it, they all heard it from me sometime. Even in elementary school, I had a classmate with whom I spent my free time, and he came to our house; a family in Linz by the name of Sebba. The last time we met we walked together through the streets of Linz, I already with the Party emblem of the N.S.D.A.P. [the Nazi Party] in my buttonhole, and he did not think anything of it."

Had Eichmann been a bit less prim or the police examination (which refrained from cross-examination, presumably to remain assured of his cooperation) less discreet, his "lack of so extraordinarily successful in arranging the "forced emigration" of Jews, he had a Jewish mistress, an "old flame" from Linz. *Rassenschande*, sexual intercourse with Jews, was probably the greatest crime a member of the S.S. could commit, and though during the war the raping of Jewish girls became a favorite pastime at the front, it was by no means common for a Higher S.S. officer to have an affair with a Jewish woman. Thus, Eichmann's repeated violent denunciations of Julius

9

Streicher, the insane and obscene editor of Der Stürmer, and of his pornographic anti-Semitism, were perhaps personally motivated, and the expression of more than the routine contempt an "enlightened" S.S. man was supposed to show toward the vulgar passions of lesser Party luminaries.

The five and a half years with the Vacuum Oil Company must have been among the happier ones in Eichmann's life. He made a good living during a time of severe unemployment, and he was still living with his parents, except when he was out on the road. The date when this idyll came to an end—Pentecost, 1933—was among the few he always remembered. Actually, things had taken a turn for the worse somewhat earlier. At the end of 1932, he was unexpectedly transferred from Linz to Salzburg, very much against his inclinations: "I lost all joy in my work, I no longer liked to sell, to make calls." From such sudden losses of Arbeitsfreude Eichmann was to suffer throughout his life. The worst of them occurred when he was told of the Führer's order for the "physical extermination of the Jews," in which he was to play such an important role. This, too, came unexpectedly; he himself had "never thought of ... such a solution through violence," and he described his reaction in the same words: "I now lost everything, all joy in my work, all initiative, all interest; I was, so to speak, blown out." A similar blowing out must have happened in 1932 in Salzburg, and from his own account it is clear that he cannot have been very surprised when he was fired, though one need not believe his saying that he had been "very happy" about his dismissal.

For whatever reasons, the year 1932 marked a turning point of his life. It was in April of this year that he joined the National Socialist Party and entered the S.S., upon an invitation of Ernst Kaltenbrunner a young lawyer in Linz who later became chief of the Head Office for Reich Security (the *Reichs-sicherheitshauptamt* or R.S.H.A., as I shall call it henceforth), in one of whose six main departments—Bureau IV, under the command of Heinrich Müller—Eichmann was eventually employed as head of section B-4. In court, Eichmann gave the impression of a typical member of the lower middle classes, and this impression was more than borne out by every sentence he spoke or wrote while in prison. But this was misleading; he was rather the déclassé son of a solid middle-class family, and it was indicative of his comedown in social status that while his father was a good fiend of Kaltenbrunner's father, who was also a Linz lawyer, the relationship of the two sons was rather cool: Eichmann was unmistakably treated by Kaltenbrunner as his social inferior. Before Eichmann entered the Party and the S.S., he had proved that he was a joiner, and May 8, 1945, the official date of Germany's defeat, was significant for him mainly because it then dawned upon him that thenceforward he would have to live without being a member of something or other. "I sensed I would have to live a leaderless and difficult individual life, I would receive no directives from anybody, no orders and commands would any longer be issued to me, no pertinent ordinances would be there to consult—in brief, a life never known before lay before me." When he was a child, his parents, uninterested in politics, had enrolled him in the Young Men's Christian Association, from which he later went into the German youth movement, the *Wandervogel*. During his four unsuccessful years in high school, he had joined the *Jungfront- kämpfeverband,* the youth section of the German-Austrian organzation of war veterans, which, though violently pro-German and anti-republican, was tolerated by the Austrian government. When Kaltenbrunner suggested that he enter the S.S., he was just on the point of becoming a member of an altogether different outfit, the Freemasons' Lodge Schlaraffia, "an association of businessmen, physicians, actors, civil servants, etc., who came together to cultivate merriment and gaiety. ... Each member had to give a lecture from time to time whose tenor was to be humor, refined humor." Kaltenbrunner explained to Eichmann that he would have to give up this merry society because as a Nazi he could not be a Freemason—a word that at the time was unknown to him. The choice between the S.S. and Schlaraffia (the name derives from *Schlaraffenland,* the gluttons' Cloud-Cuckoo Land of German fairy tales) might have been hard to make, but he was "kicked out" of Schlaraffia anyhow; he had committed a sin that even now, as he told the story in the Israeli prison, made him blush with shame: "Contrary to my upbringing, I had tried, though I was the youngest, to invite my companions to a glass of wine."

A leaf in the whirlwind of time, he was blown from Schlaraffia, the Never-Never Land of tables set by magic and roast chickens that flew into your mouth—or, more accurately, from the company of respectable philistines with degrees and assured careers and "refined humor," whose worst vice was probably an irrepressible desire for practical jokes—into the marching columns of the Thousand-Year Reich, which lasted exactly twelve years and three months. At any rate, he did not enter the Party out of conviction, nor was he ever convinced by it—whenever he was asked to give his reasons, he repeated the same embarrassed clichés about the Treaty of Versailles and unemployment; rather, as he pointed out in court, "it was like being swallowed up by the Party against all expectations and without previous decision. It happened so quickly and suddenly." He had no time and less desire to be properly informed, he did not even know the Party program, he never read *Mein Kamp.* Kaltenbrunner had said to him: Why not join the S.S.? And he had replied, Why not? That was how it had happened, and that was about all there was to it.

Of course, that was not all there was to it. What Eichmann failed to tell the presiding judge in cross-examination was that he had been an ambitious young man who was fed up with his job as traveling salesman even before the Vacuum Oil Company was fed up with him. From a humdrum life without significance and consequence the wind had blown him into History, as he understood it, namely, into a Movement that always kept moving and in which somebody like him—already a failure in the eyes of his social class, of his family, and hence in his own eyes as well—could start from scratch and still make a career. And if he did not always like what he had to do (for example, dispatching people to their death by the trainload instead of forcing them to emigrate), if he guessed, rather early, that the whole business would come to a bad end, with Germany losing the war, if all his most cherished plans came to nothing (the evacuation of European Jewry to Madagascar, the establishment of a Jewish territory in the Nisko region of Poland, the experiment with carefully built defense installations around his Berlin office to repel Russian tanks), and if, to his greatest "grief and sorrow," he never advanced beyond the grade of S.S. *Obersturmbannführer* (a rank equivalent to lieutenant colonel)—in short, if, with the exception of the year in Vienna, his life was beset with frustrations, he never forgot what the alternative would have been. Not only in Argentina, leading the unhappy existence of a refugee, but also in the courtroom in Jerusalem, with his life as good as forfeited, he might still have preferred—if anybody had asked him—to be hanged as *Obersturmbannführer a.D.* (in retirement) rather than living out his life quietly and normally as a traveling salesman for the Vacuum Oil Company.

The beginnings of Eichmann's new career were not very promising. In the spring of 1933, while he was out of a job, the Nazi Party and all its affiliates were suspended in Austria, because of Hitler's rise to power. But even without this new calamity, a career in the Austrian Party would have been out of the question: even those who had enlisted in the S.S. were still working at their regular jobs; Kaltenbrunner was still a partner in his father's law firm. Eichmann therefore decided to go to Germany, which was all the more natural because his family had never given up German citizenship. (This fact was of some relevance during the trial. Dr. Servatius had asked the West German government to demand extradition of the accused and, failing this, to pay the expenses of the defense, and Bonn refused, on the grounds that Eichmann was not a German national, which was a patent untruth.) At Passau, on the German border, he was suddenly a traveling salesman again, and when he reported to the regional leader, he asked him eagerly "if he had perhaps some connection with the Bavarian Vacuum Oil Company." Well, this was one of his not infrequent relapses from one period of his life into another; whenever he was confronted with telltale signs of an unregenerate Nazi outlook, in his life in Argentina and even in the Jerusalem jail, he excused himself with "There I go again, the old song and dance [*die alte Tour*]." But his relapse in Passau was quickly cured; he was told that he had better enlist for some military training—"All right with me, I thought to myself, why not become a soldier?"—and he was sent in quick succession to two Bavarian S.S. camps, in Lechfeld and in Dachau (he had nothing to do with the concentration camp there), where the "Austrian Legion in exile" received its training. Thus he did become an Austrian after a fashion, despite his German passport. He remained in these military camps from August, 1933, until September, 1934, advanced to the rank of *Scharführer* (corporal) and had plenty of time to reconsider his willingness to embark upon the career of a soldier. According to his own account, there was but one thing in which he distinguished himself during these fourteen months, and that was punishment drill, which he performed with great obstinacy, in the wrathful spirit of "Serves my father right if my hands freeze, why doesn't he buy me gloves." But apart from such rather dubious pleasures, to which he owed his first promotion, he had a terrible time: "The humdrum of military service, that was something I couldn't stand, day after day always the same, over and over again the same." Thus bored to distraction, he heard that the Security Service of the Reichsführer S.S. (Himmler's *Sicherheitsdienst,* or S.D., as I shall call it henceforth) had jobs open, and applied immediately.

AN EXPERT ON THE JEWISH QUESTION

In 1934, when Eichmann applied successfully for a job, the S.D. was a relatively new apparatus in the S.S., founded two years earlier by Heinrich Himmler to serve as the Intelligence service of the Party and now headed by Reinhardt Heydrich, a former Navy Intelligence officer, who was become, as Gerald Reitlinger put it, "the real engineer of the Final Solution" (*The Final Solution*, 1961). Its initial task had been to spy on Party members, and thus to give the S.S. an ascendancy over the regular Party apparatus. Meanwhile it had taken on some additional duties, becoming the information and research center for the Secret State Police, or Gestapo. These were the first steps toward the merger of the S.S. and the police, which, however, was not carried out until September, 1939, although Himmler held the double post of Reichsführer S.S. and Chief of the German Police from 1936 on. Eichmann, of course, could not have known of these future developments, but he seems to have known nothing either of the nature of the S.D. when he entered it; this is quite possible, because the operations of the S.D. had always been top secret. As far as he was concerned, it was all a misunderstanding and at first "a great disappointment. For I thought this was what I had read about in the *Münchener Illustrierten Zeitung*; when the high Party officials drove along, there were commando guards with them, men standing on the running boards of the cars. ... In short, I had mistaken the Security Service of the Reichsführer S.S. for the Reich Security Service ... and nobody set me right and no one told me anything. For I had had not the slightest notion of what now was revealed to me." The question of whether he was telling the truth had a certain bearing on the trial, where it had to be decided whether he had volunteered for his position or had been rafted into it. His misunderstanding, if such it was, not inexplicable; the S.S. or *Schutzstaffeln* had originally been established as special units for the protection of the Party leaders.

His disappointment, however, consisted chiefly in that he had to start all over again, that he was back at the bottom, and his only consolation was that there were others who had made the same mistake. He was put into the Information department, where his first job was to file all information concerning Freemasonry (which in the early Nazi ideological muddle was somehow lumped with Judaism, Catholicism, and Communism) and to help in the establishment of a Freemasonry museum. He now had ample opportunity to learn what this strange word meant that Kaltenbrunner had thrown ai aim in their discussion of Schlaraffia. (Incidentally, an eagerness to establish museums commemorating their enemies vas very characteristic of the Nazis. During the war, several services competed bitterly for the honor of establishing anti-Jewish museums and libraries. We owe to this strange craze the salvage of many great cultural treasures of European Jewry.) The trouble was that things were again very, very boring, and he was greatly relieved when, after four or five months of Freemasonry, he was put into the brand-new department concerned with Jews. This was the real beginning of the career which was to end in the Jerusalem court.

It was the year 1935, when Germany, contrary to the stipulations of the Treaty of Versailles, introduced general conscription and publicly announced plans for rearmament, including the building of an air force and a navy. It was also the year when Germany, having left the League of Nations in 1933, prepared neither quietly nor secretly the occupation of the demilitarized zone of the Rhineland. It was the time of Hitler's peace speeches—"Germany needs peace and desires peace," "We recognize Poland as the home of a great and nationally conscious people," "Germany neither intends nor wishes to interfere in the internal affairs of Austria, to annex Austria, or to conclude an *Anschluss*"—and, above all, it was the year when the Nazi regime von general and, unhappily, genuine recognition in Germany and abroad, when Hitler was admired everywhere as a great national statesman. In Germany itself, it was a time of transition. Because of the enormous rearmament program, unemployment had been liquidated, the initial resistance of the working class was broken, and the hostility of the regime, which had at first been directed primarily against "anti-Fascists"—Communists, Socialists, left-wing intellectuals, and Jews in prominent positions—had not yet shifted entirely to persecution of the Jews qua Jews.

To be sure, one of the first steps taken by the Nazi government, back in 1933, had been the exclusion of Jews from the Civil Service (which in Germany included all teaching positions, from grammar school to university, and most branches of the entertainment industry, including radio, the theater, the opera, and concerts) and, in general, their removal from public offices. But private business remained almost untouched until 1938, and even the legal and medical professions were only gradually abolished, although Jewish students were excluded from most universities and were nowhere permitted to graduate. Emigration of Jews in these years proceeded in a not unduly accelerated and generally orderly fashion, and the currency restrictions that made it difficult, but not impossible, for Jews to take their money, or at least the greater part of it, out of the country were the same for non-Jews; they dated back to the days of the Weimar Republic. There were a certain number of *Einzelaktionen,* individual actions putting pressure on Jews to sell their property at often ridiculously low prices, but these usually occurred in small towns and, indeed, could be traced to the spontaneous, "individual" initiative of some enterprising Storm Troopers, the so-called S.A. men, who, except for their officer corps, were mostly recruited from the lower classes. The police, it is true, never stopped these "excesses," but the Nazi authorities were not too happy about them, because they affected the value of real estate all over the country. The emigrants, unless they were political refugees, were young people who realized that there was no future for them in Germany. And since they soon found out that there was hardly any future for them in other European countries either, some Jewish emigrants actually returned during this period. When Eichmann was asked how he had reconciled his personal feelings about Jews with the outspoken and violent anti-Semitism of the Party he had joined, he replied with the proverb: "Nothing's as hot when you eat it as when it's being cooked"—a proverb that was then an he lips of many Jews as well. They lived in a fool's paradise, in which, for a few years, even Streicher spoke of a "legal solution" the Jewish problem. It took the organized pogroms of November, 1938, the so-called *Kristallnacht* or Night of Broken Glass, when seventy-five hundred Jewish shop windows were broken, all synagogues went up in flames, and twenty thousand Jewish men were taken off to concentration camps, to expel them from it.

The frequently forgotten point of the matter is that the famous Nuremberg Laws, issued in the fall of 1935, had failed to do the trick. The testimony of three witnesses from Germany, high-ranking former officials of the Zionist organization who left Germany shortly before the outbreak of the war, gave only the barest glimpse into the true state of affairs during the first five years of the Nazi regime. The Nuremberg Laws had deprived the Jews of their political but not of their civil rights; they were no longer citizens (*Reichsbürger*), but they remained members of the German state (*Staatsangehörige*). Even if they emigrated, they were not automatically stateless. Sexual intercourse between Jews and Germans, and the contraction of mixed marriages, were forbidden. Also, no German woman under the age of forty-five could be employed in a Jewish household. Of these stipulations, only the last was of practical significance; the others merely legalized a *de facto* situation. Hence, the Nuremberg Laws were felt to have stabilized the new situation of Jews in the German Reich. They had been second-class citizens, to put it mildly, since January 30, 1933; their almost complete separation from the rest of the population had been achieved in a matter of weeks or months—through terror but also through the more than ordinary connivance of those around them. "There was a wall between Gentiles and Jews," Dr. Benno Cohn of Berlin testified. "I cannot remember speaking to a Christian during all my journeys over Germany." Now, the Jews felt, they had received laws of their own and would no longer be outlawed. If they kept to themselves, as they had been forced to do anyhow, they would be able to live unmolested. In the words of the *Reichsvertretung* of the Jews in Germany (the national association of all communities and organizations, which had been founded in September, 1933, on the initiative of the Berlin community, and was in no way Nazi-appointed), the intention of the Nuremberg Laws was "to establish a level on which a bearable relationship between the German and the Jewish people [became] possible," to which a member of the Berlin community, a radical Zionist, added: "Life is possible under every law. However, in complete ignorance of what is permitted and what is not one cannot live. A useful and respected citizen one can also be as a member of a minority in the midst of a great people" (Hans Lamm, *Uber die Entwicklung des deutschen Judentums,* 1951). And since Hitler, in the Röhm purge in 1934, had broken the power of the S.A., the Storm Troopers in brown shirts who had been almost exclusively responsible for the early pogroms and atrocities, and since the Jews were blissfully unaware of the growing power of the black-shirted S.S., who ordinarily abstained from what Eichmann contemptuously called the "*Stürmer* methods," they generally believed that a *modus vivendi* would be possible; they even offered to cooperate in "the solution of the Jewish question." In short, when Eichmann entered upon his apprenticeship in Jewish affairs, on which, four years later, he was to be the recognized "expert," and when he made his first contacts with Jewish functionaries, both Zionists and Assimilationists talked in terms of a great "Jewish revival," a "great constructive movement of German Jewry," and they still quarreled among themselves in ideological terms about the desirability of Jewish emigration, as though this depended upon their own decisions.

Eichmann's account during the police examination of how he was introduced into the new department—distorted, of course, but not wholly devoid of truth—oddly recalls this fool's paradise. The first thing that happened was that his new boss, a certain von Mildenstein, who shortly thereafter got himself transferred to Albert Speer's *Organisation Todt*, where he was in charge of highway construction (he was what Eichmann pretended to be, an engineer by profession), required him to read Theodor Herzl's *Der Judenstaat*, the famous Zionist classic, which converted Eichmann promptly and forever to Zionism. This seems to have been the first serious book he ever read and it made a lasting impression on him. From then on, as he repeated over and over, he thought of hardly anything but a "political solution" (as opposed to the later "physical solution," the first meaning expulsion and the second extermination) and how to "get some firm ground under the feet of the Jews." (It may be worth mentioning that, as late as 1939, he seems to have protested against desecrators of Herzl's grave in Vienna, and there are reports of his presence in civilian clothes at the commemoration of the thirty-fifth anniversary of Herzl's death. Strangely enough, he did not talk about these things in Jerusalem, where he continuously boasted of his good relations with Jewish officials.) In order to help in this enterprise, he began spreading the gospel among his S.S. comrades, giving lectures and writing pamphlets. He then acquired a smattering of Hebrew, which enabled him to read haltingly a Yiddish newspaper—not a very difficult accomplishment, since Yiddish, basically an old German dialect written in Hebrew letters, can be understood by any German-speaking person who has mastered a few dozen Hebrew words. He even read one more book, Adolf Böhm's *History of Zionism* (during the trial he kept confusing it with Herzl's *Judenstaat*), and this was perhaps a considerable achievement for a man who, by his own account, had always been utterly reluctant to read anything except newspapers, and who, to the distress of his father, had never availed himself of the books in the family library. Following up Böhm, he studied the organizational setup of the Zionist movement, with all its parties, youth groups, and different programs. This did not yet make him an "authority," but it was enough to earn him an assignment as official spy on the Zionist offices and on their meetings; it is worth noting that his schooling in Jewish affairs was almost entirely concerned with Zionism.

His first personal contacts with Jewish functionaries, all of them well-known Zionists of long standing, were thoroughly satisfactory. The reason he became so fascinated by the "Jewish question," he explained, was his own "idealism"; these Jews, unlike the Assimilationists, whom he always despised, and unlike Orthodox Jews, who bored him, were "idealists," like him. An "idealist," according to Eichmann's notions, was not merely a man who believed in an "idea" or someone who did not steal or accept bribes, though these qualifications were indispensable. An "idealist" was a man who *lived* for his idea—hence he could not be a businessman—and who was prepared to sacrifice for his idea everything and, especially, everybody. When he said in the police examination that he would have sent his own father to his death if that had been required, he did not mean merely to stress the extent to which he was under orders, and ready to obey them; he also meant to show what an "idealist" he had always been. The perfect "idealist," like everybody else, had of course his personal feelings and emotions, but he would never permit them to interfere with his actions if they came into conflict with his "idea." The greatest "idealist" Eichmann ever encountered among the Jews was Dr. Rudolf Kastner, with whom he negotiated during the Jewish deportations from Hungary and with whom he came to an agreement that he, Eichmann, would permit the "illegal" departure of a few thousand Jews to Palestine (the trains were in fact guarded by German police) in exchange for "quiet and order" in the camps from which hundreds of thousands were shipped to Auschwitz. The few thousand saved by the agreement, prominent Jews and members of the Zionist youth organizations, were, in Eichmann's words, "the best biological material." Dr. Kastner, as Eichmann understood it, had sacrificed his fellow-Jews to his "idea," and this was as it should be. Judge Benjamin Halevi, one of the three judges at Eichmann's trial, had been in charge of the Kastner trial in Israel, at which Kastner had to defend himself for his cooperation with Eichmann and other high-ranking Nazis; in Halevi's opinion, Kastner had "sold his soul to the devil." Now that the devil himself was in the dock he turned out to be an "idealist," and though it may be hard to believe, it is quite possible that the one who sold his soul had also been an "idealist."

Long before all this happened, Eichmann was given his first opportunity to apply in practice what he had learned during his apprenticeship. After the *Anschluss* (the incorporation of Austria into the Reich), in March, 1938, he was sent to Vienna to organize a kind of emigration that had been utterly unknown in Germany, where up to the fall of 1938 the fiction was maintained that Jews if they so desired were permitted, but were not forced, to leave the country. Among the reasons German Jews believed in the fiction was the program of the N.S.D.A.P., formulated in 1920, which shared with the Weimar Constitution the curious fate of neve being officially abolished; it Twenty-Five Points had even been declared "unalterable" by Hitler. Seen in the light of later events, its anti-Semite provisions were harmless indeed: Jews could not be full-fledget citizens, they could not hold Civil Service positions, they were to be excluded from the press, and all those who had acquired German citizenship after August 2, 1914—the date of the outbreak of the First World War—were to be denaturalized, which meant they were subject to expulsion. (Characteristically, the denaturalization was carried out immediately, but the wholesale expulsion of some fifteen thousand Jews, who from one day to the next were shoved across the Polish border at Zbaszyn, where they were promptly put into camps, took place only five years later, when no one expected it any longer.) The Party program was never taken seriously by Nazi officials; they prided themselves on belonging to a movement, as distinguished from a party, and a movement could not be bound by a program. Even before the Nazis' rise to power, these Twenty-Five Points had been no more than a concession to the party system and to such prospective voters as were old-fashioned enough to ask what was the program of the party they were going to join. Eichmann, we have seen, was free of such deplorable habits, and when he told the Jerusalem court that he had not known Hitler's program he very likely spoke the truth: "The Party program did not matter, you knew what you were joining." The Jews, on the other hand, were old-fashioned enough to know the Twenty-Five Points by heart and to believe in them; whatever contradicted the legal implementation of the Party program ley tended to ascribe to temporary, "revolutionary excesses" of undisciplined members or groups.

But what happened in Vienna in March, 1938, was altogether different. Eichmann's task had been defined as 'forced emigration," and the words meant exactly what they said: all Jews, regardless of their desire and regardless of their citizenship, were to be forced to emigrate—an act which in ordinary language is called expulsion. Whenever Eichmann thought back to the twelve years that were his life, he singled out his year in Vienna as head of the Center for Emigration of Austrian Jews as its happiest and most successful period. Shortly before, he had been promoted to officer's rank, becoming an *Untersturmführer,* or lieutenant, and he had been commended for his "comprehensive knowledge of the methods of organization and ideology of the opponent, Jewry." The assignment in Vienna was his first important job, his whole career, which had progressed rather slowly, was in the balance. He must have been frantic to make good, and his success was spectacular: in eight months, forty-five thousand Jews left Austria, whereas no more than nineteen thousand left Germany in the same period; in less than eighteen months, Austria was "cleansed" of close to a hundred and fifty thousand people, roughly sixty per cent of its Jewish population, all of whom left the country "legally"; even after the outbreak of the war, some sixty thousand Jews could escape. How did he do it? The basic idea that made all this possible was of course not his but, almost certainly, a specific directive by Heydrich, who had sent him to Vienna in the first place. (Eichmann was vague on the question of authorship, which he claimed, however, by implication; the Israeli authorities, on the other hand, bound [as Yad Vashem's *Bulletin* put it] to the fantastic "thesis of the all-inclusive responsibility of Adolf Eichmann" and the even more fantastic "supposition that one [i.e., his] mind was behind it all," helped him considerably in his efforts to deck himself in borrowed plumes, for which he had in any case a great inclination.) The idea, as explained by Heydrich in a conference with Göring on the morning of the *Kristallnacht,* was simple and ingenious enough: "Through the Jewish community, we extracted a certain amount of money from the rich Jews who wanted to emigrate. By paying this amount, and an additional sum in foreign currency, they made it possible for poor Jews to leave. The problem was not to make the rich Jews leave, but to get rid of the Jewish mob." And this "problem" was not solved by Eichmann. Not until the trial was over was it learned from the Netherlands State Institute for War Documentation that Erich Rajakowitsch, a "brilliant lawyer" whom Eichmann, according to his own testimony, "employed for the handling of legal questions in the central offices for Jewish emigration in Vienna, Prague, and Berlin," had originated the idea of the "emigration funds." Somewhat later, in April, 1941, Rajakowitsch was sent to Holland by Heydrich in order to "establish there a central office which was to serve as a model for the 'solution of the Jewish question' in all occupied countries in Europe."

Still, enough problems remained that could be solved only in the course of the operation, and there is no doubt that here Eichmann, for the first time in his life, discovered in himself some special qualities. There were two things he could do well, better than others: he could organize and he could negotiate. Immediately upon his arrival, he opened negotiations with the representatives of the Jewish community, whom he had first to liberate from prisons and concentration camps, since the "revolutionary zeal" in Austria, greatly exceeding the early "excesses" in Germany, had resulted in the imprisonment of practically all prominent Jews. After this experience, the Jewish functionaries did not need Eichmann to convince them of the desirability of emigration. Rather, they informed him of the enormous difficulties which lay ahead. Apart from the financial problem, already "solved," the chief difficulty lay in the number of papers every emigrant had to assemble before he could leave the country. Each of the papers was valid only for a limited time, so that the validity of the first had usually expired long before the last could be obtained. Once Eichmann understood how the whole thing worked, or, rather, did not work, he "took counsel with himself" and "gave birth to the idea which I thought would do justice to both parties." He imagined "an assembly line, at whose beginnings the first document is put, and then the other papers, and at its end the passport would have to come out as the end product." This could be realized if all the officers concerned—the Ministry of Finance, the income tax people, the police, the Jewish community, etc.—were housed under the same roof and forced to do their work on the spot, in the presence of the applicant, who would no longer have to run from office to office and who, presumably, would also be spared having some humiliating chicaneries practiced on him, and certain expenses for bribes. When everything was ready and the assembly line was doing its work smoothly and quickly, Eichmann "invited" the Jewish functionaries from Berlin to inspect it. They were appalled: This is like an automatic factory, like a flour mill connected with some bakery. At one end you put in a Jew who still has some property, a factory, or a shop, or a bank account, and he goes through the building from counter to counter, from office to office, and comes out at the other end without any money, without any rights, with only a passport on which it says: 'You must leave the country within a fortnight. Otherwise you will go to a concentration camp.' "

This, of course, was essentially the truth about the procedure, but it was not the whole truth. For these Jews could not be left "without any money," for the simple reason that without it no country at this date would have taken them. They needed, and were given, their *Vorzeigegeld*, the amount they had to show in order to obtain their visas and to pass the immigration controls of the recipient country. For this amount, they needed foreign currency, which the Reich had no intention of wasting on its Jews. These needs could not be met by Jewish accounts in foreign countries, which, in any event, were difficult to get at because they had been illegal for many years; Eichmann therefore sent Jewish functionaries abroad to solicit funds from the great Jewish organizations, and these funds were then sold by the Jewish community to the prospective emigrants at a considerable profit—one dollar, for instance, was sold for 10 or 20 marks when its market value was 4.20 marks. It was chiefly in this way that the community acquired not only the money necessary for poor Jews and people without accounts abroad, but also the funds it needed for its own hugely expanded activities. Eichmann did not make possible this deal without encountering considerable opposition from the German financial authorities, the Ministry and the Treasury, which, after all, could not remain unaware of the fact that these transactions amounted to a devaluation of the mark.

Bragging was the vice that was Eichmann's undoing. It was sheer rodomontade when he told his men during the last days of the war: "I will jump into my grave laughing, because the fact that I have the death of five million Jews [or "enemies of the Reich," as he always claimed to have said] on my conscience gives me extraordinary satisfaction." He did not jump, and if he had anything on his conscience, it was not murder but, as it turned out, that he had once slapped the face of Dr. Josef Löwenherz, head of the Vienna Jewish community, who later became one of his favorite Jews. (He had apologized in front of his staff at the time, but this incident kept bothering him.) To claim the death of five million Jews, the approximate total of losses suffered from the combined efforts of all Nazi offices and authorities, was preposterous, as he knew very well, but he had kept repeating the damning sentence *ad nauseam* to everyone who would listen, even twelve years later in Argentina, because it gave him "an extraordinary sense of elation to think that [he] was exiting from the stage in this way." (Former Legationsrat Horst Grell, a witness for the defense, who had known Eichmann in Hungary, testified that in his opinion Eichmann was boasting. That must have been obvious to everyone who heard Mm utter his absurd claim.) It was sheer boasting when he pretended he had "invented" the ghetto system or had "given birth to the idea" of shipping all European Jews to Madagascar. The Theresienstadt ghetto, of which Eichmann claimed "paternity," was established years after the ghetto system had been introduced into the Eastern occupied territories, and setting up a special ghetto for certain privileged categories was, like the ghetto system, the "idea" of Heydrich. The Madagascar plan seems to have been "born" in the bureaus of the German Foreign Office, and Eichmann's own contribution to it turned out to owe a good deal to his beloved Dr. Löwenherz, whom he had drafted to put down "some basic thoughts" on how about four million Jews might be transported from Europe after the war—presumably to Palestine, since the Madagascar project was top secret. (When confronted at the trial with the Löwenherz report, Eichmann did not deny its authorship; it was one of the few moments when he appeared genuinely embarrassed.) What eventually led to his capture was his compulsion to talk big—he was "fed up with being an anonymous wanderer between the worlds"—and this compulsion must have grown considerably stronger as time passed, not only because he had nothing to do that he could consider worth doing, but also because the postwar era had bestowed so much unexpected "fame" upon him.

But bragging is a common vice, and a more specific, and also more decisive, flaw in Eichmann's character was his almost total inability ever to look at anything from the other fellow's point of view. Nowhere was this flaw more conspicuous than in his account of the Vienna episode. He and his men and the Jews were all "pulling together," and whenever there were any difficulties the Jewish functionaries would come running to him "to unburden their hearts," to tell him "all their grief and sorrow," and to ask for his help. The Jews "desired" to emigrate, and he, Eichmann, was there to help them, because it so happened that at the same time the Nazi authorities had expressed a desire to see their Reich *judenrein*. The two desires coincided, and he, Eichmann, could "do justice to both parties." At the trial, he never gave an inch when it came to this part of the story, although he agreed that today, when "times have changed so much," the Jews might not be too happy to recall this "pulling together" and he did not want "to hurt their feelings."

The German text of the taped police examination, conducted from May 29, 1960, to January 17, 1961, each page corrected and approved by Eichmann, constitutes a veritable gold mine for a psychologist—provided he is wise enough to understand that the horrible can be not only ludicrous but outright funny. Some of the comedy cannot be conveyed in English, because it lies in Eichmann's heroic fight with the German language, which invariably defeats him. It is funny when he speaks, *passim*, of "winged words" (*geflügelte Worte*, a German colloquialism for famous quotes from the classics) when he means stock phrases, *Redensarten*, or slogans, *Schlagworte*. It was funny when, during the cross-examination on the Sassen documents, conducted in German by the presiding judge, he used the phrase *"kontra geben"* (to give tit for tat), to indicate that he had resisted Sassen's efforts to liven up his stories; Judge Landau, obviously ignorant of the mysteries of card games, did not understand, and Eichmann could not think of any other way to put it. Dimly aware of a defect that must have plagued him even in school—it amounted to a mild case of aphasia—he apologized, saying, "Officialese [*Amtssprache*] is my only language." But the point here is that officialese became his language because he was genuinely incapable of uttering a single sentence that was not a cliché. (Was it these clichés that the psychiatrists thought so "normal" and "desirable"? Are these the "positive ideas" a clergyman hopes for in those to whose souls he ministers? Eichmann's best opportunity to show this positive side of his character in Jerusalem came when the young police officer in charge of his mental and psychological well-being handed him *Lolita* for relaxation. After two days Eichmann returned it, visibly indignant; "Quite an unwholesome book"—*"Das ist aber ein sehr unerfreuliches Buch"*—he told his guard.) To be sure, the judges were right when they finally told the accused that all he had said was "empty talk"—except that they thought the emptiness was feigned, and that the accused wished to cover up other thoughts which, though hideous, were not empty. This supposition seems refuted by the striking consistency with which Eichmann, despite his rather bad memory, repeated word for word the same stock phrases and self-invented clichés (when he did succeed in constructing a sentence of his own, he repeated it until it became a cliché) each time he referred to an incident or event of importance to him. Whether writing his memoirs in Argentina or in Jerusalem, whether speaking to the police examiner or to the court, what he said was always the same, expressed in the same words. The longer one listened to him, the more obvious it became that his inability to speak was closely connected with an inability to *think,* namely, to think from the standpoint of somebody else. No communication was possible with him, not because he lied but because he was surrounded by the most reliable of all safeguards against the words and the presence of others, and hence against reality as such.

Thus, confronted for eight months with the reality of being examined by a Jewish policeman, Eichmann did not have the slightest hesitation in explaining to him at considerable length, and repeatedly, why he had been unable to attain a higher grade in the S.S., that this was not his fault. He had done everything, even asked to be sent to active military duty—"Off to the front, I said to myself, then the *Standartenführer* [colonelcy] will come quicker." In court, on the contrary, he pretended he had asked to be transferred because he wanted to escape his murderous duties. He did not insist much on this, though, and, strangely, he was not confronted with his utterances to Captain Less, whom he also told that he had hoped to be nominated for the *Einsatzgruppen,* the mobile killing units in the East, because when they were formed, in March, 1941, his office was "dead"—there was no emigration any longer and deportations had not yet been started. There was, finally, his greatest ambition—to be promoted to the job of police chief in some German town; again, nothing doing. What makes these pages of the examination so funny is that all this was told in the tone of someone who was sure of finding "normal, human" sympathy for a hard-luck story. "Whatever I prepared and planned, everything went wrong, my personal affairs as well as my years-long efforts to obtain land and soil for the Jews. I don't know, everything was as if under an evil spell; whatever I desired and wanted and planned to do, fate prevented it somehow. I was frustrated in everything, no matter what." When Captain Less asked his opinion on some damning and possibly lying evidence given by a former colonel of the S.S., he exclaimed, suddenly stuttering with rage: "I am very much surprised that this man could ever have been an S.S. *Standartenführer,* that surprises me very much indeed. It is altogether, altogether unthinkable. I don't know what to say." He never said these things in a spirit of defiance, as though he wanted, even now, to defend the standards by which he had lived in the past. The very words "S.S.," or "career," or "Himmler" (whom he always called by his long official title: Reichsführer S.S. and Chief of the German Police, although he by no means admired him) triggered in him a mechanism that had become completely unalterable. The presence of Captain Less, a Jew from Germany and unlikely in any case to think that members of the S.S. advanced in their careers through the exercise of high moral qualities, did not for a moment throw this mechanism out of gear.

Now and then, the comedy breaks into the horror itself, and results in stories, presumably true enough, whose macabre humor easily surpasses that of any Surrealist invention. Such was the story told by Eichmann during the police examination about the unlucky Kommerzialrat Storfer of Vienna, one of the representatives of the Jewish community. Eichmann had received a telegram from Rudolf Höss, Commandant of Auschwitz, telling him that Storfer had arrived and had urgently requested to see Eichmann. "I said to myself: O.K., this man has always behaved well, that is worth my while … I'll go there myself and see what is the matter with him. And I go to Ebner [chief of the Gestapo in Vienna], and Ebner says—I remember it only vaguely—'If only he had not been so clumsy; he went into hiding and tried to escape,' something of the sort. And the police arrested him and sent him to the concentration camp, and, according to the orders of the Reichsführer [Himmler], no one could get out once he was in. Nothing could be done, neither Dr. Ebner nor I nor anybody else could do anything about it. I went to Auschwitz and asked Höss to see Storfer. 'Yes, yes [Höss said], he is in one of the labor gangs.' With Storfer afterward, well, it was normal and human, we had a normal, human encounter. He told me all his grief and sorrow: I said: 'Well, my dear old friend [*Ja, mein lieber guter Storfer*], we certainly got it! What rotten luck!' And I also said: 'Look, I really cannot help you, because according to orders from the Reichsführer nobody can get out. I can't get you out. Dr. Ebner can't get you out. I hear you made a mistake, that you went into hiding or wanted to bolt, which, after all, *you* did not need to do.' [Eichmann meant that Storfer, as a Jewish functionary, had immunity from deportation.] I forget what his reply to this was. And then I asked him how he was. And he said, yes, he wondered if he couldn't be let off work, it was heavy work. And then I said to Höss: 'Work—Storfer won't have to work!' But Höss said: 'Everyone works here.' So I said: 'O.K.,' I said, 'I'll make out a chit to the effect that Storfer has to keep the gravel paths in order with a broom,' there were little gravel paths there, 'and that he has the right to sit down with his broom on one of the benches.' [To Storfer] I said: 'Will that be all right, Mr. Storfer? Will that suit you?' Whereupon he was very pleased, and we shook hands, and then he was given the broom and sat down on his bench. It was a great inner joy to me that I could at least see the man with whom I had worked for so many long years, and that we could speak with each other." Six weeks after this normal human encounter, Storfer was dead—not gassed, apparently, but shot.

Is this a textbook case of bad faith, of lying self-deception combined with outrageous stupidity? Or is it simply the case of the eternally unrepentant criminal (Dostoevski once mentions in his diaries that in Siberia, among scores of murderers, rapists, and burglars, he never met a single man who would admit that he had done wrong) who cannot afford to face reality because his crime has become part and parcel of it? Yet Eichmann's case is different from that of the ordinary criminal, who can shield himself effectively against the reality of a non-criminal world only within the narrow limits of his gang. Eichmann needed only to recall the past in order to feel assured that he was not lying and that he was not deceiving himself, for he and the world he lived in had once been in perfect harmony. And that German society of eighty million people had been shielded against reality and faetuality by exactly the same means, the same self-deception, lies, and stupidity that had now become ingrained in Eichmann's mentality. These lies changed from year to year, and they frequently contradicted each other; moreover, they were not necessarily the same for the various branches of the Party hierarchy or the people at large. But the practice of self-deception had become so common, almost a moral prerequisite for survival, that even now, eighteen years after the collapse of the Nazi regime, when most of the specific content of its lies has been forgotten, it is sometimes difficult not to believe that mendacity has become an integral part of the German national character. During the war, the lie most effective with the whole of the German people was the slogan of "the battle of destiny for the German people" [*der Schicksalskarnpf des deutschen Volkes*], coined either by Hitler or by Goebbels, which made self-deception easier on three counts: it suggested, first, that the war was no war; second, that it was started by destiny and not by Germany; and, third, that it was a matter of life and death for the Germans, who must annihilate their enemies or be annihilated.

Eichmann's astounding willingness, in Argentina as well as in Jerusalem, to admit his crimes was due less to his own criminal capacity for self-deception than to the aura of systematic mendacity that had constituted the general, and generally accepted, atmosphere of the Third Reich. "Of course" he had played a role in the extermination of the Jews; of course if he "had not transported them, they would not have been delivered to the butcher." "What," he asked, "is there to 'admit'?" Now, he proceeded, he "would like to find peace with [his] former enemies"—a sentiment he shared not only with Himmler, who had expressed it during the last year of the war, or with the Labor Front leader Robert Ley (who, before he committed suicide in Nuremberg, had proposed the establishment of a "conciliation committee" consisting of the Nazis responsible for the massacres and the Jewish survivors) but also, unbelievably, with many ordinary Germans, who were heard to express themselves in exactly the same terms at the end of the war. This outrageous cliché was no longer issued to them from above, it was a self-fabricated stock phrase, as devoid of reality as those cliches by which the people had lived for twelve years; and you could almost see what an "extraordinary sense of elation" it gave to the speaker the moment it popped out of his mouth.

Eichmann's mind was filled to the brim with such sentences. His memory proved to be quite unreliable about what had actually happened; in a rare moment of exasperation, Judge Landau asked the accused: "What *can* you remember?" (if you don't remember the discussions at the so-called Wannsee Conference, which dealt with the various methods of killing) and the answer, of course, was that Eichmann remembered the turning points in his own career rather well, but that they did not necessarily coincide with the turning points in the story of Jewish extermination or, as a matter of fact, with the turning points in history. (He always had trouble remembering the exact date of the outbreak of the war or of the invasion of Russia.) But the point of the matter is that he had not forgotten a single one of the sentences of his that at one time or another had served to give him a "sense of elation." Hence, whenever, during the cross-examination, the judges tried to appeal to his conscience, they were met with "elation," and they were outraged as well as disconcerted when they learned that the accused had at his disposal a different elating cliché for each period of his life and each of his activities. In his mind, there was no contradiction between "I will jump into my grave laughing," appropriate for the end of the war, and "I shall gladly hang myself in public as a warning example for all anti-Semites on this earth," which now, under vastly different circumstances, fulfilled exactly the same function of giving him a lift.

These habits of Eichmann's created considerable difficulty during the trial—less for Eichmann himself than for those who had come to prosecute him, to defend him, to judge him, and to report on him. For all this, it was essential that one take him seriously, and this was very hard to do, unless one sought the easiest way out of the dilemma between the unspeakable horror of the deeds and the undeniable ludicrousness of the man who perpetrated them, and declared him a clever, calculating liar—which he obviously was not. His own convictions in this matter were far from modest: "One of the few gifts fate bestowed upon me is a capacity for truth insofar as it depends upon myself." This gift he had claimed even before the prosecutor wanted to settle on him crimes he had not committed. In the disorganized, rambling notes he made in Argentina in preparation for the interview with Sassen, when he was still, as he even pointed out at the time, "in full possession of my physical and psychological freedom," he had issued a fantastic warning to "future historians to be objective enough not to stray from the path of this truth recorded here"—fantastic because every line of these scribblings shows his utter ignorance of everything that was not directly, technically and bureaucratically, connected with his job, and also shows an extraordinarily faulty memory.

Despite all the efforts of the prosecution, everybody could see that this man was not a "monster," but it was difficult indeed not to suspect that he was a clown. And since this suspicion would have been fatal to the whole enterprise, and was also rather hard to sustain in view of the sufferings he and his like had caused to millions of people, his worst clowneries were hardly noticed and almost never reported. What could you do with a man who first declared, with great emphasis, that the one thing he had learned in an ill-spent life was that one should never take an oath ("Today no man, no judge could ever persuade me to make a sworn statement, to declare something under oath as a witness. I refuse it, I refuse it for moral reasons. Since my experience tells me that if one is loyal to his oath, one day he has to take the consequences, I have made up my mind once and for all that no judge in the world or any other authority will ever be capable of making me swear an oath, to give sworn testimony. I won't do it voluntarily and no one will be able to force me"), and then, after being told explicitly that if he wished to testify in his own defense he might "do so under oath or without an oath," declared without further ado that he would prefer to testify under oath? Or who, repeatedly and with a great show of feeling, assured the court, as he had assured the police examiner, that the worst thing he could do would be to try to escape his true responsibilities, to fight for his neck, to plead for mercy—and then, upon instruction of his counsel, submitted a handwritten document, containing his plea for mercy?

As far as Eichmann was concerned, these were questions of changing moods, and as long as he was capable of finding, either in his memory or on the spur of the moment, an elating stock phrase to go with them, he was quite content, without ever becoming aware of anything like "inconsistencies." As we shall see, this horrible gift for consoling himself with clichés did not leave him in the hour of his death.

DUTIES OF A LAW—ABIDING CITIZEN

So Eichmann's opportunities for feeling like Pontius Pilate were many, and as the months and the years went by, he lost the need to feel anything at all. This was the way things were, this was the new law of the land, based on the Führer's order; whatever he did he did, as far as he could see, as a law-abiding citizen. He did his *duty,* as he told the police and the court over and over again; he not only obeyed *orders,* he also obeyed the *law.* Eichmann had a muddled inkling that this could be n important distinction, but neither the defense nor the judges ever took him up on it. The well-worn coins of "superioi orders" versus "acts of state" were handed back and forth; they had governed the whole discussion of these matters during the Nuremberg Trials, for no other reason than that they gave the illusion that the altogether unprecedented could be judged according to precedents and the standards that went with them. Eichmann, with his rather modest mental gifts, was certainly the last man in the courtroom to be expected to challenge these notions and to strike out on his own. Since, in addition to performing what he conceived to be the duties of a law-abiding citizen, he had also acted upon orders—always so careful to be "covered"—he became completely muddled, and ended by stressing alternately the virtues and the vices of blind obedience, or the "obedience of corpses," *Kadavergehorsam,* as he himself called it.

The first indication of Eichmann's vague notion that there was more involved in this whole business than the question of the soldier's carrying out orders that are clearly criminal in nature and intent appeared during the police examination, when he suddenly declared with great emphasis that he had lived his whole life according to Kant's moral precepts, and especially according to a Kantian definition of duty. This was outrageous, on the face of it, and also incomprehensible, since Kant's moral philosophy is so closely bound up with man's faculty of judgment, which rules out blind obedience. The examining officer did not press the point, but Judge Raveh, either out of curiosity or out of indignation at Eichmann's having dared to invoke Kant's name in connection with his crimes, decided to question the accused. And, to the surprise of everybody, Eichmann came up with an approximately correct definition of the categorical imperative: "I meant by my remark about Kant that the principle of my will must always be such that it can become the principle of general laws" (which is not the case with theft or murder, for instance, because the thief or the murderer cannot conceivably wish to live under a legal system that would give others the right to rob or murder him). Upon further questioning, he added that he had read Kant's *Critique of Practical Reason.* He then proceeded to explain that from the moment he was charged with carrying out the Final Solution he had ceased to live according to Kantian principles, that he had known it, and that he had consoled himself with the thought that he no longer "was master of his own deeds," that he was unable "to change anything." What he failed to point out in court was that in this "period of crimes legalized by the state," as he himself now called it, he had not simply dismissed the Kantian formula as no longer applicable, he had distorted it to read: Act as if the principle of your actions were the same as that of the legislator or of the law of the land—or, in Hans Frank's formulation of "the categorical imperative in the Third Reich," which Eichmann might have known: "Act in such a way that the Führer, if he knew your action, would approve it" (*Die Technik des Staates,* 1942, pp. 15–16). Kant, to be sure, had never intended to say anything of the sort; on the contrary, to him every man was a legislator the moment he started to act: by using his "practical reason" man found the principles that could and should be the principles of law. But it is true that Eichmann's unconscious distortion agrees with what he himself called the version of Kant "for the household use of the little man." In this household use, all that is left of Kant's spirit is the demand that a man do more than obey the law, that he go beyond the mere call of obedience and identify his own will with the principle behind the law—the source from which lie law sprang. In Kant's philosophy, that source was practical reason; in Eichmann's household use of him, it was the will of the Führer. Much of the horribly painstaking thoroughness in the execution of the Final Solution—a thoroughness that usually strikes tie observer as typically German, or else as characteristic of the perfect bureaucrat—can be traced to the odd notion, indeed very common in Germany, that to be law-abiding means not merely to obey the law but to act a though one were the legislator of the laws hat one obeys Hence the conviction that nothing less than going beyond the call of duty will do.

Whatever Kant's role in the formation of "the little man's" mentality in Germany may have been, there is not the slightest doubt that in one respect Eichmann did indeed follow Kant's precepts; a law was a law, there could be no exceptions. In Jerusalem, he admitted only two such exceptions during the time when "eighty million Germans" had each had "his decent Jew": he had helped a half-Jewish cousin, and Jewish couple in Vienna for whom his uncle had intervened This inconsistency still made him feel somewhat mcomfortable, and when he .'as questioned about it during cross-examination, became openly apologetic: he had "confessed his sins" to his superiors. This uncompromising attitude toward the performance of hi murderous duties damned him in the eyes of the judges more than anything else, which was comprehensible, but in hi own eyes it was precisely what justified him, as it had once silenced whatever conscience he might have had left. No exceptions—this was the proof that he had always acted against his "inclinations," whether they were sentimental or inspired by interest, that he had always done his "duty."

Doing his "duty finally brought him into open conflict with orders from his superiors. During the last yea of the war, more than two years after the Wannsee Conference he experienced his last crisis of conscience. As the defeat approached, he was confronted by men from his own ranks who Eought more and more insistently for exceptions and, eventually, for the cessation of the Final Solution. That was the moment when his caution broke down and he began, once more, taking initiatives—for instance, he organized the foot marches of Jews from Budapest to the Austrian border after Allied bombing had knocked out the transportation system. It now was the fall of 1944, and Eichmann knew that Himmler had ordered the dismantling of the extermination facilities in Auschwitz and that the game was up. Around this time, Eichmann had one of his very few personal interviews with Himmler, in the course of which the latter allegedly shouted at him, "If up to now you have been busy liquidating Jews, you will from now on, since I order it, take good care of Jews, act as their nursemaid. I remind you that it was I—and neither Gruppenführer Müller nor you—who founded the R.S.H.A. in 1933; I am the one who gives orders here!" Sole witness to substantiate these words was the very dubious Mr. Kurt Becher; Eichmann denied that Himmler had shouted at him, but he did not deny that such an interview had taken place. Himmler cannot have spoken in precisely these words, he surely knew that the R.S.H.A. was founded in 1939, not in 1933, and not simply by himself but by Heydrich, with his endorsement. Still, something of the sort must have occurred, Himmler was then giving orders right and left that the Jews be treated well—they were his "soundest investment"—and it must have been a shattering experience for Eichmann.

Eichmann's last crisis of conscience began with his missions to Hungary in March, 1944, when the Red Army was moving through the Carpathian Mountains toward the Hungarian border. Hungary had joined the war on Hitler's side in 1941, for no other reason than to receive some additional territory from her neighbors, Slovakia, Rumania, and Yugoslavia. The Hungarian government had been outspokenly anti-Semitic even before that, and now it began to deport all stateless Jews from the newly acquired territories. (In nearly all countries, anti-Jewish action started with stateless persons.) This was quite outside the Final Solution, and, as a matter of fact, didn't fit in with the elaborate plans then in preparation under which Europe would be "combed from West to East," so that Hungary had a rather low priority in the order of operations. The stateless Jews had been shoved by the Hungarian police into the nearest part of Russia, and the German occupation authorities on the spot had protested their arrival; the Hungarians had taken back some thousands of able-bodied men and had let the other be shot by Hungarian troops under the guidance of German police units. Admiral Horthy, the country's Fascist ruler, had not wanted to go any further, however—probably due to the restraining influence of Mussolini and Italian Fascism—and in the intervening years Hungary, not unlike Italy, had become a haven for Jews, to which even refugees from Poland and Slovakia could sometimes still escape. The annexation of territory and the rickle of incoming refugees had increased the number of Jews in Hungary from about five hundred thousand before the war to approximately eight hundred thousand in 1944, when Eichmann moved in.

As we know today, the safety of these three hundred thousand Jews newly acquired by Hungary was due to the Germans' reluctance to start a separate action for a limited umber, rather than to the Hungarians' eagerness to offer asylum. In 1942, under pressure from the German Foreign Office (which never failed to make it clear to Germany's allies that the touchstone of their trustworthiness was their helpfulness not in winning the war but in "solving the Jewish question"), Hungary had offered to hand over all Jewish refugees. The Foreign Office had been willing to accept this as a step in the right direction, but Eichmann had objected: for technical reasons, he thought it "preferable to defer this action until Hungary is ready to include the Hungarian Jews"; it would be too costly "to set in motion the whole machinery of evacuation" for only one category, and hence "without making any progress in the solution of the Jewish problem in Hungary." Now, in 1944, Hungary was "ready," because on the nineteenth of March two divisions of the German Army had occupied the country. With them had arrived the new Reich Plenipotentiary S.S. Standartenführer Dr. Edmund Veesenmayer, Himmler's agent in the Foreign Office, and S.S. Obergruppenführer Otto Winkelmann, a member of the Higher S.S. and Police Leader Corps and therefore under the direct command of Himmler. The third S.S. official to arrive in the country was Eichmann, the expert on Jewish evacuation and deportation, who was under the command of Müller and Kaltenbrunner of the R.S.H.A. Hitler himself had left no doubt what the arrival of the three gentlemen meant; in a famous interview, prior to the occupation of the country, he had told Horthy that "Hungary had not yet introduced the steps necessary to settle the Jewish question," and had charged him with "not having permitted the Jews to be massacred" (Hilberg).

Eichmann's assignment was clear. His whole office was moved to Budapest (in terms of his career, this was a "gliding down"), to enable him to see to it that all "necessary steps" were taken. He had no foreboding of what was to happen; his worst fear concerned possible resistance on the part of the Hungarians, which he would have been unable to cope with, because he lacked manpower and also lacked knowledge of local conditions. These fears proved quite unfounded. The Hungarian *gendarmerie* was more than eager to do all that was necessary, and the new State Secretary in Charge of Political (Jewish) Affairs in the Hungarian Ministry of the Interior, Lászlo Endre, was a man "well versed in the Jewish problem," and became an intimate friend, with whom Eichmann could spend a good deal of his free time. Everything went "like a dream," as he repeated whenever he recalled this episode; there were no difficulties whatsoever. Unless, of course, one calls difficulties a few minor differences between his orders and the wishes of his new friends; for instance, probably because of the approach of the Red Army from the East, his orders stipulated that the country was to be "combed from East to West," which meant that Budapest Jews would not be evacuated during the first weeks or months—a matter for great grief among the Hungarians, who wanted their capital to take the lead in becoming *judenrein*. (Eichmann's "dream" was an incredible nightmare for the Jews: nowhere else were so many people deported and exterminated in such a brief span of time. In less than two months, 147 trains, carrying 434,351 people in sealed freight cars, a hundred persons to a car, left the country, and the gas chambers of Auschwitz were hardly able to cope with this multitude.)

The difficulties arose from mother quarter. Not one man but three had orders specifying that they were to help in "the solution of the Jewish problem"; each of them belonged to a different outfit and stood in a different chain of command. Technically, Winkelmann was Eichmann's superior, but the Higher S.S. and Police Leaders were not under the command of the R.S.H.A., to which Eichmann belonged. And Veeserunayer, of the Foreign Office, was independent of both. At any rate, Eichmann refused to take orders from either of the others, and resented their presence. But the worst trouble came from a fourth man, whom Himmler had charged with a "special mission" in the only country in Europe that still harbored not only a sizable number of Jews but Jews who were still in an important economic position. (Of a total of a hundred and ten thousand commercial stores and industrial enterprises in Hungary, forty thousand were reported to be in Jewish hands.) This man was Obersturmbannführer, later Standartenführer, Kurt Becher.

Becher, an old enemy of Eichmann who is today a prosperous merchant in Bremen, was called, strangely enough, as a witness for the defense. He could not come to Jerusalem, for obvious reasons, and he was examined in his German home town. His testimony had to be dismissed, since he had been shown, well ahead of time, the questions he was later called on to answer under oath. It was a great pity that Eichmann and Becher could not have been confronted with each other, and this not merely for juridical reasons. Such a confrontation would have revealed another part of the "general picture," which, even legally, was far from irrelevant. According to his own account, the reason Becher joined the S.S. was that "from 1932 to the present day he had been actively engaged in horseback riding." Thirty years ago, this was a sport engaged in only by Europe's upper classes. In 1934, his instructor had persuaded him to enter the S.S. cavalry regiment, which at that moment was the very thing for a man to do if he wished to join the "movement" and at the same time maintain a proper regard for his social standing. (A possible reason Becher in his testimony stressed horseback riding was never mentioned: the Nuremberg Tribunal had excluded the *Reiter-S.S.* from its list of criminal organizations.) The war saw Becher on active duty at the front, as a member not of the Army but of the Armed S.S., in which he was a liaison officer with the Army commanders. He soon left the front to become the principal buyer of horses for the S.S. personnel department, a job that earned him nearly all the decorations that were then available.

Becher claimed that he had been sent to Hungary only in order to buy twenty thousand horses for the S.S.; this is unlikely, since immediately upon his arrival he began a series of very successful negotiations with the heads of big Jewish business concerns. His relations with Himmler were excellent, he could see him whenever he wished. His "special mission" was clear enough. He was to obtain control of major Jewish business concerns behind the backs of the Hungarian government, and, in return, to give the owners free passage out of the country, plus a sizable amount of money in foreign currency. His most important transaction was with the Manfred Weiss steel combine, a mammoth enterprise, with thirty thousand workers, which produced everything from airplanes, trucks, and bicycles to tinned goods, pins, and needles. The result was that forty-five members of the Weiss family emigrated to Portugal while Mr. Becher became head of their business. When Eichmann heard of this *Schweinerei,* he was outraged; the deal threatened to compromise his good relations with the Hungarians, who naturally expected to take possession of Jewish property confiscated on their own soil. He had some reason for his indignation, since these deals were contrary to the regular Nazi policy, which had been quite generous. For their help in solving the Jewish question in any country, the Germans had demanded no part of the Jews' property, only the costs of their deportation and extermination, and these costs had varied widely from country to country—the Slovaks had been supposed to pay between three hundred and five hundred Reichsmarks per Jew, the Croats only thirty, the French seven hundred, and the Belgians two hundred and fifty. (It seems that no one ever paid except the Croats.) In Hungary, at this late stage of the war, the Germans were demanding payment in goods—shipments of food to the Reich, in quantities determined by the amount of food the deported Jews would have consumed.

The Weiss affair was only the beginning, and things were to get considerably worse, from Eichmann's point of view. Becher was a boom businessman, and where Eichmann saw only enormous tasks of organization and administration, he saw almost unlimited possibilities for making money. The one thing that stood in his way was the narrow-mindedness of subordinate creatures like Eichmann, who took their jobs seriously. Obersturmbannführer Becher's projects soon led him to cooperate closely in the rescue efforts of Dr. Rudolf Kastner. (It was to Kastner's testimony on his behalf that Becher later, at Nuremberg, owed his freedom. Being an old Zionist, Kastner had moved to Israel after the war, where he held a high position until a journalist published a story about his collaboration with the S.S.—whereupon Kastner sued him for libel. His testimony at Nuremberg weighed heavily against him, and when the case came before the Jerusalem District Court, Judge Halevi, one of the three judges in the Eichmann trial, told Kastner that he "had sold his soul to the devil." In March, 1957, shortly before his case was to be appealed before the Israeli Supreme Court, Kastner was murdered; none of the murderers, it seems, came from Hungary. In the hearing that followed the verdict of the lower court was repealed and Kastner was fully rehabilitated.) The deals Becher made through Kastner were much simpler than the complicated negotiations with the business magnates; they consisted in fixing a price for the life of each Jew to be rescued. There was considerable haggling over prices, and at one point, it seems, Eichmann also got involved in some of the preliminary discussions. Characteristically, his price was the lowest, a mere two hundred dollars per Jew—not, of course, because he wished to save more Jews but simply because he was not used to thinking big. The price finally arrived at was a thousand dollars, and one group, consisting of 1,684 Jews, and including Dr. Kastner's family, actually left Hungary for the exchange camp at Bergen-Belsen, from which they eventually reached Switzerland. A similar deal, through which Becher and Himmler hoped to obtain twenty million Swiss francs from the American Joint Distribution Committee, for the purchase of merchandise of all sorts, kept everybody busy until the Russians liberated Hungary, but nothing came of it.

There is no doubt that Becher's activities had the full approval of Himmler and stood in the sharpest possible opposition to the old "radical" orders, which still reached Eichmann through Müller and Kaltenbrunner, his immediatee superiors in the R.S.H.A. In Eichmann's view, people like Becher were corrupt, but corruption could not very well have caused his crisis of conscience, for although he was apparently not susceptible to this kind of temptation, he must by this time have been surrounded by corruption for many years. It is difficult to imagine that he did not know that his friend and subordinate Hauptsturmführer Dieter Wisliceny had, as early as 1942, accepted fifty thousand dollars from the Jewish Relief Committee in Bratislava for delaying the deportations from Slovakia, though it is not altogether impossible; but he cannot have been ignorant of the fact that Himmler, in the fall of 1942, had tried to sell exit permits to the Slovakian Jews in exchange for enough foreign currency to pay for the recruitment of a new S.S. division. Now, however, in 1944, in Hungary, it was different, not because Himmler was involved in "business," but because business had now become official policy; it was no longer mere corruption.

At the beginning, Eichmann tried to enter the game and play it according to the new rules; that was when he got involved in the fantastic "blood-for-wares" negotiations—one million Jews for ten thousand trucks for the crumbling German Army—which certainly were not initiated by him. The way he explained his role in this matter, in Jerusalem, showed clearly how he had once justified it to himself: as a military necessity that would bring him the additional benefit of an important new role in the emigration business. What he probably never admitted to himself was that the mounting difficulties on all sides made it every day more likely that he would soon be without a job (indeed, this happened, a few months later) unless he succeeded in finding some foothold amid the new jockeying for power that was going on all around him. When the exchange project met with its predictable failure, it was already common knowledge that Himmler, despite his constant vacillations, chiefly due to his justified physical fear of Hitler, had decided to put an end to the whole Final Solution—regardless of business, regardless of military necessity, and without anything to show for it except the illusions he had concocted about his future role as the bringer of peace to Germany. It was at this time that a "moderate wing" of the S.S. came into existence, consisting of those who were stupid enough to believe that a murderer who could prove he had not killed as many people as he could have killed would have a marvelous alibi, and those who were clever enough to foresee a return to "normal conditions," when money and good connections would again be of paramount importance.

Eichmann never joined this "moderate wing," and it is questionable whether he would have been admitted if he had tried to. Not only was he too deeply compromised and, because of his constant contact with Jewish functionaries, too well known; he was too primitive for these well-educated upper-middle-class "gentlemen," against whom he harbored the most violent resentment up to the very end. He was quite capable of sending millions of people to their death, but he was not capable of talking about it in the appropriate manner without being given his "language rule." In Jerusalem, without any rules, he spoke freely of "killing" and of 'murder," of "crimes legalized by the state"; he called a spade a spade, in contrast to counsel for the defense, whose feeling of social superiority to Eichmann was more than once in evidence. (Servatius' assistant Dr. Dieter Wechtenbruch—a disciple of Carl Schmitt who attended the first few weeks of the trial, the was sent to Germany to question witnesses for the defense, and reappeared for the last week in August—was readily available to reporters out of court; he seemed to be shocked less by Eichmann's crimes than by his lack of taste and education. 'Small fry," he said; "we must see how we get him over the hurdles—*wie wir das Würstchen über die Runden bringen.* Servatius himself had declared, even prior to the trial, that his client's personality was that of "a common mailman.")

When Himmler became "moderate," Eichman sabotaged his orders as much as he dared, to the extent at least that he felt he was "covered" by his immediate superiors. How does Eichmann dare to sabotage Himmler's orders?"—in this case, to stop the foot marches, in the fall of 1944—Kastne once asked Wisliceny. And the answer was: "He can probably show some telegram. Müller and Kaltenbrunner must have covered him." It is quite possible that Eichmann had some confused plan for liquidating Theresienstadt before he arrival of the Red Army, although we know this only through the dubious testimony of Dieter Wisliceny (who months, and perhaps years, before the end began carefully preparing an alibi for himself at the expense of Eichmann, to which he then treated the court at Nuremberg, where he was a witness for the prosecution; it did him no good, for he was extradited to Czechoslovakia, prosecuted and executed in Prague, where he had no connections and where money was of no help to him). Other witnesses claimed that it was Rolf Gunther, one of Eichmann's men, who planned this, and that there existed, on the contrary, a written order from Eichmann that the ghetto be left intact. In any event, there is no doubt that even in April, 1945, when practically everybody had become quite "moderate," Eichmann took advantage of a visit that M. Paul Dunand, of the Swiss Red Cross, paid to Theresienstadt to put it on record that he himself did not approve of Himmler's new line in regard to the Jews.

That Eichmann had at all times done his best to make the Final Solution final was therefore not in dispute. The question was only whether this was indeed proof of his fanaticism, his boundless hatred of Jews, and whether he had lied to the police and committed perjury in court when he claimed he had always obeyed orders. No other explanation ever occurred to the judges, who tried so hard to understand the accused, and treated him with a consideration and an authentic, shining humanity such as he had probably never encountered before in his whole life. (Dr. Wechtenbruch told reporters that Eichmann had "great confidence in Judge Landau," as though Landau would be able to sort things out, and ascribed this confidence to Eichmann's need for authority. Whatever its basis, the confidence was apparent throughout the trial, and it may have been the reason the judgment caused Eichmann such great "disappointment"; he had mistaken humanity for softness.) That they never did come to understand him may be proof of the "goodness" of the three men, of their untroubled and slightly old-fashioned faith in the moral foundations of their profession. For the sad and very uncomfortable truth of the matter probably was that it was not his fanaticism but his very conscience that prompted Eichmann to adopt his uncompromising attitude during the last year of the war, as it had prompted him to move in the opposite direction for a short time three years before. Eichmann knew that Himmler's orders ran directly counter to the Führer's order. For this, he needed to know no factual details, though such details would have backed him up: as the prosecution underlined in the proceedings before the Supreme Court, when Hitler heard, through Kaltenbranner, of negotiations to exchange Jews for trucks, "Himmler's position in Hitler's eyes was completely undermined." And only a few weeks before Himmler stopped the extermination at Auschwitz, Hitler, obviously unaware of Himmler's newest moves, had sent an ultimatum to Horthy, telling him he "expected that the measures against Jews in Budapest would now be taken without any further delay by the Hungarian government." When Himmler's order to stop the evacuation of Hungarian Jews arrived in Budapest, Eichmann threatened, according to a telegram from Veesenmayer, "to seek a new decision from the Führer," and this telegram the judgment found "more damning than a hundred witnesses could be."

Eichmann lost his fight against the "moderate wing," headed by the Reichsführer S.S. and Chief of the German Police. The first indication of his defeat came in January, 1945, when Obersturmbannführer Kurt Becher was promoted to *Standartenführer,* the very rank Eichmann had been dreaming about all during the war. (His story, that no higher rank was open to him in his outfit, was a half-truth; he could have been made chief of Department IV-B, instead of occupying the desk of IV-B-4, and would then have been automatically promoted. The truth probably was that people like Eichmann, who had risen from the ranks, were never permitted to advance beyond a lieutenant colonelcy except at the front.) That same month Hungary was liberated, and Eichmann was called back to Berlin. There, Himmler had appointed his enemy Becher *Reichssonderkommissar* in charge of all concentration camps, and Eichmann was transferred from the desk concerned with "Jewish Affairs" to the utterly insignificant one concerned with the "Fight Against the Churches," of which, moreover, he knew nothing. The rapidity of his decline during the last months of the war is a most telling sign of the extent to which Hitler was right when he declared, in his Berlin bunker, in April, 1945, that the S.S. were no longer reliable.

In Jerusalem, confronted with documentary proof of his extraordinary loyalty to Hitler and the Führer's order, Eichmann tried a number of times to explain that during the Third Reich "the Führer's words had the force of law" (*Führerworte haben Gesetzeskraft*), which meant, among other things that if the order came directly from Hitler it did not have to be in writing. He tried to explain that this was why he had never asked for a written order from Hitler (no such document relating to the Final Solution has ever been found; probably it never existed), but had demanded to see a written order from Himmler. To be sure, this was a fantastic state of affairs, and whole libraries of very "learned" juridical comment have been written, all demonstrating that the Führer's *words,* his oral pronouncements, were the basic law of the land. Within this "legal" framework, every order contrary in letter or spirit to a word spoken by Hitler was, by definition, unlawful. Eichmann's position, therefore, showed a most unpleasant resemblance to that of the often-cited soldier who, acting in a normal legal framework, refuses to carry out orders that run counter to his ordinary experience of lawfulness and hence can be recognized by him as criminal. The extensive literature on the subject usually supports its case with the common equivocal meaning of the word "law," which in this context means sometimes the law of the land—that is, posited, positive law—and sometimes the law that supposedly speaks in all men's hearts with an identical voice. Practically speaking, however, orders to be disobeyed must be "manifestly unlawful" and unlawfulness must "fly like a black flag above [them] as a warning reading: 'Prohibited!' "—as the judgment pointed out. And in a criminal regime this "black flag" with its "warning sign" flies as "manifestly" above what normally is a lawful order—for instance, not to kill innocent people just because they happen to be Jews—as it flies above a criminal order under normal circumstances. To fall back on an unequivocal voice of conscience—or, in the even vaguer language of the jurists, on a "general sentiment of humanity" (Oppenheim-Lauterpacht in *International Law,* 1952)—not only begs the question, it signifies a deliberate refusal to take notice of the central moral, legal, and political phenomena of our century.

To be sure, it was not merely Eichmann's conviction that Himmler was now giving "criminal" orders hat determined his actions. But the personal element undoubtedly involved was not fanaticism, it was his genuine, "boundless and immoderate admiration for Hitler" (as one of the defense witnesses called it)—for the man who had made it "from lance corporal to Chancellor of the Reich." It would be idle to try to figure on which was stronger in him, his admiration for Hitler or his determination to remain a law-abiding citizen of the Third Reich when Germany was already in ruins. Both motives came into play once more during the last days of the war, when he was in Berlin and saw with violent indignation how everybody around him was sensibly enough getting himself fixed up with forged papers before the arrival of the Russians or the Americans. A few weeks later, Eichmann, too, began to travel under an assumed name, but by then Hitler was dead, and the "law of the land" was no longer in existence, and he, as he pointed out, was no longer bound by his oath. For the oath taken by the members of the S.S. differed from the military oath sworn by the soldiers in that it bound them only to Hitler, not to Germany.

The case of the conscience of Adolf Eichmann, which is admittedly complicated but is by no means unique, is scarcely comparable to the case of the German generals, one of whom, when asked at Nuremberg, "How was it possible that all you honorable generals could continue to serve a murderer with such unquestioning loyalty?," replied that it was "not the task of a soldier to act as judge over his supreme commander. Let history do that or God in heaven." (Thus General Alfred Jodl, hanged at Nuremberg.) Eichmann, much less intelligent and without any education to speak of, at least dimly realized that it was not an order but a law which had turned them all into criminals. The distinction between an order and the Führer's word was that the latter's validity was not limited in time and space, which is the outstanding characteristic of the former. This is also the true reason why the Führer's order for the Final Solution was followed by a huge shower of regulations and directives, all drafted by expert lawyers and legal advisers, not by mere administrators; this order, in contrast to ordinary orders, was treated as a law. Needless to add, the resulting legal paraphernalia, far from being a mere symptom of German pedantry or thoroughness, served most effectively to give the whole business its outward appearance of legality.

And just as the law in civilized countries assumes that the voice of conscience tells everybody "Thou shalt not kill," even though man's natural desires and inclinations may at times be murderous, so the law of Hitler's land demanded that the voice of conscience tell everybody: "Thou shalt kill," although the organizers of the massacres knew full well that murder is against the normal desires and inclinations of most people. Evil in the Third Reich had lost the quality by which most people recognize it—the quality of temptation. Many Germans and many Nazis, probably an overwhelming majority of them, must have been tempted *not* to murder, *not* to rob, *not* to let their neighbors go off to their doom (for that the Jews were transported to their doom they knew, of course, even though many of them may not have known the gruesome details), and not to become accomplices in all these crimes by benefiting from them. But, God knows, they had learned how to resist temptation.

JEREMY BENTHAM'S ECONOMIC WRITINGS, VOL. III

(SELECTIONS)

BY JEREMY BENTHAM

Jeremy Bentham, *Jeremy Bentham's Economic Writings*, Vol III, ed. W. Stark, pp. 442. Copyright © 1954 by Allen & Unwin.

TWO

Absolute equality, is that sort of equality which would have place, if, of the several benefits, as also of the several burthens, each man had exactly the same quantity as every other man: by *practical equality*, understand whatsoever approach to absolute equality can be made, when provision as effectual as can be made has been made for those three other particular ends of superior necessity. In regard to *security*, understand likewise, that, amongst the adversaries, against whose maleficent designs and enterprizes security requires to be provided,—are not only foreign enemies and internal *malejactors* commonly so called, but moreover those members of the community, whose power affords them such facilities for producing, with impunity, and on the largest scale, those evils, for the production of which, upon the smallest scale, those who are without power are punished by them with so little reserve. As to *absolute equality*, it would be no less plainly inconsistent with *practical equality* than with *subsistence, abundance*, and *security*. Suppose but a commencement made, by the power of a government of any kind, in the design of establishing it, the effect would be—that, instead of every one's having an equal share in the sum of the objects of general desire—and in particular in the means of *subsistence,* and the matter of *abundance,* no one would have any share in it at all. Before any division of it could be made, the whole would be destroyed: and, destroyed, along with it, those *by* whom, as well as those for the sake of whom, the division had been ordained.

SHOULD MARXISTS BE INTERESTED IN EXPLOITATION?

BY JOHN ROEMER

John Roemer, "Should Marxists Be Interested in Exploitation?" *Analytical Marxism*, pp. 30-65. Copyright © 1986 by Cambridge University Press. Reprinted with permission.

THREE

> To work at the bidding and for the profit of another ... is not ... a satisfactory state to human beings of educated intelligence, who have ceased to think themselves naturally inferior to those whom they serve.
>
> J. S. Mill, *Principles of Political Economy*

> The capitalist mode of production ... rests on the fact that the material conditions of production are in the hands of non-workers in the form of property in capital and land, while the masses are only owners of the personal conditions of production, of labour power. If the elements of production are so distributed, then the present-day distribution of the means of consumption results automatically.
>
> Karl Marx, *Selected Works*

I. MOTIVATIONS FOR EXPLOITATION THEORY

Marxian exploitation is defined as the unequal exchange of labor for goods: the exchange is unequal when the amount of labor embodied in the goods which the worker can purchase with his income (which usually consists only of wage income) is less than the amount of labor he expended to earn that income. Exploiters are agents who can command with their income more labor embodied in goods than the labor they performed; for exploited agents, the reverse is true. If the concept of embodied labor is defined so that the total labor performed by a population in a certain time period is equal to the labor embodied in the goods comprising the net national product (NNP), and if the NNP is parcelled out to the members of the population in some way, then there will be (essentially) two groups: the exploiters and the exploited, as defined above. (I say "essentially" because there may be some ambiguity; an agent may be able to purchase different bundles of goods, some bundles of which embody more labor than he worked, and other bundles of which embody less labor than he worked. This gives rise to a "gray area" of agents whom we might wish to consider neither exploited nor exploiting.[1]) Thus, exploitation theory views goods as vessels of labor, and calculates labor accounts for people by comparing the "live" labor they expend in production with the "dead" labor they get back in the vessels. Exploitation is an aspect of the pattern of redistribution of labor which occurs through the process of agents "exchanging" their current productive labor for social labor congealed in goods received. It may not always be easy or even possible to *define* the content of dead labor in the vessels, as when labor is heterogeneous or joint production of many goods from the same production process exists. There is a large literature on these questions, which shall not concern me here. For this article, I assume labor is homogeneous.

It is important to note that exploitation is not defined relationally. The statement "A exploits B" is not defined, but rather "A is an exploiter" and "B is exploited." Exploitation, as I conceive it, refers to the relationship between a person and society as a whole as measured by the transfer of the person's labor to the society, and the reverse transfer of society's labor to the person, as embodied in goods the person claims.

What are the uses of exploitation theory? Why is it considered the cornerstone of Marxian social science by many writers? More directly, what positive or normative conclusions might we draw about capitalism from observing that workers are exploited under capitalism? I can identify four main uses or justifications of exploitation theory:

1. the accumulation theory: exploitation of workers explains profits and accumulation under capitalism; it is the secret of capitalist expansion.
2. the domination theory: exploitation is intimately linked to the domination of workers by capitalists, especially at the point of production, and domination is an evil.
3. the alienation theory: exploitation is a measure of the degree to which people are alienated under capitalism. The root of alienation is the separation of one's labor from oneself. If one's labor is put into goods which are produced for exchange (not for use by oneself or one's community), that constitutes alienation. Exploitation occurs because some people alienate more labor than others. It is differential alienation.
4. the inequality theory: exploitation is a measure and consequence of the underlying inequality in the ownership of the means of production, an inequality which is unjustified.

---

[1] For a discussion of the gray area of agents, see John E. Roemer, *A General Theory of Exploitation and Class* (Cambridge, MA: Harvard University Press, 1982), chap. 4.

There is another theory which is, I think, a special case of (4), and so will be numbered:

4'. the expropriation theory: exploitation is a measure of expropriation, of one agent owning part of the product which should rightfully belong to another agent.

These four (or five) proposed explanations for our interest in exploitation theory are usually confounded. They should not be, however, because they constitute different claims. Adherents to exploitation theory tend to emphasize some of (1) through (4) when others of the list become subjected to embarrassments or counterexamples. I will argue that in the general case none of (1) through (4) can be sustained; there is, in general, no reason to be interested in exploitation theory, that is, in tallying the surplus value accounts of labor performed versus labor commanded in goods purchased. My arguments against (1) through (4) are, briefly, these: (1) all commodities are exploited under capitalism, not only labor power, and so the exploitation of labor does not explain profits; concerning (2), domination is an important issue under capitalism, but exploitation is irrelevant for its study; concerning (3), differential alienation can be measured using surplus value accounts, but I do not think such alienation is interesting unless it is a consequence of unequal ownership of the means of production. We are thus led to (4) which, I think, is the closest explanation for Marxists' interest in exploitation; but in the general case, I will show inequality in ownership of the means of production, even when ethically indefensible, is not properly measured by exploitation. In particular, it can happen in theory that those who own very little of the means of production are exploiters and those who own a lot are exploited. Hence exploitation (the transfer of surplus value) is not a proper reflection of underlying property relations.

There is an apparent similarity between this iconoclastic posture toward exploitation theory, and the attacks on the labor theory of value which have accelerated in the past decade.[2] In the final section, I evaluate this similarity, and claim it is quite shallow. While the labor theory of value almost always gives incorrect insights, exploitation theory in many cases coincides with a deeper ethical position—although on its own terms it does not provide a justification for that position. My verdict will be that exploitation theory is a domicile that we need no longer maintain: it has provided a home for raising a vigorous family who now must move on.

The reader should bear in mind that throughout the article "exploit" has a technical meaning, the unequal exchange of labor. When I claim that exploitation theory is without foundation,

---

2   See, for example, Joan Robinson, *An Essay on Marxian Economics* (New York: St. Martin's Press, 1966); Michio Morishima, *Marx's Economics* (Cambridge: Cambridge University Press, 1973); Ian Steedman, *Marx after Sraffa* (London: New Left Books, 1977); John E. Roemer, *Analytical Foundations of Marxian Economic Theory* (Cambridge: Cambridge University Press, 1981); Paul A. Samuelson, "Understanding the Marxian notion of exploitation: a summary of the so-called transformation problem between Marxian values and competitive prices," *Journal of Economic Literature* 9 (1971): 339–431; Jon Elster, *Making Sense of Marx* (Cambridge University Press, forthcoming).

I do not mean capitalism is just. I believe capitalism is unjust (or ethically *exploitative*) because of sharply unequal ownership of the means of production. What I show in Section 5 is that this inequality is not necessarily coextensive with the transfer of surplus value from workers to capitalists, and therefore it is inappropriate to ground an equality-based morality on the technical measure of exploitation. If I occasionally use "exploitation" in its ethical as opposed to technical sense, the word will be italicized as above.

II. DEFINITION OF TERMS: A SIMPLE MODEL

I have outlined above an identification problem with respect to the motivation for our interest in exploitation. In this section, this identification problem will be posed as starkly and schematically as possible, by exhibiting a simple model in which exploitation emerges simultaneously with accumulation, domination, differential alienation, and inequality in ownership of the means of production. This section, therefore, serves to define terms and to pose the problem more precisely.

Imagine an economy with 1,000 persons and two goods: corn and leisure. There are two technologies for producing corn, called the Farm and the Factory. The Farm is a labor-intensive technology in which no seed capital is required, but corn is produced from pure labor (perhaps by cultivating wild corn). The Factory technology produces corn with labor plus capital—the capital is seed corn. The technologies are given by:

Farm: 3 days labor → 1 corn output
Factory: 1 day labor + 1 seed corn → 2 corn output

Corn takes a week to grow (so the seed is tied up in the ground for that long). The total stock of seed corn in this society is 500 corn, and each agent owns 1½ corn. The agents have identical preferences which are these: each wants to consume 1 corn *net* output per week. After consuming his 1 corn, the agent will consume leisure. If he can get more than 1 corn for no more labor, he will be even happier: but preferences are lexicographic in that each wishes to minimize labor expended subject to earning enough to be able to consume 1 corn per week, and not to run down his stock of capital.

There is an obvious equilibrium in this economy. The typical agent works up his ½ corn in the Factory in ½ day, which will bring him 1 corn at the end of the week. Having fully employed his seed capital, he must produce another ½ corn somewhere., to replace his capital stock: this he does by working in the Farm technology for 1½ days. Thus he works 2 days and produces 1 corn net output. Every agent does this. Indeed, 2 days is the labor time socially necessary to produce a unit of corn, given that this society must produce 1,000 corn net each week. It is the labor embodied in a unit of corn. At this equilibrium there is no exploitation, since labor expended by each agent equals labor embodied in his share of the net output. Nor is there accumulation, for society has the same endowments at the beginning of next week; nor is there domination at the point of production, since no one works for anyone else; nor is there differential alienation of labor, since there is not even trade; and, of course, there is equality in initial assets.

Now change the initial distribution of assets, so that each of 5 agents owns 100 seed corn, and the other 995 own nothing but their labor power (or, to be consistent with our former terminology, nothing but their leisure). Preferences remain as before. What is the competitive equilibrium? One possibility is that each of the 995 assetless agents works 3 days on the Farm, and each of the 5 wealthy ones works 1 day in the Factory. But this is not an equilibrium, since there is a lot of excess capital sitting around which can be put to productive use. In particular, the wealthy ones can offer to hire the assetless to work in the Factory on their capital stock. Suppose the "capitalists" offer a corn wage of 1 corn for 2 days labor. Then each capitalist can employ 50 workers, each for 2 days, on his 100 seed corn capital. Each worker produces 4 corn in the Factory with 2 days labor. Thus each capitalist has corn revenues of 200 corn: of that, 100 corn replace the seed used up, 50 are paid in wages, and 50 remain as profits. Capital is now fully employed. But this may or may not be an equilibrium wage: only $5 \times 50 = 250$ workers have been employed, and perhaps the other 745 peasants would prefer to work in the Factory for a real wage of ½ corn per day instead of slaving on the Farm at a real wage of ⅓ corn per day. If so, the real wage in the Factory will be bid down until the assetless agents are indifferent between doing unalienated, undominated labor on the Farm, and alienated, dominated labor in the Factory. Let us say, for the sake of simplicity, this equilibrating real wage is one corn for 2½ days Factory labor. (In the absence of a preference for Farm life over Factory life, the real wage will equilibrate at 1 corn for 3 days labor, that is, at the peasant's labor opportunity cost of corn, since in this economy there is a scarcity of capital relative to the labor which it could efficiently employ.) Now we have *accumulation* (or at least much more production than before, which I assume is not all eaten by the capitalists), since each capitalist gets a profit of $200 - 100 - 40 = 60$ corn net, and each worker or peasant gets, as in the first economy, 1 corn net. Hence total net product is $995 + (5 \times 60) = 1,295$ corn, instead of 1,000 corn as before. We also have *domination* since some agents are employed by others, and by hypothesis, this gives rise to domination at the point of production. *Differential alienation* has emerged, since some agents (the workers) alienate a large part of their labor to the capitalists, while the capitalists and the peasants alienate no labor (although they work different amounts of time). *Exploitation* has emerged since the workers and peasants all expend more labor than is "embodied" in the corn they get, while the five capitalists work zero days and each gets 60 corn.

Hence, the four phenomena in question emerge simultaneously with the exploitation, in the passage from the "egalitarian" economy to the "capitalist" economy. With respect to expropriation, we might also say that it has emerged in the second economy.

III. THE ACCUMULATION THEORY

The unique positive (as opposed to normative) claim among (1) through (4) is the claim that our interest in exploitation is because surplus labor is the source of accumulation and profits. Explanation (1) uses "exploit" in the sense of "to turn a natural resource to economic account; to utilize," while theories (2), (3) and (4) use "exploit" in the sense of "to make use of meanly or unjustly for one's own advantage or profit."[3] A current in Marxism maintains that exploitation is not intended as a normative concept, but as an explanation of the *modus operandi* of capitalism; the production of profits in a system of voluntary exchange and labor transfers is the riddle which must be explained, and which Marx posed in *Capital*, Volume I. The discovery that exploitation of labor is the source of profits answers the riddle. (Even though all commodities exchange "at their values," a surplus systematically emerges at one point in the labor process. For the value which labor produces is greater than what labor power is worth, and hence what it is paid.) Indeed, the claim that exploitation theory should not be construed as normative theory has its source in Marx, as Allen Wood points out.[4]

The formal theorem supporting position (1) was first presented by Okishio and Morishima,[5] and the latter coined it the Fundamental Marxian Theorem (FMT). It demonstrates that in quite general economic models, exploitation of labor exists if and only if profits are positive. The FMT is robust; the error lies in the inference that its veracity implies that profits are *explained* by the exploitation of labor. For, as many writers have now observed, *every* commodity (not just labor power) is exploited under capitalism. Oil, for example, can be chosen to be the value numeraire, and embodied oil values of all commodities can be calculated. One can prove that profits are positive if and only if oil is exploited, in the sense that the amount of oil embodied in producing one unit of oil is less than one unit of oil—so oil gives up into production more than it requires back.[6] Thus the exploitation of labor is not the explanation for profits and accumulation any more than is the exploitation of oil or corn or iron. The motivation for the privileged choice of labor as the exploitation numeraire must lie elsewhere, as I have argued in other articles.[7] In trying to locate the specialness of labor which would justify its choice as the exploitation numeraire, one is

---

3 Definitions of exploitation are from *Webster's Dictionary* (1966).
4 Allen Wood, *Karl Marx* (London: Routledge & Kegan Paul, 1981), chap. 9.
5 Morishima, *Marx's Economics*. Many authors have since studied and generalized the Fundamental Marxian Theorem.
6 This Generalized Commodity Exploitation Theorem has been proved and/or observed by many authors, including Josep Ma. Vegara, *Economia Politica y Modelos Multisectoriales* (Madrid: Editorial Tecnos, 1979); Samuel Bowles and Herbert Gintis, "Structure and practice in the labor theory of value," *Review of Radical Political Economics* 12, no. 4 (Winter 1981): 1–26; Robert P. Wolff, "A Critique and Reinterpretation of Marx's Labor Theory of Value," *Philosophy & Public Affairs* 10, no. 2 (Spring 1981): 89–120; Roemer, *General Theory*, Appendix 6.1; Paul A. Samuelson, "The Normative and Positivistic Inferiority of Marx's Values Paradigm," *Southern Economic Journal* 49, no. 1 (1982): 11–18.
7 See J. E. Roemer, "R. P. Wolff's Reinterpretation of Marx's Labor Theory of Value: Comment," *Philosophy & Public Affairs* 12, no. 1 (Winter 1983): 70–83; J. E. Roemer, "Why Labor Classes?" (U.C. Davis Working Paper, 1982).

inexorably led into arguments that labor is the unique commodity which can be "dominated" or "alienated"—the terrain of argument shifts to a defense of theories like (2) and (3). The dialogue goes something like this, where "Marxist" is defending theory (1):

Marxist: The exploitation of labor accounts for the existence of profits under capitalism. That's why we are interested in exploitation theory, not as normative theory.

Antagonist: But oil is exploited too under capitalism, and its exploitation is, as well, necessary and sufficient for profits. So labor's exploitation does not *explain* profits.

Marxist: No, you are not entitled to say oil is exploited, because oil is not dominated, oil is not alienated from its possessor in any interesting sense during production, one's oil is not a joint product with one's self, there are no problems in extracting the oil from the "oil power." Only labor has these properties and hence only labor is exploited.

Antagonist: Initially you claimed your interest in exploitation theory was as a positive theory only. But you rule out describing oil as exploited for reasons that can only imply exploitation has normative content. For surely the domination and alienation of labor and the attachment of labor to the self are germane not for evaluating whether labor is or is not used in the sense of "turning a natural resource to economic account," but only for deciding whether labor is "made use of meanly or unjustly for [one's own] advantage or profit." You claim to be interested in labor's exploitation only because labor is exploited in the first sense, but rule out calling other commodities exploited because they are not *exploited* in the second sense. I take it, then, your *true* justification for describing labor as exploited must lie in one of the normative theories of exploitation.

I conclude position (1) cannot be supported as the reason for our interest in exploitation theory.[8] Despite his avowed lack of interest in a normative justification of exploitation theory, the Marxist in the dialogue can only rescue exploitation theory from the jaws of the Generalized Commodity Exploitation Theorem by appealing to a special claim labor has on wearing the exploitation mantle,

---

8 R. P. Wolff, "A Critique and Reinterpretation," while recognizing that the exploitation of labor cannot explain profits, offers a reason other than domination and alienation to be interested in exploitation; as I have argued against his proposal elsewhere (Roemer, "R. P. Wolff's Reinterpretation of Marx's Labor Theory of Value"), I will not repeat that discussion.

a claim that seems only to be defensible on grounds of the unfairness or unjustness or nastiness of the conditions of labor's utilization. As G. A. Cohen writes, "... Marxists do not often talk about justice, and when they do they tend to deny its relevance, or they say that the idea of justice is an illusion. But I think justice occupies a central place in revolutionary Marxist belief. Its presence is betrayed by particular judgments Marxists make, and by the strength of feeling with which they make them."[9] And I would add, it is only by appealing to conceptions of justice that exploitation theory can be defended as interesting.

IV. THE DOMINATION THEORY

For the remainder of this article, my concern will be to investigate the possibility of defending an interest in exploitation theory for the light it sheds on the three issues of domination, differential alienation, and inequality in ownership of the means of production. My interest in these three issues is normative. If, for example, exploitation can be shown to imply domination of workers by capitalists, and if we argue independently that domination is unjust, then exploitation theory provides at least a partial theory of the injustice of capitalism. (Only a partial theory, since other practices besides domination might be unjust, which exploitation theory would not diagnose.) Identifying the main evil of capitalism as domination, and even extraeconomic domination, is a theme of some contemporary Marxist work.[10] It is not my purpose to evaluate this claim (with which I disagree), but rather to postulate an ethical interest in domination, and ask whether that justifies an interest in exploitation theory.

It is necessary to distinguish two types of domination by capitalists over workers, domination in the maintenance and enforcement of private property in the means of production, and domination at the point of production (the hierarchical and autocratic structure of work). The line between the two cannot be sharply drawn, but let us superscript the two types domination^1 and domination^2, respectively. I will argue that each of domination^1 and domination^2 implies exploitation, but not conversely. Hence if our interest is in domination, there is no reason to invoke exploitation theory, for the direction of entailment runs the wrong way. Domination may be a bad thing, but there is no reason to run the circuitous route of exploitation theory to make the point. In certain situations, exploitation requires domination^1, but since we cannot know these cases by analyzing the exploitation accounts alone, there is no reason to invoke exploitation if, indeed,

---

9 G. A. Cohen, "Freedom, Justice and Capitalism," *New Left Review*, no. 125 (1981). For an opposite point of view, see Wood, *Karl Marx*.
10 Ellen Meiksins Wood, "The separation of the economic and political in capitalism," *New Left Review*, no. 127 (May–June 1981); Bowles and Gintis, "Structure and Practice"; Erik Olin Wright, "The Status of the Political in the Concept of Class Structure," *Politics and Society* 11, no. 3 (1982): 321–42.

our interest in exploitation is only as a barometer of domination¹. Furthermore, our interest in domination¹ is essentially an interest in the inequality of ownership of the means of production, for the purpose of domination¹ is to enforce that ownership pattern. I maintain if it is domination¹ one claims an interest in, it is really inequality (however defined) in the ownership of the means of production which is the issue. Thus, an ethical interest in domination¹ shifts the discussion to the validity of position (4), while an interest in domination² has as its source the moral sentiments reflected in the epigraph from J. S. Mill, in the analogy implied by the term wage slavery.

Domination¹ enforces property relations in two ways. The obvious way is through police power protecting assets, preventing their expropriation by those not owning them. Clearly, since differential ownership of the means of production gives rise to exploitation, this form of domination implies exploitation. The second way domination¹ enters into property relations is to give property its value in the absence of perfect competition. A property right is not a physical asset, it is the right to appropriate the income stream flowing from a certain physical asset. (As C. B. Mac-Pherson points out, it is peculiarly under capitalism that physical assets are confused with the property rights that are related to them.[11]) In the absence of perfect competition, the value of property is not defined by the market. Under perfect competition, all agents are price (and wage) takers, no one has power to bargain or to set the terms of trade. Prices in equilibrium clear markets. Assuming the equilibrium is unique (a heroic assumption), property values are then well-defined. But in the absence of perfect competition, there is room for bargaining, and the value of one's property rights may well be determined by extraeconomic domination.[12] (It is more accurate to say values are not defined by the traditional economic data, and at present there is no accepted theory of bargaining under imperfect competition which can determine them.) This is typically the case where markets for particular assets or commodities are thin. The state or landlord which (or who) controls the irrigation canal (an indivisible commodity, with a very thin market) can exact a monopolistic price for its use, giving rise to high peasant exploitation. Due to thin credit markets in rural areas of the underdeveloped countries, local landlords are able to charge usurious interest rates to peasants for consumption loans, increasing the rate of exploitation. To the extent that one thinks incomes from different types of labor under capitalism are politically determined, in order to assert control over the work force,[13] rather than as a reflection of relative scarcities,

---

11 C. B. MacPherson, *Property: Mainstream and Critical Positions* (Toronto: University of Toronto Press, 1978), chap. 1.
12 Samuel Bowles and Herbert Gintis, "The Power of Capital: On the Inadequacy of the Conception of the Capitalist Economy as 'Private,'" *Philosophical Forum* 14, nos. 3–4 (1983) claim that even in perfect competition, if there are multiple equilibria, then property values are not well-defined and there is room for domination¹ in determining which set of equilibrium prices will prevail. This is a dubious assertion. If indeed no agent has economic power, in the sense perfect competition postulates, then which of several multiple equilibria will rule is not due to domination¹ but is simply an unanswerable question, given the information in the model.
13 See Richard Edwards, *Contested Terrain: The Transformation of the Workplace in America* (New York: Basic Books, 1979).

then domination¹ plays a role in determining exploitation. Domination¹ may determine what certificates people receive, through channeling them into different educational careers, and those certificates determine the value of the person's labor services.[14] In these cases, the peculiarity of domination¹, what contrasts it with feudal domination, is its effect on setting the value of services or assets in the *market* (and thereby influencing the degree of exploitation). Although the power relation inherent in domination¹ is finally realized through markets, contrasted with feudalism, it is similar to feudal exploitation, since one agent has *power* over another which he would not have in a fully developed, perfectly competitive market economy. Thus this exercise of domination¹ is not the essence of capitalism, if capitalism is essentially a competitive system. Certainly Marx's proclaimed task was to explain capitalism in its purest form: where the values of all commodities are explained by "fair trades," that is, values commanded on perfectly competitive markets.

In certain situations, conversely, exploitation implies domination¹; I mean the trivial observation that exploitation is the consequence of differential ownership of the means of production which, in many cases, the exploited would alter were it not for police power preventing them from doing so. (Hence, if we observe exploitation, there must be domination¹.) It has been maintained, however, that exploitation need not imply domination¹; Adam Przeworski argues that in some Western European countries workers have the power to expropriate capitalists, and hence they are not dominated¹, but they do not, because it is not in their perceived interests to do so.[15] Moreover, in Sections 4 and 5 below I show that exploitation can exist without differential ownership of the means of production; therefore, presumably exploitation can exist even though all agents accept as just the property rights, and so domination¹ (police power to protect property) need not attain. In summary, my claims concerning domination¹ are these: (a) with respect to the exercise of power under conditions of imperfect competition, domination¹ exists and is perhaps important in capitalism, and more so in less developed capitalism, but it is characteristically noncapitalist, that is, being due to imperfect competition and thin markets; (b) it implies exploitation, but that provides no reason to be interested in exploitation theory, if our concern is really with domination¹; (c) in some cases, perhaps the archetypical case, exploitation implies domination¹ in the sense of police power protecting property, but in that case it is not the domination that concerns us but the unjust inequality in the distribution of the means of production. If (c) is our reason for justifying an interest in exploitation theory, we are invoking position (4) and not position (2), since domination¹ in this case is only the means to maintain the unequal distribution of assets which is the basis for our condemnation of capitalism.

The more usual conception of domination is the second one; domination² does not involve the protection or creation of value in capitalist property, but rather the hierarchical, nondemocratic

---

14   Samuel Bowles and Herbert Gintis, *Schooling in Capitalist America* (New York: Basic Books, 1976).
15   Adam Przeworski, "Material Interests, Class Compromise and the Transition to Socialism," *Politics and Society* 10, no. 2 (1980).

relations in capitalist workplaces. Of course, this hierarchy presumably creates (additional) profits, and therefore leads to an increased valuation of capitalist property, and hence is similar to the role of domination[1]; but in discussing domination[2] I am specifically concerned with the domination of the worker's self, the relation of subordination he enters into with the capitalist when he enters the workplace. While our moral opposition to domination[1] shares its foundation with our moral opposition to feudalism, our opposition to domination[2] shares its foundation with our opposition to slavery. (The analogy is inexact, since many feudal practices involved domination[2] over the selves of serfs; for the sake of the analogy, I envisage "pure feudalism" as a system where feudal dues are paid because of extraeconomic coercion, but the serf never sees or interacts personally with the lord.)

Although domination[2] can create the conditions for profitability and therefore exploitation of labor, the converse is in general not the case. Exploitation does not imply the existence of domination[2]. I showed in my book that the class and exploitation relations of a capitalist economy using labor markets can be precisely replicated with a capitalist economy using credit markets,[16] where domination[2] does not exist. In Labor Market Capitalism, agents optimize, given their endowments of property, and end up choosing either to sell labor power, to hire labor power, or to produce for the market using their own labor power on their own account. Agents segregate themselves into five classes, based on the particular ways they relate to the labor market. The Class Exploitation Correspondence Principle demonstrates that everyone who optimizes by selling labor power is exploited, and everyone who optimizes by hiring labor is an exploiter. It was assumed in that analysis that agents make the decision to sell labor entirely on economic grounds; they do not calculate as part of their objective the disutility associated with being dominated[2], with working under a boss. In Credit Market Capitalism, there is no labor market, but a market for lending capital at an interest rate. At the equilibrium, some agents will lend capital, some will borrow capital, some will use their own capital for production. Again, agents segregate themselves into five classes defined by the particular ways they relate to the credit market. Again, the Class Exploitation Correspondence Principle holds: any agent who optimizes by borrowing capital will turn out to be exploited. Moreover, the Isomorphism Theorem states that these two hypothetical capitalisms are identical insofar as class and exploitation properties are concerned. An agent who, under Labor Market Capitalism, was a member of a labor-selling class, and was therefore exploited, will be a member of a capital-borrowing class in Credit Market Capitalism, and will be exploited. This result replays the Wicksell-Samuelson theme that it is irrelevant, for the distribution of income, whether capital hires labor or labor hires capital; the mild sin of omission of these writers was not to point out that propertyless agents are exploited in either case, whether they be

---

[16] For a detailed presentation of this material, see Roemer, *General Theory*, pts. 1 and 2. For a summary, see J. Roemer, "New Directions in the Marxian Theory of Exploitation and Class," *Politics and Society* 11, no. 3 (1982): 253–88.

the hirers or sellers of the factor. In Labor Market Capitalism there is domination[2], but in Credit Market Capitalism, there is not.[17]

Moreover, an even sharper example may be constructed of an economy possessing no labor or credit market, but only markets for produced commodities which are traded among individual producers. In such an economy exploitation will result at equilibrium, in general, if there is initial inequality in the ownership of means of production. But in this exchange and production economy, there are no relations of domination[2] of any kind; the exploitation can be accomplished through "invisible trade." It is possible to argue that there is exploitation without class in this economy, since all producers enjoy the same relation to the means of production: they work only on their own.[18] Indeed, this example may be taken as the archetype of exploitation, or unequal exchange, between countries where neither labor nor capital flows across borders. Differential initial endowments of countries will give rise to exploitation in trade, even when no relations of domination[2] through international labor migration or capital lending take place.[19]

The previous paragraphs claim to demonstrate that the existence of exploitation does not imply the existence of domination[2], and hence our putative interest in exploitation theory cannot be justified on grounds of a more basic interest in domination[2]. Here I follow Marx, in modeling capitalism as a system where there are no market frictions, but where goods exchange competitively at their market-determined prices. In particular, it seems appropriate, for this thought experiment, to assume all contracts are costlessly enforceable and can be perfectly delineated. For Marx wished to show the economic viability of capitalism in the absence of cheating: and that means contracts are well-defined and observed by all. Now the principal reason domination[2] exists is that the labor contract is not costlessly enforceable, nor can it be perfectly delineated. This point is usually put more graphically when Marxists speak of the problems of extracting the labor from the labor power. Indeed, the contemporary labor process literature addresses the methods capitalism (and perhaps socialism) has developed to solve this problem.[20] But for our thought experiment, we are entitled to assume the delivery of *labor* (not simply labor power) for the wage is as simple and enforceable a transaction as the delivery of an apple for a dime. In such a world, exploitation continues to exist, but domination[2] does not. And I claim Marxists would be almost as critical of such a perfect capitalism as they are of existing capitalism, replete as the real thing is with

---

17 I am speaking of a pure form of Credit Market Capitalism; in actual credit markets, lenders often supervise debtors if sufficient collateral is not available, or if there would be problems in enforcing collection of collateral.

18 For the details of this economy see *General Theory*, chap. 1; for a simple example, see J. E. Roemer, "Are Socialist Ethics Consistent with Efficiency?" *Philosophical Forum* 14, nos. 3–4 (1983): 369–88.

19 See J. E. Roemer, "Unequal Exchange, Labor Migration and International Capital Flows: A Theoretical Synthesis," in *Marxism, the Soviet Economy and Central Planning: Essays in Honor of Alexander Erlich*, ed. Padma Desai (Cambridge, MA: MIT Press, 1983).

20 For example, see Harry Braverman, *Labor and Monopoly Capital* (New York: Monthly Review Press, 1974) and Richard Edwards, *Contested Terrain*.

domination² due to the contract enforcement problem. Indeed, Marxists consider sharecroppers and borrowers to be *exploited* (unjustly so, that is), even when domination² is absent from those contracts. The Isomorphism Theorem I quoted was an attempt to develop this point formally, that in a world absenting deleterious domination² effects, the exploitation observed in labor markets would be indistinguishable from that observed in credit or sharecropping arrangements.[21]

A criticism of the Isomorphism Theorem can be made as follows. If one wishes to study the relationship between domination² and exploitation, then the model of the Class Exploitation Correspondence Theorem and the Isomorphism Theorem is inappropriate, because it is there assumed that domination² is not an issue to the people involved. In reply to this point, I have worked out a revised model (which is available in detail from the author) where domination² effects exist. These are captured as follows: each agent has an initial endowment of means of production, which takes on a value as finance capital at given prices. He seeks to maximize a utility function of income and work performed. It matters to him whether the work is performed in his own shop, or under a boss. Thus, the utility function has three arguments: income, labor performed on one's own account, and wage labor performed for others. Subject to his capital constraint, determined by initial asset holdings and prices, each agent maximizes utility. The domination² postulate is that every agent would rather work on his own account than for a boss, and this is reflected in the utility function. At equilibrium, agents sort themselves into five classes:

Class 1: those who only hire others
Class 2: those who hire others and work on their own account
Class 3: those who only work on their own account
Class 4: those who work on their own account and sell wage labor
Class 5: those who only sell wage labor.

I say an agent is *dominated* if he maximizes utility subject to constraint by placing himself in classes 4 or 5, and he is *dominating* if he optimizes by being in classes 1 or 2. The theorem, which can be called the Exploitation-Domination Correspondence, states that any dominated agent is exploited and any dominating agent is an exploiter. The converse, however, does not hold. In particular, agents in class position 3 will often be e. ther exploited or exploiting, but they are neither dominated nor dominating.

It is therefore difficult to justify an interest in exploitation if our real concern is domination², for two reasons. First, domination² is directly observable (simply look at who hires whom) and exploitation is not. Hence, calculating whether an agent is exploited (a difficult calculation,

---

[21] Further discussion of some of these issues can be found in J. E. Roemer, "Reply," *Politics and Society* 11, no. 3 (1982): 375–94.

necessitating all sorts of technological information to compute socially necessary labor times) would be a strangely circuitous route to concluding he is dominated[2]. Secondly, it is not true that an exploited agent is necessarily dominated or that an exploiter is necessarily dominating; the Exploitation-Domination Correspondence states the converse. Exploited (exploiting) agents who are not dominated (dominating) would have a confused ethical status if our judgment about them is made on the basis of exploitation, but our interest in exploitation is as a proxy for domination. The hardworking shopkeeper or sharecropper would have our ethical sympathy on grounds of exploitation but not domination[2]. This does not help us provide independent reason for an interest in exploitation theory, of course, which is the task at hand. Thus exploitation is a poor statistic for domination[2] on several counts.

My conclusions concerning domination[2] are: (a) our interest in exploitation theory cannot be justified on grounds that it is indicative of or a proxy for domination[2], either logically, or on pragmatic grounds; (b) although domination[2] is prevalent in existing capitalism, it is arguably a phenomenon of second order in a *Marxist* condemnation of capitalism, being associated with the imperfections in writing and enforcing contracts, while Marxist arguments should apply to a capitalism with frictionless contracts. In addition, although not argued here (as my concern is not with the evils of domination[2] but with the evils of exploitation), I think the analogy between domination[2] and slavery is ill-founded. It is arguable that the life of the small independent producer is not so marvelous compared to that of the factory worker, that the transition from poor peasant to urban proletarian is one made willingly, even gladly, and with reasonably good information, where the erstwhile independent producer is knowledgeable about the trade-offs. I say arguable, not obvious: but it is more than arguable that no population ever voluntarily committed itself to slavery willingly and gladly.

V. THE ALIENATION THEORY

To discuss properly a possible justification of an interest in exploitation theory on grounds that it is indicative of different degrees of alienation, we must separate alienation from, on the one hand, domination and on the other hand differential ownership of the means of production, as those issues are discussed separately under (2) and (4). An interest in differential alienation must be defended *per se*, even in the absence of domination and differential ownership of the means of production. Perhaps the most graphic vision of exploitation is as the extraction of surplus labor from the worker: the extraction, that is, of more labor from him than he receives back as social labor in what he consumes or can purchase with his wages. His labor is alienated from him not because he performs it for another (under conditions of domination[2]) but because it is labor performed to produce goods for exchange, not for use. More precisely, the goods produced are traded to an anonymous final recipient on a market, and thus labor becomes alienated in a way it would not have been were there a social division of labor but the final disposition of goods was in one's "community." (See B. Traven's marvelous story "Assembly Line" for a discussion of alienation.[22]) Now if everyone started off with the same endowment of means of production and had the same skills and preferences, but all agents produced goods for a market, there would be alienation of labor in this sense, but not differential alienation, since it can be shown everyone would receive back as much social labor in goods as he alienated in production for the market. Exploitation can be said to exist in a market economy when some people alienate more labor than they receive from others, and some alienate less labor than they receive back. Why might alienation be a bad thing? Perhaps because one's time is the only really valuable asset one has, and production for the market is considered to be a waste of time. Perhaps because productive labor for oneself or one's community is what constitutes the good life, but the use of labor to earn revenues solely to survive, not to produce for others directly, is a prostitution of a deep aspect of the self. Thus alienation might be bad, and differential alienation might be unjust or *exploitative*. (There are certainly other forms of alienation in Marx, but this kind of differential alienation appears to be the only kind for which exploitation as the unequal exchange of labor is an indicator.)

Any ethical condemnation of differential alienation cannot be a welfarist one, in the sense of Amartya Sen,[23] based only on the preferences of individuals. For I will outline a situation where agents with different preferences start with equal endowments of resources and voluntarily enter into relations of differential alienation (i.e., exploitation) as the way to maximize their utilities. Consider two agents, Adam and Karl, who each start off with the same amount of corn, which is the only good in the economy and can be used both as capital (seed corn) and as the consumption good. We have the same technological possibilities as in the model of Section 2.

---

22 B. Traven, *The Night Visitor and Other Stories* (New York: Hill and Wang, 1973). In the story "Assembly Line," a Mexican Indian has been offered a huge sum of money, more than he has ever dreamed of, to mass-produce little baskets for a New York department store, which he has formerly made only in small quantities for the local market. The New York buyer is astonished that the Indian is not interested in the proposal. The Indian explains: "Yes, I know that jefecito, my little chief," the Indian answered, entirely unconcerned. "It must be the same price because I cannot make any other one. Besides, señor, there's still another thing which perhaps you don't know. You see, my good lordy and caballero, I've to make these canastitas my own way and with my song in them and with bits of my soul woven into them. If I were to make them in great numbers there would no longer be my soul in each, or my songs. Each would look like the other with no difference whatever and such a thing would slowly eat my heart. Each has to be another song which I hear in the morning when the sun rises and when the birds begin to chirp and the butterflies come and sit down on my baskets so that I may see a new beauty, because, you see, the butterflies like my baskets and the pretty colors in them, that's why they come and sit down, and I can make my canastitas after them. And now, señor jefecito, if you will kindly excuse me, I have wasted much time already, although it was a pleasure and a great honor to hear the talk of such a distinguished caballero like you. But I'm afraid I've to attend to my work now, for day after tomorrow is market day in town and I got to take my baskets there."
23 See, for a definition of welfarism, Amartya Sen, "Utilitarianism and Welfarism," *Journal of Philosophy* 76, no. 9 (1979): 463–89.

Farm: 3 days labor produces 1 bushel corn
Factory: 1 day labor plus 1 bushel seed corn produces 2 bushels corn

Adam and Karl each start with ½ bushel of corn, and each will live and must consume for many weeks. (Recall, a week is the time period required in each case to bring corn to fruition, although the amount of labor expended during the week differs in the two processes.) Karl is highly averse to performing work in the present: he desires only to consume 1 bushel of corn per week, subject to the requirement that he not run down his seed stock. In the first week, he therefore works ½ day in the Factory (fully utilizing his seed corn) and 1½ days on the Farm, producing a total of 1½ bushels, one of which he consumes at harvest time, leaving him with ½ bushel to start with in week 2. Adam accumulates; he works ½ day in the Factory, utilizing his seed, and 4½ days on the Farm, producing 2½ bushels gross. After consuming 1 bushel, he has 1½ bushels left to start week 2. In week 2, Karl works up his own seed stock in ½ day in the Factory producing 1 bushel; then, instead of going to the Farm, Karl borrows or rents Adam's 1½ bushels of seed and works it up in the Factory. This takes Karl precisely 1½ days, and he produces 3 bushels gross in the factory. Of the 3 bushels he keeps ½ bushel, and returns 2½ bushels to Adam (Adam's principal of 1½ bushels plus interest of 1 bushel). Indeed, Karl is quite content with this arrangement, for he has worked for a total of 2 days and received 1½ bushels, just as in week 1, when he had to use the inferior Farm technology. Adam, on the other hand, receives a profit of 1 bushel from Karl's labor, which he consumes, and is left again to begin week 3 with 1½ bushels. He has not worked at all in week 2. This arrangement can continue forever, with Karl working 2 days each week and consuming 1 bushel, and Adam working 5 days during the first week, and zero days thereafter. Clearly there is exploitation in the sense of differential alienation in this story, in all weeks after the first, but its genesis is in the differential preferences Karl and Adam have for the consumption of corn and leisure over their lives. Thus exploitation cannot be blamed, in this story, on differential initial ownership of the means of production, nor can the situation be condemned on Paretian grounds, as no other arrangement would suit Karl and Adam more. They chose this path of consumption/leisure streams. Indeed during any week Karl could decide to work on the Farm and accumulate more seed corn, thus enabling him to cut his working hours in future weeks. (I am assuming he is *able* to do so; if he is not, then Karl is handicapped, and the ethical verdict is certainly more complicated.) But he does not.

Actually the above example does not quite rigorously make the point that differential alienation cannot be condemned on Paretian grounds: because if alienation is to be so condemned, then the agents themselves should distinguish between the performance of alienated and nonalienated labor in their utility functions. That is, each agent should prefer to perform nonalienated labor to alienated labor. If we now modify the story to include such a preference, then the above example fails, since Karl could have achieved the same outcome of 2 days labor and 1 bushel corn, each week, by continuing his autarchic program of working partly in the factory on his *own* seed corn, and then moving to the farm and working for his *own* consumption. Karl would perform no alienated labor (producing goods only for himself) and would hence be better off. Were this to occur, then Adam would have to work some in the Factory each period, since Karl refused to borrow seed capital from him. But this failure of the example can easily be fixed: simply note that Adam could work a little longer in the first week, producing a little more seed capital, and then in future weeks he could lend his seed to Karl at a sufficiently low interest rate that Karl would be compensated for his distaste in performing alienated labor by the savings in overall labor he achieves by borrowing from Adam. Thus both Adam and Karl can strictly benefit from cooperation, even if each has a distaste for performing alienated labor, so long as there is a trade-off between that distaste and the taste for leisure. Hence the claim is true: that even if alienation matters to people, an outcome of differential alienation cannot be condemned on Paretian or welfarist grounds, nor on grounds of inequality in the distribution of assets, since an example has been constructed where agents who start off with identical endowments choose to enter into relations of differential alienation. And if alienation, as I have defined it, seems unrealistic in a society of two people, then replicate the economy one millionfold, so there are a million each of Karls and Adams. Moreover, we can introduce many goods into the economy so that there is a real social division of labor, and some Adams make car fenders all day long and other Adams make pinheads all day long. But the same result can be constructed: starting from the same endowments, agents with different preferences for the various goods, leisure, and nonalienated labor, may well choose to enter into relations of differential alienation.

So if we are to conclude that differential alienation is *exploitative*, in the sense of ethically condemnable, that verdict cannot be arrived at on Paretian grounds. Indeed, the above example enables us to speak of "the impossibility of being a differential-alienation-condemning Paretian" in exactly the sense of "the impossibility of being a Paretian liberal."[24] For, as the last several paragraphs demonstrate, to avoid alienation Karl must produce only for himself (using both the Farm and the Factory), which will require Adam to work each week for himself. But in the example this is not a Pareto optimal allocation of labor. Only by engaging in differentially alienated labor can Karl and Adam take full advantage of the efficient Factory technology. Thus even the mild welfarist requirement of Pareto efficiency comes into conflict with exploitation-as-differential-alienation. There may still be grounds for calling such differential alienation *exploitative*, but it appears such grounds must be based on *rights*, not welfare outcomes as the agents see them.

We are led to ask, then, whether a person has a *right* not to perform more alienated labor than another person. We might be able to argue that one has a right not to *be forced* to perform more

---

24 On the impossibility of being a Paretian liberal, see for instance, Amartya Sen, *Collective Choice and Social Welfare* (New York: North Holland, 1979), chap. 6.

alienated labor than another: but that will lead straight into a discussion of differential ownership of the means of production, which is not the issue here.[25] For in our story Karl chooses to perform more alienated labor than Adam from a position of equality of resources and opportunity. Nobody forces him, unless we slide further down the slippery slope of defining the "resources" available to the person and argue that Karl was forced because he had no choice of the personal characteristics that gave rise to his *carpe diem* preferences. I cannot see a compelling argument for declaiming such a right, in part because I cannot see a compelling argument against the performance of alienated labor, let alone differential alienation. I think moral intuitions on this matter must take their cue from history. It is far from clear that people, in historical reality, have had an aversion to performing alienated labor. Indeed, many (including Marxists) argue that production for the market has been a liberating process for many populations, a process which they enter into willingly. (Recall, we are not concerned here with domination, of choosing to work for others, but only with alienation, of producing for a market.)

I think the argument for postulating that a person has a right not to perform more alienated labor than another person is extremely weak. Hence I cannot defend an interest in exploitation as a proxy for an interest in differentially alienated labor. The problem is that there is not necessarily anything condemnable with differentially alienated labor if it arises from differential preferences which we accept as well-formed and not like handicaps. To consider "myopic" preferences to be handicaps, we would have to argue that there is an upper bound on correct rates of time discount, and people who discount time more highly are handicapped. While in some instances the case for such a handicap can be made (typically, when a high rate of time discount is a consequence of having been severely deprived of assets in the past), in the general instance, it cannot be. The last parenthetical aside cues the most important situation where we might view differential alienation, arrived at from differential preferences, as exploitative: when those preferences are in fact learned as a consequence of differential ownership of the means of production in the past. Suppose the rich learn to save, and the poor do not; having learned such rates of time preference from their past environments, formerly rich Adam may end up accumulating and exploiting formerly poor Karl, even when the new state starts them off with clean slates by redistributing the initial endowment to one of equality between them. But in this case our justification for thinking of differential alienation as exploitative is due to the rich background of Adam and the poor one of Karl; we are reduced to an argument for an interest in exploitation as an indicator of inequality in the ownership of assets, to which I soon turn.

The possibility remains that even though nondifferentially-alienated outcomes cannot be defended on Paretian grounds, nor on grounds of rights, perhaps they can be defended for

---

25 For a discussion of why proletarians can be thought of as forced to alienate their labor, even in a world of voluntary wage contracts, see G. A. Cohen, "The Structure of Proletarian Unfreedom," *Philosophy & Public Affairs* 12, no. 1 (Winter 1983): 3–33.

perfectionist reasons. I will not attempt here to defend my position against a perfectionist attack, except to say that my defense would amplify on the point of the two previous paragraphs. It seems that differential alienation of labor, from an initial position of equal opportunity and fair division of assets, can vastly increase the welfare and life quality of people, and so a perfectionist defense of nonalienation seems remote.

VI. DIFFERENTIAL OWNERSHIP OF PRODUCTIVE ASSETS

The fourth reason to be interested in exploitation is as an index of the inequality in ownership of productive assets. This approach is represented, for example, in the epigraph from Marx. The Marxist position that socialist revolution entails redistribution or nationalization of the means of production to eliminate exploitation traces to this conception of exploitation. (In contrast, the emphasis of exploitation as domination[2] gives rise to industrial democracy as the key aspect of socialist transformation.) In my recent book and in other articles I have claimed that this is the most compelling reason to be interested in exploitation, by showing in a series of models that the existence of exploitation is equivalent to inequality in distribution of initial assets, and that the rich exploit the poor. Hence exploitation theory can be justified if we accept a presumption that initial inequality in the wealth of agents is unjust, for exploitation (in these models) is essentially equivalent to initial inequality of assets. Nevertheless this may appear to weaken the argument for being interested in exploitation (defined as I have done throughout this article), for it is probably easier to observe inequality in ownership of assets than it is to calculate exploitation accounts. Surprisingly, however, if our ethical interest is really in initial inequality of ownership of assets, the importance of Marxian *class* theory is strengthened. For in the models I investigated, class membership is closely related to wealth: the "higher" one's class position, the wealthier one is in productive assets. In particular, any agent who optimizes by hiring others is wealthy and is an exploiter, and any agent who optimizes by selling labor power is relatively poor and is exploited. Now class relations are still easier to observe than wealth, and so the Class-Wealth Correspondence enables us to conclude a great deal about the initial distribution of productive assets by observing how people relate to the hiring and selling of labor power. Class position provides a convenient proxy for the fundamental inequality in which, I claim, we are interested; but exploitation drops out as an unnecessary detour.

Still, according to this description of the results, exploitation may be thought of as an *innocuous* appendix to our true ethical concerns: innocuous because although unnecessary, surplus value accounts correspond to underlying inequality in ownership of assets in the proper way. I now go further and claim that in the general case, exploitation theory leads to results which may conflict directly with the inequality-of-productive-assets theory. And therefore, finding no other reasons to be interested in exploitation accounts, I must say exploitation theory, in the general case, is misconceived. It does not provide a proper model or account of Marxian moral sentiments; the proper Marxian claim, I think, is for equality in the distribution of productive assets, not for the elimination of exploitation.

The "general case" in which exploitation accounts and inequality accounts diverge occurs when general preferences for agents are admitted. In particular, if preferences for income versus leisure differ across agents, the divergence can occur. Indeed, the two theories can diverge even for cases when preferences are identical for all agents as I will show. In my book, I assumed preferences of all agents were the same, and of certain special forms: either all agents wanted to accumulate as much as possible, or they wanted just to subsist, two preference profiles that appear to be polar opposites. Indeed, there may be a strong case that the assumption of one of these profiles of preferences is not a bad one, historically, in which case exploitation theory might correspond empirically to Marxian ethical conceptions. But I am concerned here with the logical foundations of exploitation theory, and for that purpose general and abstract formulations with respect to admissable preference profiles are essential.

Before proceeding, it is important to correct a possible misimpression from an earlier article.[26] I argued there that a pure inequality-of-assets definition was better than the Marxian surplus value definition for characterizing exploitation; that claim is weaker than the claim here, for in that article I took the Marxian surplus value definition to mean "the extraction of surplus labor from one agent by another in a production relation." In the present paper, I am taking exploitation to be defined by "unequal exchange of labor," whether or not there is a production relation between the agents in which one "extracts" the labor of another. In the previous article, I did not argue against the "unequal exchange of labor" conception of exploitation, except to say that the inequality-of-property definition was a cleaner but equivalent characterization of the same phenomenon. I now claim that "unequal exchange of labor" is not characterized by the inequality of productive assets when we admit general preferences structures.

I shall show that if the preferences of agents do not satisfy a certain condition, then it can happen that the asset-rich are exploited by the asset-poor: the flow of surplus value goes the "wrong way." This can occur even when all agents have identical preference maps for income and leisure—but what is critical is that the agents' preference for leisure must change rather substantially, and in a particular way, as their wealth changes. Once this example is demonstrated, one can no longer claim that exploitation is a significant index of inequality of initial assets which measures the flow from the asset-poor to the asset-rich.

---

26 J. Roemer, "Property Relations vs. Surplus Value in Marxian Exploitation," *Philosophy & Public Affairs* 11, no. 4 (Fall 1982): 281–313.

I will first give a general explanation of why the correspondence between exploitation and wealth can fail. Then, a simple example will be given illustrating the phenomenon. Readers may skip directly to the example on page 58 without undue loss of comprehension.

A brief review of the Class Exploitation Correspondence Principle and the Class-Wealth Correspondence Principle is necessary. The model consists of many agents; agent i begins with a vector of impersonal assets ω^i that can be used in production, plus one unit of labor power. (I assume labor is homogeneous, as I have throughout this article. If labor is heterogeneous, then poking holes in exploitation theory is almost child's play. Homogeneity of labor at least gives the theory a fighting chance.) There is a common technology which all agents can use. Each agent has a utility function, of goods and leisure. Since we have shown that an interest in exploitation cannot be justified by an interest in domination or alienation, we need not put into the utility function any concerns with where or under whom the labor one expends is performed. *Assume all agents have identical preferences,* although they own different initial bundles ω^i. Facing a vector of commodity prices p, which I normalize by letting the wage be unity, agent i now has finance capital in amount $p\omega^i$. Given his capital constraint, he chooses how much labor to supply and how much income to earn in order to maximize his utility. An equilibrium price vector is of the usual sort, allowing all markets, including the market for labor, to clear. An agent typically has three sources of revenue in the model: wage income from selling some labor power, profit income from hiring others, and proprietary income, from working himself on his own finance capital. If we introduce a capital market, there will also be interest or rental income, but that does not change the story at all. An agent is exploited if his total revenues do not enable him to purchase goods embodying as much social labor as he chose to expend in production. Class position of agents has been discussed before, in Section IV above.

At the equilibrium prices, let us call the wealth of agent i: $W^i = p\omega^i$. Wealth is the valuation at equilibrium prices of his nonlabor assets, his finance capital. We can view the labor he decides to supply in production, by maximizing his utility, as a function, at equilibrium prices p, of this wealth. Call this labor supply function $L(W)$. If agents possessed different utility functions, then we would have to write different labor supply functions, $L^i(W)$, but by assumption, all agents have the same preferences. $L(W^i)$ can be thought of as a cross-sectional labor supply function, which tells how much labor any agent will supply at the equilibrium prices, if his wealth is W^i. Now the key lemma is this: membership in the five classes is monotonically related to the ratio $y^i = W^i/L(W^i)$ and so is exploitation status.[27] That is, the larger is the ratio y^i the higher up the class ladder agent i is, and the more of an exploiter he is. (The class ladder is described in Section 4 above.) When do class and exploitation status of agents give us a good proxy for the agent's initial

---

27 For a demonstration of this lemma, see J. Roemer, *General Theory*, p. 176. A fuller discussion is in J. Roemer, "Why Labor Classes?"

wealth of nonlabor assets? Precisely when the index y^i is monotonically related to wealth W^i. Thus exploitation and class can be indicators of our interest in wealth inequality precisely when $dy/dW > 0$, that is, when the y index increases with wealth. Taking the derivative:

$$\frac{dy}{dW} > 0 \quad \text{if and only if} \quad \frac{dL}{dW} < \frac{L}{W} \quad \text{or} \quad \frac{dL}{L} \bigg/ \frac{dW}{W} < 1.$$

This last condition is of a familiar type in economics: it says that the labor supplied by the agent is inelastic with respect to his wealth; that is, a 1 percent increase in the agent's wealth will cause him to increase his supply of labor by less than 1 percent. Summarizing:

> *Theorem:* Under identical preferences of agents, class and exploitation status accurately reflect inequality in distribution of finance capital (productive assets other than labor) if and only if the labor supplied by agents is inelastic with respect to their wealth at equilibrium prices. If preferences differ, then class and exploitation status accurately reflect wealth if and only if *cross-sectionally* labor is inelastically supplied as wealth increases.

This elasticity condition is perhaps a reasonable condition on preferences.[28] In particular, we often think of agents supplying *less* labor as their wealth increases, in which case the above condition certainly holds. The condition allows agents to increase the labor they supply with increases in wealth, so long as they do not increase the labor supplied faster than their wealth increases. However, if we allow an "unrestricted domain" of preferences for goods and leisure (even if we constrain all agents to have the same preferences!), then the relation between exploitation and class, on the one hand, and wealth on the other, is lost. It will be possible to design cases where we have an agent Karl who hires labor (and does not sell it), who will be an exploiter by the Class Exploitation Correspondence Principle, and another agent Adam who sells labor and is exploited, *but* Adam is wealthier than Karl, *and* Karl and Adam have the *same preferences* over bundles of goods and leisure. This can only happen when the elasticity condition fails, and that provides the intuition which resolves the apparent paradox. With a wealth-elastic labor supply function, Adam, who is rich, wants to work terribly hard, while Karl who is poor hardly wants to work at all. Indeed Karl does not even want to work hard enough to utilize fully his paltry stock of productive

---

28 In the two special cases I studied in *General Theory*, the correspondence between exploitation and wealth followed because the elasticity condition held. For the subsistence model, the elasticity of labor supply with respect to wealth is negative and for the accumulation model it is zero. In the subsistence model, agents desire to minimize labor performed subject to consuming a certain subsistence bundle which is independent of wealth; in the accumulation model, they desire only to accumulate, and each works as much as is physically possible (an amount assumed to be the same for all). I believed, falsely, that since these two models posed behavior representing two extremes with respect to leisure preferences that the correspondence between exploitation and wealth would hold for any preferences uniform across agents.

assets, and so he hires Adam to work up the rest of his capital for him, which Adam is willing to do, even after he has worked all he can on his substantial stock of assets. Thus poor Karl hires and, by the Class Exploitation Correspondence Principle, exploits rich Adam.

Noneconomists might think of Karl and Adam in the above example as having different preference orderings, since one wants to supply a lot of labor and the other a little. But preference orderings are defined for an individual over all bundles of labor (or leisure) and goods he might consume, and so it is perfectly consistent for Karl and Adam to have the same preference orderings yet to supply labor differentially because of their different wealths. Saying they have the same preference orderings implies they have the same utility function and the same labor supply *function,* not that they supply the same amount of labor.

We have now to consider the case where differential preferences are admitted. Then, *a fortiori,* the index $y^i = W^i/L^i(W^i)$ will in general not be monotonically correlated with wealth W^i. Now, $L^i(W^i)$ can vary with i. We cannot say the rich exploit the poor with any degree of rigor. We can only be assured that the rich exploit the poor when the elasticity condition holds cross-sectionally, that an increment in wealth implies a less than proportionate increment in labor supplied. Failing this relation, the poor can be exploiters of the rich.

Notice *cross-sectional* labor supply behavior which is wealth-elastic might be quite common if agents have different preferences for leisure and income. Indeed, it is possible for labor supply cross-sectionally to exhibit elasticity with respect to wealth, while each individual agent has a "well-behaved" wealth inelastic labor supply schedule. Those who become wealthy (in one of the versions of the neoclassical paradigm) are those who have a low preference for leisure. Hence the individuals we observe as wealthy could have gotten that way by working long hours—although their own labor supply schedules might be inelastic as their wealth increases. We might then very well observe labor supply across the population increasing faster than wealth for some interval of wealths. For an individual's labor supply to be wealth-elastic, leisure must be an inferior good for him; but for the population labor supply to be cross- sectionally wealth-elastic, this is not the case.

For the sake of concreteness, here is a simple example illustrating the divergence between exploitation and inequality of assets. It does not matter, for this example, whether the different amounts of labor which Karl and Adam supply are a consequence of different preferences or the same preferences. All that matters is that given their different initial wealths, they optimize by supplying labor in the pattern indicated. I postulate the same Farm and Factory technologies as before:

Farm: 3 days labor (and no capital) produces 1 bushel of corn
Factory: 1 day labor plus 1 bushel seed corn produces 2 bushels corn

This time, however, Karl has an initial endowment of 1 corn and Adam of 3 corn. Denote a bundle of corn and labor as (C,L). Thus $(1,1)$ represents the consumption of 1 corn and the provision of 1 day's labor. I assume, as before, that each agent is not willing to run down his initial stock of corn (because he might die at any time, and he wishes, at least, not to deprive his only child of the same endowment that his parent passed down to him). Suppose we know at least this about Adam's and Karl's preferences:

$(\frac{2}{3}, 0) \succ_K (1,1)$
$(3\frac{1}{3}, 4) \succ_A (3,3)$

(To translate, the first line says Karl would strictly prefer to consume ⅔ bushel of corn and not to work at all than to work 1 day and consume 1 bushel.) Now note that Karl can achieve (1,1) by working up his 1 corn in the Factory in 1 day; he consumes 1 of the bushels produced, and starts week 2 with his initial 1 bushel. Likewise, Adam can achieve (3,3) by working up his 3 bushels in the Factory with 3 days' labor; he consumes 3 of the 6 bushels produced, and replaces his initial stock for week 2. But this solution is not Pareto optimal. For now suppose Karl lends his 1 bushel to Adam. Adam works up the total of 4 bushels in 4 days in the Factory, produces 8 bushels, and pays back Karl his original bushel plus ⅔ bushel as interest for the loan. This leaves Adam with 3⅓ bushels, after replacing his 3 bushels of initial stock. Thus Karl can consume ⅔ bushel and work not at all, which he prefers to (1,1), and Adam consumes the bundle (3⅓,4) which he prefers to (3,3). We have a strict Pareto improvement. (The interest rate charged is the competitive one; for if Adam, instead of borrowing from Karl, worked on the Farm for an extra day he would make precisely ⅓ bushel of corn.) This arrangement may continue forever: Karl never works and lives off the interest from Adam's labor. According to the unequal exchange definition of exploitation, there is no shadow of a doubt that Karl exploits Adam. However, Adam is richer than Karl. On what basis can we condemn this exploitation? Not on the basis of domination or alienation (we have decided), and surely not on the basis of differential ownership of the means of production, since the exploitation is going the "wrong way." Indeed, eliminating inequality in the ownership of the means of production should improve the lot of the exploited at the expense of the exploiters. (That is the property relations definition I formalized in other work.[29]) But in this case an equalization of the initial assets at 2 bushels of corn for each renders the exploiter (Karl) better off, and the exploited (Adam) worse off![30]

It should be remarked that the preferences postulated in this example for Karl and Adam are not perverse in the sense that they can be embedded in a full preference relation which has convex indifference curves of the usual sort, in corn-leisure space. This is the case even when Karl and Adam possess the same (convex) preferences.

---

29   Roemer, "Property Relations vs. Surplus Value."
30   Actually, even if there is a unique equilibrium there are some perverse cases in general equilibrium models when an agent can improve his final welfare by giving away some of his initial endowment. This is not such a case.

If we have reason for calling unjust the postulated inequality in the original distribution of seed-corn assets, then it is Karl who is suffering an injustice in the previous example, and not Adam; but according to exploitation theory, Karl exploits Adam. As I have said, I think the most consistent Marxian ethical position is against inequality in the initial distribution of productive assets; when exploitation accounts reflect the unequal distribution of productive assets in the proper way (that the rich exploit the poor), that is what makes exploitation theory attractive. But if that correlation can fail, as it has, then no foundation remains for a justification of exploitation theory.

It might still be maintained that two injustices are involved when productive assets are unjustly distributed: the injustice of that distribution of stocks, and the injustice of the flows arising from them.[31] Exploitation is a statement concerning the injustice of flows, but I have invoked it only as a proxy for the underlying injustice (more precisely, inequality) of stocks. There remains the necessity for some judgment of the injustice of flows emanating from an unjust distribution of stocks: my point is that flows of labor are an imperfect proxy for that. In the Karl-Adam example, I say that Adam is unjustly gaining from the flows between him and Karl, if the initial distribution of stocks is unjust against Karl, despite the formal exploitation of Adam by Karl. In cases where exploitation does render the correct judgment on the injustice of flows, then perhaps the degree or rate of exploitation is useful in assessing the degree of injustice in the flow. But in the general case counterexamples can be supplied against this claim as well—situations where A is exploited more than B but we would agree B is more unjustly treated. It is beyond my scope here to inquire into a robust measure of the injustice of flows emanating from an unjust stock.

Another point should be made with respect to the argument of this section. It might be argued that so long as exploitation comes about, then the initial distribution of assets was not "equal." An "equal" initial distribution might be defined as one which eliminates exploitation. First, such a position is circular with respect to any attempt to vindicate exploitation theory by claiming it helps to reveal an initial inequality of assets. Secondly, such a definition of equality of initial endowments is in fact a theory of outcome equality, not a theory of resource equality. We would still be left with the question: What is wrong with exploitation?

A fifth explanation of our interest in exploitation theory, which I have enumerated (4′) as I consider it to be convincing only when it paraphrases the inequality theory, might be called the expropriation theory. The expropriation theory is summarized, for example, by G. A. Cohen,[32] as follows:

(i) The laborer is the only person who creates the product, that which has value.
(ii) The capitalist receives some of the value of the product.

---
31 I thank G. A. Cohen for pressing this point.
32 G. A. Cohen, "The Labor Theory of Value and the Concept of Exploitation," *Philosophy & Public Affairs* 8, no. 4 (Summer 1979): 338–60.

Therefore: (iii) The laborer receives less value than the value of what he creates, and
(iv) The capitalist receives some of the value of what the laborer creates.
Therefore: (v) The laborer is exploited by the capitalist.

The expropriation theory (which Cohen calls the Plain Marxian Argument) does not claim an injustice on grounds of alienation or domination, but on grounds of rightful ownership of what one has made. I think the argument is ethically defensible only when it coincides with the ine- quality-of-resources theory, that is, when the expropriation takes place because the laborer does not have access to the means of production he is entitled to. To see the unreasonableness of the expropriation theory in the general case, substitute "Karl" for "the capitalist" and "Adam" for "the laborer" in the above argument (i)–(v) where Karl and Adam are the *dramatis personae* of the last example. Statements (ii) through (iv) remain unobjectionable and perhaps statement (i) does as well; but statement (v) certainly does not follow as an *ethically* convincing statement (although *formal* exploitation exists). If we respect the ownership pattern of assets and the preferences of the agents (which, to repeat, can even be uniform preferences), I see no good reason to give exclusive ownership rights of a product to the person who has made the product. Only on grounds of alienation (which I have said is unconvincing) does it seem one's labor could confer special ownership rights over the product. Justly acquired initial resources, which the direct producer might borrow from another, must count as well in ascribing ownership of the final product. What power the expropriation theory appears to have comes from another assumption, not stated, that the capitalist starts out with a monopoly on the ownership of the means of production, unjustly acquired; it is the injustice of that monopoly which leads us to believe he has no just claim to the product of the laborer. As Cohen says, in his own criticism of the expropriation theory: "If it is morally all right that capitalists do and workers do not own the means of production, then capitalist profit is not the fruit of exploitation; and if the pre-contractual distributive position is morally wrong, then the case for exploitation is made."[33]

VII. MOLLIFYING THE VERDICT

Many writers have shown the indefensibility of the labor theory of *value*, the claim that Marxian analysis gains special insight from deducing a relationship between embodied labor values and prices.[34] There is no theory of price formation, special to Marxism, with a rigorous foundation. With the demise of the labor theory of value, various writers in the Marxian tradition have shown that the theory of exploitation can be reconstructed on a foundation which does not utilize the labor

---

33   G. A. Cohen, "More on the Labor Theory of Value," *Inquiry* (Fall 1983).
34   For a summary of the criticism of the labor theory of value see Elster, *Making Sense of Marx*, chap. 3.

theory of value.³⁵ (Marx's logic derived the theory of exploitation from the labor theory of price formation.) I have now argued there is no logically compelling reason to be interested in exploitation theory. This claim is not so destructive as might appear to the Marxian enterprise, however, for I think the reasons Marxists have been interested in exploitation theory are important and, to a large extent, distinguish Marxism from other kinds of social science: it is just that these reasons do not justify an interest in exploitation theory which is an unnecessary detour to the other concerns. First, within ethics, Marxism lays emphasis on the importance of equal access to the means of production. It regards with suspicion any large inequality in access to the means of production, while its foil in social science tends to justify such inequality on grounds of differential rates of time preference, skill, or even luck.³⁶ Having said that equality in the ownership of means of production is desirable as an initial condition, much is left to elaborate concerning inheritance, handicaps, and needs. Libertarian theorists view inheritance as a just means of acquiring resources³⁷; Ronald Dworkin, in recent work on equality of resources, does not discuss inheritance³⁸; Bruce Ackerman in recent work does attack that problem³⁹; I imagine a Marxian theory of inheritance, when elaborated, will circumscribe inheritance rights quite sharply.⁴⁰ Secondly, Marxism calls attention to domination; domination is of interest on its own, even though it provides no reason to be interested in exploitation. Interest in domination has given rise to an important literature on the labor process and technical change under capitalism, which demonstrates how a specifically Marxian question, perhaps motivated by normative concerns, can give rise to new analysis of a positive type. Another example of positive analysis related to domination and exploitation is class theory. Class position is easily observable, and class may be an excellent indicator of alliances in struggles within capitalism, for reasons closer to domination than exploitation.⁴¹ Thirdly, the concern with alienation is related

---

35 See Cohen, "The Labor Theory of Value and the Concept of Exploitation"; Roemer, *General Theory*; Morishima, *Marx's Economics*.
36 Robert Nozick, for example, considers luck to be a just method for acquiring assets (*Anarchy, State, and Utopia* [New York: Basic Books, 1974]).
37 Nozick, ibid.
38 Ronald Dworkin, "What is Equality? Part 1: Equality of Resources," *Philosophy & Public Affairs* 10, no. 4 (Fall 1981): 283–345. See n. 9, p. 313.
39 Bruce Ackerman, *Social Justice in the Liberal State* (New Haven: Yale University Press, 1980).
40 For some very tentative indications, see Roemer, "Are Socialist Ethics Consistent with Efficiency?" pt. 4.
41 I have not considered in this paper a sixth possible reason to be interested in exploitation: as an explanation of class struggle, that the exploited struggle against the exploiters. I think that if the exploited struggle against the exploiters, that is because the former are dominated, are alienated, or suffer from an unfair allocation in the distribution of assets. The unequal exchange of labor cannot be the cause of class struggle: rather, that unequal exchange must be the symptom of what must cause class struggle. (People do not calculate surplus value accounts; in fact, one of the classical Marxian points is that the surplus value accounts are masked and veiled by the market, and so the exploited do not see the true nature of the unequal exchange from which they are suffering.) But I have shown, now, that exploitation is not a useful proxy for the various injustices which may, indeed, be at the root of class struggle. Hence, my nondiscussion of exploitation as the cause of class struggle.

to the interest Marxists have had in the emergence of market economies and the proletarianization of labor forces, both in the past and the present, an interest which again leads to the posing of questions which would not otherwise have been asked. Fourthly, the concern with accumulation has given Marxists a view of capitalism as guided by a pursuit of profits which in a deep sense is anarchic and collectively irrational, while the predominant opposing view (neoclassical economics) pictures capitalism as collectively rational, as the price system harnesses profit motives to serve the needs of people.[42] While Marxists have not developed a theory of crisis and disequilibrium which is as well-founded and intellectually convincing as neoclassical equilibrium theory, one suspects the Marxian questions will eventually lead to a rigorous theory of uneven development and crisis.

Unlike the labor theory of value, the reasons for a purported interest in exploitation theory have given rise to provocative social theory. There have, on the other hand, been costs to the adherence to exploitation theory, chiefly associated with what might be called the fetishism of labor. The costs are often associated with the inappropriate application of exploitation theory in cases where some underlying deeper phenomenon, which usually coincides with exploitation, ceases to coincide with it. For example, socialist countries have exhibited a reluctant history to use material incentives and decentralizing markets. To some extent, this may result from a confusion concerning the permissibility of "exploitation" when the initial distribution of ownership or control of the means of production is just. A second cost has been the equation claimed by some Marxists between socialism and industrial democracy, the belief that hierarchical forms of production are necessarily nonsocialist. A third example, associated with an overriding concern with alienation, views the final social goal as a moneyless economy, perhaps with no detailed division of labor, in which, somehow, all of society becomes one community.[43] Strictly speaking, the last two examples do not impugn exploitation theory, but rather domination and alienation; but exploitation theory has formalized the concern with labor which reinforces this sort of misapplication.

It should be reiterated that the failure of exploitation to mirror properly the unequal distribution of the means of production is a logical one; as I noted, in what are perhaps the most important actual historical cases, preferences of agents are such that the unequal-exchange-of-labor theory coincides with the inequality-of-productive-assets theory, and so exploitation theory pronounces the "right" ethical verdict.[44]

---

42 It is this collective irrationality of capitalism which Elster, *op. cit.*, sees as the main contribution of Marxian "dialectics."

43 A fine discussion of the costs which dogmatic Marxism has imposed on developing socialist societies is in Alec Nove, *The Economics of Feasible Socialism* (London: George Allen and Unwin, 1983).

44 A striking example which suggests that labor supply may be elastic with respect to wealth, and therefore that exploitation theory is even historically wrong, is presented by Pranab Bardhan, "Agrarian Class Formation in India," *Journal of Peasant Studies* 10, no. 1 (1982), p. 78. In India, as the wealth of middle-peasant families increases, poor relations come and join the family. Viewing this extended family as the unit, it appears that labor supply increases with

Parallel to my view on the usefulness of exploitation theory as a proxy for inequality in the ownership of the means of production is George Stigler's observation concerning David Ricardo's use of the labor theory of value. Stigler writes:

> I can find no basis for the belief that Ricardo had an *analytical* labor theory of value, for quantities of labor are *not* the only determinants of relative values. ... On the other hand, there is no doubt that he held what may be called an *empirical* labor theory of value, that is, a theory that the relative quantities of labor required in production are the dominant determinants of relative values. Such an empirical proposition cannot be interpreted as an analytical theory ...

Stigler concludes with a statement which applies to my argument concerning exploitation:

> The failure to distinguish between analytical and empirical propositions has been a source of much misunderstanding in economics. An analytical statement concerns functional relationships; an empirical statement takes account of the quantitative significance of the relationships.[45]

Unlike Stigler's Ricardo, I think the labor theory of value is not a useful empirical theory. While the errors in the labor theory of value are Ptolemaic, the defects in exploitation theory are Newtonian. As an empirical statement, surplus value accounts mirror inequality in ownership of the means of production pretty well, if it is true that cross-sectional wealth- elastic labor supply behavior is as empirically inconsequential as the precession in the perihelion of the orbit of Mercury. But for the sake of clarity and consistency, I think exploitation conceived of as the unequal exchange of labor should be replaced with exploitation conceived of as the distributional consequences of an unjust inequality in the distribution of productive assets and resources. Precisely when the asset distribution is unjust becomes the central question to which Marxian political philosophy should direct its attention.

---

wealth. It is not obvious that the family labor supply increases elastically with wealth, but Bardhan's example shows, at least, there is a range of wealths for which labor supply has positive elasticity.

45 George Stigler, "Ricardo and the 93% Labor Theory of Value," *American Economic Review* 48 (June 1958): 361, 366.

A THEORY OF JUSTICE

CHAPTERS 1 AND 2

BY JOHN RAWLS

John Rawls, "Selections," *A Theory of Justice,* pp. 3-19, 52-56. Copyright © 1999 by Harvard University Press. Reprinted with permission.

FOUR

In this introductory chapter I sketch some of the main ideas of the theory of justice I wish to develop. The exposition is informal and intended to prepare the way for the more detailed arguments that follow. Unavoidably there is some overlap between this and later discussions. I begin by describing the role of justice in social cooperation and with a brief account of the primary subject of justice, the basic structure of society. I then present the main idea of justice as fairness, a theory of justice that generalizes and carries to a higher level of abstraction the traditional conception of the social contract. The compact of society is replaced by an initial situation that incorporates certain procedural constraints on arguments designed to lead to an original agreement on principles of justice. I also take up, for purposes of clarification and contrast, the classical utilitarian and intuitionist conceptions of justice and consider some of the differences between these views and justice as fairness. My guiding aim is to work out a theory of justice that is a viable alternative to these doctrines which have long dominated our philosophical tradition.

1. THE ROLE OF JUSTICE

Justice is the first virtue of social institutions, as truth is of systems of thought. A theory however elegant and economical must be rejected or revised if it is untrue; likewise laws and institutions no matter how efficient and well-arranged must be reformed or abolished if they are unjust. Each person possesses an inviolability founded on justice that even the welfare of society as a whole cannot override. For this reason justice denies that the loss of freedom for some is made right by a greater good shared by others. It does not allow that the sacrifices imposed on a few are outweighed by the larger sum of advantages enjoyed by many. Therefore in a just society the liberties of equal citizenship are taken as settled; the rights secured by justice are not subject to political bargaining or to the calculus of social interests. The only thing that permits us to acquiesce in an erroneous theory is the lack of a better one; analogously, an injustice is tolerable only when it is necessary to avoid an even greater injustice. Being first virtues of human activities, truth and justice are uncompromising.

These propositions seem to express our intuitive conviction of the primacy of justice. No doubt they are expressed too strongly. In any event I wish to inquire whether these contentions or others similar to them are sound, and if so how they can be accounted for. To this end it is necessary to work out a theory of justice in the light of which these assertions can be interpreted and assessed. I shall begin by considering the role of the principles of justice. Let us assume, to fix ideas, that a society is a more or less self-sufficient association of persons who in their relations to one another recognize certain rules of conduct as binding and who for the most part act in accordance with them. Suppose further that these rules specify a system of cooperation designed to advance the good of those taking part in it. Then, although a society is a cooperative venture for mutual advantage, it is typically marked by a conflict as well as by an identity of interests. There is an identity of interests since social cooperation makes possible a better life for all than any would have if each were to live solely by his own efforts. There is a conflict of interests since persons are not indifferent as to how the greater benefits produced by their collaboration are distributed, for in order to pursue their ends they each prefer a larger to a lesser share. A set of principles is required for choosing among the various social arrangements which determine this division of advantages and for underwriting an agreement on the proper distributive shares. These principles are the principles of social justice: they provide a way of assigning rights and duties in the basic institutions of society and they define the appropriate distribution of the benefits and burdens of social cooperation.

Now let us say that a society is well-ordered when it is not only designed to advance the good of its members but when it is also effectively regulated by a public conception of justice. That is, it is a society in which (1) everyone accepts and knows that the others accept the same principles of justice, and (2) the basic social institutions generally satisfy and are generally known to satisfy these principles. In this case while men may put forth excessive demands on one another, they nevertheless acknowledge a common point of view from which their claims may be adjudicated. If men's inclination to self-interest makes their vigilance against one another necessary, their public sense of justice makes their secure association together possible. Among individuals with disparate aims and purposes a shared conception of justice establishes the bonds of civic friendship; the general desire for justice limits the pursuit of other ends. One may think of a public conception of justice as constituting the fundamental charter of a well-ordered human association.

Existing societies are of course seldom well-ordered in this sense, for what is just and unjust is usually in dispute. Men disagree about which principles should define the basic terms of their association. Yet we may still say, despite this disagreement, that they each have a conception of justice. That is, they understand the need for, and they are prepared to affirm, a characteristic set of principles for assigning basic rights and duties and for determining what they take to be the proper distribution of the benefits and burdens of social cooperation. Thus it seems natural to think of the concept of justice as distinct from the various conceptions of justice and as being specified by the role which these different sets of principles, these different conceptions, have in common.[1] Those who hold different conceptions of justice can, then, still agree that institutions are just when no arbitrary distinctions are made between persons in the assigning of basic rights and duties and when the rules determine a proper balance between competing claims to the advantages of social life. Men can agree to this description of just institutions since the notions of an arbitrary distinction and of a proper balance, which are included in the concept of justice, are left open for each to interpret according to the principles of justice that he accepts. These principles single out which similarities and differences among persons are relevant in determining rights and duties and they specify which division of advantages is appropriate. Clearly this distinction between the concept and the various conceptions of justice settles no important questions. It simply helps to identify the role of the principles of social justice.

Some measure of agreement in conceptions of justice is, however, not the only prerequisite for a viable human community. There are other fundamental social problems, in particular those of coordination, efficiency, and stability. Thus the plans of individuals need to be fitted together so that their activities are compatible with one another and they can all be carried through without anyone's legitimate expectations being severely disappointed. Moreover, the execution of these plans should lead to the achievement of social ends in ways that are efficient and consistent with justice. And finally, the scheme of social cooperation must be stable: it must be more or less regularly complied with and its basic rules willingly acted upon; and when infractions occur, stabilizing forces should exist that prevent further violations and tend to restore the arrangement. Now it is evident that these three problems are connected with that of justice. In the absence of a certain measure of agreement on what is just and unjust, it is clearly more difficult for individuals to coordinate their plans efficiently in order to insure that mutually beneficial arrangements are maintained. Distrust and resentment corrode the ties of civility, and suspicion and hostility tempt men to act in ways they would otherwise avoid. So while the distinctive role of conceptions of justice is to specify basic rights and duties and to determine the appropriate distributive shares, the way in which a conception does this is bound to affect the problems of efficiency, coordination, and stability. We cannot, in general, assess a conception of justice by its distributive role alone, however useful this role may be in identifying the concept of justice. We must take into account its wider connections; for even though justice has a certain priority, being the most important

---

1   Here I follow H. L. A. Hart, *The Concept of Law* (Oxford, The Clarendon Press. 1961), pp. 155–159.

virtue of institutions, it is still true that, other things equal, one conception of justice is preferable to another when its broader consequences are more desirable.

2. THE SUBJECT OF JUSTICE

Many different kinds of things are said to be just and unjust: not only laws, institutions, and social systems, but also particular actions of many kinds, including decisions, judgments, and imputations. We also call the attitudes and dispositions of persons, and persons themselves, just and unjust. Our topic, however, is that of social justice. For us the primary subject of justice is the basic structure of society, or more exactly, the way in which the major social institutions distribute fundamental rights and duties and determine the division of advantages from social cooperation. By major institutions I understand the political constitution and the principal economic and social arrangements. Thus the legal protection of freedom of thought and liberty of conscience, competitive markets, private property in the means of production, and the monogamous family are examples of major social institutions. Taken together as one scheme, the major institutions define men's rights and duties and influence their life prospects, what they can expect to be and how well they can hope to do. The basic structure is the primary subject of justice because its effects are so profound and present from the start. The intuitive notion here is that this structure contains various social positions and that men born into different positions have different expectations of life determined, in part, by the political system as well as by economic and social circumstances. In this way the institutions of society favor certain starting places over others. These are especially deep inequalities. Not only are they pervasive, but they affect men's initial chances in life; yet they cannot possibly be justified by an appeal to the notions of merit or desert. It is these inequalities, presumably inevitable in the basic structure of any society, to which the principles of social justice must in the first instance apply. These principles, then, regulate the choice of a political constitution and the main elements of the economic and social system. The justice of a social scheme depends essentially on how fundamental rights and duties are assigned and on the economic opportunities and social conditions in the various sectors of society.

The scope of our inquiry is limited in two ways. First of all, I am concerned with a special case of the problem of justice. I shall not consider the justice of institutions and social practices generally, nor except in passing the justice of the law of nations and of relations between states (§58). Therefore, if one supposes that the concept of justice applies whenever there is an allotment of something rationally regarded as advantageous or disadvantageous, then we are interested in only one instance of its application. There is no reason to suppose ahead of time that the principles satisfactory for the basic structure hold for all cases. These principles may not work for the rules and practices of private associations or for those of less comprehensive social groups. They may be irrelevant for the various informal conventions and customs of everyday life; they may not elucidate the justice, or perhaps better, the fairness of voluntary cooperative arrangements or procedures for making contractual agreements. The conditions for the law of nations may require different principles arrived at in a somewhat different way. I shall be satisfied if it is possible to formulate a reasonable conception of justice for the basic structure of society conceived for the time being as a closed system isolated from other societies. The significance of this special case is obvious and needs no explanation. It is natural to conjecture that once we have a sound theory for this case, the remaining problems of justice will prove more tractable in the light of it. With suitable modifications such a theory should provide the key for some of these other questions.

The other limitation on our discussion is that for the most part I examine the principles of justice that would regulate a well-ordered society. Everyone is presumed to act justly and to do his part in upholding just institutions. Though justice may be, as Hume remarked, the cautious, jealous virtue, we can still ask what a perfectly just society would be like.[2] Thus I consider primarily what I call strict compliance as opposed to partial compliance theory (§§25, 39). The latter studies the principles that govern how we are to deal with injustice. It comprises such topics as the theory of punishment, the doctrine of just war, and the justification of the various ways of opposing unjust regimes, ranging from civil disobedience and conscientious objection to militant resistance and revolution. Also included here are questions of compensatory justice and of weighing one form of institutional injustice against another. Obviously the problems of partial compliance theory are the pressing and urgent matters. These are the things that we are faced with in everyday life. The reason for beginning with ideal theory is that it provides, I believe, the only basis for the systematic grasp of these more pressing problems. The discussion of civil disobedience, for example, depends upon it (§§55–59). At least, I shall assume that a deeper understanding can be gained in no other way, and that the nature and aims of a perfectly just society is the fundamental part of the theory of justice.

Now admittedly the concept of the basic structure is somewhat vague. It is not always clear which institutions or features thereof should be included. But it would be premature to worry about this matter here. I shall proceed by discussing principles which do apply to what is certainly a part of the basic structure. I shall then try to extend the application of these principles so that they cover what would appear to be the main elements of this structure. Perhaps these principles will turn out to be perfectly general, although this is unlikely. It is sufficient that they apply to the most important cases of social justice. The point to keep in mind is that a conception of justice for the basic structure is worth having for its own sake. It should not be dismissed because its principles are not everywhere satisfactory.

---

2 *An Enquiry Concerning the Principles of Morals,* see. III, pt. I, par. 3, ed. L. A. Setby-Bigge, 2nd edition (Oxford, 1902), p. 184.

A conception of social justice, then, is to be regarded as providing in the first instance a standard whereby the distributive aspects of the basic structure of society are to be assessed. This standard, however, is not to be confused with the principles defining the other virtues, for the basic structure, and social arrangements generally, may be efficient or inefficient, liberal or illiberal, and many other things, as well as just or unjust. A complete conception defining principles for all the virtues of the basic structure, together with their respective weights when they conflict, is more than a conception of justice; it is a social ideal. The principles of justice are but a part, although perhaps the most important part, of such a conception. A social ideal in turn is connected with a conception of society, a vision of the way in which the aims and purposes of social cooperation are to be understood. The various conceptions of justice are the outgrowth of different notions of society against the background of opposing views of the natural necessities and opportunities of human life. Fully to understand a conception of justice we must make explicit the conception of social cooperation from which it derives. But in doing this we should not lose sight of the special role of the principles of justice or of the primary subject to which they apply.

In these preliminary remarks I have distinguished the concept of justice as meaning a proper balance between competing claims from a conception of justice as a set of related principles for identifying the relevant considerations which determine this balance. I have also characterized justice as but one part of a social ideal, although the theory I shall propose no doubt extends its everyday sense. This theory is not offered as a description of ordinary meanings but as an account of certain distributive principles for the basic structure of society. I assume that any reasonably complete ethical theory must include principles for this fundamental problem and that these principles, whatever they are, constitute its doctrine of justice. The concept of justice I take to be defined, then, by the role of its principles in assigning rights and duties and in defining the appropriate division of social advantages. A conception of justice is an interpretation of this role.

Now this approach may not seem to tally with tradition. I believe, though, that it does. The more specific sense that Aristotle gives to justice, and from which the most familiar formulations derive, from pleonexia, that is from gaining some advantage for oneself by seizing what belongs to another, his property, his reward, his office, and the like, or by denying a person that which is due to him, the fulfillment of a promise, the repayment of a debt, the showing of proper respect, and so on.[3] It is evident that this definition is framed to apply to actions, and persons are thought to be just insofar as they have, as one of the permanent elements of their character, a steady and effective desire to act justly. Aristotle's definition clearly presupposes, however, an account of what properly belongs to a person and of what is due to him. Now such entitlements are, I believe,

---

3 *Nicomachean Ethics*, 1129b–1130b5. I have followed the interpretation of Gregory Vlastos, "Justice and Happiness in *The Republic*," in *Plato: A Collection of Critical Essays*, edited by Vlastos (Garden City, N.Y., Doubleday and Company, 1971), vol. 2, pp. 70f. For a discussion of Aristotle on justice, see W, F. R, Hardie, *Aristotle's Ethical Theory* (Oxford, The Clarendon Press, 1968), ch. X.

very often derived from social institutions and the legitimate expectations to which they give rise. There is no reason to think that Aristotle would disagree with this, and certainly he has a conception of social justice to account for these claims. The definition I adopt is designed to apply directly to the most important case, the justice of the basic structure. There is no conflict with the traditional notion.

3. THE MAIN IDEA OF THE THEORY OF JUSTICE

My aim is to present a conception of justice which generalizes and carries to a higher level of abstraction the familiar theory of the social contract as found, say, in Locke, Rousseau, and Kant.[4] In order to do this we are not to think of the original contract as one to enter a particular society or to set up a particular form of government. Rather, the guiding idea is that the principles of justice for the basic structure of society are the object of the original agreement. They are the principles that free and rational persons concerned to further their own interests would accept in an initial position of equality as defining the fundamental terms of their association. These principles are to regulate all further agreements; they specify the kinds of social cooperation that can be entered into and the forms of government that can be established. This way of regarding the principles of justice I shall call justice as fairness.

Thus we are to imagine that those who engage in social cooperation choose together, in one joint act, the principles which are to assign basic rights and duties and to determine the division of social benefits. Men are to decide in advance how they are to regulate their claims against one another and what is to be the foundation charter of their society. Just as each person must decide by rational reflection what constitutes his good, that is, the system of ends which it is rational for him to pursue, so a group of persons must decide once and for all what is to count among them as just and unjust. The choice which rational men would make in this hypothetical situation of equal liberty, assuming for the present that this choice problem has a solution, determines the principles of justice.

In justice as fairness the original position of equality corresponds to the state of nature in the traditional theory of the social contract. This original position is not, of course, thought of as an actual historical state of affairs, much less as a primitive condition of culture. It is understood

---

4   As the text suggests, 1 shall regard Locke's *Second Treatise of Government*, Rousseau's *The Social Contract*, and Kant's ethical works beginning with *The Foundations of the Metaphysics of Morals* as definitive of the contract tradition. For all of its greatness, Hobbes's Leviathan raises special problems. A general historical survey is provided by J. W. Gough, *The Social Contract*, 2nd ed. (Oxford, The Clarendon Press, 1957), and Otto Gierke, *Natural Law and the Theory of Society*, trans. with an introduction by Ernest Barker (Cambridge, The University Press, 1934). A presentation of the contract view as primarily an ethical theory is to be found in G. R. Grice, *The Grounds of Moral Judgment* (Cambridge, The University Press, 1967). See also §19, note 30.

as a purely hypothetical situation characterized so as to lead to a certain conception of justice.[5] Among the essential features of this situation is that no one knows his place in society, his class position or social status, nor does any one know his fortune in the distribution of natural assets and abilities, his intelligence, strength, and the like. I shall even assume that the parties do not know their conceptions of the good or their special psychological propensities. The principles of justice are chosen behind a veil of ignorance. This ensures that no one is advantaged or disadvantaged in the choice of principles by the outcome of natural chance or the contingency of social circumstances. Since all are similarly situated and no one is able to design principles to favor his particular condition, the principles of justice are the result of a fair agreement or bargain. For given the circumstances of the original position, the symmetry of everyone's relations to each other, this initial situation is fair between individuals as moral persons, that is, as rational beings with their own ends and capable, I shall assume, of a sense of justice. The original position is, one might say, the appropriate initial status quo, and thus the fundamental agreements reached in it are fair. This explains the propriety of the name "justice as fairness": it conveys the idea that the principles of justice are agreed to in an initial situation that is fair. The name does not mean that the concepts of justice and fairness are the same, any more than the phrase "poetry as metaphor" means that the concepts of poetry and metaphor are the same.

Justice as fairness begins, as I have said, with one of the most general of all choices which persons might make together, namely, with the choice of the first principles of a conception of justice which is to regulate all subsequent criticism and reform of institutions. Then, having chosen a conception of justice, we can suppose that they are to choose a constitution and a legislature to enact laws, and so on, all in accordance with the principles of justice initially agreed upon. Our social situation is just if it is such that by this sequence of hypothetical agreements we would have contracted into the general system of rules which defines it. Moreover, assuming that the original position does determine a set of principles (that is, that a particular conception of justice would be chosen), it will then be true that whenever social institutions satisfy these principles those engaged in them can say to one another that they are cooperating on terms to which they would agree if they were free and equal persons whose relations with respect to one another were fair. They could all view their arrangements as meeting the stipulations which they would acknowledge in an initial situation that embodies widely accepted and reasonable constraints on the choice of principles. The general recognition of this fact would provide the basis for a public acceptance

---

5 Kant is clear that the original agreement is hypothetical. See *The Metaphysics of Morals*, pt. I (*Rechtslehre*), especially §§47, 52; and pt. II of the essay "Concerning the Common Saying: This May Be True in Theory but It Does Not Apply in Practice," in *Kant's Political Writings*, ed. Hans Reiss and trans, by H. B. Nisbet (Cambridge, The University Press, 1970), pp. 73–87. See Georges Vlachos, *La Pensée politique de Kant* (Paris, Presses Universitaires de France, 1962), pp. 326–335; and J. G. Murphy, *Kant: The Philosophy of Right* (London, Macmillan, 1970), pp. 109–112, 133–136, for a further discussion.

of the corresponding principles of justice. No society can, of course, be a scheme of cooperation which men enter voluntarily in a literal sense; each person finds himself placed at birth in some particular position in some particular society, and the nature of this position materially affects his life prospects. Yet a society satisfying the principles of justice as fairness comes as close as a society can to being a voluntary scheme, for it meets the principles which free and equal persons would assent to under circumstances that are fair. In this sense its members are autonomous and the obligations they recognize self-imposed.

One feature of justice as fairness is to think of the parties in the initial situation as rational and mutually disinterested. This does not mean that the parties are egoists, that is, individuals with only certain kinds of interests, say in wealth, prestige, and domination. But they are conceived as not taking an interest in one another's interests. They are to presume that even their spiritual aims may be opposed, in the way that the aims of those of different religions may be opposed. Moreover, the concept of rationality must be interpreted as far as possible in the narrow sense, standard in economic theory, of taking the most effective means to given ends. I shall modify this concept to some extent, as explained later (§25), but one must try to avoid introducing into it any controversial ethical elements. The initial situation must be characterized by stipulations that are widely accepted.

In working out the conception of justice as fairness one main task clearly is to determine which principles of justice would be chosen in the original position. To do this we must describe this situation in some detail and formulate with care the problem of choice which it presents. These matters I shall take up in the immediately succeeding chapters. It may be observed, however, that once the principles of justice are thought of as arising from an original agreement in a situation of equality, it is an open question whether the principle of utility would be acknowledged. Offhand it hardly seems likely that persons who view themselves as equals, entitled to press their claims upon one another, would agree to a principle which may require lesser life prospects for some simply for the sake of a greater sum of advantages enjoyed by others. Since each desires to protect his interests, his capacity to advance his conception of the good, no one has a reason to acquiesce in an enduring loss for himself in order to bring about a greater net balance of satisfaction. In the absence of strong and lasting benevolent impulses, a rational man would not accept a basic structure merely because it maximized the algebraic sum of advantages irrespective of its permanent effects on his own basic rights and interests. Thus it seems that the principle of utility is incompatible with the conception of social cooperation among equals for mutual advantage. It appears to be inconsistent with the idea of reciprocity implicit in the notion of a well-ordered society. Or, at any rate, so I shall argue.

I shall maintain instead that the persons in the initial situation would choose two rather different principles: the first requires equality in the assignment of basic rights and duties, while the second holds that social and economic inequalities, for example inequalities of wealth and authority, are just only if they result in compensating benefits for everyone, and in particular for the least advantaged members of society. These principles rule out justifying institutions on the grounds that the hardships of some are offset by a greater good in the aggregate. It may be expedient but it is not just that some should have less in order that others may prosper. But there is no injustice in the greater benefits earned by a few provided that the situation of persons not so fortunate is thereby improved. The intuitive idea is that since everyone's well-being depends upon a scheme of cooperation without which no one could have a satisfactory life, the division of advantages should be such as to draw forth the willing cooperation of everyone taking part in it, including those less well situated. The two principles mentioned seem to be a fair basis on which those better endowed, or more fortunate in their social position, neither of which we can be said to deserve, could expect the willing cooperation of others when some workable scheme is' a necessary condition of the welfare of all.[6] Once we decide to look for a conception of justice that prevents the use of the accidents of natural endowment and the contingencies of social circumstance as counters in a quest for political and economic advantage, we are led to these principles. They express the result of leaving aside those aspects of the social world that seem arbitrary from a moral point of view.

The problem of the choice of principles, however, is extremely difficult. I do not expect the answer i shall suggest to be convincing to everyone. It is, therefore, worth noting from the outset that justice as fairness, like other contract views, consists of two parts: (1) an interpretation of the initial situation and of the problem of choice posed there, and (2) a set of principles which, it is argued, would be agreed to. One may accept the first part of the theory (or some variant thereof), but not the other, and conversely. The concept of the initial contractual situation may seem reasonable although the particular principles proposed are rejected. To be sure, I want to maintain that the most appropriate conception of this situation does lead to principles of justice contrary to utilitarianism and perfectionism, and therefore that the contract doctrine provides an alternative to these views. Still, one may dispute this contention even though one grants that the contractarian method is a useful way of studying ethical theories and of setting forth their underlying assumptions.

Justice as fairness is an example of what I have called a contract theory. Now there may be an objection to the term "contract" and related expressions, but I think it will serve reasonably well. Many words have misleading connotations which at first are likely to confuse. The terms "utility" and "utilitarianism" are surely no exception. They too have unfortunate suggestions which hostile critics have been willing to exploit; yet they are clear enough for those prepared to study utilitarian doctrine. The same should be true of the term "contract" applied to moral theories. As I have mentioned, to understand it one has to keep in mind that it implies a certain level of abstraction. In particular, the content of the relevant agreement is not to enter a given society or to adopt a

---

6   For the formulation of this intuitive idea I am indebted to Allan Gibbard.

given form of government, but to accept certain moral principles. Moreover, the undertakings referred to are purely hypothetical: a contract view holds that certain principles would be accepted in a well-defined initial situation.

The merit of the contract terminology is that it conveys the idea that principles of justice may be conceived as principles that would be chosen by rational persons, and that in this way conceptions of justice may be explained and justified. The theory of justice is a part, perhaps the most significant part, of the theory of rational choice. Furthermore, principles of justice deal with conflicting claims upon the advantages won by social cooperation; they apply to the relations among several persons or groups. The word "contract" suggests this plurality as well as the condition that the appropriate division of advantages must be in accordance with principles acceptable to all parties. The condition of publicity for principles of justice is also connoted by the contract phraseology. Thus, if these principles are the outcome of an agreement, citizens have a knowledge of the principles that others follow. It is characteristic of contract theories to stress the public nature of political principles. Finally there is the long tradition of the contract doctrine. Expressing the tie with this line of thought helps to define ideas and accords with natural piety. There are then several advantages in the use of the term "contract." With due precautions taken, it should not be misleading.

A final remark. Justice as fairness is not a complete contract theory. For it is clear that the contractarian idea can be extended to the choice of more or less an entire ethical system, that is, to a system including principles for all the virtues and not only for justice. Now for the most part I shall consider only principles of justice and others closely related to them; I make no attempt to discuss the virtues in a systematic way. Obviously if justice as fairness succeeds reasonably well, a next step would be to study the more general view suggested by the name "rightness as fairness." But even this wider theory fails to embrace all moral relationships, since it would seem to include only our relations with other persons and to leave out of account how we are to conduct ourselves toward animals and the rest of nature. I do not contend that the contract notion offers a way to approach these questions which are certainly of the first importance; and I shall have to put them aside. We must recognize the limited scope of justice as fairness and of the general type of view that it exemplifies. How far its conclusions must be revised once these other matters are understood cannot be decided in advance.

4. THE ORIGINAL POSITION AND JUSTIFICATION

I have said that the original position is the appropriate initial status quo which insures that the fundamental agreements reached in it are fair. This fact yields the name "justice as fairness." It is clear, then, that I want to say that one conception of justice is more reasonable than another, or justifiable with respect to it, if rational persons in the initial situation would choose its principles over those of the other for the role of justice. Conceptions of justice are to be ranked by their acceptability to persons so circumstanced. Understood in this way the question of justification is settled by working out a problem of deliberation: we have to ascertain which principles it would be rational to adopt given the contractual situation. This connects the theory of justice with the theory of rational choice.

If this view of the problem of justification is to succeed, we must, of course, describe in some detail the nature of this choice problem. A problem of rational decision has a definite answer only if we know the beliefs and interests of the parties, their relations with respect to one another, the alternatives between which they are to choose, the procedure whereby they make up their minds, and so on. As the circumstances are presented in different ways, correspondingly different principles are accepted. The concept of the original position, as I shall refer to it, is that of the most philosophically favored interpretation of this initial choice situation for the purposes of a theory of justice.

But how are we to decide what is the most favored interpretation? I assume, for one thing, that there is a broad measure of agreement that principles of justice should be chosen under certain conditions. To justify a particular description of the initial situation one shows that it incorporates these commonly shared presumptions. One argues from widely accepted but weak premises to more specific conclusions. Each of the presumptions should by itself be natural and plausible; some of them may seem innocuous or even trivial. The aim of the contract approach is to establish that taken together they impose significant bounds on acceptable principles of justice. The ideal outcome would be that these conditions determine a unique set of principles; but I shall be satisfied if they suffice to rank the main traditional conceptions of social justice.

One should not be misled, then, by the somewhat unusual conditions which characterize the original position. The idea here is simply to make vivid to ourselves the restrictions that it seems reasonable to impose on arguments for principles of justice, and therefore on these principles themselves. Thus it seems reasonable and generally acceptable that no one should be advantaged or disadvantaged by natural fortune or social circumstances in the choice of principles. It also seems widely agreed that it should be impossible to tailor principles to the circumstances of one's own case. We should insure further that particular inclinations and aspirations, and persons' conceptions of their good do not affect the principles adopted. The aim is to rule out those principles that it would be rational to propose for acceptance, however little the chance of success, only if one knew certain things that are irrelevant from the standpoint of justice. For example, if a man knew that he was wealthy, he might find it rational to advance the principle that various taxes for welfare measures be counted unjust; if he knew that he was poor, he would most likely propose the contrary principle. To represent the desired restrictions one imagines a situation in which everyone is deprived of this sort of information. One excludes the knowledge of those contingencies which sets men at odds and allows them to be guided by their prejudices. In this manner the veil of ignorance is arrived at in a natural way. This concept should cause no difficulty if we keep in mind the constraints on arguments that it is meant to express. At any time we can enter the original position, so to speak, simply by following a certain procedure, namely, by arguing for principles of justice in accordance with these restrictions.

It seems reasonable to suppose that the parties in the original position are equal. That is, all have the same rights in the procedure for choosing principles; each can make proposals, submit reasons for their acceptance, and so on. Obviously the purpose of these conditions is to represent equality between human beings as moral persons, as creatures having a conception of their good and capable of a sense of justice. The basis of equality is taken to be similarity in these two respects. Systems of ends are not ranked in value; and each man is presumed to have the requisite ability to understand and to act upon whatever principles are adopted. Together with the veil of ignorance, these conditions define the principles of justice as those which rational persons concerned to advance their interests would consent to as equals when none are known to be advantaged or disadvantaged by social and natural contingencies.

There is, however, another side to justifying a particular description of the original position. This is to see if the principles which would be chosen match our considered convictions of justice or extend them in an acceptable way. We can note whether applying these principles would lead us to make the same judgments about the basic structure of society which we now make intuitively and in which we have the greatest confidence; or whether, in cases where our present judgments are in doubt and given with hesitation, these principles offer a resolution which we can affirm on reflection. There are questions which we feel sure must be answered in a certain way. For example, we are confident that religious intolerance and racial discrimination are unjust. We think that we have examined these things with care and have reached what we believe is an impartial judgment not likely to be distorted by an excessive attention to our own interests. These convictions are provisional fixed points which we presume any conception of justice must fit. But we have much less assurance as to what is the correct distribution of wealth and authority. Here we may be looking for a way to remove our doubts. We can check an interpretation of the initial situation, then, by the capacity of its principles to accommodate our firmest convictions and to provide guidance where guidance is needed.

In searching for the most favored description of this situation we work from both ends. We begin by describing it so that it represents generally shared and preferably weak conditions. We then see if these conditions are strong enough to yield a significant set of principles. If not, we look for further premises equally reasonable. But if so, and these principles match our considered convictions of justice, then so far well and good. But presumably there will be discrepancies. In this case we have a choice. We can either modify the account of the initial situation or we can revise our existing judgments, for even the judgments we take provisionally as fixed points are liable to revision. By going back and forth, sometimes altering the conditions of the contractual circumstances, at others withdrawing our judgments and conforming them to principle, I assume that eventually we shall find a description of the initial situation that both expresses reasonable conditions and yields principles which match our considered judgments duly pruned and adjusted. This state of affairs I refer to as reflective equilibrium.[7] It is an equilibrium because at last our principles and judgments coincide; and it is reflective since we know to what principles our judgments conform and the premises of their derivation. At the moment everything is in order. But this equilibrium is not necessarily stable. It is liable to be upset by further examination of the conditions which should be imposed on the contractual situation and by particular cases which may lead us to revise our judgments. Yet for the time being we have done what we can to render coherent and to justify our convictions of social justice. We have reached a conception of the original position.

I shall not, of course, actually work through this process. Still, we may think of the interpretation of the original position that I shall present as the result of such a hypothetical course of reflection. It represents the attempt to accommodate within one scheme both reasonable philosophical conditions on principles as well as our considered judgments of justice. In arriving at the favored interpretation of the initial situation there is no point at which an appeal is made to self-evidence in the traditional sense either of general conceptions or particular convictions. I do not claim for the principles of justice proposed that they are necessary truths or derivable from such truths. A conception of justice cannot be deduced from self-evident premises or conditions on principles; instead, its justification is a matter of the mutual support of many considerations, of everything fitting together into one coherent view.

A final comment. We shall want to say that certain principles of justice are justified because they would be agreed to in an initial situation of equality, I have emphasized that this original position is purely hypothetical. It is natural to ask why, if this agreement is never actually entered into, we should take any interest in these principles, moral or otherwise. The answer is that the conditions embodied in the description of the original position are ones that we do in fact accept. Or if we do not, then perhaps we can be persuaded to do so by philosophical reflection. Each aspect of the contractual situation can be given supporting grounds. Thus what we shall do is to collect together into one conception a number of conditions on principles that we are ready upon due consideration to recognize as reasonable. These constraints express what we are prepared to regard as limits on fair terms of social cooperation. One way to look at the idea of the original position, therefore, is to see it as an expository device which sums up the meaning of these conditions and helps us to extract their consequences. On the other hand, this conception is also an

---

7 The process of mutual adjustment of principles and considered judgments is not peculiar to moral philosophy. See Nelson Goodman, *Fact, Fiction, and Forecast* (Cambridge, Mass., Harvard University Press, 1955), pp. 65–68, for parallel remarks concerning the justification of the principles of deductive and inductive inference.

intuitive notion that suggests its own elaboration, so that led on by it we are drawn to define more clearly the standpoint from which we can best interpret moral relationships. We need a conception that enables us to envision our objective from afar: the intuitive notion of the original position is to do this for us.[8]

11. TWO PRINCIPLES OF JUSTICE

I shall now state in a provisional form the two principles of justice that I believe would be agreed to in the original position. The first formulation of these principles is tentative. As we go on I shall consider several formulations and approximate step by step the final statement to be given much later. I believe that doing this allows the exposition to proceed in a natural way.

The first statement of the two principles reads as follows.

> First: each person is to have an equal right to the most extensive scheme of equal basic liberties compatible with a similar scheme of liberties for others.
>
> Second: social and economic inequalities are to be arranged so that they are both (a) reasonably expected to be to everyone's advantage, and (b) attached to positions and offices open to all.

There are two ambiguous phrases in the second principle, namely "everyone's advantage" and "open to all." Determining their sense more exactly will lead to a second formulation of the principle in §13. The final version of the two principles is given in §46; §39 considers the rendering of the first principle.

These principles primarily apply, as I have said, to the basic structure of society and govern the assignment of rights and duties and regulate the distribution of social and economic advantages. Their formulation presupposes that, for the purposes of a theory of justice, the social structure may be viewed as having two more or less distinct parts, the first principle applying to the one, the second principle to the other. Thus we distinguish between the aspects of the social system that define and secure the equal basic liberties and the aspects that specify and establish social and economic inequalities. Now it is essential to observe that the basic liberties are given by a list of such liberties. Important among these are political liberty (the right to vote and to hold public

---

[8] Henri Poincaré remarks: "Il nous faut une faculté qui nous fasse voir le but de loin, et, cette faculté, c'est l'intuition." *La Valeur de la science* (Paris, Flammarion, 1909), p. 27.

office) and freedom of speech and assembly; liberty of conscience and freedom of thought; freedom of the person, which includes freedom from psychological oppression and physical assault and dismemberment (integrity of the person); the right to hold personal property and freedom from arbitrary arrest and seizure as defined by the concept of the rule of law. These liberties are to be equal by the first principle.

The second principle applies, in the first approximation, to the distribution of income and wealth and to the design of organizations that make use of differences in authority and responsibility. While the distribution of wealth and income need not be equal, it must be to everyone's advantage, and at the same time, positions of authority and responsibility must be accessible to all. One applies the second principle by holding positions open, and then, subject to this constraint, arranges social and economic inequalities so that everyone benefits.

These principles are to be arranged in a serial order with the first principle prior to the second. This ordering means that infringements of the basic equal liberties protected by the first principle cannot be justified, or compensated for, by greater social and economic advantages. These liberties have a central range of application within which they can be limited and compromised only when they conflict with other basic liberties. Since they may be limited when they clash with one another, none of these liberties is absolute; but however they are adjusted to form one system, this system is to be the same for all. It is difficult, and perhaps impossible, to give a complete specification of these liberties independently from the particular circumstances—social, economic, and technological—of a given society. The hypothesis is that the general form of such a list could be devised with sufficient exactness to sustain this conception of justice. Of course, liberties not on the list, for example, the right to own certain kinds of property (e.g., means of production) and freedom of contract as understood by the doctrine of laissez-faire are not basic; and so they are not protected by the priority of the first principle. Finally, in regard to the second principle, the distribution of wealth and income, and positions of authority and responsibility, are to be consistent with both the basic liberties and equality of opportunity.

The two principles are rather specific in their content, and their acceptance rests on certain assumptions that I must eventually try to explain and justify. For the present, it should be observed that these principles are a special case of a more general conception of justice that can be expressed as follows.

> All social values—liberty and opportunity, income and wealth, and the social bases of self-respect—are to be distributed equally unless an unequal distribution of any, or all, of these values is to everyone's advantage.

Injustice, then, is simply inequalities that are not to the benefit of all. Of course, this conception is extremely vague and requires interpretation.

As a first step, suppose that the basic structure of society distributes certain primary goods, that is, things that every rational man is presumed to want. These goods normally have a use whatever a person's rational plan of life. For simplicity, assume that the chief primary goods at the disposition of society are rights, liberties, and opportunities, and income and wealth. (Later on in Part Three the primary good of self-respect has a central place.) These are the social primary goods. Other primary goods such as health and vigor, intelligence and imagination, are natural goods; although their possession is influenced by the basic structure, they are not so directly under its control. Imagine, then, a hypothetical initial arrangement in which ail the social primary goods are equally distributed: everyone has similar rights and duties, and income and wealth are evenly shared. This state of affairs provides a benchmark for judging improvements. If certain inequalities of wealth and differences in authority would make everyone better off than in this hypothetical starting situation, then they accord with the general conception.

Now it is possible, at least theoretically, that by giving up some of their fundamental liberties men are sufficiently compensated by the resulting social and economic gains. The general conception of justice imposes no restrictions on what sort of inequalities are permissible; it only requires that everyone's position be improved. We need not suppose anything so drastic as consenting to a condition of slavery. Imagine instead that people seem willing to forego certain political rights when the economic returns are significant. It is this kind of exchange which the two principles rule out; being arranged in serial order they do not permit exchanges between basic liberties and economic and social gains except under extenuating circumstances (§§26, 39).

For the most part, I shall leave aside the general conception of justice and examine instead the two principles in serial order. The advantage of this procedure is that from the first the matter of priorities is recognized and an effort made to find principles to deal with it. One is led to attend throughout to the conditions under which the absolute weight of liberty with respect to social and economic advantages, as defined by the lexical order of the two principles, would be reasonable. Offhand, this ranking appears extreme and too special a case to be of much interest; but there is more justification for it than would appear at first sight. Or at any rate, so I shall maintain (§82). Furthermore, the distinction between fundamental rights and liberties and economic and social benefits marks a difference among primary social goods that suggests an important division in the social system. Of course, the distinctions drawn and the ordering proposed are at best only approximations. There are surely circumstances in which they fail. But it is essential to depict clearly the main lines of a reasonable conception of justice; and under many conditions anyway, the two principles in serial order may serve well enough.

The fact that the two principles apply to institutions has certain consequences. First of all, the rights and basic liberties referred to by these principles are those which are defined by the public rules of the basic structure. Whether men are free is determined by the rights and duties established by the major institutions of society. Liberty is a certain pattern of social forms. The first principle simply requires that certain sorts of rules, those defining basic liberties, apply to everyone equally and that they allow the most extensive liberty compatible with a like liberty for all. The only reason for circumscribing basic liberties and milking them less extensive is that otherwise they would interfere with one another.

Further, when principles mention persons, or require that everyone gain from an inequality, the reference is to representative persons holding the various social positions, or offices established by the basic structure. Thus in applying the second principle I assume that it is possible to assign an expectation of well-being to representative individuals holding these positions. This expectation indicates their life prospects as viewed from their social station. In general, the expectations of representative persons depend upon the distribution of rights and duties throughout the basic structure. Expectations are connected: by raising the prospects of the representative man in one position we presumably increase or decrease the prospects of representative men in other positions. Since it applies to institutional forms, the second principle (or rather the first part of it) refers to the expectations of representative individuals. As I shall discuss below (§14), neither principle applies to distributions of particular goods to particular individuals who may be identified by their proper names. The situation where someone is considering how to allocate certain commodities to needy persons who are known to him is not within the scope of the principles. They are meant to regulate basic institutional arrangements. We must not assume that there is much similarity from the standpoint of justice between an administrative allotment of goods to specific persons and the appropriate design of society. Our common sense intuitions for the former may be a poor guide to the latter.

Now the second principle insists that each person benefit from permissible inequalities in the basic structure. This means that it must be reasonable for each relevant representative man defined by this structure, when he views it as a going concern, to prefer his prospects with the inequality to his prospects without it. One is not allowed to justify differences in income or in positions of authority and responsibility on the ground that the disadvantages of those in one position are outweighed by the greater advantages of those in another. Much less can infringements of liberty be counterbalanced in this way. It is obvious, however, that there are indefinitely many ways in which all may be advantaged when the initial arrangement of equality is taken as a benchmark. How then are we to choose among these possibilities? The principles must be specified so that they yield a determinate conclusion. I now turn to this problem.

SOCIAL UNITY AND PRIMARY GOODS

SECTIONS IV AND V

BY JOHN RAWLS

John Rawls, ed. Samuel Freeman, "Sections IV and V," *John Rawls: Collected Papers*, pp. 368-374. Copyright © 1999 by Harvard University Press. Reprinted with permission.

FIVE

IV

Since the discussion so far has been quite general, the next two sections elaborate what has been said by turning to several more specific matters. I begin by considering what might seem to be an objection to the use of primary goods in a well-ordered society. It may be said that when we take the two principles of justice in their simplest form, so that income and wealth is the only primary good with which the difference principle is concerned, this principle cannot be reasonable or just. This can be shown, one might argue, by two examples: special medical and health needs, and the variation of preferences between persons.[1] The economist's utility function is designed to cope with cases of this kind; but when the difference principle relies on income and wealth alone, it clearly fails, the objection continues, to make a reasonable or just allowance for citizens' different needs and preferences.

It is best to make an initial concession in the case of special health and medical needs. I put this difficult problem aside in this paper and assume that all citizens have physical and psychological capacities within a certain normal range. I do this because the first problem of justice concerns the relations between citizens who are normally active and fully cooperating members of society over a complete life. Perhaps the social resources to be devoted to the normal health and medical needs of such citizens can be decided at the legislative stage in the light of existing social conditions and reasonable expectations of the frequency of illness and accident. If a solution can be worked out for this case, then it may be possible to extend it to

---

[1] This objection, discussed in this section, was raised by K. J. Arrow in his review, "Some Ordinalist-Utilitarian Notes on Rawls's Theory of Justice," *Journal of Philosophy*, 70, no. 9 (1973): 253–254.

the hard cases. If it cannot be worked out for this case, the idea of primary goods may have to be abandoned. The point is, however, that a conception of justice need not rest on a few universal principles which apply to all cases. What is required is that from the standpoint of the original position, or some other appropriate stage, the whole family of principles can be combined into a coherent framework of deliberation.[2]

The second example bears on our present purposes. Imagine two persons, one satisfied with a diet of milk, bread, and beans, while the other is distraught without expensive wines and exotic dishes. In short, one has expensive tastes, the other does not. If the two principles of justice are understood in their simplest form (as I assume here), then we must say, the objection runs, that with equal income both are equally satisfied. But this is plainly not true. At best, citizens' income and wealth is only a rough indictor of their level of satisfaction and even an index could not be very accurate. More important, it will often be too inaccurate to be fair. The reply is that as moral persons citizens have some part in forming and cultivating their final ends and preferences. It is not by itself an objection to the use of primary goods that it does not accommodate those with expensive tastes. One must argue in addition that it is unreasonable, if not unjust, to hold such persons responsible for their preferences and to require them to make out as best they can. But to argue this seems to presuppose that citizens' preferences are beyond their control as propensities or cravings which simply happen. Citizens seem to be regarded as passive carriers of desires. The use of primary goods, however, relies on a capacity to assume responsibility for our ends. This capacity is part of the moral power to form, to revise, and rationally to pursue a conception of the good. Thus, in the case we are discussing, it is public knowledge that the principles of justice view citizens as responsible for their ends. In any particular situation, then, those with less expensive tastes have presumably adjusted their likes and dislikes over the course of their lives to the income and wealth they could reasonably expect; and it is regarded as unfair that they now should have less in order to spare others from the consequences of their lack of foresight or self-discipline.

The idea of holding citizens responsible for their ends is plausible, however, only on certain assumptions.[3] First, we must assume that citizens can regulate and revise their ends and

---

2   As the remarks in this paragraph suggest, the weights for the index of primary goods need not be established in the original position once and for all, and in detail, for every well-ordered society. What is to be established initially is the general form of the index and such constraints on the weights as that expressed by the priority of the basic liberties. Further details necessary for practice can be filled in progressively in the stages sketched in TJ, sec. 31, as more specific information is made available. When we attempt to deal with the problem of special medical and health needs, a different or a more comprehensive notion than that of primary goods (at least as presented in the text) will, I believe, be necessary, for example, Sen's notion of an index which focuses on persons' basic capabilities may prove fruitful for this problem and serve as an essential complement to the use of primary goods. See A. K. Sen, "Equality of What?" in *Tanner Lectures on Human Values,* vol. I, ed. S. McMurrin (Cambridge: Cambridge University Press, 1980), pp. 217–219.
3   This paragraph revises my brief sketch of the presuppositions of the use of primary goods, in chapter 13. I believe it now accords with Scanlon's view in "Preference and Urgency." I am grateful to Scanlon and to Samuel Scheffler for helpful discussion of these points.

preferences in the light of their expectations of primary goods. This assumption is implicit in the powers we attribute to citizens in regarding them as moral persons. But by itself this assumption does not suffice. We must also find workable criteria for interpersonal comparisons which can be publicly and, if possible, easily applied. Thus we try to show, second, how primary goods are connected with the highest-order interests of moral persons in such a way that these goods are indeed feasible public criteria for questions of justice. Finally, the effective use of primary goods assumes also that the conception of the person which lies at the basis of these two assumptions is at least implicitly accepted as an ideal underlying the public principles of justice. Otherwise, citizens would be less willing to accept responsibility in the sense required.

Thus, the share of primary goods that citizens receive is not intended as a measure of their psychological well-being. In relying on primary goods, justice as fairness rejects the idea of comparing and maximizing satisfaction in questions of justice. Nor does it try to estimate the extent to which individuals succeed in advancing their ends, or to evaluate the merits of these ends (so long as they are compatible with the principles of justice). While an index of primary goods serves some of the purposes of a utility function, the basic idea is different: primary goods are social background conditions and all-purpose means generally necessary for forming and rationally pursuing a conception of the good. The principles of justice are to ensure to all citizens the equal protection of and access to these conditions, and to provide each with a fair share of the requisite all-purpose means. The upshot is that, once an index of primary goods is made a part of the two principles of justice, the application of these principles with the index permits the characterization of what are citizens' appropriate claims to social resources. Although the shares that result must fit society's sense of justice on due reflection, this fit need not, of course, be perfect, but only close enough so that a sufficient convergence of opinion in questions of justice is achieved to sustain willing social cooperation. Thus primary goods help to provide a public standard which all may accept.[4] On the other hand, given the circumstances of justice in which citizens have conflicting conceptions of the good, there cannot be any practical agreement on how to compare happiness as defined, say, by success in carrying out plans of life, nor, even less, any practical agreement on how to evaluate the intrinsic value of these plans. Workable criteria for a public understanding of what is to count as advantageous in matters of justice, and hence as rendering some better situated than others in the relevant interpersonal comparisons, must, I believe, be founded on primary goods, or on some similar notion.

---

4   In the next to last paragraph of "Preference and Urgency," Scanlon distinguishes two interpretations of urgency, a naturalist and a conventionalist. While I should not want to call the use of primary goods a "convention," the background doctrine is not naturalistic, as the connection of primary goods with the Conception of the person, for example, makes clear. An index of these goods is closer to Scanlon's description of a conventionalist interpretation of urgency, that is, it is a "construct put together for the purposes of moral argument ... its usefulness ... stems from the fact that it represents, under the circumstances, the best available standard of justification that is mutually acceptable to persons whose preferences diverge."

V

The preceding account of primary goods shows that their use in making interpersonal comparisons in questions of justice rests on the conception of moral persons and connects with the public conception of justice in a well-ordered society. This conception includes what we may call a social division of responsibility: society, the citizens as a collective body, accepts the responsibility for maintaining the equal basic liberties and fair equality of opportunity, and for providing a fair share of the other primary goods for everyone within this framework, while citizens (as individuals) and associations accept the responsibility for revising and adjusting their ends and aspirations in view of the all-purpose means they can expect, given their present and foreseeable situation. This division of responsibility relies on the capacity of persons to assume responsibility for their ends and to moderate the claims they make on their social institutions in accordance with the use of primary goods. Citizens' claims to liberties, opportunities, and all-purpose means are made secure from the unreasonable demands of others.

We arrive, then, at the idea that citizens as free and equal persons are at liberty to take charge of their lives and each is to adapt their conception of the good to their expected fair share of primary goods. The only restriction on plans of life is that their fulfillment be compatible with the public principles of justice, and claims may be advanced only for certain kinds of things (primary goods) and in ways allowed for by these principles. This implies that strong feelings and zealous aspirations for certain goals do not, as such, give people a claim upon social resources, or a claim to design public institutions so as to achieve these goals. Desires and wants, however intense, are not by themselves reasons in matters of justice. The fact that we have a compelling desire does not argue for the propriety of its satisfaction any more than the strength of a conviction argues for its truth. Combined with an index of primary goods, the principles of justice detach reasons of justice not only from the ebb and flow of fluctuating wants and desires but even from long-standing sentiments and commitments. The significance of this is illustrated by religious toleration, which gives no weight to the strength of conviction by which we may oppose the religious beliefs and practices of others.[5]

---

5   The priority of liberty and this detachment of reasons! of justice from reasons of preference and desire are related to the Paradox of the Paretian Liberal discovered by A. K. Sen, namely , the incompatibility (given certain standard assumptions) between the Pareto principle and even a minimal assignment of individual rights. See A. K. Sen, *Collective Choice and Social Welfare* (San Francisco: Holden and Day, 1970), pp. 82–88, 87–88. Many proposed solutions to this incompatibility are surveyed in Sen, "Liberty, Unanimity and Rights," *Economka*, 43 (1976): 217–246. The problem is far too complicated to be considered here, except to say that the paradox cannot, I think, arise within justice as fairness because of the priority of liberty and the subordinate scope allowed for reasons of preference. The basic liberties are, in effect, inalienable and therefore can neither be waived nor limited by any agreements made by citizens, nor overridden by shared collective preferences. These liberties are not on the same plane as these considerations. In this respect the view of justice as fairness resembles the way Robert Nozick treats the paradox, in *Anarchy, State and Utopia* (New York: Basic Books, 1974), pp. 164–166. However, the rights which Nozick takes as fundamental are different from the

SOCIAL UNITY AND PRIMARY GOODS

The principles of justice treat all citizens with respect to their conception of the good as equals. All citizens have the same basic liberties and enjoy fair equality of opportunity; they share in the other primary goods on the principle that some can have more only if they acquire more in ways which improve the situation of those who have less. Moreover, all conceptions of the good (consistent with justice) are regarded as equally worthy, not in the sense that there is an agreed public measure of intrinsic value or satisfaction with respect to which all these conceptions come out equal, but in the sense that they are not evaluated at all from a social standpoint. The role of the conception of the person in the explanation and derivation of the two principles of justice allows us to say that these principles define a just scheme of social cooperation in which citizens are regarded as free and equal moral persons.

It remains to conclude with a few remarks on the notion of appropriate claims in questions of justice. Note first that, by relying on primaiy goods, justice as fairness asserts that for questions of justice only certain kinds of considerations are relevant. The reason is that we make interpersonal comparisons in many different contexts and for many different purposes; each context has its relevant considerations according to the appropriate ends in view. On birthdays we give things that we know are wanted, or that will please, to express affection; our gifts are chosen in the light of intimate knowledge and shared experiences. But doctors are expected to assess the situations of their patients, and teachers to judge their students, on an entirely different basis and from the standpoint of a distinct conception of their role. Thus doctors consider their patients' medical needs, what is required to restore them to good health and how urgent their treatment is; whereas deserts, in the sense of conscientious effort to learn, may be thought relevant by teachers in deciding how best to guide and encourage their students. Thus the relevant considerations depend on how a case is understood.

Now of the three kinds of considerations just mentioned (those involving desires, needs, and deserts) the idea of restricting appropriate claims to claims to primary goods is analogous to taking certain needs alone as relevant in questions of justice. The explanation is that primary goods are things generally required, or needed, by citizens as free and equal moral persons who seek to advance (admissible and determinate) conceptions of the good. It is the conception of citizens as such persons, and as normal cooperating members of society over a complete life, which

---

equal basic liberties included in the principles of justice, and his account of the basis of rights is distinct from that of the equal basic liberties in justice as fairness. Thus, these liberties are not, I think, inalienable in Nozick's view, whereas in justice as fairness any undertakings to waive or to infringe them are void *ab initio*; citizens' desires in this respect have no legal force and should not affect these rights. Nor should the desires of however many others to deny or limit a person's equal basic liberties have any weight. Preferences which would have this effect, never, so to speak, enter into the social calculus. In this way the principles of justice give force to the agreement of the parties in the original position, an agreement framed to secure their highest-order interests. Both the agreements and preferences of citizens in society are counted as hierarchically subordinate to these interests, and this is the ground of the priority of liberty. Of course, none of this rules out that justice as fairness may have its own paradoxes.

determines what they require. Since the notion of need is always relative to some conception of persons, and of their role and status, the requirements, or needs, of citizens as free and equal moral persons are different from the needs of patients and students. And needs are different from desires, wishes, and likings. Citizens' needs are objective in a way that desires are not; that is, they express requirements of persons with certain highest-order interests who have a certain social role and status. If these requirements are not met, persons cannot maintain their role or status, or achieve their essential aims. A citizen's claim that something is a need can be denied when it is not a requirement. Thus, in regarding the members of society as free and equal moral persons, we ascribe to them certain requirements, or needs, which, given the nature of these requirements and the form of rational plans of life, explain how primary goods can be used to define appropriate claims in questions of justice. In effect, the conception of the person and the notion of primary goods simply characterize a special kind of need for a conception of justice. Needs in any other sense, along with desires and aspirations, play no role.

It might seem, however, that if restricting appropriate claims to primary goods is analogous to taking certain needs alone as relevant, then justice must require distribution according to these needs. And since one might also think that the requirements of citizens as free and equal moral persons are equal, why is not an equal share of *all* primary goods the sole principle of justice? I cannot argue this question here and shall only comment that, although the parties in the original position know that the persons they represent require primary goods, it does not follow that it is rational for the parties as their representatives to agree to such a strict principle of equality. The two principles of justice regulate social and economic inequalities in the basic structure so that these inequalities work over time to the greatest benefit of the least advantaged citizens. These principles express a more rational agreement. They also express a kind of equality, since they take an equal division of primary goods as the benchmark of comparison.

A THEORY OF JUSTICE

CHAPTERS 3 AND 4

BY JOHN RAWLS

John Rawls, "Selections," *A Theory of Justice,* pp. 102-109, 118-123, 153-160, 221-227. Copyright © 1999 by Harvard University Press. Reprinted with permission.

SIX

In this chapter I discuss the favored philosophical interpretation of the initial situation. I refer to this interpretation as the original position. I begin by sketching the nature of the argument for conceptions of justice and explaining how the alternatives are presented so that the parties are to choose from a definite list of traditional conceptions. Then I describe the conditions which characterize the initial situation under several headings: the circumstances of justice, the formal constraints of the concept of right, the veil of ignorance, and the rationality of the contracting parties. In each case I try to indicate why the features adopted for the favored interpretation are reasonable from a philosophical point of view. Next the natural lines of reasoning leading to the two principles of justice and to the principle of average utility are examined prior to a consideration of the relative advantages of these conceptions of justice. I argue that the two principles would be acknowledged and set out some of the main grounds to support this contention. In order to clarify the differences between the various conceptions of justice, the chapter concludes with another look at the classical principle of utility.

THE NATURE OF THE ARGUMENT FOR CONCEPTIONS OF JUSTICE

The intuitive idea of justice as fairness is to think of the first principles of justice as themselves the object of an original agreement in a suitably defined initial situation. These principles are those which rational persons concerned to advance their interests would accept in this position of equality to settle the basic terms of their association. It must be shown, then, that the two principles of justice are the solution for the problem of choice presented by the original position. In order to do this, one must establish that, given the circumstances of the parties, and their knowledge, beliefs, and interests, an agreement on these principles is the best way for each person to secure his ends in view of the alternatives available.

Now obviously no one can obtain everything he wants; the mere existence of other persons prevents this. The absolutely best for any man is that everyone else should join with him in furthering his conception of the good whatever it turns out to be. Or failing this, that all others are required to act justly but that he is authorized to exempt himself as he pleases. Since other persons will never agree to such terms of association these forms of egoism would be rejected. The two principles of justice, however, seem to be a reasonable proposal. In fact, I should like to show that these principles are everyone's best reply, so to speak, to the corresponding demands of the others. In this sense, the choice of this conception of justice is the unique solution to the problem set by the original position.

By arguing in this way one follows a procedure familiar in social theory. That is, a simplified situation is described in which rational individuals with certain ends and related to each other in certain ways are to choose among various courses of action in view of their knowledge of the circumstances. What these individuals will do is then derived by strictly deductive reasoning from these assumptions about their beliefs and interests, their situation and the options open to them. Their conduct is, in the phrase of Pareto, the resultant of tastes and obstacles.[1] In the theory of price, for example, the equilibrium of competitive markets is thought of as arising when many individuals each advancing his own interests give way to each other what they can best part with in return for what they most desire. Equilibrium is the result of agreements freely struck between willing traders. For each person it is the best situation that he can reach by free exchange consistent with the right and freedom of others to further their interests in the same way. It is for this reason that this state of affairs is an equilibrium, one that will persist in the absence of further changes in the circumstances. No one has any incentive to alter it. If a departure from this situation sets in motion tendencies which restore it, the equilibrium is stable.

Of course, the fact that a situation is one of equilibrium, even a stable one, does not entail that it is right or just. It only means that given men's estimate of their position, they act effectively to preserve it. Clearly a balance of hatred and hostility may be a stable equilibrium; each may think that any feasible change will be worse. The best that each can do for himself may be a condition of lesser injustice rather than of greater good. The moral assessment of equilibrium situations depends upon the background circumstances which determine them. It is at this point that the conception of the original position embodies features peculiar to moral theory. For while the theory of price, say, tries to account for the movements of the market by assumptions about the actual tendencies at work, the philosophically favored interpretation of the initial situation

---

1 *Manuel d'économie politique* (Paris, 1909), ch. III, §23. Pareto says: "L'equilibre résulte précisément de cette opposition des goûts et des obstacles."

incorporates conditions which it is thought reasonable to impose on the choice of principles. By contrast with social theory, the aim is to characterize this situation so that the principles that would be chosen, whatever they turn out to be, are acceptable from a moral point of view. The original position is defined in such a way that it is a status quo in which any agreements reached are fair. It is a state of affairs in which the parties are equally represented as moral persons and the outcome is not conditioned by arbitrary contingencies or the relative balance of social forces. Thus justice as fairness is able to use the idea of pure procedural justice from the beginning.

It is clear, then, that the original position is a purely hypothetical situation. Nothing resembling it need ever take place, although we can by deliberately following the constraints it expresses simulate the reflections of the parties. The conception of the original position is not intended to explain human conduct except insofar as it tries to account for our moral judgments and helps to explain our having a sense of justice. Justice as fairness is a theory of our moral sentiments as manifested by our considered judgments in reflective equilibrium. These sentiments presumably affect our thought and action to some degree. So while the conception of the original position is part of the theory of conduct, it does not follow at all that there are actual situations that resemble it. What is necessary is that the principles that would be accepted play the requisite part in our moral reasoning and conduct.

One should note also that the acceptance of these principles is not conjectured as a psychological law or probability. Ideally anyway, I should like to show that their acknowledgment is the only choice consistent with the full description of the original position. The argument aims eventually to be strictly deductive. To be sure, the persons in the original position have a certain psychology, since various assumptions are made about their beliefs and interests. These assumptions appear along with other premises in the description of this initial situation. But clearly arguments from such premises can be fully deductive, as theories in politics and economics attest. We should strive for a kind of moral geometry with all the rigor which this name connotes. Unhappily the reasoning I shall give will fall far short of this, since it is highly intuitive throughout. Yet it is essential to have in mind the ideal one would like to achieve.

A final remark. There are, as I have said, many possible interpretations of the initial situation. This conception varies depending upon how the contracting parties are conceived, upon what their beliefs and interests are said to be, upon which alternatives are available to them, and so on. In this sense, there are many different contract theories. Justice as fairness is but one of these. But the question of justification is settled, as far as it can be, by showing that there is one interpretation of the initial situation which best expresses the conditions that are widely thought reasonable to impose on the choice of principles yet which, at the same time, leads to a conception that characterizes our considered judgments in reflective equilibrium. This most favored, or standard, interpretation I shall refer to as the original position. We may conjecture that for each traditional conception of justice there exists an interpretation of the initial situation in which its principles are the preferred solution. Thus, for example, there are interpretations that lead to the classical as well as the average principle of utility. These variations of the initial situation will be mentioned as we go along. The procedure of contract theories provides, then, a general analytic method for the comparative study of conceptions of justice. One tries to set out the different conditions embodied in the contractual situation in which their principles would be chosen. In this way one formulates the various underlying assumptions on which these conceptions seem to depend. But if one interpretation is philosophically most favored, and if its principles characterize our considered judgments, we have a procedure for justification as well. We cannot know at first whether such an interpretation exists, but at least we know what to look for.

THE PRESENTATION OF ALTERNATIVES

Let us now turn from these remarks on method to the description of the original position. I shall begin with the question of the alternatives open to the persons in this situation. Ideally of course one would like to say that they are to choose among all possible conceptions of justice. One obvious difficulty is how these conceptions are to be characterized so that those in the original position can be presented with them. Yet granting that these conceptions could be defined, there is no assurance that the parties could make out the best option; the principles that would be most preferred might be overlooked. Indeed, there may exist no best alternative: conceivably for each conception of justice there is another that is better. Even if there is a best alternative, it seems difficult to describe the parties' intellectual powers so that this optimum, or even the more plausible conceptions, are sure to occur to them. Some solutions to the choice problem may be clear enough on careful reflection; it is another matter to describe the parties so that their deliberations generate these alternatives. Thus although the two principles of justice may be superior to those conceptions known to us, perhaps some hitherto unformulated set of principles is still better.

In order to handle this problem I shall resort to the following device. I shall simply take as given a short list of traditional conceptions of justice, for example those discussed in the first chapter, together with a few other possibilities suggested by the two principles of justice. I then assume that the parties are presented with this list and required to agree unanimously that one conception is the best among those enumerated. We may suppose that this decision is arrived at by making a series of comparisons in pairs. Thus the two principles would be shown to be preferable once all agree that they are to be chosen over each of the other alternatives. In this chapter I shall consider for the most part the choice between the two principles of justice and two forms of the principle of utility (the classical and the average principle). Later on, the comparisons with perfectionism and mixed theories are discussed. In this manner I try to show that the two principles would be chosen from the list.

Now admittedly this is an unsatisfactory way to proceed. It would be better if we could define necessary and sufficient conditions for a uniquely best conception of justice and then exhibit a conception that fulfilled these conditions. Eventually one may be able to do this. For the time being, however, I do not see how to avoid rough and ready methods. Moreover, using such procedures may point to a general solution of our problem. Thus it may turn out that, as we run through these comparisons, the reasoning of the parties singles out certain features of the basic structure as desirable, and that these features have natural maximum and minimum properties. Suppose, for example, that it is rational for the persons in the original position to prefer a society with the greatest equal liberty. And suppose further that while they prefer social and economic advantages to work for the common good they insist that they mitigate the ways in which men are advantaged or disadvantaged by natural and social contingencies. If these two features are the only relevant ones, and if the principle of equal liberty is the natural maximum of the first feature, and the difference principle (constrained by fair equality of opportunity) the natural maximum of the second, then, leaving aside the problem of priority, the two principles are the optimum solution. The fact that one cannot constructively characterize or enumerate all possible conceptions of justice, or describe the parties so that they are bound to think of them, is no obstacle to this conclusion.

It would not be profitable to pursue these speculations any further. For the present, no attempt is made to deal with the general problem of the best solution. I limit the argument throughout to the weaker contention that the two principles would be chosen from the conceptions of justice on the following list.

A. The Two Principles of Justice (in serial order)
   1. The principle of greatest equal liberty
   2. (a) The principle of (fair) equality of opportunity
      (b) The difference principle
B. Mixed Conceptions. Substitute one for A2 above
   1. The principle of average utility; or
   2. The principle of average utility, subject to a constraint, either:
      (a) That a certain social minimum be maintained, or
      (b) That the overall distribution not be too wide; or
   3. The principle of average utility subject to either constraint in B2 plus that of equality of fair opportunity
C. Classical Teleological Conceptions
   1. The classical principle of utility
   2. The average principle of utility
   3. The principle of perfection

D. Intuitionistic Conceptions
   1. To balance total utility against the principle of equal distribution
   2. To balance average utility against the principle of redress
   3. To balance a list of prima facie principles (as appropriate)
E. Egoistic Conceptions (See §23 where it is explained why strictly speaking the egoistic conceptions are not alternatives.)
   1. First-person dictatorship: Everyone is to serve my interests
   2. Free-rider: Everyone is to act justly except for myself, if I choose not to
   3. General: Everyone is permitted to advance his interests as he pleases

The merits of these traditional theories surely suffice to justify the effort to rank them. And in any case, the study of this ranking is a useful way of feeling one's way into the larger question. Now each of these conceptions presumably has its assets and liabilities; there are reasons for and against any alternative one selects. The fact that a conception is open to criticism is not necessarily decisive against it, nor are certain desirable features always conclusive in its favor. The decision of the persons in the original position hinges, as we shall see, on a balance of various considerations. In this sense, there is an appeal to intuition at the basis of the theory of justice. Yet when everything is tallied up, it may be perfectly clear where the balance of reason lies. The relevant reasons may have been so factored and analyzed by the description of the original position that one conception of justice is distinctly preferable to the others. The argument for it is not strictly speaking a proof, not yet anyway; but, in Mill's phrase, it may present considerations capable of determining the intellect.[2]

The list of conceptions is largely self-explanatory. A few brief comments, however, may be useful. Each conception is expressed in a reasonably simple way, and each holds unconditionally, that is, whatever the circumstances or state of society. None of the principles is contingent upon certain social or other conditions. Now one reason for this is to keep things simple. It would be easy to formulate a family of conceptions each designed to apply only if special circumstances obtain, these various conditions being exhaustive and mutually exclusive. For example one conception might hold at one stage of culture, a different conception at another. Such a family could be counted as itself a conception of justice; it would consist of a set of ordered pairs, each pair being a conception of justice matched with the circumstances in which it applies. But if conceptions of this kind were added to the list, our problem would become very complicated if not unmanageable. Moreover, there is a reason for excluding alternatives of this kind, for it is natural to ask what underlying principle determines the ordered pairs. Here I assume that some recognizably ethical conception specifies the appropriate principles given each of the conditions. It is really

---

2 *Utilitarianism*, ch. I, par. 5.

this unconditional principle that defines the conception expressed by the set of ordered pairs. Thus to allow such families on the list is to include alternatives that conceal their proper basis. So for this reason as well I shall exclude them. It also turns out to be desirable to characterize the original position so that the parties are to choose principles that hold unconditionally whatever the circumstances. This fact is connected with the Kantian interpretation of justice as fairness. But I leave this matter aside until later (§40).

Finally, an obvious point. An argument for the two principles, or indeed for any conception, is always relative to some list of alternatives. If we change the list, the argument will, in general, have to be different. A similar sort of remark applies to all features of the original position. There are indefinitely many variations of the initial situation and therefore no doubt indefinitely many theorems of moral geometry. Only a few of these are of any philosophical interest, since most variations are irrelevant from a moral point of view. We must try to steer clear of side issues while at the same time not losing sight of the special assumptions of the argument.

THE VEIL OF IGNORANCE

The idea of the original position is to set up a fair procedure so that any principles agreed to will be just. The aim is to use the notion of pure procedural justice as a basis of theory. Somehow we must nullify the effects of specific contingencies which put men at odds and tempt them to exploit social and natural circumstances to their own advantage. Now in order to do this I assume that the parties are situated behind a veil of ignorance. They do not know how the various alternatives will affect their own particular case and they are obliged to evaluate principles solely on the basis of general considerations.[3]

It is assumed, then, that the parties do not know certain kinds of particular facts. First of all, no one knows his place in society, his class position or social status; nor does he know his fortune in the distribution of natural assets and abilities, his intelligence and strength, and the like. Nor, again, does anyone know his conception of the good, the particulars of his rational plan of life, or even the special features of his psychology such as his aversion to risk or liability to optimism or pessimism. More than this, I assume that the parties do not know the particular circumstances

---

3 The veil of ignorance is so natural a condition that something like it must have occurred to many. The formulation in the text is implicit, I believe, in Kant's doctrine of the categorical imperative, both in the way this procedural criterion is defined and the use Kant makes of it. Thus when Kant tells us to test our maxim by considering what would be the case were it a universal law of nature, he must suppose that we do not know our place within this imagined system of nature. See, for example, his discussion of the topic of practical judgment in *The Critique of Practical Reason*, Academy Edition, vol. 5, pp. 68–72. A similar restriction on information is found in J. C. Harsanyi, "Cardinal Utility in Welfare Economics and in the Theory of Risk-taking," *Journal of Political Economy*, vol. 61 (1953). However, other aspects of Harsanyi's view are quite different, and he uses the restriction to develop a utilitarian theory. See the last paragraph of §27.

of their own society. That is, they do not know its economic or political situation, or the level of civilization and culture it has been able to achieve. The persons in the original position have no information as to which generation they belong. These broader restrictions on knowledge are appropriate in part because questions of social justice arise between generations as well as within them, for example, the question of the appropriate rate of capital saving and of the conservation of natural resources and the environment of nature. There is also, theoretically anyway, the question of a reasonable genetic policy. In these cases too, in order to carry through the idea of the original position, the parties must not know the contingencies that set them in opposition. They must choose principles the consequences of which they are prepared to live with whatever generation they turn out to belong to.

As far as possible, then, the only particular facts which the parties know is that their society is subject to the circumstances of justice and whatever this implies. It is taken for granted, however, that they know the general facts about human society. They understand political affairs and the principles of economic theory; they know the basis of social organization and the laws of human psychology. Indeed, the parties are presumed to know whatever general facts affect the choice of the principles of justice. There are no limitations on general information, that is, on general laws and theories, since conceptions of justice must be adjusted to the characteristics of the systems of social cooperation which they are to regulate, and there is no reason to rule out these facts. It is, for example, a consideration against a conception of justice that, in view of the laws of moral psychology, men would not acquire a desire to act upon it even when the institutions of their society satisfied it. For in this case there would be difficulty in securing the stability of social cooperation. An important feature of a conception of justice is that it should generate its own support. Its principles should be such that when they are embodied in the basic structure of society men tend to acquire the corresponding sense of justice and develop a desire to act in accordance with its principles. In this case a conception of justice is stable. This kind of general information is admissible in the original position.

The notion of the veil of ignorance raises several difficulties. Some may object that the exclusion of nearly all particular information makes it difficult to grasp what is meant by the original position. Thus it may be helpful to observe that one or more persons can at any time enter this position, or perhaps better, simulate the deliberations of this hypothetical situation, simply by reasoning in accordance with the appropriate restrictions. In arguing for a conception of justice we must be sure that it is among the permitted alternatives and satisfies the stipulated formal constraints. No considerations can be advanced in its favor unless they would be rational ones for us to urge were we to lack the kind of knowledge that is excluded. The evaluation of principles must proceed in terms of the general consequences of their public recognition and universal application, it being assumed that they will be complied with by everyone. To say that a certain conception of justice would be chosen in the original position is equivalent to saying that rational deliberation satisfying certain conditions and restrictions would reach a certain conclusion. If necessary, the argument to this result could be set out more formally. I shall, however, speak throughout in terms of the notion of the original position. It is more economical and suggestive, and brings out certain essential features that otherwise one might easily overlook.

These remarks show that the original position is not to be thought of as a general assembly which includes at one moment everyone who will live at some time; or, much less, as an assembly of everyone who could live at some time. It is not a gathering of all actual or possible persons. If we conceived of the original position in either of these ways, the conception would cease to be a natural guide to intuition and would lack a clear sense. In any case, the original position must be interpreted so that one can at any time adopt its perspective. It must make no difference when one takes up this viewpoint, or who does so: the restrictions must be such that the same principles are always chosen. The veil of ignorance is a key condition in meeting this requirement. It insures not only that the information available is relevant, but that it is at all times the same.

It may be protested that the condition of the veil of ignorance is irrational. Surely, some may object, principles should be chosen in the light of all the knowledge available. There are various replies to this contention. Here I shall sketch those which emphasize the simplifications that need to be made if one is to have any theory at all. (Those based on the Kantian interpretation of the original position are given later, §40.) To begin with, it is clear that since the differences among the parties are unknown to them, and everyone is equally rational and similarly situated, each is convinced by the same arguments. Therefore, we can view the agreement in the original position from the standpoint of one person selected at random. If anyone after due reflection prefers a conception of justice to another, then they all do, and a unanimous agreement can be reached. We can, to make the circumstances more vivid, imagine that the parties are required to communicate with each other through a referee as intermediary, and that he is to announce which alternatives have been suggested and the reasons offered in their support. He forbids the attempt to form coalitions, and he informs the parties when they have come to an understanding. But such a referee is actually superfluous, assuming that the deliberations of the parties must be similar.

Thus there follows the very important consequence that the parties have no basis for bargaining in the usual sense. No one knows his situation in society nor his natural assets, and therefore no one is in a position to tailor principles to his advantage. We might imagine that one of the contractees threatens to hold out unless the others agree to principles favorable to him. But how does he know which principles are especially in his interests? The same holds for the formation of coalitions: if a group were to decide to band together to the disadvantage of the others, they would not know how to favor themselves in the choice of principles. Even if they could get everyone to agree to their proposal, they would have no assurance that it was to their advantage, since they cannot identify themselves either by name or description. The one case where this conclusion fails is that of saving. Since the persons in the original position know that they are contemporaries (taking the present time of entry interpretation), they can favor their generation by refusing to make any sacrifices at all for their successors; they simply acknowledge the principle that no one has a duty to save for posterity. Previous generations have saved or they have not; there is nothing the parties can now do to affect that. So in this instance the veil of ignorance fails to secure the desired result. Therefore, to handle the question of justice between generations, I modify the motivation assumption and add a further constraint (§22). With these adjustments, no generation is able to formulate principles especially designed to advance its own cause and some significant limits on savings principles can be derived (§44). Whatever a person's temporal position, each is forced to choose for all.[4]

The restrictions on particular information in the original position are, then, of fundamental importance. Without them we would not be able to work out any definite theory of justice at all. We would have to be content with a vague formula stating that justice is what would be agreed to without being able to say much, if anything, about the substance of the agreement itself. The formal constraints of the concept of right, those applying to principles directly, are not sufficient for our purpose. The veil of ignorance makes possible a unanimous choice of a particular conception of justice. Without these limitations on knowledge the bargaining problem of the original position would be hopelessly complicated. Even if theoretically a solution were to exist, we would not, at present anyway, be able to determine it.

The notion of the veil of ignorance is implicit, I think, in Kant's ethics (§40). Nevertheless the problem of defining the knowledge of the parties and of characterizing the alternatives open to them has often been passed over, even by contract theories. Sometimes the situation definitive of moral deliberation is presented in such an indeterminate way that one cannot ascertain how it will turn out. Thus Perry's doctrine is essentially contractarian: he holds that social and personal integration must proceed by entirely different principles, the latter by rational prudence, the former by the concurrence of persons of good will. He would appear to reject utilitarianism on much the same grounds suggested earlier: namely, that it improperly extends the principle of choice for one person to choices facing society. The right course of action is characterized as that which best advances social aims as these would be formulated by reflective agreement, given that the parties have full knowledge of the circumstances and are moved by a benevolent concern for one another's interests. No effort is made, however, to specify in any precise way the possible outcomes of this sort of agreement. Indeed, without a far more elaborate account, no conclusions can be drawn.[5] I do not wish here to criticize others; rather, I want to explain the necessity for what may seem at times like so many irrelevant details.

Now the reasons for the veil of ignorance go beyond mere simplicity. We want to define the original position so that we get the desired solution. If a knowledge of particulars is allowed, then

---

4 Rousseau, *The Social Contract*, bk. II, ch. IV, par. 5.
5 See R. B. Perry, *The General Theory of Value* (New York, Longmans, Green and Company, 1926), pp. 674–682.

the outcome is biased by arbitrary contingencies. As already observed, to each according to his threat advantage is not a principle of justice. If the original position is to yield agreements that are just, the parties must be fairly situated and treated equally as moral persons. The arbitrariness of the world must be corrected for by adjusting the circumstances of the initial contractual situation. Moreover, if in choosing principles we required unanimity even when there is full information, only a few rather obvious cases could be decided. A conception of justice based on unanimity in these circumstances would indeed be weak and trivial. But once knowledge is excluded, the requirement of unanimity is not out of place and the fact that it can be satisfied is of great importance. It enables us to say of the preferred conception of justice that it represents a genuine reconciliation of interests.

A final comment. For the most part I shall suppose that the parties possess all general information. No general facts are closed to them. I do this mainly to avoid complications. Nevertheless a conception of justice is to be the public basis of the terms of social cooperation. Since common understanding necessitates certain bounds on the complexity of principles, there may likewise be limits on the use of theoretical knowledge in the original position. Now clearly it would be very difficult to classify and to grade the complexity of the various sorts of general facts. I shall make no attempt to do this. We do however recognize an intricate theoretical construction when we meet one. Thus it seems reasonable to say that other things equal one conception of justice is to be preferred to another when it is founded upon markedly simpler general facts, and its choice does not depend upon elaborate calculations in the light of a vast array of theoretically defined possibilities. It is desirable that the grounds for a public conception of justice should be evident to everyone when circumstances permit. This consideration favors, I believe, the two principles of justice over the criterion of utility.

SOME MAIN GROUNDS FOR THE TWO PRINCIPLES OF JUSTICE

In this section I use the conditions of publicity and finality to give some of the main arguments for the two principles of justice. I shall rely upon the fact that for an agreement to be valid, the parties must be able to honor it under all relevant and foreseeable circumstances. There must be a rational assurance that one can carry through. The arguments I shall adduce fit under the heuristic schema suggested by the reasons for following the maximin rule. That is, they help to show that the two principles are an adequate minimum conception of justice in a situation of great uncertainty. Any further advantages that might be won by the principle of utility are highly problematical, whereas the hardship if things turn out badly are intolerable. It is at this point that the concept of a contract has a definite role: it suggests the condition of publicity and sets limits upon what can be agreed to.

The first confirming ground for the two principles can be explained in terms of what I earlier referred to as the strains of commitment. I said (§25) that the parties have a capacity for justice in the sense that they can be assured that their undertaking is not in vain. Assuming that they have taken everything into account, including the general facts of moral psychology, they can rely on one another to adhere to the principles adopted. Thus they consider the strains of commitment. They cannot enter into agreements that may have consequences they cannot accept. They will avoid those that they can adhere to only with great difficulty. Since the original agreement is final and made in perpetuity, there is no second chance. In view of the serious nature of the possible consequences, the question of the burden of commitment is especially acute. A person is choosing once and for all the standards which are to govern his life prospects. Moreover, when we enter an agreement we must be able to honor it even should the worst possibilities prove to be the case. Otherwise we have not acted in good faith. Thus the parties must weigh with care whether they will be able to stick by their commitment in all circumstances. Of course, in answering this question they have only a general knowledge of human psychology to go on. But this information is enough to tell which conception of justice involves the greater stress.

In this respect the two principles of justice have a definite advantage. Not only do the parties protect their basic rights but they insure themselves against the worst eventualities. They run no chance of having to acquiesce in a loss of freedom over the course of their life for the sake of a greater good enjoyed by others, an undertaking that in actual circumstances they might not be able to keep. Indeed, we might wonder whether such an agreement can be made in good faith at all. Compacts of this sort exceed the capacity of human nature. How can the parties possibly know, or be sufficiently sure, that they can keep such an agreement? Certainly they cannot base their confidence on a general knowledge of moral psychology. To be sure, any principle chosen in the original position may require a large sacrifice for some. The beneficiaries of clearly unjust institutions (those founded on principles which have no claim to acceptance) may find it hard to reconcile themselves to the changes that will have to be made. But in this case they will know that they could not have maintained their position anyway. In any case, the two principles of justice provide an alternative. If the only possible candidates all involved similar risks, the problem of the strains of commitment would have to be waived. This is not the case, and judged in this light the two principles seem distinctly superior.

A second consideration invokes the condition of publicity as well as that of the constraints on agreements. I shall present the argument in terms of the question of psychological stability. Earlier I stated that a strong point in favor of a conception of justice is that it generates its own support. When the basic structure of society is publicly known to satisfy its principles for an extended period of time, those subject to these arrangements tend to develop a desire to act in accordance with these principles and to do their part in institutions which exemplify them. A conception of justice is stable when the public recognition of its realization by the social system tends to bring about the corresponding sense of justice. Now whether this happens depends, of course, on the laws of moral psychology and the availability of human motives. I shall discuss these matters later on (§§75–76). At the moment we may observe that the principle of utility seems to require a greater identification with the interests of others than the two principles of justice. Thus the latter will be a more stable conception to the extent that this identification is difficult to achieve. When the two principles are satisfied, each person's basic liberties are secured and there is a sense defined by the difference principle in which everyone is benefited by social cooperation. Therefore we can explain the acceptance of the social system and the principles it satisfies by the psychological law that persons tend to love, cherish, and support whatever affirms their own good. Since everyone's good is affirmed, all acquire inclinations to uphold the scheme.

When the principle of utility is satisfied, however, there is no such assurance that everyone benefits. Allegiance to the social system may demand that some, particularly the less favored, should forgo advantages for the sake of the greater good of the whole. Thus the scheme will not be stable unless those who must make sacrifices strongly identify with interests broader than their own. But this is not easy to bring about. The sacrifices in question are not those asked in times of social emergency when all or some must pitch in for the common good. The principles of justice apply to the basic structure of the social system and to the determination of life prospects. What the principle of utility asks is precisely a sacrifice of these prospects. Even when we are less fortunate, we are to accept the greater advantages of others as a sufficient reason for lower expectations over the whole course of our life. This is surely an extreme demand. In fact, when society is conceived as a system of cooperation designed to advance the good of its members, it seems quite incredible that some citizens should be expected, on the basis of political principles, to accept still lower prospects of life for the sake of others. It is evident then why utilitarians should stress the role of sympathy in moral learning and the central place of benevolence among the moral virtues. Their conception of justice is threatened with instability unless sympathy and benevolence can be widely and intensely cultivated. Looking at the question from the standpoint of the original position, the parties would reject the principle of utility and adopt the more realistic idea of designing the social order on a principle of reciprocal advantage. We need not suppose, of course, that in everyday life persons never make substantial sacrifices for one another, since moved by affection and ties of sentiment they often do. But such actions are not demanded as a matter of justice by the basic structure of society.

Furthermore, the public recognition of the two principles gives greater support to men's self-respect and this in turn increases the effectiveness of social cooperation. Both effects are reasons for agreeing to these principles. It is clearly rational for men to secure their self-respect. A sense of their own worth is necessary if they are to pursue their conception of the good with satisfaction and to take pleasure in its fulfillment. Self-respect is not so much a part of any rational plan of life as the sense that one's plan is worth carrying out. Now our self-respect normally depends upon the respect of others. Unless we feel that our endeavors are respected by them, it is difficult if not impossible for us to maintain the conviction that our ends are worth advancing (§67). Hence for this reason the parties would accept the natural duty of mutual respect which asks them to treat one another civilly and to be willing to explain the grounds of their actions, especially when the claims of others are overruled (§51). Moreover, one may assume that those who respect themselves are more likely to respect each other and conversely. Self-contempt leads to contempt of others and threatens their good as much as envy does. Self-respect is reciprocally self-supporting.

Thus a desirable feature of a conception of justice is that it should publicly express men's respect for one another. In this way they insure a sense of their own value. Now the two principles achieve this end. For when society follows these principles, everyone's good is included in a scheme of mutual benefit and this public affirmation in institutions of each man's endeavors supports men's self-esteem. The establishment of equal liberty and the operation of the difference principle are bound to have this effect. The two principles are equivalent, as I have remarked, to an undertaking to regard the distribution of natural abilities in some respects as a collective asset so that the more fortunate are to benefit only in ways that help those who have lost out (§17). I do not say that the parties are moved by the ethical propriety of this idea. But there are reasons for them to accept this principle. For by arranging inequalities for reciprocal advantage and by abstaining from the exploitation of the contingencies of nature and social circumstance within a framework of equal liberties, persons express their respect for one another in the very constitution of their society. In this way they insure their self-respect as it is rational for them to do.

Another way of putting this is to say that the principles of justice manifest in the basic structure of society men's desire to treat one another not as means only but as ends in themselves. I cannot examine Kant's view here.[6] Instead I shall freely interpret it in the light of the contract doctrine. The notion of treating men as ends in themselves and never as only a means obviously needs an explanation. How can we always treat everyone as an end and never as a means only? Certainly we cannot say that it comes to treating everyone by the same general principles, since this interpretation makes the concept equivalent to formal justice. On the contract interpretation treating men as ends in themselves implies at the very least treating them in accordance with the principles to which they would consent in an original position of equality. For in this situation men have equal representation as moral persons who regard themselves as ends and the principles they accept will be rationally designed to protect the claims of their person. The contract view as such defines a sense in which men are to be treated as ends and not as means only.

But the question arises whether there are substantive principles which convey this idea. If the parties wish to express this notion visibly in the basic structure of their society in order to secure

---

6 See *The Foundations of the Metaphysics of Morals*, pp. 427–430 of vol. IV of *Kants Gesammelten Schriften*, Preussische Akademie der Wissenschaften (Berlin, 1913), where the second formulation of the categorical imperative is introduced.

each man's rational interest in his self-respect, which principles should they choose? Now it seems that the two principles of justice achieve this aim: for all have equal basic liberties and the difference principle interprets the distinction between treating men as a means only and treating them also as ends in themselves. To regard persons as ends in themselves in the basic design of society is to agree to forgo those gains which do not contribute to everyone's expectations. By contrast, to regard persons as means is to be prepared to impose on those already less favored still lower prospects of life for the sake of the higher expectations of others. Thus we see that the difference principle, which at first appears rather extreme, has a reasonable interpretation. If we further suppose that social cooperation among those who respect each other and themselves as manifest in their institutions is likely to be more effective and harmonious, the general level of expectations, assuming we could estimate it, may be higher when the two principles of justice are satisfied than one might otherwise have thought. The advantage of the principle of utility in this respect is no longer so clear.

The principle of utility presumably requires some who are less fortunate to accept even lower life prospects for the sake of others. To be sure, it is not necessary that those having to make such sacrifices rationalize this demand by having a lesser appreciation of their own worth. It does not follow from the utilitarian doctrine that it is because their aims are trivial or unimportant that some individuals' expectations are less. But the parties must consider the general facts of moral psychology. Surely it is natural to experience a loss of self-respect, a weakening of our sense of the value of accomplishing our aims, when we are already less favored. This is particularly likely to be so when social cooperation is arranged for the good of individuals. That is, those with greater advantages do not claim that they are necessary to preserve certain religious or cultural values which everyone has a duty to maintain. We are not here considering a doctrine of traditional order nor the principle of perfectionism, but rather the principle of utility. In this instance, then, men's self-respect hinges on how they regard one another. If the parties accept the utility criterion, they will lack the support to their self-respect provided by the public commitment of others to arrange inequalities to everyone's advantage and to guarantee the basic liberties for all. In a public utilitarian society men, particularly the least advantaged, will find it more difficult to be confident of their own worth.

The utilitarian may answer that in maximizing the average utility these matters are already taken into account. If, for example, the equal liberties are necessary for men's self-respect and the average utility is higher when they are affirmed, then of course they should be established. So far so good. But the point is that we must not lose sight of the publicity condition. This requires that in maximizing the average utility we do so subject to the constraint that the utilitarian principle is publicly accepted and followed as the fundamental charter of society. What we cannot do is to raise the average utility by encouraging men to adopt and apply non-utilitarian principles of justice. If, for whatever reasons, the public recognition of utilitarianism entails some loss of self-esteem, there is no way around this drawback. It is an unavoidable cost of the utilitarian scheme given our stipulations. Thus suppose that the average utility is actually greater should the two principles of justice be publicly affirmed and realized in the basic structure. For the reasons mentioned, this may conceivably be the case. These principles would then represent the most attractive prospect, and on both lines of reasoning just examined, the two principles would be accepted. The utilitarian cannot reply that one is now really maximizing the average utility. In fact, the parties would have chosen the two principles of justice.

We should note, then, that utilitarianism, as I have defined it, is the view that the principle of utility is the correct principle for society's public conception of justice. And to show this one must argue that this criterion would be chosen in the original position. If we like, we can define a different variation of the initial situation in which the motivation assumption is that the parties want to adopt those principles that maximize average utility. The preceding remarks indicate that the two principles of justice may still be chosen. But if so, it is a mistake to call these principles—and the theory in which they appear—utilitarian. The motivation assumption by itself does not determine the character of the whole theory. In fact, the case for the principles of justice is strengthened if they would be chosen under different motivation assumptions. This indicates that the theory of justice is firmly grounded and not sensitive to slight changes in this condition. What we want to know is which conception of justice characterizes our considered judgments in reflective equilibrium and best serves as the public moral basis of society. Unless one maintains that this conception is given by the principle of utility, one is not a utilitarian.[7]

The strains of commitment and the publicity condition, both of which we have discussed in this section, are also important. The first arises from the fact that, in general, the class of things that can be agreed to is included within, but smaller than, the class of things that can be rationally chosen. We can decide to take a chance and the same time fully intend that, should things turn out badly, we shall do what we can to retrieve our situation. But if we make an agreement, we have to accept the result; and so to give an undertaking in good faith, we must not only intend to honor it but with reason believe that we can do so. Thus the contract condition excludes a certain kind of randomizing. One cannot agree to a principle if there is a real possibility that it has any outcome that one will not be able to accept. I shall not comment further on the publicity condition except to note that it ties in with the desirability of embedding ideals in first principles (end of §26), with simplicity (§49), and with stability. The latter is examined further in what I have called the second part of the argument (§§79–82).

The form of the argument for the two principles is that the balance of reasons favors them over the principle of average utility, and assuming transitivity, over the classical doctrine as well. Thus

---

7 Thus while Brandt holds that a society's moral code is to be publicly recognized, and that the best code from a philosophical standpoint is the one that maximizes average utility, he does not maintain that the principle of utility must belong to the code itself. In fact, he denies that within the public morality the final court of appeal need be to utility. Thus by the definition in the text, his view is not utilitarian. See "Some Merits of One Form of Rule Utilitarianism," *University of Colorado Studies* (Boulder, Colo., 1967), pp. 58f.

the agreement of the parties depends on weighing various considerations. The reasoning is informal and not a proof, and there is an appeal to intuition as the basis of the theory of justice. Yet, as I have remarked (§21), when everything is tallied up, it may be clear where the balance of reasons lies. If so, then to the extent that the original position embodies reasonable conditions used in the justification of principles in everyday life, the claim that one would agree to the principles of justice is perfectly credible. Thus they can serve as a conception of justice in the public acceptance of which persons can recognize one another's good faith.

It may be helpful at this point to list some of the main grounds in favor of the two principles of justice over the principle of average utility. That the conditions of generality of principle, universality of application, and limited information are not sufficient by themselves to require these principles is clear from the reasoning for the utility principle (§27). Further assumptions must, therefore, be incorporated into the original position. Thus, I have assumed that the parties regard themselves as having certain fundamental interests that they must protect if they can; and that, as free persons, they have a highest-order interest in maintaining their liberty to revise and alter these ends (§26). The parties are, so to speak, persons with determinate interests rather than bare potentialities for all possible interests, even though the specific character of these interests is unknown to them. They must try to secure favorable conditions for advancing these definite ends, whatever they are (§28). The hierarchy of interests and its relation to the priority of liberty is taken up later (§§39, 82), but the general nature of the argument for the basic liberties is illustrated by the case of liberty of conscience and freedom of thought (§§33–35).

In addition, the veil of ignorance (§24) is interpreted to mean not only that the parties have no knowledge of their particular aims and ends (except what is contained in the thin theory of the good), but also that the historical record is closed to them. They do not know, and cannot enumerate, the social circumstances in which they may find themselves, or the array of techniques their society may have at its disposal. They have, therefore, no objective grounds for relying on one probability distribution rather than another, and the principle of insufficient reason cannot be invoked as a way around this limitation. These considerations, together with those derived from regarding the parties as having determinate fundamental interests, imply that the expectation constructed by the argument for the utility principle is unsound and lacks the necessary unity (§28).

THE KANTIAN INTERPRETATION OF JUSTICE AS FAIRNESS

For the most part I have considered the content of the principle of equal liberty and the meaning of the priority of the rights that it defines. It seems appropriate at this point to note that there is a Kantian interpretation of the conception of justice from which this principle derives. This interpretation is based upon Kant's notion of autonomy. It is a mistake, I believe, to emphasize the place of generality and universality in Kant's ethics. That moral principles are general and universal is hardly new with him; and as we have seen these conditions do not in any case take us very far. It is impossible to construct a moral theory on so slender a basis, and therefore to limit the discussion of Kant's doctrine to these notions is to reduce it to triviality. The real force of his view lies elsewhere.[8]

For one thing, he begins with the idea that moral principles are the object of rational choice. They define the moral law that men can rationally will to govern their conduct in an ethical commonwealth. Moral philosophy becomes the study of the conception and outcome of a suitably defined rational decision. This idea has immediate consequences. For once we think of moral principles as legislation for a kingdom of ends, it is clear that these principles must not only be acceptable to all but public as well. Finally Kant supposes that this moral legislation is to be agreed to under conditions that characterize men as free and equal rational beings. The description of the original position is an attempt to interpret this conception. I do not wish to argue here for this interpretation on the basis of Kant's text. Certainly some will want to read him differently. Perhaps the remarks to follow are best taken as suggestions for relating justice as fairness to the high point of the contractarian tradition in Kant and Rousseau.

Kant held, I believe, that a person is acting autonomously when the principles of his action are chosen by him as the most adequate possible expression of his nature as a free and equal rational being. The principles he acts upon are not adopted because of his social position or natural endowments, or in view of the particular kind of society in which he lives or the specific things that he happens to want. To act on such principles is to act heteronomously. Now the veil of ignorance deprives the persons in the original position of the knowledge that would enable them to choose heteronomous principles. The parties arrive at their choice together as free and equal rational persons knowing only that those circumstances obtain which give rise to the need for principles of justice.

---

8 Especially to be avoided is the idea that Kant's doctrine provides at best only the general, or formal, elements for a utilitarian or indeed for any other moral conception. This idea is found in Sidgwick, *The Methods of Ethics,* 7th ed. (London, Macmillan, 1907), pp. xvii and xx of the preface; and in F. H. Bradley, *Ethical Studies,* 2nd ed. (Oxford, Clarendon Press, 1927), Essay IV; and goes back at least to Hegel. One must not lose sight of the full scope of his view and take the later works into consideration. Unfortunately, there is no commentary on Kant's moral theory as a whole; perhaps it would prove impossible to write. But the standard works of H. J. Paton, *The Categorical Imperative* (Chicago, University of Chicago Press, 1948), and L. W. Beck, *A Commentary on Kant's Critique of Practical Reason* (Chicago, University of Chicago Press, 1960), and others need to be further complemented by studies of the other writings. See here M. J. Gregor's *Laws of Freedom* (Oxford, Basil Blackwell, 1963), an account of *The Metaphysics of Morals,* and J. G. Murphy's brief *Kant: The Philosophy of Right* (London, Macmillan, 1970). Beyond this, *The Critique of Judgment, Religion within the Limits of Reason,* and the political writings cannot be neglected without distorting his doctrine. For the last, see *Kant's Political Writings,* ed. Hans Reiss and trans. H. B. Nisbet (Cambridge, The University Press, 1970).

To be sure, the argument for these principles does add in various ways to Kant's conception. For example, it adds the feature that the principles chosen are to apply to the basic structure of society; and premises characterizing this structure are used in deriving the principles of justice. But I believe that this and other additions are natural enough and remain fairly close to Kant's doctrine, at least when all of his ethical writings are viewed together. Assuming, then, that the reasoning in favor of the principles of justice is correct, we can say that when persons act on these principles they are acting in accordance with principles that they would choose as rational and independent persons in an original position of equality. The principles of their actions do not depend upon social or natural contingencies, nor do they reflect the bias of the particulars of their plan of life or the aspirations that motivate them. By acting from these principles persons express their nature as free and equal rational beings subject to the general conditions of human life. For to express one's nature as a being of a particular kind is to act on the principles that would be chosen if this nature were the decisive determining element. Of course, the choice of the parties in the original position is subject to the restrictions of that situation. But when we knowingly act on the principles of justice in the ordinary course of events, we deliberately assume the limitations of the original position. One reason for doing this, for persons who can do so and want to, is to give expression to one's nature.

The principles of justice are also analogous to categorical imperatives. For by a categorical imperative Kant understands a principle of conduct that applies to a person in virtue of his nature as a free and equal rational being. The validity of the principle does not presuppose that one has a particular desire or aim. Whereas a hypothetical imperative by contrast does assume this: it directs us to take certain steps as effective means to achieve a specific end. Whether the desire is for a particular thing, or whether it is for something more general, such as certain kinds of agreeable feelings or pleasures, the corresponding imperative is hypothetical. Its applicability depends upon one's having an aim which one need not have as a condition of being a rational human individual. The argument for the two principles of justice does not assume that the parties have particular ends, but only that they desire certain primary goods. These are things that it is rational to want whatever else one wants. Thus given human nature, wanting them is part of being rational; and while each is presumed to have some conception of the good, nothing is known about his final ends. The preference for primary goods is derived, then, from only the most general assumptions about rationality and the conditions of human life. To act from the principles of justice is to act from categorical imperatives in the sense that they apply to us whatever in particular our aims are. This simply reflects the fact that no such contingencies appear as premises in their derivation.

We may note also that the motivational assumption of mutual disinterest parallels Kant's notion of autonomy, and gives another reason for this condition. So far this assumption has been used to characterize the circumstances of justice and to provide a clear conception to guide the reasoning of the parties. We have also seen that the concept of benevolence, being a second-order notion, would not work out well. Now we can add that the assumption of mutual disinterest is to allow for freedom in the choice of a system of final ends.[9] Liberty in adopting a conception of the good is limited only by principles that are deduced from a doctrine which imposes no prior constraints on these conceptions. Presuming mutual disinterest in the original position carries out this idea. We postulate that the parties have opposing claims in a suitably general sense. If their ends were restricted in some specific way, this would appear at the outset as an arbitrary restriction on freedom. Moreover, if the parties were conceived as altruists, or as pursuing certain kinds of pleasures, then the principles chosen would apply, as far as the argument would have shown, only to persons whose freedom was restricted to choices compatible with altruism or hedonism. As the argument now runs, the principles of justice cover all persons with rational plans of life, whatever their content, and these principles represent the appropriate restrictions on freedom. Thus it is possible to say that the constraints on conceptions of the good are the result of an interpretation of the contractual situation that puts no prior limitations on what men may desire. There are a variety of reasons, then, for the motivational premise of mutual disinterest. This premise is not only a matter of realism about the circumstances of justice or a way to make the theory manageable. It also connects up with the Kantian idea of autonomy.

There is, however, a difficulty that should be clarified. It is well expressed by Sidgwick.[10] He remarks that nothing in Kant's ethics is more striking than the idea that a man realizes his true self when he acts from the moral law, whereas if he permits his actions to be determined by sensuous desires or contingent aims, he becomes subject to the law of nature. Yet in Sidgwick's opinion this idea comes to naught. It seems to him that on Kant's view the lives of the saint and the scoundrel are equally the outcome of a free choice (on the part of the noumenal self) and equally the subject of causal laws (as a phenomenal self). Kant never explains why the scoundrel does not express in a bad life his characteristic and freely chosen selfhood in the same way that a saint expresses his characteristic and freely chosen selfhood in a good one. Sidgwick's objection is decisive, I think, as long as one assumes, as Kant's exposition may seem to allow, both that the noumenal self can choose any consistent set of principles and that acting from such principles, whatever they are, is sufficient to express one's choice as that of a free and equal rational being. Kant's reply must be that though acting on any consistent set of principles could be the outcome of a decision on the part of the noumenal self, not all such action by the phenomenal self expresses this decision as that of a free and equal rational being. Thus if a person realizes his true self by expressing it in his actions, and if he desires above all else to realize this self, then he will choose to act from principles that manifest his nature as a free and equal rational being. The missing part of the argument concerns

---

9 For this point I am indebted to Charles Fried.
10 See *The Methods of Ethics,* Appendix, "The Kantian Conception of Free Will" (reprinted from *Mind*, vol. 13, 1888), pp. 511–516, esp. p. 516.

the concept of expression. Kant did not show that acting from the moral law expresses our nature in identifiable ways that acting from contrary principles does not.

This defect is made good, I believe, by the conception of the original position. The essential point is that we need an argument showing which principles, if any, free and equal rational persons would choose and these principles must be applicable in practice. A definite answer to this question is required to meet Sidgwick's objection. My suggestion is that we think of the original position as in important ways similar to the point of view from which noumenal selves see the world. The parties qua noumenal selves have complete freedom to choose whatever principles they wish; but they also have a desire to express their nature as rational and equal members of the intelligible realm with precisely this liberty to choose, that is, as beings who can look at the world in this way and express this perspective in their life as members of society. They must decide, then, which principles when consciously followed and acted upon in everyday life will best manifest this freedom in their community, most fully reveal their independence from natural contingencies and social accident. Now if the argument of the contract doctrine is correct, these principles are indeed those defining the moral law, or more exactly, the principles of justice for institutions and individuals. The description of the original position resembles the point of view of noumenal selves, of what it means to be a free and equal rational being. Our nature as such beings is displayed when we act from the principles we would choose when this nature is reflected in the conditions determining the choice. Thus men exhibit their freedom, their independence from the contingencies of nature and society, by acting in ways they would acknowledge in the original position.

Properly understood, then, the desire to act justly derives in part from the desire to express most fully what we are or can be, namely free and equal rational beings with a liberty to choose. It is for this reason, I believe, that Kant speaks of the failure to act on the moral law as giving rise to shame and not to feelings of guilt. And this is appropriate, since for him acting unjustly is acting in a manner that fails to express our nature as a free and equal rational being. Such actions therefore strike at our self-respect, our sense of our own worth, and the experience of this loss is shame (§67). We have acted as though we belonged to a lower order, as though we were a creature whose first principles are decided by natural contingencies. Those who think of Kant's moral doctrine as one of law and guilt badly misunderstand him. Kant's main aim is to deepen and to justify Rousseau's idea that liberty is acting in accordance with a law that we give to ourselves. And this leads not to a morality of austere command but to an ethic of mutual respect and self-esteem.[11]

---

11 See B. A. O. Williams, "The Idea of Equality," in *Philosophy, Politics and Society,* Second Series, ed. Peter Laslett and W. G. Runciman (Oxford, Basil Blackwell, 1962), pp. 115f. For confirmation of this interpretation, see Kant's remarks on moral education in *The Critique of Practical Reason,* pt. II. See also Beck, *A Commentary on Kant's Critique of Practical Reason,* pp. 233–236.

The original position may be viewed, then, as a procedural interpretation of Kant's conception of autonomy and the categorical imperative within the framework of an empirical theory. The principles regulative of the kingdom of ends are those that would be chosen in this position, and the description of this situation enables us to explain the sense in which acting from these principles expresses our nature as free and equal rational persons. No longer are these notions purely transcendent and lacking explicable connections with human conduct, for the procedural conception of the original position allows us to make these ties. Of course, I have departed from Kant's views in several respects. I cannot discuss these matters here; but two points should be noted. The person's choice as a noumenal self I have assumed to be a collective one. The force of the self's being equal is that the principles chosen must be acceptable to other selves. Since all are similarly free and rational, each must have an equal say in adopting the public principles of the ethical commonwealth. This means that as noumenal selves, everyone is to consent to these principles. Unless the scoundrel's principles would be agreed to, they cannot express this free choice, however much a single self might be of a mind to adopt them. Later I shall try to define a clear sense in which this unanimous agreement is best expressive of the nature of even a single self (§85). It in no way overrides a person's interests as the collective nature of the choice might seem to imply. But I leave this aside for the present.

Secondly, I have assumed all along that the parties know that they are subject to the conditions of human life. Being in the circumstances of justice, they are situated in the world with other men who likewise face limitations of moderate scarcity and competing claims. Human freedom is to be regulated by principles chosen in the light of these natural restrictions. Thus justice as fairness is a theory of human justice and among its premises are the elementary facts about persons and their place in nature. The freedom of pure intelligences not subject to these constraints (God and the angels) are outside the range of the theory. Kant may have meant his doctrine to apply to all rational beings as such and therefore that men's social situation in the world is to have no role in determining the first principles of justice. If so, this is another difference between justice as fairness and Kant's theory.

But the Kantian interpretation is not intended as an interpretation of Kant's actual doctrine but rather of justice as fairness. Kant's view is marked by a number of deep dualisms, in particular, the dualism between the necessary and the contingent, form and content, reason and desire, and noumena and phenomena. To abandon these dualisms as he understood them is, for many, to abandon what is distinctive in his theory. I believe otherwise. His moral conception has a characteristic structure that is more clearly discernible when these dualisms are not taken in the sense he gave them but recast and their moral force reformulated within the scope of an empirical theory. What I have called the Kantian interpretation indicates how this can be done.

JUSTICE AS FAIRNESS: POLITICAL NOT METAPHYSICAL

(SELECTIONS)

BY JOHN RAWLS

John Rawls, "Justice as Fairness: Political Not Metaphysical," *Philosophy & Public Affairs*, vol. 14, pp. 226-248. Copyright © 1985 by John Wiley & Sons, Inc.. Reprinted with permission.

SEVEN

II

There are, of course, many ways in which political philosophy may be understood, and writers at different times, faced with different political and social circumstances, understand their work differently. Justice as fairness I would now understand as a reasonably systematic and practicable conception of justice for a constitutional democracy, a conception that offers an alternative to the dominant utilitarianism of our tradition of political thought. Its first task is to provide a more secure and acceptable basis for constitutional principles and basic rights and liberties than utilitarianism seems to allow.[1] The need for such a political conception arises in the following way.

There are periods, sometimes long periods, in the history of any society during which certain fundamental questions give rise to sharp and divisive political controversy, and it seems difficult, if not impossible, to find any shared basis of political agreement. Indeed, certain questions may prove intractable and may never be fully settled. One task of political philosophy in a democratic society is to focus on such questions and to examine whether some underlying basis of agreement can be uncovered and a mutually acceptable way of resolving these questions publicly established. Or if these questions cannot be fully settled, as may well be the case, perhaps the divergence of opinion can be narrowed sufficiently so that political cooperation on a basis of mutual respect can still be maintained.[2]

---

1 *Theory*, Preface, p. viii.
2 Ibid., pp. 582f. On the role of a conception of justice in reducing the divergence of opinion, see pp. 44f., 53, 314, and 564. At various places the limited aims in developing a conception of justice are noted: see p. 364 on not expecting too much of an account of civil disobedience; pp. 200f. on the inevitable indeterminacy of a conception of justice in specifying a series of points of view from

The course of democratic thought over the past two centuries or so makes plain that there is no agreement on the way basic institutions of a constitutional democracy should be arranged if they are to specify and secure the basic rights and liberties of citizens and answer to the claims of democratic equality when citizens are conceived as free and equal persons (as explained in the last three paragraphs of Section III). A deep disagreement exists as to how the values of liberty and equality are best realized in the basic structure of society. To simplify, we may think of this disagreement as a conflict within the tradition of democratic thought itself, between the tradition associated with Locke, which gives greater weight to what Constant called "the liberties of the moderns," freedom of thought and conscience, certain basic rights of the person and of property, and the rule of law, and the tradition associated with Rousseau, which gives greater weight to what Constant called "the liberties of the ancients," the equal political liberties and the values of public life. This is a stylized contrast and historically inaccurate, but it serves to fix ideas.

Justice as fairness tries to adjudicate between these contending traditions first, by proposing two principles of justice to serve as guidelines for how basic institutions are to realize the values of liberty and equality, and second, by specifying a point of view from which these principles can be seen as more appropriate than other familiar principles of justice to the nature of democratic citizens viewed as free and equal persons. What it means to view citizens as free and equal persons is, of course, a fundamental question and is discussed in the following sections. What must be shown is that a certain arrangement of the basic structure, certain institutional forms, are more appropriate for realizing the values of liberty and equality when citizens are conceived as such persons, that is (very briefly), as having the requisite powers of moral personality that enable them to participate in society viewed as a system of fair cooperation for mutual advantage. So to continue, the two principles of justice (mentioned above) read as follows:

1. Each person has an equal right to a fully adequate scheme of equal basic rights and liberties, which scheme is compatible with a similar scheme for all.
2. Social and economic inequalities are to satisfy two conditions: first, they must be attached to offices and positions open to all under conditions of fair equality of opportunity; and second, they must be to the greatest benefit of the least advantaged members of society.

Each of these principles applies to a different part of the basic structure; and both are concerned not only with basic rights, liberties, and opportunities, but also with the claims of equality; while the

---

which questions of justice can be resolved; pp. 8gf. on the social wisdom of recognizing that perhaps only a few moral problems (it would have been better to say: problems of political justice) can be satisfactorily setded, and thus of framing institutions so that intractable questions do not arise; on pp. 53, 8yff., 32of. the need to accept simplifications is emphasized. Regarding the last point, see also "Kantian Constructivism," pp. 560–64.

second part of the second principle underwrites the worth of these institutional guarantees.[3] The two principles together, when the first is given priority over the second, regulate the basic institutions which realize these values.[4] But these details, although important, are not our concern here.

We must now ask: how might political philosophy find a shared basis for settling such a fundamental question as that of the most appropriate institutional forms for liberty and equality? Of course, it is likely that the most that can be done is to narrow the range of public disagreement. Yet even firmly held convictions gradually change: religious toleration is now accepted, and arguments for persecution are no longer openly professed; similarly, slavery is rejected as inherently unjust, and however much the aftermath of slavery may persist in social practices and unavowed attitudes, no one is willing to defend it. We collect such settled convictions as the belief in religious toleration and the rejection of slavery and try to organize the basic ideas and principles implicit in these convictions into a coherent conception of justice. We can regard these convictions as provisional fixed points which any conception of justice must account for if it is to be reasonable for us. We look, then, to our public political culture itself, including its main institutions and the historical traditions of their interpretation, as the shared fund of implicitly recognized basic ideas and principles. The hope is that these ideas and principles can be formulated clearly enough to be combined into a conception of political justice congenial to our most firmly held convictions. We express this by saying that a political conception of justice, to be acceptable, must be in accordance with our considered convictions, at all levels of generality, on due reflection (or in what I have called "reflective equilibrium").[5]

The public political culture may be of two minds even at a very deep level. Indeed, this must be so with such an enduring controversy as that concerning the most appropriate institutional forms to realize the values of liberty and equality. This suggests that if we are to succeed in finding a basis of public agreement, we must find a new way of organizing familiar ideas and principles into a conception of political justice so that the claims in conflict, as previously understood, are seen in another light. A political conception need not be an original creation but may only articulate familiar intuitive ideas and principles so that they can be recognized as fitting together in a somewhat different way than before. Such a conception may, however, go further than this: it may organize these familiar ideas and principles by means of a more fundamental intuitive idea within the complex structure of which the other familiar intuitive ideas are then systematically connected and related. In justice as fairness, as we shall see in the next section, this more fundamental

---

[3] The statement of these principles differs from that given in *Theory* and follows the statement in "The Basic Liberties and Their Priority," *Tanner Lectures on Human Values*, Vol. Ill (Salt Lake City: University of Utah Press, 1982), p. 5. The reasons for the changes are discussed at pp. 46–55 of that lecture. They are important for the revisions made in the account of the basic liberties found in *Theory* in the attempt to answer the objections of H.L.A. Hart; but they need not concern us here.

[4] The idea of the worth of these guarentees is discussed ibid., pp. 4of.

[5] *Theory,* pp. 2of., 48–51, and 12of.

idea is that of society as a system of fair social cooperation between free and equal persons. The concern of this section is how we might find a public basis of political agreement. The point is that a conception of justice will only be able to achieve this aim if it provides a reasonable way of shaping into one coherent view the deeper bases of agreement embedded in the public political culture of a constitutional regime and acceptable to its most firmly held considered convictions.

Now suppose justice as fairness were to achieve its aim and a publicly acceptable political conception of justice is found. Then this conception provides a publicly recognized point of view from which all citizens can examine before one another whether or not their political and social institutions are just. It enables them to do this by citing what are recognized among them as valid and sufficient reasons singled out by that conception itself. Society's main institutions and how they fit together into one scheme of social cooperation can be examined on the same basis by each citizen, whatever that citizen's social position or more particular interests. It should be observed that, on this view, justification is not regarded simply as valid argument from listed premises, even should these premises be true. Rather, justification is addressed to others who disagree with us, and therefore it must always proceed from some consensus, that is, from premises that we and others publicly recognize as true; or better, publicly recognize as acceptable to us for the purpose of establishing a working agreement on the fundamental questions of political justice. It goes without saying that this agreement must be informed and uncoerced, and reached by citizens in ways consistent with their being viewed as free and equal persons.[6]

Thus, the aim of justice as fairness as a political conception is practical, and not metaphysical or epistemological. That is, it presents itself not as a conception of justice that is true, but one that can serve as a basis of informed and willing political agreement between citizens viewed as free and equal persons. This agreement when securely founded in public political and social attitudes sustains the goods of all persons and associations within a just democratic regime. To secure this agreement we try, so far as we can, to avoid disputed philosophical, as well as disputed moral and religious, questions. We do this not because these questions are unimportant or regarded with indifference,[7] but because we think them too important and recognize that there is no way to resolve them politically. The only alternative to a principle of toleration is the autocratic use of state power. Thus, justice as fairness deliberately stays on the surface, philosophically speaking. Given the profound differences in belief and conceptions of the good at least since the Reformation, we must recognize that, just as on questions of religious and moral doctrine, public agreement on the basic questions of philosophy cannot be obtained without the state's infringement of basic liberties. Philosophy as the search for truth about an independent metaphysical and moral order

---

6 Ibid., pp. 580–83.
7 Ibid., pp. 214f.

cannot, I believe, provide a workable and shared basis for a political conception of justice in a democratic society.

We try, then, to leave aside philosophical controversies whenever possible, and look for ways to avoid philosophy's longstanding problems. Thus, in what I have called "Kantian constructivism," we try to avoid the problem of truth and the controversy between realism and subjectivism about the status of moral and political values. This form of constructivism neither asserts nor denies these doctrines.[8] Rather, it recasts ideas from the tradition of the social contract to achieve a practicable conception of objectivity and justification founded on public agreement in judgment on due reflection. The aim is free agreement, reconciliation through public reason. And similarly, as we shall see (in Section V), a conception of the person in a political view, for example, the conception of citizens as free and equal persons, need not involve, so I believe, questions of philosophical psychology or a metaphysical doctrine of the nature of the self. No political view that depends on these deep and unresolved matters can serve as a public conception of justice in a constitutional democratic state. As I have said, we must apply the principle of toleration to philosophy itself. The hope is that, by this method of avoidance, as we might call it, existing differences between contending political views can at least be moderated, even if not entirely removed, so that social cooperation on the basis of mutual respect can be maintained. Or if this is expecting too much, this method may enable us to conceive how, given a desire for free and uncoerced agreement, a public understanding could arise consistent with the historical conditions and constraints of our social world. Until we bring ourselves to conceive how this could happen, it can't happen.

III

Let's now survey briefly some of the basic ideas that make up justice as fairness in order to show that these ideas belong to a political conception of justice. As I have indicated, the overarching fundamental intuitive idea, within which other basic intuitive ideas are systematically connected, is that of society as a fair system of cooperation between free and equal persons. Justice as fairness starts from this idea as one of the basic intuitive ideas which we take to be implicit in the public culture of a democratic society.[9] In their political thought, and in the context of public discussion of political questions, citizens do not view the social order as a fixed natural order, or as an institutional hierarchy justified by religious or aristocratic values. Here it is important to stress that from other points of view, for example, from the point of view of personal morality, or from

---

8 On Kantian constructivism, see especially the third lecture referred to in footnote 2 above.
9 Although *Theory* uses this idea from the outset (it is introduced on p. 4), it does not emphasize, as I do here and in "Kantian Constructivism," that the basic ideas of justice as fairness are regarded as implicit or latent in the public culture of a democratic society.

the point of view of members of an association, or of one's religious or philosophical doctrine, various aspects of the world and one's relation to it, may be regarded in a different way. But these other points of view are not to be introduced into political discussion.

We can make the idea of social cooperation more specific by noting three of its elements:

1. Cooperation is distinct from merely socially coordinated activity, for example, from activity coordinated by orders issued by some central authority. Cooperation is guided by publicly recognized rules and procedures which those who are cooperating accept and regard as properly regulating their conduct.
2. Cooperation involves the idea of fair terms of cooperation: these are terms that each participant may reasonably accept, provided that everyone else likewise accepts them. Fair terms of cooperation specify an idea of reciprocity or mutuality: all who are engaged in cooperation and who do their part as the rules and procedures require, are to benefit in some appropriate way as assessed by a suitable benchmark of comparison. A conception of political justice characterizes the fair terms of social cooperation. Since the primary subject of justice is the basic structure of society, this is accomplished in justice as fairness by formulating principles that specify basic rights and duties within the main institutions of society, and by regulating the institutions of background justice over time so that the benefits produced by everyone's efforts are fairly acquired and divided from one generation to the next.
3. The idea of social cooperation requires an idea of each participant's rational advantage, or good. This idea of good specifies what those who are engaged in cooperation, whether individuals, families, or associations, or even nation-states, are trying to achieve, when the scheme is viewed from their own standpoint.

Now consider the idea of the person.[10] There are, of course, many aspects of human nature that can be singled out as especially significant depending on our point of view. This is witnessed by such expressions as *homo politicus, homo oeconomicus, homo faber,* and the like. Justice as fairness starts from the idea that society is to be conceived as a fair system of cooperation and so it adopts a conception of the person to go with this idea. Since Greek times, both in philosophy and law, the concept of the person has been understood as the concept of someone who can take part in, or who can play a role in, social life, and hence exercise and respect its various rights and duties.

---

10 It should be emphasized that a conception of the person, as I understand it here, is a normative conception, whether legal, political, or moral, or indeed also philosophical or religious, depending on the overall view to which it belongs. In this case the conception of the person is a moral conception, one that begins from our everyday conception of persons as the basic units of thought, deliberation and responsibility, and adapted to a political conception of justice and not to a comprehensive moral doctrine. It is in effect a political conception of the person, and given the aims of justice as fairness, a conception of citizens. Thus, a conception of the person is to be distinguished from an account of human nature given by natural science or social theory. On this point, see "Kantian Constructivism," pp. 534f.

Thus, we say that a person is someone who can be a citizen, that is, a fully cooperating member of society over a complete life. We add the phrase "over a complete life" because a society is viewed as a more or less complete and self-sufficient scheme of cooperation, making room within itself for all the necessities and activities of life, from birth until death. A society is not an association for more limited purposes; citizens do not join society voluntarily but are born into it, where, for our aims here, we assume they are to lead their lives.

Since we start within the tradition of democratic thought, we also think of citizens as free and equal persons. The basic intuitive idea is that in virtue of what we may call their moral powers, and the powers of reason, thought, and judgment connected with those powers, we say that persons are free. And in virtue of their having these powers to the requisite degree to be fully cooperating members of society, we say that persons are equal.[11] We can elaborate this conception of the person as follows. Since persons can be full participants in a fair system of social cooperation, we ascribe to them the two moral powers connected with the elements in the idea of social cooperation noted above: namely, a capacity for a sense of justice and a capacity for a conception of the good. A sense of justice is the capacity to understand, to apply, and to act from the public conception of justice which characterizes the fair terms of social cooperation. The capacity for a conception of the good is the capacity to form, to revise, and rationally to pursue a conception of one's rational advantage, or good. In the case of social cooperation, this good must not be understood narrowly but rather as a conception of what is valuable in human life. Thus, a conception of the good normally consists of a more or less determinate scheme of final ends, that is, ends we want to realize for their own sake, as well as of attachments to other persons and loyalties to various groups and associations. These attachments and loyalties give rise to affections and devotions, and therefore the flourishing of the persons and associations who are the objects of these sentiments is also part of our conception of the good. Moreover, we must also include in such a conception a view of our relation to the world—religious, philosophical, or moral—by reference to which the value and significance of our ends and attachments are understood.

In addition to having the two moral powers, the capacities for a sense of justice and a conception of the good, persons also have at any given time a particular conception of the good that they try to achieve. Since we wish to start from the idea of society as a fair system of cooperation, we assume that persons as citizens have all the capacities that enable them to be normal and fully cooperating members of society. This does not imply that no one ever suffers from illness or accident; such misfortunes are to be expected in the ordinary course of human life; and provision for these contingencies must be made. But for our purposes here I leave aside permanent physical disabilities or mental disorders so severe as to prevent persons from being normal and fully cooperating members of society in the usual sense.

---

11 *Theory,* Sec. 77.

Now the conception of persons as having the two moral powers, and therefore as free and equal, is also a basic intuitive idea assumed to be implicit in the public culture of a democratic society. Note, however, that it is formed by idealizing and simplifying in various ways. This is done to achieve a clear and uncluttered view of what for us is the fundamental question of political justice: namely, what is the most appropriate conception of justice for specifying the terms of social cooperation between citizens regarded as free and equal persons, and as normal and fully cooperating members of society over a complete life. It is this question that has been the focus of the liberal critique of aristocracy, of the socialist critique of liberal constitutional democracy, and of the conflict between liberals and conservatives at the present time over the claims of private property and the legitimacy (in contrast to the effectiveness) of social policies associated with the so-called welfare state.

IV

I now take up the idea of the original position.[12] This idea is introduced in order to work out which traditional conception of justice, or which variant of one of those conceptions, specifies the most appropriate principles for realizing liberty and equality once society is viewed as a system of cooperation between free and equal persons. Assuming we had this purpose in mind, let's see why we would introduce the idea of the original position and how it serves its purpose.

Consider again the idea of social cooperation. Let's ask: how are the fair terms of cooperation to be determined? Are they simply laid down by some outside agency distinct from the persons cooperating? Are they, for example, laid down by God's law? Or are these terms to be recognized by these persons as fair by reference to their knowledge of a prior and independent moral order? For example, are they regarded as required by natural law, or by a realm of values known by rational intuition? Or are these terms to be established by an undertaking among these persons themselves in the light of what they regard as their mutual advantage? Depending on which answer we give, we get a different conception of cooperation.

Since justice as fairness recasts the doctrine of the social contract, it adopts a form of the last answer: the fair terms of social cooperation are conceived as agreed to by those engaged in it, that is, by free and equal persons as citizens who are born into the society in which they lead their lives. But their agreement, like any other valid agreement, must be entered into under appropriate conditions. In particular, these conditions must situate free and equal persons fairly and must not allow some persons greater bargaining advantages than others. Further, threats of force and coercion, deception and fraud, and so on, must be excluded.

---

12 Ibid., Sec. 4, Ch. 3, and the index.

So far so good. The foregoing considerations are familiar from everyday life. But agreements in everyday life are made in some more or less clearly specified situation embedded within the background institutions of the basic structure. Our task, however, is to extend the idea of agreement to this background framework itself. Here we face a difficulty for any political conception of justice that uses the idea of a contract, whether social or otherwise. The difficulty is this: we must find some point of view, removed from and not distorted by the particular features and circumstances of the all-encompassing background framework, from which a fair agreement between free and equal persons can be reached. The original position, with the feature I have called "the veil of ignorance," is this point of view.[13] And the reason why the original position must abstract from and not be affected by the contingencies of the social world is that the conditions for a fair agreement on the principles of political justice between free and equal persons must eliminate the bargaining advantages which inevitably arise within background institutions of any society as the result of cumulative social, historical, and natural tendencies. These contingent advantages and accidental influences from the past should not influence an agreement on the principles which are to regulate the institutions of the basic structure itself from the present into the future.

Here we seem to face a second difficulty, which is, however, only apparent. To explain: from what we have just said it is clear that the original position is to be seen as a device of representation and hence any agreement reached by the parties must be regarded as both hypothetical and nonhistorical. But if so, since hypothetical agreements cannot bind, what is the significance of the original position?[14] The answer is implicit in what has already been said: it is given by the

---

13 On the veil of ignorance, see ibid., Sec. 24, and the index.

14 This question is raised by Ronald Dworkin in the first part of his very illuminating, and to me highly instructive, essay "Justice and Rights" (1973), reprinted in *Taking Rights Seriously* (Cambridge, MA: Harvard University Press, 1977). Dworkin considers several ways of explaining the use of the original position in an account of justice that invokes the idea of the social contract. In the last part of the essay (pp. 173–83), after having surveyed some of the constructivist features of justice as fairness (pp. 159–68) and argued that it is a right-based and not a duty-based or a goal-based view (pp. 168–77), he proposes that the original position with the veil of ignorance be seen as modeling the force of the natural right that individuals have to equal concern and respect in the design of the political institutions that govern them (p. 180). He thinks that this natural right lies as the basis of justice as fairness and that the original position serves as a device for testing which principles of justice this right requires. This is an ingenious suggestion but I have not followed it in the text. I prefer not to think of justice as fairness as a right-based view; indeed, Dworkin's classification scheme of right-based, duty-based and goal-based views (pp. 171f) is too narrow and leaves out important possibilities. Thus, as explained in Sec. II above, I think of justice as fairness as working up into idealized conceptions certain fundamental intuitive ideas such as those of the person as free and equal, of a well-ordered society and of the public role of a conception of political justice, and as connecting these fundamental intuitive ideas with the even more fundamental and comprehensive intuitive idea of society as a fair system of cooperation over time from one generation to the next. Rights, duties, and goals are but elements of such idealized conceptions. Thus, justice as fairness is a conception- based, or as Elizabeth Anderson has suggested to me, an ideal-based view, since these fundamental intuitive ideas reflect ideals implicit or latent in the public culture of a democratic society. In this context the original position is a device of representation that models the force, not of the natural right of equal concern and respect, but of the essential elements of these fundamental intuitive ideas as identified by the reasons for principles of justice that we accept on

role of the various features of the original position as a device of representation. Thus, that the parties are symmetrically situated is required if they are to be seen as representatives of free and equal citizens who are to reach an agreement under conditions that are fair. Moreover, one of our considered convictions, I assume, is this: the fact that we occupy a particular social position is not a good reason for us to accept, or to expect others to accept, a conception of justice that favors those in this position. To model this conviction in the original position the parties are not allowed to know their social position; and the same idea is extended to other cases. This is expressed figuratively by saying that the parties are behind a veil of ignorance. In sum, the original position is simply a device of representation: it describes the parties, each of whom are responsible for the essential interests of a free and equal person, as fairly situated and as reaching an agreement subject to appropriate restrictions on what are to count as good reasons.[15]

Both of the above mentioned difficulties, then, are overcome by viewing the original position as a device of representation: that is, this position models what we regard as fair conditions under which the representatives of free and equal persons are to specify the terms of social cooperation in the case of the basic structure of society; and since it also models what, for this case, we regard as acceptable restrictions on reasons available to the parties for favoring one agreement rather than another, the conception of justice the parties would adopt identifies the conception we regard—*here and now*—as fair and supported by the best reasons. We try to model restrictions on reasons in such a way that it is perfectly evident which agreement would be made by the parties in the original position as citizens' representatives. Even if there should be, as surely there will be, reasons for and against each conception of justice available, there may be an overall balance

---

due reflection. As such a device, it serves first to combine and then to focus the resultant force of all these reasons in selecting the most appropriate principles of justice for a democratic society. (In doing this the force of the natural right of equal concern and respect will be covered in other ways.) This account of the use of the original position resembles in some respects an account Dworkin rejects in the first part of his essay, especially pp. 153f. In view of the ambiguity and obscurity of *Theory* on many of the points he considers, it is not my aim to criticize Dworkin's valuable discussion, but rather to indicate how my understanding of the original position differs from his. Others may prefer his account.

15 The original position models a basic feature of Kantian constructivism, namely, the distinction between the Reasonable and the Rational, with the Reasonable as prior to the Rational. (For an explanation of this distinction, see "Kantian Constructivism," pp. 528–32, and passim.) The relevance of this distinction here is that *Theory* more or less consistently speaks not of rational but of reasonable (or sometimes of fitting or appropriate) conditions as constraints on arguments for principles of justice (see pp. 18f., 20f., 120f., 130f., 138, 446, 516f., 578, 584f.). These constraints are modeled in the original position and thereby imposed on the parties: their deliberations are subject, and subject absolutely, to the reasonable conditions the modeling of which makes the original position fair. The Reasonable, then, is prior to the Rational, and this gives the priority of right. Thus, it was an error in *Theory* (and a very misleading one) to describe a theory of justice as part of the theory of rational choice, as on pp. 16 and 583. What I should have said is that the conception of justice as fairness uses an account of rational choice subject to reasonable conditions to characterize the deliberations of the parties as representatives of free and equal persons; and all of this within a political conception of justice, which is, of course, a moral conception. There is no thought of trying to derive the content of justice within a framework that uses an idea of the rational as the sole normative idea. That thought is incompatible with any kind of Kantian view.

of reasons plainly favoring one conception over the rest. As a device of representation the idea of the original position serves as a means of public reflection and self-clarification. We can use it to help us work out what we now think, once we are able to take a clear and uncluttered view of what justice requires when society is conceived as a scheme of cooperation between free and equal persons over time from one generation to the next. The original position serves as a unifying idea by which our considered convictions at all levels of generality are brought to bear on one another so as to achieve greater mutual agreement and self-understanding.

To conclude: we introduce an idea like that of the original position because there is no better way to elaborate a political conception of justice for the basic structure from the fundamental intuitive idea of society as a fair system of cooperation between citizens as free and equal persons. There are, however, certain hazards. As a device of representation the original position is likely to seem somewhat abstract and hence open to misunderstanding. The description of the parties may seem to presuppose some metaphysical conception of the person, for example, that the essential nature of persons is independent of and prior to their contingent attributes, including their final ends and attachments, and indeed, their character as a whole. But this is an illusion caused by not seeing the original position as a device of representation. The veil of ignorance, to mention one prominent feature of that position, has no metaphysical implications concerning the nature of the self; it does not imply that the self is ontologically prior to the facts about persons that the parties are excluded from knowing. We can, as it were, enter this position any time simply by reasoning for principles of justice in accordance with the enumerated restrictions. When, in this way, we simulate being in this position, our reasoning no more commits us to a metaphysical doctrine about the nature of the self than our playing a game like Monopoly commits us to thinking that we are landlords engaged in a desperate rivalry, winner take all.[16] We must keep in mind that we

---

16 *Theory*, pp. I38f., 147. The parties in the original position are said (p. 147) to be theoretically defined individuals whose motivations are specified by the account of that position and not by a psychological view about how human beings are actually motivated. This is also part of what is meant by saying (p. 121) that the acceptance of the particular principles of justice is not conjectured as a psychological law or probability but rather follows from the full description of the original position. Although the aim cannot be perfectly achieved, we want the argument to be deductive, "a kind of moral geometry." In "Kantian Constructivism" (p. 532) the parties are described as merely artificial agents who inhabit a construction. Thus I think R. B. Brandt mistaken in objecting that the argument from the original position is based on defective psychology. See his *A Theory of the Good and the Right* (Oxford: Clarendon Press, 1979), pp. 239–42. Of course, one might object to the original position that it models the conception of the person and the deliberations of the parties in ways that are unsuitable for the purposes of a political conception of justice; but for these purposes psychological theory is not directly relevant. On the other hand, psychological theory is relevant for the account of the stability of a conception of justice, as discussed in *Theory*, Pt. III. See below, footnote 33. Similarly, I think Michael Sandel mistaken in supposing that the original position involves a conception of the self " ... shorn of all its contingently-given attributes," a self that "assumes a kind of supra-empirical status, ... and given prior to its ends, a pure subject of agency and possession, ultimately thin." See *Liberalism and the Limits of Justice* (Cambridge: Cambridge University Press, 1982), pp. 93–95. I cannot discuss these criticisms in any detail. The essential point (as suggested in the introductory remarks) is not whether certain passages in *Theory* call for such an interpretation (I doubt that they do),

are trying to show how the idea of society as a fair system of social cooperation can be unfolded so as to specify the most appropriate principles for realizing the institutions of liberty and equality when citizens are regarded as free and equal persons.

V

I just remarked that the idea of the original position and the description of the parties may tempt us to think that a metaphysical doctrine of the person is presupposed. While I said that this interpretation is mistaken, it is not enough simply to disavow reliance on metaphysical doctrines, for despite one's intent they may still be involved. To rebut claims of this nature requires discussing them in detail and showing that they have no foothold. I cannot do that here.[17]

I can, however, sketch a positive account of the political conception of the person, that is, the conception of the person as citizen (discussed in Section III), involved in the original position as a device of representation. To explain what is meant by describing a conception of the person as political, let's consider how citizens are represented in the original position as free persons. The representation of their freedom seems to be one source of the idea that some metaphysical doctrine is presupposed. I have said elsewhere that citizens view themselves as free in three respects, so let's survey each of these briefly and indicate the way in which the conception of the person used is political.[18]

---

but whether the conception of justice as fairness presented therein can be understood in the light of the interpretation I sketch in this article and in the earlier lectures on constructivism, as I believe it can be.

17 Part of the difficulty is that there is no accepted understanding of what a metaphysical doctrine is. One might say, as Paul Hoffman has suggested to me, that to develop a political conception of justice without presupposing, or explicitly using, a metaphysical doctrine, for example, some particular metaphysical conception of the person, is already to presuppose a metaphysical thesis: namely, that no particular metaphysical doctrine is required for this purpose. One might also say that our everyday conception of persons as the basic units of deliberation and responsibility presupposes, or in some way involves, certain metaphysical theses about the nature of persons as moral or political agents. Following the method of avoidance, I should not want to deny these claims. What should be said is the following. If we look at the presentation of justice as fairness and note how it is set up, and note the ideas and conceptions it uses, no particular metaphysical doctrine about the nature of persons, distinctive and opposed to other metaphysical doctrines, appears among its premises, or seems required by its argument. If metaphysical presuppositions are involved, perhaps they are so general that they would not distinguish between the distinctive metaphysical views—Cartesian, Leibnizian, or Kantian; realist, idealist, or materialist—with which philosophy traditionally has been concerned. In this case, they would not appear to be relevant for the structure and content of a political conception of justice one way or the other. I am grateful to Daniel Brudney and Paul Hoffman for discussion of these matters.

18 For the first two respects, see "Kantian Constructivism," pp. 544f. (For the third respect, see footnote 21 below.) The account of the first two respects found in those lectures is further developed in the text above and I am more explicit on the distinction between what I call here our "public" versus our "nonpublic or moral identity." The point of the term "moral" in the latter phrase is to indicate that persons' conceptions of the (complete) good are normally an essential element in characterizing their nonpublic (or nonpolitical) identity, and these conceptions are understood as normally

First, citizens are free in that they conceive of themselves and of one another as having the moral power to have a conception of the good. This is not to say that, as part of their political conception of themselves, they view themselves as inevitably tied to the pursuit of the particular conception of the good which they affirm at any given time. Instead, as citizens, they are regarded as capable of revising and changing this conception on reasonable and rational grounds, and they may do this if they so desire. Thus, as free persons, citizens claim the right to view their persons as independent from and as not identified with any particular conception of the good, or scheme of final ends. Given their moral power to form, to revise, and rationally to pursue a conception of the good, their public identity as free persons is not affected by changes over time in their conception of the good. For example, when citizens convert from one religion to another, or no longer affirm an established religious faith, they do not cease to be, for questions of political justice, the same persons they were before. There is no loss of what we may call their public identity, their identity as a matter of basic law. In general, they still have the same basic rights and duties; they own the same property and can make the same claims as before, except insofar as these claims were connected with their previous religious affiliation. We can imagine a society (indeed, history offers numerous examples) in which basic rights and recognized claims depend on religious affiliation, social class, and so on. Such a society has a different political conception of the person. It may not have a conception of citizenship at all; for this conception, as we are using it, goes with the conception of society as a fair system of cooperation for mutual advantage between free and equal persons.

It is essential to stress that citizens in their personal affairs, or in the internal life of associations to which they belong, may regard their final ends and attachments in a way very different from the way the political conception involves. Citizens may have, and normally do have at any given time, affections, devotions, and loyalties that they believe they would not, and indeed could and should not, stand apart from and objectively evaluate from the point of view of their purely rational good. They may regard it as simply unthinkable to view themselves apart from certain religious, philosophical, and moral convictions, or from certain enduring attachments and loyalties. These convictions and attachments are part of what we may call their "nonpublic identity." These convictions and attachments help to organize and give shape to a person's way of life, what one sees oneself as doing and trying to accomplish in one's social world. We think that if we were suddenly without these particular convictions and attachments we would be disoriented and unable to carry on. In fact, there would be, we might think, no point in carrying on. But our conceptions of the good may and often do change over time, usually slowly but sometimes rather suddenly. When these changes are sudden, we are particularly likely to say that we are no longer the same person. We know what this means: we refer to a profound and pervasive shift, or reversal, in our

---

containing important moral elements, although they include other elements as well, philosophical and religious. The term "moral" should be thought of as a stand-in for all these possibilities. I am indebted to Elizabeth Anderson for discussion and clarification of this distinction.

final ends and character; we refer to our different nonpublic, and possibly moral or religious, identity. On the road to Damascus Saul of Tarsus becomes Paul the Apostle. There is no change in our public or political identity, nor in our personal identity as this concept is understood by some writers in the philosophy of mind.[19]

The second respect in which citizens view themselves as free is that they regard themselves as self-originating sources of valid claims. They think their claims have weight apart from being derived from duties or obligations specified by the political conception of justice, for example, from duties and obligations owed to society. Claims that citizens regard as founded on duties and obligations based on their conception of the good and the moral doctrine they affirm in their own life are also, for our purposes here, to be counted as self-originating. Doing this is reasonable in a political conception of justice for a constitutional democracy; for provided the conceptions of the good and the moral doctrines citizens affirm are compatible with the public conception of justice, these duties and obligations are self-originating from the political point of view.

When we describe a way in which citizens regard themselves as free, we are describing how citizens actually think of themselves in a democratic society should questions of justice arise. In our conception of a constitutional regime, this is an aspect of how citizens regard themselves. That this aspect of their freedom belongs to a particular political conception is clear from the contrast with a different political conception in which the members of society are not viewed as self-originating sources of valid claims. Rather, their claims have no weight except insofar as they can be derived from their duties and obligations owed to society, or from their ascribed roles in the social hierarchy justified by religious or aristocratic values. Or to take an extreme case, slaves are human beings who are not counted as sources of claims, not even claims based on social duties or obligations, for slaves are not counted as capable of having duties or obligations. Laws that prohibit the abuse and maltreatment of slaves are not founded on claims made by slaves on their

---

19 Here I assume that an answer to the problem of personal identity tries to specify the various criteria (for example, psychological continuity of memories and physical continuity of body, or some part thereof) in accordance with which two different psychological states, or actions (or whatever), which occur at two different times may be said to be states or actions of the same person who endures over time; and it also tries to specify how this enduring person is to be conceived, whether as a Cartesian or a Leibnizian substance, or as a Kantian transcendental ego, or as a continuant of some other kind, for example, bodily or physical. See the collection of essays edited by John Perry, *Personal Identity* (Berkeley, CA: University of California Press, 1975), especially Perry's introduction, pp. 3–30; and Sydney Shoemaker's essay in *Personal Identity* (Oxford: Basil Blackwell, 1984), both of which consider a number of views. Sometimes in discussions of this problem, continuity of fundamental aims and aspirations is largely ignored, for example, in views like H. P. Grice's (included in Perry's collection) which emphasizes continuity of memory. Of course, once continuity of fundamental aims and aspirations is brought in, as in Derek Parfit's *Reasons and Persons* (Oxford: Clarendon Press, 1984), Pt. III, there is no sharp distinction between the problem of persons' nonpublic or moral identity and the problem of their personal identity. This latter problem raises profound questions on which past and current philosophical views widely differ, and surely will continue to differ. For this reason it is important to try to develop a political conception of justice which avoids this problem as far as possible.

own behalf, but on claims originating either from slaveholders, or from the general interests of society (which does not include the interests of slaves). Slaves are, so to speak, socially dead: they are not publicly recognized as persons at all.[20] Thus, the contrast with apolitical conception which allows slavery makes clear why conceiving of citizens as free persons in virtue of their moral powers and their having a conception of the good, goes with a particular political conception of the person. This conception of persons fits into a political conception of justice founded on the idea of society as a system of cooperation between its members conceived as free and equal.

The third respect in which citizens are regarded as free is that they are regarded as capable of taking responsibility for their ends and this affects how their various claims are assessed.[21] Very roughly, the idea is that, given just background institutions and given for each person a fair index of primary goods (as required by the principles of justice), citizens are thought to be capable of adjusting their aims and aspirations in the light of what they can reasonably expect to provide for. Moreover, they are regarded as capable of restricting their claims in matters of justice to the kinds of things the principles of justice allow. Thus, citizens are to recognize that the weight of their claims is not given by the strength and psychological intensity of their wants and desires (as opposed to their needs and requirements as citizens), even when their wants and desires are rational from their point of view. I cannot pursue these matters here. But the procedure is the same as before: we start with the basic intuitive idea of society as a system of social cooperation. When this idea is developed into a conception of political justice, it implies that, viewing ourselves as persons who can engage in social cooperation over a complete life, we can also take responsibility for our ends, that is, that we can adjust our ends so that they can be pursued by the means we can reasonably expect to acquire given our prospects and situation in society. The idea of responsibility for ends is implicit in the public political culture and discernible in its practices. A political conception of the person articulates this idea and fits it into the idea of society as a system of social cooperation over a complete life.

To sum up, I recapitulate three main points of this and the preceding two sections:

First, in Section III persons were regarded as free and equal in virtue of their possessing to the requisite degree the two powers of moral personality (and the powers of reason, thought, and judgment connected with these powers), namely, the capacity for a sense of justice and the capacity for a conception of the good. These powers we associated with two main elements of the idea of cooperation, the idea of fair terms of cooperation and the idea of each participant's rational advantage, or good.

---

20 For the idea of social death, see Orlando Patterson, *Slavery and Social Death* (Cambridge, MA: Harvard University Press, 1982), esp. pp. 5–9, 38–45, 337. This idea is interestingly developed in this book and has a central place in the author's comparative study of slavery.

21 See "Social Unity and Primary Goods," in *Utilitarianism and Beyond*, eds. Amartya Sen and Bernard Williams (Cambridge: Cambridge University Press, 1982), Sec. IV. pp. 167–70.

Second, in this section (Section V), we have briefly surveyed three respects in which persons are regarded as free, and we have noted that in the public political culture of a constitutional democratic regime citizens conceive of themselves as free in these respects.

Third, since the question of which conception of political justice is most appropriate for realizing in basic institutions the values of liberty and equality has long been deeply controversial within the very democratic tradition in which citizens are regarded as free and equal persons, the aim of justice as fairness is to try to resolve this question by starting from the basic intuitive idea of society as a fair system of social cooperation in which the fair terms of cooperation are agreed upon by citizens themselves so conceived. In Section IV, we saw why this approach leads to the idea of the original position as a device of representation.

VI

I now take up a point essential to thinking of justice as fairness as a liberal view. Although this conception is a moral conception, it is not, as I have said, intended as a comprehensive moral doctrine. The conception of the citizen as a free and equal person is not a moral ideal to govern all of life, but is rather an ideal belonging to a conception of political justice which is to apply to the basic structure. I emphasize this point because to think otherwise would be incompatible with liberalism as a political doctrine. Recall that as such a doctrine, liberalism assumes that in a constitutional democratic state under modem conditions there are bound to exist conflicting and incommensurable conceptions of the good. This feature characterizes modem culture since the Reformation. Any viable political conception of justice that is not to rely on the autocratic use of state power must recognize this fundamental social fact. This does not mean, of course, that such a conception cannot impose constraints on individuals and associations, but that when it does so, these constraints are accounted for, directly or indirectly, by the requirements of political justice for the basic structure.[22]

Given this fact, we adopt a conception of the person framed as part of, and restricted to, an explicitly political conception of justice. In this sense, the conception of the person is a political one. As I stressed in the previous section, persons can accept this conception of themselves as citizens and use it when discussing questions of political justice without being committed in other parts of their life to comprehensive moral ideals often associated with liberalism, for example, the

---

22 For example, churches are constrained by the principle of equal liberty of conscience and must conform to the principle of toleration, universities by what may be required to maintain fair equality of opportunity, and the rights of parents by what is necessary to maintain their childrens' physical well-being and to assure the adequate development of their intellectual and moral powers. Because churches, universities, and parents exercise their authority within the basic structure, they are to recognize the requirements this structure imposes to maintain background justice.

JUSTICE AS FAIRNESS:

ideals of autonomy and individuality. The absence of commitment to these ideals, and indeed to any particular comprehensive ideal, is essential to liberalism as a political doctrine. The reason is that any such ideal, when pursued as a comprehensive ideal, is incompatible with other conceptions of the good, with forms of personal, moral, and religious life consistent with justice and which, therefore, have a proper place in a democratic society. As comprehensive moral ideals, autonomy and individuality are unsuited for a political conception of justice. As found in Kant and J. S. Mill, these comprehensive ideals, despite their very great importance in liberal thought, are extended too far when presented as the only appropriate foundation for a constitutional regime.[23] So understood, liberalism becomes but another sectarian doctrine.

This conclusion requires comment: it does not mean, of course, that the liberalisms of Kant and Mill are not appropriate moral conceptions from which we can be led to affirm democratic institutions. But they are only two such conceptions among others, and so but two of the philosophical doctrines likely to persist and gain adherents in a reasonably just democratic regime. In such a regime the comprehensive moral views which support its basic institutions may include the liberalisms of individuality and autonomy; and possibly these liberalisms are among the more prominent doctrines in an overlapping consensus, that is, in a consensus in which, as noted earlier, different and even conflicting doctrines affirm the publicly shared basis of political arrangements. The liberalisms of Kant and Mill have a certain historical preeminence as among the first and most important philosophical views to espouse modem constitutional democracy and to develop its underlying ideas in an influential way; and it may even turn out that societies in which the ideals of autonomy and individuality are widely accepted are among the most well-governed and harmonious.[24]

By contrast with liberalism as a comprehensive moral doctrine, justice as fairness tries to present a conception of political justice rooted in the basic intuitive ideas found in the public culture of a constitutional democracy. We conjecture that these ideas are likely to be affirmed by each of the opposing comprehensive moral doctrines influential in a reasonably just democratic society. Thus justice as fairness seeks to identify the kernel of an overlapping consensus, that is, the shared intuitive ideas which when worked up into a political conception of justice turn out to be sufficient to underwrite a just constitutional regime. This is the most we can expect, nor do we need more.[25] We must note, however, that when justice as fairness is fully realized in a well-ordered society, the

---

23 For Kant, see *The Foundations of the Metaphysics of Morals* and *The Critique of Practical Reason*. For Mill, see *On Liberty*, particularly Ch. 3 where the ideal of individuality is most fully discussed.

24 This point has been made with respect to the liberalisms of Kant and Mill, but for American culture one should mention the important conceptions of democratic individuality expressed in the works of Emerson, Thoreau, and Whitman. These are instructively discussed by George Kateb in his "Democratic Individuality and the Claims of Politics," *Political Theory* 12 (August 1984).

25 For the idea of the kernel of an overlapping consensus (mentioned above), see *Theory*, last par. of Sec. 35, pp. 22of. For the idea of full autonomy, see "Kantian Constructivism," pp. 528ff.

value of full autonomy is likewise realized. In this way justice as fairness is indeed similar to the liberalisms of Kant and Mill; but in contrast with them, the value of full autonomy is here specified by a political conception of justice, and not by a comprehensive moral doctrine.

It may appear that, so understood, the public acceptance of justice as fairness is no more than prudential; that is, that those who affirm this conception do so simply as a *modus vivendi* which allows the groups in the overlapping consensus to pursue their own good subject to certain constraints which each thinks to be for its advantage given existing circumstances. The idea of an overlapping consensus may seem essentially Hobbesian. But against this, two remarks: first, justice as fairness is a moral conception: it has conceptions of person and society, and concepts of right and fairness, as well as principles of justice with their complement of the virtues through which those principles are embodied in human character and regulate political and social life. This conception of justice provides an account of the cooperative virtues suitable for a political doctrine in view of the conditions and requirements of a constitutional regime. It is no less a moral conception because it is restricted to the basic structure of society, since this restriction is what enables it to serve as a political conception of justice given our present circumstances. Thus, in an overlapping consensus (as understood here), the conception of justice as fairness is not regarded merely as a *modus vivendi*.

Second, in such a consensus each of the comprehensive philosophical, religious, and moral doctrines accepts justice as fairness in its own way; that is, each comprehensive doctrine, from within its own point of view, is led to accept the public reasons of justice specified by justice as fairness. We might say that they recognize its concepts, principles, and virtues as theorems, as it were, at which their several views coincide. But this does not make these points of coincidence any less moral or reduce them to mere means. For, in general, these concepts, principles, and virtues are accepted by each as belonging to a more comprehensive philosophical, religious, or moral doctrine. Some may even affirm justice as fairness as a natural moral conception that can stand on its own feet. They accept this conception of justice as a reasonable basis for political and social cooperation, and hold that it is as natural and fundamental as the concepts and principles of honesty and mutual trust, and the virtues of cooperation in everyday life. The doctrines in an overlapping consensus differ in how far they maintain a further foundation is necessary and on what that further foundation should be. These differences, however, are compatible with a consensus on justice as fairness as a political conception of justice.

VII

I shall conclude by considering the way in which social unity and stability may be understood by liberalism as a political doctrine (as opposed to a comprehensive moral conception).[26]

One of the deepest distinctions between political conceptions of justice is between those that allow for a plurality of opposing and even incommensurable conceptions of the good and those that hold that there is but one conception of the good which is to be recognized by all persons, so far as they are fully rational. Conceptions of justice which fall on opposite sides of this divide are distinct in many fundamental ways. Plato and Aristotle, and the Christian tradition as represented by Augustine and Aquinas, fall on the side of the one rational good. Such views tend to be teleological and to hold that institutions are just to the extent that they effectively promote this good. Indeed, since classical times the dominant tradition seems to have been that there is but one rational conception of the good, and that the aim of moral philosophy, together with theology and metaphysics, is to determine its nature. Classical utilitarianism belongs to this dominant tradition. By contrast, liberalism as a political doctrine supposes that there are many conflicting and incommensurable conceptions of the good, each compatible with the full rationality of human persons, so far as we can ascertain within a workable political conception of justice. As a consequence of this supposition, liberalism assumes that it is a characteristic feature of a free democratic culture that a plurality of conflicting and incommensurable conceptions of the good are affirmed by its citizens.

---

26 This account of social unity is found in "Social Unity and Primary Goods," referred to in footnote 27 above. See esp. pp. 16of., 170–73, 183f.

RESOURCES, CAPACITIES, AND OWNERSHIP

THE WORKMANSHIP IDEAL AND DISTRIBUTIVE JUSTICE

BY IAN SHAPIRO

Ian Shapiro, "Resources, Capacities, and Ownership: The Workmanship Ideal and Distributive Justice," *Political Theory*, vol. 19, no. 1, pp. 47-72. Copyright © 1991 by SAGE Publications. Reprinted with permission.

EIGHT

Though the Earth, and all inferior Creatures be common to all Men, yet every Man has a *Property* in his own *Person*. This no Body has any Right to but himself. The *Labour* of his Body, and the *Work* of his hands, we may say, are properly his. Whatsoever then he removes out of the State that Nature hath provided, and left it in, he hath mixed his *Labour* with, and joyned it to something that is his own, and thereby makes it his *Property*. It being by him removed from the common state Nature placed it in, hath by his *labour* something annexed to it, that excludes the common right of other Men. For this *Labour* being the unquestionable Property of the Labourer, no Man but he can have a right to what that is once joyned to, at least where there is enough, and as good left in common for others.

John Locke, *Second Treatise of Government*, section 27

Human beings generate much of what they want and need by mixing their productive capacities with other resources, producing objects and services of value. This fact about human creativity has been incorporated into Western thinking about distributive justice via the workmanship ideal of ownership. It revolves around the conviction that as long as the resources with which people mix their productive capacities are justly acquired, they may legitimately own the product of the conjunction. Just how to organize things so that the caveat embedded in the workmanship ideal is not violated has been subject to vituperative debate for centuries, as have the meaning of and justification for the premise that people may be said to own their productive capacities in the first place. In a number of idioms both intellectual and political, the workmanship ideal sets the terms of debate about the just distribution, ownership, and even definition of property.[1]

The enduring intensity of arguments about this ideal signifies that it retains a powerful hold on the Western political imagination, and it is the hold as much as the ideal that concerns me in this essay. In a deconstructionist spirit I try to account for our collective inability to let go of the ideal, despite major conceptual difficulties it confronts. In a constructive spirit I try to adduce support for the view that, partly because of its internal tensions, the workmanship ideal can defensibly be part of our thinking about distributive justice only in a limited and conditional way; we must not expect too much from it and nor should we attribute to the rights it spawns a necessary trumping power with respect to competing requirements of social justice.

In part I, I argue that the workmanship ideal formulated by Locke was part of an internally cohesive view of just ownership that derived part of its intellectual appeal from the fact that it situated the rights of workmanship in a complex moral scheme that left room for other demands of social justice. I also argue, however, that the attractiveness and coherence of Locke's view depended on theological assumptions that have long since been jettisoned in the dominant intellectual traditions of the West. Yet because of the powerful appeal of the intuitions that drive the workmanship ideal, many have tried to formulate secular variants of it; they have sought historical linking strategies that can be used to tether legitimate property rights to the work of productive agents. Parts II and III are devoted to analysis of the two main variants of such strategies that have grown out of the Marxist and neoclassical traditions of political economy. This leads to a discussion—in part IV—of why historical linking strategies invariably fail, running into insuperable problems of overdetermination and threatening perpetually to swamp the competing values with which property regimes are bound to coexist in any intellectually compelling account of social justice. This conclusion seems naturally to counsel abandoning historical linking strategies altogether, a possibility I examine in part V via a discussion of recent attempts by John Rawls and Ronald Dworkin to displace them with socialized views of human productive capacities. But the proposal that we should abandon the workmanship ideal turns out to be as troublesome as the difficulties that result from embracing secular variants of it. In part VI, I discuss two possible ways out of the conundrum thus generated. The first involves embracing a variant of the workmanship ideal on consequentialist grounds while conceding that it rests partly on causal and moral fictions. The second, which need not be inconsistent with the first, requires us to treat the workmanship ideal as part of a democratic conception of distributive justice. I suggest briefly in conclusion that this latter course is better.

---

1 I take the term "workmanship ideal" from James Tully, *A Discourse Concerning Property* (Cambridge: Cambridge University Press, 1980).

I. THEOLOGICAL FOUNDATIONS OF THE CLASSICAL WORKMANSHIP IDEAL

Locke's theory of property was elegant, coherent, and—if one accepts the premises to which he was committed—compelling.[2] He thought human labor the main source of value, but he believed that natural resources make an independent—if comparatively minor—contribution to the value of produced goods and services.[3] Against Filmer (who insisted that God gave the world to Adam and his heirs via an hierarchical system of inheritance), Locke argued that God gave the world to mankind in common, subject to two constraints: that it not be wasted and that any individual's use of the common to produce his own property was subject to the restriction that "enough, and as good" remain available to others to use in common.[4]

Locke's treatment of human capacities was linked to his theology in a different way. It rested on his categorial distinction between natural right and natural law which explained human autonomy. Natural law, Locke tells us, "ought to be distinguished from natural right: for right is grounded in the fact that we have the free use of a thing, whereas law enjoins or forbids the doing of a thing." Right, then, is a different kind of thing from law, the former indicating a capacity for autonomous action and the latter externally imposed obligatory constraints.[5] It is through acts of autonomous making that rights over what is created come into being: Making entails ownership so that natural

---

2 The following discussion of Locke incorporates and builds on aspects of my account in *The Evolution of Rights in Liberal Theory* (Cambridge: Cambridge University Press, 1986), 86–118.

3 Locke minimizes the independent contribution of resources by arguing that the world which has been given us in common is God's "waste" and insisting that "*labour makes* the far greater part," although he is famously vague about the precise relative contributions of labor and nature. See Locke, *Two Treatises of Government* (Cambridge: Cambridge University Press, 1970), 330, 331, 337, 338, 341.

4 Ibid., 329. To this moral theory Locke added two dubious empirical claims which combined to get him from the theory of use rights to the common to something like the view of property that twentieth-century libertarians often wrongly designate as Lockean. First was the claim that with the introduction of money the injunction against waste, although not in principle transcended, for practical purposes became obsolete. Locke believed that as well as itself not being subject to physical decay, money made possible the comparatively more productive use of natural resources through trade and productive work. See Richard Ashcraft, *Locke's Two Treatises of Government* (New York: Allen & Unwin, 1987), 123–50; *Revolutionary Politics and Locke's Two Treatises of Government* (Princeton, NJ: Princeton University Press, 1986), 270–85. For the view (which Ashcraft criticizes) that Locke thought the proviso transcended with the introduction of money, see C. B. Macpherson, *The Political Theory of Possessive Individualism* (Oxford: Oxford University Press, 1962), 203–21. Second was the claim that the productivity effects of enclosing common land would be so great that the "enough, and as good" proviso could, in practice, also be dispensed with (thereby legitimating private ownership). It is possible to reject either or both of the empirical claims without rejecting Locke's basic moral argument, although any such move would jeopardize his defenses of unlimited accumulation and private property.

5 By following Hobbes and Pufendorf in this formulation of the distinction, Locke was embracing an important departure from the Thomist tradition, rooted in Grotius' revival of the Roman law conception of a right as one's *suum*, a kind of moral power or *facultas* which every man has, and which has its conceptual roots, as Quentin Skinner has established, in the writings of Suarez and ultimately Gerson and the conciliarist tradition. See *The Foundations of Modern Political Thought* (Cambridge: Cambridge University Press, 1978), vol 2, 117, 176–78. See also Richard Tuck,

law is, at bottom, God's natural right over his creation.⁶ Locke's frequent appeals to metaphors of workmanship and watchmaking in the *Two Treatises* and elsewhere make it fundamental that men are obliged to God because of his purposes in making them. Men are "the Workmanship of one Omnipotent, and infinitely wise Maker. ... They are his Property, whose Workmanship they are, made to last during his, not one another's pleasure."⁷

For Locke, human beings are unique among God's creations because he gave them the capacity to make, to create rights of their own. Natural law may dictate that man is subject to divine imperatives to live in certain ways, but, within the limits set by the law of nature, men can act—as Tully notes—in a godlike fashion: "[M]an as maker ... has analogous maker's knowledge of, and a natural right in his intentional actions." Provided we do not violate natural law, we stand in the same relation to the objects we create as God stands in to us; we own them just as he owns us.⁸ This is not to say that, for Locke, all our capacities are God-given or that their development is uninfluenced by social arrangements; he thought that productive capacities could be bought and sold in ways that increased productivity and there is some evidence that he believed workers' productivity to be influenced by mercantile workhouse discipline.⁹ Certainly there was potential for tension between these causal beliefs and the workmanship ideal; we will see later that arguments that human activity and organization shape productive capacities would eventually be pressed into the service of an explosive immanent critique of that ideal.¹⁰ But as long as human creative power was seen as a gift from God, this possibility could be staved off; even if productive capacities are influenced by human agency, this agency finds its genesis and limits in the will of a beneficent deity.

Locke conceived of the range of human activities free of God's sanctions quite broadly; certainly it included most of what is conventionally thought of as the realm of the production and

---

Natural Rights Theories (Cambridge: Cambridge University Press, 1979); John Finnis, *Natural Law and Natural Right* (Oxford; Clarendon, 1980), 207-8.

6   John Locke, *Essays on the Law of Nature,* edited by W. Von Leiden (Oxford: Clarendon, 1958), 111, 187.

7   Locke, *Two Treaties,* 311, 347. For further discussion, see Tully, *Discourse,* 35-8; John Dunn, *The Political Thought of John Locke* (Cambridge University Press, 1969), 95.

8   Tully, *Discourse,* 109-10,121.

9   Evidence that capacities may be bought and sold can be found in Locke's insistence that "the turfs my servant has cut ... become my *property,*" and his account of wage labor which states that "a free man makes himself a servant to another, by selling him for a certain time, the service he undertakes to do, in exchange for wages he is to receive." That Locke thought wage labor enhanced productivity is evident from his defense of enclosure partly on the grounds that this would replace less efficient forms of subsistence production. See *Second Treatise,* 90-97, 290, 292-93, 330, 365-66. On Locke on discipline and productivity, see Tully, "Governing Conduct," in *Conscience and Causistry in Early Modern Europe,* edited by E. Leites (Cambridge: Cambridge University Press, 1988), 12-71.

10 On the implicit tensions between the causal argument and the workmanship ideal in Locke's formulation, see David Ellerman, "On the Labor Theory of Property," *Philosophical Forum* 16 (Summer 1985): 318-22.

consumption of goods.[11] But the existence of natural law constraints on human autonomy meant that there were circumstances in which the exercise of otherwise legitimate rights of appropriation would be curtailed. If Locke's provisos were violated, for instance, the right to appropriate from nature would be limited. Likewise, someone starving and disabled would have the right to another's plenty based on the natural law requirements of the right of preservation, and someone starving and able-bodied would have the right to the means of preservation—the right to materials to work on to preserve oneself—whether by means of the workhouse system or coerced labor for a landowner. In addition there were limits, for Locke, to the reparations that a conqueror could legitimately demand in wartime having to do with the subsistence rights of the wives and children of defeated soldiers.[12]

The existence of Locke's natural law constraints thus meant that not all rights were of the same kind; property rights occupied a circumscribed space in an hierarchical system. Productive human actions issue in rights and obligations that are binding on human beings, but these are not the only types of moral claims to which Locke believed us subject. Although not independent of the workmanship model (natural law was argued to be valid as God's workmanship), these other moral claims were conceived of as prior to claims of human workmanship.[13] To be sure, there would be disputes about when and how the natural law requirements are triggered and about the degree to which they limit property rights in particular instances which the natural law theory could not by itself resolve; as Ashcraft has shown with respect to eighteenth-century English debates about poor relief, the scope of what subsistence requires could be expanded and pressed into the service of a radical Lockean critique of the claims of capital.[14] But if the theory left balancing the claims of the competing requirements of natural law and human workmanship open to interpretation and political argument at least at the margins, it also undermined the presumption that rights of human appropriation supersede competing just claims.

II. SECULARIZING THE WORKMANSHIP IDEAL: MARXISM

In many respects Marx's labor theory of value was more sophisticated than Locke's. He famously distinguished labor from labor-power, developed the concepts of abstract human labor and socially necessary labor time, and from them the theory of exploitation of labor by capital. Yet

---

11   For further discussion, see Patrick Riley, *Will and Political Legitimacy* (Cambridge, MA: Harvard University Press, 1982), 64ff.; Shapiro, *Evolution*, 105–7.
12   On the role of the provisos in the theory of individual appropriation, see Locke, *Two Treaties*, 327–44; on charity, ibid., 206; and on the natural law limits to conqueror's rights to just reparations, ibid., 438.
13   On the hierarchical priority of Locke's natural law requirements, see Ashcraft, *Locke's Two Treatises*, 123–50.
14   See Ashcraft, "Locke and Eighteenth-Century Concepts of Property: The Politics of Interpretation," Clark Lecture delivered at the UCLA Center for 17th and 18th Century Studies, November 1989.

Marx held onto the basic logic of the workmanship ideal, even though he transformed it radically by secularizing it and locating it in a dynamic theory of historical change.[15]

Since Locke's treatment of both resources and capacities had been linked to his theology, both would now have to be treated differently. For Marx, resources cease to be of independent moral significance; the value of a natural resource is determined by the socially necessary labor time required for its appropriation from nature. God is no longer needed as the giver of natural resources since they are, by definition, without value apart from the human capacities needed for their appropriation. Not until the marginalists' rejection of the labor theory of value in the late nineteenth century would natural resources reenter the explanatory and moral calculus as an independent unit of value, and by then the theory of markets would offer different conceptual tools for dealing with them.

If resources are secularized by being reconceptualized as moral proxies for capacities, what of the treatment of capacities themselves? Are we still the ultimate owners of our capacities for Marx, and if so, why? In *The Critique of the Gotha Program*, Marx offers his most elaborate discussion of his views about the ultimate basis of entitlements in the course of a discussion of fair socialist distribution. Defining the cooperative proceeds of labor as the "total social product," he argues that after various deductions have been made by the state (for the provision of public goods, welfare for indigents, and financing new production), the balance of the surplus becomes available for consumption.[16] Because distribution in the early stages of communism is "still stamped with the birth marks of the old society from whose womb it emerges," it will continue to be based on work. The individual producer receives back from society, after the deductions have been made, "exactly what he gives to it." In these circumstances, "the same principle prevails as that which regulates the exchange of commodities," but it is nonetheless an advance on capitalism because "under the altered circumstances no one can give anything except his labour," and "nothing can pass into the ownership of individuals except individual means of consumption." Thus, although "equal right" continues to mean "bourgeois right" under socialism, "principle and practice are no longer at loggerheads."[17]

Marx concedes that this principle will generate inequalities by virtue of the fact that actual work becomes the basic metric of equality. Since labor must be defined either by duration or intensity to function as a measure at all, and since people differ from one another in physical and mental capacities, the right to each according to his work is unavoidably " an unequal right for unequal labour." He also notes that these inequalities will be exacerbated by the differing social circumstances of

---

15 I skirt the question, not relevant here, of the degree to which Marx's labor theory of value was influenced by Smith's and Ricardo's.
16 Karl Marx, *Critique of the Gotha Program*, in Karl Marx and Frederick Engels, *Selected Works*, vol. 3 (Los Angeles, CA: Progress Publishers, 1970), 15–17.
17 Ibid., 17, 18.

different workers. Such defects are inevitable through the early stages of communism, but in a "higher phase" of it "after the enslaving subordination of the individual to the division of labour, and with it also the antithesis between mental and physical labour, has vanished" and the "springs of co-operative wealth flow more abundantly," then the "narrow horizon of bourgeois right" can be "crossed in its entirety" and distribution can be based on needs. The transcendence of every regime of right is seen as necessary for the triumph of genuine equality; the work-based regime of socialism is not special in this regard: It is "a right of inequality, in its content, like every right."[18]

The workmanship ideal plays a role throughout Marx's account, but it should not be confused with his formulation of the labor theory of value. This latter is the causal thesis that only living human labor power creates exchange value (which determines prices in a capitalist economy). Marx believed that it explained the phenomenon of exploitation under capitalism by generating an account of how exchange value accrues to the capitalist as a by-product of the difference between the value of wages paid to workers and the value of the products those workers produce. In Marx's hands the labor theory of value thus became a vehicle for incorporating the moral appeal of the workmanship ideal into arguments about the production and distribution of wealth in a different way than had been the case with Locke; it rested on a different variant of the labor theory of value. Yet in neither case is the workmanship ideal part of or reducible to the labor theory of value. The ideal rests on the moral thesis that the legitimate basis of entitlement lies in productive action, and it is only because of the intuitive moral appeal of this thesis that the labor theory of value was thought to be pregnant with moral significance.

It is not surprising, therefore, that Marxists who have abandoned the labor theory of value nonetheless affirm variants of the workmanship ideal. G. A. Cohen argues that exploitation under capitalism derives not from the problematical thesis that the workers alone produce value but, rather, that the workers alone produce the product.[19] Conceding that capitalists may *act productively* by investing, he distinguishes this from *producing goods* which, he argues, is exclusively done by workers. Whether Cohen is right about this we need not settle now; that he makes the argument at all exhibits his reliance on the intuitive moral pull of the workmanship ideal.[20] This reliance becomes

---

18 Ibid., 18, 19.
19 G. A. Cohen, "The Labor Theory of Value and the Concept of Exploitation," *Philosophy and Public Affairs*, 8, no. 4 (1979): 354.
20 Ibid. 355–56. Cohen does concede that in some circumstances capitalists may also work productively but not in their prototypical roles as capitalists. I do not mean to suggest that Cohen believes that the workmanship ideal is the only or most important basis for distributive entitlements. Indeed, his recent advocacy of equality of "access to advantage" suggests a different basis for distributive justice, that people should not be held responsible for unchosen disadvantages. It is not yet possible to assess how the imperatives generated by this injunction should affect other rights, including rights of workmanship, in Cohen's view because he defends equality of access to advantage only as what he dubs a weak form of egalitarianism; he explicitly refrains from saying to what extent we should equalize in his sense, or even how conflicts between his kind of equalization and other kinds that egalitarians might prize should be settled. See Cohen, "On the Currency of Egalitarian Justice." *Ethics* 99 (July 1989): 906–44; also "Equality of What? On Welfare,

explicit in two essays on the relation between self-ownership and world- ownership where Cohen advances criticisms of Robert Nozick that rely on affirming the idea that we own our productive capacities and the goods, in certain circumstances, that they are instrumental in generating.[21]

Likewise, John Roemer assumes that people own their productive capacities and defines exploitation and unfairness (for him these two are not the same) in terms of distributions of the alienable means of production that force or supply incentives to workers to produce goods that become the property of capitalists.[22] To pack any moral punch such arguments must rest on the claim that such class monopoly is unjustifiable, and when we ask why the answer turns out to rest either on the claim that the monopoly was achieved via illicit appropriation of the proceeds of the work of others or an argument that the class monopoly prevents workers' realizing at least some of the potential fruits of their own labor, or both. Thus Roemer resists the possibility that the class monopoly might have come about as a result of differences in natural abilities or propensities toward risk on historical and probabilistic grounds, and he defines unfairness and exploitation by reference to counter- factuals in which individuals or classes would produce more goods by as much or less work than is the case when the class monopoly obtains.[23]

Goods and Capabilities," forthcoming in a volume of papers presented at the WIDER Symposium on the Quality of Life and referred to here in manuscript form. Some of these issues are taken up briefly in my *Political Criticism* (Berkeley: University of California Press, 1990), 217–19.

21   G. A. Cohen, "Self-Ownership, World Ownership and Equality I," *injustice and Equality Here and Now*, edited by Frank Lucash (Ithaca, NY: Cornell University Press, 1986), 108–35; "Self-onwership, World Ownership and Equality II," *Social Philosophy and Policy*, 3 (Spring 1986): 77–96. In "Self-ownership I," Cohen appeals to the idea that "value adders merit reward" to attack Nozick's defense of private ownership of external resources by demonstrating (ingeniously) that different forms of ownership of external resources may, in some circumstances, reward value adders more often or more accurately than a private property regime of the sort Nozick advocates (see esp. 128–30). In fairness to Cohen it should be noted that in these essays he professes some discomfort with the self-ownership thesis (deriving from the inequalities it must inevitably generate given that some people are more productive than others), and he promises at a future time to show how and why the self-ownership thesis should be undermined. To say that one owns oneself is to say something broader than that one owns one's productive capacities, and it may be that both Cohen and I would eventually want to say that productive capacities should be distinguished from other dimensions of personal identity and given less, or at any rate different kinds of, protection.

22   John Roemer, "Property Relations versus Surplus Value in Marxian Exploitation," *Philosophy and Public Affairs*, 11, no. 4 (Fall 1982): 281–313. More generally, see his "Should Marxists Be Interested in Exploitation?" *Philosophy and Public Affairs*, 14, no. 1 (Winter 1985): 30–65, and *A General Theory of Class and Exploitation* (Cambridge, MA: Harvard University Press, 1982).

23   Roemer, "Property Relations," 284–92, 305–10. Roemer also insists that even when differential ownership is necessary for reasons of productivity, if it is the differential distribution of assets as such, "rather than the skills of capitalists, which brings about incentives, competition, innovation, and increased labor productivity which benefit even the workers, then the capitalists do not deserve their returns." By its terms, this reasoning concedes the moral force of the workmanship ideal: By contrary hypothesis, were it the differences in skills rather than the distribution of assets as such that accounted for greater productivity and so on, presumably the capitalist would deserve his differential benefit. Roemer does not face this possibility because he assumes equality of skill and propensity toward risk.

If the workmanship ideal is implicated in Marxist critiques of capitalist exploitation whether or not these rest on the labor theory of value, what is its role in Marx's positive argument for the superiority of socialism over capitalism and of communism over socialism? His appeal to the workmanship ideal might be interpreted as an ad hominem polemical charge that socialism is an advance on capitalism because under it, those who actually do the work are rewarded as bourgeois ideology requires. Yet to claim that what is wrong with capitalism is that it fails to live up to a standard that cannot, anyhow, be independently justified is to say less than Marx wanted or needed to say. One only has to think of other systems to which he objected—notably feudalism—that were not subject to the particular defect of hypocrisy as capitalism allegedly is, to realize that Marx's critical arguments were intended to have more far-reaching moral impact.[24] Throughout his writings human beings are described as productive creatures, creating their means of subsistence in ways that decisively shape other aspects of their lives and identities as persons.[25] Even a communist society, where the existence of a superabundance of wealth frees people from necessity, is described by the mature Marx as a society of free *producers*.[26] The workmanship ideal thus captured something in Marx's positive conception of the human condition that motivated his attack on modes of production that alienate people from their productive natures. To be sure, the ideal was much changed in his hands; it took on a dynamic character deriving from the romantic expressivist notion that human beings produce not only the means for their subsistence but also, and as a result of this fact, themselves. This meant that the distributive implications of the ideal were more complex than in Locke's mechanistic view of the relation between the producer and his product, more complex—as will become plain in part IV—than even Marx realized. But the workmanship ideal nonetheless remained the basic legitimating ideal of human ownership.[27]

Workmanship diminishes in significance for Marx when we turn attention to the argument that socialism is merely transitional to a needs-based communist regime of superabundance, although even here it retains a residual influence on his view. First there is the negative pole in Marx's implicit justificatory argument: A communist utopia is conceived of as the only possible regime in which there is no exploitation of one class by another. By thus requiring its own negation, the theory of exploitation leaves an indelible stamp on the depiction of communism and so, inevitably, does the workmanship ideal which gives the theory of exploitation its critical moral bite. Second there is the assumption driving Marx's defense of collective allocation of

---

24 See Jurgen Habermas, "Technology as Science and Ideology," *Toward a Rational Society* (Boston: Beacon, 1970), 62–80.
25 Marx and Engels, *Selected Works*, vol. 1, 20; see also 26–30, 38–50, 62–73.
26 Karl Marx, *Capital*, vol. 1 (London: Lawrence & Wishart, 1974), 82–83.
27 The difficulties inherent in trying to pin down just what work has been done by which worker in a given cycle of production have been well explored by G. A. Cohen, 'The Labor Theory of Value"; Roemer, "Property Relations versus Surplus Value" and "Should Marxists Be Interested in Exploitation?"

the productive surplus in *The Critique of the Gotha Program* and elsewhere, namely that under conditions of advanced division of labor private allocation is not defensible, and collective allocation is, on the grounds that the surplus is collectively produced.[28] This assumption has only to be stated for its reliance on the workmanship ideal to become plain. If making were not thought to entail ownership there would be no basis for arguing that the relations of mutual reliance and enhanced productivity resulting from the division of labor both reveal private appropriation as illegitimate and justify collective allocation of the collectively produced surplus. Unless we interpret superabundance to mean that a situation could arise in which no distributive choices of any kind would ever have to be made (because everyone could always have everything that they needed or wanted), Marx would presumably continue to embrace some variant of this workmanship-based defense of collective decision making.[29] In this way Marx's speculations about the postcapitalist future affirm the justificatory power of the workmanship ideal, even if he often relies on a mixture of ad hominem argument and intuitionist appeal—rather than principled justification—in its defense.

III. SECULARIZING THE WORKMANSHIP IDEAL: NEOCLASSICAL VIEWS

Like most Marxists, neoclassical political and economic theorists exhibit an abiding commitment to the workmanship ideal that has long survived the marginalists' abandonment of the labor theory of value. Indeed, the labor theory was rejected partly on the ground that since the causal story it tells was thought by the marginalists to be false, attempts to use it as a basic yardstick for thinking about distributive fairness violate the ideal; such attempts were argued not to take into account the productive contributions of capitalists. Modern neoclassicists thus retain a commitment to the notion that the act of working creates entitlements in the object or service produced by the relevant work; indeed, they typically defend acquisition of goods through exchange by reference to the claim that an agent is entitled to dispose of what she has produced however she likes. It is no accident that Nozick's critique of redistributive taxation reduces to the claim that it is "forced labor."[30]

---

28 Marx, *Selected Works,* vol. 3, 17–19; *Capital,* vol. 1, 83.
29 For reasons elaborated elsewhere, I do not regard Marx's notion of a superabundance that transcends scarcity as coherent or even consistent with his own account of human needs, nor do I regard as plausible the attempts by Cohen and others to reason about distribution without taking account of endemic scarcity by referring to the idea of "relative abundance." If I am right, those who continue to insist that the moral force of Marx's critique of capitalism depends on the possibility of a communist economy of superabundance are committed to the view that it has no force at all. See *Political Criticism,* 217–19.
30 Robert, Nozick, *Anarchy, State, and Utopia* (New York: Basic Books, 1974), 169–72, 265–68.

The principal neoclassical strategy for secularizing the workmanship ideal replaces the Lockean theology with a foundational appeal to the value of individual autonomy, whether for more or less Kantian reasons. Its proponents link property rights over the products of one's productive capacities to the preservation of autonomy, as in Nozick's claim that everyone has an inviolable right to what oneself has produced or freely been given. It is an open secret that where these rights come from is never fully accounted for in such arguments and that the freedoms they preserve are purely formal.[31] Typically, as in Nozick's case, there is some appeal to Locke, but without grappling with the issues inevitably raised once his limited defense of private appropriation is detached from its theological moorings. Thus Richard Posner embraces a variant of the Kantian claim when arguing that no injustice results from the fact that in a market system "people who lack sufficient earning power to support even a minimally decent standard of living are entitled to no say in the allocation of resources unless they are part of the utility function of someone who has wealth." He resists the Rawlsian critique of this view (taken up here in part V), insisting that treating the more and less well endowed as equally entitled to valuable resources "does not take seriously the differences between persons," and indeed that any redistributive taxation policy "impairs the autonomy of those from whom redistribution is made."

Posner concedes that this procedure implies that "if an individual happens to be bom feebleminded and his net social product is negative, he would have no right to the means of support even though there was nothing blameworthy in his inability to support himself." Yet he insists that although this conclusion might be argued to violate the autonomy of the feebleminded, there is no escape from it "consistent with any of the major ethical systems." This is a view that he shares with John Harsanyi, who asserts against Rawls and without argument that our abilities "are parts of our own inner selves and belong to us as a matter of sheer natural fact." That such declarations are deemed sufficient to bridge the fact/value gap and legitimate secular variants of the workmanship ideal is testimony to its captivating power; no principled argument is thought to be needed in their defense.[32]

---

31 Cohen usefully points out that despite the much trumpeted commitment to freedom behind libertarian thinking, in philosophies like Nozick's freedom is derivative of self-ownership. See "Self-ownership II," 77.

32 Richard Posner, *The Economics of Justice* (Cambridge, MA: Harvard University Press, 1981), 76–87; John Harsanyi, "Democracy, Equality, and Popular Consent," in *Power, inequality, and Democratic Politics*, edited by Ian Shapiro and Grant Reeher (Boulder, CO: Westview Press, 1988), 279. In the face of arguments about the prima facie moral arbitrariness of their secular variants of the workmanship ideal, neoclassical theorists often shift to consequentialist justificatory grounds, arguing that treating productive capacities and what they generate as privately owned and alienable via the market maximizes productive efficiency. See Posner, *Economics of Justice*, 81; also Nozick, *Anarchy, State, and Utopia*, 149–82, 232–76. For criticism of such consequentialist claims, see my "Richard Posner's Praxis," *Ohio State Law Journal*, 48 (1987): 999–1047.

IV. DIFFICULTIES CONFRONTING SECULAR VARIANTS OF THE WORKMANSHIP IDEAL

In both Marxist and neoclassical traditions, then, the workmanship ideal has exhibited a staying power that has long outlived both its theological origins and the labor theories of value to which it was initially linked. Yet in its secular form the workmanship ideal confronts two major types of conceptual difficulty. These combine to throw into sharp relief the difficulties of determining the nature of and limits to human-produced entitlements once we are without Locke's natural law limiting constraints such as the provisos, the requirements of charity, and the legitimate demands of dependents.

First, luck in the genetic pool and in the circumstances into which one happens to be born play substantial roles in what kinds of productive capacities people develop and are able to develop. The resulting inequalities seem to be deeply at odds with what is attractive in the logic of the workmanship ideal, since these are only the proximate result of the work of the relevant producing agent. If two people work equally hard but one is twice as productive because of having more effective natural capacities or better nurtured capacities, it seems that in a deeper sense, it is not her work but her superior genetic or nutritional luck that is the basis for such relative advantage. If differences deriving from natural capacity or social condition were traceable ultimately to the will of God, they need not seem unjustifiable nor need it be the responsibility of human society to counteract their effects. Once these differences are thought about by reference to secular understandings of workmanship, however, they are bound to become morally controversial.

Second, because human productive capacities are themselves partly produced by human work, it seems arbitrary to treat a given producing agent as the "final" owner of his productive capacities to begin with. Locke saw our productive capacities as God-given, so the question of why we might be said to own them never arose for him; indeed, their very existence was part of what marked off the ultimate moral boundaries among persons. But in the absence of a theology which dictates this assumption, defenders of secular variants of the workmanship ideal have to confront the difficulty of how to specify the morally relevant boundaries among persons qua productive creatures. In recent years American courts have begun to recognize how complex this can be in divorce settlements. The domestic labor performed in support of a spouse attaining a professional qualification is treated as part of the relevant work in creating the capacity to generate the income that the qualification brings. For this reason, the divorcing spouse who performed the domestic labor is given a property interest in the stream of future income that the now qualified divorcing spouse is newly capable of generating.[33] As a philosophical

---

33 See *O'Brien* v. *O'Brien* 66 NY2d., 576 (1985), in which the Appellate Division of the Supreme Court in the Second Judicial Department of New York upheld a decision that a husband's license to practice medicine was marital property on the grounds that "[t]he contributions of one spouse to the other's profession or career ... represent investments in

matter the intuition behind this type of example has been generalized by feminist theorists to make the point, for instance, that it was morally arbitrary for Marx to try to measure the rate of exploitation by exclusive reference to the relation between the surplus produced and the money wage paid to the worker. Any such calculation ignores the contributions of the worker's spouse to that workers' capacity to work, which is rented to the capitalist and which Marx arbitrarily takes to be the worker's "own." From this standpoint Marx's argument can be turned on the worker's relationship with one's spouse to reveal *it* in certain circumstances to be exploitative.[34] It is indeed surprising that Marxists have attended so little to the significance of produced productive capacities, both for the coherence of the self-ownership thesis which they generally embrace and for its distributive implications.[35]

In short, if the use of productive capacities generates entitlements and if productive capacities are themselves partly produced by the work of others, then tracing the moral reach of a particular productive capacity exercised in the production of a particular nonhuman object becomes exceedingly complex, arguably impossible even in principle. For the feminist point can itself be generalized: The productive capacities that a conventional wife "has" that she expends in her husband's attainment of a professional qualification were no doubt themselves partly produced by the work of others: parents, perhaps children, Sunday-school teachers who drummed into her a particular mixture of the work ethic and conventional family values, and so on. If one pushes the idea of productive capacity as the moral basis for entitlement to the limit, it seems to point in the direction of a tangled and indecipherable web of overdetermined entitlements and, indeed, to reveal a deep tension at the core of the workmanship ideal itself. The claim that we own what we make in virtue of our ownership of our productive capacities undermines the claim that we own our productive capacities, once it is conceded that those capacities are themselves produced partly by the work of others. Yet if we want to employ a variant of the workmanship ideal without pushing it to the limit, and in the absence of a theological limiting device such as Locke's, then the difficulty remains of how to do the pertinent line-drawing without inviting charges of moral arbitrariness.

---

the economic partnership of the marriage and the product of the parties' joint efforts." Thus, although New York is not a community property state, the divorcing wife was awarded 40 percent of the estimated value of the license to be paid over eleven years, and the divorcing husband was ordered to maintain a life insurance policy for the unpaid balance of the award, with the divorcing wife as the beneficiary.

34 See Nancy Folbre, "Exploitation Comes Home: A Critique of the Marxian Theory of Family Labor," *Cambridge Journal of Economics* 6 (1982): 317–29.

35 As Cohen notes in "Self-ownership I," in this respect liberals like Rawls and Dworkin, who reject self-ownership, must be accounted to the left of Marxists, who generally embrace it (pp. 113–15).

V. THE WORKMANSHIP IDEAL AND THE SOCIALIZATION OF CAPACITIES STRATEGY

These formidable difficulties lend seriousness to the suggestion that we abandon the workmanship ideal altogether. This possibility has been most fully explored by John Rawls and Ronald Dworkin in different ways in the course of contributing to a larger debate about whether resources, welfare, or some intermediate metric should form the basic unit of account of theories of distributive justice. The initial impetus for their turn to resource-based theories was the perceived defects of welfarist views like utilitarianism which seem to require either too little or too much in the way of interpersonal judgments of utility to be morally satisfying. In classical (objective) welfarism, where cardinal scales and interpersonal comparisons of utility are permitted, welfarist theories are vulnerable to the charge that they fail to take seriously the differences among persons, since paternalistic judgments may be employed to increase one person's welfare at the expense of another's. Yet if the neoclassical move toward subjective welfarism is made and interpersonal comparisons are disallowed, welfarism either requires information about mental states on which it seems impossible to rely without generating perverse incentives for the systematic misrepresentation of preferences or it is managed through the market-based theory of revealed preference. This latter strategy runs into the disquieting fact that people have different resources to express preferences in a market system, neatly summed up in Anatole France's quip that the poor are free to sleep under the bridges of Paris.[36] These difficulties with welfarism are no less intractable than are they often repeated, and resourcism is thought to be attractive partly because it appears to open up the possibility of avoiding them. Its motivating idea is that some set of instrumental goods—such as Rawls's primary goods—can be thought of as valuable for all rational individual conceptions of the good life, and it is those that should be justly distributed without reference to the mental states (or welfare otherwise construed) that they allegedly engender.[37]

Rawls and Dworkin both argue that, like other resources, human capacities should for certain purposes be regarded as social goods. This socialization of capacities strategy may be thought

---

[36] This difficulty inevitably rears its head when a theory designed for the purpose of predicting prices becomes the normative basis of arguments about distribution. I discuss this reduction at length in "Three Fallacies Concerning Majorities, Minorities, and Democratic Politics," in *NOMOS XXXII: Majorities and Minorities,* edited by John Chapman and Alan Wertheimer (New York: New York University Press, 1990), 81–94.

[37] For useful accounts of what is at issue between resourcist and welfare egalitarians, see Amartya Sen, "Equality of What?" in *The Tanner Lectures on Human Values,* edited by Sterling M. McMurrin (Salt Lake City: University of Utah Press, 1980), 197–220; Ronald Dworkin, "What Is Equality? Part I: Equality of Welfare," *Philosophy and Public Affairs,* 10 (Summer 1981): 185–246, and "What Is Equality? Part II: Equality of Resources," *Philosophy and Public Affairs,* 10 (Fall 1981): 283–345. For defense of "middle ground" metrics, intermediate between resourcism and welfarism, see Sen, "Well-being, Agency and Freedom," *the Journal of Philosophy,* 82, No. 4 (April 1985): 169–221; Richard Ameson, "Equality and Equal Opportunity for Welfare," *Philosophical Studies* 56 (1989): 77–93; and Cohen, "Currency and Egalitarian Jutsice" and "Equality of What?"

of as a mirror image of the classical Marxian one: where, for Marx, nonhuman resources cease to be of independent moral interest, being reducible to the capacities necessarily expended in their creation or their separation from nature, on this view capacities cease to be of independent moral interest: They are treated as social resources like any other. Thus Rawls argues forcibly that differences both in natural abilities and in contingencies of upbringing are morally arbitrary factors that should not, in principle, determine the rewards that people receive, usefully rendering the nature/nurture debate beside the point for arguments about distributive justice.[38] Similarly, Dworkin treats human capacities and external material resources as moral equivalents from the standpoint of distributive justice, arguing that although there may be good reasons for resisting the redistribution of physical and mental resources (insofar as this is technologically feasible), a case might nonetheless be made for compensating those with inferior physical and mental resources for their relative incapacities.[39]

Given the preceding discussion of luck and produced capacities, it might be suggested that there is no way genuinely to link entitlements to work other than via some variant of the socialization of capacities strategy, that it alone can consummate the workmanship ideal. This is true, I think, but the variant of the ideal thus saved is so thin that it dispenses with a good part of what gives it its intuitive appeal. This has to do with the psychological side of workmanship, with the sense of subjective satisfaction that attaches to the idea of making something that one can subsequently call one's own. We all know the feeling, and it is not easily argued that it can apply to a generalized notion that there is a sense in which I, along with everyone else, own everything that everyone appears at a given time and place to make. And for a species so critically reliant as is ours on productive activity for survival, it seems perverse to deny the legitimacy of so powerful a spur to productive activity as the psychic activity which producing something that one can own brings.

This is why theorists like Rawls and Dworkin balk at the implications of the socialization of capacities strategy. Rawls supplies a list of primary goods which are held to be desirable for any rational life plan, but he explicitly refuses to confront the implications of his account of the moral arbitrariness of differing capacities when he holds that the effectiveness with which people are able to use resources—or choose to use them—is not a relevant consideration in deciding how resources should be distributed. There are two different issues here, both of which raise internal tensions in the Rawlsian account. One derives from Amartya Sen's point that if what we really want justly to distribute is what people of greatly different capacities are enabled to do, then we cannot use Rawlsian primary goods; we need a different metric which takes account of how

---

38 See John Rawls, A *Theory of Justice* (Cambridge, MA: Harvard University Press, 1971), 12, 15, 72–73, 101–103, 507–11.
39 Ibid., 12, 18f., 137f., 172, 200; Dworkin, "What Is Equality I", 300–1.

different people employ capacities and resources as basic.⁴⁰ Second, there is the point made by Cohen, Nagel, Arneson, and others that different people have different preferences and goals, some more expensive and more difficult to satisfy than others. Rawls's attempt to sidestep this problem by arguing that these are not afflictions but are chosen scarcely meets the objection because, as Scanlon and others have noted, often they are not.⁴¹

Dworkin also balks at the implications of the socialization of capacities strategy. He invites us to speculate on how resources might, in principle, be equalized by use of a hypothetical auction in which all parties begin with the same finite number of bargaining chips.⁴² As part of this he argues that human capacities should be thought of as resources, yet there are two ways in which he dodges the full implications of the socialization of capacities strategy. First he claims that although capacities (his term is "physical and mental powers") are resources and, as a consequence, legitimate objects of a theory of distributive justice, they should nonetheless be treated differently from "independent material resources." With physical and mental powers, the goal should not be to strive to distribute them justly (which, for Dworkin, means equally). Instead, the problem is construed as one of discovering "how far the ownership of independent external resources should be affected by differences that exist in physical and mental powers, and the response of our theory should speak in that vocabulary."⁴³ For this reason Dworkin argues that people should be compensated by reference to a standard arrived at by our speculations concerning whether and to

---

40   See Sen, "Equality of What?" 212–20; "Well-being, Agency and Freedom," 185–221.

41   Rawls's most explicit statement of the view that people must be regarded as responsible for their preferences can be found in "Social Unity and Primary Goods," in *Utilitarianism and Beyond,* edited by Amartya Sen and Bernard Williams (Cambridge: Cambridge University Press, 1982), 168–69. For discussion of the tensions between this claim and the argument that differences in capacity are arbitrary, which Rawls defends most fully in *A Theory of Justice,* 101–104, see Thomas Scanlon, "Equality of Resources and Equality of Welfare: A Forced Marriage?" *Ethics* 97 (1986): 116–17; "The Significance of Choice," *The Tanner Lectures on Human Values,* 8 (Salt Lake City: University of Utah Press, 1988), 192–201; Richard Ameson, "Equality and Equal Opportunity for Welfare," "Primary Goods Reconsidered," *Nous,* forthcoming; Cohen, "Equality of What?" 7–10.

42   Ronald Dworkin, "What Is Equality?" parts I and II. Lack of space does not allow expounding at length on my reasons, but I think Dworkin's hypothetical auction, described in "What is Equality? II," 283–90, fails in its own terms as a device for deciding on what could count as an equal initial allocation of resources. An example of one of the difficulties, which will be intelligible only to initiates of these debates, is that in the hypothetical auction Dworkin describes, it would be quite possible for some player or players to bid up the price of some good which he or she or they did not want, but which he or she or they knew someone else had to have at all costs, such as the available stock of insulin on the island in Dworkin's example, assuming there was one diabetic. In this way the diabetic could be forced either to spend all (or at least a disproportionate quantity) of his initial resources on insulin, thereby making other bundles of goods relatively cheaper for the other inhabitants, or the diabetic might be forced to buy it at an artificially high price from whoever had bought it in the initial auction. The more general point is that Dworkin's hypothetical story assumes that people do not have different strategic resources and powers to bargain and that they will not have reasons to misrepresent their preferences during the initial auction. But there is no good reason to suppose that either of these assumptions is true, and as a result, there is no reason to believe that a hypothetical auction of the kind he describes can be a device which equalizes resources in the way that he claims.

43   Ibid., 300–1.

what extent people would, on average, have insured against the particular handicap or disability or lack of talent ex ante, assuming that insurance rates would be set in a competitive market.[44]

Notice that Dworkin supplies no principled argument for why physical and mental powers should be treated differently than material resources from the standpoint of distributive justice. The assertion that they "cannot be manipulated or transferred, even so far as technology permits" is not further explained or justified, but since Dworkin has chosen to treat powers *as* resources, an explanation is surely in order.[45] This is so not least because compensation in any amount will sometimes be inadequate to equalize a power- or capacity-deficiency (as in the case of blindness), as Dworkin elsewhere notes, yet equality of resources is his basic criterion of distributive justice. In such circumstances, compensation based on a standard set by a hypothetical insurance auction cannot be said to equalize the resources of two persons, one blind and one sighted.[46] Yet it is not always true, pace Dworkin, that their powers of sight *could not* be equalized.[47] The state might forcibly transplant one eye from a sighted person to the blind one in order to equalize their resources, or, for that matter, simply blind the sighted person. Less callous and more interesting, it might invest billions of dollars on research on and development of artificial eyes, financed by a tax on the sighted. If Dworkin is to avoid such unpalatable results, he must supply an argument for why we may be said to be entitled to our powers and capacities (and in some sense responsible for having or lacking them) in different (and trumping) ways than we can be said to be entitled to material resources, given his equation of the two. In the absence of such an argument, it is difficult to see how Dworkin can adopt the socialization of capacities strategy in principle, yet simply assert that people are entitled to, and responsible for, their capacities and incapacities in fact.

---

44 As a result, insuring against the possibility of not having an extremely rare skill would be far more expensive than insuring against the possibility of not having a widely shared capacity such as sight. In this way Dworkin hopes to come up with a theory of equality of resources that does not itself make implicit judgments about welfare and avoids the "slavery of the talented" problem which any theory that permits compensation for differences in capacities must confront. See Dworkin, ibid., 292–304. Again for initiates only: notice that for the hypothetical insurance market argument to work it has to be assumed not only that each of the ex ante choosers has equal initial resources (see note 42) but that none of them has any incapacity or absence of talent (since otherwise the question of whether or not to insure against the possibility of not having it could not arise). This latter I take to be an unthinkably incoherent speculation, given that talents and incapacities are treated as analytical equivalents from the standpoint of the hypothetical insurance market.

45 Ibid., 301.

46 Ibid., 300, where he notes in opposition to the idea that there can be a view of "normal" human powers that no amount of initial compensation could make someone born blind or mentally incompetent equal in physical or mental resources with someone taken to be "normal" in these ways.

47 Ibid., 302: "Someone who is born with a serious handicap faces his life with what we concede to be fewer resources, just on that account, than others do. This justifies compensation, under a scheme devoted to equality of resources, and though the hypothetical insurance market does not right the balance—*nothing can*—it seeks to remedy one aspect of the resulting unfairness" (italics added).

The second way in which Dworkin refuses to live with the socialization of capacities strategy that he otherwise embraces concerns his discussion of how our conception of a person should be distinguished from our conception of that person's circumstances. Dworkin argues that we need a view of distributive justice that is "ambition sensitive." It requires a view of equality by reference to which people "decide what sorts of lives to pursue against a background of information about the actual costs that their choices impose on other people and hence on the total stock of resources that may fairly be used by them." This he tries to achieve by assigning "tastes and ambitions" to the person, and "physical and mental powers" to his "circumstances," arguing that the former are not relevant considerations in deciding how resources should be distributed.[48] In this way he hopes to rescue an island of creative autonomy for the individual agent. Dworkin wants to rescue the kernel of what is intuitively attractive in the workmanship ideal: the idea that when people conceive of and put into practice productive plans, the benefits from the resulting actions should flow back to them. Yet he wants to do this without being swamped by the difficulties of overdetermination that flow from the Rawlsian claim that the distribution of physical and mental powers is morally arbitrary.[49]

Dworkin's strategy fails. The volitions that we are able to form, the ambitions that it occurs to us to develop, are greatly influenced, perhaps even determined, by our powers and capacities. To "think big," to "resolve to go for broke," to steel oneself through self-control to perform demanding acts, do these reflect ambition or capacity? When we describe someone as ambitious, are we not describing something more basic to her psychology and constitution than her tastes? There are certainly circumstances in which we would say that lack of confidence is an incapacity that prevents the formation (not just the attainment) of particular ambitions. Different people have different capacities to form different ambitions, and those different capacities must be as morally tainted from Dworkin's point of view as any other capacities. Donald Trump is able to develop more far-reaching ambitions than, say, Archie Bunker due at least partly to luck in the genetic pool and the circumstances of his upbringing.[50]

Similar arguments can be made about the different abilities to form (or refrain from forming) different kinds of tastes, whether expensive, compulsive, or both, as Dworkin is aware. The case that Dworkin considers is where a person might have an incapacitating obsession that he wishes he did not have, and Dworkin deals with this by arguing that such cravings may be thought of as handicaps and thus handled via his hypothetical insurance scheme.[51] But this is to sidestep the point being

---

48   Ibid., 288, 302, 311.
49   Ibid., 31 Iff.
50   I should not be understood here as saying that people always have the capacities to achieve their ambitions or even that we cannot develop ambitions which we know we cannot achieve, although I suspect that sustained analysis would reveal that part of the difference between an ambition and a fantasy resides in the fact that the former is generally a spur to action in a way that the latter need not be. Here, I want only to establish that it is not credible to believe that our ambitions are developed independently of our capacities, which Dworkin's categorial distinction requires.
51   Dworkin, "What Is Equality? II," 302–3ff.

made here, which is that the obsession may itself incapacitate a person from forming the relevant second- order desire to make Dworkin's hypothetical insurance solution work. Are we to say of an alcoholic, whose affliction is so severe that he cannot even form the desire not to be an alcoholic, that the preference for alcohol results from his *taste* rather than his *incapacity*? I think not.[52]

With all acquired tastes (not just the expensive), experiencing the taste is by definition conditional on the exercise of pertinent capacities. A taste for good beer or even just for beer, a taste for a particular kind of music, perhaps even for any music—these can be developed only through the exercise of relevant capacities. We would not say that a deaf person could have a taste for music of a particular sort or even a taste for music of any sort (although of course we could intelligibly say that such a person might perhaps wish that she was able to have such a taste). Likewise with beer and someone who had no functioning tastebuds or sense of smell. The idea that we form our tastes and ambitions in some way that is independent of our resources and capacities is too whiggish, as would be revealed to anyone who tried to perform a thought experiment in which she was required to decide on her future tastes and ambitions while kept in ignorance of her powers and capacities. Surely we have learned this much from two decades of debate about the veil of ignorance. What drives Dworkin's intuition here is the notion that people should be held responsible only for the choices they make in life, not for things over which they have no control. A variant of this thesis might be defensible, but Dworkin's treatment of it is unpersuasive. His replacement of the resources versus capacities distinction with the ambitions and tastes versus physical and mental powers distinction fails to rescue the Lockean notion of an autonomous agent, of whom rights and responsibilities may legitimately be predicated.

To sum up: Like Rawls, Dworkin is unable to live with the deterministic implications of the socialization of capacities strategy. This, I have suggested, is partly because when taken to its logical conclusion this strategy undermines what is attractive in the workmanship ideal. Yet reluctant as Rawls and Dworkin both are to abandon their intuitive commitments to the idea of moral agency that informs the ideal, neither has supplied an account of how this can be rendered consistent with the socialization of capacities strategy which both feel compelled to endorse. This reflects deep tensions within the secular variant of the workmanship ideal itself: It presses relentlessly toward a determinism which its very terms suggest we ought to be able to deny.

---

52   Cohen has tried to minimize the extent of such difficulties by suggesting that we should not confuse the true claim that our capacities for effort are "influenced" by factors beyond our control with the false claim that people like Nozick mistakenly attribute to egalitarians like Rawls, that those capacities are "determined" by factors beyond our control. Preserving this distinction enables Cohen to say that although not all effort deserves reward, it is not the case that no effort deserves reward, that effort "is partly praiseworthy, partly not," although he concedes that in practice "we cannot separate the parts." See Cohen, "Equality of What?" 8–10. Yet once it is conceded that the very decision to choose to expend effort is influenced by factors that are conceded to be morally arbitrary, one suspects that the difficulty becomes one of principle rather than practicality; certainly Cohen offers no account of how that component of effort meriting reward might, in principle, be singled out.

VI. PRODUCTIVE FICTIONS? CONSEQUENTIALIST AND DEMOCRATIC CONSIDERATIONS

Historical linking strategies fail to tie regimes of entitlements to the work of productive agents in morally satisfying ways, yet theorists who have explored the full implications of junking them find the consequences too threatening to the idea of personal responsibility, even of personal identity, to stomach. This is partly because once the labor theory of value has been rejected, there is no evident method to assess which work performed by whom ought to be compensated in what amount when a given object or service is produced. Liberal theorists have often argued or assumed that the market generates the appropriate system of rewards, but we saw in part III that this is not so; neoclassical variants of the workmanship ideal take for granted prevailing distributions of resources and capacities as matters of "sheer natural fact" without justificatory argument. However, the failure of the traditional contending theories to generate a metric by reference to which we might plausibly assess productive contributions does not undermine the intuition that there are productive contributions and that these should play some role in just distribution; this fact at least partly accounts for the inability of people like Rawls and Dworkin to stick consistently to the socialization of capacities strategy.

The difficulty runs deeper than a problem of measurement, however. The tensions internal to the workmanship ideal are partly reminiscent of this paradox of free will: A person may find it both rationally undeniable and psychologically impossible to accept that all of his actions are determined. In a similar spirit it might be argued that for both individual and species, some fictions about workmanship may be required for reproduction and well-being even if we know them to be fictions. The belief that autonomous productive action is possible may be indispensable to the basic integrity of the human psyche and necessary for generating and sustaining the incentive to work on which human beings are, after all, critically reliant. As a result, although facts about moral luck and produced productive capacities conspire—when confronted—to enfeeble the workmanship ideal, people may nonetheless be powerless to abandon it.

These considerations might reasonably be thought to counsel embracing a variant of the workmanship ideal on consequentialist grounds while conceding that it incorporates causal and moral fictions. There is much to be said in support of such a view, but rather than explore it at length here, I will take brief note of three difficulties that it is bound to confront. These should be evident from my repeated use of "may" and its cognates in the preceding paragraph. First, although a wide consensus might be possible on the principle of a consequentialist defense, it seems inevitable that there would be an equally wide dissensus over what it entails in practice. It is not only the labor theory of value and neoclassical price theory that fail to reward work impartially; no neutral system of rewards has ever been developed. As a consequence, whatever fiction is employed will work to the disproportionate benefit of some and be subject to endemic political controversy—as Marx noted so perspicaciously in his discussion of rights under socialism.[53]

Second, distributive questions aside, the consequentialist benefits of workmanship are not beyond legitimate controversy. If it gets out of control, the work ethic can be subversive of psychological well-being and promote morally unattractive kinds of acquisitiveness, and the realization that invisible hands can as often be malevolent as benign suggests that the consequentialist effects of embracing the workmanship ideal will not always be beneficial. A legitimating ethic that encourages productive action can easily thus become too much of a good thing, and it can have external effects (on the environment, for instance) that are bound to be controversial politically.

Third, if a variant of the workmanship ideal is embraced on consequentialist grounds, questions must arise concerning its appropriate range, given the inevitability of its conflict with other justice values. Once it is conceded that the rights of human workmanship have no natural status or special trumping moral power, then there is bound to be controversy about where they fit into a governing distributive scheme that must cope with multiple demands on scarce resources—from redressing the effects of historical disadvantage, to caring for the sick and elderly, to supporting just causes in other countries. In short, it seems unlikely that a consequentialist scheme could be developed that would or should be beyond the bounds of political controversy.

These are not intuitions about mere implementation. Once it is conceded, in a world of endemic scarcity, that there is neither a theological model nor a calculus of contribution from which correct distributive injunctions can be "read off," we have to come to grips with the primacy of politics to arguments about distributive justice. It is remarkable, in this light, that so little attention has been paid by justice theorists to how and by whom their principles should be implemented—particularly given the dismal historical records of both laissez-faire and statist distributive regimes.[54] The idea that what is just in the distribution of social goods can be reasoned

---

53 Marx and Engels, *Selected Works,* vol. 3, 15–18.
54 For instance, in his only discussion of democratic decision-making in the "Self-ownership" articles (to which he devotes a single paragraph), Cohen remarks that traditional socialist hostility to bills of rights has to be disavowed. The socialist reply to the liberal constitutionalist that "socialism is complete democracy, that it brings within the ambit of democratic decision issues about production and consumption which capitalism excludes from the public agenda" is now believed by Cohen to be inadequate. A defensible socialist constitution, he argues, "must contain a bill of individual rights, which specifies things which the community cannot do to, or demand of, any individual." The preferred reason derives from the fact that socialist democratic decisions require either a unanimous or a majority vote. If they require unanimity, then they have the potential to destroy individual freedom of action and trivialize self-ownership (since any action might require unanimous consent before legitimately being undertaken), and majority rule without a bill of rights "also legitimates unacceptable tyranny over the individual." See "Self-ownership II," 87. Yet Cohen does not address the much argued-over issues of what the content of this bill should be and how the difficulties of unanimity and majority rule should be managed in the business of constitution making. For discussion of some of these issues, see my "Three Fallacies," 81–113. In fairness to Cohen it must be said that he claims not to have done full justice to these issues, which he promises to take up more fully in the future (although, to my knowledge, he has not done so).

about independently of how such justice might practically be achieved rests on inappropriate expectations from philosophy, thrown into sharp relief by the undergraduate who insisted on knowing why, now that Rawls's difference principle "has been established," the Constitution has not yet been changed to incorporate it. Although few academic theorists will permit themselves such revealing directness, much of the debate discussed here proceeds on the assumption that there is a correct answer, that Rawls, Dworkin, Nozick, Cohen, or someone else will eventually get it right. But if the reasoning being pressed here is accepted, whether and to what degree the workmanship ideal should be institutionalized is a political not a philosophical question, and as a consequence rights of workmanship cannot fairly be thought of as anterior to the political process.

The research agenda opened up by this conclusion is to explore ways of developing and grappling with the implications of democratic distributive principles. To attempt such exploration now would take us too far from the scope of the present essay. However, let me note in conclusion that Cohen and other justice theorists may be right that in democratic systems there is the permanent possibility for tyranny of the majority, but the risks of this should be evaluated not against some unspecified ideal of a just social order (which Cohen, among others, has done much to undermine) but against the alternative feasible systems of ordering social relations.[55] In this light I would venture that the question should not be whether or not democracy carries with it the threat of majority tyranny but whether or not this threat is better to live with than systems that carry with them the threat of minority tyranny. I have suggested elsewhere that it is, a suggestion I hope in future to elaborate into a full defense of a democratic conception of social justice, conceived of as a third way between statist and market-based accounts.[56]

Ian Shapiro is Associate Professor of Political Science at Yale University and author of The Evolution of Rights in Liberal Theory *(1986) and* Political Criticism *(1990). He is currently working on a book titled* Democratic Justice.

---

55   Cohen may be wise to insist that a socialist constitution should protect individual freedoms via a bill of rights (see note 54), but as the *Lochner* era in the United States demonstrated all too clearly, bills of rights can be used to facilitate what Cohen would regard as exploitation as well as to prevent it—whatever the intentions of those who create them. This is not to say that bills of rights are undesirable, only that their benefits from the standpoint of achieving and maintaining social justice are not self-evident. Whether such bills are desirable, what their scope and content should be, and who should be empowered to alter and implement them are controversial questions that cannot be declared beyond politics (and, I would argue, beyond democratic politics). For an empirically based argument that democratic systems have best protected individual rights historically, see Robert Dahl, *Democracy and Its Critics* (New Haven, CT: Yale University Press, 1989), 135–92.

56   For the suggestion, see my *Political Criticism*, chap. 9. The first installment of the positive argument is my "Three Ways to Be a Democrat," a paper presented at the annual meeting of the American Political Science Association in San Francisco, August 1990.

ANARCHY, STATE AND UTOPIA

CHAPTERS 1–3 (SELECTIONS)

BY ROBERT NOZICK

Robert Nozick, *Anarchy, State, and Utopia,* pp. 3-17, 26-35. Copyright © 1974 by Perseus Books Group. Reprinted with permission.

CHAPTER 1: WHY STATE-OF-NATURE THEORY ?

If the state did not exist would it be necessary to invent it? Would one be *needed,* and would it have to be *invented?* These questions arise for political philosophy and for a theory explaining political phenomena and are answered by investigating the "state of nature," to use the terminology of traditional political theory. The justification for resuscitating this archaic notion would have to be the fruitfulness, interest, and far-reaching implications of the theory that results. For the (less trusting) readers who desire some assurance in advance, this chapter discusses reasons why it is important to pursue state-of-nature theory, reasons for thinking that theory would be a fruitful one. These reasons necessarily are somewhat abstract and metatheoretical. The best reason is the developed theory itself.

POLITICAL PHILOSOPHY

The fundamental question of political philosophy, one that precedes questions about how the state should be organized, is whether there should be any state at all. Why not have anarchy? Since anarchist theory, if tenable, undercuts the whole subject of *political* philosophy, it is appropriate to begin political philosophy with an examination of its major theoretical alternative. Those who consider anarchism not an unattractive doctrine will think it possible that political philosophy *ends* here as well. Others impatiently will await what is to come afterwards. Yet, as we shall see, archists and anarchists alike, those who spring gingerly from the starting point as well as those reluctantly argued away from it, can agree that beginning the subject of political philosophy with state- of-nature theory has an *explanatory* purpose. (Such a purpose is absent when epistemology is begun with an attempt to refute the skeptic.)

Which anarchic situation should we investigate to answer the question of why not anarchy? Perhaps the one that would exist if the actual political situation didn't, while no other possible political one did. But apart from the gratuitous assumption that everyone everywhere would be in the same nonstate boat and the enormous unmanageability of pursuing that counterfactual to arrive at a particular situation, that situation would lack fundamental theoretical interest. To be sure, if that nonstate situation were sufficiently awful, there would be a reason to refrain from dismantling or destroying a particular state and replacing it with none, now.

It would be more promising to focus upon a fundamental abstract description that would encompass all situations of interest, including "where we would now be if." Were this description awful enough, the state would come out as a preferred alternative, viewed as affectionately as a trip to the dentist. Such awful descriptions rarely convince, and not merely because they fail to cheer. The subjects of psychology and sociology are far too feeble to support generalizing so pessimistically across all societies and persons, especially since the argument depends upon *not* making *such* pessimistic assumptions about how the *state* operates. Of course, people know something of how actual states have operated, and they differ in their views. Given the enormous importance of the choice between the state and anarchy, caution might suggest one use the "minimax" criterion, and focus upon a pessimistic estimate of the nonstate situation: the state would be compared with the most pessimistically described Hobbesian state of nature. But in using the minimax criterion, this Hobbesian situation should be compared with the most pessimistically described possible state, including *future* ones. Such a comparison, surely, the worst state of nature would win. Those who view the state as an abomination will not find minimax very compelling especially since it seems one could always bring back the state if that came to seem desirable. The "maximax" criterion, on the other hand, would proceed on the most optimistic assumptions about how things would work out—Godwin, if you like that sort of thing. But imprudent optimism also lacks conviction. Indeed, no proposed decision criterion for choice under uncertainty carries conviction here, nor does maximizing expected utility on the basis of such frail probabilities.

More to the point, especially for deciding what goals one should try to achieve, would be to focus upon a nonstate situation in which people generally satisfy moral constraints and generally act as they ought. Such an assumption is not wildly optimistic; it does not assume that all people act exactly as they should. Yet this state-of-nature situation is the best anarchic situation one reasonably could hope for. Hence investigating its nature and defects is of crucial importance to deciding whether there should be a state rather than anarchy. If one could show that the state would be superior even to this most favored situation of anarchy, the best that realistically can be hoped for, or would arise by a process involving no morally impermissible steps, or would be an improvement if it arose, this would provide a rationale for the state's existence; it would justify the state.[1]

This investigation will raise the question of whether all the actions persons must do to set up and operate a state are themselves morally permissible. Some anarchists have claimed not merely that we would be better off without a state, but that any state necessarily violates people's moral rights and hence is intrinsically immoral. Our starting point then, though nonpolitical, is by intention far from nonmoral. Moral philosophy sets the background for, and boundaries of, political philosophy. What persons may and may not do to one another limits what they may do through the apparatus of a state, or do to establish such an apparatus. The moral prohibitions it is permissible to enforce are the source of whatever legitimacy the state's fundamental coercive power has. (Fundamental coercive power is power not resting upon any consent of the person to whom it is applied.) This provides a primary arena of state activity, perhaps the only legitimate arena. Furthermore, to the extent moral philosophy is unclear and gives rise to disagreements in people's moral judgments, it also sets problems which one might think could be appropriately handled in the political arena.

EXPLANATORY POLITICAL THEORY

In addition to its importance for political philosophy, the investigation of this state of nature also will serve explanatory purposes. The possible ways of understanding the political realm are as follows: (1) to fully explain it in terms of the nonpolitical; (2) to view it as emerging from the nonpolitical but irreducible to it, a mode of organization of nonpolitical factors understandable only in terms of novel political principles; or (3) to view it as a completely autonomous realm. Since only the first promises full understanding of the whole political realm, it stands as the most desirable theoretical alternative, to be abandoned only if known to be impossible. Let us call this most desirable and complete kind of explanation of a realm a *fundamental* explanation of the realm.

To explain fundamentally the political in terms of the nonpolitical, one might start either with a nonpolitical situation, showing how and why a political one later would arise out of it, or with a political situation that is described nonpolitically, deriving its political features from its nonpolitical description. This latter derivation either will identify the political features with those features nonpolitically described, or will use scientific laws to connect distinct features. Except perhaps for this last mode, the illumination of the explanation will vary directly with the independent glow of the nonpolitical starting point (be it situation or description) and with the distance, real or apparent, of the starting point from its political result. The more fundamental the starting point

---

1 This contrasts with a theory that presents a state's arising from a state of nature by a natural and inevitable process of *deterioration,* rather as medical theory presents aging or dying. Such a theory would not "justify" the state, though it might resign us to its existence.

(the more it picks out basic, important, and inescapable features of the human situation) and the less close it is or seems to its result (the less political or statelike it looks), the better. It would not increase understanding to reach the state from an arbitrary and otherwise unimportant starting point, obviously adjacent to it from the start. Whereas discovering that political features and relations were reducible to, or identical with, ostensibly very different nonpolitical ones would be an exciting result. Were these features fundamental, the political realm would be firmly and deeply based. So far are we from such a major theoretical advance that prudence alone would recommend that we pursue the alternative of showing how a political situation would arise out of a nonpolitical one; that is, that we begin a fundamental *explanatory* account with what is familiar within political philosophy as state-of-nature theory.

A theory of a state of nature that begins with fundamental general descriptions of morally permissible and impermissible actions, and of deeply based reasons why some persons in any society would violate these moral constraints, and goes on to describe how a state would arise from that state of nature will serve our explanatory purposes, *even if no actual state ever arose that way*. Hempel has discussed the notion of a potential explanation, which intuitively (and roughly) is what would be the correct explanation if everything mentioned in it were true and operated. Let us say that a *law-defective* potential explanation is a potential explanation with a false lawlike statement and that a *fact-defective* potential explanation is a potential explanation with a false antecedent condition. A potential explanation that explains a phenomenon as the result of a process P will be defective (even though it is neither law-defective nor fact-defective) if some process Q other than P produced the phenomenon, though P was capable of doing it. Had this other process Q not produced it, then P would have.[2] Let us call a potential explanation that fails in this way actually to explain the phenomenon a *process-defective* potential explanation.

A *fundamental* potential explanation (an explanation that would explain the whole realm under consideration were it the actual explanation) carries important explanatory illumination even if it is *not* the correct explanation. To see how, in principle, a *whole realm* could fundamentally be explained greatly increases our understanding of the realm.[3] It is difficult to say more without examining types of cases; indeed, without examining particular cases, but this we cannot

---

2 Or, perhaps yet *another* process R would have if 0 hadn't, though had R not produced the phenomenon, then P would have, or. ... So the footnoted sentence should read: P would have produced the phenomenon had no member of [Q, R, ...] done so. We ignore here the complication that what would prevent Q from producing the phenomenon might also prevent P from doing so.

3 This claim needs to be qualified. It will not increase our understanding of a realm to be told as a potential explanation what we know to be false: that by doing a certain dance, ghosts or witches or goblins made the realm that way. It is plausible to think that an explanation of a realm must present an underlying mechanism yielding the realm. (Or do something else equally productive of understanding.) But to say this is not to state precisely the deep conditions an underlying mechanism must satisfy to explain a realm. The precise qualification of the claim in the text awaits advances in the theory of explanation. Yet other difficulties call for such advances; see Jaegwon Kim, "Causation, Nomic Subsumption, and the Concept of Event," *The Journal of Philosophy*, 70, no. 8 (April 26, 1973), 217–236.

do here. Fact-defective fundamental potential explanations, if their false initial conditions "could have been true," will carry great illumination; even wildly false initial conditions will illuminate, sometimes very greatly. Law-defective fundamental potential explanations may illuminate the nature of a realm almost as well as the correct explanations, especially if the "laws" together form an interesting and integrated theory. And process- defective fundamental potential explanations (which are neither law-defective nor fact-defective) fit our explanatory bill and purposes almost perfectly. These things could not be said as strongly, if at all, about nonfundamental explanation.

State-of-nature explanations of the political realm *are* fundamental potential explanations of this realm and pack explanatory punch and illumination, even if incorrect. We learn much by seeing how the state could have arisen, even if it didn't arise that way. If it didn't arise that way, we also would learn much by determining why it didn't; by trying to explain why the particular bit of the real world that diverges from the state-of-nature model is as it is.

Since considerations both of political philosophy and of explanatory political theory converge upon Locke's state of nature, we shall begin with that. More accurately, we shall begin with individuals in something sufficiently similar to Locke's state of nature so that many of the otherwise important differences may be ignored here. Only when some divergence between our conception and Locke's is relevant to *political* philosophy, to our argument about the state, will it be mentioned. The completely accurate statement of the moral background, including the precise statement of the moral theory and its underlying basis, would require a full-scale presentation and is a task for another time. (A lifetime?) That task is so crucial, the gap left without its accomplishment so yawning, that it is only a minor comfort to note that we here are following the respectable tradition of Locke, who does not provide anything remotely resembling a satisfactory explanation of the status and basis of the law of nature in his *Second Treatise*.

CHAPTER 2: THE STATE OF NATURE

Individuals in Locke's state of nature are in "a state of perfect freedom to order their actions and dispose of their possessions and persons as they think fit, within the bounds of the law of nature, without asking leave or dependency upon the will of any other man" (sect. 4). The bounds of the law of nature require that "no one ought to harm another in his life, health, liberty, or possessions" (sect. 6). Some persons transgress these bounds, "invading others' rights and … doing hurt to one another," and in response people may defend themselves or others against such invaders of rights (chap. 3). The injured party and his agents may recover from the offender "so much as may make satisfaction for the harm he has suffered" (sect. 10); "everyone has a right to punish the transgressors of that law to such a degree as may hinder its violation" (sect. 7); each person may, and may only "retribute to [a criminal] so far as calm reason and conscience dictate, what is proportionate to his transgression, which is so much as may serve for reparation and restraint" (sect. 8).

There are "inconveniences of the state of nature" for which, says Locke, "I easily grant that civil government is the proper remedy" (sect. 13). To understand precisely what civil government remedies, we must do more than repeat Locke's list of the inconveniences of the state of nature. We also must consider what arrangements might be made within a state of nature to deal with these inconveniences—to avoid them or to make them less likely to arise or to make them less serious on the occasions when they do arise. Only after the full resources of the state of nature are brought into play, namely all those voluntary arrangements and agreements persons might reach acting within their rights, and only after the effects of these are estimated, will we be in a position to see how serious are the inconveniences that yet remain to be remedied by the state, and to estimate whether the remedy is worse than the disease.[4]

In a state of nature, the understood natural law may not provide for every contingency in a proper fashion (see sections 159 and 160 where Locke makes this point about legal systems, but contrast section 124), and men who judge in their own case will always give themselves the benefit of the doubt and assume that they are in the right. They will overestimate the amount of harm or damage they have suffered, and passions will lead them to attempt to punish others more than proportionately and to exact excessive compensation (sects. 13, 124, 125). Thus private and personal enforcement of one's rights (including those rights that are violated when one is excessively punished) leads to feuds, to an endless series of acts of retaliation and exactions of compensation. And there is no firm way to *settle* such a dispute, to *end* it and to have both parties know it is ended. Even if one party *says* he'll stop his acts of retaliation, the other can rest secure only if he knows the first still does not feel entitled to gain recompense or to exact retribution, and therefore entitled to try when a promising occasion presents itself. Any method a single individual might use in an attempt irrevocably to bind himself into ending his part in a feud would offer insufficient assurance to the other party; tacit agreements to stop also would be unstable. Such feelings of being mutually wronged can occur even with the clearest right and with joint agreement on the

---

4 Proudhon has given us a description of the *state's* domestic "inconveniences." "To be GOVERNED is to be watched, inspected, spied upon, directed, law-driven, numbered, regulated, enrolled, indoctrinated, preached at, controlled, checked, estimated, valued, censured, commanded, by creatures who have neither the right nor the wisdom nor the virtue to do so. To be GOVERNED is to be at every operation, at every transaction noted, registered, counted, taxed, stamped, measured, numbered, assessed, licensed, authorized, admonished, prevented, forbidden, reformed, corrected, punished. It is, under pretext of public utility, and in the name of the general interest, to be placed under contribution, drilled, fleeced, exploited, monopolized, extorted from, squeezed, hoaxed, robbed; then, at the slightest resistance, the first word of complaint, to be repressed, fined, vilified, harrassed, hunted down, abused, clubbed, disarmed, bound, choked, imprisoned, judged, condemned, shot, deported, sacrificed, sold, betrayed; and to crown all, mocked, ridiculed, derided, outraged, dishonored. That is government; that is its justice; that is its morality." P. J. Proudhon, *General Idea of the Revolution in the Nineteenth Century,* trans. John Beverly Robinson (London: Freedom Press, 1923), pp. 293—294, with some alterations from Benjamin Tucker's translation in *Instead of a Book* (New York, 1893), p. 26.

facts of each person's conduct; all the more is there opportunity for such retaliatory battle when the facts or the rights are to some extent unclear. Also, in a state of nature a person may lack the power to enforce his rights; he may be unable to punish or exact compensation from a stronger adversary who has violated them (sects. 123, 126).

PROTECTIVE ASSOCIATIONS

How might one deal with these troubles within a state of nature? Let us begin with the last. In a state of nature an individual may himself enforce his rights, defend himself, exact compensation, and punish (or at least try his best to do so). Others may join with him in his defense, at his call. They may join with him to repulse an attacker or to go after an aggressor because they are public spirited, or because they are his friends, or because he has helped them in the past, or because they wish him to help them in the future, or in exchange for something. Groups of individuals may form mutual-protection associations: all will answer the call of any member for defense or for the enforcement of his rights. In union there is strength. Two inconveniences attend such simple mutual-protection associations: (1) everyone is always on call to serve a protective function (and how shall it be decided who shall answer the call for those protective functions that do not require the services of all members?); and (2) any member may call out his associates by saying his rights are being, or have been, violated. Protective associations will not want to be at the beck and call of their cantankerous or paranoid members, not to mention those of their members who might attempt, under the guise of self-defense, to use the association to violate the rights of others. Difficulties will also arise if two different members of the same association are in dispute, each calling upon his fellow members to come to his aid.

A mutual-protection association might attempt to deal with conflict among its own members by a policy of nonintervention. But this policy would bring discord within the association and might lead to the formation of subgroups who might fight among themselves and thus cause the breakup of the association. This policy would also encourage potential aggressors to join as many mutual-protection associations as possible in order to gain immunity from retaliatory or defensive action, thus placing a great burden on the adequacy of the initial screening procedure of the association. Thus protective associations (almost all of those that will survive which people will join) will not follow a policy of nonintervention; they will use some procedure to determine how to act when some members claim that other members have violated their rights. Many arbitrary procedures can be imagined (for example, act on the side of that member who complains first), but most persons will want to join associations that follow some procedure to find out which claimant is correct. When a member of the association is in conflict with nonmembers, the association also will want to determine in some fashion who is in the right, if only to avoid constant and costly involvement in each member's quarrels, whether just or unjust. The inconvenience of everyone's being on call, whatever their activity at the moment or inclinations or comparative advantage, can be handled in the usual manner by division of labor and exchange. Some people will be *hired* to perform protective functions, and some entrepreneurs will go into the business of selling protective services. Different sorts of protective policies would be offered, at different prices, for those who may desire more extensive or elaborate protection.

An individual might make more particular arrangements or commitments short of turning over to a private protective agency all functions of detection, apprehension, judicial determination of guilt, punishment, and exaction of compensation. Mindful of the dangers of being the judge in his own case, he might turn the decision as to whether he has indeed been wronged, and to what extent, to some other neutral or less involved party. In order for the occurrence of the social effect of justice's being seen to be done, such a party would have to be generally respected and thought to be neutral and upright. Both parties to a dispute may so attempt to safeguard themselves against the appearance of partiality, and both might even agree upon the *same* person as the judge between them, and agree to abide by his decision. (Or there might be a specified process through which one of the parties dissatisfied with the decision could appeal it.) But, for obvious reasons, there will be strong tendencies for the above-mentioned functions to converge in the same agent or agency.

People sometimes now do take their disputes outside of the state's legal system to other judges or courts they have chosen, for example, to religious courts. If all parties to a dispute find some activities of the state or its legal system so repellent that they want nothing to do with it, they might agree to forms of arbitration or judgment outside the apparatus of the state. People tend to forget the possibilities of acting independently of the state. (Similarly, persons who want to be paternalistically regulated forget the possibilities of contracting into particular limitations on their own behavior or appointing a given paternalistic supervisory board over themselves. Instead, they swallow the exact pattern of restrictions a legislature happens to pass. Is there really someone who, searching for a group of wise and sensitive persons to regulate him for his own good, would choose that group of people who constitute the membership of both houses of Congress?) Diverse forms of judicial adjudication, differing from the particular package the state provides, certainly could be developed. Nor do the costs of developing and choosing these account for people's use of the state form. For it would be easy to have a large number of preset packages which parties could select. Presumably what drives people to use the state's system of justice is the issue of ultimate enforcement. Only the state can enforce a judgment against the will of one of the parties. For the state does not *allow* anyone else to enforce another system's judgment. So in any dispute in which both parties cannot agree upon a method of settlement, or in any dispute in which one party does not trust another to abide by the decision (if the other contracts to forfeit something of enormous value if he doesn't abide by the decision, by what agency is *that* contract to be enforced?), the parties who wish their claims put into effect will have no recourse permitted by the state's legal system other than to use that very legal system. This may present persons greatly opposed to a given state system with particularly poignant and painful choices. (If the state's legal system enforces the results of certain arbitration procedures, people may come to agree—supposing they abide by this agreement—without any actual direct contact with what they perceive to be officers or institutions of the state. But this holds as well if they sign a contract that is enforced only by the state.)

Will protective agencies *require* that their clients renounce exercising their right of private retaliation if they have been wronged by nonclients of the agency? Such retaliation may well lead to counterretaliation by another agency or individual, and a protective agency would not wish *at that late stage* to get drawn into the messy affair by having to defend its client against the counterretaliation. Protective agencies would refuse to protect against counterretaliation unless they had first given permission for the retaliation. (Though might they not merely charge much more for the more extensive protection policy that provides such coverage?) The protective agencies need not even require that as part of his agreement with the agency, a client renounce, by contract, his right of private enforcement of justice against its *other clients*. The agency need only refuse a client C, who privately enforces his rights against other clients, any protection against counterretaliation upon him by these other clients. This is similar to what occurs if C acts against a nonclient. The additional fact that C acts upon a client of the agency means that the agency will act toward C as it would toward any nonclient who privately enforced his rights upon any one of its clients (see Chapter 5). This reduces intra-agency private enforcement of rights to minuscule levels.

THE DOMINANT PROTECTIVE ASSOCIATION

Initially, several different protective associations or companies will offer their services in the same geographical area. What will occur when there is a conflict between clients of different agencies? Things are relatively simple if the agencies reach the same decision about the disposition of the case. (Though each might want to exact the penalty.) But what happens if they reach different decisions as to the merits of the case, and one agency attempts to protect its client while the other is attempting to punish him or make him pay compensation? Only three possibilities are worth considering:

1. In such situations the forces of the two agencies do battle. One of the agencies always wins such battles. Since the clients of the losing agency are ill protected in conflicts with clients of the winning agency, they leave their agency to do business with the winner.
2. One agency has its power centered in one geographical area, the other in another. Each wins the battles fought close to its center of power, with some gradient being established. People who deal with one agency but live under the power of the other either move closer to their own agency's home headquarters or shift their patronage to the other protective agency. (The border is about as conflictful as one between states.)

In neither of these two cases does there remain very much geographical interspersal. Only one protective agency operates over a given geographical area.

3. The two agencies fight evenly and often. They win and lose about equally, and their interspersed members have frequent dealings and disputes with each other. Or perhaps without fighting or after only a few skirmishes the agencies realize that such battling will occur continually in the absence of preventive measures. In any case, to avoid frequent, costly, and wasteful battles the two agencies, perhaps through their executives, agree to resolve peacefully those cases about which they reach differing judgments. They agree to set up, and abide by the decisions of, some third judge or court to which they can turn when their respective judgments differ. (Or they might establish rules determining which agency has jurisdiction under which circumstances.) Thus emerges a system of appeals courts and agreed upon rules about jurisdiction and the conflict of laws. Though different agencies operate, there is one unified federal judicial system of which they all are components.

In each of these cases, almost all the persons in a geographical area are under some common system that judges between their competing claims and *enforces* their rights. Out of anarchy, pressed by spontaneous groupings, mutual-protection associations, division of labor, market pressures, economies of scale, and rational self-interest there arises something very much resembling a minimal state or a group of geographically distinct minimal states. Why is this market different from all other markets? Why would a virtual monopoly arise in this market without the government intervention that elsewhere creates and maintains it? The worth of the product purchased, protection against others, is *relative:* it depends upon how strong the others are. Yet unlike other goods that are comparatively evaluated, maximal competing protective services cannot coexist; the nature of the service brings different agencies not only into competition for customers' patronage, but also into violent conflict with each other. Also, since the worth of the less than maximal product declines disproportionately with the number who purchase the maximal product, customers will not stably settle for the lesser good, and competing companies are caught in a declining spiral. Hence the three possibilities we have listed.

Our story above assumes that each of the agencies attempts in good faith to act within the limits of Locke's law of nature. But one "protective association" might aggress against other persons. Relative to Locke's law of nature, it would be an outlaw agency. What actual counterweights would there be to its power? (What actual counterweights are there to the power of a state?) Other agencies might unite to act against it. People might refuse to deal with the outlaw agency's clients, boycotting them to reduce the probability of the agency's intervening in their own affairs. This might make it more difficult for the outlaw agency to get clients; but this boycott will seem an effective tool only on very optimistic assumptions about what cannot be kept secret, and about the costs to an individual of partial boycott as compared to the benefits of receiving the more extensive coverage offered by an "outlaw" agency. If the "outlaw" agency simply is an *open* aggressor, pillaging, plundering, and extorting under no plausible claim of justice, it will have a harder time than states. For the state's claim to legitimacy induces its citizens to believe they have some duty to obey its edicts, pay its taxes, fight its battles, and so on; and so some persons cooperate with it voluntarily. An openly aggressive agency could not depend upon, and would not receive, any such voluntary cooperation, since persons would view themselves simply as its victims rather than as its citizens.

CHAPTER 3: MORAL CONSTRAINTS AND THE STATE

THE MINIMAL STATE AND THE ULTRAMINIMAL STATE

The night-watchman state of classical liberal theory, limited to the functions of protecting all its citizens against violence, theft, and fraud, and to the enforcement of contracts, and so on, appears to be redistributive. We can imagine at least one social arrangement intermediate between the scheme of private protective associations and the night-watchman state. Since the night-watchman state is often called a minimal state, we shall call this other arrangement the *ultraminimal state.* An ultraminimal state maintains a monopoly over all use of force except that necessary in immediate self-defense, and so excludes private (or agency) retaliation for wrong and exaction of compensation; but it provides protection and enforcement services *only* to those who purchase its protection and enforcement policies. People who don't buy a protection contract from the monopoly don't get protected. The minimal (night-watchman) state is equivalent to the ultraminimal state conjoined with a (clearly redistributive) Friedmanesque voucher plan, financed from tax revenues.[5] Under this plan all people, or some (for example, those in need), are given tax-funded vouchers that can be used only for their purchase of a protection policy from the ultraminimal state.

Since the night-watchman state appears redistributive to the extent that it compels some people to pay for the protection of others, its proponents must explain why this redistributive function of the state is unique. If some redistribution is legitimate in order to protect everyone, why is redistribution not legitimate for other attractive and desirable purposes as well? What rationale specifically selects protective services as the sole subject of legitimate redistributive activities? A rationale, once found, may show that this provision of protective services is *not* redistributive.

---

5   Milton Friedman, *Capitalism and Freedom* (Chicago: University of Chicago Press, 1962), chap. 6. Friedman's school vouchers, of course, allow a choice about who is to supply the product, and so differ from the protection vouchers imagined here.

More precisely, the term "redistributive" applies to types of *reasons* for an arrangement, rather than to an arrangement itself. We might elliptically call an arrangement "redistributive" if its major (only possible) supporting reasons are themselves redistributive. ("Paternalistic" functions similarly.) Finding compelling nonredistributive reasons would cause us to drop this label. Whether we say an institution that takes money from some and gives it to others is redistributive will depend upon *why* we think it does so. Returning stolen money or compensating for violations of rights are *not* redistributive reasons. I have spoken until now of the night-watchman state's *appearing* to be redistributive, to leave open the possibility that nonredistributive types of reasons might be found to justify the provision of protective services for some by others (I explore some such reasons in Chapters 4 and 5 of Part I.)

A proponent of the ultraminimal state may seem to occupy an inconsistent position, even though he avoids the question of what makes protection uniquely suitable for redistributive provision. Greatly concerned to protect rights against violation, he makes this the sole legitimate function of the state; and he protests that all other functions are illegitimate because they themselves involve the violation of rights. Since he accords paramount place to the protection and nonviolation of rights, how can he support the ultraminimal state, which would seem to leave some persons' rights unprotected or illprotected? How can he support this *in the name of* the nonviolation of rights?

MORAL CONSTRAINTS AND MORAL GOALS

This question assumes that a moral concern can function only as a moral *goal,* as an end state for some activities to achieve as their result. It may, indeed, seem to be a necessary truth that "right," "ought," "should," and so on, are to be explained in terms of what is, or is intended to be, productive of the greatest good, with all goals built into the good. Thus it is often thought that what is wrong with utilitarianism (which *is* of this form) is its too narrow conception of good. Utilitarianism doesn't, it is said, properly take rights and their nonviolation into account; it instead leaves them a derivative status. Many of the counterexample cases to utilitarianism fit under this objection, for example, punishing an innocent man to save a neighborhood from a vengeful rampage. But a theory may include in a primary way the nonviolation of rights, yet include it in the wrong place and the wrong manner. For suppose some condition about minimizing the total (weighted) amount of violations of rights is built into the desirable end state to be achieved. We then would have something like a "utilitarianism of rights"; violations of rights (to be *minimized)* merely would replace the total happiness as the relevant end state in the utilitarian structure. (Note that we do not hold the nonviolation of our rights as our sole greatest good or even rank it first lexicographically to exclude trade-offs, if there is some desirable society we would choose to inhabit even though in it some rights of ours sometimes are violated, rather than move to a desert island where we could survive alone.) This still would require us to violate someone's rights when doing so minimizes the total (weighted) amount of the violation of rights in the society. For example, violating someone's rights might deflect others from *their* intended action of gravely violating rights, or might remove their motive for doing so, or might divert their attention, and so on. A mob rampaging through a part of town killing and burning *will* violate the rights of those living there. Therefore, someone might try to justify his punishing another *he* knows to be innocent of a crime that enraged a mob, on the grounds that punishing this innocent person would help to avoid even greater violations of rights by others, and so would lead to a minimum weighted score for rights violations in the society.

In contrast to incorporating rights into the end state to be achieved, one might place them as side constraints upon the actions to be done: don't violate constraints C. The rights of others determine the constraints upon your actions. (A *goal-directed* view with constraints added would be: among those acts available to you that don't violate constraints C, act so as to maximize goal G. Here, the rights of others would constrain your goal-directed behavior. I do not mean to imply that the correct moral view includes mandatory goals that must be pursued, even within the constraints.) This view differs from one that tries to build the side constraints C *into* the goal G. The-side-constraint view forbids you to violate these moral constraints in the pursuit of your goals; whereas the view whose objective is to minimize the violation of these rights allows you to violate the rights (the constraints) in order to lessen their total violation in the society.[6]

The claim that the proponent of the ultraminimal state is inconsistent, we now can see, assumes that he is a "utilitarian of rights." It assumes that his goal is, for example, to minimize the weighted amount of the violation of rights in the society, and that he should pursue this goal even through means that themselves violate people's rights. Instead, he may place the nonviolation of rights as

---

6   Unfortunately, too few models of the structure of moral views have been specified heretofore, though there are surely other interesting structures. Hence an argument for a side-constraint structure that consists largely in arguing against an end-state maximization structure is inconclusive, for these alternatives are not exhaustive. (On page 46 we describe a view which fits neither structure happily.) An array of structures must be precisely formulated and investigated; perhaps some novel structure then will seem most appropriate.

The issue of whether a side-constraint view can be put in the form of the goal-without-side-constraint view is a tricky one. One might think, for example, that each person could distinguish in his goal between *his* violating rights and someone else's doing it. Give the former infinite (negative) weight in his goal, and no amount of stopping others from violating rights can outweigh his violating someone's rights. In addition to a component of a goal receiving infinite weight, indexical expressions also appear, for example, *"my* doing something." A careful statement delimiting "constraint views" would exclude these gimmicky ways of transforming side constraints into the form of an end-state view as sufficient to constitute a view as end state. Mathematical methods of transforming a constrained minimization problem into a sequence of unconstrained minimizations of an auxiliary function are presented in Anthony Fiacco and Garth McCormick, *Nonlinear Programming: Sequential Unconstrained Minimization Techniques* (New York: Wiley, 1968). The book is interesting both for its methods and for their limitations in illuminating our area of concern; note the way in which the penalty functions include the constraints, the variation in weights of penalty functions (sec. 7.1), and so on.

The question of whether these side constraints are absolute, or whether they may be violated in order to avoid catastrophic moral horror, and if the latter, what the resulting structure might look like, is one I hope largely to avoid.

a constraint upon action, rather than (or in addition to) building it into the end state to be realized. The position held by this proponent of the ultraminimal state will be a consistent one if his conception of rights holds that your being *forced* to contribute to another's welfare violates your rights, whereas someone else's not providing you with things you need greatly, including things essential to the protection of your rights, does not *itself* violate your rights, even though it avoids making it more difficult for someone else to violate them. (That conception will be consistent provided it does not construe the monopoly element of the ultraminimal state as itself a violation of rights.) That it is a consistent position does not, of course, show that it is an acceptable one.

WHY SIDE CONSTRAINTS?

Isn't it *irrational* to accept a side constraint C, rather than a view that directs minimizing the violations of C? (The latter view treats C as a condition rather than a constraint.) If nonviolation of C is so important, shouldn't that be the goal? How can a concern for the nonviolation of C lead to the refusal to violate C even when this would prevent other more extensive violations of C? What is the rationale for placing the nonviolation of rights as a side constraint upon action instead of including it solely as a goal of one's actions?

Side constraints upon action reflect the underlying Kantian principle that individuals are ends and not merely means; they may not be sacrificed or used for the achieving of other ends without their consent. Individuals are inviolable. More should be said to illuminate this talk of ends and means. Consider a prime example of a means, a tool. There is no side constraint on how we may use a tool, other than the moral constraints on how we may use it upon others. There are procedures to be followed to preserve it for future use ("don't leave it out in the rain"), and there are more and less efficient ways of using it. But there is no limit on what we may do to it to best achieve our goals. Now imagine that there was an overrideable constraint C on some tool's use. For example, the tool might have been lent to you only on the condition that C not be violated unless the gain from doing so was above a certain specified amount, or unless it was necessary to achieve a certain specified goal. Here the object is not *completely* your tool, for use according to your wish or whim. But it is a tool nevertheless, even with regard to the overrideable constraint. If we add constraints on its use that may not be overridden, then the object may not be used as a tool *in those ways. In those respects,* it is not a tool at all. Can one add enough constraints so that an object cannot be used as a tool at all, in *any* respect?

Can behavior toward a person be constrained so that he is not to be used for any end except as he chooses? This is an impossibly stringent condition if it requires everyone who provides us with a good to approve positively of every use to which we wish to put it. Even the requirement that he merely should not object to any use we plan would seriously curtail bilateral exchange, not to mention sequences of such exchanges. It is sufficient that the other party stands to gain enough from the exchange so that he is willing to go through with it, even though he objects to one or more of the uses to which you shall put the good. Under such conditions, the other party is not being used solely as a means, in that respect. Another party, however, who would not choose to interact with you if he knew of the uses to which you *intend* to put his actions or good, *is* being used as a means, even if he receives enough to choose (in his ignorance) to interact with you. ("All along, you were just *using* me" can be said by someone who chose to interact only because he was ignorant of another's goals and of the uses to which he himself would be put.) Is it morally incumbent upon someone to reveal his intended uses of an interaction if he has good reason to believe the other would refuse to interact if he knew? Is he *using* the other person, if he does not reveal this? And what of the cases where the other does not choose to be of use at all? In getting pleasure from seeing an attractive person go by, does one use the other solely as a means? Does someone so use an object of sexual fantasies? These and related questions raise very interesting issues for moral philosophy; but not, I think, for political philosophy.

Political philosophy is concerned only with *certain* ways that persons may not use others; primarily, physically aggressing against them. A specific side constraint upon action toward others expresses the fact that others may not be used in the specific ways the side constraint excludes. Side constraints express the inviolability of others, in the ways they specify. These modes of inviolability are expressed by the following injunction: "Don't use people in specified ways." An end-state view, on the other hand, would express the view that people are ends and not merely means (if it chooses to express this view at all), by a different injunction: "Minimize the use in specified ways of persons as means." Following this precept itself may involve using someone as a means in one of the ways specified. Had Kant held this view, he would have given the second formula of the categorical imperative as, "So act as to minimize the use of humanity simply as a means," rather than the one he actually used: "Act in such a way that you always treat humanity, whether in your own person or in the person of any other, never simply as a means, but always at the same time as an end."

Side constraints express the inviolability of other persons. But why may not one violate persons for the greater social good? Individually, we each sometimes choose to undergo some pain or sacrifice for a greater benefit or to avoid a greater harm: we go to the dentist to avoid worse suffering later; we do some unpleasant work for its results; some persons diet to improve their health or looks; some save money to support themselves when they are older. In each case, some cost is borne for the sake of the greater overall good. Why not, *similarly*, hold that some persons have to bear some costs that benefit other persons more, for the sake of the overall social good? But there is no *social entity* with a good that undergoes some sacrifice for its own good. There are only individual people, different individual people, with their own individual lives. Using one of these people for the benefit of others, uses him and benefits the others. Nothing more. What happens is that something is done to him for the sake of others. Talk of an overall social good covers this up. (Intentionally?) To use a person in this way does not sufficiently respect and take account of the fact that he is a separate person, that his is the only life he has. *He* does not get some overbalancing good from his sacrifice, and no one is entitled to force this upon him—least of all a state or government that claims his allegiance (as other individuals do not) and that therefore scrupulously must be *neutral* between its citizens.

LIBERTARIAN CONSTRAINTS

The moral side constraints upon what we may do, I claim, reflect the fact of our separate existences. They reflect the fact that no moral balancing act can take place among us; there is no moral outweighing of one of our lives by others so as to lead to a greater overall *social* good. There is no justified sacrifice of some of us for others. This root idea, namely, that there are different individuals with separate lives and so no one may be sacrificed for others, underlies the existence of moral side constraints, but it also, I believe, leads to a libertarian side constraint that prohibits aggression against another.

The stronger the force of an end-state maximizing view, the more powerful must be the root idea capable of resisting it that underlies the existence of moral side constraints. Hence the more seriously must be taken the existence of distinct individuals who are not resources for others. An underlying notion sufficiently powerful to support moral side constraints against the powerful intuitive force of the end-state maximizing view will suffice to derive a libertarian constraint on aggression against another. Anyone who rejects *that particular* side constraint has three alternatives: (1) he must reject *all* side constraints; (2) he must produce a different explanation of why there are moral side constraints rather than simply a goal-directed maximizing structure, an explanation that doesn't itself entail the libertarian side constraint; or (3) he must accept the strongly put root idea about the separateness of individuals and yet claim that initiating aggression against another is compatible with this root idea. Thus we have a promising sketch of an argument from moral form to moral content: the form of morality includes F (moral side constraints); the best explanation of morality's being F is p (a strong statement of the distinctness of individuals); and from p follows a particular moral content, namely, the libertarian constraint. The particular moral content gotten by this argument, which focuses upon the fact that there are distinct individuals each with his *own* life to lead, will not be the *full* libertarian constraint. It will prohibit sacrificing one person to benefit another. Further steps would be needed to reach a prohibition on paternalistic aggression: using or threatening force for the benefit of the person against whom it is wielded. For this, one must focus upon the fact that there are distinct individuals, each with his own life *to lead*.

A nonaggression principle is often held to be an appropriate principle to govern relations among nations. What difference is there supposed to be between sovereign individuals and sovereign nations that makes aggression permissible among individuals? Why may individuals jointly, through their government, do to someone what no nation may do to another? If anything, there is a stronger case for nonaggression among individuals; unlike nations, they do not contain as parts individuals that others legitimately might intervene to protect or defend.

I shall not pursue here the details of a principle that prohibits physical aggression, except to note that it does not prohibit the use of force in defense against another party who is a threat, even though he is innocent and deserves no retribution. An *innocent threat* is someone who innocently is a causal agent in a process such that he would be an aggressor had he chosen to become such an agent. If someone picks up a third party and throws him at you down at the bottom of a deep well, the third party is innocent and a threat; had he chosen to launch himself at you in that trajectory he would be an aggressor. Even though the falling person would survive his fall onto you, may you use your ray gun to disintegrate the falling body before it crushes and kills you? Libertarian prohibitions are usually formulated so as to forbid using violence on innocent persons. But innocent threats, I think, are another matter to which different principles must apply. Thus, a full theory in this area also must formulate the *different* constraints on response to innocent threats. Further complications concern *innocent shields of threats,* those innocent persons who themselves are nonthreats but who are so situated that they will be damaged by the only means available for stopping the threat. Innocent persons strapped onto the front of the tanks of aggressors so that the tanks cannot be hit without also hitting them are innocent shields of threats. (Some uses of force on people to get at an aggressor do not act upon innocent shields of threats; for example, an aggressor's innocent child who is tortured in order to get the aggressor to stop wasn't *shielding* the parent.) May one knowingly injure innocent shields? *If* one may attack an aggressor and injure an innocent shield, may the innocent shield fight back in self-defense (supposing that he cannot move against or fight the aggressor)? Do we get two persons battling each other in self-defense? Similarly, if you use force against an innocent threat to you, do you thereby become an innocent threat to him, so that he may now justifiably use additional force against you (supposing that he can do this, yet cannot prevent his original threateningness)? I tiptoe around these incredibly difficult issues here, merely noting that a view that says it makes nonaggression central must resolve them explicitly at some point.

ANARCHY, STATE AND UTOPIA

CHAPTERS 4 AND 5 (SELECTIONS)

BY ROBERT NOZICK

Robert Nozick, *Anarchy, State, and Utopia*, pp. 54-63, 78-84, 88-90, 108-119. Copyright © 1974 by Perseus Books Group. Reprinted with permission.

TEN

CHAPTER 4: PROHIBITION, COMPENSATION, AND RISK

INDEPENDENTS AND THE DOMINANT PROTECTIVE AGENCY

Let us suppose that interspersed among a large group of persons who deal with one protective agency lives some minuscule group who do not. These few independents (perhaps even only one) jointly or individually enforce their own rights against one and all, including clients of the agency. This situation might have arisen if native Americans had not been forced off their land and if some had refused to affiliate with the surrounding society of the settlers. Locke held that no one may be forced to enter civil society; some may abstain and stay in the liberty of the state of nature, even if most choose to enter (§ 95).

How might the protective association and its members deal with this? They might try to isolate themselves from the independents in their midst by forbidding anyone permission to enter their property who hadn't agreed to forgo exercising rights of retaliation and punishment. The geographical territory covered by the protective association then might resemble a slice of Swiss cheese, with internal as well as external boundaries.[1] But this would leave acute problems of relations

---

[1] The possibility of surrounding an individual presents a difficulty for a libertarian theory that contemplates private ownership of all roads and streets, with no public ways of access. A person might trap another by purchasing the land around him, leaving no way to leave without trespass. It won't do to say

with independents who had devices enabling them to retaliate across the boundaries, or who had helicopters to travel directly to wrongdoers without trespass upon anyone else's land,[2] and so on.

Instead of (or in addition to) attempts at geographically isolating independents, one might punish them for their misenforcements of their rights of retaliation, punishment, and exaction of compensation. An independent would be allowed to proceed to enforce his rights as he sees them and as he sees the facts of his situation; afterwards the members of the protective association would check to see whether he had acted wrongly or overacted. If and only if he had done so, would they punish him or exact compensation from him.

But the victim of the independent's wrongful and unjust retaliation may be not only damaged but seriously injured and perhaps even killed. Must one wait to act until afterwards? Surely there would be some probability of the independent's misenforcing his rights, which is high enough (though less than unity) to justify the protective association in stopping him until it determines whether his rights indeed were violated by its client. Wouldn't this be a legitimate way to defend their clients? Won't people choose to do business only with agencies that offer their clients protection, by announcing they will punish anyone who punishes a client without first using some particular sort of procedure to establish his right to do this, independently of whether it turns out that he *could* have established this right? Is it not within a person's rights to announce that he will not allow himself to be punished without its first being *established* that he has wronged someone? May he not appoint a protective association as his agent to make and carry out this announcement and to oversee any process used to try to establish his guilt? (Is anyone known so to lack the capacity to harm another, that others would exclude him from the scope of this announcement?) But suppose an independent, in the process of exacting punishment, tells the protective agency to get out of his way, on the grounds that the agency's client deserves punishment, that he (the independent) has a right to punish him, that he is not violating anyone's rights,

---

that an individual shouldn't go to or be in a place without having acquired from adjacent owners the right to pass through and exit. Even if we leave aside questions about the desirability of a system that allows someone who has neglected to purchase exit rights to be trapped in a single place, though he has done no punishable wrong, by a malicious and wealthy enemy (perhaps the president of the corporation that owns all the local regular thoroughfares), there remains the question of "exit to where?" Whatever provisions he has made, anyone can be surrounded by enemies who cast their nets widely enough. The adequacy of libertarian theory cannot depend upon technological devices being available, such as helicopters able to lift straight up above the height of private airspace in order to transport him away without trespass. We handle this issue by the proviso on transfers and exchanges in Chapter 7.

2   Lacking other avenues of redress, one may trespass on another's land to get what one is due from him or to give him what he deserves, provided that he refuses to pay or to make himself easily available for punishment. *B* does not violate *A*'s property rights in his wallet by touching it, or by opening its seal if *A* refuses to do so, in the course of extracting money *A* owes him yet refuses to pay or transfer over; *A* must pay what he owes; if *A* refuses to place it in *B*'s possession, as a means to maintaining his rights, *B* may do things he otherwise would not be entitled to do. Thus the quality of Portia's reasoning is as strained in holding that Shylock is entitled to take exactly one pound of flesh but not to shed a drop of Antonio's blood as is the quality of her mercy as she cooperates in requiring that to save his life Shylock must convert to Christianity and dispose of his property in a way hateful to him.

and that it's not his fault if the protective agency doesn't *know* this. Must the agency then abstain from intervening? On the same grounds may the independent demand that the person himself refrain from defending himself against the infliction of punishment? And if the protective agency tries to punish an independent who punished a client, independently of whether their client *did* violate the independent's rights, isn't the independent within his rights to defend himself against the agency? To answer these questions and hence to decide how a dominant protective agency may act toward independents, we must investigate the moral status within a state of nature of procedural rights and of prohibitions upon risky activities, and also what knowledge is presumed by principles about the exercise of rights, including especially rights to enforce other rights. To these issues, difficult ones for the natural-rights tradition, we now turn.

PROHIBITION AND COMPENSATION

A line (or hyper-plane) circumscribes an area in moral space around an individual. Locke holds that this line is determined by an individual's natural rights, which limit the action of others. Non-Lockeans view other considerations as setting the position and contour of the line. In any case the following question arises: *Are others forbidden to perform actions that transgress the boundary or encroach upon the circumscribed area, or are they permitted to perform such actions provided that they compensate the person whose boundary has been crossed?* Unravelling this question will occupy us for much of this chapter. Let us say that a system forbids an action to a person if it imposes (is geared to impose) some penalty upon him for doing the act, in addition to exacting compensation from him for the act's victims.[3] Something fully compensates a person for a loss if and only if it makes him no worse off than he otherwise would have been; it compensates person X for person Y's action A if X is no worse off receiving it, Y having done A, than X would have been without receiving it if Y had not done A. (In the terminology of economists, something compensates X for Y's act if receiving it leaves X on at least as high an indifference curve as he would have been on, without it, had Y not so acted.)[4] Shamelessly, I ignore general problems about the counterfactual "as well off (on as high an indifference curve) as X would have been if Y's action hadn't occurred." I also ignore particular difficulties; for example, If X's position was deteriorating (or improving) at the time, is the baseline for compensation where he was heading or where he was then? Are things changed If X's position would have worsened anyway the next day? But one question must be discussed. Does the compensation to X for Y's actions take into account X's best response to these

---

3 This sufficient condition for prohibiting or forbidding an action is not a necessary one. An action may be forbidden without there being any provision for its victims to be fully or at all compensated. Our purposes here do not require a general account of forbidding and prohibiting.

4 *When* is a person to be indifferent between the two situations—the time at which compensation is paid (which would encourage boundary crossing, since time heals wounds), or the time of the original act?

actions, or not? If *X* responded by rearranging his other activities and assets to limit his losses (or if he made prior provision to limit them), should this benefit *Y* by lessening the compensation he must pay? Alternatively, if *X* makes no attempt to rearrange his activities to cope with what *Y* has done, must *Y* compensate *X* for the full damage *X* suffers? Such behavior on *X*'s part may seem irrational; but if *Y* is required to compensate *X* for his full actual loss in such cases, then *X* will not be made worse off by his own noncoping, nonadaptive behavior. If so required, *Y* might lower the amount of compensation he must pay by paying *X* to respond adaptively and so to limit losses. We shall tentatively adopt another view of compensation, one which presumes reasonable precautions and adjusting activities by *X*. These activities would place *X* (given *Y*'s acts) on a certain indifference curve *I*; *Y* is required to raise *X* above his actual position by an amount equal to the difference between his position on *I* and his original position. *Y* compensates *X* for how much worse off *y*'s action would have made a reasonably prudently acting *X*. (This compensation structure uses measurement of utility on an interval scale.)

WHY EVER PROHIBIT?

A person may choose to do himself, I shall suppose, the things that would impinge across his boundaries when done without his consent by another. (Some of these things may be impossible for him to do to himself.) Also, he may give another permission to do these things to him (including things impossible for him to do to himself). Voluntary consent opens the border for crossings. Locke, of course, would hold that there are things others may not do to you by your permission; namely, those things you have no right to do to yourself. Locke would hold that your giving your permission cannot make it morally permissible for another to kill you, because you have no right to commit suicide. My nonpaternalistic position holds that someone may choose (or permit another) to do to himself *anything*, unless he has acquired an obligation to some third party not to do or allow it. This should cause no difficulty for the remainder of this chapter. Let those who disagree imagine our discussion to be limited to those actions about which (they admit) the position does hold; and we can proceed along together, having factored out that divisive and, for immediate purposes, irrelevant issue.

Two contrasting questions delimit our present concern:

1. Why is any action ever prohibited, rather than allowed, provided its victims are compensated?
2. Why not prohibit all crossings of the moral boundary that the party impinged upon did not first consent to? Why ever permit anyone to cross another's boundary without prior consent?

Our first question is too broad. For a system allowing acts *A* provided compensation is paid must prohibit at least the joint act of doing *A* and refusing to pay compensation. To narrow the issue, let us suppose there exist easy means to collect assessed compensation. Compensation is easily collected, once it is known who owes it. But those who cross another's protected boundary sometimes escape without revealing their identity. Merely to require (upon detection, apprehension, and determination of guilt) compensation of the victim might be insufficient to deter someone from an action. Why wouldn't he attempt continually to get away with it, to gain without paying compensation? True, if apprehended and judged guilty, he would be required to pay the costs of detecting, apprehending, and trying him; perhaps these possible additional costs would be sufficiently great to deter him. But they might not be. So one might be led to prohibit doing certain acts without paying compensation, and to impose penalties upon those who refuse to pay compensation or who fail to identify themselves as the crossers of certain boundaries.

RETRIBUTIVE AND DETERRANCE THEORIES OF PUNISHMENT

A person's option of crossing a boundary is constituted by a $(1 - p)$ chance of gain G from the act, where p is the probability he is apprehended, combined with the probability p of paying various costs of the act. These costs are first, the compensation to the victim over and above returning whatever transferable thing may be left from the ill-gotten gains, which we shall label C. In addition, since any nonremovable benefit from carrying out the act (for example, pleasure over fond memories) also will be exactly counterbalanced so as to leave none net, we may ignore it in what follows. Other costs are the psychological, social, and emotional costs of being apprehended, placed on trial, and so on (call them D); and the financial costs (call them E) of the processes of apprehension and trial which he must pay since they were produced by his attempt to evade paying compensation. Prospects for deterrence look dim if the expected costs of a boundary crossing are less than its expected gain; that is, if $p \times (C + D + E)$ is less than $(1 - p) \times G$. (Nevertheless, a person may refrain from a boundary crossing because he has something better to do, an option available to him with even higher expected utility.) If apprehension is imperfect, though inexpensive, additional penalties may be needed to deter crimes. (Attempts to evade paying compensation then would be made prohibited acts.)

Such considerations pose difficulties for retributive theories that set, on retributive grounds, an *upper limit* to the penalty that may be inflicted upon a person. Let us suppose (on such theories) that R, the retribution deserved, equals $r \times H$; where H is a measure of the seriousness of the harm of the act, and r (ranging between 0 and 1 inclusive) indicates the person's degree of responsibility for H. (We pass over the delicate issue of whether H represents the harm intended or the harm done or some function of both of these; or whether this varies with the type of case.)[5] When others

---

5 We also pass over whether the retribution includes a component representing the *wrongness* of the act it responds to. Those retributive theories that hold the punishment somehow should *match* the crime face a dilemma: either

will know that $r - 1$, they will believe that $R = H$. A person deciding whether to perform some harmful action then faces a probability $(1 - p)$ of gain G, and a probability p of paying out $(C + D + E + R)$. Usually (though not always) the gain from a boundary crossing is close to the loss or harm it inflicts on the other party; R will be somewhere in the neighborhood of G. But when p is small, or R is, $p \times (C + D + E + R)$ may be less than $(1 - p) \times G$, often leaving no deterrence.[6]

Retributive theory seems to allow failures of deterrence. Deterrence theorists (though they wouldn't choose to) would be in a position to gloat at retributivists' squirming over this, if they themselves possessed another theory. But "the penalty for a crime should be the minimal one necessary to deter commission of it" provides *no* guidance until we're told *how much* commission of it is to be deterred. If all commission is to be deterred, so that the crime is eliminated, the penalty will be set unacceptably high. If only one instance of the crime is to be deterred, so that there is merely less of the crime than there would be with no penalty at all, the penalty will be unacceptably low and will lead to almost *zero* deterrence. Where in between is the goal and penalty to be set? Deterrence theorists of the utilitarian sort would suggest (something like) setting the penalty P for a crime at the least point where any penalty for the crime greater than P would lead to more additional unhappiness inflicted in punishment than would be saved to the (potential) victims of the crimes deterred by the additional increment in punishment.

This utilitarian suggestion equates the unhappiness the criminal's punishment causes him with the unhappiness a crime causes its victim. It gives these two unhappinesses the same weight in calculating a social optimum. So the utilitarian would refuse to raise the penalty for a crime, even though the greater penalty (well below any retributive upper limit) would deter more crimes, so long as it increases the unhappiness of those penalized more, even slightly, than it diminishes the unhappiness of those it saves from being victimized by the crime, and of those it deters and saves from punishment. (Will the utilitarian at least always select, between two amounts of penalty that equally maximize the total happiness, the option that minimizes the unhappiness of the victims?) Constructing counterexamples to this bizarre view is left as an exercise for the reader. Utilitarian deterrence "theory" could avoid this consequence, it seems, only by giving lesser weight to the punished party's unhappiness. One would suppose that considerations of desert, which deterrence theorists had thought avoidable if not incoherent, would play a role here; one would suppose this if one weren't bewildered at how to proceed, even using such considerations, in assigning the "proper" weight to different persons' (un)happiness. The retributive theorist, on the other hand,

---

punishment fails to match the wrongness of the crime and so doesn't retribute fully, or it matches the wrongness of the crime and so is unjustified.

6 Recall that $C + D + E + R$ measures the agent's loss as compared to his initial position, not as compared to his position after gaining from the other party by inflicting damage upon him. We ignore here the question of whether the cost imposed shouldn't be $C + D + 2E + R$, with the second E deserved for attempting to impose a cost of fruitless search upon the apparatus of detection and apprehension; or rather whether the R in $C + D + E + R$ shouldn't also contain this second E as a component.

doesn't have to say that a felon's happiness is less important than his victim's. For the retributivist does not view determining the proper punishment as a task of weighing and weighting and allocating happiness at all.[7]

We can connect the retributive framework with some issues about self-defense. According to the retributive theory, the punishment deserved is $r \times H$, where H is the amount of harm (done or intended) and r is the person's degree of responsibility for bringing about H. We shall assume that the expected value of the harm to be visited upon a victim equals H (which fails to hold only if the person's intentions fail to fit his objective situation). A rule of proportionality then sets an upper limit on the defensive harm which may be inflicted in self-defense on the doer of H. It makes the upper magnitude of the permissible defensive harm some function f of H, which varies directly with H (the greater H is, the greater is $f(H)$), and such that $f(H) > H$. (Or at least, on any view, $f(H) \geq H$.) Notice that this rule of proportionality does not mention the degree of responsibility r; it applies whether or not the doer is responsible for the harm he will cause. In this respect it differs from a rule of proportionality which makes the upper limit of self-defense a function of $r \times H$. The latter sort of rule yields our judgment that, all other things being equal, one may use *more* force in self-defense against someone whose r is greater than zero. The structure we present here can yield this as follows. One may, in defending oneself, *draw against* the punishment the attacker deserves (which is $r \times H$). So the upper limit of what one may use in self-defense against a doer of harm H is $f(H) + r \times H$. When an amount A in addition to $f(H)$ is expended in self-defense, the punishment which later may be inflicted is reduced by that amount and becomes $r \times H - A$. When $r = 0$, $f(H) + r \times H$ reduces to $f(H)$. Finally, there will be some specification of a rule of necessity which requires one not to use more in self-defense than is necessary to repel the attack. If what is necessary is more than $f(H) + r \times H$, there will be a duty to retreat.[8]

---

7   We should note the interesting possibility that contemporary governments might make penalties (in addition to compensation) monetary, and use them to finance various government activities. Perhaps some resources left to spend would be yielded by the retributive penalties in addition to compensation, and by the extra penalties needed to deter because of less than certain apprehension. Since the victims of the crimes of those people apprehended are fully compensated, it is not clear that the remaining funds (especially those yielded by application of the retributive theory) must go toward compensating the victims of uncaught criminals. Presumably a protective association would use such funds to reduce the price of its services.

8   An interesting discussion of these diverse issues is contained in George P. Fletcher, "Proportionality and the Psychotic Aggressor," *Israel Law Review,* Vol. 8, No. 3, July 1973, pp. 367–390. Despite Fletcher's claim that there is no way to say *both* that one may use deadly force in self-defense against a psychotic aggressor (whose $r = 0$) *and* that we are subject to some rule of proportionality, I believe our structure presented in the text yields both these results and satisfies the diverse conditions one wants to impose.

THE PRINCIPLE OF COMPENSATION

Even when permitting an action provided compensation is paid (the second or third possibilities above) is prima facie more appropriate for a risky action than prohibiting it (the first possibility above), the issue of its being prohibited or permitted to someone still is not completely settled. For some persons will lack sufficient funds to pay the required compensation should the need arise; and they will not have purchased insurance to cover their obligations in that eventuality. May these persons be forbidden to perform the action? Forbidding an action to those not in a position to pay compensation differs from forbidding it unless compensation is paid to those actually harmed (the second possibility above), in that in the former case (but not in the latter) someone who lacks provision for paying compensation may be punished for his action even though it does not actually harm anyone or cross a boundary.

Does someone violate another's rights by performing an action without sufficient means or liability insurance to cover its risks? May he be forbidden to do this or punished for doing it? Since an enormous number of actions do increase risk to others, a society which prohibited such uncovered actions would ill fit a picture of a free society as one embodying a presumption in favor of liberty, under which people permissibly could perform actions so long as they didn't harm others in specified ways. Yet how can people be allowed to impose risks on others whom they are not in a position to compensate should the need arise? Why should some have to bear the costs of others' freedom? Yet to prohibit risky acts (because they are financially uncovered or because they are too risky) limits individuals' freedom to act, even though the actions actually might involve no cost at all to anyone else. Any given epileptic, for example, might drive throughout his lifetime without thereby harming anyone. Forbidding *him* to drive may not actually lessen the harm to others; and for all anyone knows, it doesn't. (It is true that we cannot identify in advance the individual who will turn out harmless, but why should he bear the full burden of our inability?) Prohibiting someone from driving in our automobile-dependent society, in order to reduce the risk to others, seriously disadvantages that person. It costs money to remedy these disadvantages—hiring a chauffeur or using taxis.

Consider the claim that a person must be compensated for the disadvantages imposed upon him by being forbidden to perform an activity for these sorts of reasons. Those who benefit from the reduction in risks to themselves have to "make it up" to those who are restricted. So stated, the net has been cast too broadly. Must I really compensate someone when, in self-defense, I stop him from playing Russian roulette *on me*? If some person wishes to use a very risky but efficient (and if things go well *harmless*) process in manufacturing a product, must the residents near the factory compensate him for the economic loss he suffers from not being allowed to use the possibly dangerous process? Surely not.

Perhaps a few words should be said about pollution—the dumping of negative effects upon other people's property such as their houses, clothing, and lungs, and upon unowned things which people benefit from, such as a clean and beautiful sky. I shall discuss only effects on property. It would be undesirable, and is not excluded by anything I say below, for someone to channel all of his pollution effects high above anyone's property volume, making the sky a murky grey-green. Nothing is gained by trying to transform the second type of case into the first by saying, for example, that someone who changes the way the sky looks *dumps effects on one's eyes. What follows in this note is incomplete in that it does not treat the second type of case.*

Since it would exclude too much to forbid all *polluting activities, how might a society (socialist or capitalist) decide which polluting activities to forbid and which to permit? Presumably, it should permit those polluting activities whose benefits are greater than their costs,* including within their costs their polluting effects. *The most feasible theoretical test of this net benefit is whether the activity could pay its way, whether those who benefit from it would be willing to pay enough to cover the costs of compensating those ill affected by it. (Those who favor any worthy activity that fails this test can make charitable donations to it.) For example, certain modes of airplane service impose noise pollution on homes surrounding airports. In one way or another (through lower resale value, lower rent obtainable for apartments, and so on), the economic value of these homes is diminished. Only if the benefits to air passengers are greater than these costs to airport neighbors should the noisier mode of transportation service go on. A society must have some way to determine whether the benefits do outweigh the costs. Secondly, it must decide how the costs are to be allocated. It can let them fall where they happen to fall: in our example, on the local homeowners. Or it can try to spread the cost throughout the society. Or it can place it on those who benefit from the activity: in our example, airports, airlines, and ultimately the air passenger. The last, if feasible, seems fairest. If a polluting activity is to be allowed to continue on the ground that its benefits outweigh its costs (including its polluting costs), then those who benefit actually should compensate those upon whom the pollution costs are initially thrown. The compensation might encompass paying for the costs of devices to lessen the initial pollution effects. In our example, airlines or airports might pay for soundproofing a house and then pay compensation for how much less the economic value of that house is than the value of the original unsoundproofed house in the neighborhood as it was without the additional noise.*

When each of the victims of pollution suffers great costs, the usual system of tort liability (with minor modifications) suffices to yield this result. Enforcing other people's property rights will, in these cases, suffice to keep pollution in its proper place. But the situation is changed if individual polluters have widespread and individually minuscule effects. If someone imposes the equivalent of a twenty-cent cost on each person in the United States, it will not pay for any one person to sue him, despite the great total of the cost imposed. If many persons similarly impose tiny costs on each individual, the total costs to an individual then may be significant. But since no single source significantly affects one individual, it still will not pay any individual to sue any individual polluter. It is ironic that pollution is commonly held to indicate defects in the privateness of a system of private property, whereas the problem of pollution is that high transaction costs make it difficult to enforce the private property rights of the victims of pollution. One solution might be to allow group suits against polluters. Any lawyer or law firm may act for the general public and sue, being required to distribute a proportion of the amount collected to each member of the included public who claims it from them. (Since different people are differently affected by the same polluting acts, the lawyers might be required to distribute different amounts to those in different specified groups.) The lawyers' income would come from those who do not write in to claim their due, and from earnings of the money of those who do not claim promptly. Seeing some receiving great income in this way, others would go into business as "public's agents," charging a yearly fee to collect and turn over to their clients all the pollution payments to which they were entitled. Since such a scheme gives great advantage to a lawyer who acts fast, it insures that many would be alert to protect the interests of those polluted. Alternative schemes might be devised to allow several to sue simultaneously for distinct sets of persons in the public. It is true that these schemes place great weight on the court system, but they should be as manageable as the operation of any government bureaucracy in determining and distributing costs.[9]

To arrive at an acceptable principle of compensation, we must delimit the class of actions covered by the claim. Some types of action are generally done, play an important role in people's lives, and are not forbidden to a person without seriously disadvantaging him. One principle might run: when an action of this type is forbidden to someone because it *might* cause harm to others and is especially dangerous when he does it, then those who forbid in order to gain increased security for themselves must compensate the person forbidden for the disadvantage they place him under. This principle is meant to cover forbidding the epileptic to drive while excluding the cases of involuntary Russian roulette and the special manufacturing process. The idea is to focus

---

9 The proposal I make here can, I think, be defended against the considerations adduced in Frank Michelman's sophisticated presentation of a contrasting view in his "Pollution as a Tort," an essay review of Guido Calabresi's *The Costs of Accidents*, in *Yale Law Journal*, 80 (1917), pt. V, 666–683.

I do not mean to put forth the above scheme as *the* solution to controlling pollution. Rather, I wish merely to suggest and make plausible the view that some institutional arrangement might be devised to solve the problem at a fell swoop, and to commend the task to those clever at such things. (J. H. Dales proposes, in *Pollution, Property, and Prices,* to sell transferable rights to pollute in specified amounts. This elegant proposal unfortunately involves central decision as to the desirable *total* amount of pollution.)

Popular discussions often run pollution problems together with that of conserving natural resources. Again, the clearest examples of misdirected activity have occurred where there are no clear private property rights: on *public* lands denuded by timber companies and in oil fields under separately held pieces of land. To the extent that future people (or we later) will be willing to pay for the satisfaction of their desires, including trips through unspoiled forests and wilderness land, it will be in the economic interests of some to conserve the necessary resources. See the discussion in Rothbard, *Power and Market* (Menlo Park, Calif.: Institute for Humane Studies, 1970), pp. 47–52, and in the references he cites.

on important activities done by almost all, though some do them more dangerously than others. Almost everyone drives a car, whereas playing Russian roulette or using an especially dangerous manufacturing process is not a normal part of almost everyone's life.

Unfortunately this approach to the principle places a very great burden on the scheme used to classify actions. The fact that there is *one* description of a person's action that distinguishes it from the acts of others does *not* classify it as unusual and so outside the sphere of application of the principle. Yet it would be too strong to say, on the other hand, that any action falling under some description which almost every other person also instantiates is thereby shown to be usual and to fall within the compass of the principle. For unusual activities also fall under *some* descriptions that cover actions people normally do. Playing Russian roulette is a more dangerous way of "having fun," which others are allowed to do; and using the special manufacturing process is a more dangerous way of "earning a living." Almost any two actions can be construed as the same or different, depending upon whether they fall into the same or different subclasses in the background classification of actions. This possibility of diverse descriptions of actions prevents easy application of the principle as stated.

If these questions could be clarified satisfactorily, we might wish to extend the principle to cover some unusual actions. If using the dangerous process is the only way *that* person can earn a living (and if playing Russian roulette on another with a gun of 100,000 chambers is the only way *that* person can have any enjoyment at all—I grant these are both extravagant suppositions), then perhaps this person should be compensated for the prohibition. By having *the* only way he can earn a living forbidden to him, he is disadvantaged as compared to the normal situation, whereas someone is not disadvantaged relative to the normal situation by having his most profitable alternative forbidden to him. A disadvantage as compared to the normal situation differs from being made worse off than one otherwise would be. One might use a theory of disadvantage, if one had it, in order to formulate a "Principle of Compensation": those who are *disadvantaged* by being forbidden to do actions that only *might* harm others must be compensated for these disadvantages foisted upon them in order to provide security for the others. If people's increased security from a contemplated prohibition would benefit them less than those prohibited would be disadvantaged, then potential prohibitors will be unable or unwilling to make sufficiently great compensatory payments; so the prohibition, as is proper in this case, will not be imposed.

The principle of compensation covers the cases falling under our earlier statement which involved messy problems about classifying actions. It does not avoid completely similar questions concerning the circumstances under which someone is especially disadvantaged. But as they arise here, the questions are easier to handle. For example, is the manufacturer who is prevented from pursuing his best alternative (though having other profitable alternatives) especially disadvantaged if everyone else may pursue their best alternatives, which happen not to be dangerous? Clearly not.

The principle of compensation requires that people be compensated for having certain risky activities prohibited to them. It might be objected that either you have the right to forbid these people's risky activities or you don't. If you do, you needn't compensate the people for doing to them what you have a right to do; and if you don't, then rather than formulating a policy of compensating people for your unrightful forbidding, you ought simply to stop it. In neither case does the appropriate course seem to be to forbid and then compensate. But the dilemma, "either you have a right to forbid it so you needn't compensate, or you don't have a right to forbid it so you should stop," is too short. It may be that you do have a right to forbid an action but only provided you compensate those to whom it is forbidden.

How can this be? Is this situation one of those discussed earlier, in which a border crossing is permitted provided that compensation is paid? If so, there would be some boundary line that delimits forbidding people to do certain risky acts, which it would be permissible to cross if the party trespassed upon were compensated. Even if so, since in the cases under discussion we can identify in advance the particular persons being forbidden, why are we not required instead to negotiate a contract with them whereby they agree not to do the risky act in question? Why wouldn't we have to offer them an incentive, or hire them, or bribe them to refrain from doing the act? In our earlier discussion of border crossing we noted the absence of any compelling theory of just price or compelling reason why all of the benefits of voluntary exchange should go to one of the parties. Which of the admissible points on the contract curve was to be selected, we said, was a question appropriately left to the parties involved. This consideration favored prior negotiation over posterior payment of full compensation. In the present subclass of cases, however, it *does* seem appropriate uniformly to select one extremity of the contract curve. Unlike exchanges in which both parties benefit and it is unclear how these benefits are to be divided, in negotiations over one party's abstaining from an action that will or might endanger another person, all the first party need receive is full compensation. (The payment the first party could negotiate for abstaining, were he allowed to perform the action, is *not* part of his loss due to the prohibition for which he must be compensated.)

CHAPTER 5: THE STATE

PROHIBITING PRIVATE ENFORCEMENT OF JUSTICE

An independent might be prohibited from privately exacting justice because his procedure is known to be too risky and dangerous—that is, it involves a higher risk (than another procedure) of punishing an innocent person or overpunishing a guilty one—or because his procedure isn't known not to be risky. (His procedure would exhibit another mode of unreliability if its chances were much greater of not punishing a guilty person, but this would not be a reason for prohibiting his private enforcement.)

Let us consider these in turn. If the independent's procedure is very unreliable and imposes high risk on others (perhaps he consults tea leaves), then if he does it frequently, he may make all fearful, even those not his victims. Anyone, acting in self-defense, may stop him from engaging in his high-risk activity. But surely the independent may be stopped from using a very unreliable procedure, even if he is not a constant menace. If it is known that the independent will enforce his own rights by his very unreliable procedure only once every ten years, this will *not* create general fear and apprehension in the society. The ground for prohibiting his widely intermittent use of his procedure is not, therefore, to avoid any widespread uncompensated apprehension and fear which otherwise would exist.

If there were many independents who were all liable to punish wrongly, the probabilities *would* add up to create a dangerous situation for all. Then, others would be entitled to group together and prohibit the *totality* of such activities. But how would this prohibition work? Would they prohibit *each* of the individually non-fear- creating activities? Within a state of nature by what procedure can they pick and choose which of the totality is to continue, and what would give them the right to do this? No protective association, however dominant, would have this right. For the legitimate powers of a protective association are merely the *sum* of the individual rights that its members or clients transfer to the association. No new rights and powers arise; each right of the association is decomposable without residue into those individual rights held by distinct individuals acting alone in a state of nature. A combination of individuals may have the right to do some action *C*, which no individual alone had the right to do, if *C* is identical to *D* and *E*, and persons who individually have the right to do *D* and the right to do *E* combine. If some rights of individuals were of the form "You have the right to do *A* provided 51 percent or 85 percent or whatever of the others agree you may," then a combination of individuals would have the right to do *A*, even though none separately had this right. But no individual's rights are of this form. No person or group is entitled to pick who in the totality will be allowed to continue. *All* the independents might group together and decide this. They might, for example, use some random procedure to allocate a number of (sellable?) rights to continue private enforcement so as to reduce the total danger to a point below the threshold. The difficulty is that, if a large number of independents do this, it will be in the interests of an individual to abstain from this arrangement. It will be in his interests to continue his risky activities as he chooses, while the others mutually limit theirs so as to bring the totality of acts including his to below the danger level. For the others probably would limit themselves some distance away from the danger boundary, leaving him room to squeeze in. Even were the others to rest adjacent to the line of danger so that his activities would bring the totality across it, on which grounds could *his* activities be picked out as the ones to prohibit? Similarly, it will be in the interests of any individual to refrain from otherwise unanimous agreements in the state of nature: for example, the agreement to set up a state. Anything an individual can gain by such a unanimous agreement he can gain through separate bilateral agreements. Any contract which really needs almost unanimity, any contract which is essentially joint, will serve its purpose whether or not a given individual participates; so it will be in his interests not to bind himself to participate.

THE DE FACTO MONOPOLY

The tradition of theorizing about the state we discussed briefly in Chapter 2 has a state claiming a monopoly on the use of force. Has any monopoly element yet entered our account of the dominant protective agency? *Everyone* may defend himself against unknown or unreliable procedures and may punish those who use or attempt to use such procedures against him. As its client's agent, the protective association has the right to do this for its clients. It grants that every individual, including those *not* affiliated with the association, has this right. So far, no monopoly is claimed. To be sure, there is a universal element in the content of the claim: the right to pass on *anyone's* procedure. But it does not claim to be the sole possessor of this right; everyone has it. Since no claim is made that there is some right which it and only it has, no monopoly is claimed. With regard to its own clients, however, it applies and enforces these rights which it grants that everyone has. It deems its own procedures reliable and fair. There will be a strong tendency for it to deem all other procedures, or even the "same" procedures run by others, either unreliable or unfair. But we need not suppose it excludes *every* other procedure. Everyone has the right to defend against procedures that are in fact not, or not known to be, both reliable and fair. Since the dominant protective association judges its own procedures to be both reliable and fair, and believes this to be generally known, it will not allow anyone to defend against *them;* that is, it will punish anyone who does so. The dominant protective association will act freely on its own understanding of the situation, whereas no one else will be able to do so with impunity. Although no monopoly is claimed, the dominant agency does occupy a unique position by virtue of its power. It, and it alone, enforces prohibitions on others' procedures of justice, as it sees fit. It does not claim the right to prohibit others arbitrarily; it claims only the right to prohibit anyone's using actually defective procedures on its clients. But when it sees itself as acting against actually defective procedures, others may see it as acting against what it thinks are defective procedures. It alone will act freely against what it thinks are defective procedures, whatever anyone else thinks. As the most powerful applier of principles which it grants everyone the right to apply *correctly,* it enforces its will, which, from the inside, it thinks *is* correct. From its strength stems its actual position as the ultimate enforcer and the ultimate judge with regard to its own clients. Claiming only the universal right to act correctly, it acts correctly by its own lights. It alone is in a position to act solely by its own lights.

Does this unique position constitute a monopoly? There is no right the dominant protective association claims uniquely to possess. But its strength leads it to be the unique agent acting across the board to enforce a particular right. It is not merely that it *happens* to be the only exerciser of a right it grants that all possess; the nature of the right is such that once a dominant power emerges, it alone will actually exercise that right. For the right includes the right to stop others from wrongfully exercising the right, and only the dominant power will be able to exercise this right against all others. Here, if anywhere, is the place for applying some notion of a *de facto* monopoly: a monopoly that is not *de jure* because it is not the result of some unique grant of exclusive right while others are excluded from exercising a similar privilege. Other protective agencies, to be sure, can enter the market and attempt to wean customers away from the dominant protective agency. They can attempt to replace it as the dominant one. But being the already dominant protective agency gives an agency a significant market advantage in the competition for clients. The dominant agency can offer its customers a guarantee that no other agencies can match: "Only those procedures *we* deem appropriate will be used on our customers."

The dominant protective agency's domain does *not* extend to quarrels of nonclients *among themselves.* If one independent is about to use his procedure of justice upon another independent, then presumably the protective association would have no right to intervene. It would have the right we all do to intervene to aid an unwilling victim whose rights are threatened. But since it may not intervene on paternalistic grounds, the protective association would have no proper business interfering if both independents were satisfied with *their* procedure of justice. This does not show that the dominant protective association is not a state. A state, too, could abstain from disputes where all concerned parties chose to opt out of the state's apparatus. (Though it is more difficult for people to opt out of the state in a limited way, by choosing some other procedure for settling a particular quarrel of theirs. For that procedure's settlement, and their reactions to it, might involve areas that not all parties concerned have removed voluntarily from the state's concern.) And shouldn't (and mustn't) each state allow that option to its citizens?

PROTECTING OTHERS

If the protective agency deems the independents' procedures for enforcing their own rights insufficiently reliable or fair when applied to its clients, it will prohibit the independents from such self-help enforcement. The grounds for this prohibition are that the self-help enforcement imposes risks of danger on its clients. Since the prohibition makes it impossible for the independents credibly to threaten to punish clients who violate their rights, it makes them unable to protect themselves from harm and seriously disadvantages the independents in their daily activities and life. Yet it is perfectly possible that the independents' activities including self-help enforcement could proceed without anyone's rights being violated (leaving aside the question of procedural rights). According to our principle of compensation given in Chapter 4, in these circumstances those persons promulgating and benefiting from the prohibition must compensate those disadvantaged by it. The clients of the protective agency, then, must compensate the independents for the disadvantages imposed upon them by being prohibited self-help enforcement of their own rights against the agency's clients. Undoubtedly, the least expensive way to compensate the independents would be to *supply* them with protective services to cover those situations of conflict with the paying customers of the protective agency. This will be less expensive than leaving them unprotected against violations of their rights (by not punishing any client who does so) and then attempting to pay them afterwards to cover their losses through having (and being in a position in which they were exposed to having) their rights violated. If it were *not* less expensive, then instead of buying protective services, people would save their money and use it to cover their losses, perhaps by jointly pooling their money in an insurance scheme.

Must the members of the protective agency *pay* for protective services (vis-à-vis its clients) for the independents? Can they insist that the independents purchase the services themselves? After all, using self-help procedures would not have been without costs for the independent. The principle of compensation does not require those who prohibit an epileptic from driving to pay his full cost of taxis, chauffeurs, and so on. If the epileptic were allowed to run his own automobile, this too would have its costs: money for the car, insurance, gasoline, repair bills, and aggravation. In compensating for disadvantages imposed, the prohibitors need pay only an amount sufficient to compensate for the disadvantages of the prohibition *minus* an amount representing the costs the prohibited party would have borne were it not for the prohibition. The prohibitors needn't pay the complete costs of taxis; they must pay only the amount which when combined with the costs to the prohibited party of running his own private automobile is sufficient for taxis. They may find it less expensive to compensate in kind for the disadvantages they impose than to supply monetary compensation; they may engage in some activity that removes or partially lessens the disadvantages, compensating in money only for the net disadvantages remaining.

If the prohibitor pays to the person prohibited monetary compensation equal to an amount that covers the disadvantages imposed *minus* the costs of the activity where it permitted, this amount may be insufficient to enable the prohibited party to overcome the disadvantages. If his costs in performing the prohibited action would have been monetary, he can combine the compensation payment with this money unspent and purchase the equivalent service. But if his costs would not have been directly monetary but involve energy, time, and the like, as in the case of the independent's self-help enforcement of rights, then this monetary payment of the difference will not by itself enable the prohibited party to overcome the disadvantage by purchasing the equivalent of what he is prohibited. If the independent has other financial resources he can use without disadvantaging himself, then this payment of the difference will suffice to leave the prohibited party undisadvantaged. But *if* the independent has no such other financial resources, a protective agency may *not* pay him an amount *less* than the cost of its least expensive protective policy, and so leave him only the alternatives of being defenseless against the wrongs of its clients or having to work in the cash market to earn sufficient funds to total the premium on a policy. For this financially pressed prohibited individual, the agency must make up the difference between the *monetary* costs to him of the unprohibited activity and the amount necessary to purchase an overcoming or counterbalancing of the disadvantage imposed. The prohibitor must completely supply enough, in money or in kind, to overcome the disadvantages. No compensation need be provided to someone who would not be disadvantaged by buying protection for himself. For those of scanter resources, to whom the unprohibited activity had no monetary costs, the agency must provide the difference between the resources they can spare without disadvantage and the cost of protection. For someone for whom it had some monetary costs, the prohibitor must supply the additional monetary amount (over and above what they can spare without disadvantage) necessary to overcome the disadvantages. If the prohibitors compensate in kind, they may *charge* the financially pressed prohibited party for this, up to the monetary costs to him of his unprohibited activity provided this amount is not greater than the price of the good. As the only effective supplier, the dominant protective agency must offer in compensation the difference between its own fee and monetary costs to this prohibited party of self-help enforcement. It almost always will receive this amount back in partial payment for the purchase of a protection policy. It goes without saying that these dealings and prohibitions apply only to those using unreliable or unfair enforcement procedures.

Thus the dominant protective agency must supply the independents—that is, everyone it prohibits from self-help enforcement against its clients on the grounds that their procedures of enforcement are unreliable or unfair—with protective services against its clients; it may have to provide some persons services for a fee that is less than the price of these services. These persons may, of course, choose to refuse to pay the fee and so do without these compensatory services. If the dominant protective agency provides protective services in this way for independents, won't this lead people to leave the agency in order to receive its services without paying? Not to any great extent, since compensation is paid only to those who would be disadvantaged by purchasing protection for themselves, and only in the amount that will equal the cost of an unfancy policy when added to the sum of the monetary costs of self-help protection plus whatever amount the person comfortably could pay. Furthermore, the agency protects these independents it compensates only against its own paying clients on whom the independents are forbidden to use self-help enforcement. The more free riders there are, the more desirable it is to be a client always protected by the agency. This factor, along with the others, acts to reduce the number of free riders and to move the equilibrium toward almost universal participation.

THE STATE

We set ourselves the task, in Chapter 3, of showing that the dominant protective association within a territory satisfied two crucial necessary conditions for being a state: that it had the requisite sort of monopoly over the use of force in the territory, and that it protected the rights of everyone in the territory, even if this universal protection could be provided only in a "redistributive" fashion. These very crucial facets of the state constituted the subject of the individualist anarchists' condemnation of the state as immoral. We also set ourselves the task of showing that these monopoly and redistributive elements were themselves morally legitimate, of showing that the transition from a state of nature to an ultraminimal state (the monopoly element) was morally legitimate and violated no one's rights and that the transition from an ultraminimal to a minimal state (the "redistributive" element) also was morally legitimate and violated no one's rights.

A protective agency dominant in a territory does satisfy the two crucial necessary conditions for being a state. It is the only generally effective enforcer of a prohibition on others' using unreliable enforcement procedures (calling them as it sees them), and it oversees these procedures. And the agency protects those nonclients in its territory whom it prohibits from using self-help enforcement procedures on its clients, in their dealings with its clients, even if such protection must be financed (in apparent redistributive fashion) by its clients. It is morally required to do this by the principle of compensation, which requires those who act in self-protection in order to increase their own security to compensate those they prohibit from doing risky acts which might actually have turned out to be harmless for the disadvantages imposed upon them.

We noted in beginning Chapter 3 that whether the provision of protective services for some by others was "redistributive" would depend upon the reasons for it. We now see that such provision need not be redistributive since it can be justified on other than redistributive grounds, namely, those provided in the principle of compensation. (Recall that "redistributive" applies to reasons for a practice or institution, and only elliptically and derivatively to the institution itself.) To sharpen this point, we can imagine that protective agencies offer two types of protection policies: those protecting clients against risky private enforcement of justice and those not doing so but protecting only against theft, assault, and so forth (provided these are not done in the course of private enforcement of justice). Since it is only with regard to those with the first type of policy that others are prohibited from privately enforcing justice, only they will be required to compensate the persons prohibited private enforcement for the disadvantages imposed upon them. The holders of only the second type of policy will not have to pay for the protection of others, there being nothing they have to compensate these others for. Since the reasons for wanting to be protected against private enforcement of justice are compelling, almost all who purchase protection will purchase this type of protection, despite its extra costs, and therefore will be involved in providing protection for the independents.

We have discharged our task of explaining how a state would arise from a state of nature without anyone's rights being violated. The moral objections of the individualist anarchist to the minimal state are overcome. It is not an unjust imposition of a monopoly; the *de facto* monopoly grows by an invisible-hand process and *by morally permissible means*, without anyone's rights being violated and without any claims being made to a special right that others do not possess. And requiring the clients of the *de facto* monopoly to pay for the protection of those they prohibit from self-help enforcement against them, far from being immoral, is morally required by the principle of compensation adumbrated in Chapter 4.

We canvassed, in Chapter 4, the possibility of forbidding people to perform acts if they lack the means to compensate others for possible harmful consequences of these acts or if they lack liability insurance to cover these consequences. Were such prohibition legitimate, according to the principle of compensation the persons prohibited would have to be compensated for the disadvantages imposed upon them, and they could use the compensatory payments to purchase the liability insurance! Only those disadvantaged by the prohibition would be compensated: namely, those who lack other resources they can shift (without disadvantaging sacrifice) to purchase the liability insurance. When these people spend their compensatory payments for liability insurance, we have what amounts to public provision of special liability insurance. It is provided to those unable to afford it and covers only those risky actions which fall under the principle of compensation—those actions which are legitimately prohibited when uncovered (provided disadvantages are compensated for), actions whose prohibition would seriously disadvantage persons. Providing such insurance almost certainly would be the least expensive way to compensate people who present only normal danger to others for the disadvantages of the prohibition. Since they then would be insured against the eventuation of certain of their risks to others, these actions then would not be prohibited to them. Thus we see how, if it were legitimate to prohibit some actions to those uncovered by liability insurance, and were this done, another *apparent* redistributive aspect of the state would enter by solid libertarian moral principles! (The exclamation point stands for *my* surprise.)

Does the dominant protective agency in a given geographical territory constitute the *state* of that territory? We have seen in Chapter 2 how the notion of a monopoly on the use of force is difficult to state precisely so that it does not fall before obvious counterexamples. This notion, as usually explained, cannot be used with any confidence to answer our question. We should accept a decision yielded by the precise wording of a definition in some text only if that definition had been devised for application to cases as complicated as ours and had stood up to tests against a range of such cases. No classification, in passing, by accident can answer our question in any useful manner.

Consider the following discursive description by an anthropologist:

> The concentration of all physical force in the hands of the central authority is the primary function of the state and is its decisive characteristic. In order to make this clear, consider what may not be done under the state form of rule: no one in the society governed by the state may take another's life, do him physical harm, touch his property, or damage his reputation save by permission of the state. The officers of the state have powers to take life, inflict corporal punishment, seize property as fine or by expropriation, and affect the standing and reputation of a member of the society.
>
> This is not to say that in societies without the state one may take life with impunity. But in such societies (e.g., among Bushmen, Eskimo, and the tribes of central Australia) the central authority that protects the household against wrongdoers is nonexistent, weak, or sporadic, and it was applied among the Crow and other Indians of the western Plains only as situations arose. The household or the individual is protected in societies without the state by nonexplicit means, by total group participation in suppression of the wrongdoer, by temporarily or sporadically applied force that is no longer needed (and so no longer used) when the cause for its application is past. The state has means for the suppression of what the society considers to be wrongs or crimes: police, courts of law, prisons, institutions which explicitly and specifically function in this area of activity. Moreover, these institutions are stable within the frame of reference of the society, and permanent.
>
> When the state was formed in ancient Russia, the ruling prince asserted the power to impose fines and to wreak physical pain and death, but allowed no one else to act thus. He asserted once again the monopolistic nature of the state power by withholding its power from any other person or body. If harm was done by one subject to another without the prince's express permission, this was a wrong, and the wrongdoer was punished. Moreover, the prince's power could only be explicitly delegated. The class of subject thus protected was thereby carefully defined, of course; by no means were all those within his realm so protected.

> No one person or group can stand in place of the state; the state's acts can only be performed directly or by express delegation. The state in delegating its power makes its delegate an agent (organ) of the state. Policemen, judges, jail guards derive their power to coerce, according to the rules of the society, directly from the central authority; so do the tax-collectors, the military, frontier guards, and the like. The authoritative function of the state rests on its command of these forces as its agents.

The writer does not claim that the features he lists all are necessary features of the state; divergence in one feature would not serve to show that the dominant protective agency of a territory was not a state. Clearly the dominant agency has almost all of the features specified; and its enduring administrative structures, with full-time specialized personnel, make it diverge greatly—in the direction of a state—from what anthropologists call a stateless society. On the basis of the many writings like that quoted, one would call it a state.

It is plausible to conclude that the dominant protective association in a territory is its state, only for a territory of some size containing more than a few people. We do not claim that each person who, under anarchy, retains a monopoly on the use of force on his quarter acre of property is its state; nor are the only three inhabitants of an island one square block in size. It would be futile, and would serve no useful purpose, to attempt to specify conditions on the size of population and territory necessary for a state to exist. Also, we speak of cases where almost all of the people in the territory are clients of the dominant agency and where independents are in a subordinate power position in conflicts with the agency and its clients. (We have argued that this will occur.) Precisely what percentage must be clients and how subordinate the power position of the independents must be are more interesting questions, but concerning these I have nothing especially interesting to say.

One additional necessary condition for a state was extracted from the Weberian tradition by our discussion in Chapter 2: namely, that it claim to be the sole authorizer of violence. The dominant protective association makes no such claim. Having described the position of the dominant protective association, and having seen how closely it fits anthropologists' notions, should we weaken the Weberian necessary condition so that it includes a *de facto* monopoly which is the territory's sole effective judge over the permissibility of violence, having a right (to be sure, one had by all) to make judgments on the matter and to act on correct ones? The case is very strong for doing so, and it is wholly desirable and appropriate. We therefore conclude that the protective association dominant in a territory, as described, *is* a state. However, to remind the reader of our slight weakening of the Weberian condition, we occasionally shall refer to the dominant protective agency as "a statelike entity," instead of simply as "a state."

THE INVISIBLE-HAND EXPLANATION OF THE STATE

Have we provided an invisible-hand explanation (see Chapter 2) of the state's arising within a state of nature; have we given an invisible-hand explanation of the state? The *rights* possessed by the state are already possessed by each individual in a state of nature. These rights, since they are already contained whole in the explanatory parts, are *not* provided an invisible-hand explanation. Nor have we provided an invisible-hand explanation of how the state acquires rights unique to it. This is fortunate; for since the state has no special rights, there is nothing of that sort to be explained.

We have explained how, without anyone having this in mind, the self-interested and rational actions of persons in a Lockean state of nature will lead to single protective agencies dominant over geographical territories; each territory will have either one dominant agency or a number of agencies federally affiliated so as to constitute, in essence, one. And we have explained how, without claiming to possess any rights uniquely, a protective agency dominant in a territory will occupy a unique position. Though each person has a right to act correctly to prohibit others from violating rights (including the right not to be punished unless shown to deserve it), only the dominant protective association will be able, without sanction, to enforce correctness as it sees it. Its power makes it the arbiter of correctness; *it* determines what, for purposes of punishment, counts as a breach of correctness. Our explanation does not assume or claim that might makes right. But might does make enforced prohibitions, even if no one thinks the mighty have a *special* entitlement to have realized in the world their own view of which prohibitions are correctly enforced.

Our explanation of this *de facto* monopoly is an invisible-hand explanation. If the state is an institution (1) that has the right to enforce rights, prohibit dangerous private enforcement of justice, pass upon such private procedures, and so forth, and (2) that effectively is the *sole wielder* within a geographical territory of the right in (1), then by offering an invisible-hand explanation of (2), though not of (1), we have partially explained in invisible-hand fashion the existence of the state. More precisely, we have partially explained in invisible-hand fashion the existence of the *ultraminimal* state. What is the explanation of how a *minimal* state arises? The dominant protective association with the monopoly element is morally required to compensate for the disadvantages it imposes upon those it prohibits from self-help activities against its clients. However, it actually might fail to provide this compensation. Those operating an ultraminimal state are morally required to transform it into a minimal state, but they might choose not to do so. We have assumed that generally people will do what they are morally required to do. Explaining how a state could arise from a state of nature without violating anyone's rights refutes the principled objections of the anarchist. But one would feel more confidence if an explanation of how a state *would* arise from a state of nature also specified reasons why an ultraminimal state would be transformed into a minimal one, in addition to moral reasons, if it specified incentives for providing the compensation or the causes of its being provided in addition to people's desire to do what they ought. We should note that even in the event that no nonmoral incentives or causes are found to be sufficient for the transition from an ultraminimal to a minimal state, and the explanation continues to lean heavily upon people's moral motivations, it does not specify people's objective as that of establishing a state. Instead, persons view themselves as providing particular other persons with compensation for particular prohibitions they have imposed upon them. The explanation remains an invisible-hand one.

ANARCHY, STATE AND UTOPIA

CHAPTER 7 (SELECTIONS)

BY ROBERT NOZICK

Robert Nozick, *Anarchy, State, and Utopia*, pp. 54-63, 78-84, 88-90, 108-119. Copyright © 1974 by Perseus Books Group. Reprinted with permission.

ELEVEN

DISTRIBUTIVE JUSTICE

The minimal state is the most extensive state that can be justified. Any state more extensive violates people's rights. Yet many persons have put forth reasons purporting to justify a more extensive state. It is impossible within the compass of this book to examine all the reasons that have been put forth. Therefore, I shall focus upon those generally acknowledged to be most weighty and influential, to see precisely wherein they fail. In this chapter we consider the claim that a more extensive state is justified, because necessary (or the best instrument) to achieve distributive justice; in the next chapter we shall take up diverse other claims.

The term "distributive justice" is not a neutral one. Hearing the term "distribution," most people presume that some thing or mechanism uses some principle or criterion to give out a supply of things. Into this process of distributing shares some error may have crept. So it is an open question, at least, whether *redistribution* should take place; whether we should do again what has already been done once, though poorly. However, we are not in the position of children who have been given portions of pie by someone who now makes last minute adjustments to rectify careless cutting. There is no *central* distribution, no person or group entitled to control all the resources, jointly deciding how they are to be doled out. What each person gets, he gets from others who give to him in exchange for something, or as a gift. In a free society, diverse persons control different resources, and new holdings arise out of the voluntary exchanges and actions of persons. There is no more a distributing or distribution of shares than there is a distributing of mates in a society in which persons choose whom they shall marry. The total result is the product of many individual decisions which the different individuals involved are entitled to make. Some uses of the term "distribution," it is true, do not imply a previous distributing appropriately judged by some criterion (for example, "probability distribution"); nevertheless, despite the title of this chapter, it would be best to use a terminology that clearly is neutral. We shall speak of people's holdings; a principle of justice in holdings describes (part of) what justice tells us (requires) about holdings. I shall state first what I take to be the correct view about justice in holdings, and then turn to the discussion of alternate views.

SECTION I

The Entitlement Theory

The subject of justice in holdings consists of three major topics. The first is the *original acquisition of holdings,* the appropriation of unheld things. This includes the issues of how unheld things may come to be held, the process, or processes, by which unheld things may come to be held, the things that may come to be held by these processes, the extent of what comes to be held by a particular process, and so on. We shall refer to the complicated truth about this topic, which we shall not formulate here, as the principle of justice in acquisition. The second topic concerns the *transfer of holdings* from one person to another. By what processes may a person transfer holdings to another? How may a person acquire a holding from another who holds it? Under this topic come general descriptions of voluntary exchange, and gift and (on the other hand) fraud, as well as reference to particular conventional details fixed upon in a given society. The complicated truth about this subject (with placeholders for conventional details) we shall call the principle of justice in transfer. (And we shall suppose it also includes principles governing how a person may divest himself of a holding, passing it into an unheld state.)

If the world were wholly just, the following inductive definition would exhaustively cover the subject of justice in holdings.

1. A person who acquires a holding in accordance with the principle of justice in acquisition is entitled to that holding.
2. A person who acquires a holding in accordance with the principle of justice in transfer, from someone else entitled to the holding, is entitled to the holding.
3. No one is entitled to a holding except by (repeated) applications of 1 and 2.

The complete principle of distributive justice would say simply that a distribution is just if everyone is entitled to the holdings they possess under the distribution.

A distribution is just if it arises from another just distribution by legitimate means. The legitimate means of moving from one distribution to another are specified by the principle of justice in transfer. The legitimate first "moves" are specified by the principle of justice in acquisition.[1] Whatever arises from a just situation by just steps is itself just. The means of change specified by the principle of justice in transfer preserve justice. As correct rules of inference are truth-preserving, and any conclusion deduced via repeated application of such rules from only true premises is itself true, so the means of transition from one situation to another specified by the principle of justice in transfer are justice-preserving, and any situation actually arising from repeated transitions in accordance with the principle from a just situation is itself just. The parallel between justice-preserving transformations and truth-preserving transformations illuminates where it fails as well as where it holds. That a conclusion could have been deduced by truth-preserving means from premises that are true suffices to show its truth. That from a just situation a situation *could* have arisen via justice-preserving means does *not* suffice to show its justice. The fact that a thief's victims voluntarily *could* have presented him with gifts does not entitle the thief to his ill-gotten gains. Justice in holdings is historical; it depends upon what actually has happened. We shall return to this point later.

Not all actual situations are generated in accordance with the two principles of justice in holdings: the principle of justice in acquisition and the principle of justice in transfer. Some people steal from others, or defraud them, or enslave them, seizing their product and preventing them from living as they choose, or forcibly exclude others from competing in exchanges. None of these are permissible modes of transition from one situation to another. And some persons acquire holdings by means not sanctioned by the principle of justice in acquisition. The existence of past injustice (previous violations of the first two principles of justice in holdings) raises the third major topic under justice in holdings: the rectification of injustice in holdings. If past injustice has shaped present holdings in various ways, some identifiable and some not, what now, if anything, ought to be done to rectify these injustices? What obligations do the performers of injustice have toward those whose position is worse than it would have been had the injustice not been done? Or, than it would have been had compensation been paid promptly? How, if at all, do things change if the beneficiaries and those made worse off are not the direct parties in the act of injustice, but, for example, their descendants? Is an injustice done to someone whose holding was itself based upon an unrectified injustice? How far back must one go in wiping clean the historical slate of injustices? What may victims of injustice permissibly do in order to rectify the injustices being done to them, including the many injustices done by persons acting through their government? I do not know of a thorough or theoretically sophisticated treatment of such issues. Idealizing greatly, let us suppose theoretical investigation will produce a principle of rectification. This principle uses historical information about previous situations and injustices done in them

---

1 Applications of the principle of justice in acquisition may also occur as part of the move from one distribution to another. You may find an unheld thing now and appropriate it. Acquisitions also are to be understood as included when, to simplify, I speak only of transitions by transfers.

(as defined by the first two principles of justice and rights against interference), and information about the actual course of events that flowed from these injustices, until the present, and it yields a description (or descriptions) of holdings in the society. The principle of rectification presumably will make use of its best estimate of subjunctive information about what would have occurred (or a probability distribution over what might have occurred, using the expected value) if the injustice had not taken place. If the actual description of holdings turns out not to be one of the descriptions yielded by the principle, then one of the descriptions yielded must be realized.[2]

The general outlines of the theory of justice in holdings are that the holdings of a person are just if he is entitled to them by the principles of justice in acquisition and transfer, or by the principle of rectification of injustice (as specified by the first two principles). If each person's holdings are just, then the total set (distribution) of holdings is just. To turn these general outlines into a specific theory we would have to specify the details of each of the three principles of justice in holdings: the principle of acquisition of holdings, the principle of transfer of holdings, and the principle of rectification of violations of the first two principles. I shall not attempt that task here. (Locke's principle of justice in acquisition is discussed below.)

Historical Principles and End-Results Principles

The general outlines of the entitlement theory illuminate the nature and defects of other conceptions of distributive justice. The entitlement theory of justice in distribution is *historical*; whether a distribution is just depends upon how it came about. In contrast, *current time-slice principles* of justice hold that the justice of a distribution is determined by how things are distributed (who has what) as judged by some *structural* principle(s) of just distribution. A utilitarian who judges between any two distributions by seeing which has the greater sum of utility and, if the sums tie, applies some fixed equality criterion to choose the more equal distribution, would hold a current time-slice principle of justice. As would someone who had a fixed schedule of trade-offs between the sum of happiness and equality. According to a current time-slice principle, all that needs to be looked at, in judging the justice of a distribution, is who ends up with what; in comparing any two distributions one need look only at the matrix presenting the distributions. No further information need be fed into a principle of justice. It is a consequence of such principles of justice that any two structurally identical distributions are equally just. (Two distributions are structurally identical if they present the same profile, but perhaps have different persons occupying the particular slots. My having ten and your having

---

2 If the principle of rectification of violations of the first two principles yields more than one description of holdings, then some choice must be made as to which of these is to be realized. Perhaps the sort of considerations about distributive justice and equality that I argue against play a legitimate role in *this* subsidiary choice. Similarly, there may be room for such considerations in deciding which otherwise arbitrary features a statute will embody, when such features are unavoidable because other considerations do not specify a precise line; yet a line must be drawn.

five, and my having five and your having ten are structurally identical distributions.) Welfare economics is the theory of current time-slice principles of justice. The subject is conceived as operating on matrices representing only current information about distribution. This, as well as some of the usual conditions (for example, the choice of distribution is invariant under relabeling of columns), guarantees that welfare economics will be a current time-slice theory, with all of its inadequacies.

Most persons do not accept current time-slice principles as constituting the whole story about distributive shares. They think it relevant in assessing the justice of a situation to consider not only the distribution it embodies, but also how that distribution came about. If some persons are in prison for murder or war crimes, we do not say that to assess the justice of the distribution in the society we must look only at what this person has, and that person has, and that person has, ... at the current time. We think it relevant to ask whether someone did something so that he *deserved* to be punished, deserved to have a lower share. Most will agree to the relevance of further information with regard to punishments and penalties. Consider also desired things. One traditional socialist view is that workers are entitled to the product and full fruits of their labor; they have earned it; a distribution is unjust if it does not give the workers what they are entitled to. Such entitlements are based upon some past history. No socialist holding this view would find it comforting to be told that because the actual distribution A happens to coincide structurally with the one he desires D, A therefore is no less just than D; it differs only in that the "parasitic" owners of capital receive under A what the workers are entitled to under D, and the workers receive under A what the owners are entitled to under D, namely very little. This socialist rightly, in my view, holds onto the notions of earning, producing, entitlement, desert, and so forth, and he rejects current time-slice principles that look only to the structure of the resulting set of holdings. (The set of holdings resulting from what? Isn't it implausible that how holdings are produced and come to exist has no effect at all on who should hold what?) His mistake lies in his view of what entitlements arise out of what sorts of productive processes.

We construe the position we discuss too narrowly by speaking of *current* time-slice principles. Nothing is changed if structural principles operate upon a time sequence of current time-slice profiles and, for example, give someone more now to counterbalance the less he has had earlier. A utilitarian or an egalitarian or any mixture of the two over time will inherit the difficulties of his more myopic comrades. He is not helped by the fact that *some* of the information others consider relevant in assessing a distribution is reflected, unrecoverably, in past matrices. Henceforth, we shall refer to such unhistorical principles of distributive justice, including the current time-slice principles, as *end-result principles* or *end-state principles*.

In contrast to end-result principles of justice, *historical principles* of justice hold that past circumstances or actions of people can create differential entitlements or differential deserts to things. An injustice can be worked by moving from one distribution to another structurally identical one, for the second, in profile the same, may violate people's entitlements or deserts; it may not fit the actual history.

Patterning

The entitlement principles of justice in holdings that we have sketched are historical principles of justice. To better understand their precise character, we shall distinguish them from another subclass of the historical principles. Consider, as an example, the principle of distribution according to moral merit. This principle requires that total distributive shares vary directly with moral merit; no person should have a greater share than anyone whose moral merit is greater. (If moral merit could be not merely ordered but measured on an interval or ratio scale, stronger principles could be formulated.) Or consider the principle that results by substituting "usefulness to society" for "moral merit" in the previous principle. Or instead of "distribute according to moral merit," or "distribute according to usefulness to society," we might consider "distribute according to the weighted sum of moral merit, usefulness to society, and need," with the weights of the different dimensions equal. Let us call a principle of distribution *patterned* if it specifies that a distribution is to vary along with some natural dimension, weighted sum of natural dimensions, or lexicographic ordering of natural dimensions. And let us say a distribution is patterned if it accords with some patterned principle. (I speak of natural dimensions, admittedly without a general criterion for them, because for any set of holdings some artificial dimensions can be gimmicked up to vary along with the distribution of the set.) The principle of distribution in accordance with moral merit is a patterned historical principle, which specifies a patterned distribution. "Distribute according to I.Q." is a patterned principle that looks to information not contained in distributional matrices. It is not historical, however, in that it does not look to any past actions creating differential entitlements to evaluate a distribution; it requires only distributional matrices whose columns are labeled by I.Q. scores. The distribution in a society, however, may be composed of such simple patterned distributions, without itself being simply patterned. Different sectors may operate different patterns, or some combination of patterns may operate in different proportions across a society. A distribution composed in this manner, from a small number of patterned distributions, we also shall term "patterned." And we extend the use of "pattern" to include the overall designs put forth by combinations of end-state principles.

Almost every suggested principle of distributive justice is patterned: to each according to his moral merit, or needs, or marginal product, or how hard he tries, or the weighted sum of the foregoing, and so on. The principle of entitlement we have sketched is *not* patterned.[3] There is no

---

3   One might try to squeeze a patterned conception of distributive justice into the framework of the entitlement conception, by formulating a gimmicky obligatory "principle of transfer" that would lead to the pattern. For example, the principle that if one has more than the mean income one must transfer everything one holds above the mean to persons below the mean so as to bring them up to (but not over) the mean. We can formulate a criterion for a "principle

one natural dimension or weighted sum or combination of a small number of natural dimensions that yields the distributions generated in accordance with the principle of entitlement. The set of holdings that results when some persons receive their marginal products, others win at gambling, others receive a share of their mate's income, others receive gifts from foundations, others receive interest on loans, others receive gifts from admirers, others receive returns on investment, others make for themselves much of what they have, others find things, and so on, will not be patterned. Heavy strands of patterns will run through it; significant portions of the variance in holdings will be accounted for by pattern-variables. If most people most of the time choose to transfer some of their entitlements to others only in exchange for something from them, then a large part of what many people hold will vary with what they held that others wanted. More details are provided by the theory of marginal productivity. But gifts to relatives, charitable donations, bequests to children, and the like, are not best conceived, in the first instance, in this manner. Ignoring the strands of pattern, let us suppose for the moment that a distribution actually arrived at by the operation of the principle of entitlement is random with respect to any pattern. Though the resulting set of holdings will be unpatterned, it will not be incomprehensible, for it can be seen as arising from the operation of a small number of principles. These principles specify how an initial distribution may arise (the principle of acquisition of holdings) and how distributions may be transformed into others (the principle of transfer of holdings). The process whereby the set of holdings is generated will be intelligible, though the set of holdings itself that results from this process will be unpatterned.

The writings of F. A. Hayek focus less than is usually done upon what patterning distributive justice requires. Hayek argues that we cannot know enough about each person's situation to distribute to each according to his moral merit (but would justice demand we do so if we did have this knowledge?); and he goes on to say, "our objection is against all attempts to impress upon society a deliberately chosen pattern of distribution, whether it be an order of equality or of inequality." However, Hayek concludes that in a free society there will be distribution in accordance with value rather than moral merit; that is, in accordance with the perceived value of a person's actions and services to others. Despite his rejection of a patterned conception of distributive justice, Hayek himself suggests a pattern he thinks justifiable: distribution in accordance with the perceived benefits given to others, leaving room for the complaint that a free society does not realize exactly this pattern. Stating this patterned strand of a free capitalist society more precisely,

---

of transfer" to rule out such obligatory transfers, or we can say that no correct principle of transfer, no principle of transfer in a free society will be like this. The former is probably the better course, though the latter also is true.

Alternatively, one might think to make the entitlement conception instantiate a pattern, by using matrix entries that express the relative strength of a person's entitlements as measured by some real-valued function. But even if the limitation to natural dimensions failed to exclude this function, the resulting edifice would *not* capture our system of entitlements to *particular* things.

we get "To each according to how much he benefits others who have the resources for benefiting those who benefit them." This will seem arbitrary unless some acceptable initial set of holdings is specified, or unless it is held that the operation of the system over time washes out any significant effects from the initial set of holdings. As an example of the latter, if almost anyone would have bought a car from Henry Ford, the supposition that it was an arbitrary matter who held the money then (and so bought) would not place Henry Ford's earnings under a cloud. In any event, *his* coming to hold it is not arbitrary. Distribution according to benefits to others *is* a major patterned strand in a free capitalist society, as Hayek correctly points out, but it is only a strand and does not constitute the whole pattern of a system of entitlements (namely, inheritance, gifts for arbitrary reasons, charity, and so on) or a standard that one should insist a society fit. Will people tolerate for long a system yielding distributions that they believe are unpatterned? No doubt people will not long accept a distribution they believe is *unjust,* People want their society to be and to look just. But must the look of justice reside in a resulting pattern rather than in the underlying generating principles? We are in no position to conclude that the inhabitants of a society embodying an entitlement conception of justice in holdings will find it unacceptable. Still, it must be granted that were people's reasons for transferring some of their holdings to others always irrational or arbitrary, we would find this disturbing. (Suppose people always determined what holdings they would transfer, and to whom, by using a random device.) We feel more comfortable upholding the justice of an entitlement system if most of the transfers under it are done for reasons. This does not mean necessarily that all deserve what holdings they receive. It means only that there is a purpose or point to someone's transferring a holding to one person rather than to another; that usually we can see what the transferrer thinks he's gaining, what cause he thinks he's serving, what goals he thinks he's helping to achieve, and so forth. Since in a capitalist society people often transfer holdings to others in accordance with how much they perceive these others benefiting them, the fabric constituted by the individual transactions and transfers is largely reasonable and intelligible.[4] (Gifts to loved ones, bequests to children, charity to the needy also are nonarbitrary components of the fabric.) In stressing the large strand of distribution in accordance with benefit to others, Hayek shows the point of many transfers, and so shows that the system of transfer of entitlements is not just spinning its gears aimlessly. The system of entitlements is defensible when constituted by the individual aims of individual transactions. No overarching aim is needed, no distributional pattern is required.

---

4 We certainly benefit because great economic incentives operate to get others to spend much time and energy to figure out how to serve us by providing things we will want to pay for. It is not mere paradox mongering to wonder whether capitalism should be criticized for most rewarding and hence encouraging, not individualists like Thoreau who go about their own lives, but people who are occupied with serving others and winning them as customers. But to defend capitalism one need not think businessmen are the finest human types. (I do not mean to join here the general maligning of businessmen, either.) Those who think the finest should acquire the most can try to convince their fellows to transfer resources in accordance with *that* principle.

To think that the task of a theory of distributive justice is to fill in the blank in "to each according to his _____" is to be predisposed to search for a pattern; and the separate treatment of "from each according to his _____" treats production and distribution as two separate and independent issues. On an entitlement view these are *not* two separate questions. Whoever makes something, having bought or contracted for all other held resources used in the process (transferring some of his holdings for these cooperating factors), is entitled to it. The situation is *not* one of something's getting made, and there being an open question of who is to get it. Things come into the world already attached to people having entitlements over them. From the point of view of the historical entitlement conception of justice in holdings, those who start afresh to complete "to each according to his _____" treat objects as if they appeared from nowhere, out of nothing. A complete theory of justice might cover this limit case as well; perhaps here is a use for the usual conceptions of distributive justice.

So entrenched are maxims of the usual form that perhaps we should present the entitlement conception as a competitor. Ignoring acquisition and rectification, we might say:

> From each according to what he chooses to do, to each according to what he makes for himself (perhaps with the contracted aid of others) and what others choose to do for him and choose to give him of what they've been given previously (under this maxim) and haven't yet expended or transferred.

This, the discerning reader will have noticed, has its defects as a slogan. So as a summary and great simplification (and not as a maxim with any independent meaning) we have:

> *From each as they choose, to each as they are chosen.*

How Liberty Upsets Patterns

It is not clear how those holding alternative conceptions of distributive justice can reject the entitlement conception of justice in holdings. For suppose a distribution favored by one of these non-entitlement conceptions is realized. Let us suppose it is your favorite one and let us call this distribution D_1; perhaps everyone has an equal share, perhaps shares vary in accordance with some dimension you treasure. Now suppose that Wilt Chamberlain is greatly in demand by basketball teams, being a great gate attraction. (Also suppose contracts run only for a year, with players being free agents.) He signs the following sort of contract with a team: In each home game, twenty-five cents from the price of each ticket of admission goes to him. (We ignore the question of whether he is "gouging" the owners, letting them look out for themselves.) The season starts, and people cheerfully attend his team's games; they buy their tickets, each time dropping a separate twenty-five cents of their admission price into a special box with Chamberlain's name on it. They are excited about seeing him play; it is worth the total admission price to them. Let us suppose that in one season one million persons attend his home games, and Wilt Chamberlain winds up with $250,000, a much larger sum than the average income and larger even than anyone else has. Is he entitled to this income? Is this new distribution D_2, unjust? If so, why? There is *no* question about whether each of the people was entitled to the control over the resources they held in D_1; because that was the distribution (your favorite) that (for the purposes of argument) we assumed was acceptable. Each of these persons *chose to* give twenty-five cents of their money to Chamberlain. They could have spent it on going to the movies, or on candy bars, or on copies of *Dissent* magazine, or of *Montly Review*. But they all, at least one million of them, converged on giving it to Wilt Chamberlain in exchange for watching him play basketball. If D_1 was a just distribution, and people voluntarily moved from it to D_2, transferring parts of their shares they were given under D_1 (what was it for if not to do something with?), isn't D_2 also just? If the people were entitled to dispose of the resources to which they were entitled (under D_1), didn't this include their being entitled to give it to, or exchange it with, Wilt Chamberlain? Can anyone else complain on grounds of justice? Each other person already has his legitimate share under D_1. Under D_1, there is nothing that anyone has that anyone else has a claim of justice against. After someone transfers something to Wilt Chamberlain, third parties *still* have their legitimate shares; *their* shares are not changed. By what process could such a transfer among two persons give rise to a legitimate claim of distributive justice on a portion of what was transferred, by a third party who had no claim of justice on any holding of the others *before* the transfer?[5] To cut off objections irrelevant here, we might imagine the exchanges occurring in a socialist society, after hours. After playing whatever basketball he does in his daily work, or doing whatever other daily work he does, Wilt Chamberlain decides to put in *overtime* to earn additional money. (First his work quota is set; he works time over that.) Or imagine it is a skilled juggler people like to see, who puts on shows after hours.

Why might someone work overtime in a society in which it is assumed their needs are satisfied? Perhaps because they care about things other than needs. I like to write in books that I read, and

---

5   Might not a transfer have instrumental effects on a third party, changing his feasible options? (But what if the two parties to the transfer independently had used their holdings in this fashion?) I discuss this question below, but note here that this question concedes the point for distributions of ultimate intrinsic noninstrumental goods (pure utility experiences, so to speak) that are transferrable. It also might be objected that the transfer might make a third party more envious because it worsens his position relative to someone else. I find it incomprehensible how this can be thought to involve a claim of justice. On envy, see Chapter 8.

Here and elsewhere in this chapter, a theory which incorporates elements of pure procedural justice might find what I say acceptable, *if* kept in its proper place; that is, if background institutions exist to ensure the satisfaction of certain conditions on distributive shares. But if these institutions are not themselves the sum or invisible-hand result of people's voluntary (nonaggressive) actions, the constraints they impose require justification. At no point does *our* argument assume any background institutions more extensive than those of the minimal night-watchman state, a state limited to protecting persons against murder, assault, theft, fraud, and so forth.

to have easy access to books for browsing at odd hours. It would be very pleasant and convenient to have the resources of Widener Library in my back yard. No society, I assume, will provide such resources close to each person who would like them as part of his regular allotment (under D_1). Thus, persons either must do without some extra things that they want, or be allowed to do something extra to get some of these things. On what basis could the inequalities that would eventuate be forbidden? Notice also that small factories would spring up in a socialist society, unless forbidden. I melt down some of my personal possessions (under D_1) and build a machine out of the material. I offer you, and others, a philosophy lecture once a week in exchange for your cranking the handle on my machine, whose products I exchange for yet other things, and so on. (The raw materials used by the machine are given to me by others who possess them under D_1, in exchange for hearing lectures.) Each person might participate to gain things over and above their allotment under D_1. Some persons even might want to leave their job in socialist industry and work full time in this private sector. I shall say something more about these issues in the next chapter. Here I wish merely to note how private property even in means of production would occur in a socialist society that did not forbid people to use as they wished some of the resources they are given under the socialist distribution D_1. The socialist society would have to forbid capitalist acts between consenting adults.

The general point illustrated by the Wilt Chamberlain example and the example of the entrepreneur in a socialist society is that no end-state principle or distributional patterned principle of justice can be continuously realized without continuous interference with people's lives. Any favored pattern would be transformed into one unfavored by the principle, by people choosing to act in various ways; for example, by people exchanging goods and services with other people, or giving things to other people, things the transferrers are entitled to under the favored distributional pattern. To maintain a pattern one must either continually interfere to stop people from transferring resources as they wish to, or continually (or periodically) interfere to take from some persons resources that others for some reason chose to transfer to them. (But if some time limit is to be set on how long people may keep resources others voluntarily transfer to them, why let them keep these resources for *any* period of time? Why not have immediate confiscation?) It might be objected that all persons voluntarily will choose to refrain from actions which would upset the pattern. This presupposes unrealistically (1) that all will most want to maintain the pattern (are those who don't, to be "reeducated" or forced to undergo "self-criticism"?), (2) that each can gather enough information about his own actions and the ongoing activities of others to discover which of his actions will upset the pattern, and (3) that diverse and far-flung persons can coordinate their actions to dovetail into the pattern. Compare the manner in which the market is neutral among persons' desires, as it reflects and transmits widely scattered information via prices, and coordinates persons' activities.

It puts things perhaps a bit too strongly to say that every patterned (or end-state) principle is liable to be thwarted by the voluntary actions of the individual parties transferring some of their shares they receive under the principle. For perhaps some *very* weak patterns are not so thwarted.[6] Any distributional pattern with any egalitarian component is overturnable by the voluntary actions of individual persons over time; as is every patterned condition with sufficient content so as actually to have been proposed as presenting the central core of distributive justice. Still, given the possibility that some weak conditions or patterns may not be unstable in this way, it would be better to formulate an explicit description of the kind of interesting and contentful patterns under discussion, and to prove a theorem about their instability. Since the weaker the patterning, the more likely it is that the entitlement system itself satisfies it, a plausible conjecture is that any patterning either is unstable or is satisfied by the entitlement system.

Locke's Theory of Acquisition

Before we turn to consider other theories of justice in detail, we must introduce an additional bit of complexity into the structure of the entitlement theory. This is best approached by considering Locke's attempt to specify a principle of justice in acquisition. Locke views property rights in an unowned object as originating through someone's mixing his labor with it. This gives rise to many questions. What are the boundaries of what labor is mixed with? If a private astronaut clears a place on Mars, has he mixed his labor with (so that he comes to own) the whole planet, the whole uninhabited universe, or just a particular plot? Which plot does an act bring under ownership? The minimal (possibly disconnected) area such that an act decreases entropy in that area, and not elsewhere? Can virgin land (for the purposes of ecological investigation by high-flying airplane) come under ownership by a Lockean process? Building a fence around a territory presumably would make one the owner of only the fence (and the land immediately underneath it).

Why does mixing one's labor with something make one the owner of it? Perhaps because one owns one's labor, and so one comes to own a previously unowned thing that becomes permeated with what one owns. Ownership seeps over into the rest. But why isn't mixing what I own with what I don't own a way of losing what I own rather than a way of gaining what I don't? If I own a can of tomato juice and spill it in the sea so that its molecules (made radioactive, so I can check

---

6 Is the patterned principle stable that requires merely that a distribution be Pareto-optimal? One person might give another a gift or bequest that the second could exchange with a third to their mutual benefit. Before the second makes this exchange, there is not Pareto-optimality. Is a stable pattern presented by a principle choosing that among the Pareto-optimal positions that satisfies some further condition C? It may seem that there cannot be a counterexample, for won't any voluntary exchange made away from a situation show that the first situation wasn't Pareto-optimal? (Ignore the implausibility of this last claim for the case of bequests.) But principles are to be satisfied over time, during which new possibilities arise. A distribution that at one time satisfies the criterion of Pareto-optimality might not do so when some new possibilities arise (Wilt Chamberlain grows up and starts playing basketball); and though people's activities will tend to move then to a new Pareto-optimal position, *this* new one need not satisfy the contentful condition C. Continual interference will be needed to insure the continual satisfaction of C. (The theoretical possibility of a pattern's being maintained by some invisible-hand process that brings it back to an equilibrium that fits the pattern when deviations occur should be investigated.)

this) mingle evenly throughout the sea, do I thereby come to own the sea, or have I foolishly dissipated my tomato juice? Perhaps the idea, instead, is that laboring on something improves it and makes it more valuable; and anyone is entitled to own a thing whose value he has created. (Reinforcing this, perhaps, is the view that laboring is unpleasant. If some people made things effortlessly, as the cartoon characters in *The Yellow Submarine* trail flowers in their wake, would they have lesser claim to their own products whose making didn't *cost* them anything?) Ignore the fact that laboring on something may make it less valuable (spraying pink enamel paint on a piece of driftwood that you have found). Why should one's entitlement extend to the whole object rather than just to the *added value* one's labor has produced? (Such reference to value might also serve to delimit the extent of ownership; for example, substitute "increases the value of" for "decreases entropy in" in the above entropy criterion.) No workable or coherent value-added property scheme has yet been devised, and any such scheme presumably would fall to objections (similar to those) that fell the theory of Henry George.

It will be implausible to view improving an object as giving full ownership to it, if the stock of unowned objects that might be improved is limited. For an object's coming under one person's ownership changes the situation of all others. Whereas previously they were at liberty (in Hohfeld's sense) to use the object, they now no longer are. This change in the siuation of others (by removing their liberty to act on a previously unowned object) need not worsen their situation. If I appropriate a grain of sand from Coney Island, no one else may now do as they will with *that* grain of sand. But there are plenty of other grains of sand left for them to do the same with. Or if not grains of sand, then other things.' Alternatively, the things I do with the grain of sand I appropriate might improve the position of others, counterbalancing their loss of the liberty to use that grain. The crucial point is whether appropriation of an unowned object worsens the situation of others.

Locke's proviso that there be "enough and as good left in common for others" (sect. 27) is meant to ensure that the situation of others is not worsened. (If this proviso is met is there any motivation for his further condition of nonwaste?) It is often said that this proviso once held but now no longer does. But there appears to be an argument for the conclusion that if the proviso no longer holds, then it cannot ever have held so as to yield permanent and inheritable property rights. Consider the first person Z for whom there is not enough and as good left to appropriate. The last person Y to appropriate left Z without his previous liberty to act on an object, and so worsened Z's situation. So Y's appropriation is not allowed under Locke's proviso. Therefore the next to last person X to appropriate left Y in a worse position, for X's act ended permissible appropriation. Therefore X's appropriation wasn't permissible. But then the appropriator two from last, W, ended permissible appropriation and so, since it worsened X's position, W's appropriation wasn't permissible. And so on back to the first person A to appropriate a permanent property right.

This argument, however, proceeds too quickly. Someone may be made worse off by another's appropriation in two ways: first, by losing the opportunity to improve his situation by a particular appropriation or any one; and second, by no longer being able to use freely (without appropriation) what he previously could. A *stringent* requirement that another not be made worse off by an appropriation would exclude the first way if nothing else counterbalances the diminution in opportunity, as well as the second. A *weaker* requirement would exclude the second way, though not the first. With the weaker requirement, we cannot zip back so quickly from Z to A, as in the above argument; for though person Z can no longer *appropriate*, there may remain some for him to *use* as before. In this case Y's appropriation would not violate the weaker Lockean condition. (With less remaining that people are at liberty to use, users might face more inconvenience, crowding, and so on; in that way the situation of others might be worsened, unless appropriation stopped far short of such a point.) It is arguable that no one legitimately can complain if the weaker provision is satisfied. However, since this is less clear than in the case of the more stringent proviso, Locke may have intended this stringent proviso by "enough and as good" remaining, and perhaps he meant the non-waste condition to delay the end point from which the argument zips back.

Is the situation of persons who are unable to appropriate (there being no more accessible and useful unowned objects) worsened by a system allowing appropriation and permanent property? Here enter the various familiar social considerations favoring private property: it increases the social product by putting means of production in the hands of those who can use them most efficiently (profitably); experimentation is encouraged, because with separate persons controlling resources, there is no one person or small group whom someone with a new idea must convince to try it out; private property enables people to decide on the pattern and types of risks they wish to bear, leading to specialized types of risk bearing; private property protects future persons by leading some to hold back resources from current consumption for future markets; it provides alternate sources of employment for unpopular persons who don't have to convince any one person or small group to hire them, and so on. These considerations enter a Lockean theory to support the claim that appropriation of private property satisfies the intent behind the "enough and as good left over" proviso, *not* as a utilitarian justification of property. They enter to rebut the claim that because the proviso is violated no natural right to private property can arise by a Lockean process. The difficulty in working such an argument to show that the proviso is satisfied is in fixing the appropriate base line for comparison. Lockean appropriation makes people no worse off than they would be *how?* This question of fixing the baseline needs more detailed investigation than we are able to give it here. It would be desirable to have an estimate of the general economic importance of original appropriation in order to see how much leeway there is for differing theories of appropriation and of the location of the baseline. Perhaps this importance can be measured by the percentage of all income that is based upon untransformed raw materials and given resources (rather than upon human actions), mainly rental income representing the unimproved value of land, and the price of raw material *in situ,* and by the percentage of current wealth which represents such income in the past.[7]

We should note that it is not only persons favoring *private* property who need a theory of how property rights legitimately originate. Those believing in collective property, for example those believing that a group of persons living in an area jointly own the territory, or its mineral resources, also must provide a theory of how such property rights arise; they must show why the persons living there have rights to determine what is done with the land and resources there that persons living elsewhere don't have (with regard to the same land and resources).

The Proviso

Whether or not Locke's particular theory of appropriation can be spelled out so as to handle various difficulties, I assume that any adequate theory of justice in acquisition will contain a proviso similar to the weaker of the ones we have attributed to Locke. A process normally giving rise to a permanent bequeathable property right in a previously unowned thing will not do so if the position of others no longer at liberty to use the thing is thereby worsened. It is important to specify *this* particular mode of worsening the situation of others, for the proviso does not encompass other modes. It does not include the worsening due to more limited opportunities to appropriate (the first way above, corresponding to the more stringent condition), and it does not include how I "worsen" a seller's position if I appropriate materials to make some of what he is selling, and then enter into competition with him. Someone whose appropriation otherwise would violate the proviso still may appropriate provided he compensates the others so that their situation is not thereby worsened; unless he does compensate these others, his appropriation will violate the proviso of the principle of justice in acquisition and will be an illegitimate one.[8] A theory of appropriation incorporating this Lockean proviso will handle correctly the cases (objections to the theory lacking the proviso) where someone appropriates the total supply of something necessary for life.[9]

---

7   I have not seen a precise estimate. David Friedman, *The Machinery of Freedom* (N.Y.: Harper & Row, 1973), pp. xiv, xv, discusses this issue and suggests 5 percent of U.S. national income as an upper limit for the first two factors mentioned. However he does not attempt to estimate the percentage of current wealth which is based upon such income in the past. (The vague notion of "based upon" merely indicates a topic needing investigation.)
8   Fourier held that since the process of civilization had deprived the members of society of certain liberties (to gather, pasture, engage in the chase), a socially guaranteed minimum provision for persons was justified as compensation for the loss (Alexander Gray, *The Socialist Tradition* (New York: Harper & Row, 1968), p. 188). But this puts the point too strongly. This compensation would be due those persons, if any, for whom the process of civilization was a *net loss,* for whom the benefits of civilization did not counterbalance being deprived of these particular liberties.
9   For example, Rashdall's case of someone who comes upon the only water in the desert several miles ahead of others who also will come to it and appropriates it all. Hastings Rashdall, "The Philosophical Theory of Property," in *Property, its Duties and Rights* (London: MacMillan, 1915).

A theory which includes this proviso in its principle of justice in acquisition must also contain a more complex principle of justice in transfer. Some reflection of the proviso about appropriation constrains later actions. If my appropriating all of a certain substance violates the Lockean proviso, then so does my appropriating some and purchasing all the rest from others who obtained it without otherwise violating the Lockean proviso. If the proviso excludes someone's appropriating all the drinkable water in the world, it also excludes his purchasing it all. (More weakly, and messily, it may exclude his charging certain prices for some of his supply.) This proviso (almost?) never will come into effect; the more someone acquires of a scarce substance which others want, the higher the price of the rest will go, and the more difficult it will become for him to acquire it all. But still, we can imagine, at least, that something like this occurs: someone makes simultaneous secret bids to the separate owners of a substance, each of whom sells assuming he can easily purchase more from the other owners; or some natural catastrophe destroys all of the supply of something except that in one person's possession. The total supply could not be permissibly appropriated by one person at the beginning. His later acquisition of it all does not show that the original appropriation violated the proviso (even by a reverse argument similar to the one above that tried to zip back from *Z* to *A*). Rather, it is the combination of the original appropriation *plus* all the later transfers and actions that violates the Lockean proviso.

Each owner's title to his holding includes the historical shadow of the Lockean proviso on appropriation. This excludes his transferring it into an agglomeration that does violate the Lockean proviso and excludes his using it in a way, in coordination with others or independently of them, so as to violate the proviso by making the situation of others worse than their baseline situation. Once it is known that someone's ownership runs afoul of the Lockean proviso, there are stringent limits on what he may do with (what it is difficult any longer unreservedly to call) "his property." Thus a person may not appropriate the only water hole in a desert and charge what he will. Nor may he charge what he will if he possesses one, and unfortunately it happens that all the water holes in the desert dry up, except for his. This unfortunate circumstance, admittedly no fault of his, brings into operation the Lockean proviso and limits his property rights.[10] Similarly, an

---

We should note Ayn Rand's theory of property rights ("Man's Rights" in *The Virtue of Selfishness* (New York: New American Library, 1964), p. 94), wherein these follow from the right to life, since people need physical things to live. But a right to life is not a right to whatever one needs to live; other people may have rights over these other things (see Chapter 3 of this book). At most, a right to life would be a right to have or strive for whatever one needs to live, provided that having it does not violate anyone else's rights. With regard to material things, the question is whether having it does violate any right of others. (Would appropriation of all unowned things do so? Would appropriating the water hole in Rashdall's example?) Since special considerations (such as the Lockean proviso) may enter with regard to material property, one *first* needs a theory of property rights before one can apply any supposed right to life (as amended above). Therefore the right to life cannot provide the foundation for a theory of property rights.

10 The situation would be different if his water hole didn't dry up, due to special precautions he took to prevent this. Compare our discussion of the case in the text with Hayek, *The Constitution of Liberty*, p. 136; and also with Ronald Hamowy, "Hayek's Concept of Freedom; A Critique," *New Individualist Review*, April 1961, pp. 28–31.

owner's property right in the only island in an area does not allow him to order a castaway from a shipwreck off his island as a trespasser, for this would violate the Lockean proviso.

Notice that the theory does not say that owners do have these rights, but that the rights are overridden to avoid some catastrophe. (Overridden rights do not disappear; they leave a trace of a sort absent in the cases under discussion.) There is no such external (and ad *hoc?*) overriding. Considerations internal to the theory of property itself, to its theory of acquisition and appropriation, provide the means for handling such cases. The results, however, may be coextensive with some condition about catastrophe, since the baseline for comparison is so low as compared to the productiveness of a society with private appropriation that the question of the Lockean proviso being violated arises only in the case of catastrophe (or a desert-island situation).

The fact that someone owns the total supply of something necessary for others to stay alive does *not* entail that his (or anyone's) appropriation of anything left some people (immediately or later) in a situation worse than the baseline one. A medical researcher who synthesizes a new substance that effectively treats a certain disease and who refuses to sell except on his terms does not worsen the situation of others by depriving them of whatever he has appropriated. The others easily can possess the same materials he appropriated; the researcher's appropriation or purchase of chemicals didn't make those chemicals scarce in a way so as to violate the Lockean proviso. Nor would someone else's purchasing the total supply of the synthesized substance from the medical researcher. The fact that the medical researcher uses easily available chemicals to synthesize the drug no more violates the Lockean proviso than does the fact that the only surgeon able to perform a particular operation eats easily obtainable food in order to stay alive and to have the energy to work. This shows that the Lockean proviso is not an "end-state principle"; it focuses on a particular way that appropriative actions affect others, and not on the structure of the situation that results.

Intermediate between someone who takes all of the public supply and someone who makes the total supply out of easily obtainable substances is someone who appropriates the total supply of something in a way that does not deprive the others of it. For example, someone finds a new substance in an out-of-the-way place. He discovers that it effectively treats a certain disease and appropriates the total supply. He does not worsen the situation of others; if he did not stumble upon the substance no one else would have, and the others would remain without it. However, as time passes, the likelihood increases that others would have come across the substance; upon this fact might be based a limit to his property right in the substance so that others are not below their baseline position; for example, its bequest might be limited. The theme of someone worsening another's situation by depriving him of something he otherwise would possess may also illuminate the example of patents. An inventor's patent does not deprive others of an object which would not exist if not for the inventor. Yet patents would have this effect on others who independently invent the object. Therefore, these independent inventors, upon whom the burden of proving independent discovery may rest, should not be excluded from utilizing their own invention as they wish (including selling it to others). Furthermore, a known inventor drastically lessens the chances of actual independent invention. For persons who know of an invention usually will not try to reinvent it, and the notion of independent discovery here would be murky at best. Yet we may assume that in the absence of the original invention, sometime later someone else would have come up with it. This suggests placing a time limit on patents, as a rough rule of thumb to approximate how long it would have taken, in the absence of knowledge of the invention, for independent discovery.

I believe that the free operation of a market system will not actually run afoul of the Lockean proviso. (Recall that crucial to our story in Part I of how a protective agency becomes dominant and a *de facto* monopoly is the fact that it wields force in situations of conflict, and is not merely in competition, with other agencies. A similar tale cannot be told about other businesses.) If this is correct, the proviso will not play a very important role in the activities of protective agencies and will not provide a significant opportunity for future state action. Indeed, were it not for the effects of previous *illegitimate* state action, people would not think the possibility of the proviso's being violated as of more interest than any other logical possibility. (Here I make an empirical historical claim; as does someone who disagrees with this.) This completes our indication of the complication in the entitlement theory introduced by the Lockean proviso.

MORALS AND THE CRIMINAL LAW

BY PATRICK DEVLIN

Patrick Devlin, "Morals and the Criminal Law," *The Enforcement of Morals*, pp. 66-82. Copyright © 1970 by Oxford University Press. Reprinted with permission.

TWELVE

The Report of the Committee on Homosexual Offences and Prostitution, generally known as the Wolfenden Report, is recognized to be an excellent study of two very difficult legal and social problems. But it has also a particular claim to the respect of those interested in jurisprudence; it does what law reformers so rarely do; it sets out clearly and carefully what in relation to its subjects it considers the function of the law to be.[1] Statutory additions to the criminal law are too often made on the simple principle that 'there ought to be a law against it'. The greater part of the law relating to sexual offences is the creation of statute and it is difficult to ascertain any logical relationship between it and the moral ideas which most of us uphold. Adultery, fornication, and prostitution are not, as the Report[2] points out, criminal offences: homosexuality between males is a criminal offence, but between females it is not. Incest was not an offence until it was declared so by statute only fifty years ago. Does the legislature select these offences haphazardly or are there some principles which can be used to determine what part of the moral law should be embodied in the criminal? There is, for example, being now considered a proposal to make A.I.D., that is, the practice of artificial insemination of a woman with the seed of a man who is not her husband, a criminal offence; if, as is usually the case, the woman is married, this is in

---

From *The Enforcement of Morals* by Patrick Devlin, published by Oxford University Press. © Oxford University Press 1965, reprinted by permission of the author and publisher.

1 The Committee's 'statement of juristic philosophy'(to quote Lord Pakenham) was considered by him in a debate in the House of Lords on 4 December 1957, reported in *Hansard Lords Debates,* vol. ccvi at 738; and also in the same debate by the Archbishop of Canterbury at 753 and Lord Denning at 806, The subject has also been considered by Mr. J. E Hail Williams in the *Law Quarterly Review,* January 1958, vol. lxxiv, p. 76.

2 Para. 14.

substance, if not in form, adultery. Ought it to be made punishable when adultery is not? This sort of question is of practical importance, for a law that appears to be arbitrary and illogical, in the end and after the wave of moral indignation that has put it on the statute book subsides, forfeits respect. As a practical question it arises more frequently in the field of sexual morals than in any other, but there is no special answer to be found in that field. The inquiry must be general and fundamental. What is the connection between crime and sin and to what extent, if at all, should the criminal law of England concern itself with the enforcement of morals and punish sin or immorality as such?

The statements of principle in the Wolfenden Report provide an admirable and modern starting-point for such an inquiry. In the course of my examination of them I shall find matter for criticism. If my criticisms are sound, it must not be imagined that they point to any shortcomings in the Report. Its authors were not, as I am trying to do, composing a paper on the jurisprudence of morality; they were evolving a working formula to use for reaching a number of practical conclusions. I do not intend to express any opinion one way or the other about these; that would be outside the scope of a lecture on jurisprudence. I am concerned only with general principles; the statement of these in the Report illuminates the entry into the subject and I hope that its authors will forgive me if I carry the lamp with me into places where it was not intended to go.

Early in the Report[3] the Committee put forward:

> Our own formulation of the function of the criminal law so far as it concerns the subjects of this enquiry. In this field, its function, as we see it, is to preserve public order and decency, to protect the citizen from what is offensive or injurious, and to provide sufficient safeguards against exploitation and corruption of others, particularly those who are specially vulnerable because they are young, weak in body or mind, inexperienced, or in a state of special physical, official or economic dependence.
>
> It is not, in our view, the function of the law to intervene in the private lives of citizens, or to seek to enforce any particular pattern of behaviour, further than is necessary to carry out the purposes we have outlined.

The Committee preface their most important recommendation[4]

> that homosexual behaviour between consenting adults in private should no longer be a criminal offence, [by stating the argument[5]] which we believe to be decisive, namely, the importance which society and the law ought to give to individual freedom of

---
3 Para. 13
4 Para. 62.
5 Para. 61.

choice and action in matters of private morality. Unless a deliberate attempt is to be made by society, acting through the agency of the law, to equate the sphere of crime with that of sin, there must remain a realm of private morality and immorality which is, in brief and crude terms, not the law's business. To say this is not to condone or encourage private immorality.

Similar statements of principle are set out in the chapters of the Report which deal with prostitution. No case can be sustained, the Report says, for attempting to make prostitution itself illegal.[6] The Committee refer to the general reasons already given and add: 'We are agreed that private immorality should not be the concern of the criminal law except in the special circumstances therein mentioned.' They quote[7] with approval the report of the Street Offences Committee,[8] which says: 'As a general proposition it will be universally accepted that the law is not concerned with private morals or with ethical sanctions.' It will be observed that the emphasis is on *private* immorality. By this is meant immorality which is not offensive or injurious to the public in the ways defined or described in the first passage which I quoted. In other words, no act of immorality should be made a criminal offence unless it is accompanied by some other feature such as indecency, corruption, or exploitation. This is clearly brought out in relation to prostitution: 'It is not the duty of the law to concern itself with immorality as such ... it should confine itself to those activities which offend against public order and decency or expose the ordinary citizen to what is offensive or injurious.'[9]

These statements of principle are naturally restricted to the subject-matter of the Report. But they are made in general terms and there seems to be no reason why, if they are valid, they should not be applied to the criminal law in general. They separate very decisively crime from sin, the divine law from the secular, and the moral from the criminal. They do not signify any lack of support for the law, moral or criminal, and they do not represent an attitude that can be called either religious or irreligious. There are many schools of thought among those who may think that morals are not the law's business. There is first of all the agnostic or free-thinker. He does not of course disbelieve in morals, nor in sin if it be given the wider of the two meanings assigned to it in the *Oxford English Dictionary* where it is defined as 'transgression against divine law or the principles of morality'. He cannot accept the divine law; that does not mean that he might not view with suspicion any departure from moral principles that have for generations been accepted by the society in which he lives; but in the end he judges for himself. Then there is the deeply religious person who feels that the criminal law is sometimes more of a hindrance than a help in the sphere

---

6 Para. 224.
7 Para. 227.
8 Cmd. 3231 (1928).
9 Para. 257.

of morality, and that the reform of the sinner—at any rate when he injures only himself—should be a spiritual rather than a temporal work. Then there is the man who without any strong feeling cannot see why, where there is freedom in religious belief, there should not logically be freedom in morality as well. All these are powerfully allied against the equating of crime with sin.

I must disclose at the outset that I have as a judge an interest in the result of the inquiry which I am seeking to make as a jurisprudent. As a judge who administers the criminal law and who has often to pass sentence in a criminal court, I should feel handicapped in my task if I thought that I was addressing an audience which had no sense of sin or which thought of crime as something quite different. Ought one, for example, in passing sentence upon a female abortionist to treat her simply as if she were an unlicenced midwife? If not, why not? But if so, is all the panoply of the law erected over a set of social regulations? I must admit that I begin with a feeling that a complete separation of crime from sin (I use the term throughout this lecture in the wider meaning) would not be good for the moral law and might be disastrous for the criminal. But can this sort of feeling be justified as a matter of jurisprudence? And if it be a right feeling, how should the relationship between the criminal and the moral law be stated? Is there a good theoretical basis for it, or is it just a practical working alliance, or is it a bit of both? That is the problem which I want to examine, and I shall begin by considering the standpoint of the strict logician. It can be supported by cogent arguments, some of which I believe to be unanswerable and which I put as follows.

Morals and religion are inextricably joined—the moral standards generally accepted in Western civilization being those belonging to Christianity. Outside Christendom other standards derive from other religions. None of these moral codes can claim any validity except by virtue of the religion on which it is based. Old Testament morals differ in some respects from New Testament morals. Even within Christianity there are differences. Some hold that contraception is an immoral practice and that a man who has carnal knowledge of another woman while his wife is alive is in all circumstances a fornicator; others, including most of the English-speaking world, deny both these propositions. Between the great religions of the world, of which Christianity is only one, there are much wider differences. It may or may not be right for the State to adopt one of these religions as the truth, to found itself upon its doctrines, and to deny to any of its citizens the liberty to practise any other. If it does, it is logical that it should use the secular law wherever it thinks it necessary to enforce the divine. If it does not, it is illogical that it should concern itself with morals as such. But if it leaves matters of religion to private judgment, it should logically leave matters of morals also. A State which refuses to enforce Christian beliefs has lost the right to enforce Christian morals.

If this view is sound, it means that the criminal law cannot justify any of its provisions by reference to the moral law. It cannot say, for example, that murder and theft are prohibited because they are immoral or sinful. The State must justify in some other way the punishments which it imposes on wrongdoers and a function for the criminal law independent of morals must be found.

MORALS AND THE CRIMINAL LAW

This is not difficult to do. The smooth functioning of society and the preservation of order require that a number of activities should be regulated. The rules that are made for that purpose and are enforced by the criminal law are often designed simply to achieve uniformity and convenience and rarely involve any choice between good and evil. Rules that impose a speed limit or prevent obstruction on the highway have nothing to do with morals. Since so much of the criminal law is composed of rules of this sort, why bring morals into it at all? Why not define the function of the criminal law in simple terms as the preservation of order and decency and the protection of the lives and property of citizens, and elaborate those terms in relation to any particular subject in the way in which it is done in the Wolfenden Report? The criminal law in carrying out these objects will undoubtedly overlap the moral law. Crimes of violence are morally wrong and they are also offences against good order; therefore they offend against both laws. But this is simply because the two laws in pursuit of different objectives happen to cover the same area. Such is the argument.

Is the argument consistent or inconsistent with the fundamental principles of English criminal law as it exists today? That is the first way of testing it, though by no means a conclusive one. In the field of jurisprudence one is at liberty to overturn even fundamental conceptions if they are theoretically unsound. But to see how the argument fares under the existing law is a good starting-point.

It is true that for many centuries the criminal law was much concerned with keeping the peace and little, if at all, with sexual morals. But it would be wrong to infer from that that it had no moral content or that it would ever have tolerated the idea of a man being left to judge for himself in matters of morals. The criminal law of England has from the very first concerned itself with moral principles. A simple way of testing this point is to consider the attitude which the criminal law adopts towards consent.

Subject to certain exceptions inherent in the nature of particular crimes, the criminal law has never permitted consent of the victim to be used as a defence. In rape, for example, consent negatives an essential element. But consent of the victim is no defence to a charge of murder. It is not a defence to any form of assault that the victim thought his punishment well deserved and submitted to it; to make a good defence the accused must prove that the law gave him the right to chastise and that he exercised it reasonably. Likewise, the victim may not forgive the aggressor and require the prosecution to desist; the right to enter a *nolle prosequi* belongs to the Attorney-General alone.

Now, if the law existed for the protection of the individual, there would be no reason why he should avail himself of it if he did not want it. The reason why a man may not consent to the commission of an offence against himself beforehand or forgive it afterwards is because it is an offence against society. It is not that society is physically injured; that would be impossible. Nor need any individual be shocked, corrupted, or exploited; everything may be done in private. Nor can it be explained on the practical ground that a violent man is a potential danger to others in the community who have therefore a direct interest in his apprehension and punishment as being necessary to their own protection. That would be true of a man whom the victim is prepared to forgive but not of one who gets his consent first; a murderer who acts only upon the consent, and maybe the request, of his victim is no menace to others, but he does threaten one of the great moral principles upon which society is based, that is, the sanctity of human life. There is only one explanation of what has hitherto been accepted as the basis of the criminal law and that is that there are certain standards of behaviour or moral principles which society requires to be observed; and the breach of them is an offence not merely against the person who is injured but against society as a whole.

Thus, if the criminal law were to be reformed so as to eliminate from it everything that was not designed to preserve order and decency or to protect citizens (including the protection of youth from corruption), it would overturn a fundamental principle. It would also end a number of specific crimes. Euthanasia or the killing of another at his own request, suicide, attempted suicide, and suicide pacts, duelling, abortion, incest between brother and sister, are all acts which can be done in private and without offence to others and need not involve the corruption or exploitation of others. Many people think that the law on some of these subjects is in need of reform, but no one hitherto has gone so far as to suggest that they should all be left outside the criminal law as matters of private morality. They can be brought within it only as a matter of moral principle. It must be remembered also that although there is much immorality that is not punished by the law, there is none that is condoned by the law. The law will not allow its processes to be used by those engaged in immorality of any sort. For example, a house may not be let for immoral purposes; the lease is invalid and would not be enforced. But if what goes on inside there is a matter of private morality and not the law's business, why does the law inquire into it all?

I think it is clear that the criminal law as we know it is based upon moral principle. In a number of crimes its function is simply to enforce a moral principle and nothing else. The law, both criminal and civil, claims to be able to speak about morality and immorality generally. Where does it get its authority to do this and how does it settle the moral principles which it enforces? Undoubtedly, as a matter of history, it derived both from Christian teaching. But I think that the strict logician is right when he says that the law can no longer rely on doctrines in which citizens are entitled to disbelieve. It is necessary therefore to look for some other source.

In jurisprudence, as I have said, everything is thrown open to discussion and, in the belief that they cover the whole field, I have framed three interrogatories addressed to myself to answer:

1. Has society the right to pass judgment at all on matters of morals? Ought there, in other words, to be a public morality, or are morals always a matter for private judgment?
2. If society has the right to pass judgment, has it also the right to use the weapon of the law to enforce it?

3. If so, ought it to use that weapon in all cases or only in some; and if only in some, on what principles should it distinguish?

I shall begin with the first interrogatory and consider what is meant by the right of society to pass a moral judgment, that is, a judgment about what is good and what is evil. The fact that a majority of people may disapprove of a practice does not of itself make it a matter for society as a whole. Nine men out of ten may disapprove of what the tenth man is doing and still say that it is not their business. There is a case for a collective judgment (as distinct from a large number of individual opinions which sensible people may even refrain from pronouncing at all if it is upon somebody else's private affairs) only if society is affected. Without a collective judgment there can be no case at all for intervention. Let me take as an illustration the Englishman's attitude to religion as it is now and as it has been in the past. His attitude now is that a man's religion is his private affair; he may think of another man's religion that it is right or wrong, true or untrue, but not that it is good or bad. In earlier times that was not so; a man was denied the right to practise what was thought of as heresy, and heresy was thought of as destructive of society.

The language used in the passages I have quoted from the Wolfenden Report suggests the view that there ought not to be a collective judgment about immorality *per se*. Is this what is meant by 'private morality' and 'individual freedom of choice and action'? Some people sincerely believe that homosexuality is neither immoral nor unnatural. Is the 'freedom of choice and action' that is offered to the individual, freedom to decide for himself what is moral or immoral, society remaining neutral; or is it freedom to be immoral if he wants to be? The language of the Report may be open to question, but the conclusions at which the Committee arrive answer this question unambiguously. If society is not prepared to say that homosexuality is morally wrong, there would be no basis for a law protecting youth from 'corruption' or punishing a man for living on the 'immoral' earnings of a homosexual prostitute, as the Report recommends.[10] This attitude the Committee make even clearer when they come to deal with prostitution. In truth, the Report takes it for granted that there is in existence a public morality which condemns homosexuality and prostitution. What the Report seems to mean by private morality might perhaps be better described as private behaviour in matters of morals.

This view—that there is such a thing as public morality—can also be justified by *a priori* argument. What makes a society of any sort is community of ideas, not only political ideas but also ideas about the way its members should behave and govern their lives; these latter ideas are its morals. Every society has a moral structure as well as a political one: or rather, since that might suggest two independent systems, I should say that the structure of every society is made up both of politics and morals. Take, for example, the institution of marriage. Whether a man should be allowed to take

---

10 Para. 76.

more than one wife is something about which every society has to make up its mind one way or the other. In England we believe in the Christian idea of marriage and therefore adopt monogamy as a moral principle. Consequently the Christian institution of marriage has become the basis of family life and so part of the structure of our society. It is there not because it is Christian. It has got there because it is Christian, but it remains there because it is built into the house in which we live and could not be removed without bringing it down. The great majority of those who live in this country accept it because it is the Christian idea of marriage and for them the only true one. But a non-Christian is bound by it, not because it is part of Christianity but because, rightly or wrongly, it has been adopted by the society in which he lives. It would be useless for him to stage a debate designed to prove that polygamy was theologically more correct and socially preferable; if he wants to live in the house, he must accept it as built in the way in which it is.

We see this more clearly if we think of ideas or institutions that are purely political. Society cannot tolerate rebellion; it will not allow argument about the rightness of the cause. Historians a century later may say that the rebels were right and the Government was wrong and a percipient and conscientious subject of the State may think so at the time. But it is not a matter which can be left to individual judgment.

The institution of marriage is a good example for my purpose because it bridges the division, if there is one, between politics and morals. Marriage is part of the structure of our society and it is also the basis of a moral code which condemns fornication and adultery. The institution of marriage would be gravely threatened if individual judgments were permitted about the morality of adultery; on these points there must be a public morality. But public morality is not to be confined to those moral principles which support institutions such as marriage. People do not think of monogamy as something which has to be supported because our society has chosen to organize itself upon it; they think of it as something that is good in itself and offering a good way of life and that it is for that reason that our society has adopted it. I return to the statement that I have already made, that society means a community of ideas; without shared ideas on politics, morals, and ethics no society can exist. Each one of us has ideas about what is good and what is evil; they cannot be kept private from the society in which we live. If men and women try to create a society in which there is no fundamental agreement about good and evil they will fail; if, having based it on common agreement, the agreement goes, the society will disintegrate. For society is not something that is kept together physically; it is held by the invisible bonds of common thought. If the bonds were too far relaxed the members would drift apart. A common morality is part of the bondage. The bondage is part of the price of society; and mankind, which needs society, must pay its price.

Common lawyers used to say that Christianity was part of the law of the land. That was never more than a piece of rhetoric as Lord Sumner said in *Bowman* v. *The Secular Society*.[11] What lay

---

11 (1917), A.C. 406, at 457.

behind it was the notion which I have been seeking to expound, namely that morals—and until a century or so ago no one thought it worth distinguishing between religion and morals—were necessary to the temporal order. In 1675 Chief Justice Hale said: 'To say that religion is a cheat is to dissolve all those obligations whereby civil society is preserved.'[12] In 1797 Mr. Justice Ashurst said of blasphemy that it was 'not only an offence against God but against all law and government from its tendency to dissolve all the bonds and obligations of civil society'.[13] By 1908 Mr. Justice Phillimore was able to say: 'A man is free to think, to speak and to teach what he pleases as to religious matters, but not as to morals'.[14]

You may think that I have taken far too long in contending that there is such a thing as public morality, a proposition which most people would readily accept, and may have left myself too little time to discuss the next question which to many minds may cause greater difficulty: to what extent should society use the law to enforce its moral judgments? But I believe that the answer to the first question determines the way in which the second should be approached and may indeed very nearly dictate the answer to the second question. If society has no right to make judgments on morals, the law must find some special justification for entering the field of morality: if homosexuality and prostitution are not in themselves wrong, then the onus is very clearly on the lawgiver who wants to frame a law against certain aspects of them to justify the exceptional treatment. But if society has the right to make a judgment and has it on the basis that a recognized morality is as necessary to society as, say, a recognized government, then society may use the law to preserve morality in the same way as it uses it to safeguard anything else that is essential to its existence. If therefore the first proposition is securely established with all its implications, society has a prima facie right to legislate against immorality as such.

The Wolfenden Report, not with standing that it seems to admit the right of society to condemn homosexuality and prostitution as immoral, requires special circumstances to be shown to justify the intervention of the law. I think that this is wrong in principle and that any attempt to approach my second interrogatory on these lines is bound to break down. I think that the attempt by the Committee does break down and that this is shown by the fact that it has to define or describe its special circumstances so widely that they can be supported only if it is accepted that the law *is* concerned with immorality as such.

The widest of the special circumstances are described as the provision of 'sufficient safeguards against exploitation and corruption of others, particularly those who are specially vulnerable because they are young, weak in body or mind, inexperienced, or in a state of special physical, official or economic dependence'.[15] The corruption of youth is a well-recognized ground for

---

12 *Taylor's Case*, 1 Vent. 293.
13 *R. v. Williams*, 26 St. Tr. 653, at 715.
14 *R. v. Boulter*, 72 J.P. 188.
15 Para. 13.

intervention by the State and for the purpose of any legislation the young can easily be defined. But if similar protection were to be extended to every other citizen, there would be no limit to the reach of the law. The 'corruption and exploitation of others' is so wide that it could be used to cover any sort of immorality which involves, as most do, the co-operation of another person. Even if the phrase is taken as limited to the categories that are particularized as 'specially vulnerable', it is so elastic as to be practically no restriction. This is not merely a matter of words. For if the words used are stretched almost beyond breaking-point, they still are not wide enough to cover the recommendations which the Committee make about prostitution.

Prostitution is not in itself illegal and the Committee do not think that it ought to be made so.[16] If prostitution is private immorality and not the law's business, what concern has the law with the ponce or the brothel-keeper or the householder who permits habitual prostitution? The Report recommends that the laws which make these activities criminal offences should be maintained or strengthened and brings them (so far as it goes into principle; with regard to brothels it says simply that the law rightly frowns on them) under the head of exploitation.[17] There may be cases of exploitation in this trade, as there are or used to be in many others, but in general a ponce exploits a prostitute no more than an impressario exploits an actress. The Report finds that 'the great majority of prostitutes are women whose psychological makeup is such that they choose this life because they find in it a style of living which is to them easier, freer and more profitable than would be provided by any other occupation. ... In the main the association between prostitute and ponce is voluntary and operates to mutual advantage'.[18] The Committee would agree that this could not be called exploitation in the ordinary sense. They say: 'It is in our view an over-simplification to think that those who live on the earnings of prostitution are exploiting the prostitute as such. What they are really exploiting is the whole complex of the relationship between prostitute and customer; they are, in effect, exploiting the human weaknesses which cause the customer to seek the prostitute and the prostitute to meet the demand'.[19]

All sexual immorality involves the exploitation of human weaknesses. The prostitute exploits the lust of her customers and the customer the moral weakness of the prostitute. If the exploitation of human weaknesses is considered to create a special circumstance, there is virtually no field of morality which can be defined in such a way as to exclude the law.

I think, therefore, that it is not possible to set theoretical limits to the power of the State to legislate against immorality. It is not possible to settle in advance exceptions to the general rule or to define inflexibly areas of morality into which the law is in no circumstances to be allowed to enter. Society is entitled by means of its laws to protect itself from dangers, whether from within or without. Here

---

16   Paras. 224. 285, and 318.
17   Paras. 302 and 320.
18   Para. 223.
19   Para. 306.

again I think that the political parallel is legitimate. The law of treason is directed against aiding the king's enemies and against sedition from within. The justification for this is that established government is necessary for the existence of society and therefore its safety against violent overthrow must be secured. But an established morality is as necessary as good government to the welfare of society. Societies disintegrate from within more frequently than they are broken up by external pressures. There is disintegration when no common morality is observed and history shows that the loosening of moral bonds is often the first stage of disintegration, so that society is justified in taking the same steps to preserve its moral code as it does to preserve its government and other essential institutions.[20] The suppression of vice is as much the law's business as the suppression of subversive activities; it is no more possible to define a sphere of private morality than it is to define one of private subversive activity. It is wrong to talk of private morality or of the law not being concerned with immorality as such or to try to set rigid bounds to the part which the law may play in the suppression of vice.

---

20 It is somewhere about this point in the argument that Professor Hart in *Law, Liberty and Morality* discerns a proposition which he describes as central to my thought. He states the proposition and his objection to it as follows (p. 51). 'He appears to move from the acceptable proposition that *some* shared morality is essential to the existence of any society [this I take to be the proposition on p. 75] to the unacceptable proposition that a society is identical with its morality as that is at any given moment of its history so that a change in its morality is tantamount to the destruction of a society. The former proposition might be even accepted as a necessary rather than an empirical truth depending on a quite plausible definition of society as a body of men who hold certain moral views in common. But the latter proposition is absurd. Taken strictly, it would prevent us saying that the morality of a given society had changed, and would compel us instead to say that one society had disappeared and another one taken its place. But it is only on this absurd criterion of what it is for the same society to continue to exist that it could be asserted without evidence that any deviation from a society's shared morality threatens its existence.' In conclusion (p. 82) Professor Hart condemns the whole thesis in the lecture as based on 'a confused definition of what a society is'.

I do not assert that *any* deviation from a society's shared morality threatens its existence any more than I assert that *any* subversive activity threatens its existence. I assert that they are both activities which are capable in their nature of threatening the existence of society so that neither can be put beyond the law.

For the rest, the objection appears to me to be all a matter of words. I would venture to assert, for example, that you cannot have a game without rules and that if there were no rules there would be no game. If I am asked whether that means that the game is 'identical' with the rules, I would be willing for the question to be answered either way in the belief that the answer would lead to nowhere. If I am asked whether a change in the rules means that one game has disappeared and another has taken its place, I would reply probably not, but that it would depend on the extent of the change.

Likewise I should venture to assert that there cannot be a contract without terms. Does this mean that an 'amended' contract is a 'new' contract in the eyes of the law? I once listened to an argument by an ingenious counsel that a contract, because of the substitution of one clause for another, had 'ceased to have effect' within the meaning of a statutory provision. The judge did not accept the argument; but if most of the fundamental terms had been changed, I daresay he would have done.

The proposition that I make in the text is that if (as I understand Professor Hart to agree, at any rate for the purposes of the argument) you cannot have a society without morality, the law can be used to enforce morality as something that is essential to a society. I cannot see why this proposition (whether it is right or wrong) should mean that morality can never be changed without the destruction of society, if morality is changed, the law can be changed. Professor Hart refers (p. 72) to the proposition as 'the use of legal punishment to freeze into immobility the morality dominant at a particular time in a society's existence.' One might as well say that the inclusion of a penal section into a statute prohibiting certain acts freezes the whole statute into immobility and prevents the prohibitions from ever being modified.

There are no theoretical limits to the power of the State to legislate against treason and sedition, and likewise I think there can be no theoretical limits to legislation against immorality. You may argue that if a man's sins affect only himself it cannot be the concern of society. If he chooses to get drunk every night in the privacy of his own home, is any one except himself the worse for it? But suppose a quarter or a half of the population got drunk every night, what sort of society would it be? You cannot set a theoretical limit to the number of people who can get drunk before society is entitled to legislate against drunkenness. The same may be said of gambling. The Royal Commission on Betting, Lotteries, and Gaming took as their test the character of the citizen as a member of society. They said: 'Our concern with the ethical significance of gambling is confined to the effect which it may have on the character of the gambler as a member of society. If we were convinced that whatever the degree of gambling this effect must be harmful we should be inclined to think that it was the duty of the State to restrict gambling to the greatest extent practicable.[21]

In what circumstances the State should exercise its power is the third of the interrogatories I have framed. But before I get to it I must raise a point which might have been brought up in any one of the three. How are the moral judgments of society to be ascertained? By leaving it until now, I can ask it in the more limited form that is now sufficient for my purpose. How is the law-maker to ascertain the moral judgments of society? It is surely not enough that they should be reached by the opinion of the majority; it would be too much to require the individual assent of every citizen. English law has evolved and regularly uses a standard which does not depend on the counting of heads. It is that of the reasonable man. He is not to be confused with the rational man. He is not expected to reason about anything and his judgment may be largely a matter of feeling. It is the viewpoint of the man in the street—or to use an archaism familiar to all lawyers—the man in the Clapham omnibus. He might also be called the right-minded man. For my purpose I should like to call him the man in the jury box, for the moral judgment of society must be something about which any twelve men or women drawn at random might after discussion be expected to be unanimous. This was the standard the judges applied in the days before Parliament was as active as it is now and when they laid down rules of public policy. They did not think of themselves as making law but simply as stating principles which every right-minded person would accept as valid. It is what Pollock called 'practical morality', which is based not on theological or philosophical foundations but 'in the mass of continuous experience half-consciously or unconsciously accumulated and embodied in the morality of common sense'. He called it also 'a certain way of thinking on questions of morality which we expect to find in a reasonable civilized man or a reasonable Englishman, taken at random'.[22]

---

21 (1951) Cmd. 8190, para. 159.
22 *Essays in Jurisprudence and Ethics* (Macmillan, 1882), pp. 278 and 353.

MORALS AND THE CRIMINAL LAW

Immorality then, for the purpose of the law, is what every right-minded person is presumed to consider to be immoral. Any immorality is capable of affecting society injuriously and in effect to a greater or lesser extent it usually does; this is what gives the law its *locus standi*. It cannot be shut out. But—and this brings me to the third question—the individual has a *locus standi* too; he cannot be expected to surrender to the judgment of society the whole conduct of his life. It is the old and familiar question of striking a balance between the rights and interests of society and those of the individual. This is something which the law is constantly doing in matters large and small. To take a very down-to-earth example, let me consider the right of the individual whose house adjoins the highway to have access to it; that means in these days the right to have vehicles stationary in the highway, sometimes for a considerable time if there is a lot of loading or unloading. There are many cases in which the courts have had to balance the private right of access against the public right to use the highway without obstruction. It cannot be done by carving up the highway into public and private areas. It is done by recognizing that each have rights over the whole; that if each were to exercise their rights to the full, they would come into conflict; and therefore that the rights of each must be curtailed so as to ensure as far as possible that the essential needs of each are safeguarded.

I do not think that one can talk sensibly of a public and private morality any more than one can of a public or private highway. Morality is a sphere in which there is a public interest and a private interest, often in conflict, and the problem is to reconcile the two. This does not mean that it is impossible to put forward any general statements about how in our society the balance ought to be struck. Such statements cannot of their nature be rigid or precise; they would not be designed to circumscribe the operation of the law-making power but to guide those who have to apply it. While every decision which a court of law makes when it balances the public against the private interest is an *ad hoc* decision, the cases contain statements of principle to which the court should have regard when it reaches its decision. In the same way it is possible to make general statements of principle which it may be thought the legislature should bear in mind when it is considering the enactment of laws enforcing morals.

I believe that most people would agree upon the chief of these elastic principles. There must be toleration of the maximum individual freedom that is consistent with the integrity of society. It cannot be said that this is a principle that runs all through the criminal law. Much of the criminal law that is regulatory in character—the part of it that deals with *malum prohibitum* rather than *malum in se*—is based upon the opposite principle, that is, that the choice of the individual must give way to the convenience of the many. But in all matters of conscience the principle I have stated is generally held to prevail. It is not confined to thought and speech; it extends to action, as is shown by the recognition of the right to conscientious objection in wartime; this example shows also that conscience will be respected even in times of national danger. The principle appears to me to be peculiarly appropriate to all questions of morals. Nothing should be punished by the law that does not lie beyond the limits of tolerance. It is not nearly enough to say that a majority dislike a practice; there must be a real feeling of reprobation. Those who are dissatisfied with the present law on homosexuality often say that the opponents of reform are swayed simply by disgust. If that were so it would be wrong, but I do not think one can ignore disgust if it is deeply felt and not manufactured. Its presence is a good indication that the bounds of toleration are being reached. Not everything is to be tolerated. No society can do without intolerance, indignation, and disgust; they are the forces behind the moral law, and indeed it can be argued that if they or something like them are not present, the feelings of society cannot be weighty enough to deprive the individual of freedom of choice. I suppose that there is hardly anyone nowadays who would not be disgusted by the thought of deliberate cruelty to animals. No one proposes to relegate that or any other form of sadism to the realm of private morality or to allow it to be practised in public or in private. It would be possible no doubt to point out that until a comparatively short while ago nobody thought very much of cruelty to animals and also that pity and kindliness and the unwillingness to inflict pain are virtues more generally esteemed now than they have ever been in the past. But matters of this sort are not determined by rational argument. Every moral judgment, unless it claims a divine source, is simply a feeling that no right-minded man could behave in any other way without admitting that he was doing wrong. It is the power of a common sense and not the power of reason that is behind the judgments of society. But before a society can put a practice beyond the limits of tolerance there must be a deliberate judgment that the practice is injurious to society. There is, for example, a general abhorrence of homosexuality. We should ask ourselves in the first instance whether, looking at it calmly and dispassionately, we regard it as a vice so abominable that its mere presence is an offence. If that is the genuine feeling of the society in which we live, I do not see how society can be denied the right to eradicate it. Our feeling may not be so intense as that. We may feel about it that, if confined, it is tolerable, but that if it spread it might be gravely injurious; it is in this way that most societies look upon fornication, seeing it as a natural weakness which must be kept within bounds but which cannot be rooted out. It becomes then a question of balance, the danger to society in one scale and the extent of the restriction in the other. On this sort of point the value of an investigation by such a body as the Wolfenden Committee and of its conclusions is manifest.

The limits of tolerance shift. This is supplementary to what I have been saying but of sufficient importance in itself to deserve statement as a separate principle which law-makers have to bear in mind. I suppose that moral standards do not shift; so far as they come from divine revelation they do not, and I am willing to assume that the moral judgments made by a society always remain good for that society. But the extent to which society will tolerate—I mean tolerate, not approve—departures from moral standards varies from generation to generation. It may be that over-all tolerance is always increasing. The pressure of the human mind, always seeking greater freedom of thought, is outwards against the bonds of society forcing their gradual relaxation. It may be that history is a tale of contraction and expansion and that all developed societies are on their way to dissolution. I must not speak of things I do not know; and anyway as a practical matter no society is willing to make provision for its own decay. I return therefore to the simple and observable fact that in matters of morals the limits of tolerance shift. Laws, especially those which are based on morals, are less easily moved. It follows as another good working principle that in any new matter of morals the law should be slow to act. By the next generation the swell of indignation may have abated and the law be left without the strong backing which it needs. But it is then difficult to alter the law without giving the impression that moral judgment is being weakened. This is now one of the factors that is strongly militating against any alteration to the law on homosexuality.

A third elastic principle must be advanced more tentatively. It is that as far as possible privacy should be respected. This is not an idea that has ever been made explicit in the criminal law. Acts or words done or said in public or in private are all brought within its scope without distinction in principle. But there goes with this a strong reluctance on the part of judges and legislators to sanction invasions of privacy in the detection of crime. The police have no more right to trespass than the ordinary citizen has; there is no general right of search; to this extent an Englishman's home is still his castle. The Government is extremely careful in the exercise even of those powers which it claims to be undisputed. Telephone tapping and interference with the mails afford a good illustration of this. A Committee of three Privy Councillors who recently inquired[23] into these activities found that the Home Secretary and his predecessors had already formulated strict rules governing the exercise of these powers and the Committee were able to recommend that they should be continued to be exercised substantially on the same terms. But they reported that the power was 'regarded with general disfavour'.

This indicates a general sentiment that the right to privacy is something to be put in the balance against the enforcement of the law. Ought the same sort of consideration to play any part in the formation of the law? Clearly only in a very limited number of cases. When the help of the law is invoked by an injured citizen, privacy must be irrelevant; the individual cannot ask that his right to privacy should be measured against injury criminally done to another. But when all who are involved in the deed are consenting parties and the injury is done to morals, the public interest in the moral order can be balanced against the claims of privacy. The restriction on police powers of investigation goes further than the affording of a parallel; it means that the detection of crime committed in private and when there is no complaint is bound to be rather haphazard and this is an additional reason for moderation. These considerations do not justify the exclusion of all private immorality from the scope of the law. I think that, as I have already suggested, the test of 'private behaviour' should be substituted for 'private morality' and the influence of the factor should be reduced from that of a definite limitation to that of a matter to be taken into account.

---

23 (1957) Cmd. 283.

Since the gravity of the crime is also a proper consideration, a distinction might well be made in the case of homosexuality between the lesser acts of indecency and the full offence, which on the principles of the Wolfenden Report it would be illogical to do.

The last and the biggest thing to be remembered is that the law is concerned with the minimum and not with the maximum; there is much in the Sermon on the Mount that would be out of place in the Ten Commandments. We all recognize the gap between the moral law and the law of the land. No man is worth much who regulates his conduct with the sole object of escaping punishment, and every worthy society sets for its members standards which are above those of the law. We recognize the existence of such higher standards when we use expressions such as 'moral obligation' and 'morally bound'. The distinction was well put in the judgment of African elders in a family dispute: 'We have power to make you divide the crops, for this is our law, and we will see this is done. But we have not power to make you behave like an upright man.'[24]

---

24 A case in the Saa-Katengo at Lialiu, August 1942, quoted in *The Judicial Process among the Barotse of Northern Rhodesia* by Max Gluckman (Manchester University Press, 1955), p. 172.

AFTER VIRTUE

CHAPTERS 1–3

BY ALASDAIR MACINTYRE

Alasdair MacIntyre, "Chapters 1-3," *After Virtue: A Study in Moral Theory*, pp. 1-35. Copyright © 2007 by University of Notre Dame Press. Reprinted with permission.

CHAPTER 1: A DISQUIETING SUGGESTION

Imagine that the natural sciences were to suffer the effects of a catastrophe. A series of environmental disasters are blamed by the general public on the scientists. Widespread riots occur, laboratories are burnt down, physicists are lynched, books and instruments are destroyed. Finally a Know-Nothing political movement takes power and successfully abolishes science teaching in schools and universities, imprisoning and executing the remaining scientists. Later still there is a reaction against this destructive movement and enlightened people seek to revive science, although they have largely forgotten what it was. But all that they possess are fragments: a knowledge of experiments detached from any knowledge of the theoretical context which gave them significance; parts of theories unrelated either to the other bits and pieces of theory which they possess or to experiment; instruments whose use has been forgotten; half-chapters from books, single pages from articles, not always fully legible because torn and charred. Nonetheless all these fragments are reembodied in a set of practices which go under the revived names of physics, chemistry and biology. Adults argue with each other about the respective merits of relativity theory, evolutionary theory and phlogiston theory, although they possess only a very partial knowledge of each. Children learn by heart the surviving portions of the periodic table and recite as incantations some of the theorems of Euclid. Nobody, or almost nobody, realizes that what they are doing is not natural science in any proper sense at all. For everything that they do and say conforms to certain canons of consistency and coherence and those contexts which would be needed to make sense of what they are doing have been lost, perhaps irretrievably.

In such a culture men would use expressions such as 'neutrino', 'mass', 'specific gravity', 'atomic weight' in systematic and often interrelated ways which would resemble in lesser or greater degrees the ways in which such expressions had been used in earlier times before scientific knowledge had been so largely lost. But many of the beliefs presupposed by the use of these expressions would have been lost and there would appear to be an element of arbitrariness and even of choice in their application which would appear very surprising to us. What would appear to be rival and competing premises for which no further argument could be given would abound. Subjectivist theories of science would appear and would be criticized by those who held that the notion of truth embodied in what they took to be science was incompatible with subjectivism.

This imaginary possible world is very like one that some science fiction writers have constructed. We may describe it as a world in which the language of natural science, or parts of it at least, continues to be used but is in a grave state of disorder. We may notice that if in this imaginary world analytical philosophy were to flourish, it would never reveal the fact of this disorder. For the techniques of analytical philosophy are essentially descriptive and descriptive of the language of the present at that. The analytical philosopher would be able to elucidate the conceptual structures of what was taken to be scientific thinking and discourse in the imaginary world in precisely the way that he elucidates the conceptual structures of natural science as it is.

Nor again would phenomenology or existentialism be able to discern anything wrong. All the structures of intentionality would be what they are now. The task of supplying an epistemological basis for these false simulacra of natural science would not differ in phenomenological terms from the task as it is presently envisaged. A Husserl or a Merleau-Ponty would be as deceived as a Strawson or a Quine.

What is the point of constructing this imaginary world inhabited by fictitious pseudo-scientists and real, genuine philosophy? The hypothesis which I wish to advance is that in the actual world which we inhabit the language of morality is in the same state of grave disorder as the language of natural science in the imaginary world which I described. What we possess, if this view is true, are the fragments of a conceptual scheme, pans which now lack those contexts from which their significance derived. We possess indeed simulacra of morality, we continue to use many of the key expressions. But we have—very largely, if not entirely—lost our comprehension, both theoretical and practical, or morality.

But how could this be so? The impulse to reject the whole suggestion out of hand will certainly be very strong. Our capacity to use moral language, to be guided by moral reasoning, to define our transactions with others in moral terms is so central to our view of ourselves that even to envisage the possibility of our radical incapacity in these respects is to ask for a shift in our view of what we are and do which is going to be difficult to achieve. But we do already know two things about the hypothesis which are initially important for us if we are to achieve such a shift in viewpoint. One is that philosophical analysis will not help us. In the real world the dominant philosophies of the present, analytical or phenomenological, will be as powerless to detect the disorders of moral thought and practice as they were impotent before the disorders of science in the imaginary world. Yet the powerlessness of this kind of philosophy does not leave us quite resourceless. For a prerequisite for understanding the present disordered state of the imaginary world was to understand its history, a history that had to be written in three distinct stages. The first stage was that in which the natural sciences flourished, the second that in which they suffered catastrophe and the third that in which they were restored but in damaged and disordered form. Notice that this history, being one of decline and fall, is informed by standards. It is not an evaluatively neutral chronicle. The form of the narrative, the division into stages, presuppose standards of achievement and failure, of order and disorder. It is what Hegel called philosophical history and what Collingwood took all successful historical writing to be. So that if we are to look for resources to investigate the hypothesis about morality which I have suggested, however bizarre and improbable it may appear to you now, we shall have to ask whether we can find in the type of philosophy and history propounded by writers such as Hegel and Collingwood—very different from each other as they are, of course—resources which we cannot find in analytical or phenomenological philosophy.

But this suggestion immediately brings to mind a crucial difficulty for my hypothesis. For one objection to the view of the imaginary world which I constructed, let alone to my view of the real world, is that the inhabitants of the imaginary world reached a point where they no longer realized the nature of the catastrophe which they had suffered. Yet surely an event of such striking world historical dimensions could not have been lost from view, so that it was both erased from memory and unrecoverable from historical records? And surely what holds of the fictitious world holds even more strongly of our own real world? If a catastrophe sufficient to throw the language and practice of morality into grave disorder had occurred, surely we should all know about it. It would indeed be one of the central facts of our history. Yet our history lies open to view, so it will be said, and no record of any such catastrophe survives. So my hypothesis must simply be abandoned. To this I must at the very least concede that it will have to be expanded, yet unfortunately at the outset expanded in such a way as to render it, if possible, initially even less credible than before. For the catastrophe will have to have been of such a kind that it was not and has not been—except perhaps by a very few—recognized as a catastrophe. We shall have to look not for a few brief striking events whose character is incontestably clear, but for a much longer, more complex and less easily identified process and probably one which by its very nature is open to rival interpretation. Yet the initial implausibility of this part of the hypothesis may perhaps be slightly lessened by another suggestion.

History by now in our culture means academic history, and academic history is less than two centuries old. Suppose it were the case that the catastrophe of which my hypothesis speaks had occurred before, or largely before, the founding of academic history, so that the moral and other evaluative presuppositions of academic history derived from the forms of the disorder which it brought about. Suppose, that is, that the standpoint of academic history is such that from its value-neutral viewpoint moral disorder must remain largely invisible. All that the historian—and what is true of the historian is characteristically true also of the social scientist—will be allowed to perceive by the canons and categories of his discipline will be one morality succeeding another: seventeenth-century Puritanism, eighteenth-century hedonism, the Victorian work-ethic and so on, but the very language of order and disorder will not be available to him. If this were to be so, it would at least explain why what I take to be the real world and its fate has remained unrecognized by the academic curriculum. For the forms of the academic curriculum would turn out to be among the symptoms of the disaster whose occurrence the curriculum does not acknowledge. Most academic history and sociology—the history of a Namier or a Hofstadter and the sociology of a Merton or a Lipset—are after all as far away from the historical standpoint of Hegel and Collingwood as most academic philosophy is from their philosophical perspective.

It may seem to many readers that as I have elaborated my initial hypothesis I have step by step deprived myself of very nearly all possible argumentative allies. But is not just this required by the hypothesis itself? For if the hypothesis is true, it will necessarily appear implausible, since one way of stating part of the hypothesis is precisely to assert that we are in a condition which almost nobody recognizes and which perhaps nobody at all can recognize fully. If my hypothesis appeared initially plausible, it would certainly be false. And at least if even to entertain this hypothesis puts me into an antagonistic stance, it is a very different antagonistic stance from that of, for example, modern radicalism. For the modern radical is as confident in the moral expression of his stances and consequently in the assertive uses of the rhetoric of morality as any conservative has ever been. Whatever else he denounces in our culture he is certain that it still possesses the moral resources which he requires in order to denounce it. Everything else may be, in his eyes, in disorder; but the language of morality is in order, just as it is. That he too may be being betrayed by the very language he uses is not a thought available to him. It is the aim of this book to make that thought available to radicals, liberals and conservatives alike. I cannot however expect to make it palatable; for if it is true, we are all already in a state so disastrous that there are no large remedies for it.

Do not however suppose that the conclusion to be drawn will turn out to be one of despair. *Angst* is an intermittently fashionable emotion and the misreading of some existentialist texts has turned despair itself into a kind of psychological nostrum. But if we are indeed in as bad a state as I take us to be, pessimism too will turn out to be one more cultural luxury that we shall have to dispense with in order to survive in these hard times.

I cannot of course deny, indeed my thesis entails, that the language and the appearances of morality persist even though the integral substance of morality has to a large degree been fragmented and then in part destroyed. Because of this there is no inconsistency in my speaking, as I shall shortly do, of contemporary moral attitudes and arguments. I merely pay to the present the courtesy of using its own vocabulary to speak of it.

CHAPTER 2: THE NATURE OF MORAL DISAGREEMENT TODAY AND THE CLAIMS OF EMOTIVISM

The most striking feature of contemporary moral utterance is that so much of it is used to express disagreements; and the most striking feature of the debates in which these disagreements are expressed is their interminable character. I do not mean by this just that such debates go on and on and on—although they do—but also that they apparently can find no terminus. There seems to be no rational way of securing moral agreement in our culture. Consider three examples of just such contemporary moral debate framed in terms of characteristic and well-known rival moral arguments:

1. (a) A just war is one in which the good to be achieved outweighs the evils involved in waging the war and in which a clear distinction can be made between combatants—whose lives are at stake—and innocent non-combatants. But in a modern war calculation of future escalation is never reliable and no practically applicable distinction between combatants and noncombatants can be made. Therefore no modern war can be a just war and we all now ought to be pacifists.
   (b) If you wish for peace, prepare for war. The only way to achieve peace is to deter potential aggressors. Therefore you must build up your armaments and make it clear that going to war on any particular scale is not necessarily ruled out by your policies. An inescapable part of making *this* clear is being prepared both to fight limited wars and to go not only to, but beyond, the nuclear brink on certain types of occasion. Otherwise you will not avoid war *and* you will be defeated.
   (c) Wars between the Great Powers are purely destructive; but wars waged to liberate oppressed groups, especially in the Third World, are a necessary and therefore justified means for destroying the exploitative domination which stands between mankind and happiness.
2. (a) Everybody has certain rights over his or her own person, including his or her own body. It follows from the nature of these rights that at the stage when the embryo is essentially part of the mother's body, the mother has a right to make her own uncoerced decision on whether she will have an abortion or not. Therefore abortion is morally permissible and ought to be allowed by law.
   (b) I cannot will that my mother should have had an abortion when she was pregnant with me, except perhaps if it had been certain that the embryo was dead or gravely damaged. But if I cannot will this in my own case, how can I consistently deny to others the right to life that I claim for myself? I would break the so-called Golden Rule unless I denied that a mother has in general a right to an abortion. I am not of course thereby committed to the view that abortion ought to be legally prohibited.

(c) Murder is wrong. Murder is the taking of innocent life. An embryo is an identifiable individual, differing from a newborn infant only in being at an earlier stage on the long road to adult capacities and, if any life is innocent, that of an embryo is. If infanticide is murder, as it is, abortion is murder. So abortion is not only morally wrong, but ought to be legally prohibited.

3. (a) Justice demands that every citizen should enjoy, so far as is possible, an equal opportunity to develop his or her talents and his or her other potentialities. But prerequisites for the provision of such equal opportunity include the provision of equal access to health care and to education. Therefore justice requires the governmental provision of health and educational services, financed out of taxation, and it also requires that no citizen should be able to buy an unfair share of such services. This in turn requires the abolition of private schools and private medical practice.

(b) Everybody has a right to incur such and only such obligations as he or she wishes, to be free to make such and only such contracts as he or she desires and to determine his or her own free choices. Physicians must therefore be free to practice on such terms as they desire and patients must be free to choose among physicians; teachers must be free to teach on such terms as they choose and pupils and parents to go where they wish for education. Freedom thus requires not only the existence of private practice in medicine and private schools in education, but also the abolition of those restraints on private practice which are imposed by licensing and regulation by such bodies as universities, medical schools, the A.M.A. and the state.

These arguments have only to be stated to be recognized as being widely influential in our society. They have of course their articulate expert spokesmen: Herman Kahn and the Pope, Che Guevara and Milton Friedman are among the authors who have produced variant versions of them. But it is their appearance in newspaper editorials and high-school debates, on radio talk shows and letters to congressmen, in bars, barracks and boardrooms, it is their typicality that makes them important examples here. What salient characteristics do these debates and disagreements share?

They are of three kinds. The first is what I shall call, adapting an expression from the philosophy of science, the conceptual incommensurability of the rival arguments in each of the three debates. Every one of the arguments is logically valid or can be easily expanded so as to be made so; the conclusions do indeed follow from the premises. But the rival premises are such that we possess no rational way of weighing the claims of one as against another. For each premise employs some quite different normative or evaluative concept from the others, so that the claims made upon us are of quite different kinds. In the first argument, for example, premises which invoke justice and innocence are at odds with premises which invoke success and survival; in the second, premises which invoke rights are at odds with those which invoke universalizability; in the third it is the claim of equality that is matched against that of liberty. It is precisely because there is in our society no established way of deciding between these claims that moral argument appears to be necessarily interminable. From our rival conclusions we can argue back to our rival premises; but when we do arrive at our premises argument ceases and the invocation of one premise against another becomes a matter of pure assertion and counter-assertion. Hence perhaps the slightly shrill tone of so much moral debate.

But that shrillness may have an additional source. For it is not only in arguments with others that we are reduced so quickly to assertion and counter-assertion; it is also in the arguments that we have within ourselves. For whenever an agent enters the forum of public debate he has already presumably, explicitly or implicitly, settled the matter in question in his own mind. Yet if we possess no unassailable criteria, no set of compelling reasons by means of which we may convince our opponents, it follows that in the process of making up our own minds we can have made no appeal to such criteria or such reasons. If I lack any good reasons to invoke against you, it must seem that I lack any good reasons. Hence it seems that underlying my own position there must be some non-rational decision to adopt that position. Corresponding to the interminability of public argument there is at least the appearance of a disquieting private arbitrariness. It is small wonder if we become defensive and therefore shrill.

A second, equally important, but contrasting, characteristic of these arguments is that they do none the less purport to be *impersonal* rational arguments and as such are usually presented in a mode appropriate to that impersonality. What is that mode? Consider two different ways in which I may provide backing for an injunction to someone else to perform some specific action. In the first type of case I say, 'Do so-and-so'. The person addressed replies, 'Why should I do so-and-so?' I reply, 'Because I wish it.' Here I have given the person addressed no reason to do what I command or request unless he or she independently possesses some particular reason for paying regard to my wishes. If I am your superior officer—in the police, say, or the army—or otherwise have power or authority over you, or if you love me or fear me or want something from me, then by saying 'Because I wish it' I have indeed given *you* a reason, although not perhaps a sufficient reason, for doing what it is that I enjoin. Notice that in this type of case whether my utterance gives you a reason or not depends on certain characteristics possessed at the time of hearing or otherwise learning of the utterance by you. What reason-giving force the injunction has depends in this way on the personal context of the utterance.

Contrast with this the type of case in which the answer to the question 'Why should I do so-and-so?' (after someone has said 'Do so-and-so') is not 'Because I wish it', but some such utterance as 'Because it would give pleasure to a number of people' or 'Because it is your duty'. In this type of case the reason given for action either is or is not a good reason for performing the action in question independently of who utters it or even of whether it is uttered at all. Moreover the appeal is to a type of consideration which is independent of the relationship between speaker and hearer. Its use presupposes the existence of *impersonal* criteria—the existence, independently of the preferences or attitudes of speaker and hearer, of standards of justice or generosity or duty. The particular link between the context of utterance and the force of the reason-giving which always holds in the case of expressions of personal preferences or desire is severed in the case of moral and other evaluative utterances.

This second characteristic of contemporary moral utterance and argument, when combined with the first, imparts a paradoxical air to contemporary moral disagreement. For if we attended solely to the first characteristic, to the way in which what at first appears to be argument relapses so quickly into unargued disagreement, we might conclude that there is nothing to such contemporary disagreements but a clash of antagonistic wills, each will determined by some set of arbitrary choices of its own. But this second characteristic, the use of expressions whose distinctive function in our language is to embody what purports to be an appeal to objective standards, suggests otherwise. For even if the surface appearance of argument is only a masquerade, the question remains 'Why *this* masquerade?' What is it about rational argument which is so important that it is the nearly universal appearance assumed by those who engage in moral conflict? Does not this suggest that the practice of moral argument in our culture expresses at least an aspiration to be or to become rational in this area of our lives?

A third salient characteristic of contemporary moral debate is intimately related to the first two. It is easy to see that the different conceptually incommensurable premises of the rival arguments deployed in these debates have a wide variety of historical origins. The concept of justice in the first argument has its roots in Aristotle's account of the virtues; the second argument's genealogy runs through Bismarck and Clausewitz to Machiavelli; the concept of liberation in the third argument has shallow roots in Marx, deeper roots in Fichte. In the second debate a concept of rights which has Lockean antecedents is matched against a view of universalizability which is recognizably Kantian and an appeal to the moral law which is Thomist. In the third debate an argument which owes debts to T.H. Green and to Rousseau competes with one which has Adam Smith as a grandfather. This catalogue of great names is suggestive; but it may be misleading in two ways. The citing of individual names may lead us to underestimate the complexity of the history and the ancestry of such arguments; and it may lead us to look for that history and that ancestry only in the writings of philosophers and theorists instead of in those intricate bodies of theory and practice which constitute human cultures, the beliefs of which are articulated by philosophers and theorists only in a partial and selective manner. But the catalogue of names does suggest how wide and heterogeneous the variety of moral sources is from which we have inherited. The surface rhetoric of our culture is apt to speak complacently of moral pluralism in this connection, but the notion of pluralism is too imprecise. For it may equally well apply to an ordered dialogue of intersecting viewpoints and to an unharmonious melange of ill-assorted fragments. The suspicion—and for the moment it can only be a suspicion—that it is the latter with which we have to deal is heightened when we recognize that all those various concepts which inform our moral discourse were originally at home in larger totalities of theory and practice in which they enjoyed a role and function supplied by contexts of which they have now been deprived. Moreover the concepts we employ have in at least some cases changed their character in the past three hundred years; the evaluative expressions we use have changed their meaning. In the transition from the variety of contexts in which they were originally at home to our own contemporary culture 'virtue' and 'justice' and 'piety' and 'duty' and even 'ought' have become other than they once were. How ought we to write the history of such changes?

It is in trying to answer this question that the connection between these features of contemporary moral debate and my initial hypothesis becomes clear. For if I am right in supposing that the language of morality passed from a state of order to a state of disorder, this passage will surely be reflected in—in part indeed will actually consist in—just such changes of meaning. Moreover, if the characteristics of our own moral arguments which I have identified—most notably the fact that we simultaneously and inconsistently treat moral argument as an exercise of our rational powers and as mere expressive assertion—are symptoms of moral disorder, we ought to be able to construct a true historical narrative in which at an earlier stage moral argument is very different in kind. Can we?

One obstacle to our so doing has been the persistently unhistorical treatment of moral philosophy by contemporary philosophers in both the writing about and the teaching of the subject. We all too often still treat the moral philosophers of the past as contributors to a single debate with a relatively unvarying subject-matter, treating Plato and Hume and Mill as contemporaries both of ourselves and of each other. This leads to an abstraction of these writers from the cultural and social milieus in which they lived and thought and so the history of their thought acquires a false independence from the rest of the culture. Kant ceases to be part of the history of Prussia, Hume is no longer a Scotsman. For from the standpoint of moral philosophy as *we* conceive it these characteristics have become irrelevances. Empirical history is one thing, philosophy quite another. But are we right in understanding the division between academic disciplines in the way that we conventionally do? Once again there seems to be a possible relationship between the history of moral discourse and the history of the academic curriculum.

Yet at this point it may rightly be retorted: You keep speaking of possibilities, of suspicions, of hypotheses. You allow that what you are suggesting will initially seem implausible. You are in this at least right. For all this resort to conjectures about history is unnecessary. The way in which you have stated the problem is misleading. Contemporary moral argument is rationally interminable, because *all* moral, indeed all evaluative, argument is and always must be rationally interminable. Contemporary moral disagreements of a certain kind cannot be resolved, because *no* moral disagreements of that kind in any age, past, present or future, can be resolved. What you present as a contingent feature of our culture, standing in need of some special, perhaps historical explanation, is a necessary feature of all cultures which possess evaluative discourse. This is a challenge which cannot be avoided at an early stage in this argument. Can it be defeated?

One philosophical theory which this challenge specifically invites us to confront is emotivism. Emotivism is the doctrine that all evaluative judgments and more specifically all moral judgments are *nothing but* expressions of preference, expressions of attitude or feeling, insofar as they are moral or evaluative in character. Particular judgments may of course unite moral and factual elements. 'Arson, being destructive of property, is wrong' unites the factual judgment that arson destroys property with the moral judgment that arson is wrong. But the moral element in such a judgment is always to be sharply distinguised from the factual. Factual judgments are true or false; and in the realm of fact there are rational criteria by means of which we may secure agreement as to what is true and what is false. But moral judgments, being expressions of attitude or feeling, are neither true nor false; and agreement in moral judgment is not to be secured by any rational method, for there are none. It is to be secured, if at all, by producing certain non-rational effects on the emotions or attitudes of those who disagree with one. We use moral judgments not only to express our own feelings and attitudes, but also precisely to produce such effects in others.

Emotivism is thus a theory which professes to give an account of *all* value judgments whatsoever. Clearly if it *is* true, *all* moral disagreement *is* rationally interminable; and clearly if that is true then certain of the features of contemporary moral debate to which I drew attention earlier do indeed have nothing to do with what is specifically contemporary. But is it true?

Emotivism has been presented by its most sophisticated protagonists hitherto as a theory about the meaning of the sentences which are used to make moral judgments. C.L. Stevenson, the single most important exponent of the theory, asserted that the sentence 'This is good' means roughly the same as 'I approve of this; do so as well', trying to capture by this equivalence both the function of the moral judgment as expressive of the speaker's attitudes and the function of the moral judgment as designed to influence the hearer's attitudes (Stevenson 1945, ch. 2). Other emotivists suggested that to say 'This is good' was to utter a sentence meaning roughly 'Hurrah for this!' But as a theory of the meaning of a certain type of sentence emotivism plainly fails for at least three very different reasons.

The first is that, if the theory is to elucidate the meaning of a certain class of sentences by referring to their function, when uttered, of expressing feelings or attitudes, an essential part of the theory will have to consist in an identification and characterization of the feelings or attitudes in question. On this subject proponents of the emotive theory are in general silent, and perhaps wisely. For all attempts so far to identify the relevant types of feelings or attitudes have found it impossible to avoid an empty circularity. 'Moral judgments express feelings or attitudes,' it is said. 'What kind of feelings or attitudes?' we ask. 'Feelings or attitudes of approval,' is the reply. 'What kind of approval?' we ask, perhaps remarking that approval is of many kinds. It is in answer to this question that every version of emotivism either remains silent or, by identifying the relevant kind of approval as moral approval—that is, the type of approval expressed by a specifically moral judgment—becomes vacuously circular.

It becomes easy to understand why the theory is vulnerable to this first type of criticism, if we consider two other reasons for rejecting it. One is that emotivism, as a theory of the meaning of a certain type of sentence, is engaged in an impossible task from the beginning, because it is dedicated to characterizing as equivalent in meaning two kinds of expression which, as we have already seen derive their distinctive function in our language in key part from the contrast and difference between them. I have already suggested that there are good reasons for distinguishing between what I called expressions of personal preference and evaluative (including moral) expressions, citing the way in which utterances of the first kind depend upon who utters them to whom for any reason-giving force that they may have, while utterances of the second kind are not similarly dependent for their reason-giving force on the context of utterance. This seems sufficient to show that there is some large difference in meaning between members of the two classes; yet the emotive theory wishes to make them equivalent in meaning. This is not just a mistake; it is a mistake that demands explanation. A sign of where explanation should be sought is found in a third defect of the emotive theory, considered as a theory of meaning.

The emotive theory, as we have seen, purports to be a theory about the meaning of sentences; but the expression of feeling or attitude is characteristically a function not of the meaning of sentences, but of their use on particular occassions. The angry schoolmaster, to use one of Gilbert Ryle's examples, may vent his feelings by shouting at the small boy who has just made an arithmetical mistake, 'Seven times seven equals forty-nine!' But the use of this sentence to express feelings or attitudes has nothing whatsoever to do with its meaning. This suggests that we should not simply rely on these objections to reject the emotive theory, but that we should rather consider whether it ought not to have been proposed as a theory about the *use*—understood as purpose or function—of members of a certain class of expressions rather than about their *meaning*-understood as including all that Frege intended by 'sense' and 'reference'.

Clearly the argument so far shows that when someone utters a moral judgment, such as 'This is right' or 'This is good', it does not mean the same as 'I approve of this; do so as well' or 'Hurrah for this!' or any of the other attempts at equivalence suggested by emotive theorists; but even if the meaning of such sentences were quite other than emotive theorists supposed, it might be plausibly claimed, if the evidence was adequate, that in using such sentences to *say* whatever they mean, the agent was in fact *doing* nothing other than expressing his feelings or attitudes and attempting to influence the feelings and attitudes of others. If the emotive theory thus interpreted were correct it would follow that the meaning and the use of moral expressions were, or at the very least had become, radically discrepant with each other. Meaning and use would be at odds in such a way that meaning would tend to conceal use. We could not safely infer what someone who uttered a moral judgment was doing merely by listening to what he said. Moreover the agent himself might well be among those for whom use was concealed by meaning. He might well, precisely because he was self-conscious about the meaning of the words that he used, be assured that he was appealing to independent impersonal criteria, when all that he was in fact doing was expressing his feelings to others in a manipulative way. How might such a phenomenon come to occur?

Let us in the light of such considerations disregard emotivism's claim to universality of scope; and let us instead consider emotivism as a theory which has been advanced in historically specific conditions. In the eighteenth century Hume embodied emotivist elements in the large and complex fabric of his total moral theory; but it is only in this century that emotivism has flourished as a theory on its own. And it did so as a response to a set of theories which flourished, especially in England, between 1903 and 1939. We ought therefore to ask whether emotivism as a theory may not have been both a response to, and in the very first instance, an account of *not*, as its protagonists indeed supposed, moral language as such, but moral language in England in the years after 1903 as and when that language was interpreted in accordance with that body of theory to the refutation of which emotivism was primarily dedicated. The theory in question borrowed from the early nineteenth century the name of 'intuitionism' and its immediate progenitor was G.E. Moore.

'I went up to Cambridge at Michaelmas 1902, and Moore's *Principia Ethica* came out at the end of my first year ... it was exciting, exhilarating, the beginning of a renaissance, the opening of a new heaven on a new earth.' So wrote John Maynard Keynes (quoted in Rosenbaum 1975, p. 52), and so in their own rhetorical modes Lytton Strachey and Desmond McCarthy and later Virginia Woolf, who struggled through *Principia Ethica* page by page in 1908, and a whole network of Cambridge and London friends and acquaintances. What opened the new heaven was Moore's quiet but apocalyptic proclamation in 1903 that after many centuries he had at last solved the problems of ethics by being the first philosopher to attend with sufficient care to the precise nature of the questions which it is the task of ethics to answer. What Moore believed that he had discovered by attending to the precise nature of these questions was threefold.

First that 'good' is the name of a simple indefinable property, a property different from that named by 'pleasant' or 'conducive to evolutionary survival' or any other natural property. Hence Moore speaks of good as a non-natural property. Propositions declaring this or that to be good are what Moore called 'intuitions'; they are incapable of proof or disproof and indeed no evidence or reasoning whatever can be adduced in their favor or disfavor. Although Moore disclaims any use of the word 'intuition' which might suggest the name of a faculty of intuition comparable to our power of vision, he none the less does compare good as a property with yellow as a property in such a way as to make verdicts that a given state of affairs is or is not good comparable to the simplest judgments of normal visual perception.

Secondly, Moore takes it that to call an action right is simply to say that of the available alternative actions it is the one which does or did as a matter of fact produce the most good. Moore is thus a utilitarian; every action is to be evaluated solely by its consequences, as compared with the consequences of alternative possible courses of action. And as with at least some other versions of utilitarianism it follows that no action is ever right or wrong *as such*. Anything whatsoever may under certain circumstances be permitted.

Thirdly, it turns out to be the case, in the sixth and final chapter of *Principia Ethica*, that 'personal affections and aesthetic enjoyments include *all* the greatest, and *by far* the greatest goods we can imagine . . . ' This is 'the ultimate and fundamental truth of Moral Philosophy'. The achievement of friendship and the contemplation of what is beautiful in nature or in art become certainly almost the sole and perhaps the sole justifiable ends of all human action.

We ought to notice immediately two crucial facts about Moore's moral theory. The first is that his three central positions are logically independent of each other. There would be no breach in consistency if one were to affirm any one of the three and deny the other two. One can be an intuitionist without being a utilitarian; most English intuitionists came to hold the view that there was a non-natural property of 'right' as well as of 'good' and held that to perceive that a certain type of action was 'right' was to see that one had at least a *prima facie* obligation to perform that type of action, independently of its consequences. Likewise a utilitarian has no necessary commitment to intuitionism. And neither utilitarians nor intuitionists have any necessary commitment to the values of Moore's sixth chapter. The second crucial fact is easy to see retrospectively: the first part of what Moore says is *plainly* false and the second and third parts are at the very least highly contentious. Moore's arguments at times are, it must seem now, *obviously* defective—he tries to show that 'good' is indefinable, for example, by relying on a bad dictionary definition of 'definition'—and a great deal is asserted rather than argued. And yet it is this to us plainly false, badly argued position which Keynes treated as 'the beginning of a renaissance', which Lytton Strachey declared to have 'shattered all writers on ethics from Aristotle and Christ to Herbert Spencer and Mr. Bradley' and which Leonard Woolf described as 'substituting for the religious and philosophical nightmares, delusions, hallucinations in which Jehovah, Christ and St. Paul, Plato, Kant and Hegel had entangled us, the fresh air and pure light of commonsense' (quoted in Gadd 1974).

This is great silliness of course; but it is the great silliness of highly intelligent and perceptive people. It is therefore worth asking if we can discern any clues as to why they accepted Moore's naive and complacent apocalypticism. One suggests itself. It is that the group who were to become Bloomsbury had already accepted the values of Moore's sixth chapter, but could not accept these as merely their own personal preferences. They felt the need to find objective and impersonal justification for rejecting all claims except those of personal intercourse and of the beautiful. What specifically were they rejecting? Not in fact the doctrines of Plato or St. Paul or any other of the great names in Woolf's or Strachey's catalogue of deliverance, but those names as symbols of the culture of the late nineteenth century. Sidgwick and Leslie Stephen are being dismissed along with Spencer and Bradley, and the whole of the past is envisaged as a burden that Moore has just helped them cast off. What was it about the moral culture of the late nineteenth century which made it a burden to be escaped from? That is a question to which an answer ought to be deferred, precisely because it is going to be forced on us more than once in the course of the argument and later on we shall be better equipped to answer it. But we ought to notice how dominant the theme of that rejection is in the lives and writings of the Woolfs, of Lytton Strachey, of Roger Fry. Keynes emphasized the rejection not only of the Benthamite version of utilitarianism and of Chrisitianity, but of all claims on behalf of social action conceived as a worthwhile end. What was left?

The answer is: a highly impoverished view of how 'good' may be used. Keynes gives examples of central topics of discussion among Moore's followers: 'If A was in love with B and believed that B reciprocated his feelings, whereas in fact B did not, but was in love with C, the state of affairs was certainly not as good as it would have been if A had been right, but was it worse or better than it would become if A discovered his mistake?' Or again: 'If A was in love with B under a misapprehension as to B's qualities, was this better or worse than A's not being in love at all?' How were such questions to be answered? By following Moore's prescriptions in precise fashion. Do you or do you not discern the presence or absence of the non-natural property of good in greater or lesser degree? And what if two observers disagree? Then, so the answer went, according to Keynes, either the two were focusing on different subject matters, without recognizing this, or one had perceptions superior to the other. But, of course, as Keynes tells us, what was really happening was something quite other: 'In practice, victory was with those who could speak with the greatest appearance of clear, undoubting conviction and could best use the accents of infallibility' and Keynes goes on to describe the effectiveness of Moore's gasps of incredulity and head-shaking, of Strachey's grim silences and of Lowes Dickinson's shrugs.

There is evident here precisely that gap between the meaning and purport of what was being said and the use to which utterance was being put to which our reinterpretation of emotivism drew attention. An acute observer at the time and Keynes himself retrospectively might well have put matters thus: these people take themselves to be identifying the presence of a non-natural property, which they call 'good'; but there is in fact no such property and they are doing no more and no other than expressing their feelings and attitudes, disguising the expression of preference and whim by an interpretation of their own utterance and behavior which confers upon it an objectivity that it does not in fact possess.

It is, I take it, no accident that the acutest of the modern founders of emotivism, philosophers such as F.P. Ramsey (in the 'Epilogue' to *The Foundation of Mathematics,* 1931), Austin Duncan-Jones and C.L. Stevenson, were pupils of Moore; it is not implausible to suppose that they did in fact confuse moral utterance at Cambridge (and in other places with a similar inheritance) after 1903 with moral utterance as such, and that they therefore presented what was in essentials a correct account of the former as though it were an account of the latter. Moore's followers had behaved as if their disagreements over what is good were being settled by an appeal to an objective and impersonal criterion; but in fact the stronger and psychologically more adroit will was prevailing. It is unsurprising that emotivists sharply distinguished between factual, including perceptual, disagreement and what Stevenson called 'disagreement in attitude'. But if the claims of emotivism, understood as claims about the use of moral utterance at Cambridge after 1903 and its heirs and successors in London and elsewhere rather than about the meaning of moral expressions at all times and places, seem remarkably cogent, it turns out to be for reasons which at first sight seem to undermine emotivism's universal claims and with them emotivism's apparent threat to my original thesis.

What makes emotivism convincing as a thesis about a certain kind of moral utterance at Cambridge after 1903 are certain features specific to that historical episode. Those whose evaluative utterances embodied Moore's interpretations of those utterances could not have been doing what they took themselves to be doing because of the falsity of Moore's thesis. But nothing whatsoever seems to follow about moral utterance in general. Emotivism on this account turns out to be an empirical thesis, or rather a preliminary sketch of an empirical thesis, presumably to be filled out later by psychological and sociological and historical observations, about those who continue to use moral and other evaluative expressions, as if they were governed by objective and impersonal criteria, when all grasp of any such criterion has been lost. We should therefore expect emotivist types of theory to arise in a specific local circumstance as a response to types of theory and practice which share certain key features of Moore's intuitionism. Emotivism thus understood turns out to be, as a cogent theory of use rather than a false theory of meaning, connected with one specific stage in moral development or decline, a stage which our own culture entered early in the present century.

I spoke earlier of emotivism as an account not only of moral utterance at Cambridge after 1903, but also of moral utterance 'in other places with a similar inheritance'. For it at once might be objected to my thesis that emotivism has been after all propounded in a variety of times, places and circumstances, and hence that my stress upon Moore's part in generating emotivism is mistaken. To this I should reply first that I am interested in emotivism only insofar as it has been a plausible and defensible thesis. Carnap's version of emotivism, for example—in which the characterization of moral utterances as expressions of feeling or attitude is a desperate attempt to find *some* status for them after his theory of meaning and his theory of science have expelled them from the realm of the factual and the descriptive—was based on the most meagre attention to their specific character. And secondly I should retort that there is an Oxford history beginning from Prichard's intuitionism to parallel Moore's Cambridge history and indeed that wherever something like emotivism is found to flourish it generally is the successor theory to views analogous to Moore's or Prichard's.

The scheme of moral decline which these remarks presuppose would, as I suggested earlier, be one which required the discrimination of three distinct stages; a first at which evaluative and more especially moral theory and practice embody genuine objective and impersonal standards which provide rational justification for particular policies, actions and judgments and which themselves in turn are susceptible of rational justification; a second stage at which there are unsuccessful attempts to maintain the objectivity and impersonality of moral judgments, but during which the project of providing rational justifications both by means of and for the standards continuously breaks down; and a third stage at which theories of an emotivist kind secure wide implicit acceptance because of a general implicit recognition in practice, though not in explicit theory, that claims to objectivity and impersonality cannot be made good.

Yet the very statement of this scheme is enough to suggest that the *general* claims of emotivism reinterpreted as a theory of use cannot be so easily put on one side. For a presupposition of the scheme of development which I have just sketched is that genuine objective and impersonal moral standards can in some way or other be rationally justified, even if in some cultures at some stages the possibility of such rational justification is no longer available. And this is what emotivism denies. What I have suggested to be the case by and large about our own culture—that in moral argument the apparent assertion of principles functions as a mask for expressions of personal preference—is what emotivism takes to be universally the case. Moreover it does so on grounds which require no general historical and sociological investigation of human cultures. For what emotivism asserts is in central part that there are and can be *no* valid rational justification for any claims that objective and impersonal moral standards exist and hence that there are no such standards. Its claim is of the same order as the claim that it is true of all cultures whatsoever that they lack witches. Purported witches there may be, but real witches there cannot have been, for there are none. So emotivism holds that purported rational justifications there may be, but real rational justifications there cannot have been, for there are none.

Emotivism thus rests upon a claim that every attempt, whether past or present, to provide a rational justification for an objective morality has in fact failed. It is a verdict upon the whole history of moral philosophy and as such obliterates the contrast between the present and the past embodied in my initial hypothesis. What emotivism however did fail to reckon with is the difference that it would make to morality if emotivism were not only true but also widely believed to be true. Stevenson, for example, understood very clearly that saying 'I disapprove of this; do so as well!' does not have the same force as saying 'That is bad!' He noted that a kind of prestige attaches to the latter, which does not attach to the former. What he did not note however—precisely because he viewed emotivism as a theory of meaning—is that the prestige derives from the fact that the use of 'That is bad!' implies an appeal to an objective and impersonal standard in a way in which 'I disapprove of this; do so as well!' does not. That is, if and insofar as emotivism is true, moral language is seriously misleading and, if and insofar as emotivism is justifiably believed, presumably the use of traditional and inherited moral language ought to be abandoned. This conclusion none of the emotivists drew; and it is clear that, like Stevenson, they failed to draw it because they miscontrued their own theory as a theory of meaning.

This is also of course why emotivism did not prevail within analytical moral philosophy. Analytical philosophers had defined the central task of philosophy as that of deciphering the meaning of key expressions in both everyday and scientific language; and since emotivism fails precisely as a theory of the *meaning* of moral expressions, analytical philosophers by and large rejected emotivism. Yet emotivism did not die and it is important to note how often in widely different modern philosophical contexts something very like emotivism's attempted reduction of morality to personal preference continually recurs in the writings of those who do not think of themselves as emotivists. The unrecognized philosophical power of emotivism is one clue to its cultural power. Within analytical moral philosophy the resistance to emotivism has arisen from the perception that moral reasoning does occur, that there can be logical linkages between various moral judgments of a kind that emotivism itself could not allow for ('therefore' and 'if... then ...' are obviously not used as expressions of feeling). Yet the most influential account of moral reasoning that emerged in response to this critique of emotivism was one according to which an agent can only justify a particular judgment by referring to some universal rule from which it may be logically derived, and can only justify that rule in turn by deriving it from some more general rule or principle; but on this view since every chain of reasoning must be finite, such a process of justificatory reasoning must always terminate with the assertion of some rule or principle for which no further reason can be given. 'Thus a complete justification of a decision would consist of a complete account of its effects together with a complete account of the principles which it observed, and the effect of observing those principles. ... If the enquirer still goes on asking "But why should I live like that?" then there is no further answer to give him, because we have already, *ex hypothesi,* said everything that could be included in the further answer' (Hare 1952, p. 69).

The terminus of justification is thus always, on this view, a not further to be justified choice, a choice unguided by criteria. Each individual implicitly or explicitly has to adopt his or her own first principles on the basis of such a choice. The utterance of any universal principle is in the end an expression of the preferences of an individual will and for that will its principles have and can have only such authority as it chooses to confer upon them by adopting them. Thus emotivism has not been left very far behind after all.

To this it might well be replied that I am only able to reach this conclusion by omitting to notice the wide variety of positive positions incompatible with emotivism taken within analytical moral philosophy. Such writing has characteristically been preoccupied with attempts to show that the notion of rationality itself supplies morality with a basis and a basis such that we have adequate grounds for rejecting emotivist and subjectivist accounts. Consider, it will be said, the variety of claims advanced not only by Hare, but also by Rawls, Donegan, Gert and Gewirth, to name only a few. About the arguments which are adduced in support of such claims I want to make two points. The first is that none of them in fact succeed. I shall later on—in Chapter 6—use Gewirth's argument as an exemplary case; he is to date the latest of such writers, he is self-consciously and scrupulously aware of the contributions of other analytical moral philosophers to the debate and his arguments therefore provide us with an ideal test case. If they do not succeed, that is strong evidence that the project of which they are a part is not going to succeed. And, as I shall show later, they do not succeed.

Secondly, it is very much to the point that such writers cannot agree among themselves either on what the character of moral rationality is or on the substance of the morality which is to be founded on that rationality. The diversity of contemporary moral debate and its interminability are indeed mirrored in the controversies of analytical moral philosophers. But if those who claim to be able to formulate principles on which rational moral agents ought to agree cannot secure agreement on the formulation of those principles from their colleagues who share their basic philosophical purpose and method, there is once again *prima facie* evidence that their project has failed, even before we have examined their particular contentions and conclusions. Each of them in his criticism offers testimony to the failure of his colleagues' constructions.

I therefore take it that we have no good reason to believe that analytical philosophy can provide any convincing escape from an emotivism the substance of which it so often in fact concedes, once that emotivism is understood as a theory of use rather than meaning. But it is not only analytical moral philosophy of which this is true. It also holds of certain at first sight very different moral philosophies in Germany and France. Nietzsche and Sartre deploy philosophical vocabularies which are in large part alien to the English-speaking philosophical world; and in style and rhetoric as well as in vocabulary each differs from the other as much as from analytical philosophy. Nonetheless when Nietzsche sought to indict the making of would-be objective moral judgments as the mask worn by the will-to-power of those too weak and slavish to assert themselves with archaic and aristocratic grandeur, and when Sartre tried to exhibit the bourgeois rationalist morality of the Third Republic as an exercise in bad faith by those who cannot tolerate the recognition of their own choices as the sole source of moral judgment, both conceded the substance of that for which emotivism contended. Both indeed saw themselves as by their analysis condemning conventional morality, while most English and American emotivists believed themselves to be doing no such thing. Both saw their own task as in part that of founding a new morality, but in the writings of both it is at this point that their rhetoric—very different as each is from the other—becomes cloudy and opaque, and metaphorical assertion replaces argument. The *Übermensch* and the Sartrian Existentialist-cum-Marxist belong in the pages of a philosophical bestiary rather than in serious discussion. Both by contrast are at their philosophically most powerful and cogent in the negative part of their critiques.

The appearance of emotivism in this variety of philosophical guises suggests strongly that it is indeed in terms of a confrontation with emotivism that my own thesis must be defined. For one way of framing my contention that morality is not what it once was is just to say that to a large degree people now think, talk and act *as if* emotivism were true, no matter what their avowed theoretical standpoint may be. Emotivism has become embodied in our culture. But of course in saying this I am not merely contending that morality is not what it once was, but also and more importantly that what once was morality has to some large degree disappeared—and that this marks a degeneration, a grave cultural loss. I am therefore committed to two distinct but related tasks.

The first is that of identifying and describing the lost morality of the past and of evaluating its claims to objectivity and authority; this is a task partly historical and partly philosophical. The second is that of making good my claim about the specific character of the modern age. For I have suggested that we live in a specifically emotivist culture, and if this is so we ought presumably to discover that a wide variety of our concepts and modes of behavior—and not only our explicitly moral debates and judgments—presuppose the truth of emotivism, if not at the level of self-conscious theorizing, at least in everyday practice. But is this so? To this latter issue I turn immediately.

CHAPTER 3: EMOTIVISM—SOCIAL CONTENT AND SOCIAL CONTEXT

A moral philosophy—and emotivism is no exception—characteristically presupposes a sociology. For every moral philosophy offers explicitly or implicitly at least a partial conceptual analysis of the relationship of an agent to his or her reasons, motives, intentions and actions, and in so doing generally presupposes some claim that these concepts are embodied or at least can be in the real social world. Even Kant, who sometimes seems to restrict moral agency to the inner realm of the noumenal, implies otherwise in his writings on law, history and politics. Thus it would generally be a decisive refutation of a moral philosophy to show that moral agency on its own account of the matter could never be socially embodied; and it also follows that we have not yet fully understood the claims of any moral philosophy until we have spelled out what its social embodiment would be. Some moral philosophers in the past, perhaps most, have understood this spelling out as itself one part of the task of moral philosophy. So, it scarcely needs to be said, Plato and Aristotle, so indeed also Hume and Adam Smith; but at least since Moore the dominant narrow conception of moral philosophy has ensured that the moral philosophers could ignore this task; as notably do the philosophical proponents of emotivism. We therefore must perform it for them.

What is the key to the social content of emotivism? It is the fact that emotivism entails the obliteration of any genuine distinction between manipulative and non-manipulative social relations. Consider the contrast between, for example, Kantian ethics and emotivism on this point. For Kant—and a parallel point could be made about many earlier moral philosophers—the difference between a human relationship uninformed by morality and one so informed is precisely the difference between one in which each person treats the other primarily as a means to his or her ends and one in which each treats the other as an end. To treat someone else as an end is to offer them what I take to be good reasons for acting in one way rather than another, but to leave it to them to evaluate those reasons. It is to be unwilling to influence another except by reasons which that other he or she judges to be good. It is to appeal to impersonal criteria of the validity of which each rational agent must be his or her own judge. By contrast, to treat someone else as a means is to seek to make him or her an instrument of my purposes by adducing whatever influences or considerations will in fact be effective on this or that occasion. The generalizations of the sociology and psychology of persuasion are what I shall need to guide me, not the standards of a normative rationality.

If emotivism is true, this distinction is illusory. For evaluative utterance can in the end have no point or use but the expression of my own feelings or attitudes and the transformation of the feelings and attitudes of others. I cannot genuinely appeal to impersonal criteria, for there are no impersonal criteria. I may think that I so appeal and others may think that I so appeal, but these thoughts will always be mistakes. The sole reality of distinctively moral discourse is the attempt of one will to align the attitudes, feelings, preference and choices of another with its own. Others are always means, never ends.

What then would the social world *look* like, if seen with emotivist eyes? And what would the social world *be* like, if the truth of emotivism came to be widely presupposed? The general form of the answer to these questions is now clear, but the social detail depends in part on the nature of particular social contexts; it will make a difference in what milieu and in the service of what particular and specific interests the distinction between manipulative and non-manipulative social relationships has been obliterated. William Gass has suggested that it was a principal concern of Henry James to examine the consequences of the obliteration of this distinction in the lives of a particular kind of rich European in *The Portrait of a Lady* (Gass 1971, pp. 181–90), that the novel turns out to be an investigation, in Gass's words, 'of what it means to be a consumer of persons, and of what it means to be a person consumed'. The metaphor of consumption acquires its appropriateness from the milieu; James is concerned with rich aesthetes whose interest is to fend off the kind of boredom that is so characteristic of modem leisure by contriving behavior in others that will be responsive to their wishes, that will feed their sated appetites. Those wishes may or may not be benevolent, but the distinction between characters who entertain themselves by willing the good of others and those who pursue the fulfilment of their desires without a concern for any good but their own—the difference in the novel between Ralph Touchett and Gilbert Osmond—is not as important to James as the distinction between a whole milieu in which the manipulative mode of moral instrumentalism has triumphed and one, such as the New England of *The Europeans,* of which this was not true. James was of course, at least in *The Portrait of a Lady,* concerned with only one restricted and carefully identified social milieu, with a particular kind of rich person at one particular time and place. But that does not at all diminish the importance of his achievement for this enquiry. It will in fact turn out that *The Portrait of a Lady* has a key place within a long tradition of moral commentary, earlier members of which are Diderot's *Le Neveu de Rameau* and Kierkegaard's *Enten-Eller.* The unifying preoccupation of that tradition is the condition of those who see in the social world nothing but a meeting place for individual wills, each with its own set of attitudes and preferences and who understand that world solely as an arena for the achievement of their own satisfaction, who interpret reality as a series of opportunities for their enjoyment and for whom the last enemy is boredom. The younger Rameau, Kierkegaard's 'A' and Ralph Touchett put this aesthetic attitude to work in very different environments, but the attitude is recognizably the same and even the environments have something in common. They are environments in which the problem of enjoyment arises in the context of leisure, in which large sums of money have created some social distance from the necessity of work. Ralph Touchett is rich, 'A' is comfortably off, Rameau is a parasite upon his rich patrons and clients. This is not to say that the realm of what Kierkegaard called the aesthetic is restricted to the rich and to their close neighbors; the rest of us often share the attitudes of the rich in fantasy and aspiration. Nor is it to say that the rich are all Touchetts or Osmonds or A's. But it is to suggest that if we are to understand fully the social context of that obliteration of the distinction between manipulative and non-manipulative social relationships which emotivism entails, we ought to consider some other social contexts too.

One which is obviously important is that provided by the life of organizations, of those bureaucratic structures which, whether in the form of private corporations or of government agencies, define the working tasks of so many of our contemporaries. One sharp contrast with the lives of the aesthetic rich secures immediate attention. The rich aesthete with a plethora of means searches restlessly for ends on which he may employ them; but the organization is characteristically engaged in a competitive struggle for scarce resources to put to the service of its predetermined ends. It is therefore a central responsibility of managers to direct and redirect their organizations' available resources, both human and non-human, as effectively as possible toward those ends. Every bureaucratic organization embodies some explicit or implicit definition of costs and benefits from which the criteria of effectiveness are derived. Bureaucratic rationality is the rationality of matching means to ends economically and efficiently.

This familiar—perhaps by now we may be tempted to think overfamiliar—thought we owe originally of course to Max Weber. And it at once becomes relevant that Weber's thought embodies just those dichotomies which emotivism embodies, and obliterates just those distinctions to which emotivism has to be blind. Questions of ends are questions of values, and on values reason is silent; conflict between rival values cannot be rationally settled. Instead one must simply choose—between parties, classes, nations, causes, ideals. *Entscheidung* plays the part in Weber's thought that choice of principles plays in that of Hare or Sarte. 'Values', says Raymond Aron in his exposition of Weber's view, 'are created by human decisions ...' and again he ascribes to Weber the view that 'each man's conscience is irrefutable' and that values rest on 'a choice whose justification is purely subjective' (Aron 1967, pp. 206-10 and p. 192). It is not surprising that Weber's understanding of values was indebted chiefly to Nietzsche and that Donald G. Macrae in his book on Weber (1974) calls him an existentialist; for while he holds that an agent may be more or less rational in acting consistently with his values, the choice of any one particular evaluative stance or commitment can be no more rational than that of any other. All faiths and all evaluations are equally non-rational; all are subjective directions given to sentiment and feeling. Weber is then, in the broader sense in which I have understood the term, an emotivist and his portrait of a bureaucratic authority is an emotivist portrait. The consequence of Weber's emotivism is that in his thought the contrast between power and authority, although paid lip-service to, is effectively obliterated as a special instance of the disappearance of the contrast between manipulative and non-manipulative social relations. Weber of course took himself to be distinguishing power from authority, precisely because authority serves ends, serves faiths. But, as Philip Rieff has acutely noted, 'Weber's ends, the *causes* there to be served, are means of acting; they cannot escape service to power' (Rieff 1975, p. 22). For on Weber's view no type of authority can appeal to rational criteria to vindicate itself except that type of bureaucratic authority which appeals precisely to its own *effectiveness*. And what this appeal reveals is that bureaucratic authority is nothing other than successful power.

Weber's general account of bureaucratic organizations has been subjected to much cogent criticism by sociologists who have analyzed the specific character of actual bureaucracies. It is therefore relevant to note that there is one area in which his analysis has been vindicated by experience and in which accounts of many sociologists who take themselves to have repudiated Weber's analysis in fact reproduce it. I am referring precisely to his account of *how managerial authority is justified* in bureaucracies. For those modern sociologists who have put in the forefront of their accounts of managerial behavior aspects ignored or underemphasized by Weber's—as, for example, Likert has emphasized the manager's need to influence the motives of his subordinates and March and Simon his need to ensure that those subordinates argue from premises which will produce agreement with his own prior conclusions—have still seen the manager's function as that of controlling behavior and suppressing conflict in such a way as to reinforce rather than to undermine Weber's account of managerial justification. Thus there is a good deal of evidence that actual managers do embody in their behavior this one key part of the Weberian conception of bureaucratic authority, a conception which presupposes the truth of emotivism.

The original of the character of the rich man committed to the aesthetic pursuit of his own enjoyment as drawn by Henry James was to be found in London and Paris in the last century; the original of the character of the manager portrayed by Max Weber was at home in Wilhelmine Germany; but both have by now been domesticated in all the advanced countries and more especially in the United States. The two characters may even on occasion be found in one and the same person who partitions his life between them. Nor are they marginal figures in the social drama of the present age. I intend this dramatic metaphor with some seriousness. There is a type of dramatic tradition—Japanese Noh plays and English medieval morality plays are examples—which possesses a set of stock characters immediately recognizable to the audience. Such characters partially define the possibilities of plot and action. To understand them is to be provided with a means of interpreting the behavior of the actors who play them, just because a similar understanding informs the intentions of the actors themselves; and other actors may define their parts with special reference to these central characters. So it is also with certain kinds of social role specific to certain particular cultures. They furnish recognizable characters and the ability to recognize them is socially crucial because a knowledge of the character provides an interpretation of the actions of those individuals who have assumed the character. It does so precisely because those individuals have used the very same knowledge to guide and to structure their behavior. *Characters* specified thus must not be confused with social roles in general. For they are a very special type of social role which places a certain kind of moral constraint on the personality of those who inhabit them in a way in which many other social roles do not. I choose the word 'character' for them precisely because of the way it links dramatic and moral associations. Many modern occupational roles—that of a dentist or that of a garbage collector, for example—are not *characters* in the way that that of a bureaucratic manager is; many modem status roles—that of a retired member of the lower middle class, for example—are not *characters* in the way that that of the modern leisured rich person is. In the case of a *character* role and personality fuse in a more specific way than in general; in the case of a *character* the possibilities of action are defined in a more limited way than in general. One of the key differences between cultures is in the extent to which roles are *characters*; but what is specific to each culture is in large and central part what is specific to its stock of *characters*. So the culture of Victorian England was partially defined by the *characters* of the Public School Headmaster, the Explorer and the Engineer; and that of Wilhelmine Germany was similarly defined by such *characters* as those of the Prussian Officer, the Professor and the Social Democrat.

Characters have one other notable dimension. They are, so to speak, the moral representatives of their culture and they are so because of the way in which moral and metaphysical ideas and theories assume through them an embodied existence in the social world. *Characters* are the masks worn *by* moral philosophies. Such theories, such philosophies, do of course enter into social life in numerous ways: most obviously perhaps as explicit ideas in books or sermons or conversations, or as symbolic themes in paintings or plays or dreams. But the distinctive way in which they inform the lives of *characters* can be illuminated by considering how *characters* merge what usually is thought to belong to the individual man or woman and what is usually thought to belong to social roles. Both individuals and roles can, and do, like *characters,* embody moral beliefs, doctrines and theories, but each does so in its own way. And the way in which *characters* do so can only be sketched by contrast with these.

It is by way of their intentions that individuals express bodies of moral belief in their actions. For all intentions presuppose more or less complex, more or less coherent, more or less explicit bodies of belief, sometimes of moral belief. So such small-scale actions as the mailing of a letter or the handing of a leaflet to a passer-by can embody intentions whose import derives from some large-scale project of the individual, a project itself intelligible only against the background of some equally large or even larger scheme of beliefs. In mailing a letter someone may be embarking on a type of entrepreneurial career whose specification requires belief in both the viability and the legitimacy of multinational corporations: in handing out a leaflet someone may be expressing his belief in Lenin's philosophy of history. But the chain of practical reasoning whose conclusions are expressed in such actions as the mailing of a letter or the distribution of a leaflet is in this type of case of course the individual's own; and the locus of that chain of reasoning, the context which makes the taking of each step part of an intelligible sequence, is that particular individual's history of action, belief, experience and interaction.

Contrast the quite different way in which a certain type of social role may embody beliefs so that the ideas, theories and doctrines expressed in and presupposed by the role may at least on some occasions be quite other than the ideas, theories and doctrines believed by the individual who inhabits the role. A Catholic priest in virtue of his role officiates at the mass, performs other rites and ceremonies and takes part in a variety of activities which embody or presuppose, implicitly or explicitly, the beliefs of Catholic Christianity. Yet a particular ordained individual who does all these things may have lost his faith and his own beliefs may be quite other than and at variance with those expressed in the actions presented by his role. The same type of distinction between role and individual can be drawn in many other cases. A trade union official in virtue of his role negotiates with employers' representatives and campaigns among his own membership in a way that generally and characteristically presupposes that trade union goals—higher wages, improvements in working conditions and the maintenance of employment *within* the present economic system—are legitimate goals for the working class and that trade unions are the appropriate instruments for achieving those goals. Yet a particular trade- union official may believe that trade unions are merely instruments for domesticating and corrupting the working class by diverting them from any interest in revolution. The beliefs that he has in his mind and heart are one thing; the beliefs that his role expresses and presupposes are quite another.

There are then many cases where there is a certain distance between role and individual and where consequently a variety of degrees of doubt, compromise, interpretation or cynicism may mediate the relationship of individual to role. With what I have called *characters* it is quite otherwise; and the difference arises from the fact that the requirements of a *character* are imposed from the outside, from the way in which others regard and use *characters* to understand and to evaluate themselves. With other types of social role the role may be adequately specified in terms of the institutions of whose structures it is a part and the relation to those institutions of the individuals who fill the roles. In the case of a *character* this is not enough. A *character* is an object of regard by the members of the culture generally or by some significant segment of them. He furnishes them with a cultural and moral ideal. Hence the demand is that in this type of case role and personality be fused. Social type and psychological type are required to coincide. The *character* morally legitimates a mode of social existence.

It is, I hope, now clear why I picked the examples that I did when I referred to Victorian England and Wilhelmine Germany. The Public School Headmaster in England and the Professor in Germany, to take only two examples, were not just social roles: they provided the moral focus for a whole cluster of attitudes and activities. They were able to discharge this function precisely because they incorporated moral and metaphysical theories and claims. Moreover these theories and claims had a certain degree of complexity and there existed within the community of Public School Headmasters and within the community of Professors public debate as to the significance of their role and function: Thomas Arnold's Rugby was not Edward Thring's Uppingham, Mommsen and Schmöller represented very different academic stances from that of Max Weber. But the articulation of disagreement was always within the context of that deep moral agreement which constituted the *character* that each individual embodied in his own way.

In our own time emotivism is a theory embodied in *characters* who all share the emotivist view of the distinction between rational and non-rational discourse, but who represent the embodiment of that distinction in very different social contexts. Two of these we have already noticed: the Rich Aesthete and the Manager. To these we must now add a third: the Therapist. The manager represents in his *character* the obliteration of the distinction between manipulative and nonmanipulative social relations; the therapist represents the same obliteration in the sphere of personal life. The manager treats ends as given, as outside his scope; his concern is with technique, with effectiveness in transforming raw materials into final products, unskilled labor into skilled labor, investment into profits. The therapist also treats ends as given, as outside his scope; his concern also is with technique, with effectiveness in transforming neurotic symptoms into directed energy, maladjusted individuals into well-adjusted ones. Neither manager nor therapist, in their roles as manager and therapist, do or are able to engage in moral debate. They are seen by themselves, and by those who see them with the same eyes as their own, as uncontested figures, who purport to restrict themselves to the realms in which rational agreement is possible—that is, of course from their point of view to the realm of fact, the realm of means, the realm of measurable effectiveness.

It is of course important that in our culture the concept of the therapeutic has been given application far beyond the sphere of psychological medicine in which it obviously has its legitimate place. In *The Triumph of the Therapeutic* (1966) and also in *To My Fellow Teachers* (1975) Philip Rieff has documented with devastating insight a number of the ways in which truth has been displaced as a value and replaced by psychological effectiveness. The idioms of therapy have invaded all too successfully such spheres as those of education and of religion. The types of theory involved in and invoked to justify such therapeutic modes do of course vary widely; but the mode itself is of far greater social significance than the theories which matter so much to its protagonists.

I have said of *characters* in general that they are those social roles which provide a culture with its moral definitions; it is crucial to stress that I do not mean by this that the moral beliefs expressed by and embodied in the *characters* of a particular culture will secure universal assent within that culture. On the contrary it is partly because they provide focal points for disagreement that they are able to perform their defining task. Hence the morally defining character of the managerial role in our own culture is evidenced almost as much by the variety of contemporary attacks upon managerial and manipulative modes of theory and practice as it is by allegiance to them. Those who persistently attack bureaucracy effectively reinforce the notion that it is in terms of a relationship to bureaucracy that the self has to define itself. Neo-Weberian organization theorists and the heirs of the Frankfurt School unwittingly collaborate as a chorus in the theatre of the present.

I do not want to suggest of course that there is anything peculiar to the present in this type of phenomenon. It is often and perhaps always through conflict that the self receives its social definition. This does not mean however, as some theorists have supposed, that the self is or becomes nothing but the social roles which it inherits. The self, as distinct from its roles, has a history and a social history and that of the contemporary emotivist self is only intelligible as the end product of a long and complex set of developments.

Of the self as presented by emotivism we must immediately note: that it cannot be simply or unconditionally identified with *any* particular moral attitude or point of view (including that of those *characters* which socially embody emotivism) just because of the fact that its judgments are in the end criterionless. The specifically modern self, the self that I have called emotivist, finds no limits set to that on which it may pass judgment for such limits could only derive from rational criteria for evaluation and, as we have seen, the emotivist self lacks any such criteria. Everything may be criticized from whatever standpoint the self has adopted, including the self's choice of standpoint to adopt. It is in this capacity of the self to evade any necessary identification with any particular contingent state of affairs that some modern philosophers, both analytical and existentialist, have seen the essence of moral agency. To be a moral agent is, on this view, precisely to be able to stand back from any and every situation in which one is involved, from any and every characteristic that one may possess, and to pass judgment on it from a purely universal and abstract point of view that is totally detached from all social particularity. Anyone and everyone can thus be a moral agent, since it is in the self and not in social roles or practices that moral agency has to be located. The contrast between this democratization of moral agency and the elitist monopolies of managerial and therapeutic expertise could not be sharper. Any minimally rational agent is to be accounted a moral agent; but managers and therapists enjoy their status in virtue of their membership within hierarchies of imputed skill and knowledge. In the domain of fact there are procedures for eliminating disagreement; in that of morals the ultimacy of disagreement is dignified by the title 'pluralism'.

This democratized self which has no necessary social content and no necessary social identity can then be anything, can assume any role or take any point of view, because it *is* in and for itself nothing. This relationship of the modern self to its acts and its roles has been conceptualized by its acutest and most perceptive theorists in what at first sight appear to be two quite different and incompatible ways. Sartre—I speak now only of the Sartre of the thirties and forties—has depicted the self as entirely distinct from any particular social role which it may happen to assume; Erving Goffman by contrast has liquidated the self into its role-playing, arguing that the self is no more than 'a peg' on which the clothes of the role are hung (Goffman 1959, p. 253). For Sartre the central error is to identify the self with its roles, a mistake which carries the burden of moral bad faith as well as of intellectual confusion; for Goffman the central error is to suppose that there *is* a substantial self over and beyond the complex presentations of role-playing, a mistake committed by those who wish to keep part of the human world 'safe from sociology'. Yet the two apparently contrasting views have much more in common that a first statement would lead one to suspect. In Goffman's anecdotal descriptions of the social world there is still discernible that ghostly 'I', the psychological peg to whom Goffman denies substantial selfhood, flitting evanescently from one solidly role-structured situation to another; and for Sartre the self's self-discovery is characterized as the discovery that the self is 'nothing', is not a substance but a set of perpetually open possibilities. Thus at a deep level a certain agreement underlies Sartre's and Goffman's surface disagreements; and they agree in nothing more than in this, that both see the self as entirely set over against the social world. For Goffman, for whom the social world is everything, the self is therefore nothing at all, it occupies no social space. For Sartre, whatever social space it occupies it does so only accidentally, and therefore he too sees the self as in no way an actuality.

What moral modes are open to the self thus conceived? To answer this question, we must first recall the second key characteristic of the emotivist self, its lack of any ultimate criteria. When I characterize it thus I am referring back to what we have already noticed, that whatever criteria or principles or evaluative allegiances the emotivist self may profess, they are to be construed as expressions of attitudes, preferences and choices which are themselves not governed by criterion, principle or value, since they underlie and are prior to all allegiance to criterion, principle or value. But from this it follows that the emotivist self can have no rational history in its transitions from one state of moral commitment to another. Inner conflicts are for it necessarily *au fond* the confrontation of one contingent arbitrariness by another. It is a self with no given continuities, save those of the body which is its bearer and of the memory which to the best of its ability gathers in its past. And we know from the outcome of the discussions of personal identity by Locke, Berkeley, Butler and Hume that neither of these separately or together are adequate to specify that identity and continuity of which actual selves are so certain.

The self thus conceived, utterly distinct on the one hand from its social embodiments and lacking on the other any rational history of its own, may seem to have a certain abstract and ghostly character. It is therefore worth remarking that a behaviorist account is as much or as little plausible of the self conceived in this manner as of the self conceived in any other. The appearance of an abstract and ghostly quality arises not from any lingering Cartesian dualism, but from the degree of contrast, indeed the degree of loss, that comes into view if we compare the emotivist self with its historical predecessors. For one way of re-envisaging the emotivist self is as having suffered a deprivation, a stripping away of qualities that were once believed to belong to the self. The self is now thought of as lacking any necessary social identity, because the kind of social identity that it once enjoyed is no longer available; the self is now thought of as criterionless, because the kind of *telos* in terms of which it once judged and acted is no longer thought to be credible. What kind of identity and what kind of *telos* were they?

In many pre-modern, traditional societies it is through his or her membership in a variety of social groups that the individual identifies himself or herself and is identified by others. I am brother, cousin and grandson, member of this household, that village, this tribe. These are not characteristics that belong to human beings accidentally, to be stripped away in order to discover 'the real me'. They are part of my substance, defining partially at least and sometimes wholly my obligations and my duties. Individuals inherit a particular space within an interlocking set of social relationships; lacking that space, they are nobody, or at best a stranger or an outcast. To know oneself as such a social person is however not to occupy a static and fixed position. It is to find oneself placed at a certain point on a journey with set goals; to move through life is to make progress—or to fail to make progress—toward a given end. Thus a completed and fulfilled life is an achievement and death is the point at which someone can be judged happy or unhappy. Hence the ancient Greek proverb: 'Call no man happy until he is dead.'

This conception of a whole human life as the primary subject of objective and impersonal evaluation, of a type of evaluation which provides the content for judgment upon the particular actions or projects of a given individual, is something that ceases to be generally available at some point in the progress—if we can call it such—towards and into modernity. It passes to some degree unnoticed, for it is celebrated historically for the most part not as loss, but as self-congratulatory gain, as the emergence of the individual freed on the one hand from the social bonds of those constraining hierarchies which the modern world rejected at its birth and on the other hand from what modernity has taken to be the superstitions of teleology. To say this is of course to move a little too quickly beyond my present argument; but it is to note that the peculiarly modern self, the emotivist self, in acquiring sovereignty in its own realm lost its traditional boundaries provided by a social identity and a view of human life as ordered to a given end.

Nonetheless, as I have already suggested, the emotivist self has its own kind of social definition. It is at home in—it is an integral part of—one distinctive type of social order, that which we in the so-called advanced countries presently inhabit. Its definition is the counterpart to the definition of those *characters* which inhabit and present the dominant social roles. The bifurcation of the contemporary social world into a realm of the organizational in which ends are taken to be given and are not available for rational scrutiny and a realm of the personal in which judgment and debate about values are central factors, but in which no rational social resolution of issues is available, finds its internalization, its inner representation in the relation of the individual self to the roles and *characters* of social life.

This bifurcation is itself an important clue to the central characteristics of modern societies and one which may enable us to avoid being deceived by their own internal political debates. Those debates are often staged in terms of a supposed opposition between individualism and collectivism, each appearing in a variety of doctrinal forms. On the one side there appear the self-defined protagonists of individual liberty, on the other the self-defined protagonists of planning and regulation, of the goods which are available through bureaucratic organization. But in fact what is crucial is that on which the contending parties agree, namely that there are only two alternative modes of social life open to us, one in which the free and arbitrary choices of individuals are sovereign and one in which the bureaucracy is sovereign, precisely so that it may limit the free and arbitrary choices of individuals. Given this deep cultural agreement, it is unsurprising that the politics of modern societies oscillate between a freedom which is nothing but a lack of regulation of individual behavior and forms of collectivist control designed only to limit the anarchy of self-interest. The consequences of a victory by one side or the other are often of the highest immediate importance; but, as Solzhenitzyn has understood so well, both ways of life are in the long run intolerable. Thus the society in which we live is one in which bureaucracy and individualism are partners as well as antagonists. And it is in the cultural climate of this bureaucratic individualism that the emotivist self is naturally at home.

The parallel between my treatment of what I have called the emotivist self and my treatment of emotivist theories of moral judgment—whether Stevensonian, Nietzschean or Sartrian—is now, I hope, clear. In both cases I have argued that we are confronted with what is intelligible only as the end-product of a process of historical change; in both cases I have confronted theoretical positions whose protagonists claim that what I take to be the historically produced characteristics of what is specifically modern are in fact the timelessly necessary characteristics of all and any moral judgment, of all and any selfhood. If my argument is correct we are not, although many of us have become or partly become, what Sartre and Goffman say we are, precisely because we are the last inheritors—so far—of a process of historical transformation.

This transformation of the self and its relationship to its roles from more traditional modes of existence into contemporary emotivist forms could not have occured of course if the forms of moral discourse, the language of morality, had not also been transformed at the same time. Indeed it is wrong to separate the history of the self and its roles from the history of the language which the self specifies and through which the roles are given expression. What we discover is a single history and not two parallel ones. I noted at the outset two central factors of contemporary moral utterance. One was the multifariousness and apparent incommensurability of the concepts invoked. The other was the assertive use of ultimate principles in attempts to close moral debate. To discover where these features of our discourse came from, how and why they are fashioned, is therefore an obvious strategy for my enquiry. To this task I now turn.

AFTER VIRTUE

CHAPTER 5

BY ALASDAIR MACINTYRE

Alasdair MacIntyre, "Chapter 5," *After Virtue: A Study in Moral Theory*, pp. 51-61. Copyright © 2007 by University of Notre Dame Press. Reprinted with permission.

FOURTEEN

WHY THE ENLIGHTENMENT PROJECT OF JUSTIFYING MORALITY HAD TO FAIL

So far I have presented the failure of the project of justifying morality merely as the failure of a succession of particular arguments; and if that were all that there was to the matter, it might appear that the trouble was merely that Kierkegaard, Kant, Diderot, Hume, Smith and their other contemporaries were not adroit enough in constructing arguments, so that an appropriate strategy would be to wait until some more powerful mind applied itself to the problems. And just this has been the strategy of the academic philosophical world, even though many professional philosophers might be a little embarrassed to admit it. But suppose in fact, what is eminently plausible, that the failure of the eighteenth and nineteenth-century project was of quite another kind. Suppose that the arguments of Kierkegaard, Kant, Diderot, Hume, Smith and the like fail because of certain shared characteristics deriving from their highly specific shared historical background. Suppose that we cannot understand them as contributors to a timeless debate about morality, but only as the inheritors of a very specific and particular scheme of moral beliefs, a scheme whose internal incoherence ensured the failure of the common philosophical project from the outset.

Consider certain beliefs shared by all the contributors to the project. All of them, as I noted earlier, agree to a surprising degree on the content and character of the precepts which constitute genuine morality. Marriage and the family are *au fond* as unquestioned by Diderot's rationalist *philosophe* as they are by Kierkegaard's Judge Wilhelm; promise-keeping and justice are as inviolable for Hume as they are for Kant. Whence did they inherit these shared beliefs? Obviously from their shared Christian past compared with which the divergences between Kant's and Kierkegaard's Lutheran, Hume's Presbyterian and Diderot's Jansenist-influenced Catholic background are relatively unimportant.

At the same time as they agree largely on the character of morality, they agree also upon what a rational justification of morality would have to be. Its key premises would characterize some feature or features of human nature; and the rules of morality would then be explained and justified as being those rules which a being possessing just such a human nature could be expected to accept. For Diderot and Hume the relevant features of human nature are characteristics of the passions; for Kant the relevant feature of human nature is the universal and categorical character of certain rules of reason. (Kant of course denies that morality is 'based on human nature', but what he means by 'human nature' is merely the physiological non-rational side of man.) Kierkegaard no longer attempts *to justify* morality at all; but his account has precisely the same structure as that which is shared by the accounts of Kant, Hume and Diderot, except that where they appeal to characteristics of the passions or of reason, he invokes what he takes to be characteristics of fundamental decision-making.

Thus all these writers share in the project of constructing valid arguments which will move from premises concerning human nature as they understand it to be to conclusions about the authority of moral rules and precepts. I want to argue that any project of this form was bound to fail, because of an ineradicable discrepancy between their shared conception of moral rules and precepts on the one hand and what was shared—despite much larger divergences—in their conception of human nature on the other. Both conceptions have a history and their relationship can only be made intelligible in the light of that history.

Consider first the general form of the moral scheme which was the historical ancestor of both conceptions, the moral scheme which in a variety of diverse forms and with numerous rivals came for long periods to dominate the European Middle Ages from the twelfth century onwards, a scheme which included both classical and theistic elements. Its basic structure is that which Aristotle analyzed in the *Nicomachean Ethics*. Within that teleological scheme there is a fundamental contrast between man-as-he-happens-to-be and man-as-he-could-be-if-he-realized-his-essential-nature. Ethics is the science which is to enable men to understand how they make the transition from the former state to the latter. Ethics therefore in this view presupposes some account of potentiality and act, some account of the essence of man as a rational animal and above all some account of the human *telos*. The precepts which enjoin the various virtues and prohibit the vices which are their counterparts instruct us how to move from potentiality to act, how to realize our true nature and to reach our true end. To defy them will be to be frustrated and incomplete, to fail to achieve that good of rational happiness which it is peculiarly ours as a species to pursue. The desires and emotions which we possess are to be put in order and educated by the use of such precepts and by the cultivation of those habits of action which the study of ethics prescribes; reason instructs us both as to what our true end is and as to how to reach it. We thus have a threefold scheme in which human-nature-as-it-happens-to-be (human nature in its untutored state) is initially discrepant and discordant with the precepts of ethics and needs to be transformed by the instruction of practical reason and experience into human-nature-as-it-could-be-if-it-realized-its-*telos*. Each of the three elements of the scheme—the conception of untutored human nature, the conception of the precepts of rational ethics and the conception of human-nature-as-it-could-be-if-it-realized-its-*telos*—requires reference to the other two if its status and function are to be intelligible.

This scheme is complicated and added to, but not essentially altered, when it is placed within a framework of theistic beliefs, whether Christian, as with Aquinas, or Jewish with Maimonides, or Islamic with Ibn Roschd. The precepts of ethics now have to be understood not only as teleological injunctions, but also as expressions of a divinely ordained law. The table of virtues and vices has to be amended and added to and a concept of sin is added to the Aritotelian concept of error. The law of God requires a new kind of respect and awe. The true end of man can no longer be completely achieved in this world, but only in another. Yet the threefold structure of untutored human-nature-as-it-happens-to-be, human-nature-as-it-could-be-if-it-realized-its-*telos* and the precepts of rational ethics as the means for the transition from one to the other remains central to the theistic understanding of evaluative thought and judgment.

Thus moral utterance has throughout the period in which the theistic version of classical morality predominates both a twofold point and purpose and a double standard. To say what someone ought to do is at one and the same time to say what course of action will in these circumstances as a matter of fact lead toward a man's true end and to say what the law, ordained by God and comprehended by reason, enjoins. Moral sentences are thus used within this framework to make claims which are true or false. Most medieval proponents of this scheme did of course believe that it was itself part of God's revelation, but also a discovery of reason and rationally defensible. This large area of agreement does not however survive when Protestantism and Jansenist Catholicism—and their immediate late medieval predecessors—appear on the scene. For they embody a new conception of reason. (My argument is at this and other points both deeply indebted to and rather different from that of Anscombe 1958.)

Reason can supply, so these new theologies assert, *no* genuine comprehension of man's true end; that power of reason was destroyed by the fall of man. 'Si Adam integer stetisset', on Calvin's view, reason might have played the pan that Aristotle assigned to it. But now reason is powerless to correct our passions (it is not unimportant that Hume's views are those of one who was brought up a Calvinist). Nonetheless the contrast between man-as-he-happens-to-be and man-as-he-could-be-if-he-realized-his-*telos* remains and the divine moral law is still a schoolmaster to remove us from the former state to the latter, even if only grace enables us to respond to and obey its precepts. The Jansenist Pascal stands at a peculiarly important point in the development of this history. For it is Pascal who recognizes that the Protestant-cum-Jansenist conception of reason is in important respects at one with the conception of reason at home in the most innovative seventeenth-century philosophy and science. Reason does not comprehend essences or transitions from potentiality to act; these concepts belong to the despised conceptual scheme of scholasticism. Hence anti-Aristotelian science sets strict boundaries to the powers of reason. Reason is calculative; it can assess truths of fact and mathematical relations but nothing more. In the realm of practice therefore it can speak only of means. About ends it must be silent. Reason cannot even, as Descartes believed, refute scepticism; and hence a central achievement of reason according to Pascal, is to recognize that our beliefs are ultimately founded on nature, custom and habit.

Pascal's striking anticipations of Hume—and since we know that Hume was familiar with Pascal's writings, it is perhaps plausible to believe that here there is a direct influence—point to the way in which this concept of reason retained its power. Even Kant retains its negative characteristics; reason for him, as much as for Hume, discerns no essential natures and no teleological features in the objective universe available for study by physics. Thus their disagreements on human nature coexist with striking and important agreements and what is true of them is true also of Diderot, of Smith and of Kierkegaard. All reject any teleological view of human nature, any view of man as having an essence which defines his true end. But to understand this is to understand why their project of finding a basis for morality had to fail.

The moral scheme which forms the historical background to their thought had, as we have seen, a structure which required three elements: untutored human nature, man-as-he-could-be-if-he-realized-his-*telos* and the moral precepts which enable him to pass from one state to the other. But the joint effect of the secular rejection of both Protestant and Catholic theology and the scientific and philosophical rejection of Aristotelianism was to eliminate any notion of man-as-he-could-be-if-he-realized-his-*telos*. Since the whole point of ethics—both as a theoretical and a practical discipline—is to enable man to pass from his present state to his true end, the elimination of any notion of essential human nature and with it the abandonment of any notion of a *telos* leaves behind a moral scheme composed of two remaining elements whose relationship becomes quite unclear. There is on the one hand a certain content for morality: a set of injunctions deprived of their teleological context. There is on the other hand a certain view of untutored-human-nature-as-it-is. Since the moral injunctions were originally at home in a scheme in which their purpose was to correct, improve and educate that human nature, they are clearly not going to be such as could be deduced from true statements about human nature or justified in some other way by appealing to its characteristics. The injunctions of morality, thus understood, are likely to be ones that human nature, thus understood, has strong tendencies to disobey. Hence the eighteenth-century moral philosophers engaged in what was an inevitably unsuccessful project; for they did indeed attempt to find a rational basis for their moral beliefs in a particular understanding of human nature, while inheriting a set of moral injunctions on the one hand and a conception of human nature on the other which had been expressly designed to be discrepant with each other. This discrepancy was not removed by their revised beliefs about human nature. They inherited incoherent fragments of a once coherent scheme of thought and action and, since they did not recognize their own peculiar historical and cultural situation, they could not recognize the impossible and quixotic character of their self-appointed task.

Yet perhaps 'could not recognize' is too strong; for we can rank order eighteenth-century moral philosophers in respect of how far they approached to such recognition. If we do so, we discover that the Scotsmen Hume and Smith are the least self-questioning, presumably because they are already comfortable and complacent within the epistemological scheme of British empiricism. Hume indeed had had something very like a nervous breakdown before he could come to terms with that scheme; but no hint of that breakdown remains in his writings on morality. No trace of discomfort appears either in those writings which Diderot published in his own lifetime; yet in *Le Neveu de Rameau*, one of the manuscripts which at his death fell into the hands of Catherine the Great, and which had to be smuggled out of Russia to be published in 1803, we find a critique of the whole project of eighteenth-century moral philosophy more trenchant and insightful than that of any external critic of the Enlightenment.

If Diderot is far closer to recognition of the breakdown of the project than Hume, Kant is closer than either. He does indeed look for a foundation of morality in the universalizable prescriptions of that reason which manifests itself both in arithmetic and in morality; and in spite of his strictures against founding morality on human nature, his analysis of the nature of human reason is the basis for his own rational account of morality. Yet in the second book of the second *Critique* he does acknowledge that without a teleological framework the whole project of morality becomes unintelligible. This teleological framework is presented as a 'presupposition of pure practical reason'. Its appearance in Kant's moral philosophy seemed to his nineteenth-century readers, such as Heine and later the Neo-Kantians, an arbitrary and unjustifiable concession to positions which he had already rejected. Yet, if my thesis is correct, Kant was right; morality did in the eighteenth century, as a matter of historical fact, presuppose something very like the teleological scheme of God, freedom and happiness as the final crown of virtue which Kant propounds. Detach morality from that framework and you will no longer have morality; or, at the very least, you will have radically transformed its character.

This change of character, resulting from the disappearance of any connection between the precepts of morality and the facts of human nature already appears in the writings of the eighteenth-century moral philosophers themselves. For although each of the writers we have been concerned with attempted in his positive arguments to base morality on human nature, each in his negative arguments moved toward a more and more unrestricted version of the claim that no valid argument can move from entirely factual premises to any moral or evaluative conclusion—to a principle, that is, which once it is accepted, constitutes an epitaph to their entire project. Hume still expresses this claim in the form of a doubt rather than of a positive assertion. He remarks that in 'every system of morality, which I have hitherto met with' authors make a transition from statements about God or human nature to moral judgments: 'instead of the usual copulations of propositions, *is,* and *is not,* I met with no proposition that is not connected with an *ought,* or an *ought not*' *(Treatise* III. i. 1). And he then goes on to demand 'that a reason should be given, for what seems altogether inconceivable, how this new relation can be a deduction from others, which are entirely different from it'. The same general principle, no longer expressed as a question, but as an assertion, appears in Kant's insistence that the injunctions of the moral law cannot be derived from any set of statements about human happiness or about the will of God and then yet again in Kierkegaard's account of the ethical. What is the significance of this general claim?

Some later moral philosophers have gone so far as to describe the thesis that from a set of factual premises no moral conclusion validly follows as 'a truth of logic', understanding it as derivable from a more general principle which some medieval logicians formulated as the claim that in a valid argument nothing can appear in the conclusion which was not already in the premises. And, such philosophers have suggested, in an argument in which any attempt is made to derive a moral or evaluative conclusion from factual premises something which is not in the premises, namely the moral or evaluative element, will appear in the conclusion. Hence any such argument must fail. Yet in fact the alleged unrestrictedly general logical principle on which everything is being made to depend is bogus—and the scholastic tag applies only to Aristotelian syllogisms. There *are* several types of valid argument in which some element may appear in a conclusion which is not present in the premises. A.N. Prior's counter-example to this alleged principle illustrates its breakdown adequately, from the premise 'He is a sea-captain', the conclusion may be validly inferred that 'He ought to do whatever a sea-captain ought to do'. This counter-example not only shows that there is no general principle of the type alleged; but it itself shows what is at least a grammatical truth—an 'is' premise *can* on occasion entail an 'ought' conclusion.

Adherents of the 'no "ought" from "is" view' could however easily meet part of the difficulty raised by Prior's example by reformulating their own position. What they intended to claim they might and would presumably say, is that no conclusion with substantial evaluative and moral content—and the conclusion in Prior's example certainly does lack any such content—can be derived from factual premises. Yet the problem would remain for them as to why now anyone would accept their claim. For they have conceded that it cannot be derived from any unrestrictedly general logical principle. Yet their claim may still have substance, but a substance that derives from a particular, and in the eighteenth century new, conception of moral rules and judgments. It may, that is, assert a principle whose validity derives not from some general logical principle, but from the meaning of the key terms employed. Suppose that during the seventeenth and eighteenth centuries the meaning and implications of the key terms used in moral utterance had changed their character; it could then turn out to be the case that what had once been valid inferences from or to some particular moral premise or conclusion would no longer be valid inferences from or to what *seemed* to be the same factual premise or moral conclusion. For what in some sense were the same expressions, the same sentences would now bear a different meaning. But do we in fact have any evidence for such a change of meaning? To answer this question it is helpful to consider another type of counter-example to the 'No "ought" conclusions from "is" premises' thesis. From such factual premises as 'This watch is grossly inaccurate and irregular in time-keeping' and 'This watch is too heavy to carry about comfortably', the evaluative conclusion validly follows that 'This is a bad watch'. From such factual premises as 'He gets a better yield for this crop per acre than any farmer in the district', 'He has the most effective programme of soil renewal yet known' and 'His dairy herd wins all the first prizes at the agricultural shows', the evaluative conclusion validly follows that 'He is a good farmer'.

Both of these arguments are valid because of the special character of the concepts of a watch and of a farmer. Such concepts are functional concepts; that is to say, we define both 'watch' and 'farmer' in terms of the purpose or function which a watch or a farmer are characteristically expected to serve. It follows that the concept of a watch cannot be defined independently of the concept of a good watch nor the concept of a farmer independently of that of a good farmer; and that the criterion of something's being a watch and the criterion of something's being a good watch—and so also for 'farmer' and for all other functional concepts—are not independent of each other. Now clearly both sets of criteria—as is evidenced by the examples given in the last paragraph—are factual. Hence any argument which moves from premises which assert that the appropriate criteria are satisfied to a conclusion which asserts that 'That is a good such-and-such', where 'such-and-such' picks out an item specified by a functional concept, will be a valid argument which moves from factual premises to an evaluative conclusion. Thus we may safely assert that, if some amended version of the 'No "ought" conclusion from "is" premises' principle is to hold good, it must exclude arguments involving functional concepts from its scope. But this suggests strongly that those who have insisted that *all* moral arguments fall within the scope of such a principle may have been doing so, because they took it for granted that *no* moral arguments involve functional concepts. Yet moral arguments within the classical, Aristotelian tradition—whether in its Greek or its medieval versions—involve at least one central functional concept, the concept of *man* understood as having an essential nature and an essential purpose or function; and it is when and only when the classical tradition in its integrity has been substantially rejected that moral arguments change their character so that they fall within the scope of some version of the 'No "ought" conclusion from "is" premises' principle. That is to say, 'man' stands to 'good man' as 'watch' stands to 'good watch' or 'farmer' to 'good farmer' within the classical tradition. Aristotle takes it as a starting-point for ethical enquiry that the relationship of 'man' to 'living well' is analogous to that of 'harpist' to 'playing the harp well' *(Nicomachean Ethics,* 1095a 16). But the use of 'man' as a functional concept is far older than Aristotle and it does not initially derive from

Aristotle's metaphysical biology. It is rooted in the forms of social life to which the theorists of the classical tradition give expression. For according to that tradition to be a man is to fill a set of roles each of which has its own point and purpose: member of a family, citizen, soldier, philosopher, servant of God. It is only when man is thought of as an individual prior to and apart from all roles that 'man' ceases to be a functional concept.

For this to be so other key moral terms must also have partially at least changed their meaning. The entailment relations between certain types of sentence must have changed. Thus it is not just that moral conclusions cannot be justified in the way that they once were; but the loss of the possibility of such justification signals a correlative change in the meaning of moral idioms. So the 'No "ought" conclusion from "is" premises' principle becomes an inescapable truth for philosophers whose culture possesses only the impoverished moral vocabulary which results from the episodes I have recounted. That it was taken to be a timeless logical truth was a sign of a deep lack of historical consciousness which then informed and even now infects too much of moral philosophy. For its initial proclamation was itself a crucial historical event. It signals both a final break with the classical tradition and the decisive breakdown of the eighteenth-century project of justifying morality in the context of the inherited, but already incoherent, fragments left behind from tradition.

But it is not only that moral concepts and arguments at this point in history radically change their character so that they become recognizably the immediate ancestors of the unsettlable, interminable arguments of our own culture. It is also the case that moral *judgments* change their import and meaning. Within the Aristotelian tradition to call x good (where x may be among other things a person or an animal or a policy or a state of affairs) is to say that it is the kind of x which someone would choose who wanted an x for the purpose for which x's are characteristically wanted. To call a watch good is to say that it is the kind of watch which someone would choose who wanted a watch to keep time accurately (rather than, say, to throw at the cat). The presupposition of this use of 'good' is that every type of item which it is appropriate to call good or bad—including persons and actions—has, as a matter of fact, some given specific purpose or function. To call something good therefore is also to make a factual statement. To call a particular action just or right is to say that it is what a good man would do in such a situation; hence this type of statement too is factual. Within this tradition moral and evaluative statements can be called true or false in precisely the way in which all other factual statements can be so called. But once the notion of essential human purposes or functions disappears from morality, it begins to appear implausible to treat moral judgments as factual statements.

Moreover the secularization of morality by the Enlightenment had put in question the status of moral judgments as ostensible reports of divine law. Even Kant, who still understands moral judgments as expressions of a universal law, even if it be a law which each rational agent utters to himself, does not treat moral judgments as reports of what the law requires or commands, but as themselves imperatives. And imperatives are not susceptible of truth or falsity.

Up to the present in everyday discourse the habit of speaking of moral judgments as true or false persists; but the question of what it is in virtue of which a particular moral judgment is true or false has come to lack any clear answer. That this should be so is perfectly intelligible if the historical hypothesis which I have sketched is true: that moral judgments are linguistic survivals from the practices of classical theism which have lost the context provided by these practices. In that context moral judgments were at once hypothetical and categorical in form. They were hypothetical insofar as they expressed a judgment as to what conduct would be teleologically appropriate for a human being: 'You ought to do so-and-so, if and since your *telos* is such-and-such' or perhaps 'You ought to do so-and-so, if you do not want your essential desires to be frustrated'. They were categorical insofar as they reported the contents of the universal law commanded by God: 'You ought to do so-and-so: that is what God's law enjoins.' But take away from them that in virtue of which they were hypothetical *and* that in virtue of which they were categorical and what are they? Moral judgments lose any clear status and the sentences which express them in a parallel way lose any undebatable meaning. Such sentences become available as forms of expression for an emotivist self which lacking the guidance of the context in which they were originally at home has lost its linguistic as well as its practical way in the world.

Yet to put matters in this way is to anticipate in an unjustified way. For I am apparently taking it for granted that these changes are indeed to be characterized in terms of such concepts as those of survival, loss of context and consequent loss of clarity; whereas, as I noted earlier, many of those who lived through this change in our predecessor culture saw it as a deliverance both from the burdens of traditional theism and the confusions of teleological modes of thought. What I have described in terms of a loss of traditional structure and content was seen by the most articulate of their philosophical spokesmen as the achievement by the self of its proper autonomy. The self had been liberated from all those outmoded forms of social organization which had imprisoned it simultaneously within a belief in a theistic and teleological world order and within those hierarchical structures which attempted to legitimate themselves as pan of such a world order.

Yet whether we view this decisive moment of change as loss or liberation, as a transition to autonomy or to *anomie*, two features of it need to be emphasized. The first is the social and political consequences of the change. Abstract changes in moral concepts are always embodied in real, particular events. There is a history yet to be written in which the Medici princes, Henry VIII and Thomas Cromwell, Frederick the Great and Napoleon, Walpole and Wilberforce, Jefferson and Robespierre are understood as expressing in their actions, often partially and in a variety of different ways, the very same conceptual changes which at the level of philosophical theory are articulated by Machiavelli and Hobbes, by Diderot and Condorcet, by Hume and Adam Smith and Kant. There ought not to be two histories, one of political and moral action and one of political and moral theorizing, because there were not two pasts, one populated only by actions, the other only by theories. Every action is the bearer and expression of more or less theory-laden beliefs and concepts; every piece of theorizing and every expression of belief is a political and moral action.

Thus the transition into modernity was a transition both in theory and in practice and a single transition at that. It is because the habits of mind engendered by our modern academic curriculum separate out the history of political and social change (studied under one set of rubrics in history departments by one set of scholars) from the history of philosophy (studied under quite a different set of rubrics in philosophy departments by quite another set of scholars) that ideas are endowed with a falsely independent life of their own on the one hand and political and social action is presented as peculiarly mindless on the other. This academic dualism is of course itself the expression of an idea at home almost everywhere in the modern world; so much so indeed, that Marxism, the most influential adversary theory of modern culture, presents what is just one more version of this same dualism in the distinction between basis and ideological superstructure.

Yet we also need to remember that if the self decisively separates itself from inherited modes both of thought and practice in the course of a single and unified history, it does so in a variety of ways and with a complexity that it would be crippling to ignore. When the distinctively modern self was invented, its invention required not only a largely new social setting, but one defined by a variety of not always coherent beliefs and concepts. What was then invented was the *individual* and to the question of what that invention amounted to and its part in creating our own emotivist culture we must now turn.

LIBERALISM AGAINST POPULISM

CHAPTER 5

BY WILLIAM H. RIKER

William H. Riker, "The Meaning of Social Choices," *Liberalism Against Populism: A Confrontation Between the Theory of Democracy and the Theory of Social Choice*, pp. 115-123. Copyright © 1988 by Waveland Press. Reprinted with permission.

THE MEANING OF SOCIAL CHOICES

I showed that no method of voting could be said to amalgamate individual judgments truly and fairly because every method violates some reasonable canon of fairness and accuracy. All voting methods are therefore in some sense morally imperfect. Furthermore, these imperfect methods can produce different outcomes from the same profile of individual judgments. Hence it follows that sometimes—and usually we never know for sure just when—the social choice is as much an artifact of morally imperfect methods as it is of what people truly want. It is hard to have unbounded confidence in the *justice* of such results.

It is equally hard, as I will show in this chapter, to have unbounded confidence in the *meaning* of such results. Individual persons presumably can, if they think about it deeply enough, order their personal judgments transitively. Hence their valuations mean something, for they clearly indicate a hierarchy of preference that can guide action and choice in a sensible way. But the results of voting do not necessarily have this quality. It is instead the case that *no* method of voting can simultaneously satisfy several elementary conditions of fairness and also produce results that always satisfy elementary conditions of logical arrangement. Hence, not only may the results of voting fail to be fair, they may also fail to make sense. It is the latter possibility that will be analyzed in this chapter.

5.A. ARROW'S THEOREM

Kenneth Arrow published *Social Choice and Individual Values* in 1951. Although his theorem initially provoked some controversy among economists, its profound political significance was not immediately recognized by political scientists. In the late 1960s, however, a wide variety of philosophers, economists, and political scientists began to appreciate how profoundly unsettling the theorem was and how deeply it called into question some conventionally accepted notions—not only about voting, the subject of this work, but also about the ontological validity of the concept of social welfare, a subject that, fortunately, we can leave to metaphysicians.

The essence of Arrow's theorem is that no method of amalgamating individual judgments can simultaneously satisfy some reasonable conditions of fairness on the method and a condition of logicality on the result. In a sense this theorem is a generalization of the paradox of voting (see section 1.H), for the theorem is the proposition that something like the paradox is possible in *any* fair system of amalgamating values. Thus the theorem is called the *General Possibility Theorem*.

To make the full meaning of Arrow's theorem clear, I will outline the situation and the conditions of fairness and of logicality that cannot simultaneously be satisfied. The situation for amalgamation is:

1. There are n persons, $n \geq 2$, and n is finite. Difficulties comparable to the paradox of voting can arise in individuals who use several standards of judgment for choice. Our concern is, however, *social* choice, so we can ignore the Robinson Crusoe case.
2. There are three or more alternatives—that is, for the set $X = (x_1, \ldots, x_m)$, $m \geq 3$. Since transitivity or other conditions for logical choice are meaningless for fewer than three alternatives and since, indeed, simple majority decision produces a logical result on two alternatives, the conflict between fairness and logicality can only arise when $m \geq 3$.
3. Individuals are able to order the alternatives transitively: If $x\,R_i\,y$ and $y\,R_i\,z$, then $x\,R_i\,z$. If it is not assumed that individuals are able to be logical, then surely it is pointless to expect a group to produce logical results.

The conditions of fairness are:

1. *Universal admissibility of individual orderings (Condition U).* This is the requirement that the set, D, includes all possible profiles, D, of individual orders, D_i. If each D_i is some permutation of possible orderings of X by preference and indifference, then this requirement is that individuals can choose any of the possible permutations. For example, if $X = (x, y, z)$, the individual may choose any of the following 13 orderings:

1. $x\,y\,z$	5. $z\,y\,x$	9. $z\,(x\,y)$	12. $(z\,x)\,y$
2. $y\,z\,x$	6. $y\,x\,z$	10. $(x\,y)\,z$	13. $(x\,y\,z)$
3. $z\,x\,y$	7. $x\,(y\,z)$	11. $(y\,z)\,x$	
4. $x\,z\,y$	8. $y\,(z\,x)$		

   (15–1)

The justification for this requirement is straightforward. If social outcomes are to be based exclusively on individual judgments—as seems implicit in any interpretation of democratic methods—then to restrict individual persons' judgments in any way means that the social outcome is based as much on the restriction as it is on individual judgments. Any rule or command that prohibits a person from choosing some preference order is morally unacceptable (or at least unfair) from the point of view of democracy.

2. *Monotonicity.* According to this condition, if a person raises the valuation of a winning alternative, it cannot become a loser; or, if a person lowers the valuation of a losing alternative, it cannot become a winner. The justification for monotonicity was discussed in section 3.B. Given the democratic intention that outcomes be based in some way on participation, it would be the utmost in perversity if the method of choice were to count individual judgments *negatively,* although, as I have shown, some real-world methods actually do so.

3. *Citizens' sovereignty or nonimposition.* Define a social choice as imposed if some alternative, x, is a winner for any set, D, of individual preferences. If x is always chosen, then what individuals want does not have anything to do with social choice. It might, for example, happen that x was everyone's least-liked alternative, yet an imposed choice of x would still select x. In such a situation, voters' judgments have nothing to do with the outcome and democratic participation is meaningless.

4. *Unanimity or Pareto optimality (Condition P).* This is the requirement that, if everyone prefers x to y, then the social choice function, F, does not choose y. (See Chapter 3, note 8, and Chapter 4, note 28.) This is the form in which monotonicity and citizens' sovereignty enter all proofs of Arrow's theorem. There are only two ways that a result contrary to unanimity could occur. One is that the system of amalgamation is not monotonic. Suppose in D' everybody but i prefers x to y and $y P'_i x$. Then in D, i changes to $x P_i y$ so everybody has x preferred to y; but, if F is not monotonic, it may be that x does not belong to $F(\{x, y\}), D)$. The other way a violation of unanimity could occur is for F to impose y even though everybody prefers x to y. Thus the juncture of monotonicity and citizens' sovereignty implies Pareto optimality.

Many writers have interpreted the unanimity condition as purely technical—as, for example, in the discussion of the Schwartz method of completing the Condorcet rule (see section 4.C). But Pareto optimality takes on more force when it is recognized as the carrier of monotonicity and nonimposition, both of which have deep and obvious qualities of fairness.

5. *Independence from irrelevant alternatives (Condition I).* According to this requirement (defined in section 4.H), a method of amalgamation, F, picks the same alternative as the social choice every time F is applied to the same profile, D. Although some writers have regarded this condition simply as a requirement of technical efficiency, it actually has as much moral content as the other fairness conditions (see section 4. H). From the democratic point of view, one wants to base the outcome on the voters' judgments, but doing so is clearly impossible if the method

of amalgamation gives different results from identical profiles. This might occur, for example, if choices among alternatives were made by some chance device. Then it is the device, not voters' judgments in D, that determines outcomes. Even if one constructs the device so that the chance of selecting an alternative is proportional in some way to the number of people desiring it (if, for example, two-thirds of the voters prefer x to y, then the device selects x with $p = ⅔$), still the expectation is that, of several chance selections, the device will choose x on p selections and y on $1-p$ selections from the same profile, in clear violation of Condition I. In ancient Greece, election by lot was a useful method for anonymity; today it would be simply a way to by-pass voters' preferences. Another kind of arbitrariness prohibited by the independence condition is utilitarian voting. Based on interpersonal comparisons of distances on scales of unknown length, utilitarian voting gives advantages to persons with finer perception and broader horizons. Furthermore, independence prohibits the arbitrariness of the Borda count (see section 5.F).

6. *Nondictatorship (Condition D).* This is the requirement that there be no person, i, such that, whenever $x\,P_i\,y$, the social choice is x, regardless of the opinions of other persons. Since the whole idea of democracy is to avoid such situations, the moral significance of this condition is obvious.

Finally, the condition of logicality is that the social choice is a weak order, by which is meant that the set, X, is connected and its members can be *socially* ordered by the relation, R, which is the transitive social analogue of preference and indifference combined. (This relation, as in $x\,R\,y$, means that x is chosen over or at least tied with y.) In contrast to the previous discussion, in which the method of amalgamation or choice, F, simply selected an element from X, it is now assumed that F selects repeatedly from pairs in X to produce, by means of successive selections, a social order analogous to the individual orders, D_i. And it is the failure to produce such an order that constitutes a violation of the condition of logicality.

Since an individual weak order or the relation R_i is often spoken of as individual rationality, social transitivity, or R, is sometimes spoken of as collective rationality—Arrow himself so described it. And failure to produce social transitivity can also be regarded as a kind of social irrationality.

Arrow's theorem, then, is that every possible method of amalgamation or choice that satisfies the fairness conditions fails to ensure a social ordering. And if society cannot, with fair methods, be certain to order its outcome, then it is not clear that we can know what the outcomes of a fair method mean. This conclusion appears to be devastating, for it consigns democratic outcomes—and hence the democratic method—to the world of arbitrary nonsense, at least some of the time.

Naturally there has been a variety of attempts to interpret and sidestep this conclusion. One line of inquiry is to raise doubts about its practical importance; another is to look for some theoretical adjustment that deprives the theorem of its force. The rest of this chapter is devoted to a survey of both branches of this huge and important literature, so that in Chapter 6 it will be possible to assess fully the political significance of Arrow's theorem.

I will begin with inquiries about the practical importance of the theorem. One such inquiry is an estimate of the expected frequency of profiles, D, that do not lead to a transitive order.

5.B. THE PRACTICAL RELEVANCE OF ARROW'S THEOREM: THE FREQUENCY OF CYCLES

One meaning of Arrow's theorem is that, under any system of voting or amalgamation, instances of intransitive or cyclical outcomes can occur. Since, by definition, no one of the alternatives in a cycle can beat all the others, there is no Condorcet winner among cycled alternatives. All cycled alternatives tie with respect to their position in a social arrangement in the sense that $x\ y\ z\ x, y\ z\ x\ y,$ and $z\ x\ y\ z$ have equal claims to being the social arrangement. Borda voting similarly produces a direct tie among cycled alternatives. Hence a social arrangement is indeterminate when a cycle exists. When the arrangement is indeterminate, the actual choice is arbitrarily made. The selection is not determined by the preference of the voters. Rather it is determined by the power of some chooser to dominate the choice or to manipulate the process to his or her advantage. Every cycle thus represents the failure of the voting process. One way to inquire into the practical significance of Arrow's theorem is, therefore, to estimate how often cycles can occur.

For this estimate, a number of simplifying assumptions are necessary. For one thing, majority voting (rather than positional voting or any other kind of amalgamation) is always assumed. This assumption of course limits the interpretation severely. For another thing, only cycles that preclude a Condorcet winner are of interest. Voting may fail to produce a weak order in several ways:

1. With all three alternatives, there may be a cycle: $x\ R\ y\ R\ z\ R\ x$ or simply $x\ y\ z\ x$.
2. With four or more alternatives, there may be
   a. A Condorcet winner followed by a cycle: $w\ x\ y\ z\ x$
   b. A cycle among all alternatives: $w\ x\ y\ z\ w$; or intersecting cycles: $s\ t\ w\ x\ y\ z\ w\ v\ s$
   c. A cycle in which all members beat some other alternative: $x\ y\ z\ x\ w$

If one is interested in social welfare judgments involving an ordering of all alternatives, then all cycles are significant no matter where they occur. But if one is interested in picking out a social choice, as in the voting mechanisms discussed here, then the significant cases are only 1, 2(b), and 2(c), where there is no unique social choice. (These are often called *top cycles*.) Attempts to estimate the significance of Arrow's theorem by some sort of calculation have all been made from the point of view of social choice rather than welfare judgments and have therefore concerned the frequency of top cycles.

For Arrow's theorem, Condition U allows individuals to have any weak ordering, R_i, of preference and indifference, as in (5.1). Calculation is simpler, however, based on strong orders—that is, individual preference orders, P_i, with indifference not allowed.

With m alternatives, there are $m!$ (i.e., $1 \cdot 2 \cdot \ldots \cdot m$) such linear orders possible; and, when $m = 3$, these are:

$$x\,y\,z, \quad x\,z\,y, \quad y\,x\,z, \quad y\,z\,x, \quad z\,x\,y, \quad z\,y\,x$$

Each such order is a potential D_i. When each of n voters picks some (not necessarily different) D_i a profile, D, is created. Since the first voter picks from $m!$ orders, the second from $m!$, ..., and the last from $m!$, the number of possible different profiles, D, is $(m!)^n$, which is the number of members of the set, $\mathbf{D}$, of all profiles, when voters have only strong orders.

A calculation that yields some estimate of the significance of cycles is the fraction, $p(n, m)$, of D in $\mathbf{D}$ without a Condorcet winner:

$$p(n, m) = \frac{\text{Number of } D \text{ without a Condorcet winner}}{(m!)^n}$$

If one assumes that each D is equally likely to occur (which implies also that, for each voter, the chance of picking some order is $1/m!$), then $p(n, m)$ is an a priori estimate of the probability of the occurrence of a top cycle. Several calculations have been made, as set forth in Display 5–1.[3] As is apparent from the Display, as the number of voters and alternatives increases, so do the number of profiles without a Condorcet winner. The calculation thereby implies that instances of the paradox of voting are very common. Most social choices are made from many alternatives (though often we do not realize this fact because the number has been winnowed down by various devices such as primary elections and committees that select alternatives for agendas) and by many people, so the calculations imply that Condorcet winners do not exist in almost all decisions.

But, of course, there are a number of reasons to believe that such calculations are meaningless. People do not choose an ordering with probability $1/m!$. Rather, at any particular moment, some orders are more likely to be chosen than others. The six strong orders over triples generate two cycles:

"Forward Cycle"	"Backward Cycle"	
1. $x\,y\,z$	4. $x\,z\,y$	
2. $y\,z\,x$	5. $z\,y\,x$	
3. $z\,x\,y$	6. $y\,x\,z$	(15-2)

Table 15-1.

Values of $p(n, m)$: Proportion of Possible Profiles Without a Condorcet Winner

	n = Number of Voters						
m = Number of Alternatives	3	5	7	9	11	...	Limit
3	.056	.069	.075	.078	.080		.088
4	.111	.139	.150	.156	.160		.176
5	.160	.200	.215				.251
6	.202						.315
Limit	1.000	1.000	1.000	1.000	1.000		1.000

The entry in the row for four alternatives and in the column for seven voters—namely, .150—is the ratio of the number of profiles without a Condorcet winner to the number of profiles possible when seven voters order four alternatives.

Cycles occur when voters concentrate on one or the other of these sets of three orders. But suppose voters are induced by, for example, political parties, to concentrate heavily on, say, (1), (2), and (5). Then there is no cycle. Furthermore, there is good reason to believe that debate and discussion do lead to such fundamental similarities of judgment. Calculations based on equiprobable choices very likely seriously overestimate the frequency of cycles in the natural world.

On the other hand, it is clear that one way to manipulate outcomes is to generate a cycle. Suppose that in Display 15-2 profile D exists and that person 2 realizes that his or her first choice, y, will lose to the Condorcet winner, x. Person 2 can at least prevent that outcome by generating a cycle (or a tie) by voting as if his or her preference were $y\,z\,x$ as in D'.

The tendency toward similarity may thus reduce the number $p(n, m)$, while the possibility of manipulation may increase the number. It seems to me that similarity probably reduces the number of profiles without Condorcet winners on issues that are not very important and that no one has a motive to manipulate, while the possibility of manipulation increases the number of such profiles on important issues, where the outcome is worth the time and effort of prospective losers to generate a top cycle. Neither of these influences appears in the calculations and thus renders them suspect from two opposite points of view.

Table 15–2.

The Generation of a Cycle			
D		D'	
D_1:	x y z	D'_1:	x y z
D_2:	y x z	D'_2:	y z z
D_3:	z x y	D'_3:	z x y
Note. Majoritarian ordering of D: x P y P z.		*Note.* Cycle in D' under majoritarian voting: x P y P z P x.	

In D' person 2 has reversed z and x from D, thereby generating a cycle.

5.C. THE PRACTICAL RELEVANCE OF ARROW'S THEOREM: CONDITIONS FOR CONDORCET WINNERS

Another approach to estimating the practical significance of Arrow's theorem is to inquire into what kinds of profiles are certain to produce a Condorcet winner. As in the previous approach, only majoritarian voting is considered, which limits the relevance of the inquiry to the theorem but does say something about its practical effect on this kind of decision process. For example, as can be seen in Display 15–1, for $m = n = 3$, the number of elements of $D = (m!)^n = 216$ and $p(n, m) = 12/216 = .056$. It is natural to look for the features that guarantee a Condorcet winner for 204 of the profiles in **D**. If one can generalize about the sets of preference orders that produce these results, then it may be possible to estimate the practical significance of the theorem for majoritarian voting.

THREE NORMATIVE MODELS OF DEMOCRACY

BY JÜRGEN HABERMAS

SIXTEEN

I would like to sketch a proceduralist view of democracy and deliberative politics which differs in relevant aspects from both the liberal and the republican paradigm. Let me (1) remind you the opposite features of these two established models. I will then (2) introduce a new proceduralist conception by way of a critique of the "ethical overload" of the republican view. The last part of the paper further elaborates (3) the three normative models of democracy by comparing their corresponding images of state and society.

(1) THE TWO RECEIVED VIEWS OF DEMOCRATIC POLITICS

According to the "liberal" or Lockean view, the democratic process acomplishes the task of programming the government in the interest of society, where the government is represented as an apparatus of public administration, and society as a market-structured network of interactions among private persons. Here politics (in the sense of the citizens' political will-formation) has the function of bundling together and pushing private interests against a government apparatus specializing in the administrative employment of political power for collective goals. On the "republican" view, however, politics involves more than this mediating function; it is rather constitutive for the processes of society as a whole. "Politics" is conceived as the reflective form of substantial ethical life, namely as the medium in which the members of somehow solitary communities become aware of their dependence on one another and, acting with full deliberation as citizens, further shape and develop existing relations of reciprocal recognition into an association of free and equal consociates under law. With this, the liberal architectonic of government and society undergoes an important change: in addition to the hierarchical regulations of the state and the decentralized regulations of the market, that is, besides administrative power and individual personal interests, *solidarity* and the orientation to the common good appear as a *third source* of social integration. In fact, this horizontal political will-formation aimed at mutual understanding or communicatively achieved consensus is even supposed to enjoy priority, both in a genetic and a normative sense. An autonomous basis in civil society, a basis independent of public administration and market-mediated private commerce, is assumed as a precondition for the praxis of civic self-determination. This basis preserves political communication from being swallowed up by the government apparatus or assimilated to market structures. In the republican conception, the political public sphere acquires, along with its base in civil society, a strategic significance. These competing approaches yield two contrasting images of the citizen.

According to the liberal view, the citizen's status is primarily determined according to negative rights they have vis-à-vis the state and other citizens. As bearers of these rights they enjoy the protection of the government, as long as they pursue their private interests within the boundaries drawn by legal statutes—and this includes protection against government interventions. Political rights, such as voting rights and free speech, not only have the same structure but also a similar meaning as civil rights that provide a space within which legal subjects are released from external compulsion. They give citizens the opportunity to assert their private interests in such a way that by means of elections, the composition of parliamentary bodies, and the formation of a government, these interests are finally aggregated into a political will that makes an impact on the administration.

According to the republican view, the status of citizens is not determined by the model of negative liberties to which these citizens can lay claim *as* private persons. Rather, political rights—preeminently rights of political participation and communication—are positive liberties. They guarantee not freedom from external compulsion but the possibility of participation in a common praxis, through the exercise of which citizens can first make themselves into what they want to be—politically autonomous authors of a community of free and equal persons. To this extent, the political process does not just serve to keep government activity under the surveillance of citizens who have already acquired a prior social autonomy in the exercise of their private rights and pre-political liberties. Just as little does it act as a hinge between state and society, for administrative authority is not at all an autochthonous authority; it is not something given. Rather, this authority emerges from the citizens' power produced communicatively in the praxis of self-legislation, and it finds its legitimation in the fact that it protects this praxis by institutionalizing public liberty. So, the state's *raison d'être* does not lie primarily in the protection of equal private rights but in the guarantee of an inclusive opinion- and will-formation in which free and equal citizens reach an understanding on which goals and norms lie in the equal interest of all.

The polemic against the classical concept of the legal person as bearer of private rights reveals a controversy about the concept of law itself. While in the liberal view the point of a legal order is to make it possible to determine in each case which individuals are entitled to which rights, in the republican view these "subjective" rights owe their existence to an "objective" legal order that both enables and guarantees the integrity of an autonomous life in common based on mutual respect:

> For republicans rights ultimately are nothing but determinations of the prevailing political will, while for liberals some rights are always grounded in a 'higher law' of (…) reason.[1]

Finally, the different ways of conceptualizing the role of citizen and of law express a deeper disagreement about the *nature of the political process*. In the liberal view, the political process of opinion- and will-formation in the public sphere and in parliament is determined by the competition of strategically acting collectivities trying to maintain or acquire positions of power. Success is measured by the citizens' approval, quantified as votes, of persons and programs. In their choices at the polls, voters give expression to their preferences. Their voting decisions have the same structure as the acts of choice made by participants in a market. They license access to the positions of power that political parties fight over in the same success- oriented attitude.

According to the republican view, the political opinion- and will- formation occurring in the public sphere and in parliament obeys not the structures of market processes but the obstinate structures of a public communication oriented to mutual understanding. For politics, in the sense of a praxis of civic self-legislation, the paradigm is not the market but dialogue. This dialogic conception imagines politics as contestation over questions of value and not simply questions of preference.

(2) PROCEDURALIST VS. COMMUNITARIAN VIEWS OF POLITICS

The republican model as compared to the liberal one has the advantage that it preserves the original meaning of democracy in terms of the institutionalization of a public use of reason jointly exercised by autonomous citizens. This model accounts for those communicative conditions that confer legitimating force on political opinion- and will-formation. These are precisely the conditions under which the political process can be presumed to generate reasonable results. A contest for power, if represented according to the liberal model of market competition, is determined by

---

[1] F. I. Michelman in *Florida Law Review* 41 (1989): 446 f.

the rational choice of optimal strategies. Given an indissoluble pluralism of pre-political values and interests that are at best aggregated with equal weight in the political process, politics loses all reference to the normative core of a public use of reason. The republican trust in the force of political discourses stands in contrast to the liberal skepticism about reason. Such discourses are meant to allow one to discuss value orientations and interpretations of needs and wants, and then to change these in an *insightful way.*

But contemporary republicans tend to give this public communication a communitarian reading. It is precisely this move towards an *ethical constriction* of *political discourse* that I call into question. Politics may not be assimilated to a hermeneutical process of self-explication of a shared form of life or collective identity. Political questions may not be reduced to the type of ethical questions where we, as members of a community, ask ourselves who we are and who we would like to be. In its communitarian interpretation the republican model is too idealistic even within the limits of a purely normative analysis. On this reading, the democratic process is dependent on the virtues of citizens devoted to the public weal. This expectation of virtue already led Rousseau to split the citizen oriented to the common good from the private man, who cannot be ethically overburdened. The unanimity of the political legislature was supposed to be secured in advance by a substantive ethical consensus. In contrast, a discourse-theoretic interpretation insists on the fact that democratic will- formation does not draw its legitimating force from a previous convergence of settled ethical convictions, but from both the communicative presuppositions that allow the better arguments to come into play in various forms of deliberation, and from the procedures that secure fair bargaining processes. Discourse theory breaks with a purely ethical conception of civic autonomy.

According to the communitarian view, there is a necessary connection between the deliberative concept of democracy and the reference to a concrete, substantively integrated ethical community. Otherwise one could not explain, in this view, how the citizens' orientation to the common good would be at all possible. The individual, so the argument goes, can become aware of her co-membership in a collective form of life, and therewith become aware of a prior social bond, only in a practice exercised with others in common. The individual can get a clear sense of commonalities and differences, and hence a sense of who she is and who she would like to be, only in the public exchange with others who owe their identities to the same traditions and similar formation processes. This assimilation of political discourses to the clarification of a collective ethical self-understanding does not sit well with the function of the legislative processes they issue in. Legal statutes no doubt also contain teleological elements, but these involve more than just the hermeneutic explication of shared value orientations. By their very structure laws are determined by the question of which norms citizens want to adopt for regulating their living together. To be sure, discourses aimed at achieving self-understanding—discourses in which the participants want to get a clear understanding of themselves as members of a specific nation, as members of a locale or a state, as inhabitants of a region, etc.; in which they want to determine which traditions they will continue; in which they strive to determine how they will treat each other, and how they will treat minorities and marginal groups; in short, discourses in which they want to get clear about the kind of society they want to live in—such discourses are also an important part of politics. But these questions are subordinate to moral questions and connected with pragmatic questions. Moral questions in the narrow sense of the Kantian tradition are questions of justice. The question having *priority* in legislative politics concerns how a matter can be regulated in the equal interest of all. The making of norms is primarily a justice issue and is gauged by principles that state what is equally good for all. And unlike ethical questions, questions of justice are not related from the outset to a specific collective and its form of life. The politically enacted law of a concrete legal community must, if it is to be legitimate, at least be compatible with moral tenets that claim universal validity going beyond the legal community.

Moreover, compromises make up the bulk of political processes. Under conditions of religious, or in any way cultural and societal pluralism, politically relevant goals are often selected by interests and value orientations that are by no means constitutive for the identity of the community at large, hence for the whole of an intersubjectively shared form of life. The political interests and values that stand in conflict with each other without prospects of consensus are in need of a balancing that cannot be achieved through ethical discourses—even if the outcomes of bargaining processes are subject to the proviso that they must not violate a culture's agreed-upon basic values. The required balance of competing interests comes about as a compromise between parties that may rely on mutual threats. A legitimate kind of bargaining certainly depends on a prior regulation of fair terms for achieving results, which are acceptable for all parties on the basis of their differing preferences. While debates on such regulations should assume the forms of practical discourse that neutralize power, bargaining itself well allows for strategic interactions. The deliberative mode of legislative practice is not just intended to ensure the ethical validity of laws. Rather, one can understand the complex validity claim of legal norms as the claim, on the one hand, to compromise competing interests in a manner compatible with the common good and, on the other hand, to bring universalistic principles of justice into the horizon of the specific form of life of a particular community.

In contrast to the ethical constriction of political discourse, the concept of deliberative politics acquires empirical reference only when we take account of the multiplicity of communicative forms of rational political will-formation. It is not discourse of an ethical type that could grant on its own the democratic genesis of law. Instead, deliberative politics should be conceived as a syndrome that depends on a network of fairly regulated bargaining processes and of various forms of argumentation, including pragmatic, ethical and moral discourses, each of which relies on different communicative presuppositions and procedures. In legislative politics the supply of information and the rational choice of strategies are interwoven with the balancing of interests, with the achievement of ethical self-understanding and the articulation of strong preferences, with moral justification and tests of legal coherence. Thus "dialogical" and "instrumental" politics, the two ideal-types which Frank Michelman has opposed in a polarizing fashion, do in fact interpenetrate in the medium of deliberations of various kinds.

(3) THREE IMAGES OF STATE AND SOCIETY

If we start from this proceduralist concept of deliberative politics, this reading of democracy has implications for the concept of society. Both the liberal and the republican model presuppose a view of society as centered in the state—be it the state as guardian of a market-society or the state as the self-conscious institutionalization of an ethical community.

According to the *liberal view*, the democratic process takes place exclusively in the form of compromises between competing interests. Fairness is supposed to be granted by the general and equal right to vote, the representative composition of parliamentary bodies, by decision rules, and so on. Such rules are ultimately justified in terms of liberal basic rights. According to the *republican view*, democratic will-formation takes place in the form of an ethical-political discourse; here deliberation can rely on a culturally established background consensus shared by the citizenry. Discourse theory takes elements from both sides and integrates these in the concept of an ideal procedure for deliberation and decision-making. Weaving together pragmatic considerations, compromises, discourses of self-understanding and justice, this democratic procedure grounds the presumption that reasonable or fair results are obtained. According to this proceduralist view, practical reason withdraws from universal human rights, or from the concrete ethical substance of a specific community, into the rules of discourse and forms of argumentation. In the final analysis, the normative content arises from the very structure of communicative actions. These descriptions of the democratic process set the stage for different conceptualizations of state and society.

According to the republican view, the citizens' political opinion- and will-formation forms the medium through which society constitutes itself as a political whole. Society is, from the very start, political society—*societas civilis*. Hence democracy becomes equivalent to the political self-organization of society as a whole. This leads to a polemic *understanding of politics directed against the state apparatus*. In Hannah Arendt's political writings one can see where republican argumentation directs its salvos: in opposition to the privatism of a depoliticized population and in opposition to the acquisition of legitimation through entrenched parties, the public sphere should be revitalized to the point where a regenerated citizenry can, in the forms of a decentralized self-governance, (once again) appropriate the power of pseudo-independent state agencies. From this perspective, society would finally develop into a political totality.

Whereas the separation of the state apparatus from society elicits a polemical reaction from the republican side, according to the liberal view it cannot be eliminated but only bridged by the democratic process. The regulated balancing of power and interests has need of constitutional channeling, of course. The democratic will-formation of self-interested citizens is laden with comparatively weak normative expectations. The constitution is supposed to tame the state apparatus through normative constraints (such as basic rights, separation of powers, etc.) and to force it, through the competition of political parties on the one hand and that between government and opposition on the other, to take adequate account of competing interests and value orientations. This *state-centered understanding of politics* can forego the unrealistic assumption of a citizenry capable of collective action. Its focus is not so much the input of a rational political will-formation but the output of sensible and effective administrative accomplishments. Liberal argumentation aims its salvos against the potential disturbance of an administrative power that interferes with the spontaneous forces of a self-regulating society. The liberal model hinges, not on the democratic self-determination of deliberating citizens, but on the legal institutionalization of an economic society that is supposed to guarantee an essentially nonpolitical common good by the satisfaction of private preferences.

Discourse theory invests the democratic process with normative connotations stronger than those found in the liberal model but weaker than those of the republican model. Once again, it takes elements from both sides and fits them together in a new way. In agreement with republicanism, it gives center stage to the process of political opinion- and will-formation, but without understanding the constitution as something secondary; rather it conceives the principles of the constitutional state as a consistent answer to the question of how the demanding communicative forms of a democratic opinion- and will-formation can be institutionalized. Discourse theory has the success of deliberative politics depend not on a collectively acting citizenry but on the institutionalization of the corresponding procedures and conditions of communication. Proceduralized popular sovereignty and a political system tied in to the peripheral networks of the political public sphere go hand-in-hand with the image of a *decentered society*. This concept of democracy no longer needs to operate with the notion of a social whole centered in the state and imagined as a goal-oriented subject writ large. Just as little does it represent the whole in a system of constitutional norms mechanically regulating the interplay of powers and interests in accordance with the market model.

Discourse theory altogether jettisons certain premises of the *philosophy of consciousness*. These premises either invite us to ascribe the praxis of civic self-determination to one encompassing macro-subject or they have us apply the rule of law to many isolated private subjects. The former approach views the citizenry as a collective actor that reflects the whole and acts for it; in the latter, individual actors function as dependent variables in system processes that move along blindly. Discourse theory works instead with the *higher-level intersubjectivity* of communication processes that flow through both the parliamentary bodies and the informal networks of the public sphere. Within and outside the parliamentary complex, these subjectless forms of communication constitute arenas in which a more or less rational opinion- and will-formation can take place.

Informal public opinion-formation generates "influence"; influence is transformed into "communicative power" through the channels of political elections; and communicative power is is again transformed into "administrative power" through legislation. As in the liberal model, the boundaries between "state" and "society" are respected; but in this case, civil society provides the social basis of autonomous public spheres that remain as distinct from the economic system as from the administration. This understanding of democracy suggests a new balance between the three resources of money, administrative power, and solidarity, from which modern societies meet their needs for integration. The normative implications are obvious: the integrative force of "solidarity," which can no longer be drawn solely from sources of communicative action, should develop through widely expanded and differentiated public spheres as well as through legally institutionalized procedures of democratic deliberation and decision-making. It should gain the strength to hold its own against the two other mechanisms of social integration—money and administrative power.

This view has implications for how one understands (a) legitimation and (b) popular sovereignty.

(a) On the liberal view, democratic will-formation has the exclusive function of *legitimating* the exercise of political power. Election results are the license to assume governmental power, whereas the government must justify the use of power to the public. On the republican view, democratic will-formation has the significantly stronger function of *constituting* society as a political community and keeping the memory of this founding act alive with each election. The government is not only empowered to exercise a largely open mandate, but also programmatically committed to carry out certain policies. It remains bound to a self-governing political community. Discourse theory brings a third idea into play: the procedures and communicative presuppositions of democratic opinion- and will-formation function as the most important sluices for the discursive rationalization of the decisions of an administration constrained by law and statute. Rationalization means more than mere legitimation but less than the constitution of political power. The power available to the administration changes its aggregate condition as soon as it emerges from a public use of reason and a communicative power which do not just monitor the exercise of political power in a belated manner but more or less program it as well. Notwithstanding this discursive rationalization, only the administrative system itself can "act." The administration is a subsystem specialized for collectively binding decisions, whereas the communicative structures of the public sphere comprise a far-flung network of sensors that in the first place react to the pressure of society-wide problematics and stimulate influential opinions. The public opinion that is worked up via democratic procedures into communicative power cannot "rule" of itself, but can only point the use of administrative power in specific directions.

(b) The concept of popular sovereignty stems from the republican appropriation and revaluation of the early modern notion of sovereignty initially associated with absolutist regimes. The state, which monopolizes all the means for a legitimate implementation of force, is seen as an overpowering concentrate of power—as the Leviathan. This idea was transferred by Rousseau to the will of the united people. He fused the strength of the Leviathan with the classical idea of the self-rule of free and equal citizens and combined it with his modern concept of autonomy. Despite this sublimation, the concept of sovereignty remained bound to the notion of an embodiment in the assembled, physically present people. According to the republican view, the people are the bearers of a sovereignty that in principle cannot be delegated: in their sovereign character the people cannot have others represent them. Liberalism opposes this with the more realistic view that in the constitutional state any authority originating from the people is exercised only "by means of elections and voting and by specific legislative, executive, and judicial organs."[2]

These two views would exhaust the alternatives only if we had to conceive state and society in terms of the whole and its parts—where the whole is constituted either by a sovereign citizenry or by a constitution. To the discourse theory of democracy corresponds, however, the image of a decentered society. To be sure, with the political public sphere the proceduralist model sets off an arena for the detection, identification, and interpretation of those problems that affect society as a whole. But the "self" of the self-organizing legal community here disappears in the subjectless forms of communication that regulate the flow of deliberations in such a way that their fallible results enjoy the presumption of rationality. This is not to denounce the intuition connected with the idea of popular sovereignty but to interpret it in intersubjective terms. Popular sovereignty, even if it becomes anonymous, retreats into democratic procedures and the legal implementation of their demanding communicative presuppositions only in order to make itself felt as communicatively generated power. Strictly speaking, this communicative power springs from the interactions between legally institutionalized will-formation and culturally mobilized publics. The latter for their part find a basis in the associations of a civil society quite distinct from both state and economy alike.

Read in procedural terms, the idea of popular sovereignty refers to a context that, while enabling the self-organization of a legal community, is not at the disposal of the citizens' will in any way. Deliberation is certainly supposed to provide the medium for a more or less conscious integration of the *legal community*; but this mode does not extend to the whole of society in which the political system is *embedded* as only one among several subsystems. Even

---

2 Cf. *The Basic Law of the Federal Republic of Germany*, article 20, sec. 2.

in its own proceduralist self-understanding, deliberative politics remains a component of a complex society, which as a whole resists the normative approach practiced in legal theory. In this regard the discourse-theoretic reading of democracy has a point of contact with a detached sociological approach that considers the political system neither the peak nor the center, nor even the formative model of society in general, but just one action system among others. On the other hand, politics must still be able to communicate, through the medium of law, with all the other legitimately ordered spheres of action, however these happen to be structured and steered.

DELIBERATIVE POLLING

TOWARD A BETTER-INFORMED DEMOCRACY

BY JAMES S. FISHKIN

James S. Fishkin, "Deliberative Polling," *Deliberative Polling: Toward a Better-Informed Democracy.* Copyright © 2011 by The Center for Deliberative Democracy. Reprinted with permission.

SEVENTEEN

EXECUTIVE SUMMARY

THE PROBLEM

Citizens are often uninformed about key public issues. Conventional polls represent the public's surface impressions of sound bites and headlines. The public, subject to what social scientists have called "rational ignorance," has little reason to confront trade-offs or invest time and effort in acquiring information or coming to a considered judgment.

THE PROCESS

Deliberative Polling® is an attempt to use television and public opinion research in a new and constructive way. A random, representative sample is first polled on the targeted issues. After this baseline poll, members of the sample are invited to gather at a single place for a weekend in order to discuss the issues. Carefully balanced briefing materials are sent to the participants and are also made publicly available. The participants engage in dialogue with competing experts and political leaders based on questions they develop in small group discussions with trained moderators. Parts of the weekend events are broadcast on television, either live or in taped and edited form. After the deliberations, the sample is again asked the original questions. The resulting changes in opinion represent the conclusions the public would reach, if people had opportunity to become more informed and more engaged by the issues.

HISTORY

Professor James Fishkin of Stanford University originated the concept of Deliberative Polling® in 1988. He has served as either Director or Academic Advisor for all of the Deliberative Polling® events conducted thus far. Previously he was the Director of the Center for Deliberative Polling® at the University of Texas at Austin. The Austin Center was moved to Stanford on Sept 1. 2003 and will continue under the new name Center for Deliberative Democracy. The Center will focus on research and application of Deliberative Polling®.

Deliberative Polling is a registered trademark and fees from the trademark go to the Center to support research. The Center for Deliberative Democracy has received generous support from the William and Flora Hewlett Foundation and from Stanford University.

Professor Robert C. Luskin of the Department of Government at the University of Texas in Austin is a Senior Fellow at the Center in Stanford. He is a recognized expert on public opinion and on research methodology.

The Center's Senior Advisors are Dr. Charls E. Walker and Dan Werner. Dr. Walker is a former Deputy Secretary of the Treasury. Dan Werner is President of MacNeil/Lehrer Productions and was Co-executive Producer of the National Issues Convention broadcasts.

Deliberative Polling® experiments have been conducted over twenty two times in the U.S. and abroad.

- There have been five national Deliberative Polls in Britain conducted by the television network Channel Four.

- Two national Deliberative Polls have been conducted in Australia, the first before the November 1999 referendum on Australia's possibly changing from a monarchy to a republic and the second, on reconciliation with the Aboriginals in February 2001. These events, broadcast on national television were a collaboration with Issues Deliberation Australia, involving national random samples of Australians brought to Canberra for three days of discussions in dialogue with experts and key political leaders.

- In August, 2000, we collaborated with the Danish publication <u>Monday Morning</u> and scholars at the University of Southern Denmark in Odense to mount a national Deliberative Poll before the Danish national referendum on the Euro. The weekend's proceedings were televised at length by Danish Broadcasting.

- In the U.S. there have been two events at the national level as well as ten local versions. The National Issues Convention, a collaboration of the University of Texas, PBS, MacNeil/Lehrer Productions and the National Opinion Research Center at the University of Chicago, was broadcast from Austin in January 1996. In January of 2003, the first online Deliberative Poll culminated soon after a face-to-face Deliberative Poll in Philadelphia with a national random sample of 340 participants that deliberated with the same briefing materials and took the same questionnaire.

- Eight regulated public utilities have conducted Deliberative Polls in their service territories in cooperation with the Public Utility Commission of the State of Texas—Central Power and Light (Corpus Christi), West Texas Utilities (Abilene) and South West Electric Power (Shreveport, La.), El Paso Electric (El Paso, TX), Houston Lighting and Power (Houston), Entergy (Beaumont, TX) Southwestern Public Service (Amarillo) and Texas Utilities (Dallas). The success of those polls led the PUC to require that the public be consulted on public utility policies after it has had an opportunity to become informed on the issues. In November 1999, the Nike Foundation and Oregon Public Broadcasting conducted a Deliberative Polling® process on education issues with students drawn, system-wide, from the Portland public school system. In March 2002, a local Deliberative Polling® experiment was held at Yale with the fifteen towns in the New Haven metropolitan area on regional economic cooperation between the city and suburbs.

RESULTS

Each experiment conducted thus far has gathered a highly representative sample together at a single place. Each time, there were dramatic, statistically significant changes in views. The result is a poll with a human face. The process has the statistical representativeness of a scientific sample but it also has the concreteness and immediacy of a focus group or a discussion group. Taped and edited accounts of the small group discussions provide an opportunity for the public to reframe the issues in terms that connect with ordinary people.

The weekend samples have typically ranged in size from approximately 200 in the utility polls to a high of 466 at the 1996 National Issues Convention. The process provides the data to evaluate both the representativeness of each microcosm and the statistical significance of the changes in opinion. A very partial listing of significant changes is detailed in Tab 2.

APPLICATIONS

Deliberative Polling® is especially suitable for issues where the public may have little knowledge or information, or where the public may have failed to confront the trade-offs applying to public policy. It is a social science experiment and a form of public education in the broadest sense.

DELIBERATIVE POLLING®, 1994–2000: HOW PARTICIPANTS CHANGE (SELECTED RESULTS)

Table 17–1. The National Issues Convention January 1996, Austin, Texas

	Before Deliberation %	After Deliberation %	Difference %
In favor of:			
"A tax reduction for savings"	66	83	+17
"Flat Tax"	44	30	−14
"Education and Training" (agree that we are now spending "too little")	72	86	+14
"Foreign aid" (agree that current level is "about right")	26	41	+15
"Safety net for welfare and health care" should be turned over to the states "to decide how much to give"	50	63	+13
"Make divorce harder to get" (as a way of strengthening the family)	36	57	+21
"Military cooperation with other nations to address trouble spots in the world" ("agree strongly that U.S. should continue)	21	38	+17
"Biggest problem facing the American family" is "economic pressure"	36	51	+15
"Biggest problem facing the American family" is "breakdown of traditional values"	58	48	−10

Table 17-2. Deliberative Polling® on Crime 1994 (Britain)

	Before Deliberation %	After Deliberation %	Difference %
Agree that:			
"Sending more offenders to prison" is "an effective way of fighting crime"	57	38	−19
"The rules in court should be LESS on the side of the accused	42	52	+10
"Suspects should have the right to remain silent under police questioning"	36	50	+14
Disagree that:			
"The police should sometimes be able to 'bend the rules' to get a conviction (strongly disagree)	37	46	+9
"First time burglar, aged 16" should be sent to an ordinary prison (strongly against)	33	50	+17

Table 17-3. British Deliberative Polling® on Europe 1995

	Before Deliberation %	After Deliberation %	Difference %
Agree that:			
Britain is a lot better off in the EU than out of it	45	60	+15
Closer links with EU would make Britain stronger economically	51	67	+16
If we left EU Britain would lose its best chance of real progress	40	53	+13
With single currency, Britain would lose control of its own economic policy	62	50	−12

Table 17-4. British Deliberative Polling® on the Monarchy 1996

	Before Deliberation %	After Deliberation %	Difference %
Agree that:			
"The Monarchy makes me proud to be British"	48	59	+11
"The Monarchy's role in uniting people from throughout Britain" is "very important"	32	41	+9
"The Monarchy should remain as it is"	51	39	−12
"The Monarchy should be reformed"	34	50	+16
The "Monarch should not stay head of the Church of England"	26	56	+30

Table 17-5. British Deliberative Polling® on the General Election 1997

	Before Deliberation %	After Deliberation %	Difference %
Voting Intention			
Conservative	26	19	−7
Labour	47	39	−8
Liberal Democrat	11	33	+22
Agree that:			
"Government should do more to unite fully with European Union	36	49	+13
"Unless Britain keeps its own currency, it will lose too much control over its own economic policy"	69	48	−19

Table 17-w6. Electric Utility Deliberative Polling® Conducted for CPL (Central Power and Light), WTU (West Texas Utilities) and SWEPCO (South West Electric Power) 1996

	Before Deliberation %	After Deliberation %	Difference %
Option to pursue first (to provide additional electric power to service territory):			
Renewable energy (CPL)	67	16	−51
Renewable energy (WTU)	71	35	−36
Renewable energy (SWEPCO)	67	28	−39
Invest in conservation (CPL)	11	46	+35
Invest in conservation (WTU)	7	31	+24
Invest in conservation (SWEPCO)	16	50	+34
Build fossil fuel plant (CPL)	11	29	+18
Buy and transport power (WTU)	10	18	+8
% of customers who were willing to pay at least $1 more on their monthly bill for renewable energy			
CPL	58	81	+23
WTU	56	90	+34
SWEPCO	52	84	+32

"AUSTRALIA DELIBERATES": OCTOBER 1999

A nationally representative random sample of 347 Australian voters were assembled over the weekend of October 22–24, 1999 at Old Parliament House in Canberra to discuss the issues involved in the referendum in Australia's first ever Deliberative Poll.

The event was organized by Issues Deliberation Australia, in collaboration with the Research School of Social Sciences at the Australian National University, and in consultation with the Centers for Deliberative Polling and Australian Studies at the University of Texas. It was broadcast by ABC (the Australian Broadcasting Corp) and by the "Sixty Minutes" program on the Nine Network. In addition, *The Australian* newspaper was a partner in the event.

Participants attending the Australia Deliberates were first interviewed in early September, about six weeks prior to being invited to attend the deliberations. They were then polled at the end of the weekend, following wide-ranging discussions and questioning of experts from all sides of the debate.

THE MAIN RESULTS

When Australians had the opportunity to discuss intensely the referendum on the republic, opinion shifted dramatically.

- there was a 20 percentage point increase in 'yes' voters, from 53 to 73 percent.
- support for the direct election of the President collapsed, from 50 to 19 percent.
- levels of political information increased very substantially, notably in relation to the role and powers of the President.
- 84 percent believed that the monarchy represents British interests, compared to 64 percent before the deliberations.
- fewer believed that the change is expensive or that the Referendum is a distraction from other problems
- there was a dramatic increase in the proportions who believe that the President should be non-political—up from 53 to 88 percent.
- after the weekend few believed that the Australian flag would change as a result of a yes vote at the referendum—down from 59 to 8 percent.

Support for the republican model in the referendum increased dramatically between the first poll, in early September, and the Deliberative Poll. The proportion of the participants supporting the republican model increased from 53 percent prior to the deliberations to 73 percent afterwards. Following the deliberations, there were no uncommitted voters.

On the referendum question:

Approve the proposed alteration to the constitution?

	% Before	% After	% Change
Yes	53	73	+20
No	40	27	−13
Uncommitted	7	−	−7

The referendum question involved the model of a President appointed by Parliament. But the public debate focused on direct election. Hence the Deliberative Poll probed attitudes about all three alternatives—the status quo, the appointed model and direct election. Support for the direct election model as a first choice collapsed following the weekend's deliberations, with most of the participants favoring the model in the referendum proposal. Half of the participants favored a direction election model prior to the weekend, but only 19 percent did so after they had more information. A majority (61 percent) opted for the proposed model, the appointment of the President by Parliament.

First choice model

	% Before	% After	% Change
Change to a republic with a President directly elected by the people	50	19	−31
Change to a republic with a President appointed by Parliament	20	61	+41
Not change anything, keeping the Queen and the Governor-General in their current roles	26	15	+11
None, don't know	4	5	+1

MAJOR INCREASES IN LEVELS OF POLITICAL KNOWLEDGE

During the course of the weekend, levels of basic political information increased dramatically among the participants, and this was a major factor underlying the changes in opinions noted above. Prior to the weekend, just over half believed that they had enough information to vote on the republic; after the weekend, three out of 10 believed that they had enough information.

The most dramatic change was in relation to the role of the President. Prior to the deliberations, just 16 percent understood that the Prime Minister could remove the President at any time but must obtain approval from the House of Representatives; after the deliberations, 73 percent possessed this information, an increase of 57 percentage points.

Changes in Political Knowledge

	% Before	% After	% Change
Currently know enough to be able to vote on republic	57	78	+21
Powers of president same relative to current Governor-General	61	87	+26
Queen appoints the Governor-General only on advice of Prime Minister	39	85	+46
Prime Minister can remove President at any time but must later obtain approval from the House of Representative	16	73	+57
President would be no more powerful than Governor–General is now	61	76	+15

DANISH DELIBERATIVE POLLING® ON THE EURO

On August 25–27, 2000, a national random sample of the Danish electorate gathered at the University of Southern Denmark at Odense in conjunction with **DR** (the national television network) and under the sponsorship of the publication Monday Morning. The Prime Minister, Poul Nyrup Rasmussen, the Leader of the Opposition, Anders Fogh Rasmussen, and most of the prominent advocates on both sides of the debate over joining the single currency participated in the weekend's discussions answering questions from the sample. **DR** provided five and half-hours of national broadcast on television as well as extensive radio coverage.

A representative sample of 364 participants offered the following opinions, before and after the weekend's deliberations:

	Before	After
Yes on the Euro	45%	51%
No on the Euro	36%	40%
Undecided	19%	9%
Agree that: "Being a member of the EU is positive for Denmark"	68%	75%

(Continued)		
"The single currency is a step toward 'the United States of Europe'"	68%	47%
Agree that Danish participation in The single currency:		
"weakens the Danish welfare system"	26%	35%
"Gives Denmark a stronger say in EU decisions"	57%	64%

AUSTRALIAN DELIBERATIVE POLLING® ON ABORIGINAL RECONCILIATION

On February 16–18, 2001 a national random sample of the Australian people was brought to the Old Parliament House in Canberra for a national Deliberative Poll that was broadcast on the Australian Broadcasting Corp.

The summary below is from the March 6, 2001 press conference convened by Dr. Pamela Ryan, Managing Director of Issues Deliberation Australia, the principal sponsoring organization. The Center for Deliberative Polling at the University of Texas, Austin was one of the co-sponsors of this project. More information on the Australian Deliberative Polls is available at http://www.i-d-a.com.au

SUMMARY OF MAIN FINDINGS

When Australians had the opportunity to discuss and question intensely the diverse range of issues under the general topic of Reconciliation, opinion shifted dramatically.

- Perception of reconciliation as an important issue facing the nation rose dramatically from 31% (31%) prior to deliberations to 60% (63%) following deliberations.

- Perception of disadvantage of indigenous Australians in relation to other Australians rose dramatically: from 52% (51%) prior to deliberation to 80% (82%) post deliberation.

- Levels of political knowledge in relation to indigenous issues, government services and political leaders also rose substantially, with gains in knowledge ranging from 11(9) to 50 (52) percentage points depending on the item.

Correlating significantly with changes in perceptions of the importance of the issue, changes in perceptions of levels of indigenous disadvantage and increases in levels of political knowledge, were levels of support for a range of national initiatives:

- formal acknowledgement that Australia was occupied without consent of indigenous Australians: 68% (67%) to 81% (82%);

- formal acknowledgement that indigenous Australians were the original owners of the land and waters: 73% (74%) to 81% (82%);

- an apology to the "stolen generation": 46% (45%) to 68% (70%).

- In contrast, support for some initiatives remained relatively unchanged before and after deliberations:

- a treaty or set of agreements between indigenous and non-indigenous Australians;

- allocation of special seats in parliament for indigenous Australians

Where support increased for other initiatives, such as land rights and compensation to 'the stolen generation', support was based on specific conditions, such as proof of historical/cultural links with the land, and proof of physical, emotional, financial and cultural deprivation as a result of removal.

In terms of government focus for the future: following deliberation, support for education as the key priority rose significantly from 42% to 59% (42%–55%), while health, unemployment and housing all dropped by an average of ten percentage points. [Note: first percentages quoted are those controlled for indigenous participation in group discussion, sample size = 240, percentages in parentheses are those for the complete national random sample of 344]

NEW HAVEN DELIBERATIVE POLLING® ON REGIONAL ECONOMIC COOPERATION

The New Haven Regional Dialogue, Deliberative Polling® conducted at Yale University showed dramatic changes of opinion on the issue of local revenue sharing. A randomly-selected and representative sample of residents of the fifteen towns in the New Haven region spent the weekend, March 1–3, 2002, considering regional eonomic policy. When they completed their discussions, they supported voluntary revenue sharing among towns and state provision of incentives to encourage sharing of new revenues from commercial development.

Participants moved strongly away from the proposition that "my town should maintain local control over all of its tax revenues from new businesses and industries." When first interviewed, 80 per cent agreed with this statement. After deliberation, support fell to 42%.

By contrast, voluntary agreements for sharing of incremental revenue showed a dramatic increase in support. Before deliberation 64% agreed that "my town should try for a voluntary agreement with other towns in the region to share some tax revenues from new businesses and industries." After deliberation, support rose to 81%. Support also increased from 68% to 80% for the state's providing "incentives for towns in the region to share some tax revenues for new businesses and industry."

Participants also showed increases in their levels of information. For example, before the weekend, only 8% knew that Connecticut law allows communities to share property tax revenues. After the weekend, 69% knew. The percentage who knew that the rate of job growth in the New Haven region was less than the national average during the 1990's, rose from 44% to 75%.

Evaluations of the process by the participants were strongly positive.
Large majorities, 87% thought that the members of their small groups "participated relatively equally in the discussion".
94% felt that the moderator "did not try to influence the group with his or her own views".
79% of participants gave the process an 8,9 or 10 on a 0 to 10 scale and felt that the process as a whole was highly valuable.

OPINIONS ON DELIBERATIVE POLLING®

"Deliberative Polling® is the most promising innovation in democratic practice of which I am aware. I hope that in the coming century, it will be widely adopted in the United States and other democratic countries."
    Robert A. Dahl, Sterling Professor of Political Science Emeritus, Yale University

"An innovative method for bridging the chasm between the electors and the elected"
    Walter Shapiro, *Time Magazine*

"Deliberative Polling® combines two familiar techniques—sample surveys and focus groups—into a powerful new technique for gauging informed public opinion. I think it is the most innovative approach to studying public opinion since the development of scientific polling in the 1930's"
    Norman Bradburn, Senior Vice President for Research, National Opinion Research
    Center at the University of Chicago

"From the point of view of citizenship and democratic values, the Deliberative polling® design is a delightfully fresh departure. From the scientific point of view, it holds promise of carrying us well beyond what we have learned to date from standard opinion surveys about how voters process new information bearing on their political beliefs. This is a visionary kind of inquiry."
    Philip E. Converse, Professor Emeritus, The University of Michigan and coauthor, *The American Voter.*

"An exciting concept… It has the potential to dramatically change a generally detached electorate contained in small self-indulgent pens, bounded by ignorance and cynicism, into a far-better informed and involved body of voters, unbounded in their urges to fully comprehend the issues they define and then to participate in the process to see their studied views become active reality."
    Jane Ely, Columnist, *Houston Chronicle*

"Is there not something enlightening, indeed heartening, in watching voters who mirror us all wrestling with issues, listening with respect to the views of others, trying to find consensus?…[a] promising, important, innovation in American democracy."
    Neal R. Peirce, nationally syndicated columnist

"The potential contribution [of Deliberative Polling] to a better-informed democracy is great… It is in the interest of all that it should be encouraged."
    The Independent (London) Editorial "Knowledge Can Change Minds"

"Deliberative Polling® as developed by Professor James Fishkin at the University of Texas has the potential to show policymakers and the public what well-informed citizens would think about complex issues. This potential was demonstrated at the National Issues Convention in Austin as well as in other Deliberative Polls held locally in Texas and nationally in Great Britain. In my judgment, this kind of research could be of great use to the legislative process as well as to efforts to better inform the public."
    Representative Bill Archer (R., Texas, and Chairman, House Ways and Means Committee)

"I think it's a wonderful development. And if there is anybody in this group who wonders whether or not this is going anywhere or has accomplished anything, you should stop wondering because I think it has been a tremendous success. I think you have started something great here. And I think that the great Barbara Jordan, who died this past week, should be remembered for many things, but among them should be her work in helping to make this whole event and process happen."
    Vice President Al Gore answering questions from the delegates during the National Issues Convention broadcast, January 16, 1996

CAPITALISM, SOCIALISM, AND DEMOCRACY

CHAPTERS 21 AND 22

BY JOSEPH SCHUMPETER

Joseph Schumpeter, "Chapters XXI and XXII," *Capitalism, Socialism, and Democracy*, pp. 250-273. Copyright © 1947 by HarperCollins Publishers. Reprinted with permission.

EIGHTEEN

CHAPTER 21: THE CLASSICAL DOCTRINE OF DEMOCRACY

I. THE COMMON GOOD AND THE WILL OF THE PEOPLE

The eighteenth-century philosophy of democracy may be couched in the following definition: the democratic method is that institutional arrangement for arriving at political decisions which realizes the common good by making the people itself decide issues through the election of individuals who are to assemble in order to carry out its will. Let us develop the implications of this.

It is held, then, that there exists a Common Good, the obvious beacon light of policy, which is always simple to define and which every normal person can be made to see by means of rational argument. There is hence no excuse for not seeing it and in fact no explanation for the presence of people who do not see it except ignorance—which can be removed—stupidity and anti-social interest. Moreover, this common good implies definite answers to all questions so that every social fact and every measure taken or to be taken can unequivocally be classed as "good" or "bad." All people having therefore to agree, in principle at least, there is also a Common Will of the people (=will of all reasonable individuals) that is exactly coterminous with the common good or interest or welfare or happiness. The only thing, barring stupidity and sinister interests, that can possibly bring in disagreement and account for the presence of an opposition is a difference of opinion as to the speed with which the goal, itself common to nearly all, is to be approached. Thus every member of the community, conscious of that goal, knowing his or her mind, discerning what is good and what is bad, takes part, actively and responsibly, in furthering the former and fighting the latter and all the members taken together control their public affairs.

It is true that the management of some of these affairs requires special aptitudes and techniques and will therefore have to be entrusted to specialists who have them. This does not affect the principle, however, because these specialists simply act in order to carry out the will of the people exactly as a doctor acts in order to carry out the will of the patient to get well. It is also true that in a community of any size, especially if it displays the phenomenon of division of labor, it would be highly inconvenient for every individual citizen to have to get into contact with all the other citizens on every issue in order to do his part in ruling or governing. It will be more convenient to reserve only the most important decisions for the individual citizens to pronounce upon—say by referendum—and to deal with the rest through a committee appointed by them—an assembly or parliament whose members will be elected by popular vote. This committee or body of delegates, as we have seen, will not represent the people in a legal sense but it will do so in a less technical one—it will voice, reflect or represent the will of the electorate. Again as a matter of convenience, this committee, being large, may resolve itself into smaller ones for the various departments of public affairs. Finally, among these smaller committees there will be a general-purpose committee, mainly for dealing with current administration, called cabinet or government, possibly with a general secretary or scapegoat at its head, a so-called prime minister.[1]

As soon as we accept all the assumptions that are being made by this theory of the polity—or implied by it—democracy indeed acquires a perfectly unambiguous meaning and there is no problem in connection with it except how to bring it about. Moreover we need only forget a few logical qualms in order to be able to add that in this case the democratic arrangement would not only be the best of all conceivable ones, but that few people would care to consider any other. It is no less obvious however that these assumptions are so many statements of fact every one of which would have to be proved if we are to arrive at that conclusion. And it is much easier to disprove them.

There is, first, no such thing as a uniquely determined common good that all people could agree on or be made to agree on by the force of rational argument. This is due not primarily to the fact that some people may want things other than the common good but to the much more fundamental fact that to different individuals and groups the common good is bound to mean different things. This fact, hidden from the utilitarian by the narrowness of his outlook on the world of human valuations, will introduce rifts on questions of principle which cannot be reconciled by rational argument because ultimate values—our conceptions of what life and what society should

---

1 The official theory of the functions of a cabinet minister holds in fact that he is appointed in order to see to it that in his department the will of the people prevails.

be—are beyond the range of mere logic. They may be bridged by compromise in some cases but not in others. Americans who say, "We want this country to arm to its teeth and then to fight for what we conceive to be right all over the globe" and Americans who say, "We want this country to work out its own problems which is the only way it can serve humanity" are facing irreducible differences of ultimate values which compromise could only maim and degrade.

Secondly, even if a sufficiently definite common good—such as for instance the utilitarian's maximum of economic satisfaction[2]—proved acceptable to all, this would not imply equally definite answers to individual issues. Opinions on these might differ to an extent important enough to produce most of the effects of "fundamental" dissension about ends themselves. The problems centering in the evaluation of present versus future satisfactions, even the case of socialism versus capitalism, would be left still open, for instance, after the conversion of every individual citizen to utilitarianism. "Health" might be desired by all, yet people would still disagree on vaccination and vasectomy. And so on.

The utilitarian fathers of democratic doctrine failed to see the full importance of this simply because none of them seriously considered any substantial change in the economic framework and the habits of bourgeois society. They saw little beyond the world of an eighteenth-century ironmonger.

But, third, as a consequence of both preceding propositions, the particular concept of the will of the people or the *volonté générale* that the utilitarians made their own vanishes into thin air. For that concept presupposes the existence of a uniquely determined common good discernible to all. Unlike the romanticists the utilitarians had no notion of that semi-mystic entity endowed with a will of its own—that "soul of the people" which the historical school of jurisprudence made so much of. They frankly derived their will of the people from the wills of individuals. And unless there is a center, the common good, toward which, in the long run at least, *all* individual wills gravitate, we shall not get that particular type of "natural" *volonté générale*. The utilitarian center of gravity, on the one hand, unifies individual wills, tends to weld them by means of rational discussion into the will of the people and, on the other hand, confers upon the latter the exclusive ethical dignity claimed by the classic democratic creed. *This creed does not consist simply in worshiping the will of the people as such* but rests on certain assumptions about the "natural" object of that will which object is sanctioned by utilitarian reason. Both the existence and the dignity of this kind of *volonté générale* are gone as soon as the idea of the common good fails us. And both the pillars of the classical doctrine inevitably crumble into dust.

---

[2] The very meaning of "greatest happiness" is open to serious doubt. But even if this doubt could be removed and definite meaning could be attached to the sum total of economic satisfaction of a group of people, that maximum would still be relative to given situations and valuations which it may be impossible to alter, or compromise on, in a democratic way.

II. THE WILL OF THE PEOPLE AND INDIVIDUAL VOLITION

Of course, however conclusively those arguments may tell against this particular conception of the will of the people, they do not debar us from trying to build up nother and more realistic one. I do not intend to question either the reality or the importance of the socio-psychological facts we think of when speaking of the will of a nation. Their analysis is certainly the prerequisite for making headway with the problems of democracy. It would however be better not to retain the term because this tends to obscure the fact that as soon as we have severed the will of the people from its utilitarian connotation we are building not merely a different theory of the same thing, but a theory of a completely different thing. We have every reason to be on our guard against the pitfalls that lie on the path of those defenders of democracy who while accepting, under pressure of accumulating evidence, more and more of the facts of the democratic process, yet try to anoint the results that process turns out with oil taken from eighteenth-century jars.

But though a common will or public opinion of some sort may still be said to emerge from the infinitely complex jumble of individual and group-wise situations, volitions, influences, actions and reactions of the "democratic process," the result lacks not only rational unity but also rational sanction. The former means that, though from the standpoint of analysis, the democratic process is not simply chaotic—for the analyst nothing is chaotic that can be brought within the reach of explanatory principles—yet the results would not, except by chance, be meaningful in themselves—as for instance the realization of any definite end or ideal would be. The latter means, since *that* will is no longer congruent with any "good," that in order to claim ethical dignity for the result it will now be necessary to fall back upon an unqualified confidence in democratic forms of government as such—a belief that in principle would have to be independent of the desirability of results. As we have seen, it is not easy to place oneself on that standpoint. But even if we do so, the dropping of the utilitarian common good still leaves us with plenty of difficulties on our hands.

In particular, we still remain under the practical necessity of attributing to the will of the *individual* an independence and a rational quality that are altogether unrealistic. If we are to argue that the will of the citizens *per se* is a political factor entitled to respect, it must first exist. That is to say, it must be something more than an indeterminate bundle of vague impulses loosely playing about given slogans and mistaken impressions. Everyone would have to know definitely what he wants to stand for. This definite will would have to be implemented by the ability to observe and interpret correctly the facts that are directly accessible to everyone and to sift critically the information about the facts that are not. Finally, from that definite will and from these ascertained facts a clear *and prompt* conclusion as to particular issues would have to be derived according to the rules of logical inference—with so high a degree of general efficiency moreover that one man's opinion could be held, without glaring absurdity, to be roughly as good as every other man's.[3] And all this the modal citizen would have to perform for himself and independently of pressure groups and propaganda,[4] for volitions and inferences that are imposed upon the electorate obviously do not qualify for ultimate data of the democratic process. The question whether these conditions are fulfilled to the extent required in order to make democracy work should not be answered by reckless assertion or equally reckless denial. It can be answered only by a laborious appraisal of a maze of conflicting evidence.

Before embarking upon this, however, I want to make quite sure that the reader fully appreciates another point that has been made already. I will therefore repeat that even if the opinions and desires of individual citizens were perfectly definite and independent data for the democratic process to work with, and if everyone acted on them with ideal rationality and promptitude, it would not necessarily follow that the political decisions produced by that process from the raw material of those individual volitions would represent anything that could in any convincing sense be called the will of the people. It is not only conceivable but, whenever individual wills are much divided, very likely that the political decisions produced will not conform to "what people really want." Nor can it be replied that, if not exactly what they want, they will get a "fair compromise." This may be so. The chances for this to happen are greatest with those issues which are quantitative in nature or admit of gradation, such as the question how much is to be spent on unemployment relief provided everybody favors some expenditure for that purpose. But with qualitative issues, such as the question whether to persecute heretics or to enter upon a war, the result attained may

---

3   This accounts for the strongly equalitarian character both of the classical doctrine of democracy and of popular democratic beliefs. It will be pointed out later on how Equality may acquire the status of an ethical postulate. As a factual statement about human nature it cannot be true in any conceivable sense. In recognition of this the postulate itself has often been reformulated so as to mean "equality of opportunity." But, disregarding even the difficulties inherent in the word opportunity, this reformulation does not help us much because it is actual and not potential equality of performance in matters of political behavior that is required if each man's vote is to carry the same weight in the decision of issues.

It should be noted in passing that democratic phraseology has been instrumental in fostering the association of inequality of any kind with "injustice" which is so important an element in the psychic pattern of the unsuccessful and in the arsenal of the politician who uses him. One of the most curious symptoms of this was the Athenian institution of ostracism or rather the use to which it was sometimes put. Ostracism consisted in banishing an individual by popular vote, not necessarily for any particular reason: it sometimes served as a method of eliminating an uncomfortably prominent citizen who was felt to "count for more than one."

4   This term is here being used in its original sense and not in the sense which it is rapidly acquiring at present and which suggests the definition: propaganda is any statement emanating from a source that we do not like. I suppose that the term derives from the name of the committee of cardinals which deals with matters concerning the spreading of the Catholic faith, the *congregatio de propaganda fide*. In itself therefore it does not carry any derogatory meaning and in particular it does not imply distortion of facts. One can make propaganda, for instance, for a scientific method. It simply means the presentation of facts and arguments with a view to influencing people's actions or opinions in a definite direction.

well, though for different reasons, be equally distasteful to all the people whereas the decision imposed by a non-democratic agency might prove much more acceptable to them.

An example will illustrate. I may, I take it, describe the rule of Napoleon, when First Consul, as a military dictatorship. One of the most pressing political needs of the moment was a religious settlement that would clear the chaos left by the revolution and the directorate and bring peace to millions of hearts. This he achieved by a number of master strokes, culminating in a concordat with the pope (1801) and the "organic articles" (1802) that, reconciling the irreconcilable, gave just the right amount of freedom to religious worship while strongly upholding the authority of the state. He also reorganized and refinanced the French Catholic church, solved the delicate question of the "constitutional" clergy, and most successfully launched the new establishment with a minimum of friction. If ever there was any justification at all for holding that the people actually want something definite, this arrangement affords one of the best instances in history. This must be obvious to anyone who looks at the French class structure of that time and it is amply borne out by the fact that this ecclesiastical policy greatly contributed to the almost universal popularity which the consular regime enjoyed. But it is difficult to see how this result could have been achieved in a democratic way. Anti-church sentiment had not died out and was by no means confined to the vanquished Jacobins. People of that persuasion, or their leaders, could not possibly have compromised to that extent.[5] On the other end of the scale, a strong wave of wrathful Catholic sentiment was steadily gaining momentum. People who shared that sentiment, or leaders dependent on their good will, could not possibly have stopped at the Napoleonic limit; in particular, they could not have dealt so firmly with the Holy See for which moreover there would have been no motive to give in, seeing which way things were moving. And the will of the peasants who more than anything else wanted their priests, their churches and processions would have been paralyzed by the very natural fear that the revolutionary settlement of the land question might be endangered once the clergy—the bishops especially—were in the saddle again. Deadlock or interminable struggle, engendering increasing irritation, would have been the most probable outcome of any attempt to settle the question democratically. But Napoleon was able to settle it reasonably, precisely because all those groups which could not yield their points of their own accord were at the same time able and willing to accept the arrangement if imposed.

This instance of course is not an isolated one.[6] If results that prove in the long run satisfactory to the people at large are made the test of government *for* the people, then government *by* the people, as conceived by the classical doctrine of democracy, would often fail to meet it.

---

5 The legislative bodies, cowed though they were, completely failed in fact to support Napoleon in this policy. And some of his most trusted paladins opposed it.
6 Other instances could in fact be adduced from Napoleon's practice. He was an autocrat who, whenever his dynastic interests and his foreign policy were not concerned, simply strove to do what he conceived the people wanted or needed.

III. HUMAN NATURE IN POLITICS

It remains to answer our question about the definiteness and independence of the voter's will, his powers of observation and interpretation of facts, and his ability to draw, clearly and promptly, rational inferences from both. This subject belongs to a chapter of social psychology that might be entitled Human Nature in Politics.[7]

During the second half of the last century, the idea of the human personality that is a homogeneous unit and the idea of a definite will that is the prime mover of action have been steadily fading—even before the times of Théodule Ribot and of Sigmund Freud. In particular, these ideas have been increasingly discounted in the field of social sciences where the importance of the extra-rational and irrational element in our behavior has been receiving more and more attention, witness Pareto's *Mind and Society*. Of the many sources of the evidence that accumulated against the hypothesis of rationality, I shall mention only two.

The one—in spite of much more careful later work—may still be associated with the name of Gustave Le Bon, the founder or, at any rate, the first effective exponent of the psychology of crowds *(psychologie des foules)*.[8] By showing up, though overstressing, the realities of human behavior when under the influence of agglomeration—in particular the sudden disappearance, in a state of excitement, of moral restraints and civilized modes of thinking and feeling, the sudden eruption of primitive impulses, infantilisms and criminal propensities—he made us face gruesome facts that everybody knew but nobody wished to see and he thereby dealt a serious blow to the picture of man's nature which underlies the classical doctrine of democracy and democratic folklore about revolutions. No doubt there is much to be said about the narrowness of the factual basis of Le Bon's inferences which, for instance, do not fit at all well the normal behavior of an English or Anglo-American crowd. Critics, especially those to whom the implications of this

---

This is what the advice amounted to which he gave to Eugène Beauharnais concerning the latter's administration of northern Italy.

7 This is the title of the frank and charming book by one of the most lovable English radicals who ever lived, Graham Wallas. In spite of all that has since been written on the subject and especially in spite of all the detailed case studies that now make it possible to see so much more clearly, that book may still be recommended as the best introduction to political psychology. Yet, after having stated with admirable honesty the case against the uncritical acceptance of the classical doctrine, the author fails to draw the obvious conclusion. This is all the more remarkable because he rightly insists on the necessity of a scientific attitude of mind and because he does not fail to take Lord Bryce to task for having, in his book on the American commonwealth, professed himself "grimly" resolved to see some blue sky in the midst of clouds of disillusioning facts. Why, so Graham Wallas seems to exclaim, what should we say of a meteorologist who insisted from the outset that he saw some blue sky? Nevertheless in the constructive part of his book he takes much the same ground.

8 The German term, *Massenpsychologie*, suggests a warning: the psychology of crowds must not be confused with the psychology of the masses. The former does not necessarily carry any class connotation and in itself has nothing to do with a study of the ways of thinking and feeling of, say, the working class.

branch of social psychology were uncongenial, did not fail to make the most of its vulnerable points. But on the other hand it must not be forgotten that the phenomena of crowd psychology are by no means confined to mobs rioting in the narrow streets of a Latin town. Every parliament, every committee, every council of war composed of a dozen generals in their sixties, displays, in however mild a form, some of those features that stand out so glaringly in the case of the rabble, in particular a reduced sense of responsibility, a lower level of energy of thought and greater sensitiveness to non-logical influences. Moreover, those phenomena are not confined to a crowd in the sense of a physical agglomeration of many people. Newspaper readers, radio audiences, members of a party even if not physically gathered together are terribly easy to work up into a psychological crowd and into a state of frenzy in which attempt at rational argument only spurs the animal spirits.

The other source of disillusioning evidence that I am going to mention is a much humbler one—no blood flows from it, only nonsense. Economists, learning to observe their facts more closely, have begun to discover that, even in the most ordinary currents of daily life, their consumers do not quite live up to the idea that the economic textbook used to convey. On the one hand their wants are nothing like as definite and their actions upon those wants nothing like as rational and prompt. On the other hand they are so amenable to the influence of advertising and other methods of persuasion that producers often seem to dictate to them instead of being directed by them. The technique of successful advertising is particularly instructive. There is indeed nearly always some appeal to reason. But mere assertion, often repeated, counts more than rational argument and so does the direct attack upon the subconscious which takes the form of attempts to evoke and crystallize pleasant associations of an entirely extra-rational, very frequently of a sexual nature.

The conclusion, while obvious, must be drawn with care. In the ordinary run of often repeated decisions the individual is subject to the salutary and rationalizing influence of favorable and unfavorable experience. He is also under the influence of relatively simple and unproblematical motives and interests which are but occasionally interfered with by excitement. Historically, the consumers' desire for shoes may, at least in part, have been shaped by the action of producers offering attractive footgear and campaigning for it; yet at any given time it is a genuine want, the definiteness of which extends beyond "shoes in general" and which prolonged experimenting clears of much of the irrationalities that may originally have surrounded it.[9] Moreover, under the stimulus of those simple motives consumers learn to act upon unbiased expert advice about some

---

9 In the above passage irrationality means failure to act rationally upon a given wish. It does not refer to the reasonableness of the wish itself in the opinion of the observer. This is important to note because economists in appraising the extent of consumers' irrationality sometimes exaggerate it by confusing the two things. Thus, a factory girl's finery may seem to a professor an indication of irrational behavior for which there is no other explanation but the advertiser's arts. Actually, it may be all she craves for. If so her expenditure on it may be ideally rational in the above sense.

things (houses, motorcars) and themselves become experts in others. It is simply not true that housewives are easily fooled in the matter of foods, *familiar* household articles, wearing apparel. And, as every salesman knows to his cost, most of them have a way of insisting on the exact article they want.

This of course holds true still more obviously on the producers' side of the picture. No doubt, a manufacturer may be indolent, a bad judge of opportunities or otherwise incompetent; but there is an effective mechanism that will reform or eliminate him. Again Taylorism rests on the fact that man may perform simple handicraft operations for thousands of years and yet perform them inefficiently. But neither the intention to act as rationally as possible nor a steady pressure toward rationality can seriously be called into question at whatever level of industrial or commercial activity we choose to look.[10]

And so it is with most of the decisions of daily life that lie within the little field which the individual citizen's mind encompasses with a full sense of its reality. Roughly, it consists of the things that directly concern himself, his family, his business dealings, his hobbies, his friends and enemies, his township or ward, his class, church, trade union or any other social group of which he is an active member—the things under his personal observation, the things which are familiar to him independently of what his newspaper tells him, which he can directly influence or manage and for which he develops the kind of responsibility that is induced by a direct relation to the favorable or unfavorable effects of a course of action.

Once more: definiteness and rationality in thought and action[11] are not guaranteed by this familiarity with men and things or by that sense of reality or responsibility. Quite a few other conditions which often fail to be fulfilled would be necessary for that. For instance, generation after generation may suffer from irrational behavior in matters of hygiene and yet fail to link their sufferings with their noxious habits. As long as this is not done, objective consequences, however regular, of course do not produce subjective experience. Thus it proved unbelievably hard for humanity to realize the relation between infection and epidemics: the facts pointed to it with what to us seems unmistakable clearness; yet to the end of the eighteenth century doctors did next to nothing to keep people afflicted with infectious disease, such as measles or smallpox, from mixing with other people. And things must be expected to be still worse whenever there is not only inability but reluctance to recognize causal relations or when some interest fights against recognizing them.

---

10   This level differs of course not only as between epochs and places but also, at a given time and place, as between different industrial sectors and classes. There is no such thing as a universal pattern of rationality.
11   Rationality of thought and rationality of action are two different things. Rationality of thought does not always guarantee rationality of action. And the latter may be present without any conscious deliberation and irrespective of any ability to formulate the rationale of one's action correctly. The observer, particularly the observer who uses interview and questionnaire methods, often overlooks this and hence acquires an exaggerated idea of the importance of irrationality in behavior. This is another source of those overstatements which we meet so often.

Nevertheless and in spite of all the qualifications that impose themselves, there is for everyone, within a much wider horizon, a narrower field—widely differing in extent as between different groups and individuals and bounded by a broad zone rather than a sharp line—which is distinguished by a sense of reality or familiarity or responsibility. And this field harbors relatively definite individual volitions. These may often strike us as unintelligent, narrow, egotistical; and it may not be obvious to everyone why, when it comes to political decisions, we should worship at their shrine, still less why we should feel bound to count each of them for one and none of them for more than one. If, however, we do choose to worship we shall at least not find the shrine empty.[12]

Now this comparative definiteness of volition and rationality of behavior does not suddenly vanish as we move away from those concerns of daily life in the home and in business which educate and discipline as. In the realm of public affairs there are sectors that are more within the reach of the citizen's mind than others. This is true, first, of local affairs. Even there we find a reduced power of discerning facts, a reduced preparedness to act upon them, a reduced sense of responsibility. We all know the man—and a very good specimen he frequently is—who says that the local administration is not his business and callously shrugs his shoulders at practices which he would rather die than suffer in his own office. High-minded citizens in a hortatory mood who preach the responsibility of the individual voter or taxpayer invariably discover the fact that this voter does not feel responsible for what the local politicians do. Still, especially in communities not too big for personal contacts, local patriotism may be a very important factor in "making democracy work." Also, the problems of a town are in many respects akin to the problems of a manufacturing concern. The man who understands the latter also understands, to some extent, the former. The manufacturer, grocer or workman need not step out of his world to have a rationally defensible view (that may of course be right or wrong) on street cleaning or town halls.

Second, there are many national issues that concern individuals and groups so directly and unmistakably as to evoke volitions that are genuine and definite enough. The most important instance is afforded by issues involving immediate and personal pecuniary profit to individual voters and groups of voters, such as direct payments, protective duties, silver policies and so

---

12   It should be observed that in speaking of definite and genuine volitions I do not mean to exalt them into ultimate data for all kinds of social analysis. Of course they are themselves the product of the social process and the social environment. All I mean is that they may serve as data for the kind of special-purpose analysis which the economist has in mind when he derives prices from tastes or wants that are "given" at any moment and need not be further analyzed each time. Similarly we may for our purpose speak of genuine and definite volitions that at any moment are given independently of attempts to manufacture them, although we recognize that these genuine volitions themselves are the result of environmental influences in the past, propagandist influences included. This distinction between genuine and manufactured will (see below) is a difficult one and cannot be applied in all cases and for all purposes. For our purpose however it is sufficient to point to the obvious common-sense case which can be made for it.

on. Experience that goes back to antiquity shows that by and large voters react promptly and rationally to any such chance. But the classical doctrine of democracy evidently stands to gain little from displays of rationality of this kind. Voters thereby prove themselves bad and indeed corrupt judges of such issues,[13] and often they even prove themselves bad judges of their own long-run interests, for it is only the short-run promise that tells politically and only short-run rationality that asserts itself effectively.

However, when we move still farther away from the private concerns of the family and the business office into those regions of national and international affairs that lack a direct and unmistakable link with those private concerns, individual volition, command of facts and method of inference soon cease to fulfill the requirements of the classical doctrine. What strikes me most of all and seems to me to be the core of the trouble is the fact that the sense of reality[14] is so completely lost. Normally, the great political questions take their place in the psychic economy of the typical citizen with those leisure-hour interests that have not attained the rank of hobbies, and with the subjects of irresponsible conversation. These things seem so far off; they are not at all like a business proposition; dangers may not materialize at all and if they should they may not prove so very serious; one feels oneself to be moving in a fictitious world.

This reduced sense of reality accounts not only for a reduced sense of responsibility but also for the absence of effective volition. One has one's phrases, of course, and one's wishes and daydreams and grumbles: especially, one has one's likes and dislikes. But ordinarily they do not amount to what we call a will—the psychic counterpart of purposeful responsible action. In fact, for the private citizen musing over national affairs there is no scope for such a will and no task at which it could develop. He is a member of an unworkable committee, the committee of the whole nation, and this is why he expends less disciplined effort on mastering a political problem than he expends on a game of bridge.[15]

---

13 The reason why the Benthamites so completely overlooked this is that they did not consider the possibilities of mass corruption in modern capitalism. Committing in their political theory the same error which they committed in their economic theory, they felt no compunction about postulating that "the people" were the best judges of their own individual interests and that these must necessarily coincide with the interests of all the people taken together. Of course this was made easier for them because actually though not intentionally they philosophized in terms of bourgeois interests which had more to gain from a parsimonious state than from any direct bribes.

14 William James' "pungent sense of reality." The relevance of this point has been particularly emphasized by Graham Wallas.

15 It will help to clarify the point if we ask ourselves why so much more intelligence and clear-headedness show up at a bridge table than in, say, political discussion among non-politicians. At the bridge table we have a definite task; we have rules that discipline us; success and failure are clearly defined; and we are prevented from behaving irresponsibly because every mistake we make will not only immediately tell but also be immediately allocated to us. These conditions, by their failure to be fulfilled for the political behavior of the ordinary citizen, show why it is that in politics he lacks all the alertness and the judgment he may display in his profession.

The reduced sense of responsibility and the absence of effective volition in turn explain the ordinary citizen's ignorance and lack of judgment in matters of domestic and foreign policy which are if anything more shocking in the case of educated people and of people who are successfully active in non-political walks of life than it is with uneducated people in humble stations. Information is plentiful and readily available. But this does not seem to make any difference. Nor should we wonder at it. We need only compare a lawyer's attitude to his brief and the same lawyer's attitude to the statements of political fact presented in his newspaper in order to see what is the matter. In the one case the lawyer has qualified for appreciating the relevance of his facts by years of purposeful labor done under the definite stimulus of interest in his professional competence; and under a stimulus that is no less powerful he then bends his acquirements, his intellect, his will to the contents of the brief. In the other case, he has not taken the trouble to qualify; he does not care to absorb the information or to apply to it the canons of criticism he knows so well how to handle; and he is impatient of long or complicated argument. All of this goes to show that without the initiative that comes from immediate responsibility, ignorance will persist in the face of masses of information however complete and correct. It persists even in the face of the meritorious efforts that are being made to go beyond presenting information and to teach the use of it by means of lectures, classes, discussion groups. Results are not zero. But they are small. People cannot be carried up the ladder.

Thus the typical citizen drops down to a lower level of mental performance as soon as he enters the political field. He argues and analyzes in a way which he would readily recognize as infantile within the sphere of his real interests. He becomes a primitive again. His thinking becomes associative and affective.[16] And this entails two further consequences of ominous significance.

First, even if there were no political groups trying to influence him, the typical citizen would in political matters tend to yield to extrarational or irrational prejudice and impulse. The weakness of the rational processes he applies to politics and the absence of effective logical control over the results he arrives at would in themselves suffice to account for that. Moreover, simply because he is not "all there," he will relax his usual moral standards as well and occasionally give in to dark urges which the conditions of private life help him to repress. But as to the wisdom or rationality of his inferences and conclusions, it may be just as bad if he gives in to a burst of generous indignation. This will make it still more difficult for him to see things in their correct proportions or even to see more than one aspect of one thing at a time. Hence, if for once he does emerge from his usual vagueness and does display the definite will postulated by the classical doctrine of democracy, he is as likely as not to become still more unintelligent and irresponsible than he usually is. At certain junctures, this may prove fatal to his nation.[17]

---

16 See ch. xii.
17 The importance of such bursts cannot be doubted. But it is possible to doubt their genuineness. Analysis will show in many instances that they are induced by the action of some group and do not spontaneously arise from the people.

Second, however, the weaker the logical element in the processes of the public mind and the more complete the absence of rational criticism and of the rationalizing influence of personal experience and responsibility, the greater are the opportunities for groups with an ax to grind. These groups may consist of professional politicians or of exponents of an economic interest or of idealists of one kind or another or of people simply interested in staging and managing political shows. The sociology of such groups is immaterial to the argument in hand. The only point that matters here is that, Human Nature in Politics being what it is, they are able to fashion and, within very wide limits, even to create the will of the people. What we are confronted with in the analysis of political processes is largely not a genuine but a manufactured will. And often this artefact is all that in reality corresponds to the *volonté générale* of the classical doctrine. So far as this is so, the will of the people is the product and not the motive power of the political process.

The ways in which issues and the popular will on any issue are being manufactured is exactly analogous to the ways of commercial advertising. We find the same attempts to contact the subconscious. We find the same technique of creating favorable and unfavorable associations which are the more effective the less rational they are. We find the same evasions and reticences and the same trick of producing opinion by reiterated assertion that is successful precisely to the extent to which it avoids rational argument and the danger of awakening the critical faculties of the people. And so on. Only, all these arts have infinitely more scope in the sphere of public affairs than they have in the sphere of private and professional life. The picture of the prettiest girl that ever lived will in the long run prove powerless to maintain the sales of a bad cigarette. There is no equally effective safeguard in the case of political decisions. Many decisions of fateful importance are of a nature that makes it impossible for the public to experiment with them at its leisure and at moderate cost. Even if that is possible, however, judgment is as a rule not so easy to arrive at as it is in the case of the cigarette, because effects are less easy to interpret.

But such arts also vitiate, to an extent quite unknown in the field of commercial advertising, those forms of political advertising that profess to address themselves to reason. To the observer, the anti-rational or, at all events, the extra-rational appeal and the defenselessness of the victim stand out more and not less clearly when cloaked in facts and arguments. We have seen above why it is so difficult to impart to the public unbiased information about political problems and logically correct inferences from it and why it is that information and arguments in political matters will "register" only if they link up with the citizen's preconceived ideas. As a rule, however, these ideas are not definite enough to determine particular conclusions. Since they can themselves be manufactured, effective political argument almost inevitably implies the

---

In this case they enter into a (second) class of phenomena which we are about to deal with. Personally, I do believe that genuine instances exist. But I cannot be sure that more thorough analysis would not reveal some psycho-technical effort at the bottom of them.

attempt to twist existing volitional premises into a particular shape and not merely the attempt to implement them or to help the citizen to make up his mind.

Thus information and arguments that are really driven home are likely to be the servants of political intent. Since the first thing man will do for his ideal or interest is to lie, we shall expect, and as a matter of fact we find, that effective information is almost always adulterated or selective[18] and that effective reasoning in politics consists mainly in trying to exalt certain propositions into axioms and to put others out of court; it thus reduces to the psycho-technics mentioned before. The reader who thinks me unduly pessimistic need only ask himself whether he has never heard—or said himself—that this or that awkward fact must not be told publicly, or that a certain line of reasoning, though valid, is undesirable. If men who according to any current standard are perfectly honorable or even high-minded reconcile themselves to the implications of this, do they not thereby show what they think about the merits or even the existence of the will of the people?

There are of course limits to all this.[19] And there is truth in Jefferson's dictum that in the end the people are wiser than any single individual can be, or in Lincoln's about the impossibility of "fooling all the people all the time." But both dicta stress the long-run aspect in a highly significant way. It is no doubt possible to argue that given time the collective psyche will evolve opinions that not infrequently strike us as highly reasonable and even shrewd. History however consists of a succession of short-run situations that may alter the course of events for good. If all the people can in the short run be "fooled" step by step into something they do not really want, and if this is not an exceptional case which we could afford to neglect, then no amount of retrospective common sense will alter the fact that in reality they neither raise nor decide issues but that the issues that shape their fate are normally raised and decided for them. More than anyone else the lover of democracy has every reason to accept this fact and to clear his creed from the aspersion that it rests upon make-believe.

IV. REASONS FOR THE SURVIVAL OF THE CLASSICAL DOCTRINE

But how is it possible that a doctrine so patently contrary to fact should have survived to this day and continued to hold its place in the hearts of the people and in the official language of governments? The refuting facts are known to all; everybody admits them with perfect, frequently with cynical, frankness. The theoretical basis, utilitarian rationalism, is dead; nobody accepts it as a correct theory of the body politic. Nevertheless that question is not difficult to answer.

---

18 Selective information, if in itself correct, is an attempt to lie by speaking the truth.
19 Possibly they might show more clearly if issues were more frequently decided by referendum. Politicians presumably know why they are almost invariably hostile to that institution.

First of all, though the classical doctrine of collective action may not be supported-by the results of empirical analysis, it is powerfully supported by that association with religious belief to which I have adverted already. This may not be obvious at first sight. The utilitarian leaders were anything but religious in the ordinary sense of the term. In fact they believed themselves to be anti-religious and they were so considered almost universally. They took pride in what they thought was precisely an unmetaphysical attitude and they were quite out of sympathy with the religious institutions and the religious movements of their time. But we need only cast another glance at the picture they drew of the social process in order to discover that it embodied essential features of the faith of protestant Christianity and was in fact derived from that faith. For the intellectual who had cast off his religion the utilitarian creed provided a substitute for it. For many of those who had retained their religious belief the classical doctrine became the political complement of it.[20]

Thus transposed into the categories of religion, this doctrine—and in consequence the kind of democratic persuasion which is based upon it—changes its very nature. There is no longer any need for logical scruples about the Common Good and Ultimate Values. All this is settled for us by the plan of the Creator whose purpose defines and sanctions everything. What seemed indefinite or unmotivated before is suddenly quite definite and convincing. The voice of the people that is the voice of God for instance. Or take Equality. Its very meaning is in doubt, and there is hardly any rational warrant for exalting it into a postulate, so long as we move in the sphere of empirical analysis. But Christianity harbors a strong equalitarian element. The Redeemer died for all: He did not differentiate between individuals of different social status. In doing so, He testified to the intrinsic value of the individual soul, a value that admits of no gradations. Is not this a sanction—and, as it seems to me, the only possible sanction[21]—of "everyone to count for one, no one to count for more than one"—a sanction that pours super-mundane meaning into articles of the democratic creed for which it is not easy to find any other? To be sure this interpretation does not cover the whole ground. However, so far as it goes, it seems to explain many things that otherwise would be unexplainable and in fact meaningless. In particular, it explains the believer's attitude toward criticism: again, as in the

---

20 Observe the analogy with socialist belief which also is a substitute for Christian belief to some and a complement of it to others.

21 It might be objected that, however difficult it may be to attach a *general* meaning to the word Equality, such meaning can be unraveled from its context in most if not all cases. For instance, it may be permissible to infer from the circumstances in which the Gettysburg address was delivered that by the "proposition that all men are created free and equal," Lincoln simply meant equality of legal status versus the kind of inequality that is implied in the recognition of slavery. This meaning would be definite enough. But if we ask why that proposition should be morally and politically binding and if we refuse to answer "Because every man is by nature exactly like every other man," then we can only fall back upon the divine sanction supplied by Christian belief. This solution is conceivably implied in the word "created."

case of socialism, fundamental dissent is looked upon not merely as error but as sin; it elicits not merely logical counterargument but also moral indignation.

We may put our problem differently and say that democracy, when motivated in this way, ceases to be a mere method that can be discussed rationally like a steam engine or a disinfectant. It actually becomes what from another standpoint I have held it incapable of becoming, viz., an ideal or rather a part of an ideal schema of things. The very word may become a flag, a symbol of all a man holds dear, of everything that he loves about his nation whether rationally contingent to it or not. On the one hand, the question how the various propositions implied in the democratic belief are related to the facts of politics will then become as irrelevant to him as is, to the believing Catholic, the question how the doings of Alexander VI tally with the supernatural halo surrounding the papal office. On the other hand, the democrat of this type, while accepting postulates carrying large implications about equality and brotherliness, will be in a position also to accept, in all sincerity, almost any amount of deviations from them that his own behavior or position may involve. That is not even illogical. Mere distance from fact is no argument against an ethical maxim or a mystical hope.

Second, there is the fact that the forms and phrases of classical democracy are for many nations associated with events and developments in their history which are enthusiastically approved by large majorities. Any opposition to an established regime is likely to use these forms and phrases whatever its meaning and social roots may be.[22] If it prevails and if subsequent developments prove satisfactory, then these forms will take root in the national ideology.

The United States is the outstanding example. Its very existence as a sovereign state is associated with a struggle against a monarchial and aristocratic England. A minority of loyalists excepted, Americans had, at the time of the Grenville administration, probably ceased to look upon the English monarch as *their* king and the English aristocracy as *their* aristocracy. In the War of Independence they fought what in fact as well as in their feeling had become a foreign monarch and a foreign aristocracy who interfered with their political and economic interests. Yet from an early stage of the troubles they presented their case, which really was a national one, as a case of the "people" versus its "rulers," in terms of inalienable Rights of Man and in the light of the general principles of classical democracy. The wording of the Declaration of Independence and of the Constitution adopted these principles. A prodigious development followed that absorbed and satisfied most people and thereby seemed to verify the doctrine embalmed in the sacred documents of the nation.

Oppositions rarely conquer when the groups in possession are in the prime of their power and success. In the first half of the nineteenth century, the oppositions that professed the classical

---

22 It might seem that an exception should be made for oppositions that issue into frankly autocratic regimes. But even most of these rose, as a matter of history, in democratic ways and based their rule on the approval of the people. Caesar was not killed by plebeians. But the aristocratic oligarchs who did kill him also used democratic phrases.

creed of democracy rose and eventually prevailed against governments some of which—especially in Italy—were obviously in a state of decay and had become bywords of incompetence, brutality and corruption. Naturally though not quite logically, this redounded to the credit of that creed which moreover showed up to advantage when compared with the benighted superstitions sponsored by those governments. Under these circumstances, democratic revolution meant the advent of freedom and decency, and the democratic creed meant a gospel of reason and betterment. To be sure, this advantage was bound to be lost and the gulf between the doctrine and the practice of democracy was bound to be discovered. But the glamour of the dawn was slow to fade.

Third, it must not be forgotten that there are social patterns in which the classical doctrine will actually fit facts with a sufficient degree of approximation. As has been pointed out, this is the case with many small and primitive societies which as a matter of fact served as a prototype to the authors of that doctrine. It may be the case also with societies that are not primitive provided they are not too differentiated and do not harbor any serious problems. Switzerland is the best example. There is so little to quarrel about in a world of peasants which, excepting hotels and banks, contains no great capitalist industry, and the problems of public policy are so simple and so stable that an overwhelming majority can be expected to understand them and to agree about them. But if we can conclude that in such cases the classical doctrine approximates reality we have to add immediately that it does so not because it describes an effective mechanism of political decision but only because there are no great decisions to be made. Finally, the case of the United States may again be invoked in order to show that the classical doctrine sometimes appears to fit facts even in a society that is big and highly differentiated and in which there are great issues to decide provided the sting is taken out of them by favorable conditions. Until this country's entry into the First World War, the public mind was concerned mainly with the business of exploiting the economic possibilities of the environment. So long as this business was not seriously interfered with nothing mattered fundamentally to the average citizen who looked on the antics of politicians with good-natured contempt. Sections might get excited over the tariff, over silver, over local misgovernment, or over an occasional squabble with England. The people at large did not care much, except in the one case of serious disagreement which in fact produced national disaster, the Civil War.

And fourth, of course, politicians appreciate a phraseology that flatters the masses and offers an excellent opportunity not only for evading responsibility but also for crushing opponents in the name of the people.

CHAPTER 22: ANOTHER THEORY OF DEMOCRACY

I. COMPETITION FOR POLITICAL LEADERSHIP

I think that most students of politics have by now come to accept the criticisms leveled at the classical doctrine of democracy in the preceding chapter. I also think that most of them agree, or will agree before long, in accepting another theory which is much truer to life and at the same time salvages much of what sponsors of the democratic method really mean by this term. Like the classical theory, it may be put into the nutshell of a definition.

It will be remembered that our chief troubles about the classical theory centered in the proposition that "the people" hold a definite and rational opinion about every individual question and that they give effect to this opinion—in a democracy—by choosing "representatives" who will see to it that that opinion is carried out. Thus the selection of the representatives is made secondary to the primary purpose of the democratic arrangement which is to vest the power of deciding political issues in the electorate. Suppose we reverse the roles of these two elements and make the deciding of issues by the electorate secondary to the election of the men who are to do the deciding. To put it differently, we now take the view that the role of the people is to produce a government, or else an intermediate body which in turn will produce a national executive[23] or government. And we define: the democratic method is that institutional arrangement for arriving at political decisions in which individuals acquire the power to decide by means of a competitive struggle for the people's vote.

Defense and explanation of this idea will speedily show that, as to both plausibility of assumptions and tenability of propositions, it greatly improves the theory of the democratic process.

First of all, we are provided with a reasonably efficient criterion by which to distinguish democratic governments from others. We have seen that the classical theory meets with difficulties on that score because both the will and the good of the people may be, and in many historical instances have been, served just as well or better by governments that cannot be described as democratic according to any accepted usage of the term. Now we are in a somewhat better position partly because we are resolved to stress a *modus procedendi* the presence or absence of which it is in most cases easy to verify.[24]

---

[23] The insincere word "executive" really points in the wrong direction. It ceases however to do so if we use it in the sense in which we speak of the "executives" of a business corporation who also do a great deal more than "execute" the will of stockholders.

[24] See however the fourth point below.

For instance, a parliamentary monarchy like the English one fulfills the requirements of the democratic method because the monarch is practically constrained to appoint to cabinet office the same people as parliament would elect. A "constitutional" monarchy does not qualify to be called democratic because electorates and parliaments, while having all the other rights that electorates and parliaments have in parliamentary monarchies, lack the power to impose their choice as to the governing committee: the cabinet ministers are in this case servants of the monarch, in substance as well as in name, and can in principle be dismissed as well as appointed by him. Such an arrangement may satisfy the people. The electorate may reaffirm this fact by voting against any proposal for change. The monarch may be so popular as to be able to defeat any competition for the supreme office. But since no machinery is provided for making this competition effective the case does not come within our definition.

Second, the theory embodied in this definition leaves all the room we may wish to have for a proper recognition of the vital fact of leadership. The classical theory did not do this but, as we have seen, attributed to the electorate an altogether unrealistic degree of initiative which practically amounted to ignoring leadership. But collectives act almost exclusively by accepting leadership—this is the dominant mechanism of practically any collective action which is more than a reflex. Propositions about the working and the results of the democratic method that take account of this are bound to be infinitely more realistic than propositions which do not. They will not stop at the execution of a *volonté générale* but will go some way toward showing how it emerges or how it is substituted or faked. What we have termed Manufactured Will is no longer outside the theory, an aberration for the absence of which we piously pray; it enters on the ground floor as it should.

Third, however, so far as there are genuine group-wise volitions at all—for instance the will of the unemployed to receive unemployment benefit or the will of other groups to help—our theory does not neglect them. On the contrary we are now able to insert them in exactly the role they actually play. Such volitions do not as a rule assert themselves directly. Even if strong and definite they remain latent, often for decades, until they are called to life by some political leader who turns them into political factors. This he does, or else his agents do it for him, by organizing these volitions, by working them up and by including eventually appropriate items in his competitive offering. The interaction between sectional interests and public opinion and the way in which they produce the pattern we call the political situation appear from this angle in a new and much clearer light.

Fourth, our theory is of course no more definite than is the concept of competition for leadership. This concept presents similar difficulties as the concept of competition in the economic sphere, with which it may be usefully compared. In economic life competition is never completely lacking, but hardly ever is it perfect.²⁵ Similarly, in political life there is always some competition, though perhaps only a potential one, for the allegiance of the people. To simplify matters we have restricted the kind of competition for leadership which is to define democracy, to free competition for a free vote. The justification for this is that democracy seems to imply a recognized method by which to conduct the competitive struggle, and that the electoral method is practically the only one available for communities of any size. But though this excludes many ways of securing leadership which should be excluded,²⁶ such as competition by military insurrection, it does not exclude the cases that are strikingly analogous to the economic phenomena we label "unfair" or "fraudulent" competition or restraint of competition. And we cannot exclude them because if we did we should be left with a completely unrealistic ideal.²⁷ Between this ideal case which does not exist and the cases in which all competition with the established leader is prevented by force, there is a continuous range of variation within which the democratic method of government shades off into the autocratic one by imperceptible steps. But if we wish to understand and not to philosophize, this is as it should be. The value of our criterion is not seriously impaired thereby.

Fifth, our theory seems to clarify the relation that subsists between democracy and individual freedom. If by the latter we mean the existence of a sphere of individual self-government the boundaries of which are historically variable—*no* society tolerates absolute freedom even of conscience and of speech, *no* society reduces that sphere to zero—the question clearly becomes a matter of degree. We have seen that the democratic method does not necessarily guarantee a greater amount of individual freedom than another political method would permit in similar circumstances. It may well be the other way round. But there is still a relation between the two. If, on principle at least, everyone is free to compete for political leadership²⁸ by presenting himself to the electorate, this will in most cases though not in all mean a considerable amount of freedom of discussion *for all*. In particular it will normally mean a considerable amount of freedom of the press. This relation between democracy and freedom is not absolutely stringent and can be tampered with. But, from the standpoint of the intellectual, it is nevertheless very important. At the same time, it is all there is to that relation.

Sixth, it should be observed that in making it the primary function of the electorate to produce a government (directly or through an intermediate body) I intended to include in this

---

25 In Part II we had examples of the problems which arise out of this.
26 It also excludes methods which should not be excluded, for instance, the acquisition of political leadership by the people's tacit acceptance of it or by election *quasi per inspirationem*. The latter differs from election by voting only by a technicality. But the former is not quite without importance even in modern politics; the sway held by a party boss *within his party* is often based on nothing but tacit acceptance of his leadership. Comparatively speaking however these are details which may, I think, be neglected in a sketch like this.
27 As in the economic field, some restrictions are implicit in the legal and moral principles of the community.
28 Free, that is, in the same sense in which everyone is free to start another textile mill.

phrase also the function of evicting it. The one means simply the acceptance of a leader or a group of leaders, the other means simply the withdrawal of this acceptance. This takes care of an element the reader may have missed. He may have thought that the electorate controls as well as installs. But since electorates normally do not control their political leaders in any way except by refusing to reelect them or the parliamentary majorities that support them, it seems well to reduce our ideas about this control in the way indicated by our definition. Occasionally, spontaneous revulsions occur which upset a government or an individual minister directly or else enforce a certain course of action. But they are not only exceptional, they are, as we shall see, contrary to the spirit of the democratic method.

Seventh, our theory sheds much-needed light on an old controversy. Whoever accepts the classical doctrine of democracy and in consequence believes that the democratic method is to guarantee that issues be decided and policies framed according to the will of the people must be struck by the fact that, even if that will were undeniably real and definite, decision by simple majorities would in many cases distort it rather than give effect to it. Evidently the will of the majority is the will of the majority and not the will of "the people." The latter is a mosaic that the former completely fails to "represent." To equate both by definition is not to solve the problem. Attempts at real solutions have however been made by the authors of the various plans for Proportional Representation.

These plans have met with adverse criticism on practical grounds. It is in fact obvious not only that proportional representation will offer opportunities for all sorts of idiosyncrasies to assert themselves but also that it may prevent democracy from producing efficient governments and thus prove a danger in times of stress.[29] But before concluding that democracy becomes unworkable it its principle is carried out consistently, it is just as well to ask ourselves whether this principle really implies proportional representation. As a matter of fact it does not. If acceptance of leadership is the true function of the electorate's vote, the case for proportional representation collapses because its premises are no longer binding. The principle of democracy then merely means that the reins of government should be handed to those who command more support than do any of the competing individuals or teams. And this in turn seems to assure the standing of the majority system within the logic of the democratic method, although we might still condemn it on grounds that lie outside of that logic.

---

29 The argument against proportional representation has been ably stated by Professor F.A. Hermens in "The Trojan Horse of Democracy," *Social Research*, November 1938.

II. THE PRINCIPLE APPLIED

The theory outlined in the preceding section we are now going to try out on some of the more important features of the structure and working of the political engine in democratic countries.

1. In a democracy, as I have said, the primary function of the elector's vote is to produce government. This may mean the election of a complete set of individual officers. This practice however is in the main a feature of local government and will be neglected henceforth.[30] Considering national government only, we may say that producing government practically amounts to deciding who the leading man shall be.[31] As before, we shall call him Prime Minister.

There is only one democracy in which the electorate's vote does this[32]

---

30   This we shall do for simplicity's sake only. The phenomenon fits perfectly into our schema.
31   This is only approximately true. The elector's vote does indeed put into power a group that in all normal cases acknowledges an individual leader but there are as a rule leaders of second and third rank who carry political guns in their own right and whom the leader has no choice but to put into appropriate offices. This fact will be recognized presently.

Another point must be kept in mind. Although there is reason to expect that a man who rises to a position of supreme command will in general be a man of considerable personal force, whatever else he may be—to this we shall return later on—it does not follow that this will always be the case. Therefore the term "leader" or "leading man" is not to imply that the individuals thus designated are necessarily endowed with qualities of leadership or that they always do give any personal leads. There are political situations favorable to the rise of men deficient in leadership (and other qualities) and unfavorable to the establishment of strong individual positions. A party or a combination of parties hence may occasionally be acephalous. But everyone recognizes that this is a pathological state and one of the typical causes of defeat.

32   We may, I take it, disregard the electoral college. In calling the President of the United States a prime minister I wish to stress the fundamental similarity of his position to that of prime ministers in other democracies. But I do not wish to minimize the differences, although some of them are more formal than real. The least important of them is that the President also fulfills those largely ceremonial functions of, say, the French

THE CALCULUS OF CONSENT

CHAPTER 6

BY JAMES M. BUCHANAN AND GORDON TULLOCK

James M. Buchanan and Gordon Tullock, "Chapter 6," *The Calculus of Consent: Logical Foundations of Constitutional Democracy*, pp. 63-72. Copyright © 1962 by University of Michigan Press. Reprinted with permission.

NINETEEN

A GENERALIZED ECONOMIC THEORY OF CONSTITUTIONS

> *... government is not something which just happens. It has to be "laid on" by somebody.*
>
> —T. D. Weldon, *States and Morals*

We have examined the calculus of the individual in determining the activities that shall be organized privately and collectively. As there suggested, the individual must consider the possible collectivization of all activities for which the private organization is expected to impose some interdependence costs on him. His final decision must rest on a comparison of these costs with those expected to be imposed on him as a result of collective organization itself. The costs that a collectively organized activity will impose on the individual depend, however, on the way in which collective decisions are to be made. Hence, as suggested earlier, the choice among the several possible decision-making rules is not independent of the choice as to the method of organization. In this chapter we propose to analyze in some detail the problem of individual choice among collective decision-making rules. For purposes of analytical simplicity we may initially assume that the organizational decision between collectivization and noncollectivization has been exogenously determined. We shall also assume that the specific institutional structure through which collective action is to be carried out is exogenously fixed.

THE EXTERNAL-COSTS FUNCTION

Our method will be that of utilizing the two elements of interdependence costs introduced earlier. The possible benefits from collective action may be measured or quantified in terms of reductions in the costs that the private behavior of other individuals is expected to impose on the individual decision-maker. However, collective action, if undertaken, will also require that the individual spend some time and effort in making decisions for the group, in reaching agreement with his fellows. More importantly, under certain decision-making rules, choices contrary to the individual's own interest may be made for the group. In any case, participation in collective activity is costly to the individual, and the rational man will take this fact into account at the stage of constitutional choice.

Employing the two elements of interdependence costs, we may develop two cost functions or relationships that will prove helpful. In the first, which we shall call the *external-costs function*, we may relate, for the single individual with respect to a single activity, the costs that he expects to endure as a result of the actions of others to the number of individuals who are required to agree before a final political decision is taken for the group. We write this function as:

$$C_i = f(N_a), i = 1, 2, \ldots, N \qquad (1)$$
$$N_a \leq N.$$

where C_i is defined as the present value of the expected costs imposed on the i th individual by the actions of individuals other than himself, and where N_a is defined as the number of individuals, out of the total group N, who are required to agree before final collective action is taken. Note that all of the costs represented by C_i are external costs, even though we are now discussing collective action exclusively. It is clear that, over the range of decision-making rules, this will normally be a decreasing function: that is to say, as the number of individuals required to agree increases, the expected costs will decrease. When unanimous agreement is dictated by the decision-making rule, the expected costs on the individual must be zero since he will not willingly allow others to impose external costs on him when he can effectively prevent this from happening.

This function is represented geometrically in Figure 19-1 On the ordinate we measure the present value of the expected external costs; on the abscissa we measure the number of individuals required to agree for collective decision. This curve will slope downward throughout most of its range, reaching zero at a point representing the consent of all members of the group.

Note precisely what the various points on this curve represent. Point C represents the external costs that the individual expects will be imposed on him if *any* single individual in the group is authorized to undertake action *for the collectivity*. Suppose that the decision-making rule is such

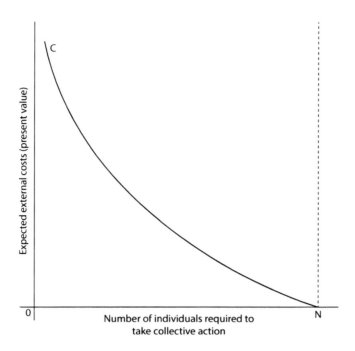

Figure 19–1.

that collective action can be taken at any time that any one member of the group dictates it. The single individual can then authorize action for the State, or in the name of the State, which adversely affects others in the group. It seems evident that under such a rule the individual must anticipate that many actions taken by others which are unfavorable to him will take place, and the costs of these actions will be *external costs* in the same sense that the costs expected from private activity might be external. The fact that collective action, under most decision-making rules, involves external costs of this nature has not been adequately recognized. The private operation of the neighborhood plant with the smoking chimney may impose external costs on the individual by soiling his laundry, but this cost is no more external to the individual's own private calculus than the tax cost imposed on him unwillingly in order to finance the provision of public services to his fellow citizen in another area. Under the extreme decision-making rule which allows any individual in the whole group to order collective action, the expected external costs will be much greater than under any private organization of activity. This is because the initial definition of property rights places some effective limits on the external effects that private people may impose on each other. By contrast, the individual rights to property against damaging state or collective action are not nearly so sharply defined in existing legal systems. The external costs that may be imposed on the individual through the collective-choice process may be much larger than those which could ever be expected to result from purely private behavior within any accepted legal framework.

Yet why must the *net* external costs expected from the various decision-making rules be positive? One of the major tasks of Part III of this book will be to demonstrate that these external costs are, in fact, positive, but a preliminary example may be quite helpful at this stage. Let us confine our discussion to the extreme decision-making rule where any individual in the group can, when he desires, order collective action. It is perhaps intuitively clear that such a rule would not be desired by the average individual, but we need to find a more rigorous proof for this intuitive observation. We shall employ a simple illustration. Assume that all local public services are financed from property-tax revenues and that the tax rate is automatically adjusted so as to cover all public expenditures. Now assume further that any individual in the municipal group under consideration may secure road or street repairs or improvements when he requests it from the city authorities. It is evident that the individual, when he makes a decision, will not take the full marginal costs of the action into account. He will make his decision on the basis of a comparison of his individual marginal costs, a part of total marginal costs only, with individual marginal benefits, which may be equal to total marginal benefits. The individual in this example will be able to secure external benefits by ordering his own street repaired or improved. Since each individual will be led to do this, and since individual benefits will exceed individual costs over a wide extension of the activity, there will surely be an overinvestment in streets and roads, relative to other public and private investments of resources. The rational individual will expect that the general operation of such a decision-making rule will result in positive external costs being imposed on him.

The decision-making rule in which *any* single individual may order collective action is useful as an extreme case in our analysis, but the model is not without some practical relevance for the real world. Specifically, such a rule is rarely encountered; but when legislative bodies, whatever the rules, respond to popular demands for public services on the basis solely of "needs" criteria, the results may approximate those which would be attained under the extreme rule discussed here. The institutional equivalent of this rule is also present in those instances where governments provide divisible or "private" goods and services to individuals without the use of pricing devices.

Before leaving the discussion of this *any person* rule, it is necessary to emphasize that it must be carefully distinguished from a rule which would identify a *unique individual* and then delegate exclusive decision-making power to him. This dictatorship or monarchy model is wholly different from that under consideration here. Requiring the identification of specific individuals within the group, the dictatorship model becomes much less general than that which we use. One or two points, however, may be noted briefly in passing. To the individual who might reasonably expect to be dictator, no external costs would be anticipated. To the individual who expects, on the other hand, to be among the governed, the external costs expected will be lower than those under the extreme *any person* rule that we have been discussing. The delegation of exclusive road-repairing decisions to a single commissioner will clearly be less costly to the average taxpayer in the community than a rule which would allow anyone in the group to order road repairs when he chooses.

As we move to the right from point C in Figure 19–1, the net external costs expected by the individual will tend to fall. If two persons in the group, *any* two, are required to reach agreement before collective action is authorized, there will be fewer decisions that the individual expects to run contrary' to his own desires. In a similar fashion, we may proceed over the more and more inclusive decision-making rules. If the agreement of three persons is required, the individual will expect lower, external costs than under the two-person rule, etc. In all cases the function refers to the expected external costs from the operation of rules in which the ultimate members of the decisive groups are not specifically identifiable. So long as there remains any possibility that the individual will be affected adversely by a collective decision, expected net external costs will be positive. These costs vanish only with the rule of unanimity. This point will be discussed in greater detail. Note, however, that by saying that expected external costs are positive, we are not saying that collective action is inefficient or undesirable. The existence of positive external costs implies only that there must exist some interdependence costs from the operation of the activity considered. These costs may be minimized by collective action, but the minimum value of interdependence need not be, indeed it will seldom be, zero.

THE DECISION-MAKING-COSTS FUNCTION

If collective action is to be taken, someone must participate in the decision-making. Recognizing this, we may derive, in very general terms, a second cost relationship or function. Any single person must undergo some costs in reaching a decision, public or private. As previously noted, however, we shall ignore these costs of reaching individual decisions, that is, the costs of the subjective effort of the individual in making up his mind. If two or more persons are required to agree on a *single* decision, time and effort of another sort is introduced—that which is required to secure agreement. Moreover, these costs will increase as the size of the group required to agree increases. As a collective decision-making rule is changed to include a larger and larger proportion of the total group, these costs may increase at an increasing rate. As unanimity is approached, dramatic increases in expected decision-making costs may be predicted. In fact, when unanimity is approached, the situation becomes radically different from that existing through the range of less inclusive rules. At the lower levels there is apt to be little real bargaining. If one member of a potential agreement asks for exorbitant terms, the other members will simply turn to someone else. As unanimity is approached, however, this expedient becomes more and more difficult. Individual investment in strategic bargaining becomes highly rational, and the costs imposed by such bargaining are likely to be high.

With the most inclusive decision rule, unanimity, each voter is a necessary party to any agreement. Since each voter, then, has a monopoly of an essential resource (that is, his consent), each person can aim at obtaining the entire benefit of agreement for himself. Bargaining, in the sense of attempts to maneuver people into accepting lower returns, is the only recourse under these circumstances, and it seems highly likely that agreement would normally be almost impossible. Certainly, the rewards received by voters in any such agreement would be directly proportionate to their stubbornness and apparent unreasonableness during the bargaining stage. If we include (as we should) the opportunity costs of bargains that are never made, it seems likely that the bargaining costs might approach infinity in groups of substantial size. This, of course, is the extreme case, but somewhat similar conditions would begin to develop as the number of parties required to approve a given project approached the full membership of the group. Thus our bargaining-cost function operates in two ranges: in the lower reaches it represents mainly the problems of making up an agreed bargain among a group of people, any one of whom can readily be replaced. Here, as a consequence, there is little incentive to invest resources in strategic bargaining. Near unanimity, investments in strategic bargaining are apt to be great, and the expected costs very high.

We may write the decision-making-costs function as:

$$D_i = f(N_a), i = 1, 2, \ldots, N \qquad (2)$$
$$N_a \leq N.$$

where D_i represents the present value of those costs that the i th individual is expected to incur while participating in the whole set of collective decisions defined by a single "activity." Figure 19–2 illustrates the relationship geometrically.

THE CHOICE OF OPTIMAL RULES

By employing these two functions, each of which relates expected individual costs to the number of persons in a group required to agree before a decision is made for the group, we are able to discuss the individual's choice of rules. These may best be defined in terms of the proportion of the total group that is to be required to earn' a decision. For a given activity the fully rational individual, at the time of constitutional choice, will try to choose that decision-making rule which will *minimize* the present value of the expected costs that he must suffer. He will do so by minimizing the *sum* of the expected external costs and expected decision-making costs, as

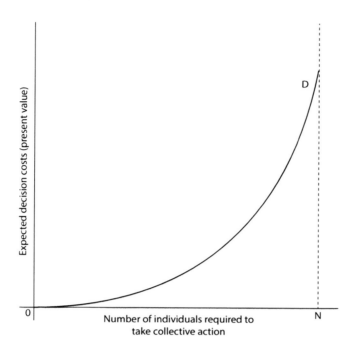

Figure 19–2.

we have defined these separate components. Geometrically, we add the two costs functions vertically. The "optimal" or most "efficient" decision-making rule, *for the individual whose expectations are depicted and for the activity or set of activities that he is considering,* will be that shown by the lowest point on the resulting curve. Figure 19–3 is illustrative: the individual will choose the rule which requires that K/N of the group agree when collective decisions are made.

A somewhat more general discussion of the manner in which the individual might reach a decision concerning the choice of a collective decision-making rule may be helpful. An external cost may be said to be imposed on an individual when his net worth is reduced by the behavior of another individual or group and when this reduction in net worth is not specifically recognized by the existing legal structure to be an expropriation of a defensible human or property right. The damaged individual has no recourse; he can neither prevent the action from occurring nor can he claim compensation after it has occurred. As we have suggested in the preceding chapter, it is the existence of such external costs that rationally explains the origin of either voluntarily organized, co-operative, contractual rearrangements or collective (governmental) activity. The individual who seeks to maximize his own utility may find it advantageous either to enter into

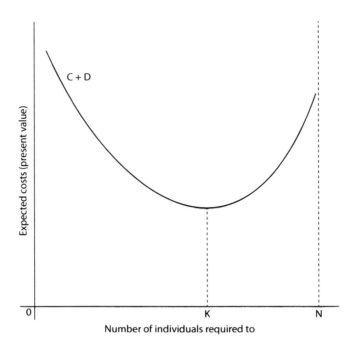

Figure 19–3.

voluntary contracts aimed at eliminating externality or to support constitutional provisions that allow private decisions to be replaced by collective decisions.

The individual will, of course, recognize that any restriction on his private freedom of action will, in certain cases, impose costs on him. Each individual will in the course of time, if allowed unrestricted freedom within the limits of the legal structure, impose certain costs on other parties; and, insofar as his own position taken alone is concerned, he will prefer to remain perfectly free to impose costs on others when he desires. On the other hand, he will recognize also that he will, on many occasions, be affected negatively by the actions of others over whom he can exert no direct control and from whom he cannot legitimately demand compensation. Knowing that he will more often be in the second situation than in the first, the fully rational individual will explore the possibility of contractual arrangements designed to protect him from external cost along with constitutional processes and provisions that may remove actions from the realm of private decision and place them within the realm of public choice.

The only means whereby the individual can insure that the actions of others will never impose costs on him is through the strict application of the rule of unanimity for all decisions, public and private. If the individual knows that he must approve *any* action before it is carried out, he will be able to remove all fear of expected external cost or damage. However, as we have already suggested, he must also consider the costs that he can expect to incur through the operation of such a rule. In small groups the attainment of general consensus or unanimity on issues thrown into the realm of collective choice may not involve overly large resource costs, but in groups of any substantial size the costs of higgling and bargaining over the terms of trade that may be required to attain agreement often will amount to more than the individual is willing to pay. The rational individual, at the stage of constitutional choice, confronts a calculus not unlike that which he must face in making his everyday economic choices. By agreeing to more inclusive rules, he is accepting the additional burden of decision-making in exchange for additional protection against adverse decisions. In moving in the opposing direction toward a less inclusive decision-making rule, the individual is trading some of his protection against external costs for a lowered cost of decision-making.

JOHN LOCKE'S DEMOCRATIC THEORY

BY IAN SHAPIRO

Ian Shapiro, "John Locke's Democratic Theory," *Two Treatises of Government*, pp. 309-333. Copyright © 2003 by Yale University Press. Reprinted with permission.

TWENTY

The democratic tradition has ancient origins, but contemporary formulations are generally traced to Jean-Jacques Rousseau's discussion of the general will in *The Social Contract*, published in 1762. Joseph Schumpeter went so far as to characterize Rousseau's account as the "classical" theory of democracy, even though his was really a neoclassical view—an eighteenth century adaptation of the ancient Greek theory in which democracy had meant ruling and being ruled in turn. Many commentators have followed Schumpeter's lead in treating Rousseau as the father of modem democratic theory, yet it is my contention that John Locke merits the distinction. He developed the elements of an account of democracy that is more realistic, far-reaching, and appealing than is Rousseau's, and it has greater continuing relevance than does Rousseau's to contemporary democratic thinking. Locke conceived of the relationship between people and ruler as one of authorship at a more fundamental level than did Rousseau, placing the authorizing people, acting collectively, at the center of his account of political legitimacy. Yet, unlike Rousseau, he did not reify collective action or the general will in ways that have since been debunked by social choice theorists. Moreover, Locke's democratic theory had other dimensions as well, ranging over accounts of the moral equality of persons, what we might today describe as a political rather than a metaphysical approach to moral and political disagreement, and a strong defense of majority rule as the wellspring of institutional legitimacy.

Some will find my suggestion jarring not so much for the invidious comparison with Rousseau as for the fact that Locke is typically portrayed as a theorist of individual rights rather than of democracy. In the debate over the ideological origins of the American Revolution, for instance, the Lockean view is contrasted, as a rights-centric one, with a civic republican interpretation of the Founders' self-understandings. There is no suggestion in this debate that Locke's view was democratic. Add to this the fact that Locke spent almost no time discussing political participation, and the case for him as a democratic theorist would seem to be rather bleak. It is my contention, however, that the deep structure of Locke's account of politics is profoundly democratic. His understanding of the moral equality of persons lends itself better to democratic than to liberal thinking, even if his is not the "strong democracy" characteristic of the participatory and deliberative democratic traditions. Moreover, as an institutional matter his defense of individual rights is nested in and subordinate to majority rule—casting his historical role as a proto-liberal rights theorist in a questionable light. This last contention is not new. As long ago as 1940 Willmoore Kendall noted that Locke's partiality to majority rule lived in tension with his account of individual rights. Kendall saw this as a deficiency of Locke's theory, whereas on my account his defense of majority rule is part of a more sophisticated view of institutional legitimacy than Kendall was able to grasp. Another way to put this is to say that although Locke was no theorist of democratic participation, he was an innovative theorist of democratic legitimacy.

Does this mean the historical Locke was a democrat? Up to a point, albeit a debated one. The gravamen of my claim here has more to do with the logic of his argument than with his intentions, but I mean to show that even they exhibited a democratic hue that has not been fully appreciated. As a matter of personal biography we know that Locke evolved over the course of his life from being a fairly conservative, or, at any rate, apolitical person in his early adult years, who gave unreflective endorsement to authoritarian political arrangements, into a political insurrectionist in Shaftesbury's circle in the 1670s and after. His political outlook expressed itself mainly in terms of the great issue of the day: is there a legitimate right to resist an illegitimate monarch to the point of removing him by force? Locke famously concluded that there is indeed such a right. This argument might be thought to have little consequence for democratic politics, dealing, as it does, with the legitimacy of revolution. Moreover, it seems clear that in some respects even the Locke of the 1680s and after distanced himself from the most radical political movements of his day. Without delving deeply into these historical controversies, I will argue that Locke's account of the conditions under which revolution is legitimate is nonetheless decidedly democratic in its assumptions, and that the ever-present possibility of legitimate revolution has significant democratic consequences for thinking about day-to-day politics.

I begin with an exploration of Locke's account of the dimensions of human moral equality, showing that his view of all human beings as equally God's property, as intrinsically rational, and as the "authors" of the state, revealed a fundamentally democratic egalitarian outlook. This is followed by a discussion of Locke's views on toleration and dissent, where I show that, in addition to embracing a comparatively capacious view of toleration for his own day, Locke's justification for the limits on toleration that he advocated was in some respects akin to the mature John Rawls in his "political, not metaphysical" mode, though Locke's political, not metaphysical stance turns out on close inspection to be more thoroughly political and less problematic than does Rawls's. This leads to a discussion of Locke's account of the relations between majority rule and institutional legitimacy, where I argue that Locke's embrace of majority rule was less starry-eyed than that of subsequent democratic theorists, but that it was by the same token more attractive given the realities of politics in diverse societies.

HUMAN MORAL EQUALITY

The first and most basic sense in which we are equal, for Locke, is as God's property. Here we need to elucidate both the senses in which we are equal and those in which we are God's property, since both turn out to be relevant to subsequent democratic understandings. Starting with the account of property, Locke's view of humans as God's property is a special case of his workmanship theory by reference to which authority, ownership, and even authentic knowledge are all rooted in acts of creative making. This theory was developed as a consequence of Locke's position on the nature and meaning of natural law. If one took the view, common among natural law theorists of his day, that natural law is eternal and unchanging, this threatened another notion many thought compelling: that God is omnipotent. By definition, an all-powerful God could not be bound by natural law. Yet if God is conceded to have the capacity to change natural law, then we cannot declare it to be timeless. Locke wrestled with this tension without ever resolving it to his own satisfaction, but in his moral and political writings he came down decisively in the voluntarist, or will-centered, camp. He could not relinquish the proposition that for something to have the status of a law, it must be the product of a will. By adopting this voluntarist view, Locke aligned himself with other will-centered theorists of the early Enlightenment, notably the German philosopher and natural law theorist Samuel von Pufendorf.

We find similar reasoning in Locke's *Essays on the Law of Nature*, delivered as lectures at Christ Church in 1663–1664. Here, Locke's treatment of human capacities was linked to his theology in a different way; it rested on his categorial distinction between natural right and natural law, which explained human autonomy. Rejecting the traditional Christian correlativities between right and law, Locke insisted instead that natural law "ought to be distinguished from natural right: for right is grounded in the fact that we have the free use of a thing, whereas law is what enjoins or forbids the doing of a thing." What humans perceive as natural law is in fact God's natural right; an expression of His will. In this sense right is prior to law in Locke's analytical scheme. Locke's theory of ownership flows naturally out of this scheme, transforming the workmanship model of knowledge into a normative theory of right. It is through acts of autonomous making that rights over what is created come into being: making entails ownership so that natural law is at bottom God's natural right over his creation. Locke's frequent appeals to metaphors of workmanship and watch making in the *Two Treatises* and elsewhere make it fundamental that men are obliged to God because of his purposes in making them. Men are "the Workmanship of one Omnipotent, and infinitely wise Maker ... they are his property, whose workmanship they are, made to last during his, not another's pleasure."

Why does this account of natural law and God's workmanship matter for the moral equality of persons? Two reasons. First, because we are all God's creatures, on Locke's account, we were all protected from being owned by one another. It might ring strange to the contemporary ear that Locke felt the need to deny that people can be one another's property, but his central preoccupation in the *First Treatise* was to refute defenses of absolutism that appealed to Adam's "right of dominion over his children." Conventional defenders of absolutism, notoriously Sir Robert Filmer, had contended "that fathers, by begetting them, come by an absolute power over their children." Locke insisted, by contrast, that God makes children and uses their parents for that purpose. Parents are "but occasions of [children's] being, and, when they design and wish to beget them, do little more towards their making, than Ducalion and his wife in the fable did towards the making of mankind, by throwing pebbles over their heads." Were parents givers of life, Locke conceded, they might have some sort of quasi-ownership claim, but they are not. Even in this hypothetical eventuality, Locke resists the absolutist case by arguing that "every one who gives another any thing, has not always thereby a right to take it away again," and he insists that because the woman "hath an equal share, if not greater" in nourishing a child, the creationist theory in any case does not justify paternal absolutism. It is "so hard to imagine the rational soul should presently inhabit the yet unformed embryo, as soon as the father has done his part in the act of generation, that if it must be supposed to derive any thing from the parents, it must certainly owe most to the mother."

In short, to give life "is to frame and make a living creature, fashion the parts, and mold and suit them to their uses; and having proportioned and fitted them together, to put into them a living soul." Parents do not fashion the child and most commonly, do not even intend to create it; they do so as a byproduct of the instinctive desires God has placed in them. In response to Filmer's claims, Locke states, "They who say the father gives life to children, are so dazzled with the thoughts of monarchy, that they do not, as they ought, remember God, who is 'the Author and Giver of Life.'" Parents have fiduciary responsibility for their children on Locke's account, but it expires upon their maturity. Parents are obliged to provide for their children "not as their own workmanship, but the workmanship of their own maker."

This is why Locke insists that although children are not born in a "state of equality, though they are born to it." Adults have "a sort of rule and jurisdiction over them when they come into the world, and for some time after; but it is a temporary one." The bonds of children's subjection "are like the Swadling Cloths they are wrapt up in, and supported by, in the weakness of their Infancy." Developing age and reason loosen these bonds, "till at length they drop quite off, and leave a man at his own free disposal." The power to command "ends with nonage." Thereafter, although "honour and respect, support and defense, and whatsoever gratitude can oblige a man to, for the highest benefits he is naturally capable of, be always due from a son to his parents; yet all this puts no sceptre into the father's hand, no sovereign power of commanding." The only legitimate sanction at the parent's disposal is the power to withhold inheritance, or "to bestow it with a more sparing or liberal hand, according as the behaviour of this or that child hath comported with his will and humor." Parents are to "inform the mind, and govern the actions of their yet ignorant nonage, till reason shall take its place, and ease them of that trouble." This treatment of children reflects an inclusive view of the right to make decisions for oneself: the only justifiable basis for paternalism is incapacity.

One reason that Locke's view of moral equality has had staying power since he wrote is that the obvious secular analogue of his claim that we are all God's property is that we are nobody's property. The workmanship model persisted in the western intellectual consciousness long after it was cut loose from its Lockean theological moorings. If we abandon the theology yet still embrace the workmanship ideal as most in the Enlightenment tradition since Locke—be they conservatives, liberals, or radicals—have done, the logic of his argument against Filmer continues to hold. Indeed, it can be extended: parents cannot own children because they do not make them, but by the same token nor can anyone else own them. In this way the egalitarian logic of his argument against Filmer extends beyond their theological disagreements.

A comparably inclusive view is reflected in Locke's discussion of women. Feminist commentators on the history of political theory note correctly that there were limits to Locke's embrace of gender equality. In the *First Treatise* he describes women as the "weaker sex," and, although he insists there is no biblical authority for men's dominion over women, that it is a matter of human law, he says "there is, I grant, a foundation in nature for it." Moreover, in the *Second Treatise,* he says that it "being necessary that the last determination, *i. e.* the rule, should be placed somewhere; it naturally falls to the man's share, as the abler and the stronger." Yet, taken in context, in both cases these statements were concessions to considerably more paternalistic views that Locke was challenging, and it should be noted that the bulk of his discussion is concerned with hemming in what Locke took to be the husband's inevitable power. We have already seen that Locke resisted patriarchalism with respect to children partly on the ground that if children were seen as human creations women's ownership claim would outweigh that of men. Beyond this, Filmer had contended that "God at the Creation gave the Sovereignty to the Man over the Woman, as being the Nobler and Principal Agent in Generation," a belief that Locke maintained is utterly inconsistent with a biblical teaching, "for God in the Scripture says, 'his father and his mother that begot him.'" Locke is equally dismissive of Filmer's claim that "'monarchical power of government [is] settled and fixed by the commandment, honour thy father and thy mother,'" since as Locke observes, "nobody will say a child may withhold honour from his mother, or, as the Scripture terms it, 'set light by her,' though his father should command him to do so; no more than the mother could dispense with him, for neglecting to *honour* his father: whereby it is plain, that this command of God, gives the father no sovereignty, no supremacy."

Perhaps more remarkably, Locke treated marriage as an egalitarian contract, grounded in the idea of mutual consent: "conjugal society is made by a voluntary compact between man and woman; and though it consist chiefly in such a communion and right in one another's bodies as is necessary to its chief end, procreation; yet it draws with it mutual support and assistance, and a communion of interests too." The husband prevails in situations of unavoidable conflict, but this nonetheless "leaves the wife in the full and free possession of what by contract is her peculiar right, and gives the husband no more power over her life, than she has over his." Indeed, the power of the husband "being so far from that of an absolute monarch, that the wife has in many cases a liberty to separate from him, where natural right or their contract allows it; whether that contract be made by themselves in the state of nature, or by the customs or laws of the country they live in; and the children, upon such Separation fall to the father's or mother's lot, as such contract does determine." In short, Locke was remarkably ahead of his time with respect to women's equality, and, as Carole Pateman and Rogers Smith have noted, the egalitarian logic of his argument is subversive of all authority relations, including those arising in marriage.

Likewise in his discussion of slavery in the *Second Treatise,* Locke insists that "The natural liberty of man is to be free from any superior power on earth, and not to be under the will or legislative authority of man, but to have only the law of nature for his rule." Human beings may not sell themselves into slavery because they are God's property. "Nobody can give more power than he has himself; and he cannot take away his own life, cannot give another power over it." Slaves may be taken as a result of legitimate victory in war on Locke's account, but only because the defeated enemy has forfeited his right to life "by some act that deserves death," and the victor "to whom he has forfeited it, may (when he has him in his power) delay to take it, and make use of him to his own service, and he does him no injury by it." Legitimate slavery is, in effect, nothing more than the continuation of a state of war between the lawful victor and the captive, who never, strictly, becomes his master's property. There can be no slave relationship among members of a legitimate political association, which has to be based on consent. We are all equally immune from being owned by other humans, and by the same token bound to recognize that we cannot own others.

In addition to our all being equally God's property', Locke argued that " 'all men by nature are equal' " due to God's decision. On Filmer's account, God had given the world to Adam and his heirs. Existing property rights and the system of political authority had allegedly passed to current owners and European monarchs in this way through primogeniture. Locke insisted, by contrast, that God gave the world to mankind in common—subject to the provisos that it not be wasted, and that "enough, and as good" remain available to others to use in common. Locke added two dubious empirical claims to his theory of inclusive use-rights to the common. The result was something like the view of property that contemporary libertarians embrace. First was that with the introduction of money the injunction against waste, although not in principle transcended, for practical purposes became obsolete. Second, Locke was convinced that the productivity effects of enclosing common land would be so great that the "enough, and as good" proviso could in practice also be dispensed with, thereby legitimating private ownership. For "he who appropriates land to himself by his labour, does not lessen, but increase the common stock of mankind."

Although Locke's theory permitted substantial inequalities to develop, it nonetheless provided the basis for an egalitarian collective constraint on them: if either of his empirical beliefs turns out not to be true, the provisos kick in with all the force of natural law behind them. In short, Locke was not a believer in equality of result, nor was he a mere proponent of equality of opportunity or what Ronald Dworkin has described as starting-gate equality. Use-rights to the common are universal and inextinguishable on Locke's account. Although he does not say this, it would thus be reasonable to infer that anyone who is deprived of access to the common due to private ownership thus has a legitimate claim to at least what he would have been able to earn from unenclosed land. If this does not "trickle down" as a byproduct of the productivity effects of enclosure, then the natural law guarantee is activated.

God's decision to treat humans as one another's peers extends beyond these natural law protections; for Locke, it is built into the nature of human agency. We are all miniature gods on his account in that, provided we do not violate natural law, we stand in the same relation to the objects we create as God stands to us. We own them just as he owns us. Natural law, or God's natural right, sets the outer boundaries to a field within which humans have divine authorization to act as little gods, creating rights and obligations of their own. And although he denies that parents create children for reasons already discussed, Locke insists that God has endowed humans with great creative power. He minimizes the independent contribution of common resources to the value of what people produce by arguing that the world which has been given us in common is God's "waste," and insisting that "labour makes the far greater part," of its value. This is why Locke was so confident of the productivity effects of enclosure. The goods produced on an acre of enclosed land are at least ten—more like a hundred—times more than those "yielded by an acre of land, of an equal richness, lying waste in common." As a result, someone who encloses ten acres "may truly be said to give ninety acres to mankind," at least.

Locke applied his workmanship model to political arrangements no less than to property. Whereas for Filmer political rulers received their authority from God, on Locke's account political institutions are the property of the human beings who create them through a social contract. Indeed, in what might seem quaint by today's criteria for knowledge, Locke held that the study of ethics and politics is superior to that of the physical world because it concerns products of the human will to which every individual has privileged access through introspection. He distinguished "ectype" from "archetype" ideas, ectypes being general ideas of substances, archetypes are constructed by man. This generated a radical disjunction between natural and conventional knowledge, underpinned by a further distinction between "nominal" and "real" essences. In substances that depend on the external world for their existence (such as trees or animals), only nominal essences can be known to man. The real essence is available only to the maker of the substance, God. In the case of archetypes, however, nominal and real essences are synonymous so that real essences can by definition be known by man. Because the social world is a function of archetype ideas, it follows that real social essences can be known by man. We know what we make. Man can thus have incontrovertible knowledge of his creations—most importantly* for our purposes, of his political arrangements and institutions.

We know what we make just as we own what we make, be it property created through individual work or a commonwealth created by collective agreement. God makes man, we are told in the *First Treatise*, " 'in his own image, after his own likeness; makes him an intellectual creature and so capable of dominion.' " Human beings are equal to one another in these endeavors because their capacity for creativity, their status as miniature gods, is both universal and God-given. It may not legitimately be given, taken away, or otherwise compromised by other human beings. Indeed, natural law requires that each person preserve himself and that "when his own preservation comes not in competition," that each person ought "as much as he can, to preserve the rest of mankind, and may not, unless it be to do justice on an offender, take away or impair the life, or what tends to the preservation of life, the liberty, health, limb or goods of another." Locke was adamant that "the state of nature has a law of nature to govern it, which obliges every one: and reason, which is that law, teaches all mankind, who will but consult it, that being all equal and independent, no one ought to harm another in his life, health, liberty, or possessions."

Reason, then, is equally available to all. Locke was quick to defuse arguments from authority by appealing to man's natural and unencumbered reasoning capacities, a view that infuses his discussion in the *Essay Concerning Human Understanding* as well as *A Letter Concerning Toleration*. So he insists in the *Essay* that it is not only those who are trained in logic that are capable of reason. "He that will look into many parts of Asia and America, will find men reason there perhaps as acutely as himself, yet who never heard of a syllogism, nor can reduce any one argument to those forms." God, Locke insists,

> has not been so sparing to men to make them barely two-legged creatures, leaving it to Aristotle to make them rational. ... He has given them a mind that can reason, without being instructed in methods of syllogizing: the understanding is not taught to reason by these rules; it has a native faculty to perceive the coherence or incoherence of its ideas, and can range them right, without any such perplexing repetitions.

Rank does not give privileged access to reason any more than education does. Locke insists in the *Letter Concerning Toleration* that although princes are born superior to other men in power, "in nature" they are equal. "Neither the right, nor the art of ruling, does necessarily carry along with it the certain knowledge of other things." And we have seen that in the *Second Treatise*, Locke avers that the laws of nature are more easily intelligible than positive laws, and in his discussion of parental authority the whole basis of his attack on Filmer is that this is limited to their children's "ignorant nonage." For Locke, adults are all assumed to be equally capable of rational behavior. He thus thought human moral equality was manifest in the Scriptures, but that it can also be seen in our rational capacities and by observing our place in nature.

TOLERATION AND DISSENT

Human beings have liberty to act as miniature gods within the constraints of natural law, but they do not have license to violate the constraints themselves. This status inevitably raises the question: What happens when people disagree about their obligations to one another, about what respecting one another's autonomy as God's creatures requires, or about whether natural law is otherwise being compromised by actions people are taking or contemplating? That which humans comprehend as reason is part God's law, as I have just noted, but Locke realized that he had to confront the possibility that people might disagree about the meaning of the Scriptures or what reason otherwise requires. One way in which he responded was by embracing a capacious doctrine of toleration.

Locke went out of his way to make toleration in general not contingent on the truth or falsity of the belief to be tolerated. We are all subject to "the duties of peace and goodwill ... as well towards the erroneous as the orthodox." In *A Letter Concerning Toleration*, he insisted that the state may not force religious conformity on anyone, for "every church is orthodox to itself; [and] to others, erroneous or heretical." A church must therefore be a voluntary association of individuals in which the magistrate both safeguards and limits, but may not regulate internally. "[T]he care of souls is not committed to the civil magistrate." His power consists in "outward force," but "true and saving religion consists in the inward persuasion of the mind."

Locke was well aware that an unqualified principle of toleration can generate paradoxes, conflicting injunctions, and self-defeating conclusions. He therefore imposed three kinds of limits on toleration. The first concerns toleration of practices inimical to the principle of toleration itself; that is, actions which, if tolerated, result in people being forced to do things they would not otherwise do. "For all force, as has often been said, belongs only to the magistrate, nor ought any private persons at any time use force unless it is in self-defense against unjust violence." "Unjust violence" seems to mean direct violation of another's will, a refusal to tolerate another's private actions. Toleration requires intolerance of anti-tolerant acts: "[F]or who could be free, when every other man's humour might domineer over him?"

Next, Locke is unequivocal in the *First Treatise* that because all people are bound by the laws of nature, they have liberty to act freely but not license to do as they please. Thus children are under the authority of parents until they are old enough to understand that law, and thus practices like cannibalism, sale of children, adultery, incest, and sodomy, all of which "cross the main intention of nature," cannot be tolerated. Leaving aside, for now, how Locke expects us to know what is and is not against the main intention of nature, he clearly expects that the civil law will uphold this law and will not tolerate transgressions against it.

Finally, actions should not be tolerated if they are prejudicial to the existence of the political order. Thus atheists ought to be suppressed not because Locke disagrees with their beliefs (though he does), but because those beliefs threaten the commonwealth. "Promises, covenants, and oaths, which are the bonds of human society, can have no hold upon an atheist." Analogous considerations lead Locke to the conclusion that Papists and "Mahometans" ought not to be tolerated because they owe allegiance to alien civil powers. "That church can have no right to be tolerated by the magistrate, which is constituted upon such a bottom, that all those who enter into it, do thereby, *ipso facto,* deliver themselves up to the protection and service of another prince."

It is difficult to know to what extent such beliefs were sincerely held by any writer in the political climate of Restoration and revolutionary England. On the subject of atheism, Locke regarded questions about the existence of God as separate from questions about alternative religions. It is clear from the *Essay* that he was convinced by versions of the cosmological proof and the argument from design. In *A Letter Concerning Toleration,* he seems to follow Hooker in invoking a version of the argument from common consent. For whatever reason, Locke regarded the existence of God as self-evident. But his decisive *political* reason for denying toleration to atheists, Catholics, and Muslims rested on his worry about their incentives for fidelity to the commonwealth. In this he was an early proponent of a view akin to John Rawls's "political, not metaphysical" outlook concerning political legitimacy. True and saving religion might consist of inward persuasion of the mind, but if the mind of an Englishman becomes persuaded of the veracity of Catholicism or Islam, or, indeed, unpersuaded of God's existence, then he is out of luck. In short, the acceptability of a belief turns on its compatibility with the legitimate political order, not on whether its veracity is demonstrable by Locke's criteria.

These constraints notwithstanding, Locke's view of toleration was a variant of the conventional Whig one in the 1680s. Since the Restoration, Charles and James had been attempting to expand toleration of Catholics and nonconformists to undermine the religious and political power of the Anglican clergy. Charles's embrace of toleration in 1662 and his declaration for indulgence a decade later met with insurmountable political opposition, but James had considerably more success with his similar declaration in 1687. James's uneasy alliance with both Catholic and Protestant nonconformists was broken at the Revolution as a result of Anglican promises to tolerate nonconformists in the general interests of Protestantism. A more liberal regime was realized to some extent in the Toleration Act of 1689, although it did little more than exempt some narrowly defined groups of dissenters from some specific penalties. The Act achieved its purposes, however. It split Protestant from Catholic dissenters, the latter being excluded from toleration legislation. Henceforth, Catholicism could be regarded as treasonable as it was in the Act Against Popery of 1700, aimed at "preventing the further growth of popery and of such treasonable, and execrable designs and conspiracies against his Majesty's person and government." Locke's view was thus in the mainstream of Whig thinking on toleration that triumphed at the Revolution, even if he advocated tolerating a wider array of dissenting groups than would most.

Locke's account of toleration was buttressed by an anti-authoritarian theory of biblical hermeneutics. Underlying his rejection of Filmer's patriarchalism was a challenge to Filmer's reading of the Scriptures, and particularly to the inherently hierarchical world view that emanates from Filmer's contention that God gave the world to Adam and his heirs. Underlying *that* rejection, as Richard Ashcraft has noted, was Locke's radical claim that where the Scriptures admit of more than one interpretation no earthly authority may declare one reading to be authoritative, Our prejudices and opinions "cannot authorize us to understand the Scripture contrary to the direct and plain meaning of the words," but where there is silence or ambiguity the reader must judge how "they may best be understood." In the course of rejecting Filmer's claim that scriptural warrant for Adam's sovereignty over Eve can generate a justification for absolute monarchical authority, Locke insists that the burden lies with whoever is advancing an interpretation to give reasons that the reader will find plausible.

Locke insisted that each reader is sovereign over what counts for him as a convincing interpretation of a text. As Locke argued in the *Letter on Toleration*, those things "that every man ought sincerely to inquire into himself, and by meditation, study, search, and his own endeavours, attain the knowledge of, cannot be looked upon as the peculiar profession of any one sort of men." When people disagree over the meaning of the Scriptures, they have to weigh the evidence for themselves. God speaks directly to every individual through the text, so that no human authority is entitled to declare one interpretation authoritative in the face of a conflicting one. This freedom to comprehend natural law by one's own lights supplied the basis for Locke's right to resist that could be invoked against the sovereign, and to which he himself appealed in opposing the English crown during the 1680s. Ashcraft captures Locke's interpretive radicalism well when he notes that it was "designed to undermine the authoritative weight of an interpretation, of the Bible advanced by any individual or group of individuals as an interpretative guide to the meaning of that work."

This is not to say that Locke believed every interpretation of the Scriptures equally valid. On the contrary, he thought that there is a correct interpretation on which reasonable people will usually agree, and he seemed confident that he could convince people that his reading of the Scriptures was consistent with their commonsense interpretations. Although God speaks with more truth and certainty than men, "when he vouchsafes to speak to men [through the Scriptures], I do not think he speaks differently from them, in crossing the rules of language in use amongst them: this would not be to condescend to their capacities, when he humbles himself to speak to them, but to lose his design in speaking what, thus spoken, they could not understand." Commonsense readings of the Scriptures must, therefore, reveal their true meaning. We have to countenance the possibility that people will continue to disagree, and protect their right to do so, but Locke did not doubt that most of the time people could be brought to agree.

I will have more to say about Locke's treatment of political disagreement anon. For now it is worth noting that there is a certain circularity to his view, parallel to that which attends Rawls in his "political, not metaphysical" mode. Rawls seeks a "political" conception of justice that "can gain the support of an overlapping consensus of reasonable religious, philosophical, and moral doctrines in a society regulated by it." He regards this as essential for people who disagree profoundly on religious, philosophical, and moral matters to "maintain a just and stable democratic society." It is not entirely clear on Rawls's account whether, in order for a religious, philosophical, or moral doctrine to be judged reasonable it must meet independently derived criteria as he sometimes claims, or whether it must be compatible with political arrangements that can be endorsed by adherents to any of the other doctrines that happen to prevail in the society—whether overlapping consensus is derived from reasonableness or the reverse.

To be sure, expansive as it was for his day, Locke's view of toleration is more restrictive than Rawls's. Yet it seems to exhibit an analogous ambiguity in that it is difficult to pin down whether he ultimately thinks commonsense interpretations of the Scriptures should be thought commonsensical because they are compatible with political arrangements that those with different readings can endorse, or rather for some independent reason. And, as with Rawls, difficulties attend both views. If there is to be an independent criterion, the question arises as to where it comes from and what is to be said to those who are unpersuaded of its basis in reason or common sense. If, on the other hand, we adopt the contingent view, there is the danger that there might not be an overlapping consensus. There might not be enough common ground between competing interpretations—say Locke's and Filmer's—to sustain any political order. After all, considerations of this kind were presumably partly what was at issue for Locke in the 1680s. In some moods at least Rawls seems to want to square the relevant circle by claiming that his proposed principles are compatible with the most diverse possible array of doctrines while still being able to sustain a stable political order. The reasons Locke gives for limiting toleration as he does suggest that analogous considerations played into his thinking, but we will see that when push comes to shove, he moves in a more decidedly democratic direction.

DEMOCRATIC FOUNDATIONS

At this point it might reasonably be asked whether Locke's view is not more liberal than democratic. After all, we have seen that it is the traditional liberal value of toleration, buttressed by a strongly individualist view of scriptural interpretation, that lies at the core of his political doctrine—a far cry from the conventional democratic commitment to participation. This is true; indeed as Kendall notes, given his doctrine, Locke is surprisingly thin on mechanisms of popular consultation. Moreover, as Ruth Grant argues convincingly in this volume, Locke did not think of day-to-day participation as a basic category of political legitimation. Closer examination reveals, however, that his underlying conception of legitimacy is democratic more than liberal, particularly once we focus on his discussion of the practical implications of disagreement over the meaning of natural law and the right to resist.

Locke's assumption that people can always be brought to agree on fundamental moral and political questions was obviously at variance with his own political experience. He acknowledged this in the most Hobbesian of terms: "For though the Law of Nature be plain and intelligible to all rational Creatures," he tells us in his discussion of the aims of political society in the *Second Treatise*, "yet men being biased by their interest, as well as ignorant for want of studying it, are not apt to allow of it as a law binding to them ... men being partial to themselves, passion and revenge is very apt to carry them too far, and with too much heat, in their own cases." For Hobbes, this view could generate a command theory of law to force men to be rational; for Rousseau, it would generate a Lawgiver to manipulate men to be "genuinely" free. Locke, however, takes the idea of consent of the governed too seriously to make an analogous move. Like the young Rawls of *A Theory of Justice*, he seems to want to reason about the legitimacy of political institutions in a way that pays homage to considerable diversity of belief yet shields it from self-interest. As is well known, Rawls deploys a "veil of ignorance" to get at this: people are assumed to be choosing institutions knowing that there is a plurality of world views and conceptions of the good but not what their particular one is. Locke, who conceived of the social contract as an actual agreement, would not have been much interested in hypothetical speculation of this kind. For him, reconciling disagreement with the view that political legitimacy is based on consent is an inescapable political problem. Whereas Rawls's "political, not metaphysical" move retains a rationalist component, Locke's is political all the way down. This is because Rawls restricts the range of acceptable views based on where they come from, whereas for Locke the decisive criterion is what they should be expected to lead to.

For Rawls, acceptable political arguments appeal only to public reason rooted in the overlapping consensus among the different views in society, not to the comprehensive religious and metaphysical doctrines to which people may be committed. This creates difficulties for him in thinking about the legitimacy of movements for political reform such as the civil rights movement.

Such movements were often avowedly religious in inspiration, manifestly rooted in the comprehensive doctrines of their adherents. Of their leaders he says that "they did not go against the ideal of public reason; or rather, they did not provided they thought, or on reflection would have thought (as they certainly could have thought), that the comprehensive reasons they appealed to were required to give sufficient strength to the political conception to be subsequently realized." The obvious question to ask Rawls is what would he say to the pro-segregationist who believes his views, though right because dictated by God, were compatible with what public reason should endorse. Because Locke focused exclusively on the political effects of beliefs in determining what should be tolerated, he did not need to indulge in such conceptual gymnastics to adjudicate among comprehensive doctrines while trying to appear not to be so doing. This consequentialist understanding of "political, not metaphysical" places him closer to Habermas than to Rawls in the contemporary debate.

The right of resistance defended in the *Second Treatise* was intensely charged politically. Locke placed himself at odds with the Whig establishment in 1689 by embracing the Lawsonian view that when James had been compelled to leave the throne an entire dissolution of government had resulted. In violating the terms of the social contract James had, in Locke's view, gone into a direct state of war with the people. Accordingly, they had the right to resist him and to remove him as king. Locke's view entailed not only that the king had been removed from office justly but also that the rule of law and the legal authority of Parliament had ended, necessitating a return of power to the general community. As a general matter, this means that, once the right to resist potentially comes into play, the political stakes cannot be higher. It also makes the issue of what to do in the face of disagreement concerning how and by whom resistance is to be deemed legitimate all the more consequential.

In the course of arguing against both mixed and limited monarchy, Filmer had noted that in either case there is no final and authoritative judge within the constitution. Neither Parliament nor any court could resolve a charge of tyranny against the king. Locke tacitly accepted this position, as Franklin notes, yet he never answered Filmer's charge that this would be an open invitation for continual resistance and even attempted revolution by anarchic individuals and groups disaffected by the actions of the king or Parliament. It was exactly this type of conflict that the Whigs wanted to avoid. Locke tried to downplay these radical implications of his view by holding that not every illegal act by the king justified revolution, "[I]t being safer for the Body, that some few private Men should be sometimes in danger to suffer, than that the head of the Republick should be easily, and upon slight occasions exposed." Unless a ruler actively places himself "into a state of war with his people, dissolve the government, and leave them to that defense which belongs to everyone in the state of nature," he may not legitimately be resisted. Indeed, in the chapter on prerogative power, Locke went so far as to maintain that the independence of the ruler is such that there may be circumstances in which he may act where there is no law, and even in some cases "against the direct letter of the law" provided this is for the public good. Wise and good princes will use this power well; others will misuse it.

This is only to push the matter back an additional step, however. Even in extreme cases—arguably especially in such cases—disagreement over whether the ruler has placed himself at war with his people has to be anticipated. Locke's instructive answer is that the "people have no other remedy in this, as in all other cases when they have no judge on earth, but to appeal to heaven." This appeal to heaven implies a resort to force. It might seem to bring Locke uncomfortably close to the Hobbesian position that although a person cannot be blamed in certain circumstances for resisting legitimate authority, such resistance is not itself legitimate—all he can do is hope that it will be recognized as valid in the life to come.

MAJORITY RULE

But Locke's view differs from Hobbes's. Locke clearly supposes that genuine cases of a government's violation of its trust will be obvious, because he expects those who are not biased by interest, who he assumes—perhaps heroically—will be most people, to converge on commonsense conclusions. The operational test of this conclusion is majoritarian for him: the right to resist does not lay "a perpetual foundation for disorder" because it "operates not, till inconvenience is so great, that the majority feel it, and are weary of it, and find a necessity to have it amended." There is no protection for minority perceptions of violations of the social contract or natural law in this scheme, or any provision to protect minorities from majority perceptions that the social contract or natural law have been violated. Given the importance Locke famously attaches to personal consent as the final legitimating mark of all political action and institutions, it might seem remarkable that at the end of the day majority rule is its only guarantor. Locke *predicts* that people will be slow to resist in fact, that the right to resist, even in circumstances of manifestly tyrannous acts, will frequently not be exercised.

> [F]or if it reach no farther than some private men's cases, though they have a right to defend themselves, and to recover by force what by unlawful force is taken from them; yet the right to do so will not easily engage them in a contest, wherein they are sure to perish; it being as impossible for one or a few oppressed men to disturb the government, where the body of the people do not think themselves concerned in it, as for a raving madman, or heady malecontent, to overturn a well-settled state; the people being as little apt to follow the one as the other.

In short, unless and until "a long train of abuses, prevarications, and artifices, all tending the same way," trigger the right to revolution, people must accept the decisions emanating from the prevailing political order. Until that threshold is crossed for a great many, even perceived violations of natural law must for all practical purposes be endured. The individual right to self-enforcement is given up on entering civil society and people can reassert it only at the risk of being executed for treason. On the other hand, if a long train of abuses, and so on, *does* convince the great majority to revolt, there is no legitimate earthly power to stop them. In these respects, Locke's account recognizes the priority of politics to disagreements about rights and laws, so that Kendall is right to insist that those who appeal to Locke as a conventional defender of rights-based liberalism are misguided.

If this were all Locke had to say on the subject of majority rule, the case for him as an early theorist of democracy would be flimsy indeed. In fact, however, he is quite explicit about the majoritarian foundations of political legitimacy. In the state of nature, "'every one has the executive power' of the law of nature," but this right is given up at the formation of civil society. Thereafter, "it being necessary to that which is one body to move one way; it is necessary the body should move that way wither the greatest force carries it, which is the consent of the majority: or else it is impossible it should act or continue one body, one community, which the consent of every individual that united into it, agreed that it should; and so every one is bound by that to be concluded by the majority." This leads Locke to defend a default presumption in favor of majority rule "in assemblies, empowered to act by positive laws, where no number is set by that positive law which empowers them." Majority rule thus has "by the law of nature and reason, the power of the whole."

Locke recognizes that the public assembly will be characterized by a "variety of opinions, and contrariety of interests, which unavoidably happen in all collections of men," and therefore, unanimity is unlikely. For Rousseau, this reality would necessitate a Lawgiver to guide and enlighten the public as to the general will. But for Locke, the determination of the majority is sufficient "for where the majority cannot conclude the rest, there they cannot act as one body, and consequently will be immediately dissolved again." It is "the consent of any number of Freemen capable of a majority to unite and incorporate into such a society" that provides the "beginning to any lawful government in the world." It may be true, as Ellen Wood has emphasized, that Locke never advocated expansion of the franchise (which was unusually wide in seventeenth century England). But the more salient point for the longer term is that his argument provides no basis for limiting the franchise. His egalitarian commitments discussed in the first half of this chapter press inexorably in the direction of universal inclusion—the only legitimate grounds for excluding people from decision-making that affects them being incapacity.

For Locke, it is majoritarian rather than individual consent that authorizes institutional arrangements. The majority may choose to retain all powers of government, thereby creating a "perfect" democracy. Alternatively, it may delegate some or all of its powers, creating various "forms of commonwealth," such as oligarchies or elective or hereditary monarchies. As Ashcraft notes, "formally, Locke is committed to the view that the majority of the community may dispose of their political power as they see fit, and this includes, of course, their power to constitute a democracy," which is the "form of government that remains closest to the institution of the political community itself." Whatever form of government is chosen, it rests ultimately on conditional delegation from the majority. The majority never relinquishes its "supreme power," which comes into play when delegated power either expires or is abused. Unless a substantial majority comes to agree that abuse has occurred, the opposition of the individual will have no practical effect. Opposition may otherwise be legitimate, but even when it is to an action that is life threatening, an individual or minority might have to wait for vindication until the next life as we have seen. In practice, in this world, natural law constrains the actions of governments only to the extent that a majority discerns it and acts on it.

But why *majority* rule? Liberal writers for whom consent supplies the basis of political legitimacy typically appeal to unanimity, not majority rule, particularly on significant questions—effectively giving everyone who might wish to withhold their consent a veto. For instance, James Buchanan and Gordon Tullock argue in *The Calculus of Consent* that people would insist on unanimity rule before collective action could be taken concerning the issues they regard as most important. Only on less consequential matters would they see the sense of accepting majority rule, or perhaps even delegation to an administrator, when they trade off the costs of participating in decision-making against the likelihood that an adverse decision will be made. Buchanan and Hillock do not supply us with criteria for distinguishing more from less consequential decisions, but it seems safe to assume that Locke's right to resist would be at or close to the top of the list. Yet, as we have seen, he protects it with majority rule only. Why?

The answer is that Locke had a more realistic view of politics than the hypothetical contract theorists of the second half of the twentieth century. As Patrick Riley has noted, "the social contract, for Locke, is necessitated by natural law's inability to be literally 'sovereign' on earth, by its incapacity to produce 'one society.'" Theorists like Buchanan and Tullock, Rawls, and Robert Nozick are often criticized for writing as if the institutions of civil association—private property, contracts, rules of inheritance—can exist independently of collective action. Locke made no such assumption and he would surely have recognized its infeasibility—after all, in his lifetime every enclosure of land required an Act of Parliament. Once we recognize that collective action is ubiquitous to civil association, then it makes little sense to assume that regimes in which change is difficult are those in which important individual freedoms will be best protected. As Locke was acutely aware, the status quo can be the source of political oppression. When this is so, obstacles to collective action will sustain that oppression. In the real world of ongoing politics, Brian Barry and Douglas Rae have shown that majority rule or something close to it is the logical rule to prefer if one assumes that one is as likely to oppose a given outcome as to support it regardless of whether it is the status quo. From this perspective the libertarian constitutional scheme is a collective action regime maintained by the state, and disproportionately financed by implicit taxes on those who would prefer an alternative regime. Locke recognized, as Laslett put it, that "it is the power that men have over others, not the power that they have over themselves, which gives rise to political authority."

In short, Locke's institutional theory differs from that of modern libertarians because he operates with a different underlying theory of power—as ubiquitous to human interaction rather than as a byproduct of collective action. As a result, unequivocal as he was that consent is the wellspring of political legitimacy, he saw majority rule as its best available institutional guarantor. Hence his concluding insistence that the "power that every individual gave the society, when he entered into it, can never revert to the individuals again, as long as the society lasts, but will always remain in the community; because without this there can be no community." And the judgment whether or not the government is at war with the community must reside with the people: "If a controversy arise betwixt a prince and some of the people, in a matter where the law is silent or doubtful, and the thing be of great consequence, I should think the proper umpire, in such a case, should be the body of the people." Common misconceptions to the contrary notwithstanding, the relation between the people and the government is not a contract. Rather, it is one of trust. Should a question arise as to whether that trust has been violated by a prince or legislature, " 'The people shall be judge;' for who shall be judge whether his trustee or deputy acts well, and according to the trust reposed in him, but he who deputes him, and must, by having deputed him, have still a power to discard him, when he fails in his trust." And the people act by majority rule.

Locke understood that the fundamental political question for human beings is not: collective action or not? Rather, it is: what sort of collective action? His presumption in favor of the supremacy of legislative authority reflects this. Legislatures are legitimate just because they embody majority rule which, in the end, is the best available guarantor of the freedoms people seek to protect through the creation of government. Although Locke perceived advantages to a separation of powers involving an independent executive and "federative" (geared to foreign affairs and to relations with those in the state of nature), he was unequivocal that these institutions are subordinate to the legislative power because it alone embodies the consent of the governed through majority rule. Even in the case of a dissolution of government there need not be a return to a state of nature. Rather, power can devolve to the people who "may constitute to themselves a new legislative, as they think best, being in full liberty to resist the force of those, who without authority would impose any thing on them." The people, acting a body by majority rule, have greater legitimacy than the alternative: individuals or arbitrary powers acting unilaterally.

Locke's recognition that power is inevitably exercised in collective life perhaps also accounts for why his discussion of tacit consent seems so cavalier, at least in comparison to a theorist like Nozick (who engages in a tortured, and ultimately unsuccessful, argument for forcibly incorporating "independents" who refuse to join the society in a manner that can be said not to undermine their consent). Locke insists that "every man, that hath any possessions, or enjoyment of any part of the dominions of any government, doth thereby give his tacit consent, and is as far forth obliged to obedience to the laws of that government, during such enjoyment, as any one under it." His claim that their tacit consent is reasonably taken for granted because they are free to leave is obviously belied by most people's circumstances. Yet if one takes the view that even those who have given express consent must inevitably expect often to be at odds with actions of the government then this seems less troubling. Only from the unrealistic perspective of someone who thinks it possible to live in a form of political association with others in which one's consent is never violated does it seem troubling that one's only protection is majority rule. No other decision rule provides better protection.

It is sometimes said this is why constitutional courts and bills of rights are needed to protect individuals and minorities from the vicissitudes of democratic politics. At least since Mill's and Tocqueville's time, it has been characteristic for liberal constitutionalists to worry about majority tyranny, but as Robert Dahl has recently reminded us, history has revealed these worries to be misplaced. Since the advent of the universal franchise, political freedoms have turned out to be safer in democracies than in non-democracies by a considerable margin. In 1956 Dahl had registered skepticism that, even within democracies, constitutional courts and judicial review could be shown to have a positive effect on the degree to which individual freedoms are respected. Subsequent scholarship has shown skepticism to be well founded. It seems that Locke's underlying institutional commitment to majority rule was more indeed far-sighted than critics such as Kendall appreciated. Indeed, there are reasons to think that the popularity of independent courts in the contemporary world may have more in common with die popularity of independent banks than with the protection of individual freedoms. They operate as devices to signal foreign investors and international creditors that the capacity of elected officials to engage in redistributive policies or interfere with property rights will be limited. That is, they may be devices for limiting domestic political opposition to unpopular policies by taking them off the table.

That said, it might nonetheless be objected that Locke's insistence that majority rule is the ultimate guarantor of the entitlements human beings create for themselves, the agreements human beings make with one another, and the natural law constraints on all their actions, has few—if any—implications for day-to-day politics. This is partly what Kendall has in mind when complaining that Locke's commitment to majoritarianism is not buttressed by any mechanism of popular consultation. There is truth to this, but two points should be noted in mitigation. First, Locke's account looks a good deal more plausible if we think of the reality of democratic systems rather than participatory democratic ideals. Actual democratic systems involve a mix of decision-making mechanisms, considerable delegation to administrative agencies, and many empower courts to conduct judicial review. But these different mechanisms are all subservient to majoritarian political decision-making in various ways, whether through systems of appointment, control of funding and jurisdiction, oversight, or some combination of these. Constitutional systems sometimes limit democracy's range, to be sure, particularly in separation-of-powers systems such as those of the United States. But constitutions generally contain entrenched guarantees of democratic government as well. Moreover, they are themselves revisable at constitutional conventions or via amendment procedures whose legitimacy is popularly authorized. Even liberal constitutionalists like Brace Ackerman agree that critical moments of constitutional founding and change require popular democratic validation if they are to be seen as legitimate over time. In short the practice in modem democracies is consistent with Locke's picture of various institutional arrangements—some more participatory than others—existing against a backdrop of popular sovereignty.

There is a second and more specific sense in which Locke might be seen as being more prescient about democracy than Kendall gives him credit for having been, linked to the reality that mechanisms of popular consultation turn out to be fraught with difficulty. Modem social choice theory has taught us that it is doubtful that there can be any such thing as a Rousseauian general will in even minimally diverse societies. As a result, we should think of democracy as a way of ensuring that, however inclusive decision-making can be made to be, the possibility of opposition from those whose interests may be harmed by the exercise of power is an important discipline. Majority rule is less a system of representation from this point of view as "flexing muscles," as Adam Przeworski puts it, "a reading of the chances in the eventual war." Though he did not intend it thus, it would be difficult to conjure up a more apposite expression of the sentiment behind the discussion of majority rule in chapter XIX of the *Second Treatise*. That Locke fails to provide for mechanisms of popular consultation looks less worrisome, from this perspective, as does the objection that his right to resist issues in a theory of revolution more than one of government. All governments live in the shadow of possible revolution. The way for them to avoid it is to be responsive to the interests of the majority, who might otherwise conclude that their trust has been violated. This may be a more sober view of democratic politics than those that have enthralled many theorists since Locke's time. At the same time, however, Locke's view has done better over the long run—and with good reason.

THE LIMITS OF CONSENSUAL DECISION

BY DOUGLAS W. RAE

Douglas W. Rae, "The Limits of Consensual Decision," *American Political Science Review,* vol. 69, pp. 1270-1294. Copyright © 1975 by Cambridge University Press. Reprinted with permission.

TWENTY-ONE

The idea that governments should function by some approximate consensus—unanimous agreement as a condition to action—has deep intuitive and analytic roots in liberal thought: in the myth of the social contract, in the doctrine of consent, in the structure of markets, in the utilitarian ethic which survives economic theory under the title of efficiency.[1] It is everywhere understood that consensus—this is the way with ideals—has serious practical limits, but these hardly disqualify it from service as a normative criterion to be approximated in experience. Yet, if I am right, we should not say merely that consensus *cannot* be duplicated in practice, we should say that it *should not* be approximated in practice. This, because consensual decision displays structural defects which, for any society requiring politics, spoil its normative promise. I will try at some length to explain this vague slander.

The paper argues three main theses. First, that consensual decision does indeed have deep roots in liberalism, of which the deepest run toward consent

---

1 I presuppose at the outset that consensual decision does not emerge as a self-enforcing norm of collective action. There are structures for which this may be expected: ones in which the defection of any denies the reward of cooperation at all. This so-called "essential coalition" problem has its historical instances: in the cartel, the minimal parliamentary coalition, the Western marriage, the isolated exchange of goods and services, the international alliance between approximate equals. The European Economic Community, especially in light of the Luxembourg Accords (1966), also seems a case of this sort. And in all these cases, consensus is self-enforcing: disagreement opens the prospect of defection, which in turn denies the rewards of joint action to others. But the nation-state deviates decisively from the "essential coalition" ideal for at least three reasons: (1) relations of authority and *control* permit the repression of deviance, (2) *slack* permits the toleration of at least minor deviance and defection and (3) *substitution* permits the recruitment of alternative collaborators in collective action when deviance does occur. For all these reasons, it is no historical surprise that consensual decision, like substantive equality, serves as a normative ideal raised in protest against experience.

of the governed and toward utilitarian efficiency. This is the rather thin history[2] presented as Part I. Second, that neither consensual decision nor any other structure can conceivably grant an unconditional right of consent to persons living together in political society. Part II thus argues that some outcome to any decision must portend a violation of consent.[3] Third, that the new political economy—Knut Wicksell, Buchanan and Tullock[4]—is wrong in claiming that consensual decision leads toward social efficiency. They would be right only for a society requiring no politics. This is the burden of Part III. A final section offers one general and perhaps ironic conclusion.

I. HISTORICAL PLACE OF THE CONSENSUS DOCTRINE

At least so far as it is a theory of public life, liberalism has always been committed to a fundamental symmetry among individuals—in John Schaar's phrase, to "men of standard size and shape."[5] This is a kind of equality which sleeps, in practice and theory, with partners as inequalitarian as Hobbes's *Leviathan* or as divisive as the class differences which attend private capital and managerial or technical expertise. Its fundamental meaning is that relevantly similar individuals must be treated with relevant similarity, and its central implication for argument is that men may be distinguished by ability and the social utility of their work, but not by their formal value as persons. This in turn constricts normative analysis to general or symmetrical judgments: to the consent of *all* relevant subjects, to utility measured across a whole community.[6]

---

2 This account is admittedly preliminary and covers a large sweep of arguments: Locke on consent, through Godwin, Mill, Calhoun, to the new political economy on the best structure for governmental decision.

3 The argument here is addressed mainly to Calhoun's doctrine of "concurrent majorities," Wicksell's *laissez faire* consensus, and Robert Paul Wolff's "direct unanimous democracy." Cf. J. C. Calhoun, *A Disquisition on Government*, ed. Gordon Post (Indian-apolis: Bobbs-Merrill, 1973); Knut Wicksell, "Ein neues Prinzip der gerechten Besteuerung," *Finanztheoretische Untersuchungen* (Jena, 1896), abridged and translated as "A New Principle of Just Taxation," by J. M. Buchanan in Classics in the Theory of Public Finance, ed. Richard A. Musgrave and Alan T. Peacock (New York: St. Martins Press, 1964) pp. 72–118; and Robert Paul Wolff, *In Defense of Anarchism* (New York: Harper & Row, 1970).

4 James M. Buchanan and Gordon Tullock, *The Calculus of Consent* (Ann Arbor: University of Michigan Press, 1962).

5 John H. Schaar, "Some Ways of Thinking About Equality," *Journal of Politics*, 26 (November, 1964) 867–95.

6 This universality defines a nearly constant element of political reform in Europe and the United States from the early nineteenth century forward, as rules of exclusion based on property, race, sex, and religion are constricted and overturned. "All" comes closer and closer to meaning all, even if "consent" does not come closer and closer to meaning consent. In moral philosophy, its analog is the principle of universalizability, e.g., roughly, answers to the question "what if everyone did that?" See, for example, R. M. Hare, *Freedom and Reason* (London: Oxford University Press, 1963).

IA. CONSENT IN POLITICAL REGIME OR THEIR DECISIONS

The fundamental idea of government by *consent,* enveloped from its beginning in this equalitarian symmetry,[7] became important for a quite specific historical purpose: the rationalization of liberal revolution. Locke's *Second Treatise* was, in part, an attempt to discredit Stuart absolutism as against a parliamentary alternative in the paradigm case of 1688.[8] And its central dogma is government by consent. For our purposes, two facts about Locke and his ideological task seem important.

First, like all of the great liberal constitutionalists, Locke was reacting against a structure of power—a structure which permitted some to take actions whose consequences fell upon others. This was a particular species of power—autocracy—and the doctrine of consent was shaped by it. In particular, it was *asymmetric* and *public.* By "asymmetric" I mean that it matched elite against subject public, so that authority flowed in one direction and not the other. The contrasting case, symmetrical power, was not faced by Locke's doctrine of consent. It was "public" in the sense that it had a necessary and explicit relation to the choice of policy by government: Locke did not choose to emphasize the alternative cases of anomic and civil power.[9] It is, at least in part, this attention to the special case of autocracy (and its parliamentary alternative) which underlies the peculiar quality of Locke's central fiction, a social contract in which "free, equal, and independent" men agree with one another—consent—to a government by majorities:

> When any number of men have so consented to make one community or government, they are thereby presently incorporated and make one body politic wherein the majority have a right to act and conclude the rest.[10]

This is not the least bit odd as a weapon of parliamentary revolution, and it carried a certain ideological weight in the later revolutions of 1776 and 1789. But it is an odd idea if one looks *backward* from the experience of democratic societies.[11] It attaches the ideal of consent to *regimes,* and it was clear enough that Stuart absolutism had its objectors at that level. But once regimes are legitimated, the question of consent turns on particular *decisions,* and there exists no self-evident

---

7   Were it not enveloped in such a symmetry, its value as an assault on monarchy and aristocracy would of course seem slight. If one asymmetry, why not another?
8   It is not altogether certain that Locke saw his book in this light. Cf. John Plamenatz, *Man and Society*, Vol. I (London: Longman's, 1963), 209 ff.
9   By "anomic power" I have in mind coercion which does not rely on a public code, as in Hobbes's state of nature or many contemporary cities; by "civil" or "private" power I have in mind control over others based on the use of public codes, as with the rights of ownership.
10   Locke, of course, goes on to develop a very loose doctrine of consent for "later," historical acts of government, thus avoiding the issue raised by Godwin and others as discussed below.
11   See in particular Willmoore Kendall, *John Locke and the Doctrine of Majority-Rule* (Urbana: University of Illinois Press, 1941).

link between (1) a fictional (or, for that matter, historical) consent in regimes, and (2) an actual consent in government policy. If I am governed by some approximate democracy, and find my own will trampled by its law, government by consent may seem a shallow artifice. And, save perhaps Rousseau, no major theorist escapes the inference that consent—or self-government—may be threatened by the symmetry of democratic decision just as it may be threatened by the asymmetry of autocracy. We are bound, that is, to honor the nonconsenting minority as a legitimate problem of value. This is the second point about Locke's invocation of consent as a doctrine: it arose in one quarrel, but survived to haunt parties to very different quarrels.

The line of argument which brings us to the doctrine of consensual decision is faced by this later problem, by the ideological heritage of consent and the persistent historical importance of less-than-unanimous decisions by parliamentary regimes. As early as 1798, before the democracies had got very democratic, William Godwin was able to debunk the transition from consent in regimes to consent in policies:

> ... if government be founded in the consent of the people, it can have no power over any individual by whom that consent is refused. If a tacit consent be not sufficient, still less can I be deemed to have consented to a measure upon which I put an express negative. This immediately follows from the observations of Rousseau. If the people, or the individuals of whom the people is constituted, cannot delegate their authority to a representative; neither can any individual delegate his authority to a majority, in an assembly of which he is himself a member. That must surely be a singular species of consent, the external indications of which are often to be found, in an unremitting opposition in the first instance, and compulsory subjection in the second.[12]

Partly, no doubt, his temperament, but equally important his position as an outsider, carry Godwin toward anarchism, not consensus. As we will see (Part IIE), this is not so great a leap—from anarchism to consensus—as it may seem. The later view of Mill embodies essentially the same observation:

> It was now perceived that such phrases as "self-government," and "the power of the people over themselves" do not express the true state of the case. The "people" who exercise the power are not always the same people with those over whom it is exercised; and the "self-government" spoken of is not the government of each by himself, but of each by all the rest. The will of the people, moreover, practically means the will

---

12 William Godwin, *Enquiry Concerning Political Justice* (edition of 1798), 3 Vols., F. E. L. Priestley (Toronto: University of Toronto Press, 1946), book III, chap. 2, p. 193. In his reference to Rousseau, Godwin evidently has in mind the argument that sovereignty is indivisible as it appears in chaps. 1 and 2 of Book II in the *Social Contract*.

of the most numerous or the most active *part* of the people; the majority, or those who succeed in making themselves accepted as the majority; the people, consequently, *may* desire to oppress a part of their number; and precautions are as much needed against this as against any other abuse of power.[13]

Mill's response is essentially libertarian: to argue that the common good compels a highly constrained use of state authority, confining prohibitions to acts that harm others,[14] mandates to acts whose omission would do similar harm. The resulting economy of liberty is notoriously complex. We should note, for future reference, that this argument is at least ostensibly built on an hypothesis connecting restraint from coercion with aggregate social utility:

I forego any advantage which could be derived to my argument from the idea of abstract right, as a thing independent of utility. ...

Mankind are greater gainers by suffering each to live as seems good to themselves, than by compelling each to live as seems good to the rest.[15]

This claim later becomes the cornerstone on which the most sophisticated case for consensual decision is built. Mill himself, however, comes no closer to consensual decision than his advocacy of Mr. Hare's scheme of proportional representation: giving minorities voices if not vetoes over state policy.[16] It was for J. C. Calhoun to "remedy" these difficulties with a full doctrine of consensual decision. His recognition of symmetrical coercion is especially clear in his account of representative government:

If the whole community had the same interests so that the interests of each and every portion would be so affected by the action of the government that the laws which oppressed or impoverished one portion would necessarily oppress or impoverish all others—or the reverse—then the right of suffrage, of itself, would be all-sufficient to counteract the tendency of the government to oppression and abuse of its powers, and, of course, would form, of itself, a perfect constitutional government. ... But such is not the case. On the contrary, nothing is more difficult than to equalize the action of

---

13   John Stuart Mill, *On Liberty* in *Utilitarianism, Liberty,* and *Representative Government*, Everyman edition (New York: E. P. Dutton and Co.; and London: J. M. Dent and Sons, 1951), chap. 1, p. 88.
14   "As will become apparent, in III below, acts of private harm, combined with static government policy, are critical to the present analysis.
15   "Mill, p. 97, p. 100. I have perhaps unfairly juxtaposed two sentences separated by nearly one hundred lines, but I think they give the main sense of Mill's view as briefly as possible.
16   Mill's further proposal for a second Chamber composed of intellectuals is meant, evidently, as a method of moral persuasion, not a center of countervailing power against parliament. Cf. *Representative Government*, ch. 13.

the government in reference to the various and diversified interests of the community; and nothing more easy than to pervert its powers into instruments to aggrandize and enrich one or more interests by oppressing and impoverishing the others; and this, too, under the operation of laws couched in general terms and which, on their face, appear fair and equal.[17]

Calhoun, perhaps more than any other theorist, speaks for a defensive minority, for the Southern planter after the Tariff of 1828, during the rise of Yankee industrialism, at the ascendance of abolitionism. It is this, perhaps, which leads his excellent imagination to a doctrine of consensual decision by "concurrent majority":

... the government of the concurrent majority, where the organism is perfect, excludes the possibility of oppression by giving to each interest, or portion, or order—where there are established classes—the means of protecting itself by its negative against all measures calculated to advance the peculiar interests of others at its expense. Its effect, then, is to cause the different interests ... to desist from attempting to adopt any measure calculated to promote the prosperity of one, or more, by sacrificing that of others: and thus to force them to unite in such measures only as would promote the prosperity of all, as the only means to prevent the suspension of the action of government, and, thereby, to avoid anarchy, the greatest of all evils.[18]

Calhoun's interests are partly sinister, and his sociology is Panglossian, but his doctrine is nevertheless a prime historical leap from the concern with symmetrical conflict to the ideal of consensus.[19] American readers, reared on *Federalist 10*, may imagine that I have slighted James Madison or perhaps Alexander Hamilton here. But any careful reading of that great essay and its companions reveals a mistrust of consensual decision, born partly of experience with *immobilism* under the Articles of Confederation:

---

17 "Calhoun, p. 13.
18 Calhoun, p. 30.
19 Two antecedents to this argument deserve notice. There is some evidence that the earliest European equivalents for positive law in our sense of that term were made by something like unanimity among local elites. Cf. Max Weber, *On Law in Economy and Society*, transl., Edward Shils and Max Rheinstein, ed. Max Rheinstein (Cambridge, Massachusetts: Harvard University Press, 1954), especially, p. 84. This perhaps corresponds to the "essential coalition" problem, footnote 1 above. A second antecedent is in the doctrine of separation of powers, in its less pragmatic formulations. Cf. Moses Mather, *America's Appeal to an Impartial World* (Hartford, 1775) especially p. 8, where he writes of estates "... armed with a power of self-defense against the encroachments of the other two, by being enabled to put a negative upon any or all of their resolves. ..."
Cited in Bernard Bailyn, *The Ideological Origins of the American Revolution* (Cambridge: Harvard University Press, 1967) p. 57, 73. The explicit veto makes the parallel to Montesquieu or *Federalist 51* less clear.

> ... What at first sight may seem a remedy, is, in reality, a poison. To give a minority a negative upon a majority (which is always the case where more than a majority is requisite to a decision) is, in its tendency, to subject the sense of the greater number to that of the lesser.[20]

This might seem momentary opportunism, were it not a sample from a substantial theme, and were not its sense backed up by the partial record we have of the 1787 Convention.[21]

It is Calhoun, then, who draws the relevant consequence of government by consent when we consider policies rather than regimes: consent *in policy* is assured only by a regime requiring consensus, not majoritarian democracy or its representational approximation. In Part II, this claim will be tested, and found partly incorrect. First, it is important to note that it is open to the most obvious objections as it stands.

IB. IMMEDIATE OBJECTIONS

The doctrine of consensual decision would be frail indeed if it had maintained a direct connection with the theory of consent in the nationstate. It can be shown, first, that consensus is less than optimal if one begins from the ideas of consent and formal equality. For example, we may interpret "consent" as a matching problem between individual preferences and policy outcomes: the optimum, among simple voting schemes, is majority rule if we make one set of assumptions, and will be consensual decision only if we make the evidently strong assumption that changes of policy opposed by individuals are *a priori* very much more costly than continuances of policy opposed by individuals. Similarly, it can be very simply shown that majority decision minimizes the maximum number of voters who can possibly be dissatisfied with such outcomes.[22] And, from the view of equality, it is evident that consensual decision favors negative minorities over positive majorities—"weights" them unevenly: " ... unless government policy responds to the preferences of the greater number, the preferences of some individuals (the lesser number) must be weighted more heavily than the preferences of some

---

20 Alexander Hamilton, *Federalist* 22. All quotations from the *Federalist* are as in the edition by Benjamin Fletcher Wright (Cambridge, Massachusetts: Harvard University Press, 1961).
21 See *Federalists* 45 and 58 by Madison, in Wright, and consult Max Farrand, *The Records of the Federal Convention*, 4 vols. (New Haven: Yale University Press, 1937). Particularly revealing are the internal organization of the convention (majority rule by states) and the reaction against the Articles.
22 Douglas W. Rae, "Decision Rules and Individual Values in Constitutional Choice," and "Political Democracy as a Property of Political Institutions," both, *American Political Science Review*, 63 (March, 1969), 40–56 and 65 (March, 1971), 111–19.

other individuals (the greater number). But to weight preferences in this way is to reject the goal of political equality."[23]

Moreover, the doctrine is easy prey to the charge that defensive minorities may use their special leverage—the potential cost of their votes to those who want change—as a means to exploit others. Indeed, there seem to be incentives for persons indifferent or even modestly favorable to change to falsify their preferences as a means of extortion. This is the sense of Ben Franklin's opposition to executive veto as he recounts his experience with the colonial Governor of Pennsylvania for the Convention of 1787:

> The negative of the Governor was constantly made use of to extort money. No good law whatever could be passed without a private bargain with him. An increase of his salary, or some donation, was always made a condition; till at last it became the regular practice, to have orders in his favor on the Treasury, presented along with the bills to be signed, so that he might actually receive the former before he should sign the latter.[24]

This no doubt betrays the liberty of an aging wit, and has the special structural feature of monopoly: only one actor could singlehandedly threaten veto. But, it is easy to show that the same may happen where veto rights are symmetrical, and, perhaps worse, that bluffing may lead to the rejection of policies which would in fact have benefited everyone.[25]

There is also the intuitive historical sense that consensual decision may saddle societies with policies designed to meet circumstances which no longer exist, making it all but impossible to cope with present exigencies:

> When the concurrence of a large number is required by the Constitution to the doing of any national act, we are apt to rest satisfied that all is safe, because nothing improper will be likely *to be done;* but we forget how much good may be prevented, and how much ill may be produced, by the power of hindering the doing what may be necessary from being done, and of keeping affairs in the same unfavorable posture in which they may happen to stand at particular periods.[26]

---

23 Robert A. Dahl and Charles E. Lindblom, *Politics, Economics and Welfare* (New York: Harper & Row, 1953) p. 44. A more formal argument with similar implications is K. O. May, "A Set of Independent Necessary and Sufficient Conditions for Simple Majority Decision," *Econometrica*, 20 (October, 1952), 680–684. See also, Neal Reimer, "The Case of Bare Majority Rule," Ethics, 62 (October, 1951), 16–32.
24 As reported by Madison's notes, in Farrand, p. 99.
25 Brian Barry, *Political Argument* (London: Routledge and Kegan Paul, 1965), pp. 245–250.
26 Hamilton, *Federalist 22*. Hamilton's example demonstrates an almost clairvoyant intuition for what is now the recent past: "Suppose, for instance, we were engaged in a war, in conjunction with one foreign nation, against another.

This criticism is in the end decisive, but in much altered form. This is because other developments lead toward a far subtler account of consensual decision and its relation to the public good.

IC. UTILITARIAN EFFICIENCY AND THE MARKET ANALOGY

These developments, emerging during about the same historical era, center on a doctrine, utilitarianism, and an institution, the market. From them rises a theory of social value—utilitarian efficiency—which unites the practice of consensus, the doctrine of consent, and a withered residue of utilitarian philosophy.

Benthamite utilitarianism seems to have codified a kind of enlightened common sense for a civilization whose institutions had only just begun to accommodate the notion of formal equality: if each is to count for one, class and standing aside, what could be more sensible than a grand addition of welfare in social decision? Yet the doctrine has always displayed singular vulnerabilities. One of these is the leap from an ostensibly descriptive idea of greatest happiness to a prescriptive judgment that it ought to be pursued, even where the happiness fails to accrue to the person who must decide. The question, quite simply, "Why?" is not answerable within the unamended utilitarian doctrine.[27] For our argument, however, the real relevance of the greatest-good idea is precisely that some important analysts *have* made that transition. If one studies a scheme of partial conflict, where the goals of groups and individuals cross one another, and one simultaneously claims a measure of neutrality, then a plausible and impersonal criterion is required. One can then attach judgments to it—"If you want that, do this ... "—and produce a prudential science which avoids at least the most obvious forms of special pleading. This was the position of 19th-century political economy, and the parts of it which remained liberal seem at least tacitly to have taken this line. The greatest happiness idea thus becomes an underlying axiom of analysis.[28] Its apogee is no doubt to be found in the quite incredible pages of F. Y. Edgeworth's *Mathematical Psychics*,[29] Although

---

Suppose the necessity of our situation demanded peace, and the interest or ambition of our ally lead him to seek the prosecution of the war, with views that might justify us in making separate terms. In such a state of things, this ally of ours would evidently find it much easier, by his bribes and intrigues, to tie up the hands of government from making peace..."

27 Cf. John Plamenatz, *Man and Society*, 2 vols. (New York: McGraw-Hill, 1963), vol. II, chap. 1, pp. 1–36. A related difficulty, worth noting, is the blindness of the utilitarian doctrine to fair distribution. We will touch on this later, but a particularly useful attempt to offer an alternative doctrine, sensitive to fairness, is John Rawls, *A Theory of Justice* (Cambridge: Harvard University Press, 1971).

28 It would perhaps be more accurate to call it a "tacit assumption" than an axiom, since the present economic theory of utility is reducible in principle to an entirely formal schema.

29 *Mathematical Psychics* (London: Kegan Paul, 1881). Despite the elegance of his analysis, Edgeworth's contribution is flawed by Victorian prejudice: he manages to use the utilitarian calculus to justify nearly all the major inequalities of his time. See especially pp. 74, 77–82.

the doctrine has grown less fashionable with time, its at least tacit acceptance seems essential to an understanding of what followed.

Three major difficulties are at once encountered if one proposes to apply a utilitarian ethic: (1) for a given individual, it seems impossible to "measure" utiles cardinally;[30] (2) if such measurements are possible, it seems impossible to aggregate them among individuals—at least not with arithmetic precision; and (3) it has never been clear how to conceive the underlying "stuff" of utility apart from the subjective preferences of individuals. These difficulties, taken together, have three important implications. First, they seem to undermine direct utilitarian engineering; for example, the "leveling" of real income to maximize aggregate utility as suggested by a line of analysts stretching from Mill to Abba Lerner in our own time.[31] Second, they offer a line of resistance against arguments predicated on ethics of distribution—equality, fairness, justice—especially as these are used in attacks upon market institutions. Finally, they define the analytic challenge met by the normative *principle of efficiency* as we know it today.

This notion of efficiency arises indirectly from the astonishingly recent discovery, dating apparently to the work of Adam Smith, that exchange *itself* is a source of utility. If Peter gives X to Paul and receives Y from him in return, both acting voluntarily,[32] does it not follow that both have gained utility? Is not Y worth more than X to Peter and X worth more than Y to Paul? How else to explain the constituents of market behavior? Both analytically and normatively, this has become a central pillar in the theory of the market. Moreover, its modest methodological requirements ingratiate themselves nicely with the caveats against utilitarianism noted a moment ago.

If we accept those caveats, we are entitled to precisely two inferences about individual utility: (1) if a person successfully chooses to alter his position, he has gained utility, and (2) if he is unwillingly compelled to change his position, he has lost utility. We can, of course, drop "utility" and reduce this to a discussion of indifference curves, but the important point is this: we can neither quantify gains and losses for an individual, nor compare those of two individuals. It follows, and this is critical, that *any event in which some persons gain and some lose is indeterminate with respect to aggregate welfare.* We cannot, on this view, decide whether losses outweigh gains or vice versa: such inferences are impossible within the analytic scheme. Two things follow immediately. First, if (say by majority voting) n − 1 people gain and one loses, we cannot claim to have done the group a good turn.[33]

---

30   Apart from the Von Neumann-Morgenstem system on the assumption that risk does not affect utility.
31   *The Economics of Control* (New York: Macmillan, 1944). See also Kenneth Arrow, "A Utilitarian Approach to the Concept of Equality in Public Expenditure," *Quarterly Journal of Economics*, 85 (August, 1971), 409–15.
32   And as rational egoists who know what's good for them.
33   This of course raises the "intensity problem" from democratic theory. Cf. Robert A. Dahl, *A Preface to Democratic Theory* (Chicago: University of Chicago Press, 1956), especially chap. 4; Willmoore Kendall and George M. Carey, "The 'Intensity' Problem and Democratic Theory," *American Political Science Review*, 62 (March, 1968), 5–24; Douglas Rae and Michael Taylor, "Some Ambiguities in the Concept of Intensity," *Polity*, 1 (Spring, 1969), 298–308. Notice the devastating effect of the present position on any utilitarian argument for majority rule.

Second, what is somewhat improperly called the "Pareto principle"[34] takes center stage: we will call it the "efficiency rule."

Let us define the efficiency rule as we will use it later.[35] Suppose we have a "policy set," consisting of possible outcomes to a particular social decision. In the market case, these would be bundles of goods associated to owners. One of these outcomes may be distinguished as the status quo. We have a community of people whose welfare is relevant to the selection of an outcome from the policy set. Each of these people entertains preferences about outcomes which are at least sufficient to produce a three-cell division of this set: (1) *a preference set* of outcomes which he would substitute for the status quo, (2) *a rejection set* of outcomes against which he would retain the status quo, and (3) an *indifference set* for which neither (1) nor (2) holds. Each person has such a division for any given status quo point, and it is ostensibly based on a weak ordering of all alternatives. The efficiency rule has two relevant provisions:

1. If an outcome belongs to at least one preference set and no rejection set, its substitution for the status quo is efficient.
2. If no outcome meets requirement (1), the status quo is efficient (or "Pareto optimal").

The efficiency rule is subject to at least four misunderstandings. First, a transaction, considered as a whole, may meet (1), although its component elements do not: this is true for simple market exchange, as well as more complex cases. Second, provision (2) usually defines a very large, sometimes infinite, set of outcomes, all of them efficient. If this is so, many, perhaps most, social choices are "undecidable" from the standpoint of efficiency. What should we do about undecidable cases? This question is central to our analysis of the consensus argument later. Third, the efficiency criterion is blind to both distributive and perfectionist morals. As Amartya Sen has it,

> An economy can be optimal in this sense even when some people are rolling in luxury and others are near starvation as long as the starvers cannot be made better off without cutting into the pleasures of the rich. If preventing the burning of Rome would have made Emperor Nero feel worse off, then letting him burn Rome would have been Pareto-optimal. In short, a society or an economy can be Pareto-optimal and still be perfectly disgusting.[36]

---

34 "Improperly" because it appears that Pareto did not intend the use presently given to his criteria. Cf. Talcott Parsons, *The Structure of Social Action*, Vol. 1 (New York: The Free Press, 1937, 1968), 241-249, and, less importantly, Vincent J. Tarascio, *Pareto's Methodological Approach to Economics* (Chapel Hill: University of North Carolina Press, 1968).
35 Cf. III below.
36 *Collective Choice and Social Welfare* (San Francisco: Holden-Day, 1970), p. 22.

Last, the efficiency rule is extremely "brittle" in its sensitivity to the status quo: Once he ignites the curtains, Nero must be bribed to desist; before he does so, the Romans must be bribed to have their city burned. In the case of economic exchange, this makes property rights pivotal, and where they are ambiguous—as with external diseconomies not contemplated by existing civil law[37]—the criterion itself is ambiguous. We will find this difficulty in exacerbated form when we come to political decision.

These difficulties, important as they are, fail to deny the efficiency rule its enormous influence. Its immediate effect is to make the connection between consent and utility (vouchsafed by efficiency) a tautology. How do we know a change is efficient? By the consent of the parties, by their willingness to consent in the substitution. How do we know a status quo is efficient? By someone's unwillingness to substitute any alternative for it. Apart from the special case of "hypothetical compensation,"[38] this analytic seam is airtight. And one need not be the least bit cynical to see that it has enormous ideological value to people well placed in society, for no redistribution can be justified without the consent of those who stand to lose, even if they are numerically overwhelmed by prospective beneficiaries.

We are in the midst of a chain relationship. If we retain a tacit loyalty to Benthamite utilitarianism, then the utility caveats draw us toward the efficiency rule. This in turn renders the utility-consent hypothesis we earlier attributed to Mill an analytic inevitability. Finally, this gives market exchange a normatively privileged position. My consent is my willingness to deal, and if you and I are rational egoists, the market's rules lead us to act out the doctrine "automatically," by trading efficiently until an efficient outcome is reached. It is the voluntary quality of market exchange that makes this possible, and—for the doctrine of consensual decision—this is a momentous fact. For *we should now imagine the market as a normative ideal, against which ordinary political decisions look "sub-optimal" at best.*

The critical inference is a simple one: the normative virtue of markets lies in the voluntariness of exchange, and this voluntariness is guaranteed by the consensual structure of market exchange. Leaving aside external diseconomies and the occasional prospect of blackmail, we can represent the choice-structure of market transactions thus,

---

37 For a brilliant analysis of such cases see R. H. Coase, "The Problem of Social Cost," *Journal of Law and Economics*, 3 (October, 1960), 1–44.

38 Hypothetical compensation undoes the connection because it lets me carry out a change so long as I gain enough from it that I *could have* compensated you for your losses. The idea, implicit in Wicksell (see below), is formalized by N. Kaldor, "Welfare Propositions of Economics and Interpersonal Comparisons of Utility," *Economic Journal*, 49 (September, 1939), 549, which is excellently discussed in I. D. Little, *A Critique of Welfare Economics* (London: Oxford University Press, 1950), p. 88 ff; and E. J. Mishan, *Welfare Economics* (Amsterdam: North Holland, 1969), p. 38–51; and Sen, pp. 30–32. A further difficulty, evidently proved by Skitovski, is that the criterion gives intransitive results. Its importance, for us, is that it brings the practical implications of "efficiency" very nearly full circle to the Benthamite position.

Coalitions that can impose exchanges:
  ((seller & buyer))
Coalitions that can veto exchanges:
  ((seller) or (buyer))

Which is, formally at least, homologous with

Coalitions that can change public policy
  ((A & B & C ... & N)
Coalitions that can veto changes of public policy
  ((A) or (B) ... or (N)

The market analogy" is that, for both market exchange and consensual decision, anyone can prevent action, so that no party can be damaged by it.[39] This provides the background for Knut Wicksell's claim (in his account of taxation) that

> provided the expenditure in question holds out any prospect at all of creating utility exceeding costs, it will always be theoretically possible, and approximately so in practice, to find a distribution of costs such that all parties regard the expenditure as beneficial and may therefore approve it unanimously. Should this prove altogether impossible, I would consider such failure as an *a posteriori*, and the sole possible, proof that the state activity under consideration would not provide the community with utility corresponding to the necessary sacrifice and should hence be rejected on rational grounds.[40]

We will later examine Wicksell's argument more closely, but here it is necessary merely to see that this is a very strong new case for consensual decision, and that it completes the complex development we have been sketching. Very nearly the same claim is offered by James Buchanan and Gordon Tullock, as they write,

> ... we admit as "better" only those changes that are observed to be approved unanimously by all members of the group. Any change that secures unanimous support is clearly "desirable," and we can say that such a change is "in the public interest." Few

---

39 Ironically, the idea of the social contract seems to have an at least intuitive relation to this analogy in pre-Lockean thought. This is suggested by the multiple contract theory of Althusius' *Politica Methodice Diogesta* (1603), as analyzed by Kendall, John Locke, pp. 46–9. The explicit analogy reappears in Buchanan and Tullock, p. 250 ff.
40 Wicksell, pp. 89–90.

would, we suspect, dispute this half of our criterion for evaluating social changes. However, we go further and state that for *any* change *in* the public interest, unanimous support can be achieved.[41]

It is evident that these authors entertain a utilitarian conception of the public interest. And they seem to have combined a constrained version of this philosophy with the consent of the governed.

ID. SUMMARY

This completes an admittedly fragmentary historical sketch, which leaves us, I think, with three important facts. First, that the ideology of parliamentary revolution—most of all a symmetrical doctrine of government by consent—left liberal ideology with an enormous leap to be made: from Active consent in regimes to actual consent in their policies. Second, that a plausible response to this leap is to be found in a doctrine of consensual decision. Finally, that the additional doctrine of efficiency and the "market analogy" offer an apparent synthesis of these two—consent and utilitarianism.

My purpose from this point is to offer an analytic appraisal for these conjectures. I begin with the contention that consensual decision would, at least in theory, guarantee the consent of the governed.

II. CONSENSUS AND THE CONSENT OF THE GOVERNED

The most fundamental claim for consensual decision is also the simplest: that consensus implies consent. That is, if an outcome is adopted under a system of consensual decision, we are entitled to assume that everyone has given his consent to it. This is *not* a mere tautology, and it is not always true. Let me begin by looking briefly at two arguments which have this consent-consensus hypothesis as their cornerstones.

IIA. THE CONSENSUAL SYSTEMS PROPOSED BY CALHOUN AND WOLFF

Calhoun is central to the consensus doctrine. His scheme for concurrent majority decision is an effort to approximate consensual decision in the face of large numbers and the resulting escalation of decision-making costs.[42] Summarized very simply, Calhoun's plan is this:[43]

---

41 Buchanan and Tullock, p. 285.
42 A concept owing to Buchanan and Tullock, cf. III below.
43 Calhoun, *Disquisition*, pp. 19–23, 27–31, 35–54.

THE LIMITS OF CONSENSUAL DECISION

1. The community is to be divided into a set of mutually exclusive classes.
2. These classes are to be homogeneous with respect to the effects of government policy.
3. For any proposal of government policy, each such class is to make a separate decision: approve or disapprove.
4. Given homogeneity (2), and some rationality assumption, the method of class decision (3) is not very important: majority rule will do.
5. If a government policy is to be enforced, every class must agree.

This presupposes a cleavage structure without cross-cutting: a "pillar society," such as the Dutch are said to have. And, more demanding still, this structure must remain essentially constant through time, else repeated constitutional crisis. Calhoun is obviously thinking about the southern planters as a class, and is tactically willing to permit other classes to fall as they may. If the required assumptions be granted, I believe the concurrent majorities must be admitted as a valid approximation to consensual decision. The question however remains: Does this guarantee consent ? Let me return to that momentarily.

A more recent analysis is Robert Paul Wolff's *In Defense of Anarchism*.[44] This author writes from the American moral left during the Vietnam era; he is concerned with the moral autonomy of citizens as it is threatened by government authority. And the overall structure of his argument is straightforward: (1) each citizen should do as he thinks best, (2) the state necessarily entails authority, which requires that citizens do as someone else thinks best; (3) these are incompatible, so that (4) there ought to be no states. This argument is compelling only on the unlikely supposition that the abolition of states would be attended by no other form of coercion. Buried within this larger argument, however, is the proposition that states would be acceptable if only it were practicable to organize them consensually. This position may be summed up as follows:[45]

1. Citizens should do as they think best.
2. This is possible if they must obey only laws and policies to which they have each given their consent.
3. If government authority were exercised only by unanimous direct democracy, (2) would obtain and (1) would therefore be possible.

---

44 In *Defense of Anarchism* (New York: Harper and Row, 1970).
45 Wolff, pp. 22–27. Notice the similarity to Rousseau's search for " ... a form of association which may defend and protect with the whole force of the community the person and property of each associate, and by means of which each, coalescing with all, may nevertheless *obey only himself*, and remain free as before." (Emphasis added.) Social Contract, book I, chap. VI. Rousseau does propose consensus as the basis of a Active social contract, but urges that "the citizen consents to all the laws, even to those which are passed in spite of him ... " (book IV, chap. II). The sense of this consent has always escaped me.

399

Wolff imagines that this scheme would in principle resolve his normative dilemma:

> The solution is a direct democracy—that is, a political community in which every person votes on every issue—governed by a rule of unanimity. Under unanimous direct democracy, every member of society wills freely every law which is actually passed. Hence, he is only confronted as a citizen with laws to which he has consented. Since a man who is constrained only by the dictates of his own will is autonomous, it follows that under the directions of unanimous direct democracy, men can harmonize the duty of autonomy with the commands of authority.[46]

Now Wolff must be aware that each citizen is born into a society with a history; that this history will have deposited a residue of laws; that each of these laws cannot be conditionally revoked at the birth of each fresh infant, pending his yes vote during the morning of his eighteenth birthday. Yet this difficulty alone would seem sufficient to shatter his hypothesis that consensus implies autonomy (which is, of course, a species of consent).[47]

IIB. A REVISED MARKET ANALOGY

To avoid this difficulty, one would have to change the "market analogy" (IC above) so that it looked like this:

Coalitions that can impose exchanges:
((seller & buyer))
Coalitions that can veto exchanges:
((seller & buyer))

and analogously,

Coalitions that can impose new policies:
((A & B, ... & N))
Coalitions that can retain old policies:
((A & B, ... & N))

---

46 Wolff, p. 23.
47 Godwin's response to the myth of the social contract seems appropriate to the point: How am I obliged? "Surely not upon the contract into which my father entered before I was born?" *Enquiry*, book III, chap. 2, p. 189. In his assault on the Pareto principle, I. D. Little makes essentially the same observation in *A Critique*, p. 94.

Thus, each would hold a right of veto over every policy, including old laws in politics and the nonexchange outcome in the market. But there is something very wrong here, for these structures open the prospect that *every* outcome will be blocked by some coalition. In the market case, this would suggest that you and I might neither exchange nor fail to exchange certain bundles of goods, in politics that we might neither retain nor rid ourselves of a law. Both prospects are in some fundamental way preposterous, and important foundations are missing from the analysis. These are supplied by a simple and very partial account of public choices (IIC), and a criterion of robustness for the structures by which they are resolved (IID).

IIC. FORCED CHOICE

The full policy of a government at any moment will be some historical combination of outcomes to specific issues. Suppose we treat issues, $X_1, X_2, \ldots, X_n$, as sets of mutually exclusive government policies. Each such issue, or "policy set" X_i thus contains a collection of policy outcomes which exclude one another, $X_i = (x_1, x_2, \ldots, x_{mi})$. On any such issue, at any given time, there must be some status quo, whether explicit or tacit. So we can represent a full public policy as an n-tuple of alternatives for $x_1 \ldots x_n$, and mark their standing as status quo outcomes with a bar:

$$\bar{x}_{i1}, \bar{x}_{j2}, \bar{x}_{k3}, \ldots, \bar{x}_{ln}.\text{[48]}$$

This account carries the implication that each issue involves a *forced choice* among alternative outcomes. Forced in two senses (1) not more than one outcome can be the status quo, and (2) some outcome must be the status quo. This applies to issues, and by an obvious extension to the n-tuples of issues which define public policies.

Here are some classes of issues which illustrate the forcing of choice:

1. Even if government chooses to permit market decision makers to establish it, a society must have some given social product over any interval of time, and must have some set of rules for its allocation.
2. Consider any given public good[49] which any given government might produce: it must always be producing it at some level, even if that level be zero.
3. Consider the public law as a compound of triples in the form:

---

48 E.g., the *i*th outcome to the first issue, the *j* th to the second, etc.
49 E.g., a good for which exclusion is impossible or expensive, so that its distribution follows the pattern "if any then all," or at least, "if some then others." Mancur Olson's Logic of Collective Action (Cambridge: Harvard University Press, 1965) offers a classic analysis of the incentive problems raised by public goods.

[(subject class) (norm-operator) (action class)] and think of three norm-operators (must, may, must-not).⁵⁰ Then, for any pair of subject and action classes, there must be *one and only one* effective norm-operator. For example, let the subject class be "persons living in California" and the action class be "deliberately kill other people": the law must either prohibit or command or permit this pattern of behavior for those people. It is shallow at best to imagine that such legal choices can be put off: to "not decide" must imply one of two outcomes:

(a) tacit permission, *nullum crimen sine lege*,

or

(b) continuance of an explicit status quo mandate, prohibition or permission.

To see the point's obviousness, try to devise a way of effectively postponing a decision on the legality of abortion which can be explained to a pregnant woman.

4. In the choice of candidates for office, either someone is elected or nobody is (yet) elected at any given moment: a final choice can be put off only by accepting an interval of indeterminancy or "provisional" control which is a very real outcome (consider the Greek colonels or the Portuguese Communists).

5. International agreements can be put off, but a very real and often painful status quo remains to be experienced.

These cases suggest a ubiquitous forcing of choice:⁵¹ even when explicit outcomes can be postponed, tacit ones are *ipso facto* chosen. In the schemes proposed by Calhoun and Wolff, this suggests that *some* outcomes and not others are subject to the requirement of unanimity. If *all*

---

50 This three-operator analysis is controversial, but our point would hold for the four- or n-operator case as well. Cf. Georg Henrik von Wright, *Norm and Action* (London: Routledge & Kegan Paul, 1963) or Alf Ross, *Directives and Norms* (New York. Humanities Press, 1968). I myself believe von Wright is correct in claiming that these three operators are sufficient to express the content of any law or other rule, given the auxiliary privilege of negation.

51 " ... government *inaction* is as much a choice of policy as government action," Dahl and Lindblom, Politics, *Economics and Welfare*, p. 338. See also IV below. Two contrary observations need mention. First, it has been suggested that this choice from mutually exclusive alternatives rules out compromise and creates a zero-sum constraint on outcomes. This is simply incorrect: the compromise outcome *is* an alternative, and *does* exclude other outcomes. Second, there is no reason whatever to imagine a zero-sum constraint for mutually exclusive alternatives. Consider, for example, an Edgeworth box for two traders. Its points are in the end mutually exclusive, but choices among them are certainly not zero-sum. These erroneous views are expounded by Buchanan and Tulllock, *The Calculus of Consent*, p. 253 ff. Second, some decisions suggest the possibility of multiple outcomes. Say we are awarding medals to national heroes: awarding one may deflate the value of awarding another, but surely does not exclude it. This is correct, but rather superficial. The effective alternatives are lists of national heroes. With n candidates, there would be 2^n possible lists. But any one list does rule out any other list. A more important example: public works projects as authorized by the American Congress. At the margin, when each new project is considered, it seems irrelevant that others have been approved already, so each may be treated as a separate issue. But the choices are nonetheless forced in two ways: (1) each must be approved in some form or rejected, and (2) one grand list of projects must emerge from each Congress. The current proposal for centralizing the appropriations process in Congress would make this latter point clear even as each project was considered.

outcomes were subject to unanimity, then we would risk the position in which we both refused to change policy and refused to keep it the same. This brings us to a somewhat more exact account of policy decisions.

Considering any single issue, we are confronted with a status quo, and some alternatives to it. Assuming m alternatives in X_1, and repressing the subscript which identifies the issue, we have a list of possible status quo points as the left column of the matrix below. We also have a list of alternatives to each of these, as shown in the top row of the matrix. Notice that the status quo is included as "an alternative to itself," in order to display the rejection of change as a choice:

$$
\begin{array}{c|cccc}
 & \multicolumn{4}{c}{\text{to these alternatives}} \\
X_1 & x_1 & x_2 & \ldots & x_m \\
\hline
x_1 & D_{11} & D_{12} & & D_{1m} \\
x_2 & D_{21} & D_{22} & & D_{2m} \\
\ldots & & & & \\
x_m & D_{m1} & D_{m2} & & D_{mn} \\
\end{array}
$$

(from these possible status quo policies)

Society's problem is to pick a *transition* from the alternatives thus offered. Decision D_{11}, for example, means retaining outcome x_1. By contrast, D_{12} represents the substitution of outcome x_2 for x_1. We will operate always in a single row of the matrix, as defined by the particular status quo we confront. We can therefore confine our attention to a single arbitrary row with status quo Xi:

$$
\begin{array}{c|ccc}
\text{moving from } \bar{x}_i \text{ to} & x_j \cdots x_i \cdots x_m \\
\hline
\text{is decision} & D_{ij} \quad D_{ij} \quad D_{im} \\
\end{array}
$$

We can define consent, consensus, and the criterion of robustness over the choice so defined.

IID. ROBUSTNESS, CONSENT, AND WHY CONSENSUS MUST BE CONDITIONAL

A *control-structure* defines the coalitions which can impose decisions. An arbitrary decision D_{ij} can be imposed by one or more minimally sufficient coalitions, and the set of such coalitions is labelled C_{ij}. Thus, for example, we might let x_i and x_j represent arbitrary imputations of goods to two traders, A and B. Then the normal rules of market exchange would display the structure,

$$\begin{array}{c|cc} & x_i & x_j \\ \hline x_i & C_{ij} = ((A) \text{ or } (B)) & C_{ij} = ((A \ \& \ B)) \end{array} \qquad (1)$$

so that the nonexchange decision D_{ij} can be imposed by either; exchange decision D_{ij} only by both.

A given actor enjoys a *right of consent* in decision Da only if he belongs to every minimally sufficient coalition in C_{ij}. Both A and B enjoy such a right for the exchange outcomes; neither enjoys such a right for the nonexchange outcome. Similarly, a control structure is *consensual for a specific decision* if and only if every relevant actor enjoys a right of consent in that outcome. The market is consensual for exchange but not for nonexchange outcomes.

Earlier observations (IIC) suggest that society must always be prepared to choose exactly one outcome. It is therefore inadmissible to have a structure which could deny us *any* decision, any location for the status quo. Such a structure could be workable in exactly the same way that sugar could be "insoluble"—until, that is, it was wet. In our case, that means until there is a conflict in which coalitions at once block all decisions. I have in mind a concept of *robustness*. Here is the peculiar market structure mentioned in IIB.

$$\begin{array}{c|cc} & x_i & x_j \\ \hline x_i & C_{ii} = ((A \ \& \ B)) & C_{ij} = ((A \ \& \ B)) \end{array} \qquad (2)$$

This scheme has two properties. First, it is unconditionally consensual: each person enjoys a right of consent in each outcome. Second, it is non-robust. Intuitively: what if A blocks the nonexchange outcome and B blocks the exchange outcome(s)? Precisely: a structure is robust if it meets the following requirement:

1. Consider a coalition (*) which is insufficient to impose any decision (impotent)
2. For every coalition (*) there must exist at least one other coalition (*') with two properties:
   (a) it is disjoint with (*)—no members in common
   (b) it is potent—can impose some outcome

Ordinary market exchange (1) meets this requirement. Neither (A) nor (B) nor (AB) is impotent. The emply set $(\emptyset)$ is impotent like (*). But all three of the other coalitions just mentioned satisfy (ii) by being disjoint with (ø) and potent. Now consider the special market exchange system defined by (2). The coalition (A) is impotent like (*). The coalitions (B) and (ø) are disjoint with (A), but both are impotent. The coalition (AB) is non-impotent, but is not disjoint with (A). Thus this odd scheme is nonrobust. It permits failure to adopt any outcome.

More generally, consider a structure which is unconditionally consensual and therefore gives a universal right of consent to all decisions,

$$\begin{array}{c|ccc} & x_i & x_j & \ldots & x_j \\ \hline \bar{x}_i & C_{ii} = ((\forall)) & C_{ij} = ((\forall)) & C_{im} = ((\forall)) \end{array} \quad (3)$$

where ($\forall$) represents the coalition of all relevant actors. No other structure is unconditionally consensual and gives an unconditional right of consent. But this structure is nonrobust. Any proper subset of ($\forall$) is impotent like (*). Some other subset of ($\forall$) may be disjoint with this impotent coalition, but will itself be impotent. Only ($\forall$) is nonimpotent, but it can hardly be disjoint with its own subset. Therefore, this structure and all its concrete analogs are nonrobust.

The choice of structure is then between robustness and unconditional consensus with its correspondingly perfect right of consent. We do not choose robustness; necessity chooses it for us. We therefore can choose at most a conditional form of consensus and correspondingly conditional right of consent. If there are m decisions available, as many as $m-1$ may be consensual, but *at least one must not be consensual.*

IIE. ANARCHIC CONSENSUS: CALHOUN AND WOLFF

Calhoun seems to have known this. Notice that he attributes a motive for agreement to his actors: they must come to unanimous agreement on positive policy " … as the only means to prevent the suspension of the action of the government, and, thereby, to avoid anarchy, the greatest of all evils."[52] The structure seems to be this:

$$\begin{array}{c|ccc} & x_i & x_j & \ldots & x_0 \\ \hline \bar{x}_i & C_{ii} = ((\forall)) & C_{ij} = ((\forall)) & C_{i0} = ((\exists)) \end{array}$$

---

52 Calhoun, *Disquisition*, p. 30, as cited above, IA.

To sustain the status quo requires unanimity;[53] to substitute another positive policy requires unanimity; but to block either course of action and thereby suspend all positive policy (D_{i0}) requires only a single class (let ∃ be any single class). In other words, each class can impose anarchy, which functions as the nonconsensual outcome and preserves the robustness of the concurrent majorities as a structure. If we classify conditional (hence, robust) schemes of consensus by their "escape" decisions, this might be termed *anarchic consensus.* It is, so far as I can tell, precisely the scheme which answers to Godwin's objection against government: insofar as Calhoun's structure imposes any status quo save anarchy, it does so by a functional equivalent of unanimous consent. Calhoun's system—or the more general structure of anarchic consensus—abandons consent in regimes and imposes direct consent in policy.

However fanciful this may seem, it forces the question: should we *choose* the prospect of being bound by government without our own consent ? In other words, should we reject universal consent in policy as a normative criterion? Calhoun avoids this deeper issue. From his vantage, remember, the force of government was used to bind one large class—the blacks—without their consent or even a gesture in that direction. Calhoun clearly *would not* have liked to part with this leverage by universalizing his concurrent majorities to include the blacks as a class. Calhoun clearly *would* have liked to gain new leverage by extending the concurrent majorities to the class of southern planters, in their conflict with other sectors of the society, notably the industrial North. Since the blacks do not qualify as citizens, he is able to finesse the obvious contradiction.

But if one is bound by symmetry of argument, then the fundamental dilemma is unavoidable. Let "Ego" and "Alter" be any two persons or classes. Then symmetry implies that if Ego would bind Alter by governmental decision, against his will, he too must face the prospect of being bound unwillingly by Alter. Calhoun's proposal, read symmetrically, is a mutual agreement to rule out such binding. It is clear that both must surrender any right of consent in the ungoverned action of the other. If Alter chooses to aggress against Ego, directly or indirectly, Ego cannot invoke a governmental constraint against him. *The effect of Calhoun's proposal is to repeat the social contract position at the level of policy.* Each governmental decision is like a fresh social contract, and each such contract is subject to unilateral revocation at any time.[54] We purchase unconditional consent in government by surrendering any further right of consent in the behavior of others.

---

53 This critical point of interpretation is perhaps counterintuitive, but fits well with the text of Calhoun's essay and is consistent with his tactical position. Calhoun, it will be recalled, had taken a "nullificationist" position against federal tariff policy on behalf of South Carolina in 1828. And, during the 1840s when the present theory was concocted, his region found itself at an increasing disadvantage in federal policy. Only a doctrine which at once offered a defense against further damage *and* a recourse against existing policy would suit his need. I believe he found this in the "anarchic consensus" theory as interpreted here.
54 I draw this inference in full knowledge that Calhoun rejected the social contract as an historical doctrine, in *Disquisition,* pp. 3–4. His analytic motive for this seems obvious.

Robert Paul Wolff's *In Defense of Anarchism* carries this facet of Calhoun's theory to its conclusion. We should seek a society in which each does as he thinks best, thus enjoys autonomy by consent in all decisions. This could be accomplished if all decisions were taken by direct unanimous democracy. But we could achieve this unanimous democracy only if we *already* had " … substantial agreement among *all* members of a community on all matters of major importance."[55] Wolff thus points to a problem (autonomy or consent); proposes a solution (consensual decision); and cautions that it will work only if we haven't got the problem in the first place (e.g., no real disagreements exist). It is as if we had contrived a medicine useful only to the well.

It is worth noticing that this exercise should lead, as it does in Wolff, to a doctrine of philosophical anarchism only if a stateless society promises a better approximation to a condition of universal autonomy. This might mean that we asked everyone to internalize the interests of others under a universal principle of just action so that no part of society would ever choose to act in a way unacceptable to others. And, as Wolff admits by way of footnote, unanimous agreement is a useful mental experiment in choosing the principle which would be so internalized.[56] But this is not to be confused with the problem of political structure—with the rules under which public decisions are in fact to occur. Here, Wolff's analysis offers very little. For suppose that either (1) a principle of just action has become the guide to action by all or (2) that it hasn't. In the first case, anarchism will work but so will everything else; in the second case anarchism won't work—won't function as an approximation to universal autonomy.

It can indeed be shown that *no* structure of decision unanimity—majority-rule, combat, dice-throwing, oracular contemplations, or the reading of coffee grounds—can of itself unhinge the fundamental problem of *political vulnerability:* unanimous universal consent has the logical form of the square circle.

IIF. STASIS CONSENSUS: BUCHANAN AND TULLOCK

An especially important consensual structure, argued by Buchanan and Tullock, has this shape,

	x_i	x_j
$\bar{x}_i$	$C_{ii} = ((\exists))$	$C_{ij} = ((\forall))$

---

55 Wolff, p. 24.
56 See, for a main example, John Rawls, *A Theory of Justice* (Cambridge: Harvard University Press, 1971).

The *stasis consensus* has the status quo as its non-consensual outcome, offering a universal right of consent only in change. This is the version of consensus which fits the "market analogy," and the version which goes to the doctrine of utilitarian efficiency: if a new outcome is adopted, must not this change benefit society? It evidently cannot have damaged society if nobody objects and blocks its adoption. But the issue is more subtle, and I postpone it for Part III below.

IIG. LAISSEZ FAIRE CONSENSUS: WICKSELL

Yet another structure is Knut Wicksell's *laissez faire* consensus.[57] Here, the policy which removes least from the private sector can be imposed unilaterally by anyone, or at least by a small minority. Unless it also happens to be the *laissez faire* solution, the status quo enjoys no special privilege, and all spending is open to what might be called the "Earl Landgrebe syndrome"[58] in which all activity is vetoed. Wicksell thus asks us to accept the rules of a market society—property, contract, rights of disposition—nonconsensually, and to offer a right of consent in any deviation from them.

IIH. IMPLICATIONS OF CONSENSUS ANALYSIS

The right of consent cannot be unconditionally vouchsafed by any workable structure. For any issue, there must be at least one outcome against which no universal right of consent is available. If we follow Calhoun's anarchic consensus, this is the "no-policy" solution, which leaves people free to act as they can and will without governmental intervention. We would never be freighted with positive policies against our will, but the price is measured in the events which might occur without governmental intervention. Calhoun, in effect, asks us to surrender the right to coerce others through government in return for freedom from coercion by them through government. Whether this is an appropriate idealization depends on an estimate for the consequences of anarchy. It should be noted in closing that only the anarchic consensual system resolves the problem of consent in policy left open by Locke's initial argument. Any alternative structure must leave some positive

---

57 Wicksell. Since Wicksell's system is not symmetrical with respect to the status quo, its structure must be represented in two matrix rows, as follows:

	x_i	cost-minimal x_j	other x_j
cost-minimal $\bar{x}_i$	(θ)	$(?)$	$(\&)$
other $\bar{x}_i$	$(\&)$	(θ)	$(?)$

Unanimity is thus required to increase or sustain spending. The system is undefined for cases in which spending is not a relevant variable.

58 Landgrebe is Congressman from the Indiana 2nd District and claims to have voted against every nonmilitary appropriation in the 92nd Congress.

policy which may be imposed nonconsensually, be it the status quo created by an earlier generation, the bare market solution, or the law whose first word stands highest in alphabetical order.

III. CONSENSUS AND UTILITARIAN EFFICIENCY

Bearing in mind, then, that all viable structures offer an at most conditional right of consent, we may at last test the central dogma of the new political economy: that consensual decision leads to utilitarian efficiency. For this purpose, we put aside the objections already raised (Part I), and begin with a spatial interpretation for the rule of efficiency.

IIIA. THE EFFICIENCY RULE

Consider an N-space, each of whose dimensions corresponds to the utility of a single individual, and each of whose points is defined by an n-tuple of individual utilities. The dimensions are "elastic," and distance is meaningless: only direction is determinate. This corresponds to the caveats against cardinality and interpersonal comparison of utility. Each dimension is an individual weak ordering, and each point is defined by the intersect of n such orderings. In Figure 21.1, we have picked one two-dimensional slice from this space and use it to depict the intersection between the orderings of two arbitrary individuals A and B. These allow us to define efficiency and its alternatives spatially.

The weak ordering attributed to A defines three sets with respect to a status quo at $\bar{x}_i$: (1) a preference set north of A—A', (2) an indifference set *on* A—A', and (3) a rejection set south of A—A'. Line B—B' defines analogous sets for B. From $\bar{x}_i$, according to our earlier definitions, we can identify the set of *efficiency dominant changes* as those north, east, or northeast of $\bar{x}_i$ (the set defined inclusively by line B'—x_i—A'). These bestow gains without losses. *Counterefficient changes*, if we may be permitted such a barbarism, are defined inclusively by the southwesterly set bounded at A—x_i—B. These bestow losses without gains. *Undecidable changes* are located in the sets exclusively defined by A—$\bar{x}_i$—B' and B—$\bar{x}_i$—A'—northwest and southeast of x. Notice that such undecidable substitutions may be very tempting: as with x_k, which seems to offer a great gain to A at small cost to B. In Calhoun's terms, this seems a profitable sacrifice of one interest to another. But within the present frames of reference, we need not argue against it from consent, since *we are not entitled to the inference itself*.[59] That is, we cannot distinguish x_k from a point

---

59 A limitation which rules out a very great deal: any compromise with consensual decision (agreement by $n - 1$ members, say) is, in this light, qualitatively indistinguishable from majority-rule or a personal dictatorship. In policy terms, it also entitles me to retain my twenty-seventh fur coat against the feeding of your sick child unless I choose to part with the coat.

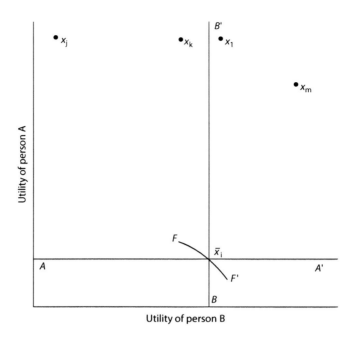

Figure 21-1. The Efficiency Rule

like x_j, cannot know that we are making a "social dividend" by this change. We can, of course, construct a *new* alternative, like x_1, perhaps by side-payment from A to B or log-rolling—either simultaneously with a "rider" or by promise of future votes. But this is not the same as moving to x_k (no more the same than selling me a car is the same as giving it to me.)

Suppose, for the moment, that line F—F' defines a possibility frontier passing through $\bar{x}_i$. This means there can be no efficient substitutions for $\bar{x}_i$ (the sector bounded by B'—$\bar{x}_i$—A' being entirely out of reach). In this case, the rule tells us that $\bar{x}_i$ is an *efficiency maximum*. We may reformulate the efficiency rule in strong terms: *Make substitutions if and only if they are efficiency dominant.* This is precisely what a well-functioning market does if each person behaves as a rational egoist. If certain other conditions are also met, the market moves toward an efficient outcome: an equilibrium from which no further efficient progress is possible. We wish to analyze the claim that consensual political decision will function similarly. The detailed implications would seem to be as follows:

1. Only efficient changes occur.
2. All efficient changes occur, and
3. Efficiency equilibria will be attained.

IIIB. STASIS CONSENSUS AND EFFICIENT DECISION

We want to see whether consensual decision will produce these results. We consider a stasis consensual system which I believe embodies the most attractive features of the account given by Buchanan and Tullock.[60] This is sufficiently determined by the following model:

1. Each person whose utility may be affected by a decision either has a vote or is faithfully represented by an agent who does.[61]
2. Each such person's vote is determined as follows:
   (a) If a substitute outcome is in his preference set, a yes vote,
   (b) if a substitute outcome is in his rejection set, a no vote,
   (c) if a substitute policy is in his indifference set an abstention.
3. A substitute for the status quo is imposed if and only if there is at least one yes vote and no no votes.

This scheme is a sophisticated cousin of the consent theories with which we began. Does it fulfill the requirements we have adduced for the efficiency principle? This would seem to be the minimum implication of the claim made by Buchanan and Tullock as they set unanimity as a necessary and sufficient condition to change.[62]

Implication (a) is confirmed for this model: only efficient changes occur. Suppose a policy change is undecidable or counterefficient. Someone loses from the substitution, and the policy belongs to one or more rejection sets. A no vote follows, and the necessary condition for change is violated. Thus, only efficient changes occur. With side-payments, this may mean the adoption of complex packages, efficient in aggregate but composed of inefficient elements (e.g., an inefficient policy outcome and an inefficient side-payment to make an efficient package). This is consistent with our hypothesis, which we confirm for this model.

Now implication (b): that all efficient changes occur. Assume, first, a fixed and fully visible set of efficient alternatives to the status quo. Each of these will be adopted against the status quo. Thus in Figure 21.1, either D_{i1} or D_{im} would substitute x_1 or x_m for x_i under the stasis consensual system. Notice, however, that once either was adopted, the other would *become* an efficiency-undecidable proposal for change, and would be rejected under our model. In other words, we should say, *any* rather than all efficient changes will be adopted. The significance of this is both distributive and

---

60 See Buchanan and Tullock, *The Calulus of Consent*, especially pp. 63–96, 249–262; and section IIG above.
61 Wicksell imagines this as achieved by parliamentary decision with decision with proportional representation (pp. 96–97), while Buchanan and Tullock focus mainly on direct decision. The word *each* is very important, for the logic of the efficiency argument collapses even under minor deviations.
62 Buchanan and Tullock, p. 285; above, p. 1276–1277.

tactical. A would rather move to x_1 and B to x_m. Each may well be tempted to express insincere preferences so that *both* outcomes are rejected. A may try to impose x_1 by alleging that x_m belongs to his rejection set for $\bar{x}_i$, and B may take the obverse strategy. It is, then, evident that *neither* outcome may be adopted: decisions D_{i1} and D_{im}, both efficient, may be rejected in favor of the status quo choices D_{ii}. This suggests that the model contains within itself incentives for departure from the voting rule (2). This is a serious practical limitation, despite the formal result implied if the model is faithfully acted out. This point of brittleness is already well understood.[63]

A second difficulty: suppose we do not imagine a fixed set of visible alternatives, but assume that only a few of the many possible outcomes are searched out and proposed. This would seem realistic. It follows immediately that an efficient substitution (say D_{im}) may be omitted. It should, nevertheless, be noted that the model contains strong incentives for search: somebody inevitably stands to gain from any efficient substitution. A plausible supposition would be that each participant will search up to some personal threshold of "satisficing,"[64] so that this omission would be less serious than one might imagine. Yet, it is also plausible to imagine large inequalities of information and technical competence which would lead to search biased toward large gains for some minorities and not others.[65] Partial and possibly biased search, then, adds a second caveat to our confirmation of implication (b).

IIIC. UTILITARIAN MAXIMA, EQUALITY, AND THE LIMITS OF EFFICIENCY

Suppose, next, that we go along way beyond implications (a) and (b), and begin to engage in loose talk about the maximization of aggregate utility. We might allege that our confirmation of (a) and (b) supports Wicksell's conjecture that "[failure to reach unanimity provides] an *a posteriori*, and the sole possible, proof that the state activity under consideration would not provide the community with utility corresponding to the necessary sacrifice. ... "[66] Consider a redistributive program, whose incidence for two arbitrary individuals is to reduce the difference between their

---

[63] Barry, pp. 245–250. Also hamilton, *Federalist 22*, and Franklin as cited above, and William Baumol, *Welfare Economics and the Theory of the State* (Cambridge: Harvard University Press, 2nd ed., 1965) p. 42ff.
[64] The nation is Herbert Simon's. See, for example, "Theories of Decision-Making in economics and Behavioral Science," *American Economic Review*, 49 (June, 1995), 253–283.
[65] Notice that no *sinister* motive need be attributed to an elite under this account; a merely self-centered search for alternatives will suffice. It is to Calhoun's credit that he sees the possibility of extractive outcomes without recourse to evil motive: *Disquisition*, especially pp. 3–7. The classic formulation is Robert Michels, *Political Parties*, trans. Eden and Cedar Paul (1915; rpt., New York: Dover Books, 1959), especially pp. 377–392.
[66] Wicksell, as quoted above, p. 1276. Wicksell has a different consensus structure in mind, but this happens to coincide exactly with the stasis structure under consideration for the present case: both the status quo and the *laissez faire* solutions would leave real incomes undisturbed.

THE LIMITS OF CONSENSUAL DECISION

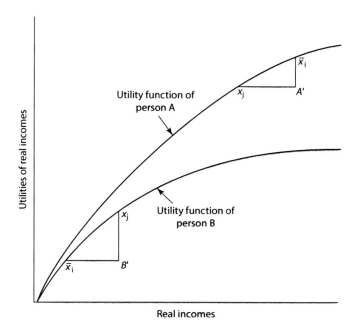

Figure 21-2. An Inefficient Increase of Aggregate Utility by Redistributive Decision D_{ij}

real incomes. Person A loses a given increment of real income $(A'-x_j$ in Figure 2) and Person B gains the same amount $(B'-\bar{x}_i$ in Figure 21.2). Clearly, this package is efficiency-unde- cidable[67] and will be rejected consensually if (a) holds: Person A will withhold his consent. Does this entitle us to claim that the redistribution would therefore have failed to increase aggregate utility? Not at all. Following the common supposition that real income yields a decreasing marginal utility, an opponent could claim that this downward redistribution would increase aggregate utility.[68] Suppose he conjectures utility functions for real income shown as Figure 21.2. Since B' utility gain (x_j-B') exceeds A's loss $(\bar{x}_i-A')$, his case is good: this has nothing to do with the labeling of the two functions, and his argument would actually be stronger if the two curves were reversed. His argument does violate our utility caveats, but so does any refutation we may offer.

This digression has four consequences for the larger analysis. First, efficiency and consensual decision (so far as it is efficient), are blind to distributive equality. Blind twice: (1) because equality as ordinarily conceived requires interpersonal comparisons, and (2) because consensus gives the privileged a right of consent in reform. If then, the object is to reduce inequalities, we must either

---

[67] In the spatial interpretation given as Figure 21.2, it is analogous to decision D_{ik} or D_{ij}.
[68] Lerner and Arrow give far subtler arguments. The simple case made here appears in Christopher Jencks et al., *Inequality* (New York: Basic Books, 1972), p. 5ff.

reject consensual choice or hope fervently for the good will of the rich. It is, in short, clear that equalitarians, with or without utilitarian roots, have good reason to reject efficient consensus as an ideal. Conversely, Wicksell has suggested this as an advertisement for his scheme of consensus to the rich.[69] Second, if our underlying normative position is utilitarian, it follows that consensual decision may exact serious *opportunity costs* precisely because it respects implication (1) of the efficiency rule, rejecting efficiency-undecidable decisions (like D_{ij} in Figure 21.2). This in turn modifies the normative sense of implication (2): that we adopt any *efficiency*-improvement does not imply that we adopt any *utility*-improvement. We are sheltered from this conjecture by the fact the utilitarian case for redistribution requires interpersonal comparisons, which permits us to deny that any valid evidence could even in principle be displayed for the hypothesis that leveling increases aggregate utility. By the same stroke, of course, it denies us any claim to the falsification of that hypothesis.

Both of these difficulties are overcome by a political economy of abundance. If the total supply of real income expands inexorably, then we need not face the harsh trade-off between "haves" and "have nots." This optimism has deep roots in American thought, and is elegantly caricatured by David Potter in its contrast to the European alternative,

> … Europe has always conceived of redistribution of wealth as necessitating the expropriation of some and the corresponding aggrandizement of others; but America has conceived of it primarily in terms of giving to some without taking from others … without necessarily treating one class as the victim or even, in an ultimate sense, the antagonist of another.[70]

This permits us to look past these objections to consensus. First, we can "level up"[71] by giving dividends of growth to the poor while allowing the rich to maintain their position. Second, we need not take the opportunity costs of consensual decision very seriously: the future presents a steady supply of fresh (and painless) opportunities. This optimism is expressed in the market analogy itself: Since traders trade, they are surely doing themselves a good turn; since citizens accept change (if they do), they too are doing themselves a good turn.[72]

But this line of escape seems to me increasingly implausible. There is every reason to suspect that the future does not promise boundless economic growth, at least not at a price we ought to be willing to pay.[73] If (by grace) the future does offer such a prospect, another difficulty must

---

69 Wicksell, p. 95–96. Given a *lassiz, faire* status quo, his argument would apply to the stasis consensual scheme as well.
70 *People of Plenty* (Chicago: University of Chicago Press, 1954), p. 113.
71 The phrase is Potter's, *People of Plenty*, p. 121.
72 Cf. Buchanan and Tullock, pp. 249–262.
73 The literature of pessimistic economics grows daily. I have in mind, for example, the Committee of Rome's argument as expressed in Danella H. Meadows et al., *The Limits to Growth* (New York: Universe Books, 1972). A very

be faced. We have so far tacitly supposed independence in the utility of real income. Thus, the case goes, if *A* gets more while *B* stands pat, gross utility must have increased. But there is some evidence that the utility of real income is defined *invidiously*: If you gain in real income, the utility of my real income is diminished by invidious comparison. This ancient supposition is supported by intuition: Why else are "poor" Americans, whose incomes excel more than 90 per cent of the world's population, poor? Partly, to be sure, because the structure of everyday life presses high demands for consumption in a society like our own. But partly also because they *are* poor in relation to the rest of us. It is also supported by some contemporary research: deprivation is relative, and the utility of income varies not with its absolute amount but with its placement in specific social distributions.[74] If this is so, then "leveling up" is chimerical: if it is possible to level up real incomes, it may still be impossible to level up welfare.

A third implication returns us to the doctrine of consensus itself. If governmental decisions were taken without side-payments, consensual decision would clearly be vulnerable to Hamilton's objection, would make adaptive change all but impossible. The open use of bribes is the punch behind the market analogy, and only Victorian prissiness would suggest that it is an inherently bad idea.[75] The present digression on equality and redistribution, however, calls to mind a distressing prospect. Suppose that, under the status quo, persons are well stocked with side-payments valued by others, and some other persons are utterly without such side-payments. Let *A* represent a "fat cat" and *B* represent a "pauper." Suppose then that a policy change advantaging *A* arises: he can make it an efficiency improvement by giving *B* a sufficient bribe, and it will be adopted. But the reverse case is distressing: a measure advantaging *B* arises, but he cannot lay hands on a sufficient bribe for *A*. If side-payments have diminishing marginal utility, this effect will be magnified, since *A* will set less store on a bribe of fixed size than *B* will. Neither as utilitarians nor as equalitarians are we apt to rest happily with the fact that *A*'s proposal goes through while *B*'s does not. Insofar as we escape Hamilton's objection, then, the case for consensual decision must *presuppose* a relatively equalitarian and fluid distribution of transferable, valuable goods.

Finally, this case once again calls into question our commitment to the idea of unanimous consent in government policy. The consent assumption, built into the argument from efficiency, here rises and falls with that doctrine. We have suggested three reasons—utilitarian opportunity costs, distributive fairness, and the distribution of side-payments—to hold the doctrine of efficiency at

---

concise and pointed analysis of material limits on growth is Earl Cook, "Energy for Millenium Three," *Technology Review,* 75 (December, 1972), 16–23.

74 See, for example, W. G. Runciman, *Relative Deprivation and Social Justice* (Berkeley: University of California Press, 1966) and Richard A. Easterlin, "Does Money Buy Happiness?", *The Public Interest,* 30 (Winter, 1973), 3–10.

75 The institutionalization of side-payments is discussed in James S. Coleman, "Political Money," *American Political Science Review,* 64 (December, 1970), 1074–87, and Buchanan and Tullock, pp. 265–81.

arm's length. Here, as before, we are given cause to deny that the right of consent in change should always be honored in governmental decision.[76]

IIID. CONSENSUAL DECISION AND PROGRESS TOWARD EFFICIENCY MAXIMA

We have yet to examine implication (3)—the achievement of efficiency equilibria—for our consensual model. This line of analysis leads, if I am not mistaken, to a serious objection against the consensus doctrine even in this sophisticated form. Let us proceed on the supposition that implications (1) and (2) are essentially correct: consensual decision makes only efficient substitutions of policy, and makes such substitutions whenever they are visible.

If this were so, we might expect to find "histories" of the kind suggested by Figure 21–3. Possibility frontier $F—F'$ defines an efficiency equilibrium set: once such a point is achieved, no efficient changes are possible. Policies $x_1, x_2, \ldots, x_5$ define a hierarchy of efficiency, each an improvement over its predecessors. It follows that decisions D_{12}, D_{23}, D_{45} represent a "history" of progress toward equilibrium. Each narrows the remaining set of efficiency improvements, defined by the nested sectors radiating from each policy point (the dotted lines in Figure 21.3). The status quo plods toward equilibrium, as these sets of remaining improvements diminish with each decision.[77] Now, if consensual decision displays this sort of sequence, we are entitled to imagine a steady progress and enjoy a strong objection against "risky" deviations from consensual efficiency. Moreover, we have given real substance to the earlier doctrine of consent: each citizen is free from any loss of welfare. But is this what we ought to expect?

Consider a scenario which seems to confirm the optimistic history just outlined.[78] I have in mind the famous Pigouvian chimney:

---

76 It should be clear that these shortcomings are not *unique* to consensual decision. It is obvious that implication (1) does not hold for other structures: All other structures permit changes opposed by some persons and thus brook the possibility that efficiency-undecidable choices will result. Implication (2) is also violated by other structures: efficiency-dominant outcomes may be passed up. Biased search is perhaps universal; many structures, such as majority voting, invite strategic manipulation. (See, for instance, Robin Farquharson, *A theory of Voting* (New Haven: Yale University Press, 1969). Finally, other structures fail to enforce equalitarian outcomes even welfare. See William riker, "Bargaining in a Three Person Game," *American Political Science Review,* 61 (September, 1967), 642–56. For an introduction to the related "games of fair division" problem, see Duncan Luce and Howard Raiffa, *Games and decision* (New York: John Wiley, 1967) pp. 363°68.

77 Notice that this history is exactly the "market case" in which successive gains from trade drive partners toward a contract locus from which further gains are impossible. This is the very heart of the "market analogy."

78 Here is the account given by Buchanan and Tullock, p. 91:

> ... if decisionmaking costs are neglected, this test [consensus] must be met if collective action is to be judged "desirable" by any rational individual calculus at the constitutional level. We may illustrate this point by the classical example of Pigouvian welfare economics, the case of the smoking chimney. Smoke from an industrial plant fouls the air and imposes external costs on residents in the surrounding areas. If

THE LIMITS OF CONSENSUAL DECISION

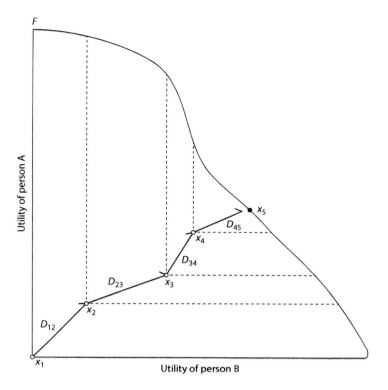

Figure 21.3. A Sequence of Efficiency Improvements Approaching Equilibrium

1. A chimney emits smoke, reducing the welfare of people living nearby.
2. The victims of this diseconomy would gain from its elimination, but the chimney owners would lose from its elimination.

---

this represents a genuine externality, either voluntary arrangements will emerge to eliminate it or collective action with unanimous support can be implemented. If the externality is real, *some* collectively imposed scheme through which the damaged property owners are taxed and the firm's owners are subsidized for capital losses incurred in putting in a smoke-abatement machine can command the assent of all parties. If no such compensation scheme is possible (organizing costs neglected), the externality is only apparent and not real. The same conclusion applies to the possibility of voluntary arrangements being worked out. Suppose that the owners of the residential property claim some smoke damage, however slight. If this claim is real, the opportunity will always be open for them to combine forces and buy out the firm in order to introduce smoke-abatement devices. If the costs of organizing such action are left out of account, such an arrangement would surely be made. All externalities of this sort would be eliminated through either voluntary organized action or unanimously supported collective action, with full compensation paid to parties damaged by the changes introduced by the removal of the externalities." This is an unconventional use of "externality." But, as will be seen momentarial, it is also incorrect analytically.

3. It is proposed that government eliminate the smoke by simple prohibition. This is rejected (implication 1).
4. It is proposed that government eliminate the smoke by the combination of a prohibition and a tax on former victims sufficient to make this a gain for the chimney owners. This is accepted (implication 2).

This is a happy story. We reject an efficiency-undecidable reform at step (3), and simultaneously honor the chimney owner's right of consent in the alteration of government policy. Notice that we do *not* honor the victims' right of consent in the retention of status quo policy, but put this aside (momentarily) as inconsequential. Better yet, we are able to achieve an efficiency improvement by combining two (efficiency undecidable) changes in a single package of reform which is accepted by everyone. In step (4), that is, we have made an efficiency improvement. And we have done so without violating anyone's right of consent. This move would be analogous to a decision in Figure 21.4, say D_{12}, where A is a smoke victim and B is a chimney owner. But what if we had rejected the reform package at (4)? This would suggest that the package was not an efficiency improvement, perhaps because the tax-bribe was insufficient compensation to the chimney owners. Again, all is well and good for the optimistic history: we have here one of its constituent elements.

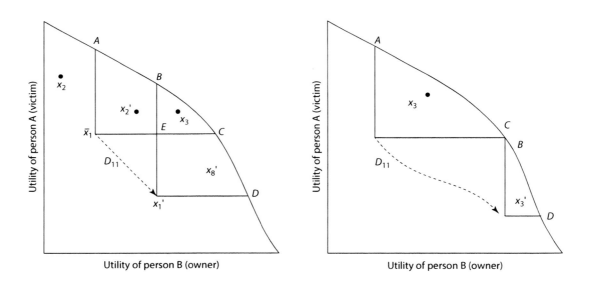

Figure 21–4. The Difference between Aggregate and Incremental Efficiency

Notice that this telling might founder on any of several difficulties noted already. First, the reform might never be proposed for the lack of a sufficient search, especially if the victims of the smoke lacked the confidence or skill to seek it out and communicate the result to the owners. Second, it might be rejected not for its inefficiency, but out of strategic misrepresentation. The chimney owners, for example, might calculate thus: (1) the tax-bribe offered is acceptable to the smoke victims, so (2) they must therefore enjoy a margin of improved welfare from its adoption; but (3) why not obtain some of this margin for ourselves by demanding a higher level of compensation? The result might be the rejection of an efficiency improvement. Third, the story offers no hint of fairness. Fourth, we have no assurance that a rejected alternative might not constitute an effi-ciency-undecidable gain of aggregate utility. This would be an especially tempting hunch if there were far more victims than chimney owners. Finally, it might happen that the victims simply did not have the assets required to offer sufficient compensation. For all these reasons, we have no right to propose the story as an historical probability or to take unambiguous satisfaction in its occurrence.

IIIF. DRIFT AND THE DETACHMENT OF INCREMENTAL FROM AGGREGATE EFFICIENCY

But all of these difficulties are less serious than the ones which arise from the effort to extend the analysis *backward* in time.[79] The telling we have so far given *begins* with the existence of an external diseconomy. But suppose we supply step (O) as follows:

> O. Government policy permits industrial siting in the neighborhood, and then the owners site their chimney so that the smoke begins to fall on the neighborhood.

This suggests two relevant inferences. First, government policy is a *partial* constraint on action: government decisions only partially determine social states. From this a second point follows: it is possible for people to suffer welfare losses *within* a given status quo policy. Let us define the "private sector" rather unconventionally as the sum total of action within any fixed government policy. Then we may divide the class of all possible private sectors in two: (1) uniformly efficient private sectors, and (2) sometimes inefficient private sectors. The former will *never* impose welfare losses, and corresponds to a "market society" without external diseconomies (like the smoke in our example). The latter corresponds to society as we know it. I will discuss this more generally below, but let us apply it to the smokestack immediately.

---

79 See Barry, p. 256 ff, in connection with this and succeeding criticisms of Buchanan and Tullock.

Consider x_i to be a permissive government policy. Perhaps the permission is tacit, *nullum crimen*, because nobody has anticipated the social cost of chimneys. In the initial position, we map $\bar{x}_1$ onto the welfare surface of A and B as we have it in Figure 21-4. Then the chimney's prospective owners, acting within $\bar{x}_1$, site their factory and it begins to belch smoke. They have, we assume, gained from this enterprise. If B is an owner, this is reflected as an eastward shift in the space defined by Figure 4. But, again within $\bar{x}_1$ some local residents have lost utility. If A is one of these victims, this is accounted as a southerly shift in Figure 4. The result is a *drift in the utility of the status quo policy*. The drift, which is itself efficiency undecidable, is traced by the stasis outcome, D_{11}. It is *a change in social welfare without a change in government policy*. On this new telling, the story begins not at $\bar{x}_1$ but at $\bar{x}_1'$, in Figure 21.4. This detail destroys the optimistic history.

The consensus-efficiency hypothesis is split by this. In Figure 21-4, we begin at $\bar{x}_1$ (no smoke, no prohibition). Overall or *aggregate* efficiency, therefor, is defined with respect to the shaded set of outcomes bounded by $A—\bar{x}_1—C—A$. Only by achieving outcomes in this set, and avoiding outcomes elsewhere, can we claim aggregate conformity to the efficiency principle. And, only by this result can we give substance to the notion of consent—protecting citizens from coercive losses of welfare. But efficiency also has a marginal or *incremental* interpretation. We find ourselves at $\bar{x}_1'$, and efficient increments from here are bounded by the line $B—\bar{x}_1'D—B$, so that precisely the confirmation of implications (i) and (ii) for (incremental) governmental action detaches the effect of action from the prospect of aggregate efficiency.

This analysis forces us to revise our earlier claims. First, what does it mean that consensual decision rejects efficiency undecidable changes as per implication (i)? Suppose, in our chimney story, that a proposal is rejected. Perhaps the rejected decision is an order to close the chimney along with compensation which the owners judge inadequate. By hypothesis, this must be something other than an efficiency improvement in incremental terms. In Figure 4, it therefore lies outside $B—\bar{x}_1'—D$. There are two normatively relevant locations for the rejected proposal in the remaining space. Like x_2, it may be an efficient change in neither the incremental nor the aggregate sense. Its rejection is therefore appropriate But, it may also resemble x_2': conforming to aggregate but not incremental efficiency. In this case, its rejection will violate implication (ii): failing, that is, to adopt an efficiency improvement (in the aggregate). The troublesome set of rejected alternatives (like x_2') have the following property: they assure both A and B their pre-drift utility levels, but fail to assure B his post-drift utility level. The set is bounded by $A—\bar{x}_1—E—B$ in Figure 4a. Consensual decision permits B to veto these policy changes, and therefore *denies us the inference that any aggregate improvement of efficiency will be selected*. In other words, *implication (ii) holds in the increment but not the aggregate for a society whose private sector permits efficiency-undecidable drift*.

But consider the converse case. According to implication (ii) consensus will lead to the adoption of any alternative which is an efficiency improvement. We re-examine this inference from the view of aggregate efficiency. Suppose an outcome is adopted. Perhaps a sufficient bribe for the chimney's closure. By hypothesis, this outcome is incrementally efficient, and thus lies within $B-x_1'-D$ in Figure 4a. There are again two relevant possibilities. Like x_3, the new outcome may be an aggregate improvement. This is good. But, like x_3', it may be efficiency-undecidable in the aggregate. This will be so if B equals or surpasses his post-drift utility level but A fails to reach his predrift level. The embarrassing set of outcomes with this property is bounded by $E-\bar{x}_1'D-C$ in Figure 4a. Consensual decision withholds from A the authority to impose his initial level of utility, and therefore *denies us the inference that adopted consensual decisions will be efficient in the aggregate. Implication (ii) is therefore false in the aggregate for societies whose private sectors permit efficiency-undecidable drift.*

The chimney case is in fact even more distressing than this analysis indicates. If there is to be any hope of aggregate efficiency within incremental consensus, then there must be a non-empty set of outcomes which are improvements over both $\bar{x}_1'$ and $\bar{x}_1$. The test for membership in that set: an outcome must exceed each person's utility threshold both before *and* after drift occurs. The critical edge of this is in our case: A must reach his pre-drift level without B going below his postdrift level. The set of such points would be $B-E-C$ in Figure 4a. Consider the common solution:[80] A and his fellow victims pay B and his fellow owners a sufficient bribe. If this is offered, it must exceed A's post-drift level of utility, but will it also exceed his pre-drift level? Surely not, for he loses something he values (his share of the bribe), but gains only what he had in the first place (clean air). Only if he derives the side-payment from some effect of the chimney's operation—a job in the factory?—does it seem so much as possible that aggregate efficiency will be achieved. Indeed, if such a byproduct is ruled out, there seems every reason to think Figure 4b is appropriate: the drift is sufficient to collapse the set of incrementally and aggregately efficient points: $B-E-C$ has evaporated. If this is so, we are forced to the still more pessimistic conclusion that *the consensual outcome cannot possibly be an aggregate improvement of efficiency.* In Figure 4a, will be rejected against $\bar{x}_1'$, and this stasis outcome, $D_{1'1'}$, is not efficient in aggregate. But x_3' will be adopted. The latter, efficient in the increment, is not efficient in the aggregate. Since this depends on special features of the example chosen, we will not claim any generality for it. We do, however, note it as a prospect, and insist that it denies any guarantee that successive movements will return the outcome to aggregate efficiency.

If we commit the (remissable) sin of interpersonal comparison, a further difficulty emerges. Suppose A initiates a change within the status quo which gains him a little, say 1 International Utile. The social cost may be very great, perhaps 5 International Utiles from each of a thousand persons. If this is so, and an appropriate medium of exchange happens to exist, it may become evident that no change can return us to aggregate efficiency even if we are willing to expropriate

---

80 See note 79.

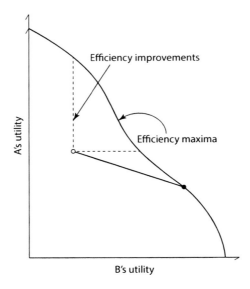

Figure 21–5. Reaching an Efficiency Maximum by an Efficiency-Undecidable Change

assets corresponding to A's full gain of 1 utile. There is nothing in the doctrine of consensual decision to refute this conjecture. Except, of course, the denial of interpersonal comparison. But this leads to more serious difficulty still. Suppose only one person is damaged by the drift in question. The chimney's shadow ruins a rose garden. Without interpersonal comparison, we cannot claim that $n - 1$ gains—it is perhaps a People's Chimney—will balance out this single loss. Surely, this is not a satisfying response to the difficulties we have been exploring.

It may be argued that we have missed our own point. We began with the hypothesis that efficiency maxima will be achieved consensually, but we have discussed only transitions from one sub- maximal point to another. Granting that consensus will not assure aggregate efficiency in such transitions, it may be argued that maxima will nevertheless be achieved. Indeed it is easily possible to reach an efficient equilibrium by a decision which violates implication (i) by imposing an efficiency-undecidable change that turns out to reach a maximum. (See Figure 21–5.)

This may of course happen, but then consensual decision holds no special distinction: majority- rule,[81] dictatorship, or perhaps the Oracle of Delphi might also accomplish the same result. Indeed drift itself might press the community to an efficient maximum. These possibilities suggest that the maximum criterion by itself implies neither consensual decision nor any fixed right of

---

[81] Buchanan and Tullock, p. 186 recognize this prospect where side-payments are available.

consent in policy. But consensual decision still holds two distinctions. First, *if* it follows implications (1) and (2) in aggregate, then consensus offers us a "safe" line of travel toward maxima. This is the idea of our optimistic history in Figure 3. Second, ask yourself how we are to *know* that a maximum has been achieved. Assuming that the number of possible states is very large or infinite, we will not be able to identify efficiency maxima by any casual inspection. Nor can we use the shortcut assumptions of economics since we lack goods of the kind they consider. Under the complex conditions of government decision, the fact that an outcome is a maximum will emerge as an *inference from experience*. Even *with* drift, stasis consensus offers the appropriate laboratory: if protracted search produces no acceptable change, we are entitled to the practical hunch that a maximum has already been achieved. Of course we will not *stay* at a maximum merely because we fail to change policy, which renders this slight comfort.

IIIG. BUCHANAN AND TULLOCK ON THE ELIMINATION OF EXTERNAL COST

Let us pause to formulate this in the "external cost" language proposed by Buchanan and Tullock. An external cost is what " … the individual expects to endure as a result of the actions of others over which he has no direct control."[82] Like Locke—and Calhoun and Wolff and Wick-sell—these authors are thinking mainly about the threat posed by *public* power over the individual: the cost of action through government. They do not say so, but it is otherwise impossible to comprehend their most fundamental conclusion: "Only the unanimity rule will insure that all external effects will be eliminated by collectivization."[83] Or, " … only if the consent of all members of the group is required will he be free of all expectations of external costs."[84] This is the punch behind the general claim with which we began—consensus as a means of utilitarian efficiency.[85]

The claim that consensus eliminates external cost is equivalent to claiming that implication (1) is fulfilled: only efficient changes occur.[86] (This is because other changes will damage some people and therefore exact external costs.) With some qualification, we have accepted this as a property of consensual decision in the increment. But, critically, we have shown it not to hold in the aggregate, unless the private sector is "perfect." If we confine our attention to the former case, what Buchanan and Tullock say is correct. If we consider the latter, what they say is not correct. In this latter instance, we are compelled to consider *two* forms of external cost, two classes

---

82   Buchanan and Tullock, p. 45.
83   *Ibid*., p. 39.
84   *Ibid*.
85   Above, Section IC, or Buchanan and Tullock, p. 285.
86   *Ibid*., pp. 43–62.

of harmful acts over which we lack direct control. First, changes of government policy may be carried over our objection. This is eliminated by consensus. Second, private or civil actions, consistent with existing government policy, may damage our interests. If we cannot control these by governmental initiative, surely they are relevant external costs. Precisely because it rules out the first sort of cost, consensus permits those who benefit from these actions and the resulting "drift" to veto our efforts at government intervention.

It follows immediately that Buchanan and Tullock err when they offer the conclusion that unanimity excludes external costs—even if decision-making costs are ignored. Yet it may be claimed that the private sector *is* perfect, permitting no efficiency-undecidable drift. But in this case, the same authors would have urged that the activity in question not be subject to governmental decision.[87] They propose that government consider only imperfect portions of the private sector, but these are exactly the sectors in which the relevant difficulty occurs. Moreover, as Olson has suggested this seems to imply the optimality of an anarchic solution similar to Calhoun's.[88] But this is a slight exaggeration. At what point would a man expecting to eliminate future external costs agree to the sort of consensual government decision we have been discussing? At the point when he believed that existing government policy, with no further change, would eliminate all external effects occasioned by the private conduct of others; when, in other words, a code corresponding to a perfect private sector was in hand.

IIIH. PERFECTION OF PRIVATE SECTOR AS A CONDITION OF CONSENSUAL EFFICIENCY

A perfect private sector—a society in which no harm was done to others except by action of government—is historically implausible. I cannot explore the point fully here, but three observations seem at once obvious and important. First, let us suppose I claim that some present public code brooks no imperfection. How are we to test my hypothesis? Presumably by waiting for someone to claim that his welfare has been diminished under existing policy. Apart from the sheer statistical brittleness of the hypothesis,[89] and allowing that the status quo would include a court

---

87 *Ibid.*
88 Mancur Olson, Jr., "The Principle of 'Fiscal Equivalence': the Division of Responsibilities among Different Levels of Government," *The Ameican Economic Review*, Papers and Proceedings, 59 (May, 1969), 479–87, the point in question is at p. 480.
89 If the probability of an exception is some small number, p, and there are n citizens with independent chances of being harmed, I should expect the hypothesis to stand in only one out of $(1-p)^n$ trials. With p greater than, say, .01, and n greater than 1,000, this comes to practically nothing. And regardless what non-zero value p takes, the relevant function approaches zero as n increases toward infinity.

system capable of absorbing small and middle-sized exceptions,[90] we still confront an appalling epistemo-logical dilemma: How are we to judge the accuracy of any claims which do arise? Suppose Smith is the claimant: Am I to be the judge? Or are we to poll the society? Or is Smith alone to judge? If we choose any but the last alternative, we confront the prospect of disagreement, perhaps a Smith-Rae debate. How is this to be settled? I know no way which is consistent with consensual decision, and that seems the appropriate criterion unless our activity is an idle one. If our hypothesis is politically relevant—its violation having some relevance to policy—we should resolve it consensually. But if the alternatives become "Smith is right" or "Rae is right," then one disputant must prevail over the other, probably Smith over Rae, yet this is hardly consensual.

Second, unless the citizenry is dull as dirt or the makers of the public code utterly clairvoyant, it seems to me very nearly certain that innovation will occur, creating relations not proscribed by present policy, which are nonetheless misfortunes for some groups and individuals. The Pigouvian chimney is an example, but an easy one readily faced down by the simplest of zoning ordinances. Here are some general categories which illustrate the point.[91]

1. Changes in the technology of productive activity imposing material diseconomies on others, including the marginalization of workers.
2. Pecuniary diseconomies resulting from market transactions, such as wage inflation or the price fluctuation of goods under changing demand by third parties.
3. Declines of welfare resulting from static codes of behavior in the face of generational change in values.
4. Declines of welfare arising from static policy and changes in the size or distribution of population.
5. Declines of welfare resulting from changing patterns of personal decision with complementarity between individual behaviors.
6. Historical change in the material environment brought about by the cumulative effect of past and present human behavior.

All these patterns will occasion "drift" of the sort analyzed in IIIF unless they are fully anticipated by government policy. This is simply implausible as a long-term proposition. And once

---

90 But such a system of courts would be odd: judges could not make law, and could not therefore cope with ambiguity. This suggests, however, either that the courts would be virtually inert or that the law would be very different from any law we presently know. It would be utterly mechanical and lack "open texture" of the sort H. L. A. Hart describes so interestingly in *The Concept of Law* (Oxford: Oxford University Press, 1961).
91 The relevant literature is stupendous. Two at once entertaining and informative analyses are offered by William F. Baxter, "A Parable," *Stanford Law Review*, 23 (May, 1971), 973–77, and Thomas Schelling, "Hockey Helmets, Concealed Weapons, and Daylight Saving," Kennedy School Discussion Paper No. 9, 1972. Schelling's famous paper, "On the Ecology of Micromotives," *Public Interest*, 25 (Fall, 1971), 61–98, is also worth consulting, alone with Barry p. 256ff.

the drift occurs, we have seen that stasis consensual decision will not necessarily protect us by achieving aggregate efficiency.

Finally, the analysis given here is unfair to the doctrine of consensus. The critique of its claim to efficiency does not, strictly speaking, apply to consensual decision *itself*. It applies rather to the combination of consensual decision in government policy and the lack of consensual decision for behavior within government policy. If *everything* were decided consensually, then incremental and aggregate efficiency would coincide, and would be at least approximated by consensual decision. Drift would not occur, for each action would require unanimous consent. The private sector would be perfectly efficient precisely because it would be empty: everything would be a governmental policy. This is wildly implausible sociologically, and utterly unattractive to the liberal conscience. It is the odd suggestion that consensual decision will achieve its stated relation to utilitarian efficiency precisely as the government's agenda becomes total.[92]

III-I. FREE EXIT AND THE FAILURE OF THE MARKET ANALOGY

A main conclusion: *Consensual decision will cash its guarantee—assure utilitarian efficiency—precisely where politics itself seems unnecessary—i. e., in a perfect private sector.* This last, however improbable, would make politics a risky luxury: If no harm can befall me under static policy, yet losses can be inflicted by governmental action, why should I not choose to end political history?

But what has become of the "market analogy?" I am afraid the answer is that the relation between market transactions and governmental choices of policy will not bear so strong an assertion of similarity. The distinguishing property of free exchange is ease of escape: a well-functioning market permits each trader to *exit* any relationship he finds odious. Suppose it didn't: I could buy salt only from you. You could of course use your veto over the exchange outcome to exact a blackmail price from me, because of the market's consensual structure—because, that is, I have no right of consent in the status quo. The voluntary quality of the market arises from the freedom of exit and the ready availability of substitute partners.[93] But government is another matter: one can typically escape governments only at a high price, measured in material and psychic dislocation. If the government chooses to sell me salt at monopoly prices—some have—my line of escape is clogged, and the right of consent in a *change* of policy far from helpful. "Drift" of the kind discussed above can be escaped cheaply by traders, but not by citizens. And it is at just this point that the market analogy fails.

---

92 The nearest historical approximation seems to occur within certain small utopian communities such as the Hutterite colonies of Western Canada. Cf. Victor Peters, *All Things Common* (Minneapolis: University of Minnesota Press, 1965).
93 See Albert Hirschmann, *Exit, Voice and Loyalty* (Cambridge, Mass.: Harvard University Press, 1970).

With it goes the marriage of consent and utility in consensual efficiency. It is no comfort that increments of governmental change honor this union if aggregates of social change abuse it. And this last must be expected in a world which needs politics and in that way resembles our own experience. I turn now to a finishing conjecture.

IV. ONE IMPLICATION

I will withstand the (very slight) temptation to repeat the essay's main points, and finish instead a single line of conjecture which leads to an odd conclusion. We began with consent as a response against autocracy. The critical transition from consent in regimes to consent in their policies, presents an historical embarrassment, and the doctrine of consensual decision speaks in answer to it. The doctrine has grown subtler, but retains the mark of its birth: a single-minded attention to *public* power and a corresponding inattention to its alternatives. If it were possible to put these aside by granting an unconditional right of consent to everyone, then the doctrine of consensual decision would be an appropriate ideal for government decision. It is not possible to do so. I do not mean to raise the sociological difficulties occasioned by entrenched elites, or the division of labor in politics, or the mere costs of talk and newsprint. If the obstacles to unconditional consensus were of this order, it would provide an intelligent guide to reform—an optimum to be approximated in the face of difficulty. The objection is a deeper one which arises from the inner structure of decision making itself: choices must have outcomes, and the structures by which they are made must contain points of vulnerability so that these may be achieved. These in turn deny a universal right of consent, no matter what configuration society takes. If this is so, then any unconditional ideal of consensual decision must present an *inherently* unreachable structure which cannot be approximated by actual institutions.

Whatever practical ideal of consensual decision is available must therefore be conditional: must leave open a nonconsensual path to some outcomes. In the theories considered by this essay, the line of escape leads to private as opposed to public forms of power. With Calhoun's anarchic consensus, we are vulnerable—without a right of consent—to the nullification of positive government policy. The *laissez-faire* proposal of Wicksell leaves us vulnerable to the bare market outcome. The stasis consensual system of Buchanan and Tullock leaves us vulnerable to action within the status quo. I personally believe these proposals should be rejected because their points of vulnerability are more than a little unattractive under the historical circumstances of 20th-century society. Others may of course disagree, but I hope at least that the analysis clarifies the central question. If we are to decide by an approximation of consensus for some outcomes, we must surrender that right for other outcomes: What should they be?

There is, in fact, exactly one structure of decision which escapes this choice. Such a structure would grant somebody an unconditional right of consent in *every* outcome for every issue. This cannot be a scheme which grants more than one person a right of consent in some incomplete class of outcomes—like the structures examined here. It likewise cannot be a nonconsensual structure like majority-rule democracy. Given the criterion of robustness, it can brook no disagreement within the consenting class. A moment's reflection suggests that the only such structure for the formation of policy in society is pure autocracy.

ELEMENTS OF DEMOCRATIC JUSTICE

BY IAN SHAPIRO

TWENTY-TWO

Democratic movements derive much of their moral authority from the hope they hold out of displacing unjust social arrangements. This reflects the fact that the promise of democracy and that of social justice are intimately linked in the modern political imagination. The great democratic movements of the nineteenth century were less concerned to implement an abstract democratic ideal than, as John Dewey observed, "to remedy evils experienced in consequence of prior political institutions."[1] One only has to think of the ways in which the lack of democracy and the presence of social injustice were fused in the ideologies of opposition to communism in the Soviet bloc and the apartheid in South Africa to see that, in the twentieth century no less than in the nineteenth, many people blame social injustice on the lack of democracy and assume that democracy is an important weapon in replacing unjust social relations with just ones.

Yet this popular expectation is at variance with much academic orthodoxy, which recognizes that achieving political democracy guarantees nothing about the attainment of social justice.[2] In countries where the basic democratic institutions of popularly elected governments based on universal franchise prevail, wealth may or may not be redistributed, minorities may or may not be respected, opportunities

---

1 John Dewey, *The Public and Its Problems* (New York: Henry Holt, 1927), 84–5.
2 See, for example, Guiseppe Di Palma, *To Craft Democracies: An Essay on Democratic Transitions* (Berkeley: University of California Press, 1990), 23, for defense of the view that the democratic ideal should be disengaged "from the idea of social progress" if it is to endure, and Samuel P. Huntington, *The Third Wave: Democratization in the Late Twentieth Century* (Norman: University of Oklahoma Press, 1991), 165–9, for the argument that political leaders who sell out on their constituents' demands for social justice are more likely to succeed in consolidating democratic institutions than those who do not.

may or may not be open to all, and religious dissent may or may not be tolerated. Far from necessarily promoting it, then, democracy can actually undermine whatever social justice might be thought to require, and it is partly for this reason that bills of rights and other constitutional restraints on democratic politics are argued to be worthwhile. They limit the possibility of social injustice by constraining what can be done by those who wield state power in democracy's name.

Once it is held that democracy should be constrained by the requirements of social justice, a difficulty arises, however. There are many competing theories of social justice and no evident way to choose among them. Elsewhere I have argued that the standard attempts to resolve this difficulty fail, and that the apparent tensions between democracy and justice need to be rethought along lines that have more in common with popular expectations than with academic orthodoxy. On my view, although democracy is not sufficient for social justice, arguments about democracy and social justice are more deeply entwined with one another than the conventional opposition suggests. The mutual dependence of these two ideals is signaled by the fact that, on the one hand, most arguments for democracy rest at bottom on intuitions about what is just, and, on the other, if we dig deeply enough into arguments about social justice we frequently discover that they rest on appeals to democratic moral intuitions. This is not to say that commitments to democracy and to social justice entail one another; it is to say, however, that no account of either that undermines one's moral intuitions about the other is likely to be judged satisfactory.[3]

Drawing out the implications of this observation, I have sought to develop a view of social justice in which democratic considerations play a three-part foundational role: in the definition of social goods, in the determination of principles by which conflicts over goods should be resolved, and in the appropriate stance toward implementing principles of justice in the actual world of day-to-day politics.[4] These three ways to be a democrat set the basic terms of the view that I characterize as *democratic justice*, in contrast to liberal, socialist, conservative, and communitarian views that are in wide academic currency today. Although my view is conceived of as an alternative to these, I mean to make it attractive to many of their proponents because it depends less on alternative sets of assumptions about social justice and more on making explicit the implications of democratic moral intuitions to which many of them, on reflection, will find themselves committed. My earlier defenses of democratic justice have been ground-clearing and programmatic, amounting to a downpayment, at best, on a positive argument for democratic justice. My aim here is to deliver on the first installment of the constructive account.

Three preliminary points: First, democracy as I defend it is a subordinate good. By this I mean that although democracy is necessary for ordering social relations justly, we should resist every

---

3 See my "Three Ways to Be a Democrat," *Political Theory* 22 (February 1994): 124–51.
4 I should say at the outset that by using the term *foundational* I do not mean to take up a position here in debates about the nature of knowledge and existence. In describing a commitment to democracy as foundational, I mean only to suggest that no prior or more basic political commitment rightly commands our common allegiance.

suggestion that it is sufficient, that it is the highest human good, that it is the only human good, or that it should dominate the activities in which we engage. Democracy operates best when it sets the terms for our civil interactions without thereby determining their course. Our lives require much else as well to be satisfactory, and it is wrongheaded to expect democracy to deliver those other things. This conception follows from the thought that because power relations form part—but not all—of most collective activities, democracy appropriately conditions those activities but it does not appropriately displace them. Although we should aspire to get on with our collective lives in democratic ways on my account, we should nonetheless aspire to get on with them. The creative political challenge is to devise mechanisms of institutional governance that can make this possible.

Second, my argument for democratic justice is semicontextual in that it varies partly, but only partly, with time and circumstance. Aspects of what democratic justice might reasonably be thought to require may change over time and vary both across the domains of civil society and from culture to culture. This means that a satisfying elaboration of the argument can only be developed as its injunctions are explored through a variety of contexts. Shouldering that burden is the central task of the larger project on which I am engaged. In the present article my attention is confined to exploring aspects of the argument for democratic justice that can be defended in general terms.

Third, in making the case for democratic justice my central focus is on the procedural and institutional level of analysis, not on matters concerning higher order human interests and questions of ultimate justification. In this regard my approach is similar to Rawls's in his "political, not metaphysical" mode, although Rawls seems to me to press implausibly far the claim that a political conception of justice can be developed independently of controversial philosophical commitments.[5] The account developed here rests on skepticism toward the absolutist epistemologies and ontologies that a Platonist or a classical Marxist might embrace, but this skepticism is political rather than metaphysical; I take no position on whether or not the accounts are true, only on whether or not it is wise to allow our lives to be governed by their injunctions. This is not the same thing as philosophical neutrality, however, because partisans of such absolutist views are likely to find their political aspirations frustrated by the politics I am advocating in ways that many philosophical fallabilists, pragmatists, empiricists, realists, and philosophical antifoundationalists will not. My claim is that given the impossibility of neutrality among ultimate philosophical commitments, the democratic conception of social justice that I describe is the most appropriate foundational political commitment.

---

5   John Rawls, "Fairness to Goodness," *Philosophical Review* 82 (1973): 228, and "Justice as Fairness: Political not Metaphysical," *Philosophy and Public Affairs* 14, no. 3 (1985): 223–51, esp. 223–6.

It might be said that, having conceded that neutrality about questions of higher order interests and ultimate justification is not possible, one is not free to turn to the institutional and procedural level of analysis without first defending the higher order assumptions on which a given analysis rests. This conclusion seems to me to be unwarranted for three related reasons. It is true, first, that every political theory rests on higher order assumptions, but it is also true that all such assumptions are controversial. Consequently, if we put off the questions of institutional design until the higher order questions are settled, we may get to them at the time of Godot's arrival. In the meantime, however, life goes on and we need grounds for preferring some institutional arrangements over others. Second, although it is common to think that we should start with general matters because people are more likely to agree on them and then move to more specific and divisive matters—to the details wherein the devil is thought to lurk—exactly the opposite is often true, as Cass Sunstein has usefully noted. A faculty may be able to reach agreement that a particular person should be granted tenure even though its members could never agree on the reasons why. By extension, in arguing about the merits of different political arrangements, it is often wise to avoid—or at least minimize—attention to controversial questions of higher order interests and ultimate justification.[6] That is the assumption behind the present discussion. Last, because no one can do everything, it behooves practitioners in different disciplines to reflect on where they are most likely to make a useful contribution. In my view normative political theorists best devote attention to analyzing how to structure the power-dimensions of human interaction, leaving to psychologists, moral philosophers, and metaphysicians full analysis of higher order interests and issues of ultimate justification. Although every intellectual division of labor will be unsatisfactory from some defensible point of view, choices inevitably have to be made in this regard. The reader must judge whether I have made the right ones here.

TWO DIMENSIONS OF DEMOCRATIC JUSTICE

Democrats are committed to rule by the people. They insist that no aristocrat, monarch, bureaucrat, expert, or religious leader has the right, in virtue of such status, to force people to accept a particular conception of their proper common life. People should decide for themselves, via appropriate procedures of collective decision, what their collective business should be. They may reasonably be required to consult and take account of one another, and of others affected by their actions, but beyond this no one may legitimately tell them what to do. The people are sovereign; in all matters of collective life they rule over themselves.

---

6 See Cass Sunstein, "On Legal Theory and Legal Practice," in *Nomos XXXVII: Theory and Practice*, ed. Ian Shapiro and Judith Wagner DeCew (New York: New York University Press, 1995), 267–87.

ELEMENTS OF DEMOCRATIC JUSTICE

Although this is less often commented on in the academic literature, democracy is as much about opposition to the arbitrary exercise of power as it is about collective self-government. In this connection Barrington Moore remarks that historically democracy has been a weapon "of the poor and the many against the few and the well-to-do." Those who have actively sought it in organized political movements "have wanted it as a device to increase their share in political rule and weaken the power and authority of those who actually rule."[7] In the modern world at least, democratic movements have derived much of their energy and purpose from opposition to socioeconomic, legal, and political hierarchies that seemed capricious from a democratic point of view. Rooted in the remnants of feudal and absolutist regimes and shaped by the vicissitudes of conquest and chance, the political orders of eighteenth- and nineteenth-century Europe and North America seemed to the dispossessed to personify arbitrary hierarchy and domination. This reality, as much as anything else, motivated working-class and other democratic movements. The English philosophic radicals, the French and American revolutionaries, the nineteenth-century Chartists, and the anticolonial movements in the third world after the Second World War all wanted to free themselves from hierarchical orders for which they could see no rationale or justification. It was to this oppositional dimension of the democratic ideal that Nelson Mandela appealed at his sentencing for treason by a South African court in 1961. Conceding that he had disobeyed the law by inciting resistance to the government, he nonetheless wondered whether "the responsibility does not lie on the shoulders of the government which promulgated that law, knowing that my people, who constitute the majority of the population of this country, were opposed to that law, and knowing further that every legal means of demonstrating that opposition had been closed to them by prior legislation, and by government administrative action."[8]

Mandela's formulation might be taken to embody the conventional view that democracy is primarily about collective self-government and only secondarily about opposition. Part of his claim, after all, is that he should not be bound by "a law which neither I nor any of my people had any say in preparing."[9] But he insists also that the law lacks legitimacy because every avenue of legal opposition to it has been sealed off. In a world of ideal political institutions a derivative view of the place of opposition in democratic politics might be sustainable. But in the actual world, where social orders come to be what they are in morally arbitrary ways, and where all procedures of government turn out on close inspection to be flawed, opposition must enjoy a more independent

---

7 Barrington Moore, Jr., *Liberal Prospects under Soviet Socialism: A Comparative Historical Perspective* (New York: The Averell Harriman Institute, 1989), 25.
8 Nelson Mandela, "Address to Court before Sentencing," in *Ideologies of Liberation in Black Africa 1856–1970*, ed. J. Ayo Langley (London: Rex Collins, 1979), 665. On the Chartists, see Dorothy Thompson, *The Chartists* (London: Temple Smith, 1984). Generally see Elie Halevy, *The Growth of Philosophic Radicalism* (New York: Kelley, 1972).
9 Langley, *Ideologies of Liberation*, 664.

and exalted status in a persuasive account of just democratic politics. Or so I will argue; but first let us attend to the governance side of the equation.

COLLECTIVE SELF-GOVERNMENT

If democracy is understood to require that the people be sovereign over their collective goals, it exhibits considerable overlap with liberalism as a political ideology. Both are rooted in antivanguardist conceptions of the good; their proponents resist the idea that values should be imposed on people against their wishes in the name of some greater social good. The reasons for affirming this antivanguardist stance vary: they can range from commitments to variants of philosophical skepticism, pragmatism, and antifoundationalism, to beliefs in the psychological value of critical reflection and contested authority, to the conviction that a degree of pluralism about values is sociologically or politically desirable. Liberals and democrats do not divide predictably over these foundational matters, but for most of both some combination of them issues in a principled resistance to moral vanguardism.[10]

Liberals and democrats do divide predictably, however, over the institutional implications they draw from their moral antivanguardism. Liberals, who typically regard individual freedom as the greatest good, characteristically focus on devices to protect the individual from the realm of collective action. Democrats, by contrast, try to structure collective action appropriately to embody the preferences of the governed. Liberals characteristically resist this logic on the grounds that no procedure can fairly embody the preferences of all the governed. For liberals, democratic decision rules all too readily become devices by which phantom majorities—sometimes even manipulative minorities—tyrannize over individuals.[11]

Although there is merit to the liberal argument, it rests on flawed assumptions about the nature of politics and about the limits of collective action. Concerning the first, the characteristic liberal mistake is to focus on the forms of tyranny performed by and through government as the only—certainly the principal—kind of tyranny that should worry political theorists. Liberal commitments to negative freedom, conventional constructions of public/private dichotomies,

---

10 Nor do all liberals agree with one another, any more than all democrats do, over which of these, combinations of these, or combinations of these and other, reasons they invoke for adhering to antivanguardist conceptions of the good.
11 For one conventional statement of this view, see William Riker, *Liberalism against Populism* (Prospect Heights, IL: Waveland, 1982). It might be objected that the depiction of liberalism in the text is something of a caricature in that it deals with academic rather than popular conceptions, and only a subset of academic conceptions of liberalism at that. This is conceded, though I would contend that it is an expansive subset, ranging at least from the fears of majority tyranny expressed through the state that can be found in Mill's *On Liberty* (1859; reprint, Indianapolis, IN: Hackett, 1978) and de Tocqueville's *Democracy in America* (1832; reprint, Garden City, NY: Doubleday, 1969), through the libertarian liberalisms of Riker, Nozick, and Buchanan and Tullock discussed in the text, and the nonlibertarianism antistatism embraced by Judith N. Shklar, *Ordinary Vices* (Cambridge, MA: Harvard University Press, 1984).

and arguments for limited government are all shaped by this governmentalist view of politics. Governmental power is one potential site of domination, but there are many others that permeate the different domains of "private" life. Government can be an instrument for mitigating domination as well as a source of its generation. As a result, the choices and tradeoffs that can minimize domination throughout society will likely defy such simplifying formulae as "the government that governs least governs best."

The liberal view is flawed also because its proponents tend to think that whether or not our lives should be governed by collective institutions is an intelligible question about politics. Hence Robert Nozick's remark that the fundamental question of political theory "is whether there should be any state at all."[12] This view is misleading because the institutions of private property, contract, and public monopoly of coercive force that its proponents characteristically favor were created and are sustained by the state, partly financed by implicit taxes on those who would prefer an alternative system. In the modern world, Nozick's assertion makes as much sense as would a claim that the fundamental question of astronomy is whether or not there ought to be planets. A characteristic liberal sleight of hand involves trying to naturalize or otherwise obscure liberal institutional arrangements in order to disguise this reality. Such subterfuges have received more attention than they deserve in the recent history of political theory; they cannot any longer detain us.[13]

This is not to say that the liberal fear of majority rule is groundless. It is to say that we need a different response to it than the conventional liberal one. We can begin to develop this by noting, first, that there is no reason to think that there is one best rule of collective decision. Different rules will be appropriate in different domains of social life, depending on the nature of the domain in question, the importance of the decision to participants, the potential costs of decisions to third parties, and related contingent factors. Such a plural attitude about decision rules flows naturally out of the view that civil society is made up of domains of social action that differ qualitatively from one another.[14]

Few liberals would deny this last claim, but they usually regard unanimity rule as the best default option, the decision rule most likely to protect individuals against violations of their rights. This is at least partly why liberals so often find markets attractive. Markets embody unanimity rule in that every transaction requires the consent of both parties. On the liberal view, classically advocated in *The Calculus of Consent*, it is always *departures* from unanimity that stand

---

12 Robert Nozick, *Anarchy, State, and Utopia* (New York: Basic Books, 1974), 4.
13 For extensive discussion of this question, see my *The Evolution of Rights in Liberal Theory* (New York: Cambridge University Press, 1986), chaps. 4–6, and "Three Fallacies Concerning Majorities, Minorities, and Democratic Politics," in *Nomos XXXII: Majorities and Minorities*, ed. John Chapman and Alan Wertheimer (New York: New York University Press, 1990), 79–125.
14 See Michael Walzer, *Spheres of Justice* (New York: Basic Books, 1983), 3–20, and Alasdair MacIntyre, *After Virtue*, 2d ed. (Notre Dame, IN: University of Notre Dame Press, 1984), 181–203.

in presumptive need of justification, whether on efficiency or other grounds. James Buchanan and Gordon Tullock argue in that work that, under conditions of a hypothetical social contract, rational individuals concerned to safeguard their interests would insist on a hierarchy of decision rules, starting with unanimity rule for constitutional matters. Next come "those possible collective or public decisions which modify or restrict the structure of individual human or property rights after these have once been defined and generally accepted by the community." Foreseeing that collective action may "impose very severe costs on him," the individual will tend "to place a high value on the attainment of his consent, and he may be quite willing to undergo substantial decision-making costs in order to insure that he will, in fact, be reasonably protected against confiscation." He will thus require a decision rule approaching unanimity. Last is the class of collective actions characteristically undertaken by governments. For these "the individual will recognize that private organization will impose some interdependence costs on him, perhaps in significant amount, and he will, by hypothesis, have supported a shift of such activities to the public sector." Examples include provision of public education, enforcement of building and fire codes, and maintenance of adequate police forces. For such "general legislation" an individual at the constitutional stage will support less inclusive decision rules, though not necessarily simple majority rule, and indeed, within this class, different majorities might be agreed on as optimal for different purposes. "The number of categories, and the number of decisionmaking rules chosen, will depend on the situation which the individual expects to prevail and the 'returns to scale' expected to result from using the same rule over many activities."[15]

This story is intuitively plausible only if we take the contractualist metaphor on which it rests seriously, assuming a prepolitical status quo where there is no collective action and then a series of consensual moves that lead to the creation of what we know of as political society. But, as Brian Barry, Douglas Rae, and others have pointed out, once this assumption is jettisoned there is no particular reason to regard unanimity rule as the most appropriate default decision rule.[16] In the real world of ongoing politics, if I assume that I am as likely to oppose a given policy as to support it regardless of whether it is the status quo, then majority rule or something close to it is the logical rule to prefer. Once we move from majority toward unanimity rule, we begin to privilege the status quo. This will rightly seem arbitrary in a world that has not evolved cooperatively from

---

15 James Buchanan and Gordon Tullock, *The Calculus of Consent: Logical Foundations of Constitutional Democracy* (Ann Arbor, MI: Ann Arbor Paperbacks, 1962), 77,73–6.
16 Brian Barry, *Political Argument* 2d ed., (1965; reprint, Herefordshire: Harvester Wheat-sheaf, 1990); Douglas W. Rae, "Decision-Rules and Individual Values in Constitutional Choice," *American Political Science Review* 63, no. 1 (1969): 40–56, 51; Michael Taylor, "Proof of a Theorem on Majority Rule," *Behavioral Science* 14 (May 1969): 228–31. When the number of voters is odd, the optimal decision rule is majority rule, n over two, plus one-half; when n is even, the optimal decision rule is either majority rule (n over two plus one), or majority rule minus one (simply n over two). Generally, see Dennis C. Mueller, *Public Choice II* (New York: Cambridge University Press, 1989), 96–111.

a precollective condition. In short, other things being equal tyranny of the majority is something that people should rationally fear, but not as much as they should fear tyranny of the minority.[17]

The preceding discussion reinforces the suggestion that there is no single best decision rule for democratic governance. In domains of social life where relations really do tend to approximate the contractualist story—in that they are both created *ex nihilo* by the participants and are basically cooperative in character—a presumptive commitment to unanimity rule is defensible. One might think of marriage in contemporary America as a paradigm case. It is created consensually, usually with the expectation that in important matters day-to-day governance will also be consensual. (Indeed, with the advent of no-fault divorce since the 1970s, we see an unusually strong form of the unanimity requirement at work. In most American states either spouse can insist—subject to a brief waiting period—on a divorce unilaterally: the marriage continues only so long as both parties agree. Far from privileging the status quo, this variant of unanimity rule makes it perpetually vulnerable, since the rule is not defined by reference to the status quo but by in effect recreating the conditions antecedent to it at the wish of either party.)[18]

Many social relationships do not approximate the contractualist ideal; they are not created *ex nihilo* in the sense that contemporary American marriages usually are, and they are to a high degree structured by forces other than the wills of the participants. Even childless marriages involve the generation of reliances and externalities that can undermine their exclusively consensual character. These are questions of degree, however. Social relations are often not contractualist to anything like the extent that marriage is, even when such reliances are taken into account; most obviously, think of parent-child relations. Constitutional political arrangements are often pointed to as presumptively contractualist because of their foundational character and their place in the social contract tradition. Such arrangements might once have been consented to by the relevant parties, although even in the American founding a narrowly circumscribed class agreed in fact—and then not unanimously. Generations later, whatever contractualist element these arrangements once exhibited has receded into the mists of time. In such circumstances (and no doubt there are others) there is no evident reason to regard unanimity rule as best on the grounds that it embodies the consent of the governed.

---

17   Even if we accept the contractualist metaphor, the logic of Buchanan's and Tullock's defense of unanimity rule can be shown to break down once time and externalities are taken into account. See Douglas W. Rae, "The Limits of Consensual Decision," *American Political Science Review* 69 (1975): 1270–94.

18   It might appear that no-fault divorce destroys the marriage contract qua contract entirely, since it is terminable at the will of either party. But such a conclusion (i) ignores the fact that conventional unanimity rule operates in marriages unless and until they reach the point of dissolution, and (ii) conflates the *grounds* for divorce with the *terms* of divorce (and in particular the distribution of costs that courts will impose on divorcing parties). In fact many countries, and some American states, that embrace some form of no-fault divorce do not go all the way with it. Instead they insist that the court find that "irretrievable breakdown" has occurred, for which purpose the judge may take various factors including the wishes of both parties into account. See Mary Ann Glendon, *Abortion and Divorce in Western Law* (Cambridge, MA: Harvard University Press, 1987), 64–81.

Nor are there good reasons to think that some alternative decision rule should appropriately govern all relations where a contractualist element is either missing or overdetermined by other factors. As the examples just mentioned indicate, this is a heterogeneous class. In some domains, the sort Rae evidently has in mind, majority rule is prima facie the best decision rule. These include relations typically characterized by arms-length transactions, where substantial aspects of the collective action in question are competitive rather than cooperative, and where there are no obvious reasons to countenance paternalistic decision making. They are also often circumstances in which people are either born into structural relations that cannot easily be escaped, or, if there is a contractualist element to their participation, it is accompanied by a good deal of what Marxists like to think of as "structural coercion." Whatever the surface appearances, the relations in question are not substantially voluntary. Arguments for workplace democracy in which majority rule plays a substantial role generally appeal to some combination of these characteristics in justifying their appeal; Rae's logic supplies us with reasons for accepting them.[19]

Not every noncontractualist or minimally contractualist form of association should be governed by majority rule, however. Both Buchanan and Tullock's and Rae's reasoning take it for granted that, ceteris paribus, decision-making costs should be minimized, for which they have sometimes been criticized by participatory democrats.[20] Rather than follow the participatory democrat's reasoning (which creates difficulties of its own),[21] the argument here is that participation must itself be thought about in a context-sensitive way. In some circumstances participation is no more than a cost to be minimized, subject to achieving or preventing a particular outcome. Anyone who has sat through enough faculty meetings will know what at least one of those circumstances is. In other situations, institutions may reasonably be structured to maximize participation. Juries are an obvious example. Unanimity is generally required just because it forces discussion and joint deliberation, which, in turn, are believed most likely to lead to discovery of the truth in trial courts, and that is the point of the exercise. Parent-child relations are also noncontractualist relations (since the child does not ask to be born, let alone to be born to the parent in question) that do not lend themselves to governance by majority rule, at least not on many questions. In these relations more flexibility is necessary in delineating the appropriate scope for participation by different parties, because they include the total dependence of young children on their parents, relations among more-or-less equal adults, and relations between adults and their aging parents. And since human beings are developmental creatures for whom decision making has to be learned over time, there has to be space for regimes of domestic governance to adapt to peoples' changing capacities and dependencies. To be appropriate, the decision rules governing domestic relations must be able to respond to this complex reality.

---

19 See Robert Dahl, *A Preface to Economic Democracy* (Berkeley: University of California Press, 1985), 111–35.
20 See Elaine Spitz, *Majority Rule* (Chatham, NJ: Chatham House, 1984), 135–215.
21 See my "Three Ways to Be a Democrat," 142–4.

Taking note of such complexities lends credence to the suggestion that when they can be discovered and made to work, local solutions to local problems are to be preferred. The kinds of knowledge that are pertinent to democratizing an activity will often be disproportionately available to insiders because of their hands-on experience and their participants' understanding of the activity in question. In this respect the argument of democratic justice is compatible with the aspirations of many who think of themselves as communitarians. Notice, however, that there will be circumstances in which no local decision rule can be made to work effectively from the standpoint of democratic self-government, the most obvious being when the obstacles to exit are insuperable for some yet easily overcome for others. The American history of white flight from inner-city school districts since the 1960s stands as eloquent testimony to that fact. Whether the substantially white middle-class population opts out of the public school system, moves out of the inner city (or both, to avoid both using and paying for the inner-city schools), its ability to leave undermines democracy in educational provision. Local majority rule promotes white flight, but local unanimity rule gives disaffected individuals veto power that enables them to avoid contributing to the provision of public education. In this type of circumstance, the presence of collective action problems suggests that constraints other than choosing one local decision rule over another should come into play.

The decision rules appropriate to different walks of life vary, then, with the activity in question and the purposes around which it is organized. Yet to say this is to solve one problem by raising another, because these activities and purposes are never fixed and there is usually, perhaps endemically, disagreement about them.[22] How can we say that the nature of the activity in question makes one decision rule more appropriate than another, having conceded that those purposes and activities are inevitably in contention? Whereas most liberals would say that all social relations should be redesigned to approximate the contractualist ideal as much as possible (regardless of how they are currently organized), the subordinate character of the democratic commitment in the argument for democratic justice precludes my defending an analogous claim. Instead it recommends a more pragmatic approach that is antivanguardist in method as well as substance, because we should neither accept things as they have evolved nor aspire to redesign them, tabula rasa. Rather, the goal should be to take social relations as we find them and discover ways to democratize them as we reproduce them. Democratic justice thus has a Burkean dimension, but this is tempered by the aspiration to create a more democratic world over time. Prevailing ways of doing things reasonably make a partial claim on our allegiance, but this claim is conditional and always subject to revision in democratic ways; the inertial legitimacy of existing modes of governance can never achieve a status greater than that of a rebuttable presumption. The creative

---

22 This is discussed at length in my *Political Criticism* (Berkeley: University of California Press, 1990), 252–61.

challenge is to devise methods of governance that both condition existing ways of doing things democratically and open the way to their reévaluation over time.

Although there is no best decision rule for the governance of different domains of civil society, a general constraint for thinking about decision rules follows from what has been said so far: everyone affected by the operation of a particular domain of civil society should be presumed to have a say in its governance. This follows from the root democratic idea that the people appropriately rule over themselves. To require that everyone affected should have a say is not to require that this presumption be conclusive or that every say should necessarily be of equal weight. There are often—but not always— good reasons for granting outsiders to a domain (who may be subject to its external effects) less of a say than insiders concerning its governance, and even within a domain there may be compelling reasons to distribute governing authority unequally, and perhaps even to disenfranchise some participants in some circumstances. What these circumstances are cannot be specified in general, but we can say that we begin with a presumption of universal inclusion.

We can also say that proposals to undermine universal inclusion reasonably prompt suspicion, whatever their source. In the limiting case, if someone sells herself into slavery, her agreement should be regarded as void *ab initio*. Most incursions on inclusion are considerably less radical than selling oneself into slavery is. As a consequence, evaluating policies and practices that limit the nature and extent of the governed's participation in decisions that affect them is more difficult (and controversial) from the standpoint of democratic justice than is the case with slavery. In the ongoing world of everyday politics there will often be circumstances in which inclusion is reasonably traded off against other imperatives. But the general argument counsels suspicion of these tradeoffs; the burden of persuasion lies with those who advocate them.

Although the requirements of the principle of universal inclusion will vary with circumstances, it is possible to defend at least one constraint on it in general terms that goes beyond the limiting case of slavery: Participation by one individual or group in ways that render the participation of other legitimate participants meaningless is unacceptable. For instance, it is estimated that in the United States the health care and medical insurance industries spent upward of $50 million in 1993–4 on advertising and lobbying to kill the Clinton Administration's proposed health care reform legislation, and that they would have spent whatever was necessary to achieve this result.[23] Granting, *arguendo*, this account of the facts, we can say that an understanding of participation that permits such a result goes too far. It gives one set of interests affected by the proposal the power to obliterate the participation of others, and to determine the result more or less unilaterally.

---

23 The $50 million figure is reported by Tim Rinne, "The Rise and Fall of Single-Payer Health Care in Nebraska," *Action for Universal Health Care* 3, no. 10 (May 1995): 4–5. See also Tom Hamburger and Ted Marmor, "Dead on Arrival: Why Washington's Power Elites Won't Consider Single Payer Health Reform," *The Washington Monthly* (September 1993): 27–32.

To be sure, this does not tell us which types of limitations on lobbying and political speech are appropriate, but it sets an outer constraint on the debate.

The account of collective self-government defended here is causally based. The right to participate comes from one's having an interest that can be expected to be affected by the particular collective action in question. In this respect the argument for democratic justice differs from liberal and communitarian views, both of which tend to regard membership of the relevant community as a trump (liberals by assumption, communitarians by express argument).[24] Once the contractualist way of thinking has been dethroned, it is difficult to see any principled basis for regarding membership as primary. On the view advanced here, the structure of decision rules should follow the contours of power relations, not those of political memberships. Adopting the causally based view has implications for a host of issues relating to intergenerational justice and the handling of externalities. In a world in which international military and environmental questions increasingly dominate political agendas, whether or not one adopts it can be expected to be consequential over an expanding portion of the political landscape.

It will be objected that serious difficulties arise in determining who is affected by a particular decision and who is to determine whose claims about being affected should be accepted. To provide a full defense of the causally based view here would take us too far afield, but two points should be noted. First, although who is affected by a decision is bound to be controversial, this fact scarcely distinguishes causally based arguments from membership-based arguments about social justice. Who is to decide, and by what authority, who is to be a member is as fraught with conceptual and ideological baggage as who is to decide, and by what authority, who is causally affected by a particular collective decision. These difficulties should not therefore count as decisive against the causally based view if the membership-based view is seen as the alternative. Second, there is considerable experience with causally based arguments in tort law. Although tort actions are often concerned with the causal effects of individual rather than collective decisions, in dealing with them courts have developed mechanisms for determining whose claims should be heard, for sorting genuine claims from frivolous ones, and for distinguishing weaker from stronger claims to have been adversely affected by an action and shaping remedies accordingly. This is not an argument for turning politics into tort law; the point of the comparison is rather to illustrate that in other areas of social life institutional mechanisms have been developed to assess and manage conflicting claims of being causally affected by actions. They may be imperfect mechanisms, but

---

24 Liberals take the basic unit of the nation state for granted, treating it as a kind of Lockean voluntary association writ large, as has often been pointed out in criticism of Rawls. See John Rawls, *A Theory of Justice* (Cambridge, MA: Harvard University Press, 1971), 371–82, and his "The Law of Peoples," *Critical Inquiry* 20 (Autumn 1993): 36–68. No doubt this is often a consequence of the liberal proclivity for thinking in contractualist terms. For an illustration of the communitarian view of membership as the basic trumping good, see Walzer, *Spheres of Justice*, 29, 31–63.

they should be evaluated by reference to the other imperfect mechanisms of collective decision making that actually prevail in the world, not by comparison with an ideal that prevails nowhere.[25]

INSTITUTIONALIZING OPPOSITION

Barrington Moore contends that "the existence of a legitimate and, to some extent effective, opposition" is the defining criterion of democracy. One need not go all the way with him to be persuaded that institutions fostering "loyal" opposition are essential to democratic life.[26] This is true for several related reasons. First, opposition institutions perform the functional role of providing sites for potential alternative leaderships to organize themselves, making possible periodic turnovers of power that are necessary—though not sufficient—for democratic governance. Second, opposition institutions help legitimate democracy by attracting social dissent toward antigovernment forces within the regime, rather than directing it at the regime's foundations. Anger and disaffection can thus be directed at particular power holders, without endangering the democratic order's legitimacy. Third, opposition institutions serve the public interest by ensuring that there are groups and individuals who have incentives to ask awkward questions, shine light in dark corners, and expose abuses of power. The importance of these considerations should not be minimized, but there is a more basic reason why the possibility of effective opposition is an essential requirement of democratic justice. Unless people can challenge prevailing norms and rules with the realistic hope of altering them, the requirement that the inherited past not bind us unalterably would be empty. The Burkean dimension of democratic justice could not be tempered in the ways that democratic justice requires.

Below I argue that the imperative to make effective opposition possible leads to three conditioning constraints on the exercise of power. Procedurally, it suggests that rules of governance should be deemed unacceptable if they render revision of the status quo impossible. Mechanisms should always exist, therefore, through which opposition can be articulated. Procedural guarantees need to be backed up by permissive freedoms of speech, petition, and association if they are to be effective, but even then they may often be insufficient to ensure meaningful opposition. Some have suggested that "substantive" democracy is the appropriate remedy for this malady,

---

25 My contention that the causally based view is more defensible than the going alternatives is compatible with a number of recent arguments whose purpose is to decenter membership-based sovereignty as the decisive determinant of participation, and to replace it with systems of overlapping jurisdiction in which different groups of persons are seen as sovereign over different classes of decisions. See Thomas Pogge, "Cosmopolitanism and Sovereignty," *Ethics* 103 (October 1992): 48–75; Alexander Wendt, "Collective Identity-Formation and the International State," *American Political Science Review* 88, no. 2 (June 1994): 384–96; and William Antholis, "Liberal Democratic Theory and the Transformation of Sovereignty" (Ph.D. diss., Yale University, 1993).

26 Barrington Moore, Jr., *Liberal Prospects*, 8. See also Archibald S. Foord, *His Majesty's Opposition 1714–1830* (Oxford: Oxford University Press, 1964).

and although I resist this conclusion, I do defend a quasi-substantive constraint on the exercise of power: that hierarchies should generally be presumed suspect because of their propensity to atrophy into systems of domination. The presumption against hierarchy should be rebutted in many circumstances, some of which I explore via a series of queries that democratic justice bids direct at hierarchical arrangements. But the burden of justification appropriately falls on defenders of particular hierarchies.

Since there are no perfect decision rules, the products of even the best democratic procedures will leave some justifiably aggrieved. Libertarian writers draw from this the implication that it is better to have as little collective action as possible, but in a world of ubiquitous power relations, I argued earlier, that option is neither satisfying nor plausible. To point this out is not to deny that democratic decision rules can lead to the imposition of outcomes on one group by another, or that the justification for those impositions classical democratic theorists believed available is not.[27] Rather, it leads to the suggestion that procedures for expressing opposition should be thought valuable no matter what the prevailing mechanisms of collective decision. Recognizing that life goes on and decisions have to be made, we should seek the most appropriate rules of democratic governance for every circumstance. But people should nonetheless remain free to oppose what has been decided, and try to change it.

To require that meaningful opposition be tolerated is frequently to require more than dominant groups want to accept, since it can weaken their control of collective values and purposes. Accordingly, they often seek to oppose opposition or render it ineffective. Part of the challenge of democratic justice is to institutionalize ways to stop them, and it seems safe to assume that, on their own, procedural guarantees of the freedom to oppose will not secure this goal. Democratic theorists who value effective opposition, such as Huntington, have long recognized that unless procedural guarantees are backed up by permissive civil and political freedoms of speech, press, assembly, and organization, they are all too easily rendered meaningless.[28] The history of sham democracies during the communist era illustrates what can happen when permissive freedoms are not honored. Democrats would be unwise ever to think them dispensable.

Although permissive freedoms are often essential to securing the space for opposition and fostering it, it would be a mistake to conclude that in general they will be sufficient. To see why this is so, notice that permissive freedoms can actually undermine the possibility of challenging the status

---

27 Even before the advent of the modem literature on public choice, Schumpeter had exposed the logical flaws in the Rousseauist idea of a general will, concluding that "though a common will or public opinion of some sort may still be said to emerge from the infinitely complex jumble of individual and group-wise situation, volitions, influences, actions and reactions of the 'democratic process,' the result lacks not only rational unity but also rational sanction." Joseph Schumpeter, *Capitalism, Socialism and Democracy* (New York: Harper and Row, 1942), 253.

28 Huntington regards at least two turnovers of power following elections as necessary for a country's being democratic. See *The Third Wave*, 6–7. See also Robert Dahl, *Polyarchy: Participation and Opposition* (New Haven, CT: Yale University Press, 1971).

quo, as my earlier discussion of the proposed Clinton health care reform indicated. Inequalities in control over the resources needed to transform permissive freedoms into the service of effective opposition can mean that strategically powerful groups, when committed to prevailing arrangements, may be able to block all attempts to alter them. Thus, although permissive freedoms are reasonably deemed valuable for their propensity to permit and even foster opposition, they are not a panacea. When those committed to the status quo have unmatched access to information, wealth, and organizational resources, they may actually be able to use permissive freedoms to cement their advantages in place.

Awareness of the combined impact of imperfect decision rules and differential control over political resources has led some commentators to defend "substantive" conceptions of democracy over "procedural" ones, usually by appeal to some variant of Justice Stone's celebrated fourth footnote in *United States v. Carotene Products Co.* Noting that well-functioning democratic processes might lead to the domination of "discrete and insular minorities," Stone countenanced the possibility that their operation might reasonably be limited when this occurs. Stone dealt with a circumscribed class of cases. But his point is a general one, and others have employed his reasoning more expansively.[29] For instance, John Hart Ely defended much of the judicial activism of the Warren Court by reference to *Carolene Products* reasoning.[30] Likewise, Charles Beitz has pressed the same considerations into an argument that the quantitative fairness of equal voting power will never ensure substantively democratic outcomes.[31] In Beitz's view, a truly democratic system of "qualitative fairness" requires a prior system of "just legislation," since mere equal voting power can never be relied upon to produce fair outcomes.[32]

Substantively democratic views merely have to be stated for the difficulty with them to be plain: How can Ely know what democratic processes ought to have achieved had they not been corrupted

---

29 Stone focused his attention on "statutes directed at particular religious ... or racial minorities" and circumstances that tend "seriously to curtail the operation of those political processes ordinarily to be relied upon to protect minorities," *United States v. Carolene Products Co.*, 304 U.S. 144 (1938), 152 n. 4.

30 John Hart Ely, *Democracy and Distrust* (Cambridge, MA: Harvard University Press, 1980). Ely described his argument as purely procedural, designed to repair defects of democratic process. But as critics have pointed out and the discussion below makes clear, it is obviously a substantive argument. See R. Smith, *Liberalism and American Constitutional Law* (Cambridge, MA: Harvard University Press, 1985), 89–91,170–4.

31 Charles Beitz, "Equal Opportunity in Political Representation," in *Equal Opportunity*, ed. Norman E. Bowie (Boulder, CO: Westview, 1988), 155–74. It should not be thought that *Carolene Products* logic is the exclusive preserve of the political left. For instance, Riker and Weingast employ it to criticize taxation of property: "What protection is there against members of today's majority from providing private, redistributive benefits to themselves under the guise of public purposes and at the expense of some minority of owners and the efficiency of production? Why is the abridgement of a minority's economic rights less troubling than an abridgement of the same minority's political rights?" William H. Riker and Barry R. Weingast, "Constitutional Regulation of Legislative Choice: The Political Consequences of Judicial Deference to Legislatures," The Hoover Institution, Stanford University, *Working Paper Series* (December 1986), 6.

32 Beitz, "Equal Opportunity," 168.

by the *Carolene* problem? Whence the theory of just legislation against which Beitz will evaluate the results of voting procedures? Writers like Ely and Beitz have little to say to those who are unpersuaded by their respective conceptions of "equal concern and respect" and "qualitative fairness." If, as I maintain, there is no criterion for justice that is anterior to what democracy generates, this should not be surprising. To say this is not, however, to respond to the difficulty that motivates *Carolene*-type reasoning: There are no perfect decision rules and those who are better placed to translate permissive freedoms into political power should be expected, ceteris paribus, to get their way. The problem is real but the proffered solutions overreach, suggesting the desirability of finding a middle ground. "More than process, less than substance" might be an appropriate slogan.

My suggestion is that we stake out the middle ground with the proposition that hierarchies should be presumed suspect. The reason is that although hierarchies can exist for many legitimate purposes, by definition they contain both power inequalities and truncated opportunities for opposition. Power, as Lord Acton said, tends to corrupt. Even, and perhaps especially, when they acquire it legitimately, power-holders all too easily convince themselves that their authority should expand in space and time, that critics are ignorant or irresponsible, and that subordinates lack the requisite ability to ascend from inferior roles. The allure of power can thus divert power-holders within hierarchies from their legitimate goals, leading to the reduction of hierarchies to their power dimensions. The comparatively limited scope for opposition within hierarchies makes it difficult to block or check their atrophy into systems of domination; indeed as atrophy advances the possibilities for opposition are likely to be increasingly constrained. It is for this reason that democrats should keep a skeptical eye on all hierarchical arrangements, placing the burden of justification on their defenders. Power need not be abused but it often is, and it is wise for democrats to guard against that possibility.

The preceding observations do not imply that all hierarchies should be eliminated, even if this could be achieved.[33] Rather, they suggest that there are good grounds for prima facie suspicion of them, even when they result from democratic collective decisions. Too often, avoidable hierarchies masquerade as unavoidable ones, involuntary subordination is shrouded in the language of agreement, unnecessary hierarchies are held to be essential to the pursuit of common goals, and fixed hierarchies are cloaked in myths about their fluidity. Democratic justice suggests mistrust of prevailing hierarchies; it invites us to look for institutional and other structuring devices to limit them and to mitigate their unnecessary and corrosive effects. Such devices may be thought of as contributing to the evolving frameworks of democratic constraints within which people should be free to negotiate and renegotiate the terms of their cooperation and conflict.

---

33   The quixotic political commitments that follow from the injunction to overthrow all hierarchy everywhere have been explored in Roberto Unger's multivolume *Politics* (New York: Cambridge University Press, 1987). For criticism of his argument, see my "Constructing Politics," *Political Theory* 17 (August 1989): 475–82.

To say that hierarchies are suspect is not to say anything about what is to count as sufficient to rebut the presumption. Nor is it to say anything about what kinds of constraints on hierarchies should be employed in different circumstances, or about how these constraints should be enforced. By itself, the general argument cannot answer these questions. But it does generate a series of appropriate queries about hierarchies; ways of probing them in the name of democratic justice.

The first concerns the degree to which a given hierarchy is inevitable. Consider the differences between adult domestic relations and parent-child relations. Both have taken a multiplicity of forms, even in the recent history of the West, yet almost all of these have been explicitly hierarchical in character. It is evident, however, that parent-child relations are inevitably hierarchical in ways that adult domestic relations are not. If a relationship is not inevitably hierarchical, the first question that arises is why should it be hierarchical at all? There may be justifiable reasons for a particular inessential hierarchy (that it is comparatively efficient, that it has been chosen, that the relevant people like it, or some other), but from the standpoint of democratic justice the presumption is against hierarchy and the proponent of such reasons should adopt the burden of persuasion.

When relations are inevitably hierarchical a different class of considerations becomes relevant. We begin by asking: is it necessary that the relations in question be maintained at all? Parent-child relations of some kind must exist, but not all inevitably hierarchical relations are of this sort. To consider a limiting case once again, history has shown that the institution of slavery need not exist. If an inescapably hierarchical relationship is unnecessary, it immediately becomes suspect—a kind of surplus hierarchy—from the standpoint of democratic justice. Slavery thus fares badly from this standpoint quite apart from its incompatibility with the presumption of universal inclusion.

A second class of appropriate inquiries about hierarchies concerns their pertinence to the activity at hand: are the hierarchical relations that exist appropriately hierarchical? Parent-child relations, for example, may be more hierarchical than they need to be in many instances and they may include unnecessary kinds of hierarchical authority. They may also be maintained for a variety of reasons, ranging from the convenience of parents to desires to dominate, that have nothing to do with the interests of their charges. Of alterable hierarchies we should thus always inquire: in whose interests are they sustained? Those who would sustain a hierarchy of a particular kind, or sustain it for longer than necessary, take on the burden of establishing that this operates in the interests of those who are subjected to the relevant hierarchy. For this reason one would be unmoved by the argument advanced by Amish parents in the *Wisconsin v. Yoder* litigation, namely, that they should be free not to send their teenage children to school because experience had taught them that this induced in the teenagers the desire to leave the Amish community, which interfered with their (i.e., the parents') rights of free religious exercise.[34]

---

34 *Wisconsin v. Yoder*, 406 U.S. 205 (1972). From the standpoint of democratic justice, *Yoder* was thus wrongly decided, although it would have been a more difficult case had the parents pressed their best understandings of their children's interests rather than their own.

Democratic justice also bids us to attend to the degree to which hierarchies are ossified or fluid. We should distinguish self-liquidating hierarchies, as when children become adults or students graduate, from non-self-liquidating hierarchies such as caste systems and hierarchies constituted by hereditary transmissions of wealth and power. We should also distinguish hierarchical orders in which anyone can in principle ascend to the top from those where that is not so. No woman can aspire to become Pope, a fact that makes the Catholic religion less attractive than some others from the standpoint of democratic justice on this score. In general the argument tells us to prefer fluid hierarchies over ossified ones, other things being equal. Fluid hierarchies may not create permanently subordinated classes whereas ossified hierarchies will. Of course other things seldom are equal; nonetheless the requirement is a useful starting point. It tells us what the presumption is and by whom the burden of persuasion should be carried.

Similarly, asymmetrical hierarchies are questionable whereas symmetrical ones are not necessarily so. Polygamous marriages are generally asymmetrical, for example, and as such suspect from the standpoint of democratic justice: a husband can have many wives but a wife cannot have many husbands.[35] If these polygamous regimes were symmetrical, or had their members practiced "complex marriage" as did the nineteenth-century Oneida perfectionist community (in which any number of men could marry any number of women), they would not be questionable by reference to this aspect of the argument for democratic justice. Again, there may be other reasons rooted in democratic justice for objecting to such arrangements, but their symmetry would count in their favor.[36]

Closely related to questions about the relative fluidity and symmetry of hierarchies are questions about the degree to which they are imposed. Did the people who are subjected to them elect to be thus subjected? What were their other realistic options at the time? Whether or not they chose to enter, what degree of freedom to exit now exists? Generally nonimposed

---

35 This is not to say that all polygamous regimes fare equally poorly from the standpoint of democratic justice. Polygamous regimes from which there is no realistic chance of escape (as when they are enshrined in a country's legal system as the only available form of marriage) fare worse than polygamous regimes that are tolerated but not obligatory, and from which escape is legally possible and not prohibitively expensive. Even in these circumstances there is always the possibility that voluntary adherents have been brainwashed, of course, and arguments to this effect cannot be dismissed out of hand. But their proponents will have to come to grips with the eloquently reasoned denials of this that have been put forward by some Mormon women. It has been argued, for instance, that polygamous marriage makes it possible for women to have both a career and a family so that polygamy "is good for feminism." See Elizabeth Joseph, "My Husband's Nine Wives," *New York Times*, April 9, 1991, A22.

36 The Oneida Perfectionists, founded in 1848 in Oneida, New York, by John Henry Noyes, rejected all forms of private property, and extended their belief in community property to community property in persons. Like the Mormon polygamists, they were persecuted by the state, eventually abandoning their commitment to complex marriage in 1879. See Carol Weis- brod, "On the Breakup of Oneida," *Connecticut Law Review* 14 (Summer 1982): 717–32. In fact, the community was run in an authoritarian manner by Noyes, who decided unilaterally who could marry, suggesting that the community would have been suspect on a number of grounds from the standpoint of democratic justice. See Spenser Klaw, *Without Sin* (New York: Allen Lane, 1993).

hierarchies fare better than imposed ones, and less imposed hierarchies fare better than more imposed ones. If someone elected to participate at the bottom of a hierarchical relationship when she had alternative nonhierarchical (or less hierarchical) options in front of her, the fact of her choice confers some presumptive legitimacy on the state of affairs. Analogously, if someone remains in a hierarchical order when we are fairly confident that she has the resources to leave, we have less reason to be troubled from the standpoint of democratic justice than when this is not the case.

Finally, the general argument for democratic justice directs us to attend to the relative insularity of hierarchies. To what extent do they consist of self-contained groups of people minding their own business who want to be left alone by outsiders? Withdrawing sects like the Old Order Amish, or migrating groups like the Mormons who went to Utah in the nineteenth century to escape persecution in the east, have at least prima facie valid claims that they should be able to set the terms of their association unimpeded. Such groups do not proselytize, or seek to shape the world outside their communities (as religious fundamentalists, e.g., often do). Hierarchical and undemocratic as these groups might be in their internal organization, they are of little consequence to the outside world. By contrast, a hierarchical established church whose influence on outsiders could not be escaped without substantial cost would not enjoy the same prima facie claim to be left alone. Relatively insular groups may be objectionable from the standpoint of democratic justice on some of the other grounds just discussed, but the fact of their insularity diminishes any externality-based claim by outsiders to restructure or abolish them.

SOME DIFFICULTIES CONSIDERED

The preceding elaboration of the two central dimensions of democratic justice is a first installment; as such it raises many questions that it fails to answer. In the space that remains I will say something about what seems to me to be the most important of these, having to do with the complex character of democratic justice, tensions between it and other goods, and the appropriate role for the state that is implied by the general argument.

CONFLICTS INTERNAL TO DEMOCRATIC JUSTICE

Any argument for an internally complex set of principles must confront the possibility that they cannot be satisfied simultaneously. The question then arises: how are conflicts among the different injunctions to be resolved? One response to this question is to come up with a system of meta-rules for resolving conflicts when they occur. For instance Rawls's theory of justice consists of a number of principles that, he argues, should be lexically ranked: In the case of conflicts the principles that are higher in his lexical ordering trump those that are lower.[37]

It is evident that democratic justice exhibits an analogous potential for internal conflict. What the general argument recommends as the appropriate system of governance in a domain may conflict with the presumptive suspicion of hierarchy. People might choose to create a hierarchy by voluntary action or majority rule. Likewise, the various injunctions against hierarchy might produce contradictory prescriptions as far as a particular practice is concerned. The insular character of withdrawing sects, such as Mormons and the Amish, counsels leaving them alone, yet their internally hierarchical practices prompt suspicion from the standpoint of democratic justice. How should conflicts of this kind be resolved?

The two alternatives here are either to try to come up with a system of meta-principles analogous to Rawls's lexical rules or to supply a principled defense of a more underdetermined view. To try to come up with a complete system of meta-principles that would resolve every possible tension that could arise out of the complexities of the general argument seems to me to be so demanding a task that it would almost certainly fail.[38] The range of circumstances that can arise is exceedingly large, if not infinite, and the complexity of the social world is such that there will always be challenges to the logic internal to democratic justice. This is less troubling than might at first appear to be the case. For one thing, the lack of a complete system of meta-principles does not silence democratic justice in every circumstance. We can still say, for example, that a practice that runs up against a great many of democratic justice's presumptions is correspondingly more suspect for that reason. Slavery is an easy case for democratic justice just because this is so. It violates basic principles of collective self-governance and it is on the wrong side of every presumption about hierarchy that I discussed: it is unnecessary, it is not usually entered into voluntarily, it is hard or impossible to escape, it is both asymmetrical and non-self-liquidating, and it has external effects that permeate through the social world. By the same token a practice that turns out to be on the right side of every presumption will be equally easy to deal with.

The more difficult and interesting cases are those that are less clear-cut. In many of these instances it may be possible to find accommodations among conflicting injunctions. For instance, in the case of the Amish one might take the view that the withdrawing character of the group and the absence of a threat posed by it to the rest of society counsels against any attempt to interfere with its existence, but that the state should nonetheless insist that Amish children be educated so that they have the capacities to function outside the Amish community in the

---

37 Rawls, *A Theory of Justice*, 42–5, 61–5, 82–9, 151–61.
38 It is not difficult, for example, to demonstrate the existence of contradictory imperatives flowing from Rawls's lexical rankings. See T. M. Scanlon, "Rawls's Theory of Justice," in *Reading Rawls,* ed. Norman Daniels (Bristol, UK: Basil Blackwell, 1975), 169–205; H.L.A. Hart, "Rawls on Liberty and Its Priority," idem, 230–52; and Benjamin Barber, "Justifying Justice: Problems of Psychology, Politics and Measurement in Rawls," idem, 292–318.

event that they decide to leave. Thus while on this view one would not tolerate all Amish educational practices, in other respects they would be left alone.[39] Likewise, although the ossified and non-self-liquidating hierarchies in the Catholic Church contravene some of the presumptions of democratic justice, the history of domination that has accompanied established churches might also counsel that there is wisdom in an especially wide latitude of tolerance as far as religious matters are concerned. A government guided by the principles of democratic justice might nonetheless attach some costs to religions that contravene them, such as denying tax-exempt status to those in which some offices are reserved for men, persons of a particular race, or any other group that is defined in a morally arbitrary way. The governing body of the religion in question would then be free to decide whether to live with the sanctions in question or to adjust its practices to avoid them.[40]

These examples indicate that once we recognize that there is a range of possible sanctions and of feasible responses to them, apparently conflicting imperatives can be managed in a variety of ways that can, over time, be expected to encourage civil institutions to evolve in comparatively democratic directions. To some even this approach will sound like opening the way for dangerously radical interference with freedom of religious worship. But reflection on our current laws concerning racially exclusionary organizations, and on the distinctions we comfortably draw between religions and cults and between education and brainwashing, should reveal that we routinely make many judgments of this kind, however implicitly. These examples also underline the fact that when we value more than one commitment we sometimes have either to live with tensions among them or to come up with creative solutions to the tensions. This is no less true of the world in which we actually live than it would be in a world in which democratic justice furnished the basic principles of governance. The imperatives that follow from the constituent parts of the United States constitution and its amendments generate many tensions, and just as courts and legislatures have to order, rank, and accommodate them in particular contexts, so the same would have to be done in a world governed by considerations derived from the general argument for democratic justice. Admittedly, to say this is not to resolve any specific tensions, but it does perhaps indicate the limits of what it is reasonable to expect from a general statement of principles.

A different objection to the internally complex character of democratic justice is that it is unnecessarily complex. My claim that freedom to oppose collective outcomes is not derivative

---

39 This is the view defended in Richard Ameson and Ian Shapiro, "Democracy and Religious Freedom: A Critique of *Wisconsin v. Yoder,*" in *Nomos XXXVIII: Political Order,* ed. Ian Shapiro and Russell Hardin (New York: New York University Press, forthcoming).

40 From the standpoint of democratic justice, the Supreme Court thus reached the right result in *Bob Jones University v. United States,* 461 U.S. 574 (1983), when it held that the federal government may legitimately deny tax-exempt status to institutions that would otherwise qualify but which engage in racial discrimination.

of rights to inclusive participation might be granted, but, if this freedom is valued regardless of whether decisions were made democratically, then why value democratic decision-making? Is not democracy, on my account, reducible to opposition? My answer is that although inclusive participation and freedom to oppose are valuable independently of one another, the ways in which they are exercised are not without mutual implications. In particular, I propose the following injunction: The more democratically those who win in battles over collective decisions conduct themselves in victory, the stronger is the obligation on the defeated to ensure that their opposition is loyal rather than disloyal—and vice versa. Processes of inclusive consultation, meaningful hearings, good-faith consideration of how to mitigate external effects of decisions, and willingness to consider alternatives all build legitimacy for democratic decision making, and they should. No less appropriately, their opposites breed cynicism and mistrust on the part of losers, which erode democracy's legitimacy in predictable ways. By linking the obligation to make opposition loyal to how democratically those in power conduct themselves, protagonists on all sides are reminded of the imperfection of the rules that give present winners their victories and losers their losses. In addition, if the two are linked, both winners and losers have incentives to search for mechanisms that can diminish the distances between them.

TRADEOFFS BETWEEN DEMOCRATIC JUSTICE AND OTHER GOODS

Additional sources of tension arise from my argument being premised on the notion that democracy is a conditioning good—subordinate to the activities whose pursuit it regulates. This means that there can and most likely will be tensions between the requirements of democratic justice and the activities it is intended to condition. In the limiting case, there will be activities that operate in flat contradiction with the principles I have described. Apart from the case of parent-child relations to which some attention has already been devoted, there are football teams, armies, and many other organizational forms whose purposes seem to defy democratic governance. No doubt one can always challenge the proposition that such organizational forms must necessarily be undemocratic, and as the rich literature on the governance of the firm indicates, we should always be open to creative possibilities for the democratic management of institutions that seem inherently undemocratic.[41] Yet one has to confront the possibility that there will be circumstances in which there are inescapable tradeoffs between democratic control and the pursuit of a particular good, be it the gathering of military intelligence, the running of a professional sports team, or other valuable activity.

---

41 For a useful summary of recent literature, see Henry Hansman, "When Does Worker Ownership Work?" *Yale Law Journal* 99 (June 1990): 1749–816.

One response is to deal with tradeoffs of this kind in the same way that tensions internal to democratic justice are handled, by recognizing that when there is more than one thing we value at times we will have to choose among them. But this should be the last response, not the first. Although there is never a guarantee that tradeoffs between democratic justice and other goods can be avoided, the argument for democratic justice bids us to try to find ways to avoid them. Consider the two examples just mentioned. Congress has devised oversight mechanisms that, however imperfectly, ensure some democratic accountability of intelligence agencies consistent with their secret purposes. No doubt we pay a price for them and they could be improved upon, but the outcome of the Cold War scarcely suggests that our system fared worse than the Soviet system, in which there was virtually no democratic accountability of any sort, or indeed that it fared less well than other systems in the West that until recently have had little or no democratic oversight.[42] As far as professional sports are concerned, there too the situation is less clear-cut than might at first sight appear to be the case. Although one would not want everyone on the team calling plays, there are many areas in professional sports where a measure of democratic control can be achieved without compromise of athletic purpose. Pay and working conditions are the most obvious areas; no doubt there are others. To reiterate, the general point is that the presumption is against undemocratic ways of doing things. It is only a presumption and it can be overcome, but reasons should be demanded and the burden of persuasion should always lie with those who would limit democracy's operation.

COMPETING DEMANDS OF DIFFERENT DOMAINS

Yet other potential tensions arise, for democratic justice, out of the fact that it is simultaneously concerned with many domains of civil society. It may be the case that pursuing democratic justice in one domain makes it more difficult, perhaps even impossible, to pursue it in other domains. For instance, participating in governance is part of what democratic justice requires. Yet there are limits to how much time people have available, so that increased participatory involvement in one domain may mean diminished participation in others. This is what Carmen Sirianni has characterized as the "paradox of participatory pluralism." It arises for anyone who both values democratic participation and embraces a view of politics that ranges throughout civil society. We cannot simultaneously maximize participation over all domains.[43]

---

[42] Robert Dahl has argued that analogous skepticism is in order toward claims that democratic control of nuclear arsenals and development interferes with their efficient deployment. See *Controlling Nuclear Weapons: Democracy versus Guardianship* (Syracuse, NY: Syracuse University Press, 1985), 33–51.

[43] Carmen Sirianni, "Learning Pluralism: Democracy and Diversity in Feminist Organizations," in *Nomos XXXV: Democratic Community*, ed. John Chapman and Ian Shapiro (New York: New York University Press, 1993), 283–312.

The paradox is inescapable for participatory democrats like Sirianni (who offers no solution to it), but the argument for democratic justice suggests avenues for dealing with it. Participation is not valuable for its own sake on my view; rather, it is valuable only as it is pursued in conjunction with the goods that it conditions. Collective self-governance is important in every domain of civil society but it is never the most important thing; adherents of democratic justice should thus always be open to timesaving and other novel devices to conserve participatory resources. For instance, since the 1970s a number of writers have explored the use of "deliberative polls": randomly selected groups that are paid to debate public issues from the selection of presidential candidates to the governance of school districts.[44] Experience with deliberative polls suggests that they may provide useful mechanisms for both exerting democratic control and solving the difficulty, pointed to by Sartori and others, that "knowledge—cognitive competence and control—becomes more and more the problem as politics becomes more and more complicated."[45] Randomly selected lay groups, that have no particular vested interest in the outcome in a given area, can invest the time and energy needed to make informed decisions. Such groups can gather data and listen to expert witnesses, making use of esoteric knowledge without being held hostage to it. The decisions they render could be advisory or even binding, at least for certain matters. From the standpoint of democratic justice the possibilities offered by deliberative polls are worth exploring because they provide a potential way out of Sirianni's paradox: they combine citizen control with the possibility of sophisticated decision making in a complex world, and they do it in a way that takes account of the economy of time.[46]

Earlier I suggested that from the standpoint of democratic justice participation should be seen neither in purely instrumental terms nor as the point of the exercise in politics. Such devices as the deliberative poll are attractive because they are an example of a creative institutional response to the goal of trying to occupy a middle ground between these two views. Everyone might be expected to participate in some deliberative polls, just as everyone is expected to sit on some conventional juries. Everyone would know that, in the bodies they are not involved in, other randomly selected bodies were sitting with no particular agendas or interest groups of their own that were being advanced. Everyone would also know that no matter how complex and technical decisions were becoming, a meaningful element of lay control would nonetheless be present in all collective decision making. This is essential for democratic justice.

---

44 See James Fishkin, *Democracy and Deliberation: New Directions for Democratic Reform* (New Haven, CT: Yale University Press, 1991).

45 Giovanni Sartori, *The Theory of Democracy Revisited*, vol. 1 (Chatham, NJ: Chatham House, 1987), 119–20.

46 Deliberative polls must confront the difficulty that whoever sets the agenda may exert disproportionate influence on the outcome, but this is a difficulty that every decision-making procedure must confront. It is not the weakness in democratic theory that proponents of deliberative polls are intending to resolve, though they, like proponents of other decision-making mechanisms, need to be concerned about it.

THE ROLE FOR THE STATE

Apart from the extremes of limiting cases like slavery, the general argument for democratic justice does not provide conclusive assessments of particular decision rules or mechanisms of opposition. Instead, as we have seen, it generates presumptions and distributes burdens of persuasion in various ways. That is as it should be. Since the general argument is a semicontextual, particularities of context are needed to decide when burdens have been appropriately carried and when presumptions have been rebutted. Democratic justice generates determinate conclusions in particular contexts only.

To say this is not, however, to deliver on everything that should reasonably be expected of the general argument. Invoking the language of presumptions and burdens of persuasion immediately raises the question: who is to judge when burdens have been carried and presumptions rebutted? Since the evidence will often be inconclusive and opinion about it must be expected often to be divided, just where decision-making authority should be located is, and is bound to remain, an important general question. The answer is also partly contextual; different authorities are appropriate in different kinds of circumstances. But the answer is only partly contextual; from the standpoint of democratic justice, some general considerations apply.

ANTIVANGUARDISM AND ITS LIMITS

Whenever anyone claims to know how to get to democracy undemocratically, skepticism is in order for two reasons, one practical and one normative. The practical reason is that it is doubtful that they can know that they are right. Just because democratic reforms are typically reactive responses to particular evils that chart new courses into the future, it is usually difficult to know what their full consequences will be or what new problems the reforms will create. For instance, changes in the structure of American family law, making marriage more of a contract and less of a status, have been motivated by a desire to undermine the patriarchal family. But it has since become evident that one of the net effects of these changes has been to render women increasingly vulnerable to the greater economic power of men in marriage.[47] As this becomes apparent, other ways of democratizing family life will be sought and new experiments tried and modified as and when the obstacles they generate come into view. Democratizing family life will likely require changes in the organization of the economy, and perhaps other changes that are yet to be thought of. Likewise with the debate on democracy in the workplace, there is now considerable disagreement on which are more effective in undermining alienating hierarchy: strategies of worker self-management or plans for employee ownership or part-ownership that leave the structure of management comparatively

---

47 See Susan Okin, *Justice, Gender, and the Family* (New York: Basic Books, 1989), 134–69.

untouched. Many varieties of both have been tried in different industries. It seems certain that no single model will turn out to be generally applicable and that new possibilities are yet to be tried.[48]

To take an example from the realm of institutional governance, during the nineteenth century reasonable salaries and working conditions for politicians were rightly seen as essential to undermining a system in which government was a part-time activity for the wealthy. But these improvements have brought with them new brands of ossified power in the form of professional politicians with lifetime career aspirations in government. In the United States, electoral politics have become dependent on money to such a degree that political elites manage to maintain themselves in positions of power for life in ways that are at odds with democracy's hostility toward entrenched hierarchy.[49] As a response to this, new democratic reforms are being called for, geared toward limiting the number of terms politicians can serve and better regulating the role of money in electoral politics.[50]

It defies credulity to suppose that in any of these instances democratic reformers could have understood social processes profoundly enough, or seen sufficiently far into the future, to have anticipated all the problems and possibilities that lay ahead. Yet these cases are not exceptional; life has more imagination than we do, and it will often defeat our best efforts and present unexpected obstacles and opportunities. The fabric of social life and the dynamics of historical change are complex and little understood; that is the reality with which we have to live. Designing democratic institutional constraints is thus bound to be a pragmatic business, best pursued in context-sensitive and incremental ways. New activities come into being, technological change, experience, and the evolution of other causally linked activities all present fresh problems and generate novel possibilities for democratic governance. There are good reasons to be skeptical of anyone who denies this, whether they harbor a hidden agenda that is being obscured by their vanguardist pretensions or they are acting out of misplaced faith in their own prescient abilities.

---

48 See Charles Sabel and Jonathan Zeitlin, "Historical Alternatives to Mass Production," *Past and Present* 108 (1986): 133–76; and Hansman, "When Does Worker Ownership Work?"
49 See Herbert Alexander, *Financing Politics: Money, Elections and Political Reform* (Washington, DC: Congressional Quarterly Press, 1976) and Frank J. Sorauf, *Inside Campaign Finance* (New Haven, CT: Yale University Press, 1992).
50 In this connection a small but not insignificant victory was achieved for democracy in March 1990 in *Austin v. Michigan State Chamber of Commerce,* 110 S. Ct. 1391, when the Supreme Court cut back on the *Buckley v. Valeo* 424 U.S. 1 (1976) rule, which had held that although contributions to political campaigns may be limited by legislation, limiting expenditures constitutes a violation of the free speech clause of the First Amendment. In *Austin* the Court held that some corporate expenditures on political speech may be regulated. As far as term limits are concerned, there is considerable scholarly debate as to how bad the incumbency problem is and whether or not term limits would be a solution to the problem of the ossification of power in professional hands. They might, for example, lead to a net transfer of power from politicians to bureaucrats, as Morris Fiorina suggests in *Divided Government* (London: Macmillan, 1992), 53–9.

Means/ends dichotomies are suspect, also, for the normative reason that they undermine the spirit of democratic justice. Although I have argued that we should resist the participatory democrat's contention that participation is valuable for its own sake, we should be no less wary of purely instrumental conceptions of democracy. Democratic means are never the point of the exercise, but they are usually of more than mere instrumental value. There is value to doing things democratically, and there is value to struggling with how to do things democratically while still achieving one's other goals. Democratic habits of self-restraint and attention to the needs and aspirations of others have to be learned through democratic practice; succumbing to the authoritarianism inherent in means/ends dichotomies should be expected to undermine it. In this connection, Dewey penned the right maxim for democratic justice over half a century ago: "Our first defense is to realize that democracy can be served only by the slow day by day adoption and contagious diffusion in every phase of our common life of methods that are identical with the ends to be reached."[51]

The principled refusal to impose solutions from above can provoke the argument that unless this is done they will not be implemented at all, and there are, indeed, at least three important classes of exceptions to the initial presumption against vanguardism. The first concerns the provision of public goods. As my earlier discussion of education revealed, when the provision of public goods is at issue and there are differential capacities for exit, no local decision rule will likely be effective in diminishing injustice. This amounts to saying that effective policies will have to be imposed from above.[52] Proponents of "shock therapy" in the transition from communism to capitalism seem often to take an analogous view. Adam Przeworski argues, for example, that during transitions from authoritarianism to democracy unless economic reforms are rammed through from above, those who are adversely affected by them will mobilize their opposition to them through the democratic process, scuttling the reforms. Consequently, fledgling democratic governments "face the choice of either involving a broad range of political forces in the shaping of reforms, thus compromising their economic soundness, or trying to undermine all opposition to the [reform] program." In Przeworski's view, any government "that is resolute must proceed in spite of the clamor of voices that call for softening or slowing down the reform program." Because reformers "know what is good" all political conflicts become no more than a waste of time. Przeworski goes on to point out that every instance of successful market reform during democratic transitions on record was implemented by executive decree, remarking that "[t]his potential is inherent in the very conception of market reforms."[53]

---

51 John Dewey, "Democratic Ends Need Democratic Methods for Their Realization," *New Leader* 22 (October 1939) reprinted in John Dewey, *The Political Writings*, ed. Debra Morris and Ian Shapiro (Indianapolis, IN: Hackett, 1993), 206.

52 For elaboration, see Jennifer Hochschild, *The New American Dilemma: Liberal Democracy and School Desegregation* (New Haven, CT: Yale University Press, 1984).

53 Adam Przeworski, *Democracy and the Market* (Cambridge, England: Cambridge University Press, 1991), 183–4. See also Janos Komai, *The Road to a Free Economy: Shifting from a Socialist System* (New York: Norton, 1990); and

From the standpoint of democratic justice, the critical question is whether the reformers really do "know what is good" and pursue it in fact. Much of what is presented by economic reformers as uncontroversially good might in fact be controversial, and many economic reforms that are described as public goods do not meet the technical criteria that require both joint supply and nonexcludability.[54] Whether the sorts of privatization and stabilization policies that such political economists as Przeworski, Janos Kornai, Jeffrey Sachs, and others advocate lead to the supply of public goods in this sense is debatable. No doubt parts of what is provided are public goods, but other aspects of these policies may amount to little more than mechanisms for raiding public treasuries by strategically well-placed groups, generating little or no benefit for anyone else. In such instances, the pursuit of private benefit may be cloaked in the language of public goods, and opposition to them that is really a reflection of zero-sum distributive conflict will masquerade as a collective action problem. What are billed as solutions to it will actually be partisan policies that help some sectors and hurt others. Democrats who suspect this is the case with substantial parts of postcommunist privatizations are bound to find themselves ambivalent, at least, about the "bitter pill" strategies that depend on "initial brutality, on proceeding as quickly as possible with the most radical measures," and implementing reforms either by administrative fiat or ramming them through legislatures.[55]

In circumstances where one does not doubt that a public good is being supplied, one's democratic moral intuitions are not troubled by decisive action from above. For instance in the South African constitutional negotiations that led up to the April 1994 elections, it gradually became clear that—desirable as multiparty roundtable negotiations sounded—they were not going to produce an agreement on a democratic constitution. Too many groups had too many incentives to pursue private agendas at the expense of ensuring that the public good was provided. Consequently, it became evident that, if a democratic political order was to be put in place, it would have to be hammered out as an elite pact and then imposed on the society. This is what transpired in fact, and the reason that democrats the world over applauded as opponents to the transition were so effectively either marginalized or co-opted was that almost no one doubted that what the elites proposed to impose—a democratic constitutional order—was in fact a public good.[56]

Jeffrey Sachs, "The Transformation of Eastern Europe: The Case of Poland" (The Frank E. Seidman Lecture, Rhodes College, Memphis, Tennessee, September 26, 1991); Boris Pleskovic and Jeffrey Sachs, "Political Independence and Economic Reform in Slovenia," in *The Transition in Eastern Europe,* ed. Oliver Blanchard, Kenneth Froot, and Jeffrey Sachs, vol. 1 (Chicago: University of Chicago Press, 1994), 191–220.

54 "A pure public good has two salient characteristics: jointness of supply, and the impossibility or inefficiency of excluding others from its consumption, once it has been supplied by some members of the community." Mueller, *Public Choice II,* 11.

55 Przeworski, *Democracy and the Market,* 183–4.

56 On the collapse of the roundtable negotiations and the emergence of an elite pact between the National Party and ANC leaderships, see my "Democratic Innovation: South Africa in Comparative Context," *World Politics* 46, no. 1 (October 1993): 138–41.

Distinguishing the provision of genuine public goods from spurious ones is a difficult and controversial business. Often the two will be mixed, making it even more difficult, as is almost certainly the case with most privatization plans. Even in the case of the South African constitution it seems clear that the elites who committed themselves to providing the public good in question sprinkled in a few benefits for themselves, notably a system of electoral and parliamentary rules that greatly weakens backbenchers vis-à-vis leaderships, as well as bribes to particular interest groups to insulate them from the new political order.[57]

From the standpoint of democratic justice, the extent to which policies may legitimately be imposed from above varies with the degree to which genuine public goods are being provided. As the preceding remarks indicate, this will often be hotly disputed and ideologically charged, not least because there will be those who have an interest in obscuring the matter. It may also be genuinely unclear in certain circumstances. When either of these things is the case, what we are witnessing is not a failure in the argument for democratic justice. Rather, it is a failure in understanding of, or agreement about, whether or not something constitutes a public good. This is not to diminish the normative importance of the matter, it is only to say that it would be to expect the wrong kind of thing from any political theory to ask of it that it resolve contentious empirical questions of political economy. The argument for democratic justice can be expected to counsel what to do when a certain fact pattern obtains; it cannot be expected to tell us whether or not the fact pattern really does obtain. The general argument does, however, counsel us to regard claims to be providing public goods with suspicion, and to subject them to what lawyers think of as "strict scrutiny." American courts typically subject legislative action to this most demanding level of constitutional scrutiny when the proposed action interferes with a "fundamental" liberty, usually a freedom protected by the Bill of Rights. Strict scrutiny requires a showing that the governmental objective is unusually important—that a "compelling" state interest is at stake—and that it cannot be accomplished in a less intrusive way.[58] By analogy we might say that the undemocratic imposition of a public good is justified only when the good in question is essential to the operation of a democratic order and cannot be attained in any other way. Because those who claim to provide public goods may have ulterior motives, and because private goods

---

57 As far as political elites sprinkling in benefits for themselves is concerned, the 1993 constitution requires that any member of parliament who ceases to be a member of his or her political party will also cease to be a member of parliament, being replaced by someone else from the party's parliamentary list. As for bribes, all civil service jobs and salaries were guaranteed for at least five years following the transition, and in the last weeks before the election President de Klerk transferred some three million acres of land to Zulu king Goodwill Zwelitini in order to prevent their falling under the control of the new national government following the April 1994 elections. *New York Times*, May 24, 1994, A6. For further discussion, see Courtney Jung and Ian Shapiro, "South Africa's Negotiated Transition: Democracy, Opposition, and the New Constitutional Order," *Politics & Society* 23, no. 3 (September 1995): 269–308.
58 See Laurence H. Tribe, *American Constitutional Law,* 2d ed. (New York: Foundation, 1988), 251–75.

can often masquerade as public goods, the strong presumption should always be against their imposition from above.

A second class of exceptions to the general presumption against vanguardism arises when illegitimate hierarchies have been maintained by the state. For example, in the West the disadvantaged status of women in family life was sustained by the common law and other active policies of the state for centuries. One dramatic legacy of this history is that as recently as the 1950s throughout the United States a husband could not be prosecuted for raping his wife. By the mid-1990s spousal rape was a prosecutable felony during an ongoing marriage in well over a third of American jurisdictions, the product of a concerted feminist campaign in state legislatures and courts.[59] It would have been impossible for such changes to have come about without the state's active involvement, since it is the policies of the state that were at the root of the injustice in question. Likewise, it took the passage of the married women's property acts (the first wave of which began in the 1840s) to destroy the common law rule that had given the husband control, and sometimes title, to the wife's property and possessions during marriage.[60]

In such circumstances it will be necessary, and justifiable from the standpoint of democratic justice, for the state to be centrally involved in dismantling the unjust system it has created. Women would have been morally misguided as well as politically shortsighted had they not sought to enlist public institutions in this struggle to refashion the terms of their domestic association. Since the unjust hierarchies to which they had been subjected were direct products of state policies and sustained by the legal order, it was reasonable to require the state to play an active role in dismantling the injustices in question. Likewise, the effects of the Group Areas Act in South Africa, which led to the forced removals of millions of blacks from viable communities to desolate deserts, are properly responded to by remedial action from a democratic South African state.[61] The general point here is that the more antidemocratic practices have been underwritten by the state, the more powerful is the case for the involvement of state institutions in remedying the unjust status quo.[62]

A third class of exceptions arises when domination within a domain is not a direct product of state action, but it is nonetheless sustained by forces external to that domain that can be removed

---

59 On the changing law of marital rape in the United States, see Michael Freeman, "If You Can't Rape Your Wife, Who[m] Can You Rape? The Marital Rape Exception Re-examined," *Family Law Quarterly* 15, no. 1 (Spring 1981): 1–29; Deborah Rhode, *Justice and Gender* (Cambridge, MA: Harvard University Press, 1989), 249–51; Rene I. Augustine, "Marriage: The Safe Haven for Rapists," *Journal of Family Law* 29, no. 3 (1990-1): 559–90; Sandra Ryder and Sheryl Kuzmenka, "Legal Rape: The Marital Exception," *John Marshall Law Review* 24 (1992): 393–421. On the English evolution of the exception, see P. M. Bromley and N. V. Lowe, *Family Law*, 7th ed. (Salem, NH: Butterworths, 1987), 109–12.
60 See H. H. Clark, *The Law of Domestic Relations in the United States*, 2d ed. (Saint Paul, MN: West, 1988), 589.
61 For an account of the extent and effects of these policies, see Helen Suzman, *In No Uncertain Terms* (New York: Knopf, 1993), 65–212.
62 This says nothing about which state institutions are most appropriate for the purpose, whether courts, legislatures or executive agencies. See below.

only by state action. This is what Michael Walzer has described as "dominance," the transfer of power in one domain of social life where it may be legitimate into another where it is not. Walzer contends, for instance, that economic inequality is not objectionable as such, and that it may be justified in the sphere of production for its incentive and other efficiency effects. What is objectionable is that disparities in income and wealth are all too easily translatable into disparities in the political domain, the domestic domain, the educational domain, and other areas where they have no evident rationale.[63] This happens because the resources necessary to exercise power tend to be fungible across domains, and Walzer sees it as one of the appropriate tasks of a democratic state to limit this fungibility. On this view, laws against buying and selling votes for money can be defended, for example, even though such laws are inefficient in the economist's sense. Similarly, refusals by courts to enforce antenuptial agreements that leave divorcing spouses destitute amount to a refusal by the state to allow economic disparities that may be justifiable outside the domestic domain to set the terms of life within it.

From the standpoint of democratic justice Walzer's intuition about this class of cases is defensible, if for different reasons than those that he supplies. Whereas for Walzer the reason for trying to prevent domination within a sphere by those who control goods external to it is rooted in shared meanings about which goods are appropriate in which domains, from the present standpoint the justification is rooted in considerations drawn from the political economy of power.[64] I said earlier that the shape of decision rules should follow the contours of power relations, not those of memberships. It follows that when obstacles to democracy within a domain are externally sustained, it is an appropriate use of state power that it be used to remove such obstacles. To deny this would amount to abandoning democratic justice in particular domains to those who have imperial control of fungible resources. In short—*pace* Walzer—because causal effects rather than shared membership within a domain are decisive in legitimating a right to democratic control, it follows that state action that crosses the boundaries of domains can be justified when this is necessary to achieve democratic justice within a domain.[65]

Action by the state to advance democratic reform can be justified, then, but not as part of any missionary quest on democratic justice's behalf. There is no secular analogue to "Christianizing the infidels" to justify such action, whether by courts, legislatures, or invading armies. Rather, external involvement can be justified by three principal classes of reasons. First, when provision of a public good is at stake, imposed solutions may be justifiable, subject to the caveats I have mentioned. This we might think of as a market-failure justification. Second, the state may often

---

63 Walzer, *Spheres of Justice*, 3–30.
64 I have noted elsewhere that the appeal to shared meanings fails because these are invariably in contention. "Three Ways to Be a Democrat," 130–5.
65 It should be evident from my earlier discussion of public goods and state culpability that I also think Walzer is mistaken in thinking that preventing dominance is the only legitimate basis for the imposition of solutions by the state.

have an affirmative obligation to help foster democracy flowing from its historical culpability in creating and sustaining injustice. Last, when external sources of domination within a domain can be removed only by state action, this can be justified by reference to the argument from causal legitimacy.

LEGISLATURES VERSUS COURTS

The aspiration to avoid imposed solutions suggests that the presumption should generally be in favor of doing things through representative institutions rather than courts or other agencies, for the conventional reason that legislatures are comparatively more democratically accountable. There will be exceptions to this, but it is the exceptions that stand in need of justification. In this connection the argument for democratic justice exhibits an elective affinity with the approaches to constitutional adjudication that have been defended in recent years by Ruth Bader Ginsburg and Robert Burt, and it will be useful to end with some discussion of their views.

Burt conceives of a constitutional democracy as inescapably committed to two principles—majority rule and equal self-determination—that have the potential to conflict with one another. If majoritarian processes are employed to promote domination of some by others, the contradiction latent in democratic politics becomes manifest. In such circumstances democracy goes to war with itself and an institutional mechanism is needed to resolve the conflict. This is supplied, on Burt's account, by judicial review, understood as "a coercive instrument extrinsic to the disputants" in a political struggle. Burt sees judicial review as a "logical response to an internal contradiction between majority rule and equal self-determination. It is not a deviation from that theory."[66]

If the court's legitimate role in a democracy is rooted in this logic of preventing domination through democratic process, then it follows on Burt's view that its activities should be limited to dealing with the consequences of the democratic contradiction. And since preventing domination is the goal, it also follows that courts should not take up sides in disputes that are by-products of the democratic contradiction (effectively imposing the wishes of one group on another). Rather, they should declare the domination that has emerged from the democratic process unacceptable and insist that the parties try anew to find an accommodation. Thus in contrast to what many have seen as the altogether too timid approach taken by the U.S. Supreme Court in the school desegregation cases of the 1950s and after, on Burt's view the Court took the right stand. In *Brown v. Board of Education* the justices declared the doctrine of "separate but equal" to be an unconstitutional violation of the equal protection clause, but they did not describe schooling conditions that would be acceptable.[67] Rather, they turned the problem back to Southern state

---

66 Robert A. Burt, *The Constitution in Conflict* (Cambridge, MA: Harvard University Press, 1992), 29.
67 *Brown v. Board of Education I*, 347 U.S. 483 (1954).

legislatures, requiring them to fashion acceptable remedies themselves.[68] These remedies came before the Court as a result of subsequent litigation, were evaluated when they did, and were often found to be wanting.[69] But the Court avoided designing the remedy itself, and with it the charge that it was usurping the legislative function.

Ginsburg, too, has made the case that when courts try to step beyond a reactive role they undermine their legitimacy in a democracy. Although she thinks that it is sometimes necessary for the court to step "ahead" of the political process to achieve reforms that the Constitution requires, if it gets too far ahead it can produce a backlash and provoke charges that it is overreaching its appropriate place in a democratic constitutional order.[70] She and Burt both think that the sort of approach adopted by Justice Blackmun in *Roe v. Wade* exemplifies this danger.[71] In contrast to the *Brown* approach in *Roe* the Court did a good deal more than strike down a Texas abortion statute. The majority opinion laid out a detailed test to determine the conditions under which any abortion statute could be expected to pass muster. In effect, Justice Blackmun authored a federal abortion statute of his own. As Ginsburg put it, the court "invited no dialogue with legislators. Instead, it seemed entirely to remove the ball from the legislators' court" by wiping out virtually every form of abortion regulation then in existence.[72]

On the Ginsburg-Burt view, the sweeping holding in *Roe* diminished the Court's democratic legitimacy at the same time as it polarized opinion about abortion and put paid to various schemes to liberalize abortion laws that were under way in different states. Between 1967 and 1973 statutes were passed in nineteen states liberalizing the permissible grounds for abortion. Many feminists had been dissatisfied with the pace and extent of this reform. This is why they mounted the campaign that resulted in *Roe*. Burt concedes that in 1973 it was "not clear whether the recently enacted state laws signified the beginning of a national trend toward abolishing all abortion restrictions or even whether in the so-called liberalized states, the new enactments would significantly increase access to abortion for anyone." Nonetheless, he points out that "the abortion issue was openly, avidly, controverted in a substantial number of public forums, and unlike the regimen extant as recently as 1967, it was no longer clear who was winning the battle."[73] Following the *Brown* model, the Court might have struck down the Texas abortion statute in *Roe* and remanded the matter for further action at the state level, thereby setting limits on what legislatures might do in the matter of regulating abortion without involving the Court directly in designing that regulation. On the

---

68 *Brown v. Board of Education II*, 349 U.S. 294 (1955).
69 Burt, *Constitution in Conflict*, 271–310.
70 Ruth Bader Ginsburg, "Speaking in a Judicial Voice" (Madison Lecture, New York University Law School, March 9, 1993, mimeo), 30–8. See also *Nomination of Ruth Bader Ginsburg to Be an Associate Justice of the United States Supreme Court: Report Together with Additional Views*, Exec. Report 103-6-93-1 United States Senate.
71 *Roe v. Wade*, 410 U.S. 113 (1973).
72 Ginsburg, "Speaking in a Judicial Voice," 32.
73 Burt, *Constitution in Conflict*, 348.

Ginsburg-Burt view, this would have left space for democratic resolution of the conflict, ensuring the survival of the right to abortion while at the same time preserving the legitimacy of the Court's role in a democracy.[74]

Although the tensions that arise within democratic justice differ from those that motivate Burt and Ginsburg, in three important respects their view of the appropriate role for courts in a democratic order fits comfortably within the general argument developed here. First, they articulate an appropriate institutional response to the injunction that rather than impose democracy on collective activities the goal should be to try to structure things so that people will find ways to democratize things for themselves. By placing courts in a nay-saying stance of ruling out practices as unacceptable when they violate the strictures of democratic justice, courts can force legislatures and the conflicting parties they represent to seek creative solutions to their conflicts that can pass constitutional muster. Second, the Ginsburg-Burt view is attractive because it is reactive but directed; it exemplifies the creative pragmatism that motivates democratic justice. It involves accepting that there is an important—if circumscribed—role for courts in a democracy, yet it does not make the unmanageable administrative demands on courts that accompany more proactive views of adjudication. On this view a court might reasonably hold that a given policy should be rejected without stating (indeed, perhaps without having decided) what policy would pass muster. "This is unacceptable for reasons *a, b, c* ... ; find a better way" is seen as an appropriate stance for a constitutional court. Finally, by recognizing the relatively greater legitimacy of legislatures and treating courts as institutional mechanisms for coping with legislative failure, the Ginsburg-Burt view takes account of the fact that no decision-making mechanism is flawless. Yet it does so in a way that is rooted in the idea that democratic procedures should be made to operate as well as possible, and, when they fail, remedies should be no more intrusive on the democratic process than is necessary to repair them.

Some will object to this as too minimal a role for reviewing courts, but democrats have to concern themselves not only with courts that aspire to advance the cause of democratic justice, as

---

74 Ibid., 349–52. The Ginsburg-Burt approach was finally adopted by the Supreme Court in *Planned Parenthood of Pennsylvania v. Casey,* 112 S. Ct. 2791 (1992). By affirming the existence of a woman's fundamental constitutional right to an abortion, recognizing the legitimacy of the state's interest in potential life, and insisting that states may not pursue the vindication of that interest in a manner that is unduly burdensome to women, the Court set some basic parameters within which legislatures must now fashion regulations that govern abortion. The *Casey* dissenters are right to point out that there will be a degree of unpredictability and confusion as different regulatory regimes are enacted in different states and tested through the courts; 112 S. Ct. 2791, at 2866 (1992). On views of adjudication that encourage efficiency and clarity above all else this will appear to be a reprehensible invitation to further litigation. On the Ginsburg-Burt view, however, that *Casey* invites litigation may be a cost worth paying. It places the burden of coming up with modes of regulating abortion that are not unduly burdensome on democratically elected legislatures, and forces them to do this in the knowledge that the statutes they enact will be tested through the courts and thrown out if they are found wanting. These issues are taken up further in my introduction to *Abortion: The Supreme Court Decisions* (Indianapolis, IN: Hackett, 1995), 1–23.

they might reasonably be thought to have done in *Brown* and *Roe*, but also with courts that do not, as was the case in *Dred Scott*, the *Civil Rights Cases*, and *Lochner v. New York*[75] Insulated from any further review and lacing, at least in the American context, in democratic accountability, courts can put decisions of this kind in place that may not be reversed for decades or even generations. Although it may thus be wise from the standpoint of democratic justice to embrace an activist role for a constitutional court, it is equally wise to limit courts to a circumscribed and negationist activism.

CONCLUDING REMARKS

My aim in this essay has been to render plausible the case for a democratic conception of social justice. This I have sought to do by building on the popular view, in which considerations of democracy and justice are intimately linked, rather than conventional academic views of them as fundamentally distinct and mutually antagonistic. The account that I offer rests on the twin commitments to government and opposition in democratic theory, suggesting that there should always be opportunities for those affected by the operation of a collective practice both to participate in its governance and to oppose its results when they are so inclined. These two injunctions should reasonably be expected to have different implications in different cultures and, within the same culture, to evolve over time and play themselves out differently in different domains. They are best thought of as conditioning constraints, designed to democratize social relations as they are reproduced, rather than as blueprints for social justice.

This view contains internal tensions, to be sure, but I have tried to show that these come with the territory in reflecting about the justness of social arrangements, and to indicate something about how these tensions might best be coped with consistent with the spirit of the general argument. Beyond this, I have sought to indicate the main outlines of a view of the state that follows from my view, and to develop some of its implications for the provision of public goods and for the state's appropriate role in advancing democratic justice more generally. I have sketched the basic principles that should guide state action, as well as the fitting nature and place for judicial review in the argument for democratic justice. No doubt these arguments raise as many questions as they settle, but I hope, nonetheless, that I have characterized the central argument and its motivation sufficiently fully to cast it in an attractive light.

In 1918 Dewey remarked that any philosophy animated by the striving to achieve democracy "will construe liberty as meaning a universe in which there is real uncertainty and contingency, a

---

75 *Dred Scott v. Sandford*, 60 U.S. 393 (1856); *In re Civil Rights Cases*, 109 U.S. 3 (1883); and *Lochner v. New York,*, 198 U.S. 45 (1905).

world which is not all in, and never will be, a world which in some respects is incomplete and in the making, and which in these respects may be made this way or that according as men judge, prize, love and labor. To such a philosophy any notion of a perfect or complete reality, finished, existing always the same without regard to the vicissitudes of time, will be abhorrent."[76] Democratic justice is conceived of in a similar contingent and pragmatic spirit. Just as there are no blueprints, there are no final destinations. Social practices evolve, as do technologies of government and opposition, often presenting fresh injustices and novel possibilities for dealing with them. The challenge is to confront the injustices and take advantage of the possibilities in a principled and satisfying way. Democratic justice is intended to help in that endeavor.

---

76 From an address to the Philosophical Union of the University of California in November 1918, reprinted in Dewey, *The Political Writings*, 44.

CPSIA information can be obtained
at www.ICGtesting.com
Printed in the USA
LVOW09s2240260118
563675LV00009B/12/P